Using Windows™ 3.1
Special Edition

RON PERSON
KAREN ROSE

D1208939

Using Windows 3.1, Special Edition

Copyright© 1993 by Que® Corporation.

All rights reserved. Printed in the United States of America. No part of this book may be used or reproduced in any form or by any means, or stored in a database or retrieval system, without prior written permission of the publisher except in the case of brief quotations embodied in critical articles and reviews. Making copies of any part of this book for any purpose other than your own personal use is a violation of United States copyright laws. For information, address Que Corporation, 11711 N. College Ave., Carmel, IN 46032.

Library of Congress Catalog No.: 92-81758

ISBN: 1-56529-109-3

This book is sold *as is*, without warranty of any kind, either express or implied, respecting the contents of this book, including but not limited to implied warranties for the book's quality, performance, merchantability, or fitness for any particular purpose. Neither Que Corporation nor its dealers or distributors shall be liable to the purchaser or any other person or entity with respect to any liability, loss, or damage caused or alleged to be caused directly or indirectly by this book.

95 94 93   4

Interpretation of the printing code: the rightmost double-digit number is the year of the book's printing; the rightmost single-digit number, the number of the book's printing. For example, a printing code of 92-1 shows that the first printing of the book occurred in 1992.

Screen reproductions in this book were created by means of the program Collage Plus from Inner Media, Inc., Hollis, NH.

This book is based on Microsoft Windows Version 3.1 and Microsoft Windows for Workgroups.

Publisher: Lloyd J. Short

Associate Publisher: Rick Ranucci

Operations Manager: Sheila Cunningham

Publishing Plan Manager: Thomas H. Bennett

Aquisitions Editor: Chris Katsaropoulos

Book Designer: Scott Cook

Production Team: Debra Adams, Jeff Baker, Julie Brown, Paula Carroll, Laurie Casey, Michelle Cleary, Brook Farling, Bob LaRoche, Laurie Lee, Cindy L. Phipps, Caroline Roop, Linda Seifert, Sandra Shay, Tina Trettin, Phil Worthington

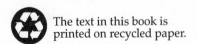 The text in this book is printed on recycled paper.

Ron Person has written more than 12 books for Que Corporation, including *Using Excel 4 for Windows*, Special Edition; *Using Microsoft Windows 3*, 2nd Edition; *Windows 3 QuickStart*; and *Using Word for Windows 2*, Special Edition. Ron is the principal consultant for Ron Person & Co. He has an M.S. in physics from The Ohio State University and an M.B.A. from Hardin-Simmons University.

Karen Rose is a senior trainer for Ron Person & Co. She has written five books for Que Corporation, including *Using Microsoft Windows 3*, 2nd Edition; *Using Word for Windows 2*, Special Edition; and *Using WordPerfect 5.0/5.1*. Karen teaches Word for Windows and desktop publishing for Ron Person & Co. and has taught for the University of California, Berkeley Extension, and Sonoma State University.

Ron Person & Co., based in San Francisco, has attained Microsoft's highest rating for Microsoft Excel and Word for Windows consultants—Microsoft Consulting Partner. The firm helps corporations nationwide in consulting and developing in-house programming and support skills with the embedded macro languages in Microsoft Excel, Word for Windows, and Microsoft Access. The firm's macro and embedded BASIC developer's courses have enabled many corporations to develop their own powerful financial, marketing, and business analysis systems in a minimum amount of time. If your company plans to develop applications using Microsoft's macro or embedded BASIC languages, you will gain significantly from the courses taught by Ron Person & Co. For information on course content, on-site corporate classes, or consulting, contact Ron Person & Co. at the following address:

Ron Person & Co.
P.O. Box 5647
Santa Rosa, CA 95402

(415) 989-7508   voice
(707) 539-1525   voice
(707) 538-1485   fax

CREDITS

Title Manager
Walter R. Bruce, III

Product Director
Timothy S. Stanley

Production Editors
H. Leigh Davis
Kelly D. Dobbs

Editors
Jo Anna Arnott
William A. Barton
Elsa M. Bell
Robin Drake
Donald R. Eamon
Diana Moore
Colleen Totz

Technical Editors
Raymond A. Elseth
Bob Eidson
Roger Jennings
David R. Rorabaugh

Formatter
Jill Stanley

Composed in Garamond and MCPdigital by Que Corporation

ACKNOWLEDGMENTS

Using Windows 3.1, Special Edition, was created through the work and contributions of many professionals. We want to thank the people who contributed to this effort.

Thanks to everyone at Microsoft. Their energy and vision have opened new frontiers in software—software that is more powerful, yet easier to use. Windows has changed the face of computing. Thanks to Christie Gersiche for keeping us in touch and informed.

Thanks to the software consultants and trainers who helped us write *Using Windows 3.1*, Special Edition.

> Robert Voss, Ph.D., applied his knowledge of many Windows applications to the chapters on Windows accessories, Windows Graph, the Microsoft applets, Mail, and Schedule+. Again, Robert has done a conscientious and in-depth job. Robert is a senior trainer in Microsoft Excel and Word for Windows for Ron Person & Co.

> Don Roche is the DOS and Windows expert who wrote chapters on working with DOS applications under Windows. Don is a very experienced technical writer and computer consultant in Austin, Texas. Don does technical writing and support for corporations.

> Doug Bierer contributed the networking portions of the book. Doug is a Certified Netware Instructor and Engineer (CNI/CNE). He's been working with Netware, Banyan, and LANtastic for approximately seven years. Doug currently works for Vitek Systems Distribution, Systems Education, in Sacramento.

> Ralph Soucie, long time contributing editor to *PC World* and author of a popular book on Microsoft Excel, is also a Microsoft Excel consultant. Ralph works out of Tualatin, Oregon. Ralph wrote the chapters on Program Manager and File Manager.

> Toby Wraye, a professional technical writer and magazine editor in Santa Rosa, California, has extensive knowledge of many electronic mail systems. Toby wrote the Mail chapter.

Matt Fogarty is the talented artist who drew the pictures of the guitarist and pelicans using PaintBrush and of the horse race and the old man's character study using Microsoft Draw. Matt is a student at Santa Rosa High School in Santa Rosa, California.

Technical editing was done by David R. Rorabaugh, Raymond A. Elseth, and Roger Jennings; however, the responsibility for any errors that may have slipped through their knowledgeable gaze lies solely with us. Our thanks to their keen eyes.

The skillful pens of our editors ensure that our books are consistent and easy to read. That they succeed in their jobs is evident by the comments of our corporate clients on the quality and value of Que books.

Tim Stanley, product development specialist, brought his years of technical experience to the book to ensure that *Using Windows 3.1*, Special Edition, had the structure and content to help readers.

Kelly D. Dobbs, senior editor, worked with us daily to ensure that we didn't get too far behind schedule and to give us feedback on style and content. We're grateful to Kelly for her patience and for the many late nights and long weekends she devoted to this book.

With the rush of consulting, training, and book development going on in our office, we could not have kept our heads above the diskettes and client folders were it not for our assistant, Wilma Thompson.

Introduction

The phenomenal success of Windows, which came of age with the release of Version 3.0, surprised many people. The success didn't surprise the engineers and evangelists at Microsoft, who have praised Windows since the beginning, and it didn't surprise users who have appreciated the benefits of a graphical interface, multitasking, and connectivity between applications for years. Windows' success, however, surprised people accustomed to the command-line interface of DOS and who never really thought computers should be easy to use. Computers, after all, are serious business tools.

The following reasons demonstrate why a PC running Windows is a *very* serious business tool:

- Windows is easier to use than DOS: Windows commands are listed in menus that you can pick from easily, not hidden in some technical tome. Because commands are easier to find and understand, you will use more of them.

- If you need further assistance, most Windows applications provide a Help command that displays on-screen documentation.

- Windows applications are consistent: the point-and-pick principles of operating Windows extend to all Windows applications.

- Because learning one application moves you well along the way toward using any other Windows application, you will be comfortable using more applications, and you will learn the applications faster.

■ Windows offers multitasking: each Windows application runs in its own *window*, and you can have many windows on-screen at the same time. To move from one application to another, point to the window containing the application you want to use and click (or press a key combination if you don't use a mouse). Running two applications side-by-side is easy.

■ With Windows, you can share data between applications: copying and moving data within and between Windows applications is simple. You can forge links between applications so that updating one file updates all those files linked to it. You can even create compound documents that enable you to start one application from within another.

Not only are Windows and Windows applications easier to use than DOS and DOS applications, they also are very powerful. The word processing program Word for Windows includes advanced capabilities for formatting documents, creating and editing tables, adding tables of contents and indexes, using reference tools like bookmarks and annotations, proofing documents with a spell checker and a thesaurus, automatically creating bulleted and numbered lists, quickly printing envelopes, and much more. The worksheet program Microsoft Excel includes formatting and charting capabilities that rival annual report quality. Excel has more math, scientific, and finance functions than any other worksheet and includes a robust programming language. With its toolbars, drag-and-drop techniques, and help system, however, Excel is easy to use. Powerful applications also exist for database management, presentation development, illustration, photo editing, desktop publishing, multimedia production, accounting, and more. Many of these Windows applications outperform their DOS counterparts.

Besides being easier to use and very powerful, many Windows applications are highly customizable as well. They are packed with features right out of the box but also can be enhanced to meet your specific needs. Word for Windows and Microsoft Excel, for example, include built-in programming languages that far surpass the capabilities of simple macros. Both applications also include customizable toolbars displaying icons that you can click for instant access to commands you use frequently.

Windows 3.1

Windows 3.1, released in the Spring of 1992, adds many features to the already powerful Windows 3.0. To make the upgrade easy, all Windows 3.0 applications are completely compatible with Windows 3.1. You have to upgrade only Windows—not your applications.

The most important new features of Windows 3.1 include TrueType font technology, object linking and embedding (OLE), a new File Manager, drag-and-drop moving and copying, and built-in multimedia extensions.

TrueType is a revolutionary new technology that will bring the magic of fonts to anyone who owns a computer and a printer. In brief, TrueType provides outline fonts that can be scaled to any size and used on both your screen and your printer—at any resolution. With TrueType, you do not need expensive PostScript, and you do not need downloadable fonts that take up a great deal of space on your hard disk and are slow. TrueType is discussed in Chapter 8.

Object linking and embedding (OLE) augments (and greatly expands) what Windows 3.0 knew as *dynamic data exchange*, or DDE. To understand OLE, you need to understand that an *object* is anything—data, picture, or chart—that becomes associated with an application other than the application used to create it; *linking* is including an object within a different application but leaving the object linked to the application used to create it so that the linked object is updated when the original changes; *embedding* puts data from a server application within the document of a client application. This leaves all the data in the final document—data is not linked back to its original application. Through OLE, you can create compound documents made up of objects created by diverse applications. Object linking and embedding is discussed in Chapter 6.

If the new File Manager included with Version 3.1 had added only much greater speed, it would be a hit with veteran Windows users. Besides being considerably faster, however, the new File Manager also offers a whole new look and new features. Its split window shows the contents of a disk on one side and the contents of a selected directory on the other. You can open multiple File Manager windows and display a different drive or directory in each. Using Windows' drag-and-drop feature to move or copy files between drives or directories is easy in Version 3.1. You can learn more about File Manager in Chapter 5.

The new drag-and-drop feature is useful in File Manager and in many Windows applications. In the new File Manager, you can drag a data file onto its application icon to start the application and load the file;you can drag a data file or application file onto the Program Manager to create a program item icon; you can drag a data file onto the running Print Manager to print the file; and as before, you can drag files of any type onto a disk or directory icon to copy or move the files. The drag-and-drop feature also is evident in many Windows applications. You read about the drag-and-drop feature throughout this book.

New multimedia extensions enable you to turn your PC into a musical composition workstation, into a video production studio, or into a reference library. Multimedia means the integration of many media; therefore, a multimedia presentation may consist of text, animation, music, and voice. You can create your own multimedia productions, or you can purchase them pre-made. You need special equipment to turn your PC into a multimedia workstation: a CD-ROM drive, a sound board, and speakers. Learn the details of multimedia in Chapter 17.

Many other aspects of Windows also have been improved with the release of Version 3.1; you read about these changes throughout the book.

 # Windows for Workgroups

By the fall of 1992, more than one million new people were using Windows each month. But many faced problems with communicating and sharing data between people working on the same projects or working in the same organization.

Although Windows 3.1 and its applications gave individuals more productivity, it did nothing to aid the productivity of people working together in groups. People were forced to walk a diskette of files across a building, send internal messages that the company mail room routes through Siberia, and deal with a general lack of coordination. One solution to these problems was to put Windows 3.1 on a network. But most networks require money, a lot of time, and technical expertise.

Microsoft's solution to increasing the productivity of groups of Windows users who work together is Windows for Workgroups. Windows for Workgroups is Windows 3.1 with enhancements that give it networking capability and features to help people work together.

Windows for Workgroups is based on the idea that most work gets done in small groups of people. These groups are usually organized around performing a common task, reaching a common goal, or having a common flow of work and communication. Windows for Workgroups helps these groups by giving them a low-cost, easy-to-install network and application that help people share and communicate. (Appendix B describes in greater detail these three ways to organize workgroups.)

Windows for Workgroups makes connecting a network of computers almost as easy as installing Windows 3.1 by itself. Most networks require one computer to act as a dedicated *server* that controls the network, but Windows for Workgroups shares the networking overhead between all the computers on the network. This reduces the cost of the network. Most networks also require a system administrator who has had technical training. In the peer-to-peer network used by Windows for Workgroups, each user is responsible for his own password, and each user controls who can and can't access her files and printer.

In addition to creating an easy-to-install network, Windows for Workgroups adds features to Windows 3.1 that are designed to help groups of people work together. If you are familiar with Windows 3.1, you will recognize the File Manager and Print Manager in Windows for Workgroups, but these features have been enhanced. With the Windows for Workgroups File Manager and Print Manager, you can share your directories and printers with others in your workgroup. These *shared resources* can even have two levels of sharing so that you can give different people different levels of use.

Windows for Workgroups also includes three powerful applications to help you and your workgroup work together:

> Mail is a message passing system. People in your workgroup can send messages, memos, and files to others in the workgroup. A network *postoffice* stores and forwards mail so that you can pick up your mail when it is convenient to you.

> Schedule+ is a personal or group scheduling application. It will help you manage your time and appointments and monitor when groups of people are available for a meeting. It ties into Mail so that you can notify people of a meeting and confirm when the meeting time is added to their schedule.

> Clipbook enables everyone in your workgroup to share data. It acts like a central scrapbook for everyone in the workgroup. Workgroup users can paste or link data from the Clipbook into their documents. When the chart, table, or data in the Clipbook changes, everyone in the workgroup gets the updated version.

Windows for Workgroups also recognizes when one of its workgroup members is attached to other networks, such as LAN Manager and Novell, and gives you access to the other network. If you need to expand the horizons of Windows for Workgroups, you can buy Microsoft Mail and Schedule+ Extensions, a product from Microsoft, which enables you to link Windows for Workgroups to large networks, mainframes, or off-site (remote) Windows users.

How This Book Is Organized

This book is divided into six parts, beginning with the most basic information and progressing to the most advanced. At the end of the book are two appendixes that describe how to install Windows and Windows for Workgroups.

Part I

Part I, "Getting Started," includes two chapters for those who are new to Windows. If you have never used Windows, these two chapters are a must, because they contain basic information on operating Windows, menus, and dialog boxes. This information is not repeated in individual chapters. Even if you have been using Windows for a while, you may want to scan Chapters 1 and 2 for tips.

Chapter 1, "Operating Windows," teaches you how to perform basic Windows functions. You learn how to start Windows and about the two different modes of running Windows. You also learn how to start an application and how to use its menus and dialog boxes. You learn how to run multiple applications simultaneously and how you can cut and paste information between documents in different applications. You also learn that many things you do in one Windows application are the same in all Windows applications, making it easier to become familiar with more Windows applications.

Chapter 2, "Quick Start: Operating Windows," teaches you the basics of operating Windows. In this quick start, you learn by doing. A sample business scenario enables you to practice while you are learning how to use Windows applications.

Part II

Part II, "Managing Your Windows Work Session," includes chapters that detail the essential elements of Windows, including how to get help, how to use the File Manager, and how to use the Control Panel. In these chapters, you learn how to customize Windows and how to use features shared by all Windows applications.

Chapter 3, "Getting Help," begins with an overview of the application's features and commands. Many Windows applications, including the Windows accessories, include easy-to-use on-line documentation in the form of Help files. You can access Help through a menu, and the Help files in each application work similarly. Windows Help also enables you to search for information by choosing from an index of key topics.

Chapter 4, "Controlling Applications with the Program Manager," presents the Program Manager, which is the heart of Windows. When you start Windows, the Program Manager is what you see on-screen. This highly customizable manager of your Windows session includes several group windows, each containing a group of program item icons that you use to start applications. You can create your own program item icons, and you can organize them inside your own custom windows.

Chapter 5, "Managing Files with the File Manager," shows how you can use the File Manager to copy or move files or groups of files. You also learn to delete or rename files, create or remove directories, format disks, view files in almost any order, and search for files that meet specified criteria. This new, faster File Manager makes extensive use of Windows' drag-and-drop feature to manage files.

If you are using Windows for Workgroups, you will learn to share your directories with other members of the workgroup. You also see how to get information from the shared directories of other members of the workgroup.

Chapter 6 "Embedding and Linking," introduces object linking and embedding, or OLE, which is another exciting Windows innovation. OLE breaks down the barriers between applications, enabling you to create compound documents made up of pieces from several applications. Importantly, linked objects retain their connection to their originating applications, so they can be automatically updated. You can edit and update embedded objects from within the document where they are embedded. For OLE to work, you need a server application (used to create an object) and a client application (where the object is embedded or linked).

If you are part of a workgroup using Windows for Workgroups, you learn to reduce work among the groups members by using the Clipbook. The Clipbook is like a scrapbook in which you can store your personal clippings. But the workgroup Clipbook can share text, tables, and charts with anyone in your workgroup. If workgroup members link to data in the Clipbook, then their document updates whenever the data in the Clipbook updates. The Clipbook makes it easy to keep a group document up-to-date.

Chapter 7, "Customizing with the Control Panel," shows how to take control of the Control Panel, which includes a suite of applications you can use to customize your Windows environment. A Colors application enables you to choose screen colors; a Desktop application enables you to choose background patterns and a screen saver; and a Sounds application enables you to assign sounds to events. A Fonts application enables you to easily install new fonts, and a Printers application enables you to install and connect printers. You can customize your keyboard, your mouse, and your numeric formats. You can set the time and date, install multimedia drivers, and establish network connections. The Network application in the Control Panel gives you the capability to change or control how Windows works within your network.

Chapter 8, "Managing Fonts," introduces one of Windows' most exciting new features—TrueType, a font technology that provides you with high-quality fonts on any printer. TrueType scalable font outlines adapt to screen and any printer that Windows supports (at any resolution) and are instantly available to Windows and Windows applications. To preserve your investment in other types of fonts, TrueType works seamlessly with existing font technologies, such as downloadable and PostScript fonts.

Chapter 9, "Using the Print Manager," shows you how to use the Print Manager to *spool* print jobs. When you print a file from a Windows application, you don't have to wait impatiently until your printer is finished printing before you can start using your computer again. Instead, the Print Manager spools print jobs to the printer, taking over management of printing functions while you continue working. You also can use the Print Manager to install new printers.

When you are printing in Windows for Workgroups, you can use the Print Manager to monitor your print job even if it is printing on a printer located at someone else's computer.

Part III

Part III, "Using Windows Accessories," teaches you how to use the free accessory applications that come with Windows. Windows accessory applications include a word processor, a painting application, a communications application, a macro recorder, multimedia applications, and others. You can use these applications to *accessorize* your primary applications.

Chapter 10, "Using Mail with Windows for Workgroups" discusses Mail, which is a full-featured electronic mail system that comes as part of Windows for Workgroups. By using Mail, you can send, receive, and store messages over the network. You can even attach files to messages so that you can send a message that includes the backup document, spreadsheet, or charts.

Chapter 11, "Using Schedule+ with Windows for Workgroups" discusses how to help you and everyone in your workgroup schedule your time, meetings, and common resources, such as meeting rooms. Schedule can be used as a personal scheduler to help you keep appointments. It will even print schedules in standard time management notebook sizes. Schedule is also designed to work with Mail to make it easy to review when a group of people have a common block of time available for a meeting. Mail incorporates a note for scheduling and confirming group meetings.

Chapter 12, "Using Windows Write," discusses Windows Write, a simple but powerful word processing application that comes free with Windows. In Write, you can enter, edit, and format text just as in any word processor, and you can add tabs, headers, and footers. Write lacks advanced features like spell checking and automatic tables of contents but is upward-compatible with more powerful word processors like Word for Windows, making Write a perfect springboard for moving up to an advanced word processor. Write is an OLE client, into which you can embed objects.

Chapter 13, "Using Windows Paintbrush," discusses Windows Paintbrush, a fun and colorful painting program you can use to create illustrations in a rainbow of colors and shades. Use Paintbrush's many painting tools to create fanciful works of art or serious illustrations for business use. Paintbrush is an OLE server that you can use to create objects embedded in client documents

Chapter 14, "Using Windows Terminal," shows how you can use Windows Terminal (if your computer is equipped with a modem) to manage your communications. For easy access to modems or on-line services that you use frequently, such as CompuServe, you can create files containing all the information you need to make a connection. Use Terminal to connect to another computer and to upload and download files.

Chapter 15, "Using Windows Recorder," shows how many of the tasks you perform over and over can be automated using a macro. The Recorder records as a macro a series of steps that you perform in one or more Windows applications. With the Recorder application running, you can play back your macro to instantly duplicate the keystrokes and mouse movements you recorded.

Chapter 16, "Using Desktop Accessories," describes each of the smaller accessory programs that come with Windows. Using the Cardfile, you can keep track of names and addresses in a file that looks like a stack of indexed cards. You can even automatically dial a phone number on a cardfile card, if your computer has a modem. The Calendar provides you with a visual calendar into which you can schedule your appointments for years to come. You can mark important appointments with a beep to remind you when it is time for your appointment. Start up the Calculator to do quick calculations, or complex scientific calculations, and copy the results into your primary application. Use the clock when you need to watch the time, minimizing the clock to an icon at the bottom of your screen.

If you are using Windows for Workgroups, you have three additional accessories to help you use the network. Chat is a simple two-way typing screen on which you and anyone else in your workgroup can type simultaneously. You can *chat* back and forth in Chat and get more immediate results than sending a message by Mail.

The other two accessories are used to help you manage your computer on the Windows for Workgroups network. Unlike most other networks, you have full control over your computer on the network. The WinMeter accessory shows how your computer's time is being spent between your applications and its network housekeeping duties. The Net Watcher accessory lets you see who is using the files, directories, and printers that you are sharing with others in your workgroup.

Chapter 17, "Multimedia," introduces the two accessory programs new with Windows 3.1 that you can use with your multimedia equipment. Sound Recorder enables you to create your own music, blend and mix tunes, and record your own voice. Media Player enables you to play existing music files, and Windows comes equipped with two 2-minute tunes that sound pretty amazing, coming out of your computer. To take advantage of multimedia, you need to equip your PC with a sound board, a CD-ROM drive, and speakers. Optionally, you can add a MIDI-based keyboard, a microphone, a VCR, and other equipment. With a multimedia-equipped PC (or MPC), you can create your own multimedia productions or take advantage of animated, speaking stories and reference libraries available for purchase.

Part IV

Part IV, "Using Windows Applets," includes chapters that describe how to use the *applets* or mini-applications that come free with some Windows applications such as Word for Windows, Microsoft Excel, and Microsoft Publisher. Applets create objects embedded within a document and can be opened only from within another application.

Chapter 18, "Using Microsoft Draw," concentrates on Microsoft Draw, one of several OLE-based *applets*, or mini-applications that comes free with some Windows applications like Word for Windows, Microsoft Publisher, and PowerPoint. Draw is a drawing program that creates editable, layerable, colorful objects. As an object-oriented application, which creates lines, squares, and shapes that you can resize, move, or reshape, Draw is a good complement to Paintbrush, which is a bit-map application that creates paintings in one layer. As an applet, Draw can be used only from within a client application, such as Word for Windows or Microsoft Excel.

Chapter 19, "Using Microsoft Graph," demonstrates the benefits of easy-to-use graphing that Microsoft Excel users have enjoyed for years. All the power of Excel is available to owners of applications like Word for Windows which include, for free, the Microsoft Graph applet. You can use Graph to create line, bar, column, pie, scatter, combination, and 3-D graphs in a variety of styles, and you can type the data you want to use as the basis for your graph, or you can copy or import existing data. Like Draw, Graph is an applet that you can use only from within an OLE-capable client application.

Chapter 20, "Using WordArt," shows you how to use WordArt, a simple applet, to create logos and fancy typography. You can use WordArt to turn, twist, and stretch words into almost any shape. Many different fonts are available, and you can type words in any color that your computer can produce. You can add a shadow effect to characters or include a colored or shaded background. As an applet, WordArt works only from within a client application. Like all applets, although WordArt comes free with only some applications (such as Word for Windows), after it is on your computer, WordArt is available to any application that supports OLE.

Chapter 21, "Using the Equation Editor," shows you how to use the Equation Editor that comes free with Word for Windows. If you create scientific papers or mathematical treatises, you will be grateful for the Equation Editor, which solves the problem of how to include mathematical and scientific symbols in your document by presenting you with a range of symbols from which you can choose. You can include numbers and letters with your symbols to create a working equation. As an applet, Equation Editor works only from within client applications.

Part V

Part V, "Running Applications," teaches you how to use Windows applications together and how to use DOS applications in Windows.

Chapter 22, "Using Windows Applications Together," teaches you about Windows' powerful capability to share data between applications. You can run more than one application, switch between applications, and exchange data between applications. Tips help you integrate some of the most commonly used Windows applications such as Microsoft Excel, Word for Windows, and others.

Chapter 23, "Running DOS Applications," demonstrates how you can use your existing DOS applications during a Windows work session. You can run DOS applications in a special window and can copy and paste data between DOS and Windows applications using simple Windows techniques.

Chapter 24, "Customizing PIFs," shows you how to optimize the performance of DOS applications by customizing PIFs. A PIF is a program information file that contains technical specifications. Although a PIF already exists for many DOS applications, you can improve performance by optimizing the PIF for your own computer configuration. In this chapter, you also learn how to create a PIF for DOS applications that don't have one.

Part VI

Part VI, "Customizing and Tuning Windows," gives you the information to fine-tune Windows for optimal performance and teaches you how to set up Windows to run on a network. A chapter on troubleshooting lists some of the most common problems with Windows.

Chapter 25, "Enhancing Windows Performance," shows you how to improve performance with a few simple adjustments to the configuration information integrated into Windows files when you install the program. Turn to this chapter to get the most out of your computer and Windows.

Chapter 26, "Enhancing DOS Application Performance," shows you tuning techniques for DOS applications that can help you get the best performance from your DOS applications.

 Chapter 27, "Networking with Windows for Workgroups," begins with a short description and definitions to help you understand how networks work. It then shows you how to get on and off the network and how to share such resources as disk drives and printers with other members of your work group. Because groups of people and networks are dynamic, you also learn how to change workgroup and user names and change your password. This chapter also presents tips on improving performance when using Windows for Workgroups.

Chapter 28, "Networking Windows," teaches you how Windows works with common networks, such as Novell. If you are setting up Windows to run on a network, turn to this chapter.

Chapter 29, "Troubleshooting," provides solutions to the problems that everyone runs into with their computer now and then. Many times, you will find that the fix is simpler than you expect.

Chapter 30, "Help, Support, and Resources," teaches you who to call to get answers to pressing questions and where to turn for on-going support. Despite all your best efforts at finding the answer yourself, sometimes you need help.

Appendixes

Appendix A, "Installing Windows," tells you how to install Windows 3.1 if it is still sitting in a box on your desk. You will find the installation easier than you may expect.

Appendix B, "Installing Windows for Workgroups" has a few more steps than installing Windows, but once the network adaptor cards are installed, installing Windows for Workgroups is no more difficult than normal Windows. In Appendix B, you learn about network cards and cabling and the system requirements for Windows for Workgroups. You also learn about the decisions you need to make before you begin the process of installing Windows for Workgroups.

How To Use This Book

To use this book, start with Part I, especially if you are a beginner. To get right to work, go to the specific chapters that interest you. To become more familiar with Windows, focus on Part II, where you can learn the details of working with Windows.

Two important reference tools begin and end the book: a table of contents and an index. When you are not sure exactly what you want to learn, browse through the table of contents at the beginning of the book to get an overview of Windows features and applications. Then turn to the chapter that seems most relevant. If you know exactly what you want to find, look it up in the index at the end of the book. After you become familiar with Windows, take some time to browse through the table of contents to look for features you may have passed over when you were a beginner. You are likely to learn some valuable tips.

Tip boxes appear at appropriate locations throughout the book to provide information that increases your productivity or improves your understanding. These boxes also provide important information you need to ensure that you do not make an error, lose data, or damage software or equipment.

T I P

The icon depicting a handshake indicates information for users of Windows for Workgroups.

Where To Find More Help

You can get additional information about Windows and products designed for Windows from Que, the leading publisher of personal computer books for business. Some of the Windows and Windows application books available from Que include the following:

Connecting Windows 3.1 for Workgroups
Windows 3.1 QuickStart
Windows 3.1 Quick Reference
Upgrading to Windows 3.1
Using Word for Windows 2, Special Edition
Look Your Best with Word for Windows
Easy Word for Windows
Using Excel 4 for Windows, Special Edition
Excel Trade Secrets for Windows
Excel 4 for Windows QuickStart
Using PageMaker 4 for Windows
Using WordPerfect for Windows, Special Edition
Look Your Best with WordPerfect for Windows
Using 1-2-3 for Windows
Using Microsoft Works for Windows, Special Edition
Using Paradox for Windows
Using Quattro Pro for Windows

For more information about ordering Que books, call 1-800-428-5331.

Getting Started

PART

1

OUTLINE

Operating Windows

Windows is a graphical working *environment* that makes it easier to use your computer. Under Windows, each application runs in a *window* on your screen that you can open or close. You can run multiple applications at the same time, each in its own window, and you easily can switch between applications. Your knowledge of one application transfers to each new application you use because each Windows application operates in a similar way.

What you learn in this chapter and the next will help you operate any Windows application. Both chapters contain important information about operating Windows but present the information in different ways. This chapter gives full explanations and suggests alternative ways of accomplishing tasks. In Chapter 2, you actually start Windows and perform basic procedures but with a minimum of explanation. After completing these chapters, you should learn how to start and manage applications with the Program Manager as described in Chapter 4 and how to manage your disk and files with the File Manager as described in Chapter 5. From there, you can jump to any other chapter in this book.

In this chapter, you learn that Windows is easy to operate and that operating one Windows application is similar to operating another. This "learning carry-over" is important—when you start a new Windows application, you already understand most of the concepts necessary to operate it. You know how to choose, find, and use most commands.

This chapter shows you how to control the location, size, and status of windows that contain applications. You also learn the three methods of choosing commands and working with applications. The first method uses a mouse and is excellent for graphics applications and for learning new applications. The second method uses the keyboard—touch typists usually prefer this method of choosing commands and entering data. The third method uses shortcut key combinations and improves everyone's efficiency.

Starting Windows

If you have not yet installed Windows, turn to the Appendix to learn how. After installed, Windows is easy to start:

1. Type *C:* or the drive designator of the drive where you installed Windows.

2. Press Enter.

3. Type *WIN* and press Enter.

   If your computer displays the prompt that designates the drive containing Windows (such as C:), you need only this step to start Windows.

When you start Windows, the Program Manager appears on your screen as a window that contains other windows and icons (see fig. 1.1). The windows inside the Program Manager window, such as the open *Main* window in the figure, contain icons that represent applications. The icons (pictures with names below them) at the bottom of the Program Manager window represent closed windows.

When you first install Windows, you see that the Program Manager contains the Main window, which includes utilities to help you manage files, work with DOS, customize Windows, and install new printer drivers. The Program Manager also includes the Accessories window, which includes applications you can use to accessorize your main applications; the Games window, which contains two games you can use to learn how to use Windows; and, if Windows detects existing Windows applications, an Applications window, which contains your Windows and DOS applications.

As you'll learn in this chapter and in Chapter 4, you can customize your Windows start-up screen in many ways. You can create new windows and new icons to go in the windows. Each icon can represent an application or an application and a data file (so that when you start the application the data file opens automatically). The applications and files can be located in different directories on your disk, and different icons can represent the same application in different windows. If you customize your Program Manager, windows and icons different from those shown in figure 1.1 may appear when you start Windows on your computer.

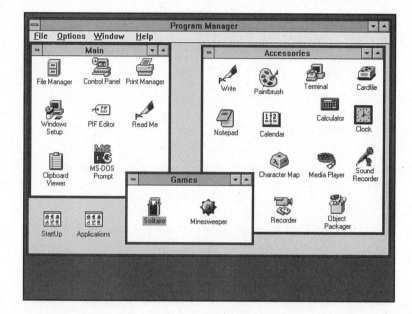

FIG. 1.1

The Program Manager with the Main, Accessories, and Games groups.

You can start Windows *and* an application from the DOS prompt by typing *WIN*, a space, and the application name and then pressing Enter. To start Windows and Word for Windows, for example, type *WIN WINWORD* at the DOS prompt and then press Enter. The application name and the path to the subdirectory containing your application must be listed in your AUTOEXEC.BAT file. (Most applications automatically update the AUTOEXEC.BAT file when installed.)

T I P

For Related Information:

▸▸   See "Starting Windows," p. 66.

FROM HERE...

Choosing an Operating Mode

Windows runs in one of two modes—standard or 386-enhanced. Your ability to use 386-enhanced mode depends on your equipment. When you start Windows, the application examines your PC and then runs in the mode best suited for your equipment. (You can force your PC to start in the standard mode, however, by typing WIN/S at the DOS prompt, and you can force it to start in 386-enhanced mode by typing WIN/3 at the DOS prompt.) Each mode has different operating capabilities and uses memory differently. Standard mode operates in extended memory; 386-enhanced mode operates in extended memory and accesses the virtual memory functions built into the 386 processor, so your PC seems to have more memory than is actually installed.

Windows starts in 386-enhanced mode if you have a 386 or 486 PC with more than 2M of memory. This default is meant for people who are running some DOS applications under Windows. If you are not running any DOS applications, you are better off running Windows in standard mode. In 386-enhanced mode, Windows creates *virtual machines* of memory, which often are about 640K (but are determined by settings in the PIF) because many DOS applications cannot use more than 640K, for the DOS applications to use. This is restrictive for Windows applications that don't have the memory restriction and can use any amount of memory available to them. To start Windows in standard mode, type *WIN/S* (or *WIN/2*) at the DOS prompt. You can set up your PC so that you start Windows in standard mode by creating a batch file called WIN.BAT that includes only one command: WIN/S. (If you need to start a Windows session in which you will use DOS applications, you can override the batch file and start in 386-enhanced mode by typing *WIN/3* at the DOS prompt.)

FROM HERE...

For Related Information:

▶▶ To learn more about operating modes, see "Understanding How Windows Uses Memory," p. 965 and "Operating DOS Applications Efficiently," p. 982.

▶▶ See also "Using Memory Efficiently," p. 962.

Working in the Windows Environment

Windows uses concepts that, for many people, make computers easier to use. The basic organizational concept is that all applications run on a desktop, and each application runs in its own window. Windows can run multiple applications just as you may have stacks of papers on your desk from more than one project. You can move the windows and change their size just as you can move and rearrange the stacks of papers on your desk.

Just as you can cut, copy, and paste parts between papers on your real desktop, Windows enables you to cut or copy information from one application and paste the information into another. Some Windows applications even share *live* information; when you change data in one application, Windows automatically updates linked data in other applications.

Making entries, edits, and changes to information is similar in all Windows applications. The basic procedure is as follows:

1. Activate the window containing the desired application.

2. Select the text or graphics object you want to change.

3. Choose a command from the menu at the top of the application.

4. Select options from a dialog box if one appears and complete the command by choosing OK or pressing Enter.

Learning the Parts of the Windows Screen

Figure 1.2 shows a Windows desktop containing multiple applications, each in its own window. The parts of a typical Windows screen are labeled in the figure.

With the *mouse pointer*, you can control Windows applications quickly and intuitively. It enables you to choose commands, select options, and move on-screen items. When you move the mouse, the mouse pointer moves accordingly. The mouse pointer changes shape at different locations on-screen to indicate that it has different capabilities at that point. You select items on-screen by positioning the pointer on the item to be selected and then pressing or holding down the mouse button. You use three actions to control the pointer in Windows: *clicking*, *double-clicking*, and *dragging* (see table 1.1 later in this chapter).

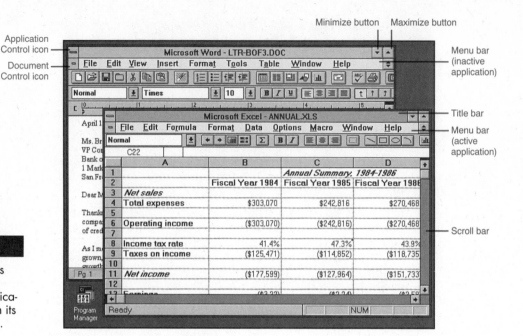

FIG. 1.2

The Windows
desktop with
multiple applica-
tions, each in its
own window.

The *Control icon* opens a menu that contains commands to control window location, size, and status (open or closed). Each application and
each document window has its own Control icon and menu. The *application Control icon* appears at the left edge of the application title bar.
The *document Control icon* appears at the left edge of the document title
bar (if the document window is smaller than full-screen) or at the left
edge of the menu bar (if the document window is full-screen). To open
an application Control menu, press Alt, space bar; to open a document
Control menu, press Alt, hyphen (-). You can open either menu by clicking the pointer on the Control icon.

The *title bar* at the top of each window contains the name of the application. After you save a file, the title bar also shows the file name. The
title bar is one color when the window is active and another color when
the window is inactive. (The *active window* is the window on top; it
contains the currently running application.)

Menu names are located in the *menu bar* directly under the title bar.
Windows applications use the same menu headings for common functions (such as File, Edit, Window, and Help) to make it easy for you to
learn new applications. Select a menu by clicking on it with the left
mouse button or by pressing Alt and then the underlined letter in the
menu name. (This book shows the letter you press in **bold** type: for
example, File.)

Icons are small pictorial representations. Some icons in Windows represent applications in memory that do not currently occupy a window. Icons appear along the bottom of the desktop or within the Program Manager window. To reduce the clutter of a filled desktop, you can minimize windows to icons. When you want to work with the application, restore icons into windows by using mouse techniques or the Control menu.

Application windows are the windows containing applications. *Document windows* appear inside application windows and contain documents. In many (but not all) applications, you can have several document windows open at a time; you switch between them by pressing Ctrl+F6 or by selecting the document you want from the **W**indow menu.

In applications, you use *scroll bars* to move up and down in a document or from left to right in documents wider than the screen.

You can *maximize* a window by clicking on the Maximize button—an upward pointing arrow at the top right of the window—so that it occupies the full screen, or you can *minimize* a window by clicking on the Minimize button—a downward pointing icon at the top right of a window. Double-click the minimized icon to return it to a window. (When a window is maximized, you can *restore* it to its previous size.) You also can minimize, maximize, and restore windows by choosing commands from the application or document Control menu.

You can resize a window by dragging its *window border* with the mouse or by choosing the **S**ize command from the Control menu. You can move a window without resizing by dragging its title bar with the mouse or by choosing the Move command from the Control menu.

Using the Mouse and the Keyboard

The *mouse* is a hand-held pointing device that controls the position of a pointer on-screen. As you move the mouse across your actual desktop or mouse pad, the pointer moves across the screen in the same direction. The mouse acts as an extension of your hand, enabling you to point to objects on-screen. The mouse works well for people unfamiliar with a keyboard, for new users, or for people using graphics and desktop publishing applications.

To use a mouse, hold it so that the cable extends forward from your fingers and the mouse's body nestles under the palm of your hand. Place your index finger and second finger on the buttons. Move the mouse on your desk to move the pointer on-screen; click the left mouse button to make a selection. (Windows and Windows applications use the left button to indicate most selections, but you can use the Control

Panel to make the right button the selector button if you find that button more convenient.) The most common use of the mouse is to select menus, commands, text, graphics objects, or windows so that you can change them with a command. In graphics applications and desktop publishing applications, you usually use the mouse to select menus, options, and icons and to select and move objects on-screen.

The mouse senses movement through the rotating ball on its undercarriage. To use a mouse, your desktop surface must be smooth and clean. If possible, do not run the mouse on paper or cardboard surfaces; the lint from paper or cardboard can clog the ball and cause the pointer to skip. The ideal surface is a specially-designed mouse pad. If you have an optical or laser mouse, you may have a special surface on which you must move your mouse.

To use a mouse, you need a clear area on your desk next to the keyboard. You don't have to clean your whole desktop—you only need a six- or eight-inch square of space for the mouse. Using the Control Panel, you can increase or decrease the sensitivity of the mouse so that you need a smaller or larger area to move the mouse.

To select an object or menu item using the mouse, follow these steps:

1. Move the mouse so that the tip of the mouse pointer, usually an arrow, is on the name, graphics object, or text you want to select.

2. Quickly press and release the left mouse button.

Throughout this book, this two-step process is called *clicking*. Clicking the mouse button twice in rapid succession while pointing is called *double-clicking*. Double-clicking produces an action different from clicking. In a word processing application, for example, you click to position the insertion point, but you double-click to select a word.

You also can use the mouse for *dragging*. Dragging selects multiple text characters or moves graphic objects such as windows. In figure 1.3, a sentence in the Write word processor is selected.

To drag with the mouse, follow these steps:

1. Move the mouse so that the tip of the pointer is on the object or at the beginning of the text you want to select. (When over text, the pointer appears as an I-beam.)

2. Press and hold down the mouse button.

3. While holding down the mouse button, move the mouse. If you are dragging a graphical object, the object moves when you move the mouse. If you are selecting text, the highlighted text area expands when you move the mouse.

4. Release the mouse button.

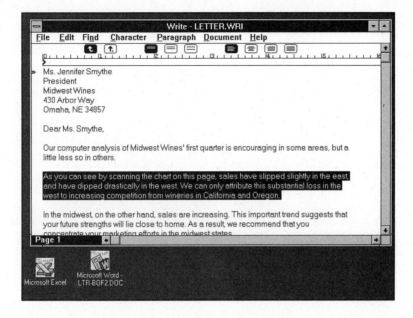

FIG. 1.3

Selected text.

The mouse is a useful tool, but you can use the keyboard to do nearly everything you can do with the mouse. (Table 1.1 describes keyboard actions in detail.) The mouse and the keyboard work as a team for controlling Windows applications. You can perform some tasks more easily with the mouse and some more easily with the keyboard. Most Windows applications can perform all functions with either. Experiment with the mouse and the keyboard and use each where it works best for you.

For Related Information:

FROM HERE...

▶▶ To learn more about working with groups, see "Customizing Groups," p. 119.

▶▶ To learn more about the File Manager, see " Understanding the File Manager's Display," p. 141.

Understanding Windows Terminology

Table 1.1 introduces terms, mouse actions, and keystrokes that describe certain actions. The first part of the table contains general terms describing Windows actions. The next part defines keystrokes and mouse actions that produce consistent results in most Windows applications. Refer to this table as you continue reading *Using Windows 3.1, Special Edition.*

Table 1.1 Basic Terminology of Windows and of This Book

Term	Definition
Special Terms Used in Windows	
Choose	Execute a command or complete a dialog box.
Select	Select an item to activate it so that you can change it. Selecting a command or option turns it on but does not complete it. Selected options show a black dot or an *X*. Selected text appears in reversed type. Selected graphics appear enclosed by a dashed line or fenced in by boxes known as *handles.*
Unselect or Deselect	Remove the selection.

Mouse Terms

Note: A comma indicates that you release the first key before pressing the second key. A plus (+) indicates that you press and hold down the first key and then press the second key.

Term	Definition
Point	Move the mouse so that the arrow pointer is on the desired menu name, command name, or graphic object, or so that the I-beam pointer (used in text) is where you want the insertion point (cursor) to be.
Pointer	The on-screen symbol controlled by the mouse. As you move the mouse on the desk, the pointer moves on-screen. The pointer changes shape to indicate the current status and the type of functions and selections available. An arrow means that you can select menus, commands, or objects. An I-beam means that the pointer is over text that you can edit. A two-headed or four-headed arrow means that you can move the edge or item. An hourglass means that you must wait while the application works. A crosshair means that you can draw.

Term	Definition
I-beam	When the mouse pointer is in an area of text that you can edit, the pointer appears as a vertical I-beam. Reposition the flashing insertion point (cursor) by positioning the I-beam and clicking.
Mouse button	The mouse usually has two buttons. (Some mice have three.) Normally, clicking the left button completes an action; clicking the center or right button does nothing in Windows. (Clicking the right mouse button performs a specific function in some Windows applications.) You can switch the action of the left and right buttons through the Control Panel.
Click	Quickly press and release the mouse button as you point to the item indicated. Clicking is used to reposition the insertion point in text, select a menu, choose a command from a menu, or select an option from a dialog box.
Drag	Select multiple text characters or move objects by pointing to them and holding down the left mouse button as you move the mouse.
Double-click	Rapidly press and release the left mouse button twice as you point to the indicated item. Double-clicking on an icon or file name opens an application or window related to that icon or file name.
Shift+click	Press and hold down the Shift key as you click. Use Shift+click to select multiple consecutive file names or to select text between the current insertion point and where you press Shift+click.
Ctrl+click	Press and hold down the Control (Ctrl) key as you click. Use Ctrl+click to select multiple nonconsecutive file names or item choices.

Keyboard Actions

Note: A comma indicates that you release the first key before pressing the second key. A plus (+) indicates that you press and hold down the first key and then press the second key.

Alt, *letter*	Press and release the Alt key and then press *letter*. This action opens a menu without choosing a command.
Alt+*letter*	Press and hold down the Alt key as you press *letter*. This action opens a menu or selects an option in a dialog box.

continues

Table 1.1 Continued

Term	Definition
Letter	Press the indicated letter to choose a command in a menu. To choose a command, press the letter in the command that is <u>underlined</u> on-screen (this book shows the letter you are to press in **bold** type). Press **M**, for example, to choose the **M**ove command. You can press the uppercase or lowercase letter.
Arrow key	Press the appropriate directional arrow key.

Keystrokes To Control Windows

Note: A comma indicates that you release the first key before pressing the second key. A plus (+) indicates that you press and hold down the first key and then press the second key.

Alt+Esc	Activate the next application window or icon on the desktop. Pressing Alt+Esc does not restore icons into windows.
Alt+Tab	Activate the *next* application window or icon. Restores icons into windows. Only the application's title bar or a box displaying the application's name shows until you release Alt+Tab, making it faster to cycle through application windows than to use Alt+Esc.
Alt+Shift+Tab	Activate the *previous* icon or application. Restore icons into a window. Only the application's title bar or a box displaying the application's name shows until you release Alt+Tab.
Ctrl+F6	Activate the next document window (if an application has multiple document windows open).
Ctrl+Tab	Activate the next group window within the Program Manager.
Ctrl+Esc	Display the Task List window, from which you can activate an application by selecting from a list of currently running applications.
Alt+space bar	Select the Control menu for the active application icon or window so that you can control the location, size, and status of the window.
Alt+hyphen (-)	Select the Control menu for the active *document* window within the *application* window so that you can control the location, size, and status of the document window.

Term	Definition

Keystrokes To Control the Menus

Note: A comma indicates that you release the first key before pressing the second key. A plus (+) indicates that you press and hold down the first key and then press the second key.

Alt	Activate the menu bar.
Alt, *letter*	Select the menu indicated by *letter* (*letter* is <u>underlined</u> on-screen; *letter* is displayed in **bold** in this book).
Letter	Choose (execute) the command in the menu indicated by *letter*.
Arrow keys	Select but do not choose the next menu (use the right or left arrows) or the next command (use the up or down arrows).
Enter	Choose (execute) the selected command in the menu.
Esc	Close the current menu without making a choice. Press Esc a second time to deactivate the menu bar and return to the document.

Keystrokes To Control Dialog Boxes

Note: See table 1.2 in the up-coming section, "Selecting Options from Dialog Boxes," for more information.

Arrow keys	Select or scroll file names in a list box. Select round option buttons in a group.
Tab	Select the next text box, list box, group of options, or button.
Shift+Tab	Select the *previous* text box, list box, group of options, or button.
Alt+*letter*	Select the option, text box, or list box specified by *letter* (*letter* is <u>underlined</u> on-screen; *letter* is displayed in **bold** in this book).
Space bar	Select or deselect the active check box or button.
Enter	Choose the bold or outlined button (usually the OK button). This action completes the command or opens another dialog box.
Esc	Close an open dialog box without making any changes.

Controlling the Windows in Windows

Just as you move papers on your desktop, you can move and reorder windows on-screen. In fact, you can resize windows, expand them to full size, shrink them to a small icon to save space, and restore them to their original size.

All these activities take place by choosing options on a Control menu or with a mouse action. Every application and document window has a Control menu icon located at the left edge of the window's title bar. Figure 1.4 shows an open application Control menu.

FIG. 1.4

The Paintbrush Control menu.

In an application window, the Control menu icon looks like a space bar in a box. To activate it with the keyboard, press Alt, space bar. In a document window in an application, the Control menu icon looks like a hyphen in a box. To activate it with the keyboard, press Alt, hyphen (-). To activate either Control menu with the mouse, click on the Control menu icon.

Many of the commands in a document Control menu are the same as those in an application Control menu. The application Control menu, however, controls the application window; the document Control menu controls the document window within the application. The commands in a Control menu are given in the following chart.

Command	Action
Restore	Restores an icon or maximized window to its *previous* window size. The shortcut-key combination is Ctrl+F5 (for a document window).
Move	Moves the currently selected icon or window to a new location when you press the arrow keys. The shortcut-key combination is Ctrl+F7 (for a document window).
Size	Resize a window by moving its edge. The shortcut-key combination is Ctrl+F8 (for a document window).
Mi**n**imize	Minimize a window into an icon. In most cases, this command applies only to application windows.
Ma**x**imize	Increase an application window or icon to its full size. The shortcut-key combination is Ctrl+F10 (for a document window).
Close	Exits an application or closes a document window. If changes were made to the current file since the last save, the application asks whether you want to save the file. The shortcut-key combinations are Alt+F4 (for an application window) and Ctrl+F4 (for a document window).
S**w**itch To	Displays the Task List so that you can switch to a different application. The shortcut-key combination is Ctrl+Esc.
Next Window	Activates the next document window in applications that enable multiple documents to run simultaneously; works only when multiple document windows are open. The shortcut-key combination is Ctrl+F6.

When you size or move a window using the mouse pointer, the mouse pointer changes appearance to indicate what change you can make. The different mouse-pointer appearances are listed and described in the following chart.

Pointer Appearance	Mouse Action
⟷	Drag the edge left or right.
↕	Drag the edge up or down.
⬂	Drag the corner in any direction.
✛	Drag the window to a new location.

Moving a Window or an Icon

With Windows, you can move a window to any location on-screen. You can arrange applications on your Windows desktop as neatly or as messily as your real desktop.

To move a window with the mouse, activate the window by clicking on it; then place the pointer on the window's title bar, press and hold down the mouse button, drag the outline of the window to the new location, and release the button. Move icons in the same way.

To move a window with the keyboard, activate the window you want to move by pressing Alt+Tab or Alt+Esc until the window is active. Select the Control menu by pressing Alt, space bar or Alt, hyphen; then choose **M**ove. A four-headed arrow appears, and the window borders turn gray. Press the arrow keys to move the shadowed borders to where you want the window and then press Enter.

To move a program or group icon with the keyboard, press Alt+Esc to select the icon. Press Alt, space bar to display the Control menu and then select **M**ove from the Control menu. Press the arrow keys until the icon is where you want it.

You cannot move a maximized window (if you open the Control menu in a maximized window, the Move command is dimmed—unavailable). To move a maximized window, you must restore it to a smaller size (see the following section).

Changing the Size of a Window

To change the size of a window with the mouse, activate the window by clicking on it. Move the pointer to one edge or corner of the window until the pointer changes into a two-headed arrow (see the preceding chart). Press and hold down the mouse button and drag the double-headed arrow to move the edge or corner of the window and resize the window. When the window is the size you want, release the mouse button.

To change the size of a window with the keyboard, press Alt+Tab or Alt+Esc to activate the window you want to resize. Choose the Control menu and select **S**ize to display a four-headed arrow in the window. Press the arrow key that points to the edge you want to resize. A double-headed arrow jumps to the edge you selected. Press the appropriate arrow key to move the selected edge. When the window is the size you want, press Enter. To return the window to its original size, press Esc while the edges are shadowed.

You cannot size a maximized window (if you open the Control menu in a maximized window, the Size command is dimmed—unavailable). To size a maximized window, you must restore it to a smaller size (see the following sections on maximizing, minimizing, and restoring).

Moving Two Edges at the Same Time
To move two edges at once with the mouse, move the pointer to the corner of a window so that the pointer becomes a two-headed arrow tilted at a 45-degree angle. Drag the corner to its new location and release the mouse button.

To move two edges at once with the keyboard, choose the Control Size Command so that a four-headed arrow appears. Press the arrow key that points to the first edge you want to move (for example, press the left arrow to select the left edge); then press the arrow key that points to the second edge of the corner. A double-headed arrow appears pointing to the corner you selected. Press the arrow keys to move that corner to its new location; press Enter to fix the corner.

Maximizing a Window to Full Size

When you are working in an application, you may find it convenient to maximize the application window so that it fills the screen. If the application includes document windows, you can maximize the document windows so that they fill the entire inside of the application window. When you maximize a window, you hide other windows and icons, but they are still active.

To maximize a window with the mouse pointer, click the Maximize button at the top right of the window (the up arrow) or double-click in the title bar. Restore the window to its previous size by clicking the Restore icon that appears at the top right of the window (the double arrow that appears only in a maximized window) or by double-clicking in the maximized window's title bar.

You can maximize or restore windows with the keyboard by choosing the Control Maximize or Control Restore command. When a window is already restored, the Restore command is unavailable (appears in gray) in the menu.

You cannot move or size a maximized window.

Minimizing and Restoring Windows and Icons

When you have too many windows on-screen, you can clean up the screen by changing windows into icons. As you know, *icons* are small pictorial representations of an application (or, in the Program Manager, of a closed group window). Usually, application icons are stored at the bottom of the screen (see fig. 1.5). Icons usually show a name, symbol, or shape that indicates the application they represent. They also can show their active file or document. The icons at the bottom of figure 1.5 are for the Excel, Paintbrush, Recorder, Terminal, Program Manager, File Manager, Clock, and Calendar applications. In the figure, Word for Windows and its document are sized and positioned at less than the maximum so that you have immediate access to the applications shown as icons at the bottom of the screen.

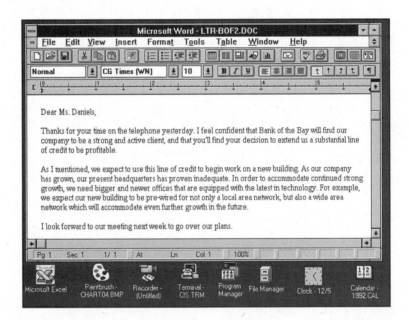

FIG. 1.5

Icons representing applications available in memory that are not in a window.

Application icons represent applications that are in memory but not in a window. Windows applications can continue running even when minimized into an icon. The Clock application, for example, continues to tell time.

With a mouse, you can reduce a window to an icon by clicking on the Minimize button (the down-arrow located at the right edge of the application's title bar). Restore an icon into a window by double-clicking on the icon (if you cannot see the icon, move the window covering it). You also can restore an icon to a window by activating the Task List and selecting the application from the list (to activate the Task List, double-click on the desktop background or press Ctrl+Esc) .

From the keyboard, you can minimize windows into icons by pressing Alt, space bar to display the Control menu and then choosing **Mi**nimize. To restore an icon to its previous size with the keyboard, choose **R**estore from the Control menu. Or, press and hold down Alt+Tab until the icon is selected. When you release Alt+Tab, the selected icon restores itself into a window.

To select an icon but not restore it, press Alt+Esc until the icon is selected. Press Alt, space bar to display the Control menu for that application. Choose any of the Control commands such as **R**estore, **Ma**ximize, or **C**lose.

You can close an application by choosing the Control **C**lose command. If you made changes to the file since the last save, you are asked whether you want to save the changes. Some DOS applications require special closing procedures. For full details on DOS applications, refer to Chapter 23.

For Related Information:

▶▶ To learn more about working with groups, see "Customizing Groups," p. 119.

FROM HERE...

Using Menus and Dialog Boxes

Every Windows application operates in a similar way. As you have already learned, you can move and resize all windows the same way in every application. You also execute commands in the same way in all Windows applications. Commands are listed in menus whose names appear at the top of the window. You can choose commands from a menu by using the mouse or the keyboard (many timesaving shortcuts exist for choosing commands, too). If a command needs information from you, a dialog box appears after you choose the command. You can use the mouse or the keyboard to choose options or enter values in dialog boxes.

Choosing Menus and Commands

When a menu is selected as shown in figures 1.6 and 1.7, its commands appear in a list. If you're not sure where to find a command, try browsing through the menus until you find the command you need. Many applications use similar commands for similar actions—a practice that makes learning multiple Windows applications easier.

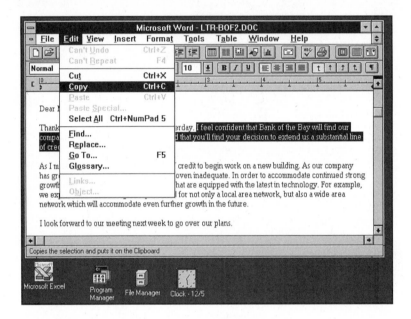

FIG. 1.6

Microsoft Word's Edit menu.

To choose a command with the mouse, follow these steps:

1. Position the tip of the mouse pointer on the menu name in the menu bar and click the left mouse button.

2. Click on the command name in the menu.

To choose a command with the keyboard, follow these steps:

1. Press and release the Alt key to activate the menu bar.

2. Type the underlined letter in the name of the menu you want.

3. Type the underlined letter in the name of the command you want.

   or

   Press the down arrow to select the command you want and then press Enter.

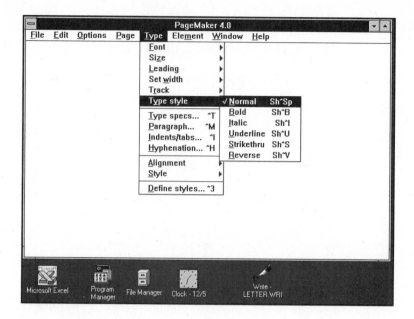

FIG. 1.7

PageMaker 4.0's
Type menu with
a submenu
displayed.

Another way to choose commands with the keyboard is to press Alt,
Enter to open the first menu, press the left and right arrows to open
adjacent menus, and then press the up and down arrows to select the
command you want from the open menu. Press Enter to choose the
selected command.

You can choose commands that appear in a menu in solid black (bold)
type. You performed all the steps necessary to activate a command
that appears in bold.

You cannot choose commands that appear in gray in a menu. You can
see the gray command, but you cannot choose it. If a command you
want to choose appears in gray, you probably forgot a step that is required before you can choose it. For the **Edit C**opy command to appear
in bold type, for example, you must select what you want to copy.

Command names followed by an ellipsis (...) display an additional dialog box or window from which you can choose options or enter data. If
you choose **Edit F**ind... from a Windows application, for example, a box
appears in which you type the word you want to find.

Commands with a check mark to the left are commands that toggle on
and off. A check mark indicates the command is on; no check mark
indicates the command is off. In Windows Write, for example, a check
mark next to the **B**old command in the **C**haracter menu indicates that
bold is *on* for the currently selected text.

Commands with key combinations listed to the right have shortcuts. In Word for Windows, for example, the Edit Copy command lists a shortcut of Ctrl+C. To copy text, you can choose Edit Copy or press Ctrl+C.

Commands with an arrowhead next to them, as in figure 1.7, have cascading menus that list additional commands. In Aldus PageMaker, the Font command in the Type menu has a triangle to its right, indicating that a list of all available fonts appears when you choose the Type Font command. You must choose the font you want from this list.

If you don't want to make a choice after displaying a menu, click the pointer a second time on the menu name or click outside the menu. If you are using the keyboard, press Esc to back out of a menu without making a choice and press Esc a second time to return to the document.

Backing Out of Menus, Edits, and Dialog Boxes
When you are in doubt about the command you are about to choose or the edit you are about to make, you can escape. Press the Esc key to cancel the current dialog box or edit. Press the Esc key to close the open menu but leave the menu bar active; press Esc a second time to leave the menu bar and return to your document. If you are in a dialog box, you can choose the Cancel button to cancel selections you made. Clicking on the Cancel button or pressing Esc closes the dialog box.

Many Windows applications have an Undo command. If you complete a command and then decide you want to undo it, check under the Edit menu for an Undo command.

Many commands have associated key combinations, many of which appear to the right of the command on the pull-down menu. Figure 1.6 shows the shortcut key combinations available under the Edit menu in the Word for Windows application. You can press Ctrl+C to copy selected text, for example, or press F5 to go to a specific page. (Notice that some of the commands are gray and therefore unavailable.)

Selecting Options from Dialog Boxes

Some commands need additional information before you can complete them. To use the Format Number command in Excel, for example, you must specify which predefined or custom numeric and date formats you want to use. The command displays a dialog box containing a list from which you can choose existing predefined or custom formats and a text box in which you can type new custom formats.

Commands that require more information display a *dialog box*—a window similar to those shown in figures 1.8 and 1.9. Dialog boxes like the one in figure 1.8 have areas for you to enter text (see the File **Name** text box) or to select from a scrolling list of choices (see the **Directories** list). Many applications also include drop-down list boxes with lists that appear only when you select the box and press the down-arrow key or click on the down arrow on the right side of the window. Figure 1.9 shows that dialog boxes can have round option buttons and square check boxes. The round option buttons are clustered in groups, and you can select only one of the options. The square check boxes, like the Parity Chec**k** box in figure 1.9, are by themselves, and you can turn each on or off. After you select options or make text entries, you accept the contents of the dialog box by choosing the OK button (press Enter); you can cancel the dialog box by choosing the Cancel button (press Esc).

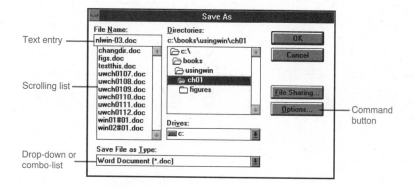

FIG. 1.8

The Save As dialog box with text-entry boxes, scrolling-list boxes, drop-down list boxes, and command buttons.

The five areas of a dialog box are summarized in table 1.2.

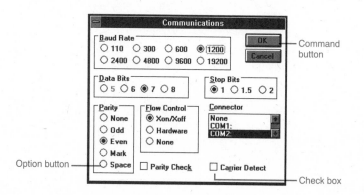

FIG. 1.9

The Communications dialog box in the Terminal application, with round option buttons and square check boxes.

If a dialog box hides something that you want to see on-screen, you can move the dialog box with the mouse by dragging the dialog box by its title bar to a new position. With the keyboard, press Alt, space bar to open the dialog Control menu and then choose **Move**. The arrow turns into a four-headed arrow; press any arrow key to use the four-headed arrow to move the dialog box. Press Enter when the dialog box is where you want it. (You can cancel the move before you press Enter by pressing Esc.)

Using the Mouse in Dialog Boxes

To select an option button or check box, click on it. Clicking on a check box the first time puts an *X* in it, signifying that the check box is selected. Clicking on a check box a second time turns off the *X*. To turn off a round option button, click on one of the other buttons in the group.

To select command buttons such as OK, Cancel, Yes, or No, click on them.

Table 1.2 Areas of a Dialog Box

Area	Use
Text box	Type text entries manually. Press the Backspace key to erase characters if you make a mistake.
List box	Select a listed item by scrolling through the list and selecting one item. The selected item appears in highlighted text (and also may appear in the text box above the list).
Drop-down or combo list box	Display the list by selecting the list and then pressing the down-arrow key, or clicking the arrow on the right side of the list. Press the down-arrow to select the item you want from the list or click on the item you want to select.
Option button	Select one option from a group of option buttons. (You can select only one option button in each group.) Option buttons are round and have darkened centers when selected. To remove a selection, select a different option in the same group.

Area	Use
Check box	Select multiple options from a group of check boxes. Check boxes are square and contain an *X* when selected. To deselect a check box, select it a second time.
Command button	Complete the command, cancel the command, or open an additional dialog box for more alternatives. Pressing Enter chooses the command button that appears in bold.

To select a text box so that you can type in it, click in the box. Reposition the cursor by moving the I-beam to a new location and clicking. The flashing insertion point is where your typed characters or edits appear. Select multiple characters by holding down the mouse button and dragging the I-beam across the text you want selected. (Text entry and editing is described in "Editing Text in Text Boxes," later in this chapter.)

To select from a scrolling-list box, select the list box by clicking in it. Scroll through the list by clicking on the up or down arrow in the scroll bar at the right side of the box. Make large jumps through the list by clicking in the shaded area of the scroll bar. Drag the square in the scroll bar to new locations for long moves. When the desired selection appears in the list box, click once on that selection.

Some Windows applications use drop-down list boxes. These list boxes appear like figure 1.10 when closed and like figure 1.11 when opened. To select from a drop-down list box, click on the down arrow to the right side of the text box. When the scrolling list appears, select from it in the same way you select from any scrolling-list box—click on the item you want.

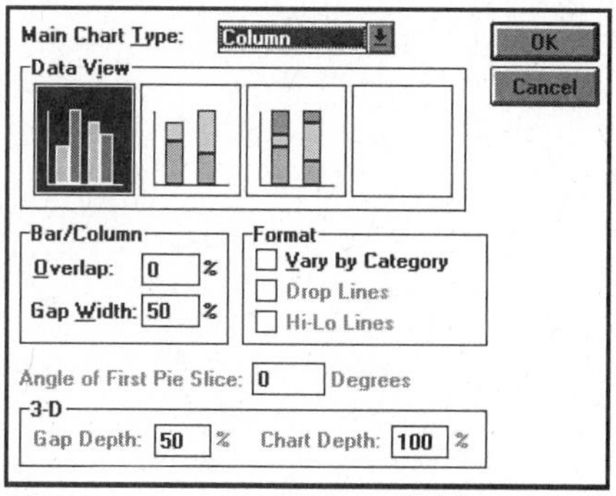

FIG. 1.10

A closed drop-down list box.

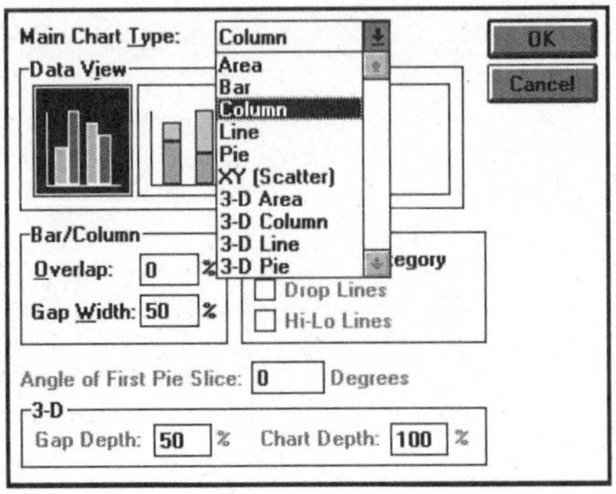

FIG. 1.11

An opened drop-down list box.

Mouse Shortcut in Dialog Boxes
In some dialog boxes, double-clicking on an option button or an item in a list selects that option and simultaneously chooses the OK command button. In the Open dialog box, for example, you can double-click on a file name to select and open the File. Experiment with the dialog boxes in your applications to determine whether double-clicking is a viable shortcut.

Using the Keyboard in Dialog Boxes

With the keyboard, you can select from dialog boxes in one of two ways. With the faster method, you use Alt+*letter*. You press and hold down Alt while you press the underlined letter in the name of the item you want. With the second method, you move among items in a dialog box by pressing Tab.

To select from a group of round option buttons, access the group of option buttons by pressing Alt+*letter*, where *letter* is the underlined letter in the name of the group of option buttons. A dashed line encloses the active option button. Move the selection to another button in the same group by pressing the arrow keys. For example, in the Communications dialog box shown in figure 1.9, press Alt+B to select the **B**aud Rate group and then press arrow keys to select the baud rate you want.

To select a check box, press Alt+*letter*, where *letter* is the underlined letter in the name of the check box. Each time you press Alt+*letter*, you toggle the check box between selected and deselected. An *X* appears in the check box when the box is selected. You also can toggle the active check box between selected and deselected by pressing the space bar.

A dashed line encloses the active check box. In the Communications dialog box in figure 1.9, press Alt+k to select the Parity Check option; press Alt+k again or press the space bar to deselect the option.

To make an entry in a text box, select the text box by pressing Alt+*letter*, where *letter* is the underlined letter in the name of the text box. Press Alt+N, for example, to select the File **N**ame text box in the Save As dialog box shown in figure 1.8. Type a text entry or edit the existing entry by using the editing techniques described in the up-coming section, "Editing Text in Text Boxes."

To select from a list of alternatives in a scrolling-list box, select the list box by pressing Alt+*letter*, where *letter* is the underlined letter in the name of the list box. When the list box is active, use the up- or down-arrow key or PgUp or PgDn to move through the list. The text in reversed type is selected. (To display a drop-down scrolling list by using the keyboard, press Alt+*letter* to activate the list and then press Alt+down-arrow to drop the list. Select items by pressing the up- or down-arrow keys.)

To select a command button, press Tab or Shift+Tab until a dashed line encloses the name of the button you want. Press the space bar to select the active button shown by the dashed enclosure. You can select the button in bold, usually the OK button, at any time by pressing Enter. Press Esc to choose the Cancel button and escape from a dialog box without making any changes.

Changing Directories in a List Box

In many Windows applications, the Save As and Open dialog boxes contain hierarchical **D**irectories and Dri**v**es lists with icons (other dialog boxes used for locating files may have similar lists). See figure 1.12 for an example. To change the directory, you must navigate through this hierarchical list.

The topmost entry in the **D**irectories list represents the current drive. To its left is an icon that represents an open folder, indicating that the contents of the drive are displayed. The entries below it represent directories. They have closed folder icons, indicating that the directory contents are not listed, or they have open folder icons, indicating that the directory contents are listed. To see what's in a directory, you must open this folder.

When you open a folder, any subdirectories contained within the directory are listed below the directory in the **D**irectories list, and any files contained in the directory are listed in the File **N**ame list. Figure 1.12 shows the Windows Write Save As dialog box; other dialog boxes may have lists that look slightly different or have different list names.

To open a directory or subdirectory in a **D**irectories list, follow these steps:

1. Select the **D**irectories list.

2. Scroll the **D**irectories list to display the directory you want to open.

    Mouse: Click on the down arrow. (Click and hold down the down arrow to scroll continuously.)

    Keyboard: Press Tab to advance to the Directories list; press the down or up arrows to scroll the list.

3. Select and open the directory.

    Mouse: Double-click on the directory you want to open.

    Keyboard: Select the directory by pressing the up or down arrow. Press Enter or choose OK to open the directory.

4. Open the subdirectory in a directory by using the same technique as for opening a directory.

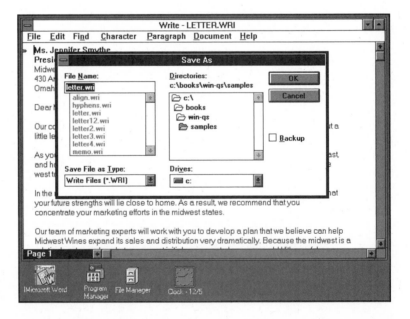

FIG. 1.12

A hierarchical
Directories list.

You can close a subdirectory by using the reverse procedure: select an open directory higher in the hierarchy than the subdirectory you want to close and press Enter (or double-click on the higher directory).

Editing Text in Text Boxes

You can use the text-editing techniques you learn in this section in all Windows applications. These editing techniques are described for text boxes inside dialog boxes, but they also work when editing text in other locations in Windows applications.

To edit text in a text box with the keyboard, select the text box by pressing Alt+*letter* or by pressing Tab until the text box is selected. (All text inside the box usually is selected.) To replace selected text, begin typing; the new characters you type replace the selected text.

To edit text in the text box with the mouse, position the I-beam pointer over the text where you want the insertion point to be and click. To delete multiple characters, drag across the characters so that they are selected and then press Del.

To deselect text in the text box, click somewhere else in the text or press End, Home, or the right or left arrow. When you select text, the characters you type are inserted at the insertion point. (The insertion point is the vertical flashing bar.)

To delete a character to the right of the flashing insertion point, press Del. Press Backspace to delete a character to the left of the insertion point.

Replace existing text with new text by selecting the text you want to replace and then typing. To select text with the keyboard, move the insertion point to the left of the first character, press and hold down Shift, and press the right arrow. Select with the mouse by dragging the I-beam across the text as you hold down the mouse button.

When you are editing text in an application, you can use **E**dit commands such as **U**ndo, **C**opy, and **P**aste, but these commands do not work in dialog boxes. However, the keystroke equivalents Ctrl+C, Ctrl+X, and Ctrl+V do work.

For Related Information:

▸▸ To learn more about the Program Manager, see "Operating the Program Manager," p. 116.

FROM HERE...

Starting, Using, and Quitting Applications

When you start Windows, the Program Manager appears. With the Program Manager, which is always running in Windows, you can easily start applications which you work with frequently.

The Program Manager usually contains one or more open windows, called *group windows.* The Program Manager also usually contains one or more *group icons,* which are closed group windows (refer to the earlier section, "Controlling the Windows in Windows," to learn how to open and close group windows). Inside each group window are one or more *program item icons.* A program item icon represents an application (and sometimes an associated data file).

Shortcut Keys for Editing
Some Windows applications include shortcut keys for editing text. These keys may work in some parts of the application, such as a formula bar, but may not work in others. Experiment to find the shortcuts that can help you.

Key	Action
Shift+left-arrow or Shift+right-arrow	Adds the next adjacent character to the selection
Shift+down-arrow	Selects to next line
Shift+up-arrow	Selects to preceding line
Shift+PgUp or Shift+PgDn	Selects to top or bottom of page or screen
Shift+Home	Selects to beginning of line
Shift+End	Selects to end of line
Ctrl+Shift+left-arrow or Ctrl+Shift+right-arrow	Selects a word each time you press the left or right arrow

Key	Action
Ctrl+Shift+Home	Selects to start of document
Ctrl+Shift+End	Selects to end of document

With the mouse, you can click where you want to begin to select text, press and hold down the Shift key, and click where you want the selected text to end. The text between the clicks is selected. In some applications, such as Word for Windows and Excel, you can select a word by double-clicking anywhere within the word.

The easiest way to start an application is from its program item icon. You can start your application by using the mouse or the keyboard. You also can start an application with the File Manager, whether or not the application has a program item icon (described in Chapter 5).

When you run multiple applications, you will want to switch easily among them. You can cycle through running applications by pressing shortcut keys, or you can use the Task List to switch to the application you need.

When you are finished using an application, exit it before you exit Windows (especially with DOS-based applications). The procedure for exiting is similar in most Windows applications. Exit DOS applications by using the appropriate technique for that application—even though the DOS application is running under Windows.

T I P

If the Program Manager does not appear when you start Windows, someone may have customized Windows so that the Program Manager displays as an icon at the bottom of the screen. Double-click on the Program Manager icon or press Alt+Tab enough times to display the Program Manager window or a box showing its name. When you release the Alt and Tab keys, the Program Manager window opens.

If you cannot see the Program Manager because Windows is customized so that an application starts when you start Windows, minimize the application (by choosing the Control Minimize command or clicking on the Minimize button—the downward-pointing arrow at the top right of your screen). After you minimize the application so that it appears as an icon at the bottom of your screen, you can see the Program Manager.

48

Starting Applications

When you installed Windows, you had the choice of assigning Windows and DOS applications to groups. *Group windows* store all applications related to a specific task together. With group windows, you can find and start applications and get data for a job you do frequently. Chapter 4 goes into depth about setting up group windows in the Program Manager.

If you requested it during the installation, Windows made program item icons for each application and put them in an Applications group. This group appears within the Program Manager as a group window or a group icon at the bottom of the window. If you open the group icon into a window, the program item icons are displayed. You can start the applications from the icons. Figure 1.13 shows the Program Manager with group windows, group icons, and program item icons. Application icons appear at the bottom of the screen to represent running applications.

If you did not install the applications into a group (or if you added a new application to your system or want to regroup your applications), read Chapter 4 and create your own customized program item icons to hold applications.

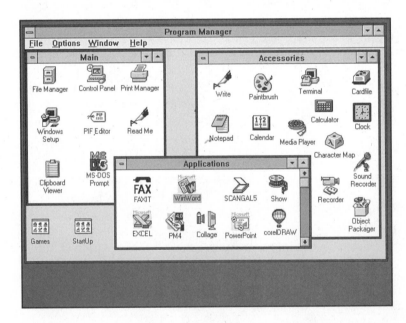

FIG. 1.13

Grouping applications and data together in the Program Manager.

To learn how to start applications from the File Manager, read Chapter 5.

Starting Applications from Icons

To start an application from a program item icon, follow these steps:

1. Open the Program Manager. It usually is open when you start Windows. If you just installed Windows, the Main group window appears open in the Program Manager window. If the Program Manager is not open, follow the appropriate instructions:

   Mouse: Double-click on the desktop. When the Task List appears, double-click on the name Program Manager. If you can see the Program Manager icon, double-click the icon to open it into a window.

   Keyboard: Press Ctrl+Esc. When the Task List appears, press the arrow keys to select the name Program Manager, and then press Enter. As an alternative, press Alt+Tab until you see the Program Manager, then release both keys.

2. Open the group icon or activate the group window that contains the application you want to start.

   Mouse: In the Program Manager window, click on the group window you want. If the correct group window is not open, double-click on the group icon you want in the Program Manager window.

   Keyboard: Press Ctrl+Tab until the group window you want activates. If the application is inside a group icon, press Ctrl+Tab to select the icon and then press Enter.

3. Start the program item that contains the application or the application and document you want.

   Mouse: Double-click on the program item icon containing the application or application and document you want to start.

   Keyboard: Press the arrow keys to select the program item icon you want to start and press Enter.

Starting Applications with Commands

You may not want applications you use infrequently to clutter the
Program Manager. Instead of starting applications from icons, you can
start applications and their related data documents by using the **File
R**un command in the Program Manager. To start an application by using **File R**un, follow these steps:

1. Choose the **File R**un command from the menu bar. The Run dialog
   box appears (see fig. 1.14).

```
┌─────────────────────────────────────────────────┐
│ ▭              Run                                │
├─────────────────────────────────────────────────┤
│                                      ┌────────┐   │
│ Command Line:                        │   OK   │   │
│ ┌─────────────────────────────────┐  └────────┘   │
│ │ c:\windows\excel.exe budget.xls │  ┌────────┐   │
│ └─────────────────────────────────┘  │ Cancel │   │
│ ☐ Run Minimized                      └────────┘   │
│                                      ┌────────┐   │
│                                      │ Browse.│   │
│                                      └────────┘   │
│                                      ┌────────┐   │
│                                      │  Help  │   │
│                                      └────────┘   │
└─────────────────────────────────────────────────┘
```

2. Type the full path name and application name in the **C**ommand
   Line text box.

3. To open a document with the application, type a space after the
   application name and type the name of the document. If the document is in a different directory from the application, also specify
   the path name of the document. For example, type the first of the
   following lines to start Excel, which is located in the EXCEL directory, and open the file BUDGET.XLS, also in the EXCEL directory.
   Type the second of the following lines if the file BUDGET.XLS is in
   the FINANCE directory:

   C:\EXCEL\EXCEL.EXE BUDGET.XLS

   C:\EXCEL\EXCEL.EXE C:\FINANCE\BUDGET.XLS

4. If you want the application to shrink to an icon when it starts,
   select the Run **M**inimized check box.

5. Choose OK or press Enter.

If you are not sure of the path or name of the application you want to
start from the Run dialog box, choose the **B**rowse button and select the
program from the Browse dialog box. When you choose OK or press
Enter, the application's path and name appear in the **C**ommand Line
text box. You can return to the DOS prompt while you run Windows. To
start the DOS prompt from the Program Manager, open the Main group
window. Select the DOS Prompt icon with arrow keys and press Enter,
or double-click on it. When you are finished working from the DOS
prompt, type **EXIT** at the prompt and press Enter to return to Windows
and the Program Manager.

> **Do Not Run CHKDSK with the /F Argument**
> You must not run some DOS commands and utilities from
> Windows. These commands and utilities change the DOS file-
> allocation table (FAT) or close files that Windows expects to re-
> main open. If you run these commands, Windows can freeze, or
> you can lose data. A DOS command that causes this problem is
> CHKDSK /F (used to unfragment disks). You can use CHKDSK by
> itself to check disk and memory, but you must not use the /F argu-
> ment. Other utilities that can cause problems are file-compression
> utilities, disk-optimizer utilities, and undelete-file utilities. To use
> these types of utilities, exit Windows and run them directly from
> the DOS prompt. When using Windows and DOS 5, you get the
> message CHKDSK/F cannot be done in a Windows /DOS Shell
> Command Prompt.

Working with Applications

Many operations are similar from application to application in Windows. Nearly all Windows applications, for example, start with the File
and Edit menus. The File menu includes commands for opening, closing, saving, and printing files. The Edit menu includes commands for
cutting, copying, and pasting and other editing commands specific to
the application. Operating menus and dialog boxes is the same in all
applications and is the same in applications as in Windows itself; you
learned these techniques in the earlier section on Learning Windows
Techniques. Selecting text and objects also is similar in most Windows
applications.

Opening, Saving, Printing, and Closing Files

When first started, many applications present you with a new, empty
document—a blank page, if the application is a word processing or
graphics or desktop publishing application; an empty worksheet, if the
application is a spreadsheet application. If you finish working on one
file, you can start a new file by choosing the File New command. Your
application may ask you for information about the type of new file to
start.

To open an existing file, choose the File Open command. An Open dialog box similar to the one shown in figure 1.15 appears. In the Drives
box, select the drive that contains your file. In the Directories box, select the directory containing your file and choose OK to display the list

of files in that directory. From the list of files presented in the File Name text box, select the file you want to open and choose OK or press Enter. (The File Name text box lists only files with the application's extension; to list other types of files, type a different extension in the File Name text box.)

The File menu contains two commands for saving files: Save As and Save. Use the File Save or File Save As command the first time you save a file so that you can tell Windows where to save it and so that you can name your file. You also can choose Save As to create a new version of an existing file by giving the file a new name. The Save As dialog box is often similar to the Open dialog box shown in the preceding figure; in it, you must specify the drive and directory to which you want to save your file and name the file. File names are limited to eight characters with a three-character extension, usually supplied by the application. After you type the file name, choose OK or press Enter to save the file. After you name your file, you can choose the File Save command to save the file without changing its name or location. This command replaces the original file.

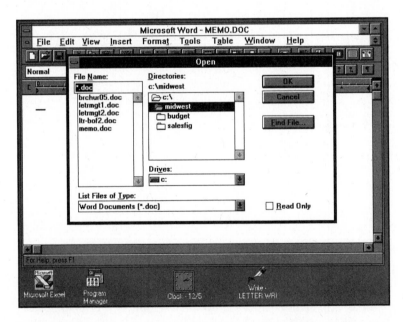

FIG. 1.15

The Open dialog box in a Windows application.

Printing your file may take two steps. Often you first must make some choice about the printer by using a command in the File menu named something like Print Setup or Target Printer. Use this command to identify the printer you want to use or to change the paper orientation.

(After you make these selections, you need not access this menu again until you want to change the setting.) After you identify the printer you will use, you can choose the **File** **P**rint command to print your document. You are presented with a dialog box that asks for details about the print job: how many copies to print; what range of pages to print; and other options depending on the application. Make your selections and then choose OK or press Enter. In some applications, like Windows Write and Aldus PageMaker, you can change the printer setup by choosing a special "Setup" command in the Print dialog box.

To close a file, you often can choose the **File** **C**lose command. Applications that don't allow more than one document to be open at once, however, usually don't include a **File** **C**lose command; instead, to close the current file, you open a new file or exit the application. If you choose **File** **E**xit, you exit the application. When you close or exit, most Windows applications prompt you to save any changes you made since you last saved your document.

Scrolling in a Document

Most applications include scroll bars at the right and bottom edges of the screen. You can use the vertical scroll bar at the right to scroll up and down in your document. You can use the horizontal scroll bar to scroll left and right. To scroll a small distance, click on the arrow at either end of either scroll bar; you will scroll in the direction the arrow points. To scroll a larger distance, click in the grey area next to the arrow or drag the scroll bar box to a new location. In many applications, the scroll bars are optional: if you want more working space, you can turn them off.

You can scroll using the keyboard by pressing the arrow keys to move a character or line at a time or by pressing the PgUp or PgDn keys to move a screen at a time. The Home key usually scrolls you to the left margin, and the End key takes you to the end of the line or the right side. Holding down the Ctrl key when you press any other scrolling key extends the scroll: Ctrl+Home, for example, takes you to the beginning of your file; Ctrl+End takes you to the end of the file; Ctrl+the left- or right-arrow key moves you a word at a time instead of a character at a time. Most applications have many shortcuts for scrolling.

If you scroll by using the scroll bars, the insertion point does not move; it remains where it was before you scrolled. If you scroll by using the keyboard, the insertion point moves as you scroll. Scroll bars are shown in figure 1.16.

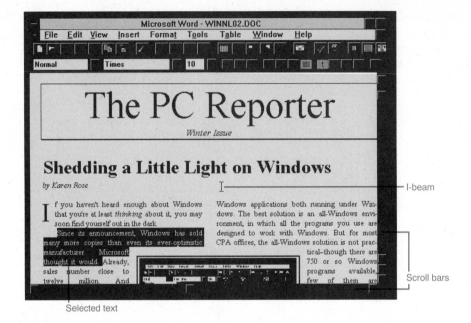

I-beam

Scroll bars

FIG. 1.16

Selected text
appears
reversed.

Selected text

Using Simple Editing Techniques

Editing text and objects is similar in all Windows applications. When you're working with text, in your document or in a dialog box, the mouse pointer turns into an I-beam when you move it onto editable text. You can use the I-beam to move the insertion point and to select text. The flashing vertical insertion point is where text appears when you type.

You can use the mouse or the keyboard to move the insertion point. To use the mouse, position the I-beam where you want the insertion point to move and click the left mouse button. (If you cannot see the insertion point, it may be under the I-beam; move the mouse a little to move the I-beam.) To use the keyboard to move the insertion point, press the arrow keys. For a complete description of how the arrow keys work, refer to the box on page 46, earlier in this chapter. Many keyboard shortcuts also are listed in the table.

To insert text at the insertion point, type. Most applications push existing text to the right to make room for the new text (though some applications allow you to select an *overtype* mode). To delete text to the left of the insertion point, press the Backspace key. To delete text to the right of the insertion point, press the Delete key.

Most applications contain an "oops" function: the **Edit U**ndo command. This command undoes your most recent edit—use it when you make an edit you instantly regret.

T I P

Selecting Text and Objects

You can sum up one of the most important editing rules in all Windows applications in three simple words: *Select, then Do.* You must select text or an object before you can do anything to it (if you don't select first, the application doesn't know where to apply your command).

To select text and objects, you can use the mouse or the keyboard. To select text with the mouse, position the I-beam at the beginning of the text you want to select, click and hold down the left mouse button, drag to the end of the text you want to select, and release the mouse button. To select text with the keyboard, position the insertion point at the beginning of the text you want to select, press and hold down the Shift key, use arrow keys to move to the end of the text to select, and then release the Shift key. Selected text appears reversed, as shown in figure 1.16.

Many shortcuts exist for selecting. To select a word with the mouse, double-click on the word. To select a word using the keyboard, hold down Ctrl+Shift while you press the left- or right-arrow key. To select a length of text with the mouse, you can drag until you touch the end of the screen, which causes the screen to scroll. To select a length of text with the keyboard, position the I-beam where you want the selection to start, hold down the Shift key, and scroll to the end of the selection by using any keyboard scrolling technique.

After you select a word, you can turn it bold or change its font. In most applications, typing replaces the selection, so you can replace text by selecting it and typing the new text. If a graphic is selected, you can resize it.

To select an object, such as a picture, with the mouse, click on the object. (To select multiple objects, hold down Shift while you click on each one in turn.) To select with the keyboard, position the insertion point beside it, hold down Shift, and press an arrow key to move over the object. Selected objects, such as graphics, usually appear with *selection handles* on each side and corner.

Copying and Moving

After you select text or an object, you can use the Edit menu to copy or move it. The commands all Windows applications use to copy and move are **Edit Cut**, **Edit Copy**, and **Edit Paste**. The **Edit Cut** command removes the selection from your document; **Edit Copy** duplicates it. Both commands transfer the selection to the Clipboard, a temporary holding area. The **Edit Paste** command copies the selection out of the Clipboard into your document at the insertion point's location. Your selection remains in the Clipboard until you replace it with another selection.

To copy a selection, choose **Edit Copy**, move the insertion point where you want the selection duplicated, and choose **Edit Paste**. To move a selection, choose **Edit Cut**, move the insertion point where you want it moved, and choose **Edit Paste**. Many shortcuts exist for copying and moving. Shift+Delete usually cuts a selection, and Shift+Insert usually pastes the Clipboard's contents. Many Windows applications also take advantage of Windows' *drag and drop* feature: you can use the mouse to drag a selection to its new location and drop it into place.

Because the Clipboard is shared among all applications running under Windows, you can move or copy a selection between documents and between applications as easily as you can move and copy within the file you are working in. The next two sections explain how to switch between documents and applications.

Switching between Document Windows

In many—but not all—Windows applications, you can open more than one file and switch between the files easily. Use these techniques when you want to copy or move information from one document to another. To open multiple files, choose the **File Open** command multiple times. If your application doesn't support multiple documents, it closes the current file, asking you whether you want to save any changes you made since you last saved.

If your application supports multiple documents, each document opens in its own document window as shown in figure 1.17. You can use the document control menu, at the left of the menu bar, to control the size and position of the document window. You also can control the document window using the restore, minimize, and maximize buttons that appear at the right end of the menu bar.

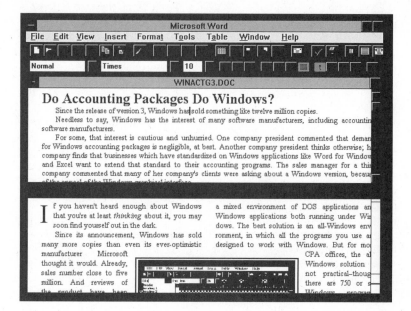

FIG. 1.17

Multiple document windows.

You will find the document Control menu icon in one of two places. If the document is maximized in the application window, the document Control menu icon is found to the left of the menu bar. However, if the document window is not maximized—appears as a window in the application window—the document Control menu icon can be found at the left end of the document title bar. Click on the box or press Alt+hyphen to open the document Control menu.

The file you opened most recently is the active file; usually it appears in the top window, and it may hide the other document windows. In some applications, such as Word for Windows, you can use the **W**indow **A**rrange All command to arrange your document windows so that they all are visible (if you have many files open, the windows may be very small).

To switch between document windows with the mouse, click on the window you want to activate. If the window you want to activate is not visible, you may need to move or size the active window on top (move a window by dragging its title bar; size it by dragging its border). To switch between document windows with the keyboard, choose the **W**indow menu and select the document you want from the list of open windows. In most applications, you can hold down Ctrl while you press the F6 key to switch between open document windows within an application.

Switching between Applications

When you run several applications, you need an easy way to switch between the windows.

If you are using a mouse, *activate* another window (or bring it to the top of the stack of windows) by clicking on it. If you cannot see the window of the application you want, use a keyboard technique or move the top windows as described in the earlier section, "Controlling the Windows in Windows." If the application you want is in an icon, double-click on the icon to open it into an active window.

If you are using the keyboard, press and hold down Alt+Tab to cycle through the application windows. A dialog box appears on-screen showing the name and icon of the next application. As you hold down the Alt key, each time you press Tab, the next icon and application name appear in the box. Release the Alt+Tab keys when the title of the application you want appears. You also can press Alt+Esc to cycle through application windows, but this method is slower because each window must be completely redrawn before the next window appears.

Whether you use the mouse or the keyboard, you can use the Task List to switch among many applications (see fig. 1.18). The Task List shows which applications are currently running. You can switch between applications by choosing the one you want from the list.

FIG. 1.18

The Task List window.

To switch among applications using the Task List, follow these steps:

1. Activate the Task List.

   Mouse: Double-click on the desktop background.

   Keyboard: Press Ctrl+Esc; or press Alt, space bar and choose the Switch To command.

2. Choose the application you want active.

   Mouse: Double-click on the application you want active.

   Keyboard: Press the down arrow to select the application you want and then press Enter.

The following chart lists the command buttons in the Task List window.

Command Button	Action
Switch To	Activates the selected application in the Task List.
End Task	Exits the selected application in the Task List.
Cancel	Exits the Task List without making a choice.
Cascade	Arranges all open application windows in an overlapping cascade from top left to bottom right.
Tile	Arranges all open application windows to fill the screen with equal-sized windows.
Arrange Icons	Arranges all application icons along the bottom of the desktop.

Quitting Windows Applications

Most Windows applications abide by the same design rules. Fundamental commands such as saving and quitting are common across different applications. To quit a Windows application, follow these steps:

1. Activate the application by following the appropriate instructions:

   Mouse: Click on the application window.

   Keyboard: Press Alt+Tab until the application appears; or press Ctrl+Esc to display the Task List, press the down-arrow key to select the name of the desired application, and then press Enter.

2. Choose the File Exit command from the application's menu.

You also can exit an application by selecting the application Control menu (press Alt, space bar) and choosing Close or by double-clicking on the Control menu icon. For most applications, the shortcut key for Control Close is Alt+F4.

If you alter documents without saving them, you are prompted to save your changes before the application quits.

To run a non-Windows (DOS) application from Windows, follow the normal procedure to quit or exit that application. Make sure that you save before quitting because you may or may not be prompted to save your work before the application quits. Depending on your Windows settings and on how the DOS application was started, you may return immediately to Windows, or you may return to an empty (inactive) window. If you return to an inactive window, press Alt, space bar to display the Control menu. Choose the **C**lose command to close the window and return to normal Windows operation.

FROM HERE...

For Related Information:

▶▶ See "Starting an Application from the Program Manager," p. 75.

▶▶ See "Starting Applications from a Group Window," p. 118.

▶▶ To learn how to link objects between applications, see Chapter 22, "Using Windows Applications Together," p. 847.

▶▶ To learn how to use DOS applications in Windows, see "Loading and Running DOS Applications," p. 886.

Exiting Windows

To exit Windows and return to DOS, close the Program Manager window by choosing the **F**ile **E**xit Windows command or pressing Alt+F4. Windows gives you the chance to cancel this command and remain in Windows. If Windows applications are running, Windows closes them. If you changed documents in the applications since they were last saved, you are prompted to save them.

In the following explanation of how to quit Windows, the convention *Alt+key* indicates that you should hold down the Alt key as you press the indicated letter or key. When you are asked to click on an object, move the pointer so that the tip is on the object and then quickly press the left mouse button.

To exit Windows when applications are running, follow these steps:

1. Activate the Program Manager if its window is not open and on top of the other windows by following the appropriate instructions:

   Mouse: Click on any exposed part of the Program Manager window or double-click on the Program Manager icon to open the Program Manager window.

   Keyboard: Press Ctrl+Esc to display the Task List. Press the up or down arrow to highlight the name Program Manager and then press Enter.

2. Choose the **File Exit** Windows command to close the Program Manager and exit Windows. Choose this command by using the appropriate instructions:

> **Mouse:** Click on the **F**ile menu and then click on the **E**xit Windows command.

> **Keyboard:** Press Alt, **F**, and then **X**. As a keyboard shortcut, you can press Alt+F4 to exit the Program Manager and Windows.

3. Choose OK when the message advising you that This will end your Windows session appears.

> **Mouse:** Click on the OK button.

> **Keyboard:** Press Enter.

If you don't want to exit Windows, choose Cancel instead of OK.

4. If a Windows application is still running with a document containing unsaved changes, you are prompted to save your changes. Choose **Y**es to save changes, **N**o to discard changes, or Cancel to return to Windows. If you choose Yes to save changes to an unnamed file, the application's Save As dialog box appears, and you must name and save the file. If a DOS application is still running, Windows tells you to return to the application and quit it in the usual way before you can exit Windows.

You also can quit Windows from the Program Manager's Control menu. The Control menu is the square icon at the left edge of the Program Manager title bar. Normally, you use the Control menu to close an application's window; however, when you close the Program Manager window, you also close Windows. To close Windows from the Program Manager's Control menu, follow these steps:

1. Save any documents and quit all applications.

2. Open the Program Manager's Control menu.

> **Mouse:** Click on the Control menu icon.

> **Keyboard:** Press Alt, space bar.

3. Choose the **C**lose command.

> **Mouse:** Click on the **C**lose command.

> **Keyboard:** Type **C**.

4. Choose OK from the alert box that says This will end your Windows session, or choose Cancel to return to Windows.

5. If an application is still running that contains a file with unsaved changes, you are prompted to save changes.

An alternative method for closing the Program Manager and closing Windows is to press the Alt+F4 key combination.

T I P   Double-clicking on the Control menu icon that appears at the top left corner of each document or application window closes that window. If you made changes in the document or application since the last save, you are asked whether you want to save the changes. Double-clicking on the Control menu icon at the left corner of the Program Manager's title bar closes the Program Manager window *and* closes Windows.

FROM HERE...

For Related Information:

▶▶ See "Exiting Applications and Windows," p. 93.

▶▶ To learn how to customize Windows, see "Customizing Windows with Color," p. 255 and "Customizing the Desktop," p. 260.

▶▶ To learn how to use the Program Manager to start applications and create program item icons, see "Operating the Program Manager," p. 116 and "Starting Applications from a Group Window," p. 118.

▶▶ See also "Operating in Windows," p. 67 and "Operating Applications," p. 77.

Chapter Summary

In this chapter, you learned how to start Windows and how to understand the terms used in Windows. You learned the parts of the Windows screen, and you learned that you can choose from menus by activating the menu bar with the Alt key and then pressing the underlined letter of the command or by clicking with the pointer on the menu name and then on the command name. You also learned how to choose options from dialog boxes, which appear for commands that need additional information. You can choose options in dialog boxes by holding down the Alt key and pressing the underlined letter for that option or by clicking with the pointer on that option.

Windows gets its name from the way the screen looks and works: each application appears in a window that you can size, move, minimize, or maximize by using a mouse or the keyboard.

All Windows' applications work similarly. Techniques you learn for operating Windows carry through to the applications, and techniques you learn for operating one application are similar in all applications. You can use multiple applications at the same time.

To get started using Windows, turn to the quick start in Chapter 2. The quick start gives you hands-on practice using Windows and several of the accessory applications that come with Windows. By experimenting with these applications, you learn a great deal about how most fully featured Windows applications work. Part III of the book includes chapters detailing use of these accessory applications.

Windows applications are built to work together—especially true of the OLE-based *applets* that can be shared among Windows applications. To learn about OLE, or object linking and embedding, read Chapter 6; to learn about applets, refer to Part IV.

When you are comfortable running the desktop applications, you will want to run fully featured Windows and DOS applications and exchange data between them. When you reach that level of involvement with Windows, read the chapters in Parts V and VI. They explain how to integrate Windows applications so that they pass and share data; the chapters also explain how to run non-Windows—or DOS—applications within a window.

Quick Start: Operating Windows

This chapter is a short step-by-step, hands-on session designed to help you understand the general principles of operating Windows and Windows applications. For detailed discussions of operating Windows, refer to Chapter 1.

A quick start gives you the chance to practice as you learn. After you complete this chapter, you should be quite comfortable using Windows techniques. Because these techniques hold true throughout Windows and throughout all Windows applications, the time you spend practicing in this chapter will serve you well as you continue to other chapters in this book and to other Windows applications.

Quick Starts and Stops
This hands-on session should take less than an hour to complete, but you can skip to the last section of this chapter and follow the procedures for exiting applications and Windows to stop earlier.

Starting Windows

You can run Windows in one of two modes (standard and 386-enhanced), depending on the processor in your computer and how much memory your computer has. Unless you specify otherwise, Windows selects the mode automatically. Sometimes you can force Windows to run in a different mode.

To start Windows, follow this procedure:

1. Turn on your PC. If necessary, change to the drive containing Windows. (If your PC defaults to drive C, for example, and Windows is on drive D, at the C: prompt type *D*: and press Enter.)

2. Type *CD C:\WINDOWS* and press Enter to change to the directory that contains Windows.

3. Type *WIN* and press Enter to start Windows.

These instructions have you change to the WINDOWS directory before you start Windows, but if you let Windows modify the AUTOEXEC.BAT file during installation, you can turn on your PC and type *WIN* to start Windows.

When Windows starts, it displays the Program Manager application and opens the Main group window (see fig. 2.1). If you do not see the Program Manager, Windows has been customized to start with the Program Manager minimized as an icon. To start the Program Manager, double-click on the Program Manager icon or hold down the Alt key, press Tab enough times to select the Program Manager icon, and then release the Alt key to open the Program Manager window.

The Program Manager acts as the coordinator of frequently used applications and data documents. In the Program Manager window are windows that contain groups of applications and associated documents. The Main group is one of these windows.

The *icons*, or small pictures, in each group window are known as *program item icons*. Each program item icon starts one application and optionally one data document. Grouping program item icons together in a group window makes it easy for you to work with applications and data used for a specific task. Chapter 4 describes how to create your own custom program item icons and group windows.

You can create your own customized group windows (as described in Chapter 4), but the Program Manager comes with some group windows already created. Figure 2.1 shows the Main group and the Accessories group. The program item icons in the Main group are utilities and the File Manager. The Accessories group contains small desktop applications such as a miniature word processor, calculator, clock, and calendar.

FIG. 2.1

The Program
Manager with
the Main and
Accessories
group windows.

Other groups are shown in figure 2.1 as icons at the bottom of the Program Manager window. These icons are *minimized* (closed) group windows. The Games group contains two games. You may see other group icons at the bottom of the Program Manager window that you created or that you requested when you installed Windows. The Applications group icon in figure 2.1 is one such customized group.

For Related Information:

◄◄ See "Starting Windows," p. 18.

◄◄ To learn how to start in a mode other than the default, see "Choosing an Operating Mode," p. 20.

►► To learn about the different operating modes and their advantages, see "Using Memory Efficiently," p. 962.

FROM HERE...

Operating in Windows

Windows applications run on a screen background known as the *desktop*. The desktop is a metaphor for *your desk*. The applications and their documents are like reports on your desk. You can run many different applications and documents on the desktop at the same time.

Within Windows are two types of windows: application windows and document windows (see fig. 2.2). An application window contains the application itself. In figure 2.2, the application window has the title Microsoft Excel. The menu bar that controls the application is always at the top of the application window underneath the application's title. Depending on the type of processor and amount of memory you have, you can run multiple applications at one time in Windows. Each application appears in its own application window.

A document window is located in an application window. In figure 2.2, the two document windows have the titles MW-WINES.XLS and MW-WINES.XLC. Document windows contain the data or document on which the application works. Some applications, such as Windows Write or Aldus PageMaker, can have only one document window open at a time. With other applications, such as Microsoft Excel and Word for Windows, you can have multiple document windows open at a time.

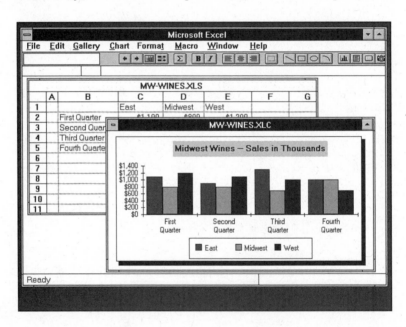

FIG. 2.2

Multiple document windows open within the Excel application window.

Controlling with Mouse or Keyboard

Most Windows applications can be controlled by mouse, keyboard, function keys, shortcut keys, or a combination of these. Do not feel that you must use one method to the exclusion of the others. Use them together to maximize efficiency and productivity.

Use the mouse to move the mouse pointer on-screen. When you hold the mouse, hold it in a relaxed but firm grip with two fingers resting on the buttons, the mouse's "body" under your palm, and the tail (wire) pointing in the same direction as your fingers. When you press a mouse button, do not move the mouse; just click the button.

Don't choke the mouse. Relax!

The following chart describes the three types of mouse actions.

Mouse Action	Meaning
Click	Move the mouse pointer so that the tip points to what you want to select and then quickly press and release the left mouse button.
Double-click	Move the mouse pointer so that the tip points to what you want to select and then press and release the left mouse button twice in rapid succession.
Drag	Move the mouse pointer so that the tip points to what you want to move or resize. Hold down the left mouse button and move the mouse pointer to the new location. Release the mouse button.

The mouse pointer appears differently depending on where you are working. In the Program Manager, the mouse pointer appears as an arrow. When you work with text, the mouse pointer appears as an *I-beam* which you can use to select text or position the insertion point for editing. When you move or resize a window, the mouse pointer appears as a four-headed or double-headed arrow.

With the keyboard, you use different keys in combination, as explained in the following chart.

Key Combination	Meaning
letter	Press the indicated letter. In menus, commands, and dialog boxes, the indicated letters are underlined. In this book, the letters are in bold type.
Alt, *letter*	Press *and release* the Alt key and then press and release the indicated letter.
Alt+*letter*	Press *and hold down* the Alt key as you press and release the indicated letter.
Ctrl+*key*	Press and hold down the Ctrl key as you press and release the indicated key. The *key* may be a key such as the left-arrow key or one of the function keys.

Controlling Windows and Icons

Figure 2.3 shows the parts of windows. Knowing these different window parts enables you to move windows, scroll through their contents, maximize them to fill the screen, or minimize them into an icon. To change windows or icons with a mouse, move the mouse pointer to different locations on a window and perform a mouse action. With the keyboard, use the application or document Control menu to change windows or icons.

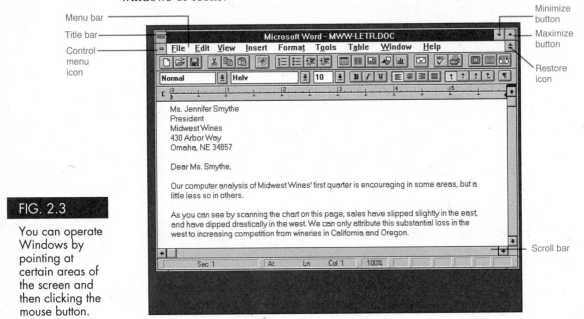

FIG. 2.3

You can operate Windows by pointing at certain areas of the screen and then clicking the mouse button.

Although you can have several windows open on your desktop, only one is active at any time. You can activate a window with the mouse by clicking on the window. You can activate a window with the keyboard using two techniques—depending on the type of window. To activate an application window, such as the Program Manager or Microsoft Word, press Alt+Tab until you see the application name. To activate a document window (such as the Main window inside the Program Manager), press Ctrl+Tab. The active window appears on top and has a solid or colored title bar.

You use the *Control menu* to control windows with the keyboard. Notice that figure 2.3 shows two Control menu icons. One is for the application window and one is for the document window. The application Control menu is to the left of the application title bar; the document

Control menu is to the left of the document title bar. Applications that contain only one document do not have a document Control menu.

You use the *maximize*, *minimize*, and *restore icons* to control windows with a mouse. These icons are shaped like arrowheads and are located at the top right corner of the application and document windows. The restore icon (a double arrowhead) appears only when a window is maximized to its full size.

Moving an application or document window is especially helpful when you have multiple windows on-screen and want to see more than one of them.

The Program Manager is like any other application window. For the following exercise, move your Program Manager window to the top left corner of the desktop (the screen background) by following the appropriate instructions:

Mouse: To move the window by dragging, position the tip of the mouse pointer on the Program Manager title bar, press and hold down the left mouse button, and move the mouse. Release the mouse button when the window is in position.

Keyboard: To move the Program Manager window by choosing the application Control Move command, press Alt, space bar to open the application Control menu. Type *M* to choose the **M**ove command. Press the arrow keys to move the window. Press the Enter key when the window is in position.

Key Combinations for the Two Control Menus
Notice that the application Control menu is in the application title bar and is shaped like a box with a space bar in it. To open the application Control menu, press Alt, space bar.

The document Control menu is in the document title bar and is shaped like a box that contains a hyphen (-). To open the document Control menu, press Alt, hyphen.

Both control menus control the window. The application control menu controls the application window; the document control menu controls the document window.

Practice resizing the document window that contains the Main group so that it is smaller (see fig. 2.4). Follow the appropriate instructions to resize the window:

72

Mouse: To drag the right edge of the document window inward, move the mouse pointer over the right edge of the Main group window. When the pointer changes to a double-headed arrow, press and hold down the left mouse button and move the mouse to the left. Release the mouse button so that the edge hides one or more of the program item icons. You can resize most window edges or corners in this manner.

Keyboard: Press Alt, hyphen (-) to select the document Control menu, type **S** to choose the **S**ize command, and press the right-arrow key to indicate that you want to move the right window edge. Press the left-arrow key to move that edge to the left. Press Enter to freeze the edge of the window.

Scroll bars —

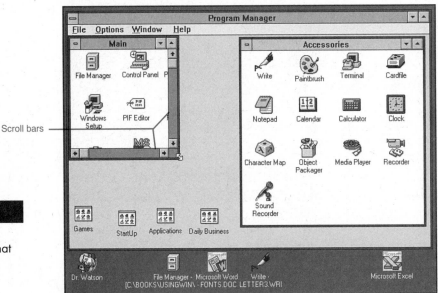

FIG. 2.4

Resizing a window so that not all of its contents are visible.

Notice that when the window becomes too small to show all the icons, *scroll bars* appear at the right and bottom sides of the window (depending on how small you make the window, only one scroll bar may appear). The horizontal scroll bar enables you to scroll left and right through the window contents. You use vertical scroll bars to scroll vertically through data.

To use the horizontal scroll bar in the resized Main group window, follow the appropriate instructions:

Mouse: Click on the right-pointing arrowhead located at the right side of the horizontal scroll bar. The window scrolls to the right. Click on the left arrowhead to scroll back to the left.

Keyboard: The keyboard doesn't scroll the window, but pressing the right or left arrow moves the selection in the window between program item icons. As the selection moves to an icon outside the window, the window scrolls to show the icon. Windows in typing or graphics programs work in a similar fashion.

You can minimize application windows so that they become small icons on the desktop. You also can minimize some document windows so that they become small icons in the application's window.

To minimize the Main group window to become an icon, follow the appropriate instructions:

Mouse: Click on the document minimize button (the down arrow-head to the right of the Main group title bar). Make sure that you click on the minimize button for the Main group window and not for the Program Manager. (If you accidentally minimize the Program Manager, it shrinks to an icon at the bottom of your screen. Double-click on the icon to restore it to a window.)

Keyboard: Activate the Main window and press Alt, hyphen (-) to access the Control menu and then type **N** for Minimize.

Figure 2.5 shows how the Main group window becomes an icon within the Program Manager window. Minimizing unused windows into icons leaves them accessible but reduces the amount of screen space they use.

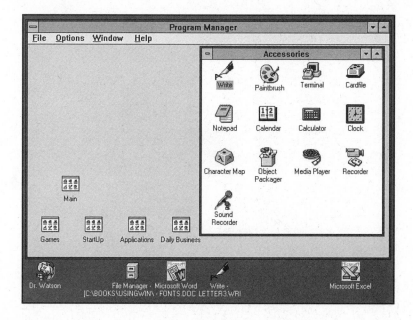

FIG. 2.5

Reducing document windows to icons at the bottom of the Program Manager window.

To work with a document or application that you reduced to an icon, restore it to a window by following the appropriate steps:

Mouse: Double-click on the Main group icon.

Keyboard: Press Ctrl+Tab until the name of the Main group icon is highlighted. Press Enter.

When you want a document to fill the inside of an application window, maximize the group window so that this window fills the Program Manager and resembles figure 2.6 by following the appropriate instructions:

Mouse: Click on the maximize button at the far right of the Main group window title bar.

Keyboard: Activate the Main group window, choose the document Control Maximize command by pressing Alt, hyphen (-), and then press X.

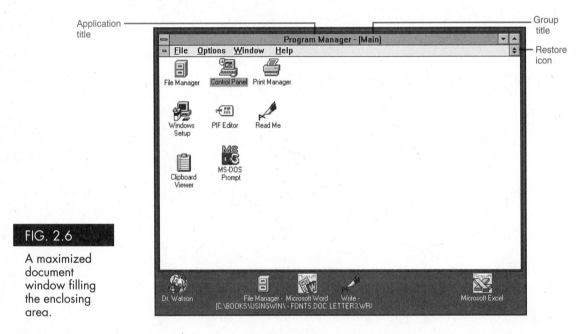

FIG. 2.6

A maximized document window filling the enclosing area.

Notice that when you maximize a document window, all the other document windows and group icons are hidden.

By using the maximize button in an application's title bar, you can maximize an application window so that it fills the entire desktop (screen background). This technique is useful in applications that require a large working area. Even if a window is maximized, you can switch between applications if more than one is running.

Restore the Main group window so that other groups show within the Program Manager by following these steps:

Mouse: Click on the double-headed restore icon at the top right corner of the Program Manager window (see fig. 2.6). The double-headed restore icon belongs to the group window and is underneath the minimize and maximize buttons that belong to the Program Manager window.

Keyboard: Choose the document Control **R**estore command: press Alt, hyphen (-) and then press **R**.

> You cannot move or resize a maximized window. Before you can move or resize a maximized window, you must restore it to a movable window.

T I P

What you have learned about moving, sizing, maximizing, and minimizing windows and icons applies to application windows and the document windows within them, as well as to group windows.

For Related Information:

◀◀ To learn more about navigating Windows, see "Working in the Windows Environment," p. 21; "Understanding Windows Terminology," p. 26; and "Controlling the Windows in Windows," p. 30.

◀◀ See also "Using Menus and Dialog Boxes," p. 35.

FROM HERE...

Starting an Application from the Program Manager

In this section of the quick start, you learn how to start an application from the Program Manager. Before starting an application, the group window containing the application must be open. In the following steps, you activate or open the Accessories group window that contains the desktop applications that come with Windows. From that group, you open Microsoft Write, a simple word processor.

To activate the open Accessories group window inside the Program Manager, follow these steps:

Mouse: Click on the Accessories window.

Keyboard: If the Program Manager window is not selected, press Alt+Tab to select it. Press Ctrl+Tab until the Accessories group window is active.

If the Accessories group window is minimized to an icon, follow these instructions to open it:

Mouse: Double-click on the Accessories icon.

Keyboard: If the Program Manager window is not selected, press Alt+Tab to select it. Press Ctrl+Tab until the Accessories icon is selected, and then press Enter.

The Accessories group window appears (see fig. 2.7). If several windows are open on your desktop, the active window is the one on top (usually the one with a solid or colored title bar).

FIG. 2.7

The Accessories group window.

The Accessories group window displays all the applications it contains. Descriptions and in-depth instructions for these desktop applications can be found in Chapters 12 through 16.

To start the Microsoft Write application, follow the appropriate instructions:

Mouse: Double-click on the Write program item icon.

Keyboard: Press the left or right arrow until the Write program item is selected and then press Enter.

For Related Information:

◄◄ See "Starting, Using, and Quitting Applications," p. 46.

►► See "Starting Applications from a Group Window," p. 118.

►► To learn more about the File Manager, see "Using the File Manager's Drag and Drop Feature," p. 191.

FROM HERE...

Operating Applications

When the Write application starts, it appears in a separate application window (see fig. 2.8). No document windows are in the Write application window because you cannot work on multiple documents at the same time with the Write application. The insertion point that marks where typed characters will appear is a flashing vertical line at the top left of the screen. (The *insertion point* is known as the *cursor* in DOS applications.)

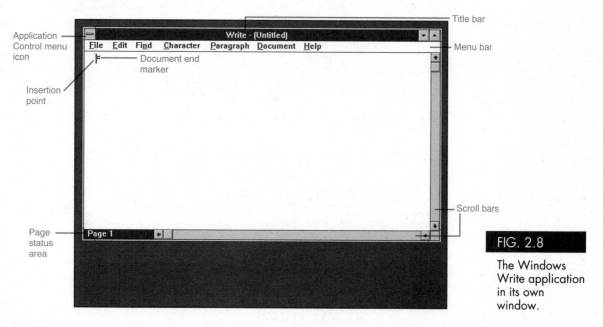

FIG. 2.8

The Windows Write application in its own window.

Moving the Insertion Point with the Mouse

When you use the mouse in Windows applications, the mouse pointer may change shape in some areas of the screen. When the mouse pointer is over a text-entry area, for example, the pointer changes to the shape of an I-beam. This I-beam is the mouse pointer—not the insertion point that marks where typed characters appear. To reposition the insertion point with the I-beam, move the I-beam where you want the insertion point and then click. Move the I-beam away so that you can see the repositioned flashing insertion point. You also can move the insertion point by pressing the left-, right-, up-, and down-arrow keys on your keyboard.

Editing Text

Typing and editing text is the same in nearly every Windows application. After you practice the techniques described in this section, you can type and edit text in other applications.

In the following steps, you type a list and make a simple editing correction to it. Follow the steps and remember to include the misspelled word *Raketball*.

1. Type the following lines and press Enter at the end of each line:

   Things to do today:

   Complete cash flow analysis

   Plan next quarter's goals

   Raketball at 7:00

2. Change *Raketball* to *Racquetball* by following the appropriate instructions:

   Mouse: Move the I-beam pointer between the *k* and the *e* in *Raketball* and click once. The flashing insertion point should now be between the *k* and *e*. Press the Backspace key to delete the letter *k* and type *cqu*.

   Keyboard: Press the arrow keys to move the flashing insertion point between the *k* and *e* in *Raketball*. Press the Backspace key to delete the letter *k* and type *cqu*.

   The result of your typing is shown in figure 2.9.

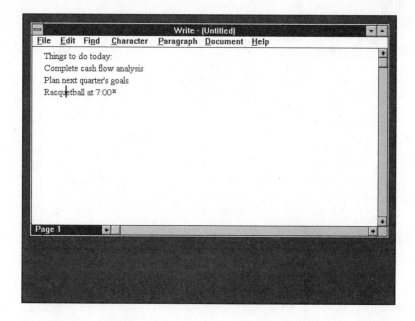

FIG. 2.9

The Write word processor with the corrected list.

What you have learned about editing text in Write applies to editing text in all Windows applications and text-entry boxes. You can learn much more, however, that will save you time. Windows applications have many shortcuts for editing, cutting, and pasting text. These shortcuts are briefly described in Chapter 1 and are described in more detail in Chapter 12.

Choosing Menus and Commands

Every Windows application lists its commands in menus. The menus are listed at the top of the application Window, just below the title bar. You can choose commands by using the keyboard or the mouse or sometimes by using shortcut keys.

Figure 2.10 shows the Find menu selected so that its commands show. Follow the appropriate instructions to select the Find menu:

Mouse: Click on the menu name Find.

Keyboard: Press the Alt key to activate the menu bar and then press the letter **n** (the underlined letter in the menu name).

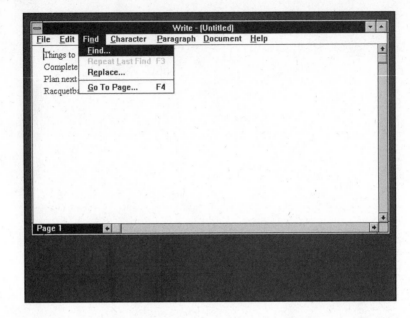

FIG. 2.10

A Windows menu with available commands in bold; commands that lead to dialog boxes with ellipses.

Commands that appear in solid type in a pull-down menu are available for selection; all the requirements necessary for you to select the command have been fulfilled. In the Find menu, Repeat Last Find F3 is shaded gray (see fig. 2.10). A shaded command in a Windows menu is momentarily unavailable. The command may be unavailable because a required preceding step has not been completed or because the command is not appropriate for the type of document active in the application. The F3 to the right of the Repeat Last Find command is the shortcut key for that command. Some shortcut keys are combinations such as Ctrl+C. (Ctrl+C is the shortcut key for the Edit Copy command. This shortcut is executed by holding down the Ctrl key as you press the C key.)

Notice that the Replace command is followed by an ellipsis (...). When you choose a command followed by an ellipsis, you see a dialog box. A *dialog box* is a pop-up box that asks you to select additional options or make entries.

To exit from a menu without executing a command, follow the appropriate instructions:

Mouse: Click anywhere outside the menu or click the menu name a second time.

Keyboard: Press the Esc key once to close the menu and a second time to leave the menu bar and return to the document.

To change something in a Windows application, you *select* the text, graphical object, or data cell, and then *do* something to the selection by choosing a command. In most applications, if you do not select specific text or objects before you choose the command, the command applies only to the location of the insertion point.

In the following steps, you complete a menu command that boldfaces the heading of the list you typed. Before you can make the *Things to do today:* heading bold, you must select it. To select the heading as shown in figure 2.11, follow the appropriate instructions:

Mouse: Position the I-beam pointer to the left of the *T* in *Things*, and then drag to the right by holding down the mouse button as you move the mouse to the right. When the mouse is at the end of the word *today:*, release the mouse button. If you don't get it right the first time, just try again.

Keyboard: Position the flashing insertion to the left of the *T* in *Things*; press and hold down the Shift key as you press the right-arrow key. Holding down the Shift key selects text as the insertion point moves.

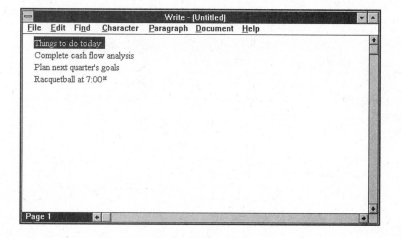

FIG. 2.11

Selected text to be changed by the next edit or character-formatting command.

This book uses the phrase *choose the menuname commandname command* to instruct you to complete a command. In this phrase, *menuname* refers to the name on the menu bar, and *commandname* refers to the name of the command on the pull-down menu. The phrase *choose the Find Find command*, for example, means that you should select the **Fin**d menu and then choose the **Find** command from that menu.

T I P

When the text you want to change has been highlighted, choose the **Character Bold** command by following the appropriate instructions:

> **Mouse:** Click on **Character** and then click on **Bold.**

> **Keyboard:** Press Alt, **C, B** or use the shortcut key, Ctrl+B.

Windows applications include an **Undo** command that undoes the last editing action you took. If you look at the command in the **Edit** menu now, it reads **Undo Formatting** because the last action you took was to format some text in bold. The **Undo** command changes to names such as **Undo Typing,** depending on the last action you took.

Explore Unfamiliar Menus
You can find out what commands are available in a Windows application by selecting a menu and closing it without making a choice. To see the commands in a menu adjacent to the open menu, press the left-arrow or right-arrow key.

Selecting Options from a Dialog Box

Dialog boxes appear when a command needs additional information. They enable you to type data entries and select options for the command. Dialog boxes provide four ways of selecting options or making data entries:

- Square check boxes enable you to choose one or multiple options.

- Round option buttons enable you to select one option from a group of options.

- Scrolling lists enable you to choose a named selection from a list of alternatives.

- Text boxes give you a space in which to type numbers or text.

In the following steps, you change the document format for the list you typed earlier in this chapter. A set of option buttons and text boxes will appear. Chapters 12 and 13 go into more detail about the uses of scrolling lists and check boxes.

Select the *optionname* Option

This book uses the phrase *select the optionname option* to instruct you to turn on an option or move the insertion point into an option. In this phrase, *optionname* refers to the name of the option button, check box, text box, or scrolling list. The phrase *select the Inch option in the Page Layout dialog box*, for example, means that you should turn on that option so that a dot appears in the circle to the option's left.

To deselect a round option button so that the black dot does not appear in it, select a different option from the group that button is in. To deselect a square check box so that the *X* disappears, select the check box a second time.

Mouse: To select an option button with the mouse, a check box, or a text box, click inside the button or box.

Keyboard: To select an item in a dialog box with the keyboard, hold down the Alt key and type the underlined letter of the option or box name.

To change the document layout of the document you typed earlier, follow these steps:

1. Choose the **Document Page** Layout command to display the Page Layout dialog box.

   Mouse: Click on **Document** and then click on **Page**.

   Keyboard: Press Alt, **D**, **P**.

   When the Page Layout dialog box first appears, the number in the Start Page Numbers At text box is selected (see fig. 2.12). The contents of the text box are highlighted, or the flashing insertion point is in the text box. To replace the selected number 1, type text or a number.

```
┌─────────────────────────────────────┐
│ ▬            Page Layout             │
│                                      │
│ Start Page Numbers At:  [1]   [ OK ] │
│                               [Cancel]│
│ Margins:                             │
│                                      │
│ Left:  [1.25"]   Right:  [1.25"]     │
│                                      │
│ Top:   [1"]      Bottom: [1"]        │
│                                      │
│ Measurements:                        │
│  ◉ inch  ○ cm                        │
└─────────────────────────────────────┘
```

FIG. 2.12

The Page Layout dialog box.

2. Select the **cm** measurement option.

> **Mouse:** Click on the **cm** button.
>
> **Keyboard:** Press Alt+C.

Notice that the selected option button has a black dot. A dashed line encloses the button name when you first select it.

3. Select the **inch** measurement option.

> **Mouse:** Click on the **inch** button.
>
> **Keyboard:** Press Alt+I.

4. Select the **T**op margin text box and type *2* for a 2-inch top margin. (Because inches are the default unit of measurement, you don't have to type the " symbol.)

> **Mouse:** Click between the 1 and " characters in the **T**op margin text box and press Backspace to remove the 1. Type *2*. You also can drag the mouse pointer across the contents of the text box and type *2*, or you can double-click in the text box and type *2*.
>
> **Keyboard:** Press Alt+T to select the contents of the **T**op margin text box. Press Del or Backspace to delete the selected measurement and type *2* to replace it. You also can type the number *2* to replace the selected number 1. To use the insertion point to edit the selected contents of a text box, press the left- or right-arrow key or click the I-beam cursor where you want the insertion point to appear.

5. Choose the OK button or press Enter.

> **Mouse:** Click on the OK button to complete your selections and execute the command.
>
> **Keyboard:** Press the Enter key to complete your selections and execute the command.

Saving Files

You can save the document containing your list so that you can add to it later. Follow these steps to save the list:

1. Choose **F**ile Save **A**s.

> **Mouse:** Click on **F**ile and then click on Save **A**s.
>
> **Keyboard:** Press Alt, **F**, **A**.

A File Save As dialog box appears with the flashing insertion point at the beginning of the File **N**ame text box.

2. Type the file name *TODO* (see fig. 2.13).

3. Choose OK or press Enter.

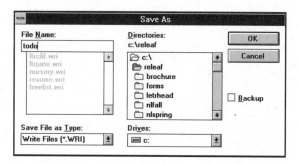

FIG. 2.13

The Save As
dialog box.

You do not have to type a file name extension because Write automatically adds the extension WRI. Notice that after you save the file, the file name, TODO.WRI, displays in the title bar of the Write window.

Getting Help

Most Windows applications include a **H**elp menu. You can display a window containing a list of the contents of Help by choosing the **H**elp **C**ontents command or by pressing the F1 key. You even can use the command **H**elp **H**ow to Use Help to explain how to use Help. Figure 2.14 shows the Help contents for Windows Write.

To display helpful information about any topic listed in the Help contents, click on the underlined item in which you are interested. With the keyboard, press Tab to move forward through items; press Shift+Tab to move backward through items. When the item you want is selected, press Enter.

To close and exit the Help window, choose the **F**ile **Ex**it command in the Help window or press Alt+F4, the shortcut key that exits an application.

For Related Information:

▶▶ To learn more about working with multiple applications, see "Integrating Windows Applications," p. 850 and "Copying and Linking between DOS and Windows Applications," p. 869.

▶▶ See "Troubleshooting Windows Applications," p. 1064.

FROM HERE...

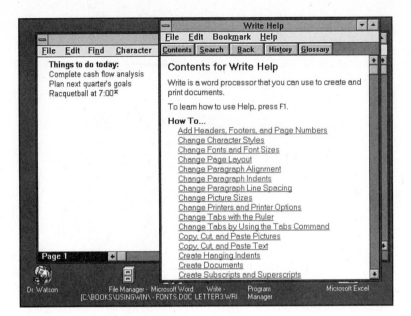

FIG. 2.14

Extensive on-line help is available from the Help Contents command.

Operating the File Manager

The File Manager is an application that comes with Windows and enables you to manage your files and disks.

The File Manager window initially includes one document window (see fig. 2.15). The document window is divided into two areas. On the left side, the File Manager displays your disk directories in a tree-like structure called the directory tree. On the right side, the files contained in the selected directory are listed. You can sort files by name, type, size, and date. You can use the File Manager to copy files or entire directories, start applications, and format new disks. With a mouse, you can drag a file or directory from one location and drop it into another location.

If you just finished the preceding exercise, Windows Write is active onscreen. To open the File Manager application, you must activate the Main group window. To activate the Main group window within the Program Manager and then start the File Manager, follow these steps:

1. Activate the Program Manager.

   Mouse: Click on the Program Manager window if you can see it. (Use the following keyboard technique if you cannot see the Program Manager window.)

Keyboard: Press Alt+Tab until the Program Manager window appears.

Notice that the Write window may still be visible behind the Program Manager. Both applications are available to you in memory; you can switch between them quickly.

2. Activate the Main group window within the Program Manager. Your screen should resemble figure 2.16.

   Mouse: Click on the Main window if you can see it or double-click on the Main group icon.

   Keyboard: Press Ctrl+Tab until the Main group window appears on top of the other windows on the desktop. If the Main group window is closed so that it appears as an icon, press Ctrl+Tab to select the Main group icon and then press Enter.

3. Start the File Manager program item icon.

   Mouse: Double-click on the File Manager icon.

   Keyboard: Press the arrow keys until the File Manager icon is selected as shown in figure 2.16 and then press Enter.

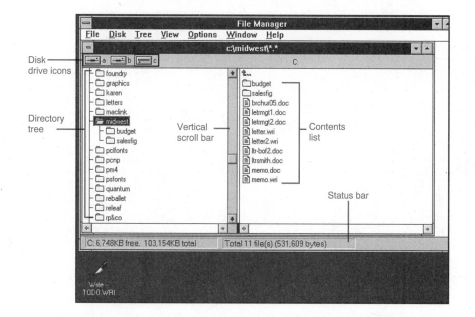

FIG. 2.15

The File Manager with the directory tree in the left window and the contents of a selected directory in the right window.

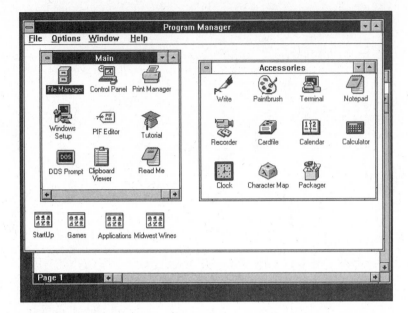

FIG. 2.16

Starting the File Manager application from the Main group window.

The File Manager appears in its own window and displays the directory tree of your hard disk (similar to that of fig. 2.15). The selected drive icon at the top of the File Manager window indicates which drive you are viewing. The list on the left shows the contents of the drive; the list on the right shows the contents of the selected directory. Chapter 5 describes how to expand the directory tree to see all levels and how to manage your files with this labor-saving application.

T I P   If the directory tree does not show the drive you want, change to a different drive by pressing Ctrl+*driveletter*, where *driveletter* is the letter of the drive you want active. To display the contents of drive D:, for example, press Ctrl+D. If you are using a mouse, click once on the disk-drive icon you want active.

Follow these steps to open the WINDOWS directory (if it is not open already):

1. Select the WINDOWS directory in the Directory Tree window on the left. If you cannot see the Windows directory, scroll the window until you can by clicking the down arrow or up arrow in the vertical scroll bar on the right side of the directory tree or press the PgDn or PgUp keys.

Mouse: Click on the WINDOWS directory name.

Keyboard: Press the down arrow until the WINDOWS directory is highlighted.

2. Open the WINDOWS directory and display its contents.

Mouse: Double-click on the WINDOWS directory name.

Keyboard: Press Enter with the WINDOWS directory selected.

The status bar at the bottom of the window shows information about available memory, directory space, or file size.

For Related Information:

▶▶ See "Understanding the File Manager's Display," p. 141 and "Operating the File Manager," p. 143.

FROM HERE...

Starting an Application from the File Manager

So far you have two applications running: Windows Write and File Manager. In this section, you start a third application, the Calendar application, from the File Manager.

You can start applications from the File Manager if you know the directory in which they are located. To start the Calendar application, follow these steps:

1. Select the CALENDAR.EXE file from the WINDOWS directory window (right side of the File Manager window). If you cannot see the file, scroll until you can.

Mouse: Click on the CALENDAR.EXE file.

Keyboard: Press the arrow keys to select CALENDAR.EXE.

Notice that when you select a file, the status bar at the bottom of the File Manager window shows you how many files are in the window and the size of the file you selected.

2. Start the Calendar application.

>   **Mouse:** Double-click on CALENDAR.EXE.

>   **Keyboard:** Press Enter with CALENDAR.EXE selected.

FROM HERE...

For Related Information:

▶▶ See "Starting Applications and Documents," p. 188.

▶▶ See "Using the File Manager's Drag and Drop Feature," p. 191.

Using Multiple Applications

With Windows, you can run multiple Windows or DOS applications and switch between them. You even can copy and paste data between applications. You can copy tables or charts from a spreadsheet application, for example, and paste them into a word processing report or copy drawings from a design application and paste them into a desktop publishing application. The following section takes you through a simple example that copies the racquetball appointment from Write and pastes it into the Calendar.

Switching between Applications

You can switch between multiple applications by clicking on an application's window if the window is visible. With the keyboard, switch between applications by pressing Alt+Tab.

If you have many applications running, you can use the Task List to switch between applications that are running. The Task List is a window that shows all the applications that are running (see fig. 2.17). To switch applications, select the name of the application you want to switch to from the list.

To display the Task List with the mouse, double-click on any exposed area of the desktop (outside of any open window). To display the Task List with the keyboard, press Ctrl+Esc.

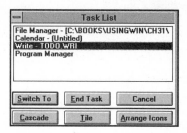

FIG. 2.17

The Task List
dialog box.

The Windows Write application is open but in an inactive window. To activate it, follow these steps:

1. Display the Task List.

   Mouse: Double-click on any part of the desktop.

   Keyboard: Press Ctrl+Esc.

2. Select and activate the Write application.

   Mouse: Double-click on the name Write in the list box.

   Keyboard: Press the down arrow to select the name Write and press Enter.

The Write application window is activated and overlaps the other windows.

Transferring Data between Applications

With Windows, you can transfer data and graphics between Windows applications. You also can use Windows to transfer data and graphics between some DOS applications. A reserved area of memory, known as the *Clipboard*, temporarily stores copied data. If you cut or copy another piece of data, the new data replaces the old data in the Clipboard. To transfer information, copy the data from one application, switch to the other application, position the insertion point, and paste in the data.

If you completed the steps in the preceding section, the To-Do list in Write should be active. To copy the 7:00 racquetball appointment to the Calendar, follow these steps:

1. Select the statement *Racquetball at 7:00*.

   Mouse: Click to the left of the *R* in *Racquetball*. Hold down the mouse button and drag the I-beam pointer across the phrase to select the entire phrase.

Keyboard: Use arrow keys to move the insertion point to the left of the *R* in *Racquetball.* Press and hold down the Shift key while you press the right arrow. As the insertion point moves, it selects the text. Continue until the entire phrase is selected.

2. Choose the **Edit C**opy command.

    Mouse: Click on **E**dit and then click on **C**opy.

    Keyboard: Press Alt, **E**, **C**.

3. *Activate* (switch to) the Calendar application.

    Mouse: If the Calendar window is visible, click on it; you also can use the Task List.

    Keyboard: Press Alt+Tab until the Calendar window is active.

4. Select the 7:00 time period on the Calendar.

    Mouse: Click on the down arrow in the vertical scroll bar until 7:00 PM is displayed; click to the right of 7:00 PM.

    Keyboard: Press the down arrow until the insertion point is to the right of 7:00 PM.

5. Choose the **Edit P**aste command.

    Mouse: Click on **E**dit and then click on **P**aste.

    Keyboard: Press Alt, **E**, **P**.

The phrase you copied from Write is pasted into the Calendar (see fig. 2.18).

Some Windows applications can link data to other Windows applications. You usually create these links by using **E**dit **C**opy to copy from the server application and **E**dit **P**aste **L**ink to paste the shared data into the client application. When data in the server application changes, the linked data in the client application changes. To link data in this way, you use Windows' object linking and embedding (OLE) capability, which is described more fully in Chapter 6. With OLE, you also can embed an object created in one application inside a file created in another application. You can edit the embedded object in the file where you embedded it, but you use the same application you used to create the embedded object.

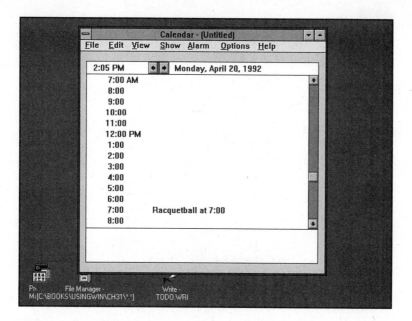

FIG. 2.18

Copying information from one Windows application and pasting it into another.

For Related Information:

▶▶ See also, "Understanding the Methods of Integration," p. 848.

▶▶ To learn more about working with multiple applications, see "Integrating Windows Applications," p. 850 and "Copying and Linking between DOS and Windows Applications," p. 869.

FROM HERE...

Exiting Applications and Windows

You can save your work in each application before closing the application by activating the application and then choosing the File Save As command like you did in "Saving Files" earlier in this chapter. In this section, you learn how to exit applications *and* Windows. If you try to exit an application or Windows, and a document has been changed but not saved, Windows asks whether you want to save the document. You must respond to this request before you can close the application.

Follow these steps to exit the Calendar:

1. Choose the **F**ile E**x**it command from the Calendar. The dialog box shown in figure 2.19 appears, asking whether you want to save changes to the document.

2. Choose **Y**es or press Enter. Because this document has not been saved before, the File Save As dialog box appears. (If you previously saved the file, choosing **Y**es or pressing Enter saves the document to its previous file name.)

3. Type a file name of 1 to 8 characters. Use letters and numbers but don't use spaces.

4. Choose OK or press Enter.

The Calendar window disappears.

A dialog box that asks whether you want to save documents that have changed before you exit an application.

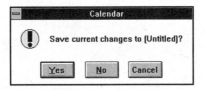

To close all the applications at once, activate and then close the Program Manager. Follow these steps to accomplish this task:

1. Activate the Task List.

   Mouse: Double-click anywhere *on the desktop* (not in a window or on an icon).

   Keyboard: Press Ctrl+Esc.

2. Activate the Program Manager.

   Mouse: Double-click on the name Program Manager in the list.

   Keyboard: Press the down-arrow key to select Program Manager and then press Enter.

3. Exit the Program Manager to exit Windows and all applications.

   Mouse: Double-click on the Program Manager Control icon at the left edge of the Program Manager title bar.

   Keyboard: Choose the **F**ile E**x**it Windows command by pressing Alt, **F**, **X**. You also can use the shortcut key Alt+F4.

4. The Exit Windows dialog box appears. Choose OK or press Enter to exit Windows and all Windows applications.

You are returned to the DOS prompt.

For Related Information:

FROM HERE...

◄◄ See "Exiting Windows," p. 60.

►► To learn how the Program Manager works, see "Operating the Program Manager," p. 116.

►► To learn how to use the File Manager to manage your disk and to start applications not in a group window, see "Operating the File Manager," p. 143 and "Starting Applications and Documents," p. 188.

Chapter Summary

With Windows, you are not limited to using the mouse or the keyboard. You can use any combination of mouse, touch typing, function keys, and shortcut keys. Use what you feel comfortable with and what best fits the task. Other ways to complete tasks are described in Chapter 1, "Operating Windows"; refer to that chapter as you begin using Windows.

To learn more about the many desktop accessories that come with Windows—including the accessories described in this chapter—read the chapters in Part III, "Using Windows Accessories."

PART

II

OUTLINE

Managing Your Windows Work Session

Getting Help

Windows applications and accessories have extensive Help screens to help you find information on procedures, commands, techniques, and terms. The tools in Windows Help enable you to search for topics, print Help information, annotate the Help screens with your own notes, and copy information from the Help screens to the Clipboard for use in other applications.

Although different Windows applications come from different software manufacturers, most manufacturers use the Help application supplied by Microsoft, the manufacturer of Windows. The Help applications in many different programs, therefore, all work similarly. You can learn the basics of using Help in one application and translate what you know to all your other Windows applications.

Although Help is part of your Windows application, Help also is a separate application. As such, Help runs in a separate window that overlays your application window. If you expect to use it frequently, you can leave Help open and easily switch between your application and the Help window. You also can minimize Help to an easily accessible icon at the bottom of your screen.

This chapter uses the Help screens in Notepad as examples. Many Windows accessories and applications use the same kinds of commands and procedures as the Notepad Help. Each application's Help screens are different, however, and you can learn how to use an application's Help by selecting the How to Use Help command from the Help menu.

Understanding Windows Help

You start Help by choosing a command from the **Help** menu or by pressing the F1 key. Figure 3.1 shows the Help pull-down menu for the Notepad accessory. Different Windows applications may have more or fewer Help menus or buttons.

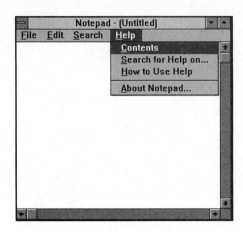

FIG. 3.1

Help pull-down menu for the Notepad application.

The following list defines the commands you find in the **Help** menu:

Contents	A table of contents of all Help topics
Search for Help on	Enables you to search the Help information for specific topics
How to use Help	Basic instructions for using Help
About...	Information about the current application, including copyright, the licensed user information, and the current Windows mode and memory and system resources information

To start Help, follow these steps:

1. Choose the **Help** menu.

2. Select the Contents command to display the Help contents (fig. 3.2).

   or

   Select the **S**earch for Help on command to display the Search dialog box (see fig. 3.4).

In most applications, you also can start Help by pressing the F1 key.

When you start Help by choosing the **Help Contents** command, the Help window usually has three sections: the menu bar, the button bar, and the Help text area. Figure 3.2 shows the Notepad's Help window.

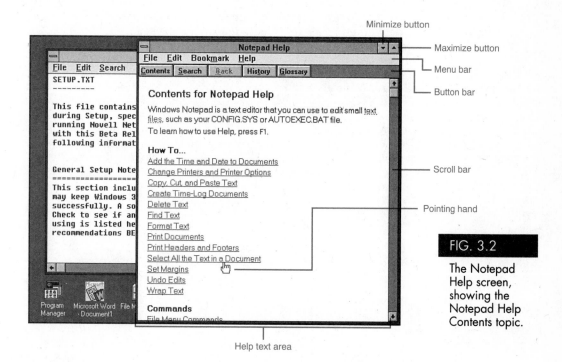

Minimize button
Maximize button
Menu bar
Button bar
Scroll bar
Pointing hand

FIG. 3.2

The Notepad Help screen, showing the Notepad Help Contents topic.

Help text area

Jumping between Topics in Help

The underlined topics listed in the Help Contents window are known as :hotspots and are used to display additional information about the topic. Some Help screens may contain graphic hotspots, which appear in a second color. When you move the mouse cursor over a hotspot on a Help screen, the mouse pointer changes to a pointing hand, as shown in figure 3.2. Selecting a hotspot shows additional information about the item in a text window or displays a Help screen about the topic.

To select a hotspot by using a mouse, just move the mouse over a hotspot, and the mouse pointer changes to a hand icon. Click once to select the item. To select a hotspot by using the keyboard, press the Tab key to move to the next hotspot or press Shift+Tab to move to the previous hotspot and then press the Enter key.

Displaying a Definition

Some Help topics contain words underlined with a dashed line. The dashed line indicates that a definition is linked to this word. To display the word's definition, click on the word. Click a second time to remove the definition box. If you are using a keyboard, press the Tab key until the dashed underline is selected and then press Enter to display the definition box. Press Enter a second time to remove the box.

Getting Help for a Dialog or Alert Box

Many Windows applications are designed to give you help as you work. When a dialog box or alert box with which you are unfamiliar appears, try pressing the F1 function key. This action may display *context-sensitive help*, or information related to what you are doing at the moment.

In many applications, if you press F1 when a dialog box appears, you see the definitions of what each item in the dialog box does.

If you Press F1 when an alert or error box appears, you see an explanation of the cause of—and possibly a solution for—the error.

Getting Help Quickly with the Button Bar

Help screens may have buttons on a button bar. (Some applications may use different Help buttons.) These buttons enable you to jump to a specific Help screen or perform other functions. Some buttons you may see are **C**ontents, **S**earch, **B**ack, His**t**ory, <<, >>, and **G**lossary.

You choose a button by clicking with the mouse pointer or by pressing the underlined key.

Seeing Help's Table of Contents

Selecting the **C**ontents command in the **H**elp pull-down menu or pressing F1 in a Windows application opens the Help Contents window. Figure 3.3 shows the Notepad Help Contents screen.

The Help window uses the standard Windows controls: scroll bars (vertical and horizontal as needed), minimize/maximize buttons, and the application control button in the upper left corner. The Help window can be resized as needed.

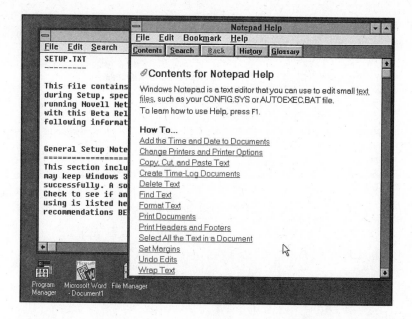

FIG. 3.3

Notepad Help
Contents screen;
the underlined
topics are known
as hotspots.

The Contents screen typically shows a short description of the screen's contents, and the major topics (How To... and Commands) for the screen. Each major topic is divided into subtopics, which are shown as underlined text in a different color. You can jump to the underlined topic by clicking on the topic's name or by tabbing to the spot and pressing Enter.

Searching for Topics by Key Word

You can use Help's **S**earch button to quickly find information on a particular topic. By using *keywords*—words associated with Help topics—you can display on-screen a list of topics that contains information about the keyword.

To search for a Help topic, follow these steps:

1. In the Help Button Bar, choose the **S**earch button.

2. From the Search dialog box shown in figure 3.4, select a phrase or word from the Type a **w**ord list or type the word for which you are searching in the text box; the list box scrolls to the first entry that most closely matches the characters that you type.

3. Choose **S**how Topics or double-click on the desired topic in the list box.

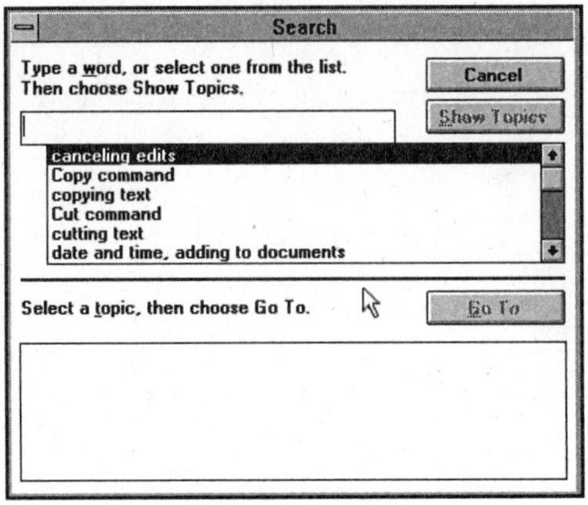

FIG. 3.4

The Search
dialog box.

4. The lower topic list box shows a list of all topics that you can
   select.

5. Select a topic and then choose **G**o To to display the Help screen
   for this topic.

   To cancel the search, select Close or press the Esc key.

Retracing Your Path through Help

If you move through different Help topics or search on different keywords, you may occasionally want to retrace this path to see where
you have been and to review previous topics. You can perform this
step by choosing the **B**ack button to see the Help topic you previously
viewed. Help tracks the topics that you previously viewed; using the
Back button shows these topics in reverse order until the Help Contents screen appears.

You use the << and >> (Previous and Next) buttons in many applications (such as Word for Windows and Excel) to move to the previous or
next topic in the Help file. These topics usually are related until you
reach the end of a series of Help topics; then the topic may become
unrelated. The Previous and Next buttons are useful when you want to
go through a series of Help screens about a particular topic. With the
keyboard, you can use the < and > keys.

Reviewing Previous Help Screens

To see a list of all the topics you covered, and even jump back to a previous topic, use the History button. The History button presents a list of up to 40 previously viewed Help screens. You can jump quickly to a Help topic from this list. To use the History button, follow these steps:

1. Choose the History button. The History window displays up to the last 40 topics viewed.

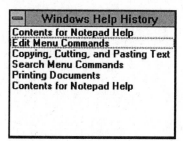

Windows Help History
Contents for Notepad Help
Edit Menu Commands
Copying, Cutting, and Pasting Text
Search Menu Commands
Printing Documents
Contents for Notepad Help

FIG. 3.5

The History
dialog box.

2. Choose a topic by double-clicking on (or pressing arrow keys to select) the topic and then pressing Enter.

Because the history list appears in a window and not a dialog box, this list remains visible until closed. Windows handles the history list in this way so that you can keep the list visible until you no longer need to select previously used Help screens. To close the history list, press Alt+F4 or double-click on the Control menu icon at the top left corner of the window.

Reviewing Terms with the Glossary Button

Some Help button bars include a **G**lossary button that shows a list of defined Windows terms. When you select an item in the glossary, a pop-up window presents the definition of the word or phrase. The **G**lossary button may be unavailable in some Help files.

Customizing Help for Your Work

Help is more than just a list of procedures or word definitions. You can print Help screens, copy screens into word processors, and even annotate your notes so that Help becomes customized to the kind of work you do.

Adding Custom Notes to Help Topics

You can customize Help information in a Windows application to make Help information more useful to you or to co-workers. You may want to include your company's default settings, for example, in a Help window on document formatting, or you may want to attach a note that names the templates for mailing labels to a built-in Help window that describes creating mailing labels. You can use Annotations to add these notes.

A Help window is marked as having annotated text by showing a paper clip icon next to the topic. To create an annotation, follow these steps:

1. Display the topic that you want to annotate.

2. Choose the **Edit Annotate** command from the menu bar. The Annotate dialog box appears, (see fig. 3.6).

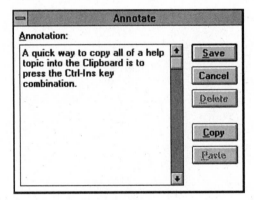

FIG. 3.6

The Annotate dialog box.

3. Type in notes or choose the **Paste** button to paste text you previously cut or copied to the Clipboard. By default, text wraps as you type. Press the Enter key to start a new line.

4. To copy text in the Annotation text box, select the text and then choose the **Copy** button.

5. Choose the **Save** button.

   A paper clip icon appears to the left of the topic title in the Help window.

To view an annotation, follow these steps:

1. Select the topic with an annotation.

2. With the mouse, click on the paper clip icon or use the Tab key to highlight the paper clip icon and press Enter.

3. Make all changes to the annotation and choose the **S**ave button. To return to the topic without making changes, choose Cancel.

To remove an annotation, follow these steps:

1. Select the topic with the annotation.

2. Click on the paper clip icon with the mouse or use the Tab key to highlight the paper clip icon and press Enter.

3. Choose the **D**elete button in the Annotate window.

The paper clip icon disappears from the Help topic, and the Annotate window is deleted.

Marking Special Places in Help

Bookmarks enable you to mark Help topics that you frequently reference. A bookmark is a named location. By assigning a bookmark to a location in Help, you can choose this bookmark's name from a list at any time to quickly go to the location.

To create a bookmark, follow these steps:

1. Display the Help topic that you want to add to the bookmark list.

2. Choose the Bookmark **D**efine command from the menu bar.

   The Bookmark Define dialog box, shown in figure 3.7, shows a list of existing bookmarks.

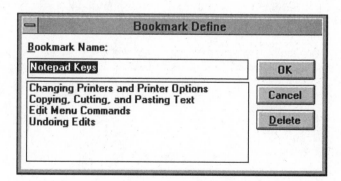

FIG. 3.7

The Bookmark Define dialog box.

3. In the **B**ookmark Name text box, type a bookmark description or accept the default topic.

4. Choose OK or press Enter.

To quickly go to a location you previously marked with a bookmark, follow these steps:

1. Choose the Bookmark menu.

2. From the lower part of the menu, select the bookmark name you entered. With the mouse, click on the desired bookmark. With the keyboard, press the number associated with the bookmark. If more than nine bookmarks are available, select **More** to see the next group of nine bookmarks.

To delete a bookmark, follow these steps:

1. Choose the Bookmark **D**efine command.

2. Select the name of the bookmark to delete.

3. Choose the **D**elete button.

Running Help for Other Applications

In some Help windows (especially those for newer applications), you can read Help information for more than just the application in which you are currently working. From within a Help window, you can open other applications' help files, or you can use the File Manager to open Help for an application.

After you start Help, you can open another application's help window by following these steps, with the Help window active:

1. Choose the **File O**pen command. The Open dialog box appears (see fig. 3.8).

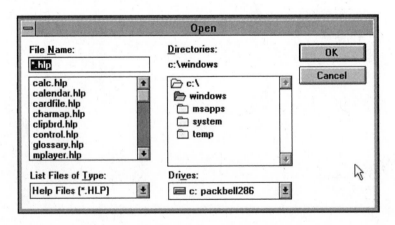

FIG. 3.8

The Open dialog box.

2. Select or type in the File **N**ame list box the filename with an HLP extension to view.

3. Choose OK or press Enter.

Printing Help Information

Often, having a printed copy of the Help topic in which you are interested can help you more clearly understand the topic. When the topic for which you want information is in the Help window, choose the **F**ile **P**rint Topic command to print the topic on the current printer. The entire text for the current Help topic prints. Choose the **F**ile **P**rint Setup command to select a printer or to change printer options.

> Some of the handiest information you can print or copy from Help is an application's shortcut keys. If you didn't get a shortcut keystroke template for the keyboard attached to your computer, look under the Help contents for a topic called Keyboard Shortcuts, or a similar name. Copy these topics to a word processor and reorganize them or print the topics directly from Help. You then can use a photocopier to reduce the printouts for pasting onto 3x5 cards for easy reference.

T I P

Copying Help Information to Another Application

You can create a collection of Help topics by copying Help information and pasting this data into a word processor document file. You can copy and paste into another application any information you see in a Help window. The information transfers as editable text.

Depending on the Windows application you are using, you can copy information from a Help window in two ways. In some applications, you are limited to copying all the text information in a Help window. To perform this operation, display the Help topic in which you are interested and choose the **E**dit **C**opy command from the menu bar. The full text of the window is copied to the Clipboard so that you can paste text into another application.

In other Help applications you can selectively copy Help information. To perform this action, take the following steps:

1. Display the Help topic you want to copy and choose the **Edit Copy** command. The Copy dialog box appears (see fig. 3.9).

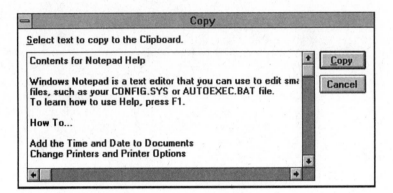

FIG. 3.9

The Copy dialog box.

To copy the entire Help topic, press Ctrl+Ins rather than choosing the **Edit Copy** command. Then skip to step 4. The entire topic is copied to the Clipboard.

2. Select the portion of the text that you want to copy. With the mouse, drag across desired text; with the keyboard, move the insertion point to the beginning of the selection and then use Shift+arrow key to select.

3. Choose the **Copy** button to copy the selected text to the Clipboard.

4. Switch tothe application in which you want to paste the information, position the insertion point, and then choose the **Edit Paste** command.

Shortcut Keys in Help

Several shortcut keys are available in Windows Help, which also are common to many Windows applications:

F1   In an application, starts the Help application and displays the Help contents for that application. If the Help window is active, the Contents for How to Use Help topic appears.

Shift+F1	In many applications, including Word for Windows and Excel, turns the mouse pointer into a question mark. To get information, you then can click on a command, screen region, or press a key combination.
Tab	Moves to the next hotspot (underlined topic) in the Help window.
Shift+Tab	Moves to the previous hotspot in the Help window.
Ctrl+Tab	Highlights all hotspots in a topic.
Ctrl+Ins	Copies the current Help topic to the Clipboard.
Shift+Ins	Pastes the Clipboard contents in the Annotate dialog box.
Alt+F4	Closes the Help window.

Exiting Help

While using the Help screens, you can minimize the Help window to an icon, or you can exit Help. To minimize Help to an icon, click on the minimize button or choose the Control Minimize command.

To exit Help, choose the File Exit command or press Alt+F4.

For Related Information:

◄◄ To learn more about getting around in Windows, see "Starting, Using, and Quitting Applications," p. 46.

◄◄ See also, "Operating in Windows," p. 67.

Chapter Summary

Help in Windows applications is a useful feature. Not only can you learn about individual commands, many applications also include numbered lists to help you with complex procedures.

An important aid to learning more about many Windows applications is to press F1 when a dialog box or alert box appears. The Help window that appears describes the options available in the dialog box. In some dialog boxes, you can get Help by choosing a Help button.

Some Windows applications even include help to aid you in changing from one application to another. Microsoft Excel, for example, contains a keystroke Help feature that accepts Lotus 1-2-3 keystrokes and then uses those keystrokes to demonstrate how to do the equivalent feature in a Microsoft Excel worksheet. You can learn as you work. Word for Windows has a similar feature that enables you to learn Word for Windows, even as you use WordPerfect keystrokes and commands.

Controlling Applications with the Program Manager

The Program Manager is the application and document coordinator for Windows. The Program Manager helps you keep together software applications and their associated data by organizing related applications and data into groups.

With the Program Manager, you can group applications and files together according to the way you work, and you can start an application and (optionally) an associated data file.

The Program Manager contains windows and icons that help you quickly find and run applications and documents you use frequently. The Program Manager contains the following parts:

Part	Definition
Program item icon	An icon that represents an application or an application with an associated document. Opening such an icon starts the application and opens the document (if one is associated with the icon). You can have a program item icon for each task you perform with an application—in other words, you can have multiple program item icons for the same application. Program item icons can be copied and moved to different group windows. The Windows Write icon in the Chapter 2 quick start is an example of a program item icon. Create your own program item icons by following the steps in "Adding Applications and Documents to a Group," later in this chapter.
Group icon	An icon that represents a collection of program item icons. Opening such an icon displays the group window where you can see the program item icons belonging to that group.
Group window	A window in the Program Manager containing a collection of program item icons. Usually a group window contains program item icons that relate to a specific type of work. A group window can contain multiple program item icons that start the same application. Group windows save you time by grouping together similar program item icons, making it easy to start applications and documents related to that group. Create your own group window by following the steps in "Creating Groups of Applications and Documents," later in this chapter.

The Program Manager opens as soon as you start Windows and remains as a running application while Windows runs. Closing or quitting the Program Manager closes Windows. The Program Manager remains ready for you to choose the group of applications and documents you want to work with. The Main group window, shown in figure 4.1, appears inside the Program Manager when Windows starts for the first time. After you begin using Windows, you probably will customize your Program Manager to fit your own work habits. If you do, the Program Manager will look different from the figure when you start Windows.

At the bottom of figure 4.1 you can see other groups. You can create groups like these that contain the applications and documents you use. When you installed Windows, you had the option of letting Windows create the Applications group for you from applications that Windows found on your hard disk. Regardless of whether you had this group created, you still have the Main group, the Startup group, the Accessories group, and a Games group. Following is a list of the contents of these groups.

Group	Contents
Main group	Includes system applications that help you control files, control printing, set up peripherals, customize the desktop, and manage files.
Startup group	Includes applications that Windows activates immediately on startup.
Accessories group	Includes desktop accessories that come with Windows, such as a simple word processor, calendar, calculator, and so on.
Games group	Includes two games, Solitaire and Minesweeper, to help relieve the stress of working for long hours at your computer.

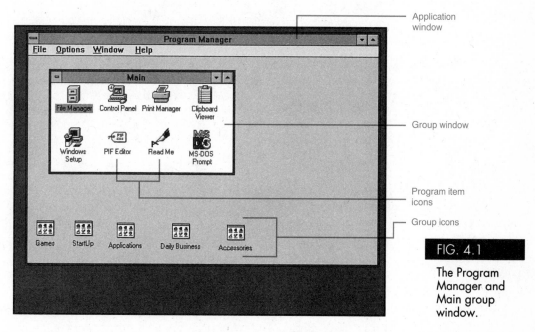

Application window

Group window

Program item icons

Group icons

FIG. 4.1

The Program Manager and Main group window.

Operating the Program Manager

Learning how to operate the Program Manager gives you the power to group applications and documents together in the same way you work with them. You also can start applications and documents quickly.

Figure 4.1 shows the four major parts of the Program Manager. Because the Program Manager is a Windows application, it resides in its own application window. The Program Manager window can contain many group windows or group icons. A *group window* and a *group icon* are two different views of a group of applications and data. A group window reveals all the program item icons. Group windows can be minimized to group icons; group icons can be changed back (restored) to group windows.

In figure 4.1, the Main group window is inside the Program Manager window. The Main group window contains program item icons that represent applications.

Figure 4.2 shows another group window, called Daily Business, opened on top of the Main group window. The Daily Business group contains program item icons referencing applications such as Excel, Word for Windows, and PageMaker; a single document that is used on a daily basis is associated with each application. Each of these applications and its associated document is represented by a program item icon. Each program item icon can contain one application and one associated document. That is why you see several Excel and Word for Windows icons—each contains a different associated document.

Each program item icon represents an application and an associated document. Program item icons in the Daily Business group have been given names such as Letter Template, Fax Template, Graphics, Invoice, Invoice Data, and Newsletter. When you create your own groups and program item icons, you can name them to fit the task they perform.

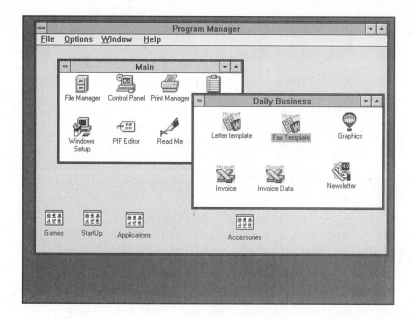

FIG. 4.2

Customized groups containing applications and documents.

Icons of applications that are running can be dragged on top of the Program Manager window or on top of one of the group windows. These icons may appear to be in the Program Manager, but they really are not; they merely overlap the Program Manager in the same way that windows overlap. If you reselect the Program Manager window by clicking it or pressing Ctrl+Esc, you see the Program Manager window without the overlapping icon.

T I P

You can start applications from the program item icons in a group window or from the File Manager (discussed in Chapter 5). Once an application is running, it occupies its own window. Applications also can be shown as icons on the desktop, but you should not confuse these icons with program item icons. The easiest way to tell them apart is that program item icons appear *inside* the Program Manager window, while icons that represent running applications appear *outside* the Program Manager window (unless you drag the icon on top of the Program Manager window). You can switch between applications that are running in a couple of ways, as described in Chapter 1.

Starting Applications from a Group Window

When you open a group window in the Program Manager, you see program item icons. Each icon refers to an application and, optionally, an associated *document,* or file of data. Sometimes the associated document is simply a new, empty document.

To open a group window, follow these steps:

1. Open the Program Manager (if it isn't open) by double-clicking the Program Manager icon or by pressing Ctrl+Esc and choosing the Program Manager from the Task List.

2. Activate the group window or open the group icon containing the program item you want to start. Click a group window to activate it; double-click a group icon to open it; or press Ctrl+Tab until the icon or window is selected (then press Enter if you need to open a group icon).

You can start an application in the active group window with a mouse by double-clicking the program item icon. If you are working with the keyboard, however, follow these steps:

1. Select the icon in the active group window by pressing the arrow keys until the program item name is highlighted.

2. Press Enter.

Moving an application to the Startup group causes Windows to start the application automatically when you start Windows. You can add any application you like to the Startup group (for details, see the section "Adding Applications and Documents to a Group").

Check the Program Item Properties

If you try to start a program item but the application does not start, or the application starts but the document cannot be found, check the program item's properties. The name or directory path to the application or document files may be incorrect. Files may have been moved, renamed, or erased.

To check the path and file name, activate the Program Manager and the appropriate group window. Select the program item icon and then choose the **File Properties** command. Change the path, application file name, or document file name in the **Command Line** text box. You can use **Browse** to find the correct path and file name for the application. The File Properties command is described in more detail in "Creating Groups of Applications and Documents," later in this chapter.

For Related Information:

◀◀ To learn more about navigating Windows, see "Working in the Windows Environment," p. 21 and "Controlling the Windows in Windows," p. 30.

◀◀ See "Starting, Using, and Quitting Applications," p. 46.

▶▶ See "Starting Applications and Documents," p. 188 and "Using the File Manager's Drag and Drop Feature," p. 191.

FROM HERE...

Customizing Groups

You don't have to limit yourself to the Windows Applications group that may have been created automatically for you. You can create your own customized groups to match the way you work, putting together applications and associated documents that you use to do specific jobs.

Creating and Deleting Groups

You can create your own groups to fit the way you work. Your groups can contain collections of applications and documents you use together for a task. The applications and documents can be located in different locations on your disk, yet they appear together in the group window. Items in a group can contain just an application or an application and one associated document.

> **Program Items Contain One Application and Document**
> Each program item contains either one application and no associated document, or one application and one associated document. Groups can contain many program items that start the same application but have different documents. For some applications like Word for Windows and Excel, however, each program item starts a different instance of the same application. This arrangement results in multiple copies of the application—a waste of memory when the application is large. (Not all applications will run multiple copies. You can have multiple program item icons for applications that will only run a single copy, such as Aldus PageMaker, and each icon can have a unique associated document, but only one copy of the program will run.)
>
> If you want an application to start with multiple documents, create an auto-opening macro that runs from the document specified by the program item. When the application and that document start, the auto-opening macro loads the other documents that are also needed. In Microsoft Excel 4, for example, you can create a Workbook that Windows associates with Excel. The Workbook opens all worksheets, charts, and macros that were open when you last selected File Save Workbook from Excel. Auto-opening macros and worksheets for Microsoft Excel are described in *Using Excel 4 for Windows,* Special Edition; auto-opening macros for Word for Windows are described in *Using Word for Windows 2,* Special Edition. Both books are published by Que Corporation.

Creating Groups of Applications and Documents

Before creating groups, imagine the tasks you perform each day. Divide those tasks into related groups, such as writing proposals, managing a project timeline and budget, or contacting clients and sending follow-up letters. Each of these groups of tasks can become a group window. Within each group window, you add program item icons representing the applications and documents needed to get that work done.

To create your own group, start with the Program Manager window active and follow these steps:

1. Choose the **File New** command.

2. Select the Program **Group** option.

3. Choose OK or press Enter. The Program Group Properties dialog box appears (see fig. 4.3).

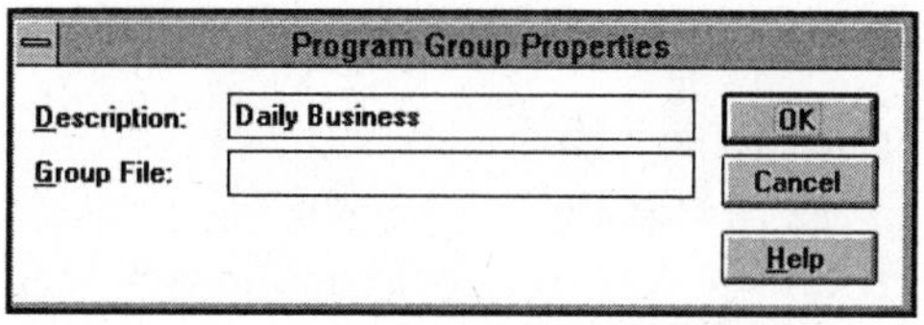

Program Group Properties

Description: Daily Business

Group File:

OK

Cancel

Help

FIG. 4.3

The Program Group Properties dialog box.

4. Type in the **D**escription text box the title you want under the group icon or as the title of the group window. Do not make an entry in the **G**roup File text box; Program Manager automatically creates a GRP file for the group you are creating.

5. Choose OK or press Enter.

The new group window you have created remains open on-screen. If you want to add applications and data to the window, leave it open. If you want to minimize the group window so that it appears as an icon, double-click the Control menu icon of the new group window. As a shortcut, press Ctrl+F4 to change the group window to an icon.

Protecting a Program Group

If you want to prevent changes to a group, designate it as a "read-only" group. Start the File Manager, select the group file (usually this is a file located in your Windows directory with a GRP extension), and choose the File **P**roperties command. In the Properties dialog box, select the **R**ead Only option from the Attributes group.

When you make a program group read-only, you can make no further changes to the Group window, unless you remove the read-only attribute. For example, you cannot add new program items to or delete program items from the protected group. You also cannot move or rearrange the program item icons in the protected group.

Adding Applications and Documents to a Group

Once you create and title a new group window, include in the window the applications and documents you use in this group. The applications and documents you put in a group are called *program items*; they appear as item icons in the group window.

T I P   Microsoft recommends that you do not include more than 40 program items in a single group.

To add items, applications, and documents associated with an application to a new or existing group, follow these steps:

1. Select the group window that will contain the program item.

2. Choose the **File New** command.

3. Select Program **I**tem from the New Program Object dialog box.

4. Choose OK or press Enter. The Program Item Properties dialog box appears (see fig. 4.4).

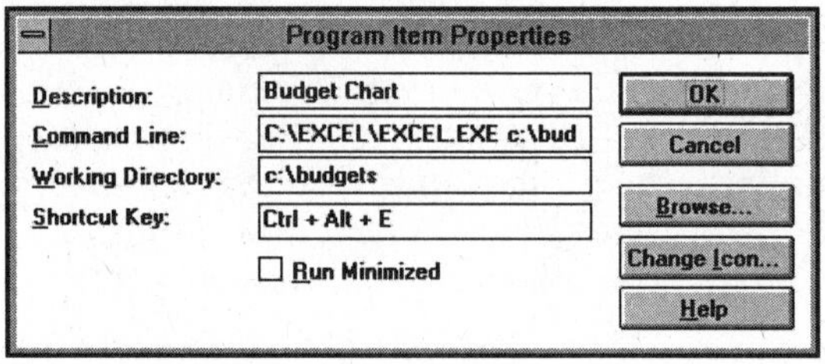

FIG. 4.4

The Program Item Properties dialog box.

Program Item Properties

Description:	Budget Chart
Command Line:	C:\EXCEL\EXCEL.EXE c:\bud
Working Directory:	c:\budgets
Shortcut Key:	Ctrl + Alt + E
	☐ Run Minimized

OK
Cancel
Browse...
Change Icon...
Help

5. Select the **D**escription text box and type the title you want to appear under the program item icon.

6. Select the **C**ommand Line text box and type the path name, file name, and extension of the program for this item. If you are unsure of the path and program file name, choose **B**rowse to display a list of files and directories (see fig. 4.5). Select the directory containing the application from the **D**irectories list, select the application from the File Name list, and choose OK. (To open a higher, or *parent*, directory, select the parent directory in the **D**irectories list—the one indicated by an "open folder" icon—and choose OK.) When you choose OK, the Program Item Properties dialog box reappears with the path and application name copied into the **C**ommand Line text box.

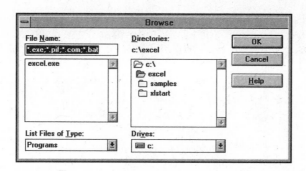

FIG. 4.5

The Browse
dialog box.

7. If you want a document such as a spreadsheet, letter, or data file
   to open with the application, type a space after the file name in
   the **C**ommand Line text box and then type the path and file name
   of the document. A completed command line where the application and document are in separate directories might look like this:

   C:\EXCEL\EXCEL.EXE C:\BUDGETS\JUNE.XLS

8. In the **W**orking Directory text box, enter the directory you want to
   be active when you start this application (your program defaults
   to this directory when opening or saving files).

9. Select the **S**hortcut Key text box and press Shift, Shift+Ctrl, or Ctrl
   while you type a character or function key. You see a shortcut key
   combination such as Ctrl+Alt, plus your character; press this key
   combination to switch to the application if it is running.

10. Normally, Windows chooses an icon to represent the program
    item you are creating. If more than one icon is available to repre-
    sent the item, the Change Icon button turns bold. Choose the
    Change **I**con button and select the icon you want to represent the
    application and document. Move through the icons using the
    scroll bar below the icon window. Choose OK or Cancel to return
    to the Program Item Properties dialog box.

11. Select the **R**un Minimized icon if you want the application to be
    minimized to an icon upon start-up.

12. Choose OK or press Enter.

To use icons other than those shown, choose Change **I**con to display   **T I P**
the Change Icon dialog box. In the File Name text box, enter
PROGMAN.EXE or MORICONS.DLL, including the full path where
those files are located (usually your Windows directory). To
access icons in the MORICONS.DLL file, for example, enter
C:\WINDOWS\MORICONS.DLL. You also can choose the **Browse**
button to locate these files.

Figure 4.6 shows a Program Item Properties dialog box that has been filled out to start Word for Windows and one document template. A program item can have only one document associated with an application.

FIG. 4.6

A Program Item Properties dialog box that specifies an application and one document.

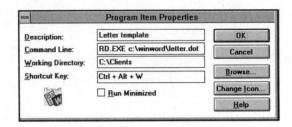

By default, the Browse window initially shows only application files (files with the extensions EXE, COM, BAT, or PIF). To see all the files in the directory, select the All Files option from the List Files of **Type** box in the Browse dialog box.

Creating a Program Item Icon

Another way you can create a program item icon is to run the File Manager and the Program Manager side by side, locate in the File Manager the application for which you want to create an icon, and drag the file name from the File Manager into the Program Manager. A program item icon appears in the group window where you drop the file name. You can use the **File Properties** command (described in the next section, "Redefining Groups and Program Items") to associate a document to the application.

Redefining Groups and Program Items

When you gain experience with groups and program items, you may want to change the names you have assigned them or change the document associated with a specific program item. You can make these changes easily.

To change the title of a group, follow these steps:

1. Select the group icon whose name you want changed (you cannot change the name of an open group window).

2. Choose the **File Properties** command.

3. Select the **Description** text box and type a new description. This text becomes the new title.

4. Choose OK or press Enter.

When you want to change the title of a program item icon, or when you want to change the application associated with an application, follow these steps:

1. Select the program item icon you want to change.

2. Choose the **File Properties** command.

3. Change the icon title in the **Description** text box or change the application or document name in the **Command Line** text box.

4. Choose OK or press Enter.

If you have used Version 3.0 of Windows, you may notice that some of the group and application names look different. Version 3.1 limits the width of names on the screen by "wrapping" the text to additional lines. This word-wrap feature is helpful because it can create names up to four lines long. But you may have to shorten some of the group and item names to avoid obscuring other icons beneath them in the window.

Deleting Groups

If you no longer use any of the program items in a group, or if you find a group unnecessary, you can delete the entire group so that it no longer appears in the Program Manager window. Deleting the group removes the group window and its program items from the Program Manager window; it does not delete the application files or data files from disk. To delete a group, follow these steps:

1. If the group window is open, minimize it to an icon by clicking its minimize button or by pressing Ctrl+F4.

2. Select the group icon you want to delete by clicking it or by pressing Ctrl+Tab until the group icon is selected.

3. Choose the **File Delete** command or press the Del key.

4. Choose **Yes** to delete the group.

Deleting Program Items

As your job changes, or as you become more familiar with Windows and groups, you frequently will want to keep a group but move or delete a program item in that group. Deleting the program item only removes the icon from the group window; it does not delete the application or data file from disk. To delete program items, follow these steps:

1. Open the group window containing the program item.

2. Select the program item by clicking it or by pressing an arrow key to select it.

3. Choose the File Delete command or press the Del key.

4. Choose Yes when asked to verify deletion.

Moving and Copying Program Items

As you become more familiar with your work habits in Windows, you may want to change the contents of your groups. That may mean copying or moving program items between groups. You also may find that one program item can be useful in more than one group window (you can use it repeatedly for different jobs). If that happens, don't re-create the program item in the multiple groups; instead, move or copy the existing program item to other groups where it is needed.

To move a program item to another group using a mouse, open the group window containing the program item and drag the program item onto the destination group window. You also can drag a program item from one group onto a group icon, but you have no control over where the program item is positioned in the destination window.

To move a program item using the keyboard, open the group window containing the program item. Select the program item to be moved by pressing the arrow keys. Choose File Move (or press F7); when the Move Program Item dialog box appears, select the name of the destination group window and choose OK or press Enter.

To copy a program item to another group using a mouse, follow these steps:

1. Open the group window containing the program item. Open the destination group window if you want to position the icon in a specific place or position the destination group icon where you can see it.

2. Press and hold down the Ctrl key and drag the program item icon where you want it in the destination group window or over the destination group icon.

3. Release the mouse button.

To copy a program item to another group using the keyboard, follow these steps:

1. Open the group window containing the program item.

2. Use the arrow keys to select the program item to be copied.

3. Choose the **File Copy** command.

4. Select the destination group's name from the **To** Group list in the Copy Program Item dialog box.

5. Choose OK or press Enter.

Duplicating a Program Item
To duplicate a program item in a group window, hold down the Ctrl key and use the mouse to drag the program item to a new position in the same group window. Release the mouse button to copy the program item in the original group window.

For Related Information:

▶▶ See "Using the File Manager's Drag and Drop Feature," p. 191.

◀◀ See "Operating in Windows," p. 67.

FROM HERE...

Controlling the Program Manager

The Program Manager is always available in Windows. It may appear on-screen in its own window or as the Program Manager icon. Activate the window or the icon to use the Program Manager.

If you can see the Program Manager or its icon, you can activate it by clicking anywhere on the Program Manager window, by double-clicking the Program Manager icon, or by pressing Alt+Tab until the Program Manager icon or window is selected and then releasing both keys.

If you cannot see the Program Manager window or icon, you can activate it by pressing Ctrl+Esc or double-clicking the desktop to activate the Task List. The Task List is shown in figure 4.7. From the Task List, select the Program Manager by clicking its name or by pressing the up- or down-arrow key. Choose the **S**witch To button or press Enter to activate the Program Manager.

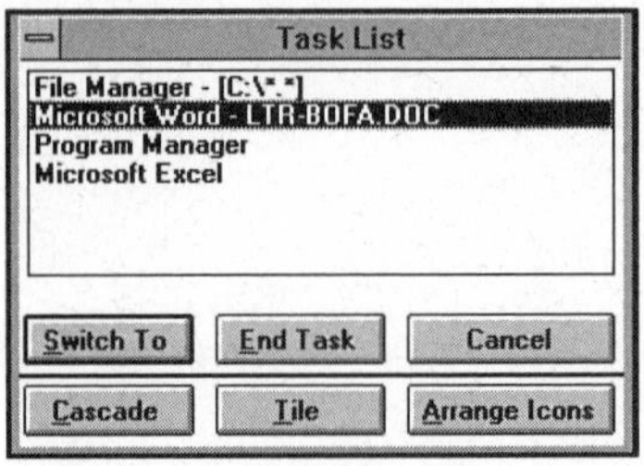

FIG. 4.7

The Task List
window.

Using Menu Commands
with the Program Manager

You can operate the Program Manager by using menus, mouse actions, or shortcut keys. The menu commands for the Program Manager are as follows:

Command	Action
File New	Adds a new group item to a group or creates a new group
File Open	Starts the selected program item and its associated document
File Move	Moves a program item to another group
File Copy	Copies a program item to another group
File Delete	Deletes a group or program item
File Properties	Changes the description, program name, document name, or icon for a program item
File Run	Starts the application whose name you enter, with or without a document (the application does not have to be a program item)
File Exit Windows	Quits Windows
Options Auto Arrange	Rearranges icons automatically in the selected group window when you change the window
Options Minimize on Use	Shrinks the Program Manager window to an icon when another application starts
Options Save Settings on Exit	When a check mark appears next to this item, Windows will save all changes to window sizes and positions to preserve the current environment for your next Windows session.

Command	Action
Window Cascade	Arranges windows in an overlapping cascade so that titles remain visible
Window Tile	Arranges windows side by side so that each window is visible
Window Arrange Icons	Arranges all group icons in a row at the bottom of the screen or all program item icons into neat rows in a selected group window
Window # (group names)	Selects a group and opens or activates its window
Help	Defines Program Manager terms and explains its operation

Using the Mouse with the Program Manager

By using the mouse you can open different groups, activate windows, and start items quickly. If you are familiar with how the mouse works in Windows, you can guess how most of the Program Manager operates. Following are some of the basic mouse actions:

Mouse Action	Result
Click an item in the active window	Selects the item
Click a window	Activates the window
Double-click a program item icon	Starts the program item (the application and its associated document)
Double-click a Group icon	Opens the Group icon to a Group window
Drag an item or window title	Moves the item within its group window or moves the group window within the Program Manager window

Using Shortcut Keys with the Program Manager

Although the mouse is the most intuitive method of operating the Program Manager, you can touch-type your way through almost any Windows application—including the Program Manager. Following are the shortcut keys you can use to operate the Program Manager:

Key	Result
Arrow keys	Moves the selection between items in the active group window
Ctrl+F6 or Ctrl+Tab	Moves selection to the next group window or icon
Enter	Starts the selected program item (the application and its associated document) or opens the selected group icon
Shift+F4	Arranges group windows in tiles
Shift+F5	Arranges group windows in a cascade
Ctrl+F4	Closes the active group window
Alt+F4	Exits Windows (You are given a chance to cancel the action.)

Minimizing the Program Manager to an Icon for Easy Access

Figure 4.8 shows the Windows desktop with the Program Manager minimized to an icon in the lower left corner. Whenever you need room on the desktop or want to remove visual clutter, minimize the Program Manager window to an icon. When the Program Manager shrinks to an icon, all the group windows remain "inside" the Program Manager icon. To minimize the Program Manager, click the minimize button (the down triangle) at the right edge of the Program Manager title bar. If you use the keyboard, follow these steps to minimize the Program Manager window:

1. Select the Program Manager Control menu (press Alt+space bar).

2. Choose the Minimize command.

To restore the Program Manager from an icon to a window, double-click the icon. If you use the keyboard, follow these steps:

1. Press Ctrl+Esc to display the Task List.

2. Press the up- or down-arrow key to select the Program Manager from the list.

3. Press Enter.

You can specify that the Program Manager minimize to an icon automatically whenever you start an application. To make this specification, choose the **O**ptions **M**inimize on Use command from the Program

Manager's menu bar. A check mark appears next to the **M**inimize on Use option when it is selected. To turn off this command, choose it again.

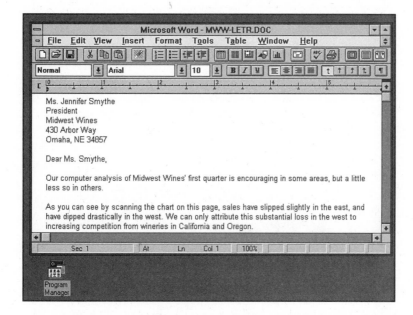

FIG. 4.8

The Program Manager has been shrunk to an icon to give more space on the desktop.

Opening Group Windows

Before you can open program items (applications and their associated documents), you must open the group window that contains the items. Group windows usually are stored as icons at the bottom of the Program Manager window (see fig. 4.9). The name of the icon appears below each icon.

If you are using a mouse, double-click the group item icon to open it into a window.

If you are using the keyboard, select and then open an icon by pressing Ctrl+F6 or Ctrl+Tab until the group icon you want is selected. Once it is selected, press Enter. If you find it difficult to read the names under each group icon, choose the **W**indow command in the menu bar and then select the group name from the list at the bottom of the menu.

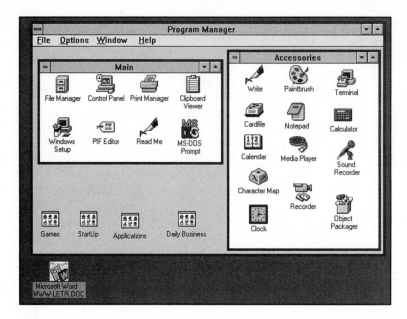

FIG. 4.9

The icons that represent groups stored at the bottom of the Program Manager window.

Sizing Group Windows

When you have multiple windows, you may want to change their sizes to see multiple groups or to maximize one group window so that it fills the inside of the Program Manager. You can resize a group window using the same window-sizing principles you learned in Chapter 1. If you are unfamiliar with window sizing, minimizing, and maximizing, you may want to review Chapter 1 or the quick start in Chapter 2.

To resize a group window with a mouse, move the pointer to a window edge until the pointer changes to a two-headed arrow. Drag the window edge to a new location and release the mouse button. To resize a group window with the keyboard, press Alt and the hyphen (-) to access the document Control menu; choose the **S**ize command. Press the arrow key that points to the edge you want to move and then press the arrow keys to move the edge. When the window is sized as you want it, press Enter.

Maximizing a Group Window
Double-click the title bar of a group window to maximize the window. You can restore a maximized window to its previous window size by clicking the restore icon (a double-headed arrow in the upper right corner of the window).

You can maximize, minimize, and restore group windows in the Program Manager just as you can do with windows (described in Chapters 1 and 2). To maximize, minimize, and restore with the mouse, click the arrowhead icons located at the right edge of each group window's title bar. The up arrowhead maximizes a window; the down arrowhead minimizes the window to an icon; the double arrowhead restores a maximized window to its previous size.

If you have many group windows, you may find it easier to move between groups if you minimize group windows you are not using. Another method of minimizing a group window with the mouse is to double-click the document Control menu icon. This icon is located at the left edge of the title bar of each group window. If you double-click this icon in an application window, you close the application window; but because group windows cannot be closed, they become icons when you double-click the document Control menu icon.

Arranging Group Windows and Icons

You can arrange group windows and icons manually, or you can use commands in the Program Manager to arrange them. If you want to manually move a group window, drag its title bar with the mouse pointer. To move a group window with the keyboard, press Alt and the hyphen (-), choose **M**ove, move the group window with the arrow keys, and press Enter.

If you want a cascading arrangement of overlapping group windows, like that shown in figure 4.10, choose **W**indow **C**ascade or press Shift+F5.

Cascading group windows are useful when you are working with primarily one group, when you have a large number of program items in each window, or when you have so many group windows that tiling produces small windows. When you have too many group windows to fit in a single cascade, Windows overlaps cascades. (The window that was active before you issued the command is the window on the top of the cascade.)

You can arrange group windows in tiles so that you can see a portion of all open group windows (see fig. 4.11). To achieve this arrangement, choose **W**indow **T**ile or press Shift+F4. Tiling group windows is useful if you need access to the program items from multiple groups. To tile multiple group windows, choose the **W**indows **T**ile command.

You can arrange group icons in the Program Manager window. If you want to move a group icon to a new location, drag the icon with the mouse to its new location. If you are using the keyboard, press Ctrl+Tab until the group icon is selected, press Alt and the hyphen (-) to open the document Control menu, choose the **M**ove command, press the arrow keys to move the group icon, and press Enter when you want to fix the icon's location. To arrange all the group icons at the bottom of the Program Manager window, first select any group icon and then choose the **Window Arrange Icons** command.

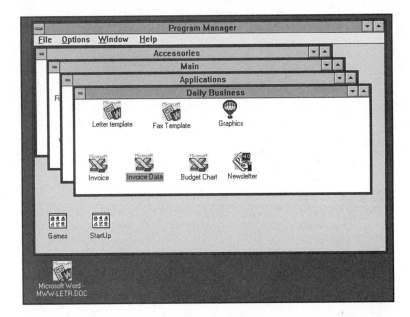

FIG. 4.10

Using **W**indow **C**ascade to overlap group windows.

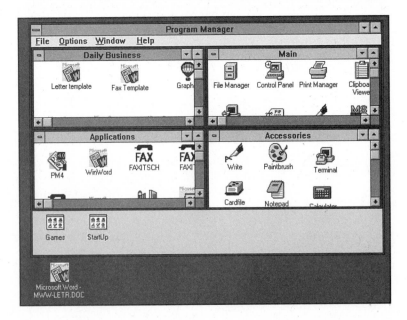

FIG. 4.11

Using **W**indow **T**ile to fill the Program Manager with a portion of all group windows.

To arrange the program item icons in a group window, select the group window and then choose the **Windows Arrange Icons** command. If you want Windows to automatically arrange program item icons whenever you open or resize a window, choose the **Options Auto Arrange** command. A check mark appears next to the **Auto Arrange** command when it is on. Choose the command again to turn it off.

Changing Groups with the File Manager

You can perform many of the operations you just learned from the File Manager. You also can use the File Manager to prevent accidental or unauthorized changes, such as deletions of program items. You learn how to do this in Chapter 5.

Restoring the Program Manager

If you have been running an application, the Program Manager may have been minimized to an icon. If you want to restore the Program Manager icon to a window, double-click the Program Manager icon if you can see it.

If you cannot see the icon or are using a keyboard, press Ctrl+Esc to display the Task List (see fig. 4.7). The Task List enables you to activate applications that are running in Windows but that are not visible (and Program Manager is always running when Windows is running). From the Task List, press the up- or down-arrow keys until Program Manager is highlighted; press Enter to start the Program Manager.

Quitting the Program Manager and Windows

Be careful when you quit the Program Manager. The Program Manager is always running and available because it is the central coordinator for any applications running in Windows. When you close or quit the Program Manager, you also quit Windows.

When you are ready to quit Windows, follow these steps:

1. Save the data in your application and then quit the application.

2. Activate the Program Manager, opening the icon into a window, if necessary.

3. Choose the **File Exit** command.

4. Choose OK or press Enter.

A quick way to quit any application—including the Program Manager—is to press Alt+F4.

FROM HERE...

For Related Information:

◀◀ To learn more about window sizing, minimizing, and maximizing, see "Controlling the Windows in Windows," p. 30.

◀◀ See also "Operating Applications," p. 77.

▶▶ To learn how to integrate applications so that you can pass data between them and use multiple applications for new business solutions, see "Integrating Windows Applications," p. 850.

▶▶ To learn how you can make your DOS applications run efficiently under Windows, see "Understanding How Windows Handles DOS Applications," p. 879 and "Controlling DOS Applications," p. 890.

Chapter Summary

In this chapter, you learned how the Program Manager can help you organize your applications and their associated documents into groups that match the way you work. You can use the Program Manger to create groups for each different type of work you do.

From here, you will want to learn how to manage the files on your disk: how to copy, move, and erase the files as well as how to create new directories. The File Manager displays trees showing the files in each directory and showing how directories are organized. The File Manager also displays the corresponding file lists next to the tree. Copying or moving with a mouse is as easy as dragging a file name to the disk or directory where you want it to go and dropping it in. With the File Manager, you may find that managing your hard disk and floppy disks can actually be fun.

Managing Files with the File Manager

The File Manager in Windows is a well-designed tool that acts like an office manager to help you see how files are organized; to manage disks; to copy, move, and erase files; and to start applications. When you first start the File Manager, you see a window divided into left and right sides. The directory tree area on the left shows the tree-like structure in which directories and subdirectories are organized on a hard disk. The right side of the window shows the files and subdirectories found within the directory selected on the left side. You can have multiple directory windows open—each showing the contents of a different directory in the contents list segment.

With the File Manager, you can view and maintain files and directories more easily than you can with DOS commands. If you have a mouse, for example, you can copy all the files in a directory to a diskette by dragging the directory's icon on top of the diskette drive icon and releasing the mouse button. Figure 5.1 shows the different parts of the File Manager.

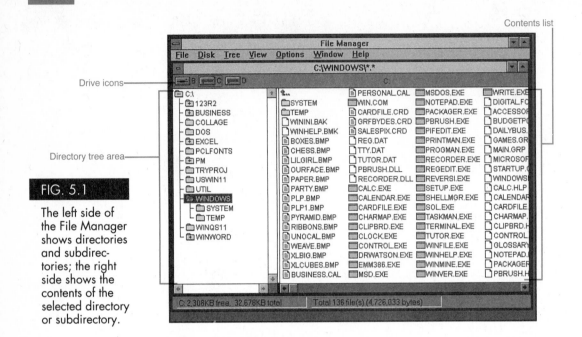

Contents list

Drive icons

Directory tree area

FIG. 5.1

The left side of the File Manager shows directories and subdirectories; the right side shows the contents of the selected directory or subdirectory.

If you are working with Windows for Workgroups, you can connect to *shared* directories on other computers on your network. Likewise, you can designate directories on your hard disk as shared so that other users can access the files in those directories. You use File Manager to connect to shared directories and also to share directories on your computer.

In addition to the commands associated with working with shared directories, the File Manager in Windows for Workgroups is different from the File Manager in Windows 3.1 in a few other ways. The most noticeable difference is the toolbar in the File Manager in Windows for Workgroups (see fig. 5.2). The toolbar gives you ready access to frequently used commands. There are a few other minor differences, which are indicated in the appropriate sections in this chapter. Features unique to the File Manager in Windows for Workgroups are designated with the Windows for Workgroups icon.

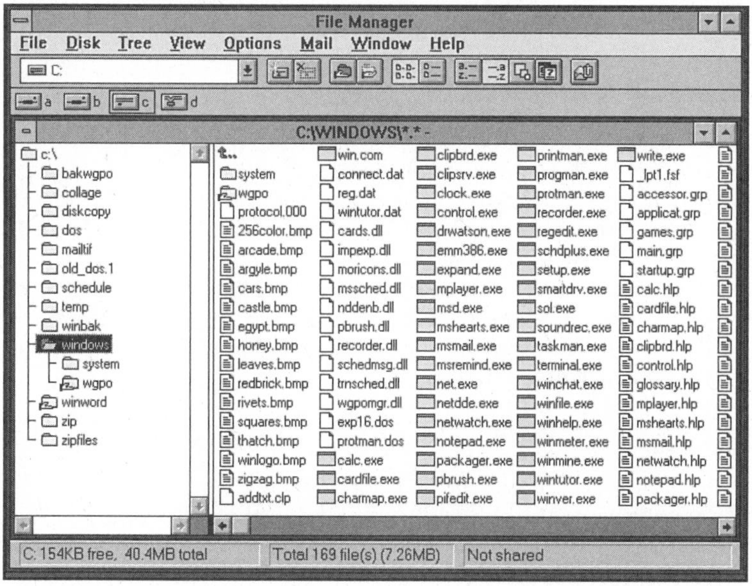

File Manager

FIG. 5.2

The File Manager window in Windows for Workgroups includes a toolbar for accessing frequently used command.

T I P

With DOS, you may have used or created batch files that executed multiple commands to copy directories, erase diskettes, and so on. You can automate the File Manager to reproduce many of these procedures by using the Windows Recorder. The Recorder records the keystrokes you press so that the process can be repeated upon request.

When you make a recording to delete, copy, or move files, do not use the mouse. Instead, use keystroke commands, File Manager menus, and explicit file names or DOS wild cards in file names. Doing so enables the Recorder to reproduce actions exactly. If you record mouse movements, the Recorder may not duplicate the action you want if windows or files are positioned differently on-screen. Refer to Chapter 15 for more information about the Recorder.

For Related Information:

▶▶ To continue using existing DOS batch files with Windows, see "Running DOS Memory-Resident Applications," p. 884 and "Understanding Why Windows Uses PIFs," p. 886.

FROM HERE...

Understanding Storage, Memory, Files, and Directories

The computer does all calculations and work in electronic *memory*. (Electronic memory is known as *RAM*, Random-Access Memory.) RAM is where Windows and your applications work. The data you work on also resides in RAM. If the computer loses electrical power, the data, application, and Windows are lost from memory. Because electronic memory is limited in size and disappears when electrical power is removed, the computer needs a way to store large amounts of data and applications for long periods of time.

You use *magnetic storage* to store applications and data for long periods of time or when the computer is turned off. Magnetic-storage media are floppy disks (which are removable and don't contain much space) or hard disks (which are internal to the computer and have vast amounts of space). When you start an application or open a data file, the computer places a *copy* of the information stored in magnetic storage (on floppy disks or a hard disk) into electronic memory (RAM). If power is lost, the magnetic copy still is available.

You save the work in magnetic *files*, which store the data on a floppy disk or hard disk. Over time, you may have hundreds or even thousands of files. Searching for a specific file among the thousands of file names that the File Manager displays could be very time-consuming.

To make the job of finding files easier, hard disks usually are organized into *directories*. If you think of the hard disk as a filing cabinet, directories are like the drawers in the filing cabinet. In a filing cabinet, each drawer can hold a different category of document. In a hard disk, each directory can hold a different category of file. The files in a directory can be *applications* (also known as *programs*) or *documents*.

Within a filing-cabinet drawer, you can further segment the drawer with file folders. Within a hard disk, you can segment a directory by putting subdirectories under it. *Subdirectories* also hold files.

The process of organizing a hard disk is similar to organizing a filing cabinet. With File Manager commands, you can create, name, and delete directories and subdirectories. (Some networks, however, may prevent you from altering or creating directory structures.) For example, you may want a WINWORD directory for word processing jobs. Within the WINWORD directory, you may want subdirectories with names such as BUDGETS, SCHEDULE, LETTERS, and REPORTS.

Large computers and networks have multiple hard disks, each disk with its own drive letter. In figure 5.1, there are three disks, as shown by the icons for drives B, C, and D. Each disk acts like a separate filing cabinet and can have its own unique directories and subdirectories.

For Related Information:

▶▶ To learn more about memory, see "Using Memory Efficiently," p. 962 and "Solving Memory Conflicts," p. 1072.

▶▶ To learn more about managing your hard disk, see "Optimizing Hard Disk Performance," p. 969.

FROM HERE...

Understanding the File Manager's Display

Before you use File Manager, you will find it helpful to understand the different characteristics of the File Manager display. Recognizing the display features enables you to more quickly perform file management tasks like listing the contents of a directory or finding the total space used by a group of files.

For those of you using Windows for Workgroups, you will find File Manager very similar to the Windows 3.1 File Manager. However, for some of the added features that you get with Windows for Workgroups File Manager, see the section "Windows for Workgroups File Manager Display."

Windows 3.1 File Manager Display

When you first start the File Manager, the *directory window* is divided into two parts. In figure 5.3, the *directory tree*, with the expanded structure of directories and subdirectories on drive C, occupies the left portion of the window. The *contents list* on the right shows the files in the C:\EXCEL\LIBRARY directory.

The plus and minus signs shown in the directory tree designate expandable and collapsible branches. The directory icons in the directory tree do not display plus and minus signs by default. To display them, select the Tree Indicate Expandable Branches command. At the top of the directory window (just below the menu bar) are icons that represent the available *disk drives*. The title bar shows the *directory path* for the currently selected directory.

Directory path

Selected subdirectory

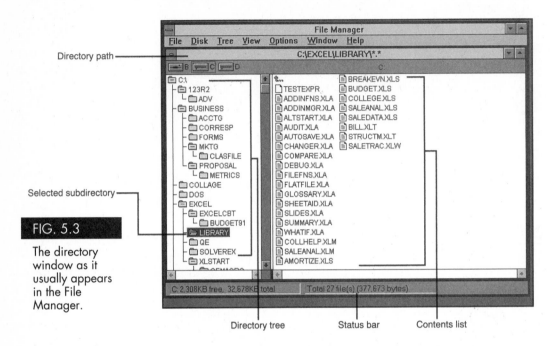

FIG. 5.3

The directory window as it usually appears in the File Manager.

Directory tree   Status bar   Contents list

Notice the *status bar* at the bottom of the File Manager. At right, the bar always displays the number and sum total size of the files on the selected subdirectory. When the directory tree portion of the window is active, the left portion of the bar shows the available storage on the active disk. When the contents list is active, this area shows the total size in bytes of the selected files. Scroll bars appear on the right and bottom sides of the directory tree and at the bottom of the contents list. If either segment contains more information than it can show at once, the scroll bar is shaded.

The directory tree contains miniature folder icons, which represent directories and subdirectories. The contents list shows files as miniature icons that represent documents. The first time you start the File Manager, a plus sign (+) in a directory or subdirectory icon indicates that additional subdirectories are inside the icon. A minus sign (-) in a subdirectory icon indicates that the directory can be collapsed inside its parent directory. A folder icon without a plus or minus sign indicates that it is the lowest level of subdirectory. (If you cannot see pluses and minuses, choose the **T**ree **I**ndicate Expandable Branches command to display them.)

When a directory or subdirectory icon is expanded, as shown in figure 5.3, you can see the underlying subdirectories. Notice the vertical lines and indentations that show how directories and subdirectories are dependent. When a directory or subdirectory is open, its icon changes to look like an open folder, and its contents are displayed in the contents list.

At any given time, the File Manager's *focus* is on only one area of the window: the drive bar, the directory tree, or the contents list. The area that has a selection with a highlighted background has the focus. In the area with the focus, you can use the arrow keys on the keyboard to change the selection. Press Tab to move the focus between areas.

The File Manager can display multiple directory windows at one time to show the file contents of any directory or subdirectory you select. To make comparing disk contents or copying or deleting files easy, open multiple directory windows onto different disks and directories.

Windows for Workgroups File Manager Display

The File Manager in Windows for Workgroups is slightly different in appearance from the File Manager in Windows 3.1 (see fig. 5.4). Just below the menu bar is the *toolbar*. The *buttons* on the toolbar enable you to quickly access several frequently used File Manager commands. Each button represents one of the menu commands. You can customize the toolbar so that it includes buttons for whatever commands you want (see "Customizing the Toolbar"). See "Using the Toolbar with the File Manager" in this chapter to learn how to use the toolbar.

Also located on the toolbar (at the left end) is a drop-down list of all the drives available for you to use, including *network drives*, which are directories being *shared* by other users. The *share name* and a *computer name* may appear next to the names of network drives in this list (see "Working with Networks in Windows for Workgroups").

When a directory is shared, it is represented in the directory tree as a folder with a hand underneath it (see fig. 5.4). The BUSINESS and COLLAGE directories in the figure show that they are shared.

Operating the File Manager

As with most Windows applications, you can operate the File Manager with the mouse, by touch typing, or with shortcut keys. Use the method that is most convenient for you. A combination of mouse actions and typing is fast and flexible.

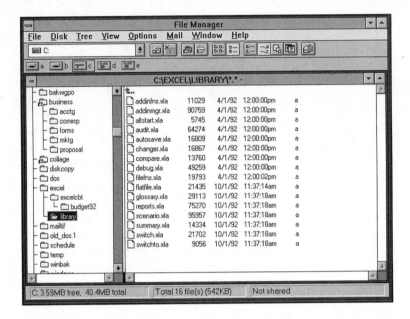

FIG. 5.4

The directory window in the File Manager in Windows for Workgroups includes a toolbar.

Using Commands with the File Manager

Table 5.1 lists the commands available in the File Manager. You can select these commands with either the keyboard or mouse.

Table 5.1 File Manager Commands

Command	Description
Disk Copy Disk	Copies the contents of one diskette to another diskette of the same capacity
Disk Format Disk	Formats a diskette
Disk Label Disk	Creates or changes the volume label on disks or diskettes
Disk Make System Disk	Formats a disk and includes the system files for diskette start-up
Disk Net Connections	Connects to a particular network drive (only displayed if you are on a network)

Command	Description
Disk Connect Network	Connects the computer to a network Drive (only displayed if you are on a network)
Disk Disconnect Network	Disconnects the computer from a Drive (only displayed if you are on a network)
Disk Select Drive	Selects a different disk drive
File Associate	Associates a selected document file with an application so that you can open a document in an application by opening only the document file
File Copy	Copies selected files or directories to a new location
File Create Directory	Creates a directory or subdirectory within the currently selected directory or subdirectory
File Delete	Deletes selected files or directories
File Exit	Exits and closes the File Manager
File Move	Moves selected files or directories from one location to another
File Open	Starts the selected application, opens a directory window of the selected directory, or opens the selected document and starts the application associated with the document
File Print	Prints the selected text file to the current printer
File Properties	Displays some information about a selected file and allows changes to a file's Read Only, Hidden, Archive, and System attributes
File Rename	Renames selected file or directory
File Run	Starts a selected application with a data file (if one is associated) or with a start-up argument (if one is associated)
File Search	Searches for file or directory names that meet naming patterns you set. You can search the entire disk with this command.

continues

Table 5.1 Continued

Command	Description
File Select Files	Selects files and directories in the active directory window
Mail Send Mail	Sends a mail message with selected files attached to the message (see Chapter 10, "Using Mail with Windows for Workgroups")
Options Customize Toolbar	Adds, removes, and rearranges the buttons on the toolbar
Options Drivebar	Displays a bar with drive buttons for each drive connected to your computer. Selecting a drive button displays the contents of that drive in the File Manager window.
Options Font	Changes the font, font style, and font size used to display directory and file information
Options Minimize on Use	Minimizes the File Manager to an icon when you start an application
Options Save Settings	Enables the automatic saving of current on Exit settings of all options in the Options menu
Options Status Bar	Displays the status bar at the bottom of the File Manager for information about the selected files or directories
Options Toolbar	Displays the toolbar at the top of the File Manager with buttons for quickly carrying out several File Manager commands
Tree Collapse Branch	Collapses the lower level subdirectories into the selected directory
Tree Expand All	Expands all directories and subdirectories; files are not shown.
Tree Expand Branch	Expands the selected directory to show all lower subdirectories
Tree Expand One Level	Expands the selected directory to show the next level
Tree Indicate	Uses plus (+) and minus (-) symbols Expandable Branches to indicate whether or not a directory contains subdirectories

Command	Description
View **All** File Details	Shows all information about the files and file attributes (name, size, date and time most recently edited, and attributes)
View by File **Type**	Limits the files displayed to the specified types and/or to files whose names match specified parameters
View Directory **Only**	Displays the contents list only
View **Name**	Shows the file and directory name in the current directory window
View **Partial** Details	Shows selected information about the files. (You select what you want to show.)
View Sort by **Date**	Sorts file names by last modification date (oldest dates first)
View **S**ort by Name	Sorts file names by name (alphabetical order)
View Sort by **Size**	Sorts file names by size (from largest to smallest)
View Sort **by** Type	Sorts file names by type (alphabetically by extension name)
View S**p**lit	Moves the dividing line between the directory tree and the contents list
View T**r**ee and Directory	Displays the directory tree on the left and the contents list on the right
View T**r**ee Only	Displays the directory tree only
Window #	Activates the indicated window. All open windows' names are assigned a number in the list.
Window Arrange Icons	Arranges minimized directory windows icons in a row at the bottom of the screen.
Window **C**ascade	Arranges windows so that they cascade in overlapping fashion from top left to lower right
Window New Window	Opens a new directory window
Window **R**efresh	Rereads the disk and updates the active window to match the disk contents

continues

Table 5.1 Continued

Command	Description
Window Tile	Arranges windows to fill the File Manager so that the contents of all windows are visible
Window Tile Horizontally	Arranges open windows horizontally so that the contents of all windows are visible
Window Tile Vertically	Arranges open windows vertically so that the contents of all windows are visible

Using the Keyboard with the File Manager

To operate the File Manager by using keystrokes, use this section as a quick reference. This section lists the keyboard shortcuts; complete instructions for procedures using these keystrokes are in following sections.

When you are in the *drive icon area*, use the keystrokes in the following list:

Keystroke	Action
Tab or F6	Moves the active area between the disk-drive icons, the directory tree, and the contents list
Ctrl+*letter*	Selects and opens the drive specified by *letter*. For example, Ctrl+C selects drive C and displays the directories on this drive in the directory tree area.
← or →	Moves the selection among the drive icons if you have tabbed into the drive area of the window
Enter	Opens the selected drive and displays the contents of the drive in the directory-tree area of the window

When you are in the *directory tree area*, use the following keystrokes:

Keystroke	Action
↑ or ↓	Moves the selection to a directory or subdirectory above or below the currently selected directory in the directory-tree section of the window
→	Selects the first subdirectory (the daughter) within the currently selected and open directory when you are in the directory-tree section of the window
←	Selects the directory that contains the current subdirectory (the parent) when you are in the directory-tree section of the window
Ctrl+↑ or Ctrl+↓	Restricts selections to a subdirectory level within the current directory
PgUp	Selects the directory one window up
PgDn	Selects the directory one window down
Home	Selects the root directory for the disk
End	Selects the last directory in the window
letter	Selects the next directory or subdirectory, beginning with *letter*
- (hyphen)	Collapses the selected directory. (The minus sign key also works.)
+ (plus)	Expands the selected directory one level
* (asterisk)	Expands all branches in the selected directory
Ctrl+*	Expands all branches on the disk

When you are in the *contents list area*, use the keystrokes in the following list:

Keystroke	Action
PgUp	Selects the file or directory one window up

continues

Keystroke	Action
PgDn	Selects the file or directory one window down
Home	Selects the first file or directory in the window
End	Selects the last file or directory in the window
letter	Selects the first file or directory beginning with *letter*
Shift+arrow	Selects all files or directories over which you move the selection highlight
Shift+F8	Selects nonadjacent files; keeps current selections as you move the selection highlight without selecting additional files. Press the space bar to select or deselect files; press Shift+F8 to return the arrow keys to normal.
Ctrl+/ (slash)	Selects all items
Ctrl+\ (backslash)	Deselects all items except the one that was selected when you started
↑,↓	Moves the selection between files or directories
←,→	Scrolls the contents window left or right
space bar	Selects or deselects the current file or directory when moving the selection with Shift+F8
Enter	Opens a directory if the directory is selected or starts an application if an application or the associated data file is selected

Using the Mouse with the File Manager

If you have a mouse, the File Manager can be much easier to use. The mouse makes selecting and copying nonadjacent files very easy. The following chart lists some activities and the mouse actions you do to achieve them.

Activity	Mouse Action
Select a directory	Click on a directory in the directory tree area
Select a file	Click on a file in the contents list
Select multiple and adjacent files	Click on the first file; press and Shift+click on the last file
Select multiple nonadjacent files	Ctrl+click on each file
Start an application or open a document file	Double-click on the application file or an associated document file
Expand a directory one level	Double-click on the icon with the plus sign (+) to the left of the directory you want to expand
Collapse a directory one level	Double-click on the icon with the minus sign (-) on the open folder icon above the directory you want to collapse
Copy a file	Drag the file name onto another disk drive
Move a file	Drag a file name into a different directory on the same disk drive

For Related Information:

FROM HERE...

◄◄ To learn more about navigating the File Manager, see "Understanding Windows Terminology," p. 26; "Controlling the Windows in Windows," p. 30; and "Using Menus and Dialog Boxes," p. 35.

◄◄ See also "Operating the File Manager," p. 86.

Using the Toolbar with the File Manager

If you are working with File Manager in Windows for Workgroups, you can quickly execute many File Manager commands with the toolbar, which is located immediately below the menu bar. To execute a command, click the button on the toolbar for that command. File Manager comes with a default set of buttons in the toolbar, which are described in the following table. The table lists the icons in left to right order as they appear in File Manager. You can also customize the toolbar so that it includes buttons for the commands you use most frequently (see "Customizing the Toolbar").

Icon	Button Name	Description
	Connect Network Drive	For connecting to a network drive
	Disconnect Network Drive	For disconnecting from a network drive
	Share As	For sharing a directory with other users on a network (this button is only available when you are running in 386-enhanced mode)
	Stop Sharing	Stops the sharing of a directory with other users (this button is only available when you are running in 386-enhanced mode)
	View Name	Changes display to show file names only
	View All File Details	Changes display to show all file details
	Sort By Name	Sorts files alphabetically by file name
	Sort By Type	Sorts files alphabetically by file name extension
	Sort By Size	Sorts files by size, from largest to smallest
	Sort By Date	Sorts files by date, starting with most recent files
	Send Mail	Sends a mail message with selected files attached to the message

Selecting and Opening Files and Directories

File Manager follows the primary rule of all Windows applications: *Select, then Do.* When you want to work on a file or directory in the File Manager, you first must find and select the file or directory. After you select a file, you can display information about the file and start, copy, move, or delete the file. After you select a directory, you can find information about the directory contents, copy or move the directory, or open the directory to see the subdirectories or files it contains.

Selecting a New Disk Drive

Before you can work with files and directories, you must be in the correct disk drive. The disk drives available in the computer appear as icons under the directory window title bar. The currently selected drive appears outlined. If the focus is on the drive icon bar, the currently selected drive also displays with a dark background. To change to a new drive with the mouse, click on the drive icon you want to activate.

When using the keyboard to change to a new drive, first notice whether the focus is in the drive icon area of the window. Press the Tab key to move the focus among the three screen areas.

If the focus is in the drive icon bar, change to a new drive by pressing the left- or right-arrow key to move the focus to a different drive; then press Enter. The highlight moves behind the drive you selected.

If the focus is in the directory tree or contents list area of the window, press Ctrl+*letter* to change to a different drive, where *letter* is the drive's letter. (If you change to a diskette drive containing an unformatted disk, File Manager prompts you to format the diskette. Refer to the later section, "Formatting Diskettes," to learn how.)

In Windows for Workgroups' File Manager, you can also select the drive you want to work with by using the drop-down list at the left end of the toolbar (see fig. 5.5). The advantage to using the drop-down list is that you can easily see the shared directory associated to the drive letter.

To open this list, click the down arrow to the right of the list or press F2. Click the drive you want to activate or use the up- or down-arrow keys to select the drive you want to activate and press Enter.

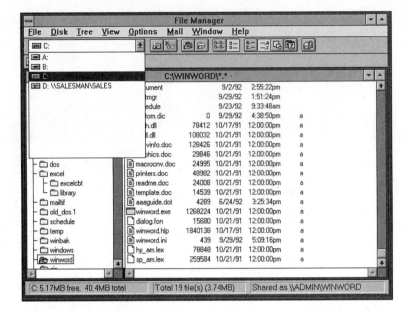

FIG. 5.5

Selecting a drive using the drive list on the toolbar.

Selecting, Expanding, and Collapsing Directories

The directory window, shown in figure 5.6, always displays in the File Manager window. It may be either in its own window or in an icon at the bottom of the File Manager window. The directory tree area in the left half of the File Manager shows the hierarchical structure of the area of the disk you are currently examining.

> **Select One Directory at a Time**
> You can select only one directory at a time in a given directory window. You can, however, open multiple directory windows, each displaying a different directory. Open more than one directory when you want to see the contents of multiple directories at one time. Copying files between directories is easier when you open a source-directory window and a destination-directory window. To learn how to open a second File Manager window, refer to the upcoming section, "Opening and Selecting Directory Windows."

To select a directory using the mouse, click on the directory or sub-directory you want. If you cannot see the directory, use the vertical

scroll bar on the directory tree area to scroll it into sight before clicking. If you need files in a subdirectory, open the directory above the
desired subdirectory first, as described later in this section.

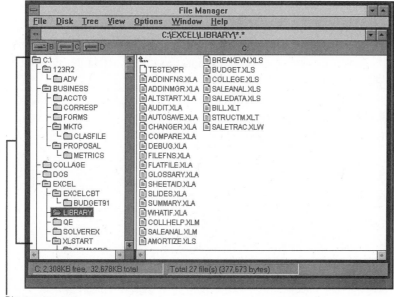

Directory tree area

FIG. 5.6

The directory tree
area.

To select a directory using the keyboard, follow these steps:

1. Press Tab if necessary to move the focus to the directory tree
   area of the window.

2. Press Ctrl+*letter* to change to the drive that contains the files you
   want.

3. Select a directory from the tree with the keys described in "Using
   the Keyboard with the File Manager," earlier in this chapter.

After you select a specific directory, you may want to see the subdirectories beneath it. Or you may want to collapse the fully expanded
directory structure so that you can see the directories at a higher level.
Figure 5.6 shows a directory structure with directories expanded. The
BUSINESS directory is a parent directory that has been expanded to
show the ACCTG, CORRESP, FORMS, MKTG, and PROPOSAL
subdirectories beneath it. Collapsed directories do not show the
subdirectories they contain.

Directory icons appear as file folders. If a directory icon contains a
+ (plus) sign, the directory contains subdirectories. If a directory icon

contains a - (minus) sign, the directory can be collapsed so as not to display its subdirectories. If the directory icon does not contain a + (plus) sign, no subdirectories are contained within this directory (or the plus and minus signs are hidden—to display them, choose the Tree Indicate Expandable Branches command).

To expand or collapse a directory or subdirectory with the mouse, use one of the following mouse actions:

- Double-click on the + (plus) sign in a directory icon if you want to expand the directory one level.

- Double-click on the - (minus) sign in a directory icon if you want to collapse the directory.

To expand or collapse a directory or subdirectory with the keyboard, follow these steps:

1. Select the directory or subdirectory.

2. Press one of the following keys:

Key	Action
- (hyphen)	Collapses the selected directory
+ (plus)	Expands the selected directory one level
* (asterisk)	Expands all subdirectories in the selected directory
Ctrl+* (asterisk)	Expands all subdirectories on the disk

To expand or collapse directories with the menu commands, follow these steps:

1. Select the directory or subdirectory.

2. Choose one of the following commands:

Command	Action
Tree Expand One Level	Expands the selected directory to show all subdirectories at the next lower level
Tree Expand Branch	Expands the selected directory to show all lower subdirectories
Tree Expand All	Expands all subdirectories on the disk
Tree Collapse Branch	Collapses the lower level subdirectories into the selected directory

Opening and Selecting Directory Windows

You can have many directory windows that show the contents of individual directories. Figure 5.7 shows the File Manager with numerous directory windows. Notice that each directory window displays a different directory—and even different disks. For any directory window, you have the option of displaying just the directory tree, just the list of files in the directory, or both. Use the View command to select one of these three options. As you see later in this chapter, having multiple windows open onto different directories and disks is a convenient way to copy or move files with a mouse.

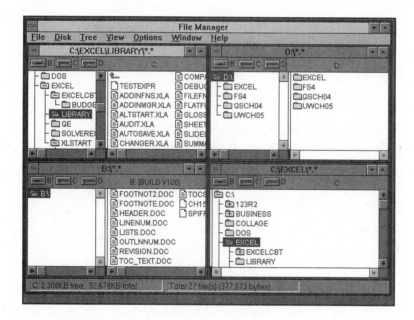

FIG. 5.7

Directory windows, each displaying the contents of different directories.

To open a new directory window, choose the **W**indow **N**ew Window command. The new window will display the path name of the previously active window in the title bar, followed by a colon and 2, which indicates that the window is the second one associated with this particular directory. When you choose another directory, however, the path name in the new window changes.

T I P   To cycle through all the open directory windows, press Ctrl+F6. To arrange all the directory windows on-screen, choose the **Window Cascade** command or the **Window Tile** command.

Each file within a directory window displays an icon that helps identify its type of file. These file shapes are shown in the following list.

Icon	Type of File
Directory Tree Icons	
📂	Open directory or subdirectory
📁	Closed directory or subdirectory
Contents List icons	
▭	Application or batch file having the extension EXE, COM, PIF, or BAT (choosing one of these files may start an application)
📄	Document file associated with an application (choosing one of these files starts the application that created the file)
📄	Other files
Shared directory icon	
📁	Directory that is shared with other users

Suppose that you have multiple directory windows open and want a specific window to be active. If you are using a mouse and can see the window you want, click on a portion of this window to make it active. If you are using a keyboard, press Ctrl+F6 until the window you want is active or select the **Window** menu and choose the name of the window you want from the menu. (If you have more than nine windows open, the **More Windows** command appears at the bottom of the **Window** menu. Choose it to select from a scrolling list of open windows.)

T I P   A quick way to open a new window in File Manager is to double-click on a disk drive icon. Double-click on the icon for diskette drive A, for example, to open a new window displaying the contents of a diskette in drive A. Double-click on the current drive icon to duplicate the window currently displayed. Often, follow this step by tiling your windows so that you can see the contents of all open windows. A shortcut to tiling your windows vertically is to press Shift+F4.

Changing or Closing Directory Windows

Each directory window usually contains both a directory tree and a contents list. However, you can change this to another View option for any given window. You might be doing some intensive disk management, for example, and need to display multiple directory windows for easier moving and copying. To save screen space, you can display one directory tree together with multiple contents lists. To do this, follow these steps:

1. With a single directory window open, choose the **View Tree** Only command.

2. For each directory whose contents you want to see on the screens, open a new window.

3. Select each window in turn and choose the **View Directory O**nly command. Leave one window in tree-only format and use it for quick perusals of the directory structure.

4. Choose **W**indow **T**ile if you want to see all the open directory windows at all times. If you have more than a few windows open, you might need to maximize the File Manager window to work effectively.

Directory windows are document windows, so you can use the mouse or document Control menu to resize, move, or close each window. Activate the window you want to change by clicking on it or by pressing Ctrl+F6 until it is on top of the other windows.

To close the active directory window using a shortcut key, press Ctrl+F4.

To control the active window with the keyboard, press Alt+hyphen (-) to display the Control menu. The Control menu lists all the commands necessary to move, resize, or close the window.

For Related Information:

◀◀ To learn more about how to control document windows using the mouse or keyboard, see "Controlling the Windows in Windows," p. 30 and "Controlling with Mouse or Keyboard," p. 68.

FROM HERE...

Selecting More Than One File or Directory

Before you can act on a file, you must select it. In some cases—when copying or deleting files, for example—you may want to select multiple files before choosing any command.

To select a single file with the mouse, click on the file name. To select multiple adjacent files, click on the first file, press and hold down the Shift key, and click on the last file. All files between the two files you clicked on are selected. To select nonadjacent files, click on the first file and hold down the Ctrl key as you click on other files. If you want to retain current selections but deselect a file, Ctrl+click on the file you no longer want selected.

To select a single file with the keyboard, press the arrow keys to move the selection to the file name you want. To select multiple adjacent files, move the selection to the first file, press and hold down the Shift key, and press an arrow key. To select nonadjacent files, select the first file, press Shift+F8, press an arrow key to move to the next file to be selected, and press the space bar. Move to the additional files you want to select and press the space bar. To deselect a file and retain other selections, move to the selected file and press the space bar. Press Shift+F8 to return to normal mode (selecting a single file at a time).

If you want to select all files in a directory window with a given extension, select a contents list window and choose the **F**ile **S**elect Files command. The dialog box shown in figure 5.8 appears.

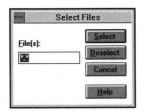

FIG. 5.8

The Select Files dialog box with *.* specified.

In the **F**iles text box, type the name for the file you want to select. You can use a pattern of DOS wild cards in the file name.

Use wild cards, such as * and ?, to search for a group of files or directory names or to search when you don't know the exact name of the file or directory. In the example shown in figure 5.9, the pattern E*.XLS searches for all file names beginning with E and having the extension XLS (an Excel worksheet). Although the file name must begin with E, the rest of the file name can be any group of letters (as specified by *).

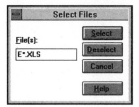

FIG. 5.9

The Select Files
dialog box with
E*.XLS specified.

To select all files in the window, choose the **S**elect button while the
Files text box displays *.*. If you want to deselect certain files, change
the **F**iles parameter and choose **D**eselect. Choose Close when you finish
making the selection(s).

> A quick way to select all the files in a selected contents list is to
> press Ctrl+/. To deselect all files but one, press Ctrl+\.

T   I   P

Canceling Selections

If you select the wrong file or directory, you can cancel any selection
you do not want. To cancel a single selection with the mouse, click on
another file or directory. If you select multiple files and want to cancel
one but retain the others, press and hold down the Ctrl key as you click
on the file you want to deselect.

To cancel a single selection with the keyboard, press an arrow key to
select another file or directory. If you select multiple files or directories
and want to cancel one but retain the others, press Shift+F8, press the
arrow keys to enclose the incorrect selection with the dashed focus
line, and press the space bar. Deselect any other incorrect selections
and press Shift+F8 to return to normal selection mode.

To cancel a selection while the Select Files dialog box is on-screen,
change the Files parameter to *.* and choose the **D**eselect button.

Searching for Files or Directories

Losing a file is frustrating and wastes time. With Windows, you can
search disks or directories for file names similar to the file you have
misplaced. To search for a file by its name or part of its name, follow
these steps:

1. Select the disk drive you want to search.

2. Select the directory (if you want to search a single directory).

    If you do not know the specific directory that contains a file, select the parent directory of all subdirectories that might contain the file.

3. Choose the **File Search** command. The Search dialog box appears (see fig. 5.10).

FIG. 5.10

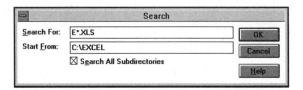

4. Type in the **Search** For text box the name of the file for which you are searching. You can use a pattern of DOS wild cards in the file name.

5. To search all directories on the current disk, specify the root directory in the Start **From** text box. By default, Windows searches all subdirectories beneath the directory you select. To search the specified directory only, turn off the **Search** All Subdirectories option.

6. Choose OK or press Enter.

A Search Results window, like the one shown in figure 5.11, displays the paths and file names of all files that match the pattern you were seeking. When you see the file or application you want in the Search Results window, start the document or application by double-clicking on it with the mouse or by selecting it and pressing Enter. You can start documents and applications together if the document has been associated with an application, as explained in "Associating Documents with an Application," later in this chapter.

When you use wild cards in a name pattern, remember that the * wild-card character finds any group of characters in the file name in the same or following positions. The ? wild-card character matches any single character within the file name that is in the same position as ?.

Suppose that you know the directory in which a file is located and the date or time at which the file was last saved, but you don't know the file name. You can display the time and date of all the files in the directory window to help you locate that specific file. Choose the View **All** File Details command to show the time and date on which files were last saved. This command also indicates file attribute(s) at the right.

FIG. 5.11

The Search Results window.

If you want to save screen space, you can choose the **View P**artial Details command and specify which particular file details to display in the Partial Details dialog box (see fig. 5.12).

FIG. 5.12

The Partial Details dialog box.

To sort the files in the directory window by name, type, size, or date, choose the corresponding Sort By command under the **View** menu. Figure 5.13 shows a directory window after choosing the **View** Sort By **D**ate command.

T I P

Some Windows applications, such as Word for Windows, can search through their document files and return a list of all files that contain specific words or phrases. An application's search facility can be more effective and precise than the File Manager's search command.

For Related Information:

FROM HERE...

◀◀ To learn more about operating Windows, see "Using Menus and Dialog Boxes," p. 35 and "Starting, Using, and Quitting Applications," p. 46.

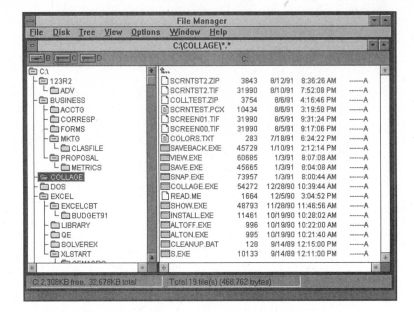

FIG. 5.13

A directory window sorted by date (the newest files are displayed first).

Controlling File Manager Windows and Displays

You can arrange the windows and files in a way that makes it easy to get work done, whether copying files between directories, making backup copies to disk, or deleting files. The following sections explain how to manipulate the appearance of the Windows display screen.

Arranging Directory Windows and Icons

You can arrange directory windows and icons in three ways. You can arrange them by manually sizing and positioning them, by cascading them to show all the window titles, or by placing them in tiles to show each window's contents. You also can minimize windows so that they appear as icons.

To arrange directory windows in a cascade like that shown in figure 5.14, choose the **Window Cascade** command or press Shift+F5. The active window becomes the top window in the cascade.

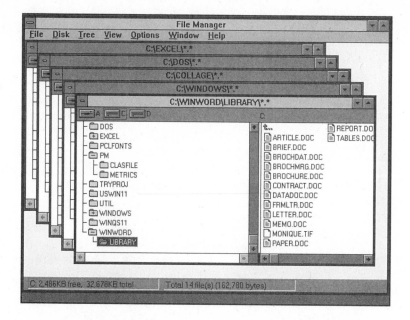

FIG. 5.14

Windows in
a cascade
arrangement.

To arrange directory windows in tiles so that the screen is evenly divided among the windows (see fig. 5.15), choose the **Window Tile** command or press Shift+F4. The active window becomes the window at the
top left of the screen.

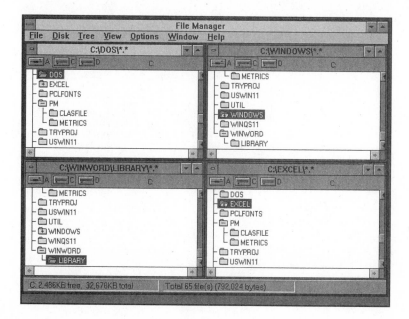

FIG. 5.15

Windows in a
tile arrangement.

In Windows for Workgroups, File Manager provides two ways to arrange directory windows in tiles. Choose the **Window** Tile **H**orizontally command to distribute directory windows in tiles that are arranged one on top of the other. Choose **Window** Tile Vertically to distribute directory windows in tiles that are arranged side by side.

When windows are arranged by cascading or by tiling, you still can use each directory window's Control menu to move a window. Chapters 1 and 2 describe how to use the Control menu to move a window.

T I P

You can save time if you minimize to icons directory windows that you use frequently (see fig. 5.16). When you want to work with the directory contained within the icon, maximize the icon. To minimize a directory window into an icon, click on the minimize button (the down arrow at the top right of the window). Alternatively, press Alt+hyphen (-), N (for Minimize). To maximize a directory icon into a window, double-click on the icon; alternatively, select the icon by pressing Ctrl+F6 and then press Alt+hyphen (-), X (for Maximize). Remember that you move among icons with the keyboard by pressing Ctrl+F6 or Ctrl+Tab. Chapter 1, "Operating Windows," describes how to minimize windows, maximize icons, and move both windows and icons.

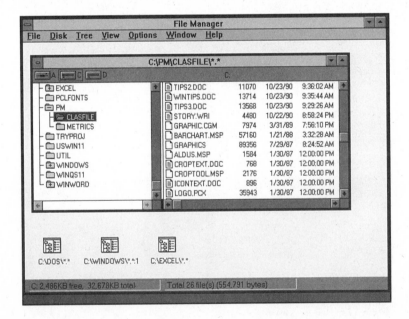

FIG. 5.16

Directory icons keep frequently used directory windows available.

Specifying File-Display Details

You can specify what file information appears in the directory window. **View Name** shows only the file names and extensions. **View All File Details** shows all file information. The **View Partial Details** command enables you to select the information you want displayed. To display file information, follow these steps:

1. Activate the directory window you want to change. If you want to change the display of all subsequent windows you open, activate the directory tree area.

2. Choose the appropriate command. The following chart lists the commands that affect the window display.

Command	Description
View Name	Displays only names and directories
View All File Details	Displays the name, size, date and time last saved, and file attributes
View Partial Details	Selects a custom display showing one or more of the following file characteristics:
	Size—displays the file size in bytes
	Last Modification Date—displays the last date the file was modified and saved
	Last Modification Time—displays the last time the file was modified and saved
	File Attributes—displays one of the following letters for different attributes:
	A Archive
	S System
	H Hidden
	R Read Only

3. If you chose **View Partial Details**, choose OK or press Enter after you select one or more of the options.

You can sort the directory window by any of the characteristics displayed. Use the **View Sort By** commands as explained later in this section. If you want to change a file's attributes, use the **File Properties** command, described later in this chapter.

Figure 5.17 shows the Partial Details dialog box from which you can select the different file characteristics you want to display. Figure 5.18 shows two directory windows, each displaying different sets of file characteristics.

FIG. 5.17

The Partial Details dialog box.

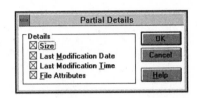

FIG. 5.18

Two directory windows, each showing different file characteristics.

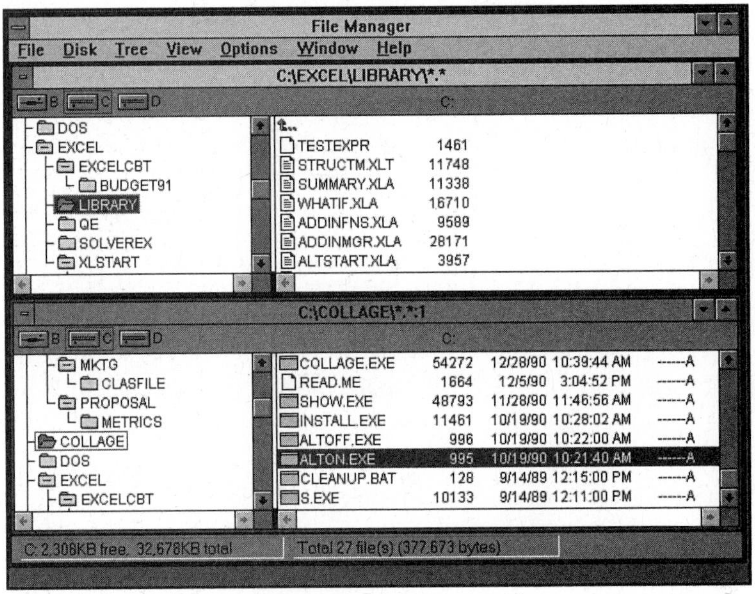

Hiding the Status Bar

You can change some characteristics of the File Manager window. For example, you can hide the status bar at the bottom of the File Manager window.

Leave the Status bar turned on to see available storage and the number of files. The status bar displays important information about the active window. If the directory tree is selected, the status bar shows the available storage on the disk and the number of files in the current directory. If the contents list is selected, the disk storage information is replaced by the number of selected files and the total size of the selected files.

If you want to find out how much room you have on a disk, change to that disk and look at the status bar.

You may want to remove the status bar from the bottom of the File Manager so that you can display more files. In general, however, you should display the status bar so that you can monitor the available disk storage. To turn on the status bar, choose the **O**ptions **S**tatus Bar command. A check mark appears next to the command when the option is on. Choose the command again to turn off the status bar. (This action also removes the check mark.) All directory windows you open subsequently also omit the status bar.

Hiding the Toolbar and Drivebar

You can choose to display or not display the toolbar and drivebar. If you need more room to display files, or do not use the toolbar, you may want to turn off one or both of these options. To turn off the toolbar, choose the **O**ptions **T**oolbar command. Choose the command again to turn the toolbar on. To turn off the drivebar, choose the **O**ptions **D**rivebar command. Choose the command again to turn the drivebar on. A check mark appears next to these commands when the options are on. When you turn off the option, the check mark is removed.

Changing the Font

By default, File Manager displays directory and file names in 8-point MS Sans Serif font. This small font is generally optimal for displaying as many entries as possible while still remaining readable. You can change the font, however, with the **O**ptions **F**ont command.

Choose **O**ptions **F**ont; then select the desired font (typeface), font style, and size from the appropriate list boxes. As you make selections, the Sample box changes to reflect the current state of the File Manager display font. When you are satisfied, choose OK or press Enter.

By default, characters in the File Manager appear in upper- and lower-case letters—exactly as you enter them. If you want text in the File Manager window to display in uppercase letters, choose the **O**ptions **F**ont command. The dialog box shown in figure 5.19 appears. Turn off the **L**owercase option to display file and directory names in uppercase letters.

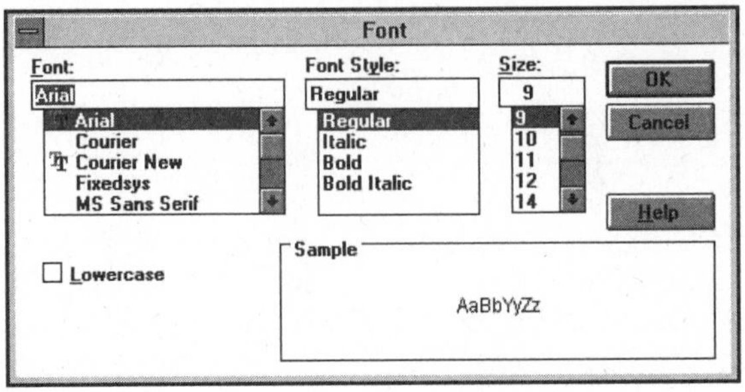

FIG. 5.19

The Font dialog box.

Updating a File Manager Window

You may need to update a directory window. For example, you may have switched diskettes. As a result, you may activate the File Manager and not see a file you have just saved—a scenario that is more than a little disconcerting. Don't panic; the file is there. All you have to do is to choose the **Window Refresh** command (as a shortcut, press F5). If you still cannot find the file in the directory in which you thought you saved the file, you may have saved it to a different directory or disk. Use the **File Search** command to find the file.

Sorting the Display of Files and Directories

Finding files or directories is much easier if you rearrange the contents of a directory window. You can order the window contents alphabetically by file name, alphabetically by file extension, by file size, or by the last date the file was saved. To reorder a window's contents, choose one of the commands in the following chart to sort the window.

Command	Description
View **S**ort by Name	Sorts alphabetically by file name
View Sort **by** Type	Sorts alphabetically by file extension
View Sort by **S**ize	Sorts by file size from largest to smallest
View Sort by **D**ate	Sorts by last date modified, most recent first

You don't have to display the file date or size in the directory window to sort by those attributes. If you want to see the file's date and size in the directory window, use the View **A**ll File Details or View **P**artial Details command.

Filtering Out Unwanted Files from the Display

Another way to easily find a specific type of file in a directory window is to limit the number of files displayed. You can set criteria to filter files so that only files of the type you want are displayed. Specify the type of file to be displayed when you want to see only application files or only document files that end with a specific extension.

To include in the directory window only the files you want, follow these steps:

1. Activate the directory window in which you want to specify the type of file you want to display.

2. Choose the **View By File Type** command. The dialog box shown in figure 5.20 appears.

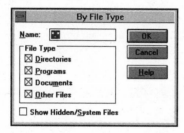

FIG. 5.20

The View By File Type dialog box.

3. Select the **Name** text box and type a file pattern to display only the files matching the pattern you specify (you can use the wild cards * and ?). Alternatively, select one of the following options:

Option	Description
Directories	Displays only directories or subdirectories
Programs	Displays only files with file extensions of EXE, COM, PIF, or BAT
Documents	Displays document files and files that have been associated with an application with the **File Associate** command
Other Files	Displays all other files that are not directories, applications, or documents
Show Hidden/**S**ystem files	Displays hidden files or system files

4. Choose OK or press Enter.

Changing a File's Attributes

Each file on a disk has a set of *attributes*, or descriptive characteristics. Attributes describe whether the file has been backed up, is part of the DOS system, is hidden from normal viewing, or can be read but not written over. With the File Manager, you can display file attributes and change them.

You can display the file attributes in the current directory window by choosing the View All File Details command. If you want to see only the attributes, choose the View Partial File Details command and select the attributes option. This process is described in "Specifying File-Display Details," earlier in this chapter.

To change a file's attributes, select the file or files you want to change and then choose the File Properties command. The Properties dialog box appears. Select the attribute you want changed and choose OK or press Enter. The following is a list of the attributes you can change.

Attribute	Description
Read Only	Sets the R or read-only attribute, which prevents a file from being changed or erased. Set this attribute for a file when you want to prevent someone from accidentally changing a master template or erasing a file critical to system operation.
Archive	Sets the A or archive attribute. Marks with an A any file that has changed since being backed up using the DOS BACKUP, RESTORE, or XCOPY commands. If no A appears, the file has not changed since you backed it up.
Hidden	Sets the H or hidden attribute, which prevents files from displaying.
System	Sets the S or system attribute, which prevents files from displaying. Some files that belong to DOS are hidden so that they aren't accidentally erased.

Reducing the Chance of Erasing Critical Files
If you want to ensure that a file isn't accidentally changed or erased, set the attributes to Read Only and Hidden or System. These attributes prevent the file from being changed and hide the file from standard display.

> **Display Hidden or System Files with the View Include Command**
> Assigning the Hidden or System attribute to hide files is a good
> way to prevent tampering or accidental erasure. As an experi-
> enced Windows user, however, you may need to see these files to
> change, erase, or copy them. To display files with the Hidden or
> System attribute, choose the **View By File Type** command and
> select the Show Hidden/**S**ystem Files check box.

Viewing the Properties of a File or Directory

You can view the properties of a file or directory in the Properties dialog box. The file name, path, file size, and the date and time the file or
directory was last changed are displayed.

The Properties dialog box in File Manager in Windows for Workgroups
includes more information. For example, you also will find information
on the version number, copyright, and company name of a program if
the selected item is a program file.

Displaying Warning Messages

During some File Manager operations, a warning message appears and
asks you to confirm the action about to take place. If you select a directory and choose **File Delete**, for example, you may be asked to confirm
the deletion of each file and the removal of the directory. If you find the
confirmation messages annoying, you can turn them off—but remember that these warning messages appear to prevent you from making
mistakes. If you turn off the messages, you have no warning for potentially hazardous actions!

Turn off warning messages by choosing the **Options Confirmation** command and deselecting the desired options from the Confirmation dialog
box (see fig. 5.21). Choose OK or press Enter after choosing an option.
Turn a confirmation message back on by reselecting the option so that
the check box contains an X.

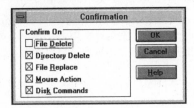

The following is a list of the options in the Confirmation dialog box and the messages whose display they control.

Option	Action Confirmed by Message
File **D**elete	Each file being erased
D**i**rectory Delete	Each directory being erased
File **R**eplace	One file being copied or moved over another
Mouse Action	Any mouse action involving moving or copying
Dis**k** Commands	Each disk being copied over or formatted

As you gain more experience and confidence with the computer, you may want to turn off these messages. If you are a beginner or have difficulty accurately positioning the mouse, you may want to leave these messages on.

Customizing the Toolbar

The toolbar comes with a default set of buttons for quickly accessing some of the more commonly used File Manager commands. However, you can add and remove buttons from the toolbar so that the commands you use most frequently are accessible from the toolbar. There is a button available for every File Manager command. You can remove buttons that you do not use, add buttons for the commands you use frequently, and move buttons around to arrange them in whatever order you want. You can also return to the default set of buttons at any time.

Adding a Toolbar Button

To add a button to the toolbar, follow these steps:

1. Double-click anywhere on the background of the toolbar.

    or

    Choose the **O**ptions Customize Tool**b**ar command.

The dialog box shown in figure 5.22 appears. All available toolbar buttons are listed in the Available Buttons list on the left side of the dialog box. All buttons currently displayed on the toolbar are listed in the Toolbar Buttons list on the right.

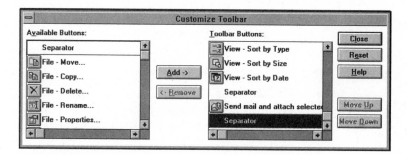

FIG. 5.22

Customize your toolbar in the Customize Toolbar dialog box.

2. Select the button you want to add from the Available Buttons list. Use the scroll bar to find the button you want, if necessary.

3. Choose the Add button. The button will be added to the Toolbar Buttons list on the right side of the dialog box.

   The button will be inserted immediately above the button that was selected in the Toolbar Buttons list when the Add button was chosen. Use the Move Up and Move Down buttons to locate the button wherever you want on the toolbar.

4. Repeat steps 2 and 3 to add buttons you desire.

5. Choose the Close button.

   If you run out of room to add more buttons, you must remove buttons for commands that you use less often.

Removing a Toolbar Button

To quickly remove a toolbar button when you are using a mouse, put the tip of the mouse pointer on the button on the toolbar, hold down the Shift key, and drag the button off the toolbar. When the toolbar button is off the toolbar, release the mouse button.

To remove a toolbar button using the Customize Toolbar dialog box, follow these steps:

1. Choose the Options Customize Toolbar command or double-click in the background of the toolbar.

   This displays the Customize Toolbar dialog box shown in figure 5.22.

2. Select the button you want to remove from the Toolbar Buttons list.

3. Choose the **R**emove button.

4. Repeat steps 2 and 3 for each button you want to remove.

5. Choose the Close button.

Rearranging Toolbar Buttons

To quickly move a toolbar button to a new location when you are using a mouse, put the tip of the mouse pointer on the button on the toolbar, hold down the Shift key, and drag the button to its new location on the toolbar, then release the mouse button.

You can arrange the buttons on the toolbar in any order you want. To move a toolbar button using the Customize Toolbar dialog box, follow these steps:

1. Choose the **O**ptions Customize Tool**b**ar command or double-click in the background of the toolbar to display the Customize Toolbar dialog box shown in figure 5.22.

2. Select the button from the Toolbar Buttons list that you want to move.

3. Choose the Move **U**p button to move the button up the list. This action will move the button to the left on the toolbar.

   or

   Choose the Move **D**own button to move the button down the list. This action will move the button to the right on the toolbar.

4. Repeat steps 2 and 3 for each button you want to move.

5. Choose the Close button.

Restoring the Default Toolbar

You can restore the default toolbar by following these steps:

1. Double-click anywhere on the background of the toolbar.

   or

   Choose the **O**ptions Toolbar command.

   This displays the Customize Toolbar dialog box.

2. Choose the Reset button.

3. Choose the Close button.

For Related Information:

◄◄ To learn more about managing windows, see "Controlling the Windows in Windows," p. 30.

FROM HERE...

Managing Files and Disks

Working with a hard disk, which can store thousands of files, can be confusing. Problems arise if you do not erase unnecessary files or do not make backup copies of files in case the hard disk fails.

In this section, you see how easy it is to erase unwanted files, copy files to other disks, or move files between directories. You also learn how to create directories so that you can organize a disk to fit your work and data.

Copying Files or Directories

Copying files is an important part of keeping work organized and secure. When organizing files, you may want to copy a file to make it accessible in two different locations. A more important reason for copying files is security.

The hard disk on which you store files is a mechanical device and has one of the highest failure rates among computer components. Should the hard disk fail, the cost of replacing the disk is insignificant compared to the cost of the hours you worked accumulating data on the disk. One way to prevent the loss of this data is to make a set of duplicate files on backup diskettes.

If you have copied files with DOS commands, you will find copying files and directories much more fun with Windows and a mouse. All you do is drag the files you want to copy from one location in the File Manager to another.

T I P   Before you copy multiple files or a directory full of files, make sure that you have enough storage space on the destination disk. To do this, select the destination disk-drive icon, activate the directory tree area, and check the amount of available storage displayed in the status bar at the bottom of the screen. Then activate the directory window that contains the files you want to copy and select the files. (If you are copying an entire directory, you must select all the files in the directory.) Check the status bar again to see how much storage these files occupy. Compare the amount of space occupied by the files you want to copy with the amount of space left on the destination disk to make sure that the destination disk can receive all the files.

Follow these steps to copy files with a mouse:

1. Make sure that both the source and destination are visible.

   The *source* is the item you want to copy. It can be a file in the contents list or a directory from the contents list or the directory tree.

   The *destination* can be a directory icon in the directory tree or the contents list. It also can be a directory icon at the bottom of the File Manager window or a disk drive icon at the top of the File Manager window.

2. Activate the part of the File Manager screen that contains the source file or directory. If you are copying an entire directory, you can activate the directory tree or the contents list.

3. Select the file(s) or directory to be copied.

   If you want to copy more than one file, select multiple files. You can select only one directory at a time from the directory tree area, but you can select multiple directories in the contents list. When you copy a directory, you copy all the files and subdirectories in the directory.

4. To copy the files, drag the directory or the individual files to the destination (see fig. 5.23). Press and hold down the Ctrl key if the destination is on the same disk as the source files. Do not hold down the Ctrl key if the destination is on a different disk from the source files.

   You cannot drag a window to copy it, but you can use keyboard techniques to copy an entire window.

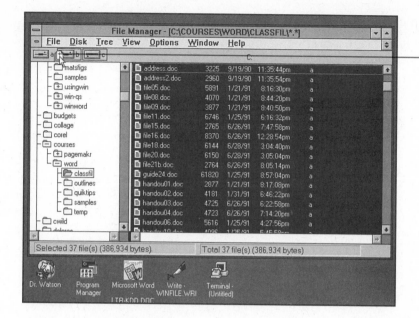

File copy icon

FIG. 5.23

Dragging files
to a disk or
directory to make
copies.

5. When the file icon is over the destination, release the mouse
   button; release the Ctrl key if you were using the Ctrl key.

   If the destination has a file with the same name as the file you are
   copying, you are asked to confirm that the destination file can be
   replaced by the copy.

Copying Many Files into Multiple Directories
A directory icon can serve as the destination for a file or files that
you copy. If you want to copy files into several different directories quickly, this technique is useful. For each directory into
which you want to copy the file or files, open a window by selecting the directory in the directory tree and then choosing the Window New Window command. Minimize each new window to an
icon at the bottom of the File Manager screen by clicking the minimize button at the top right of the window. (Make sure that your
original directory window is smaller than the File Manager window so that you can see the icons.) Then drag the files you want
to copy onto the directory icons.

To copy files with the keyboard, follow these steps:

1. Activate the window that contains the files or directories you want to copy.

2. Select the files or directories you want to copy. If you want to select a large number of files, you can use DOS wild cards in step 4.

3. Choose the **File Copy** command or press F8. The Copy dialog box appears (see fig. 5.24).

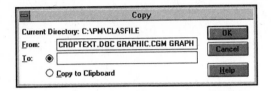

4. If you want to specify a group of files to copy, type a file-name pattern in the **From** text box. Use the DOS wild cards * and ? to specify groups of similar file names. To specify an entire directory, type the directory path, such as *C:\BUDGET*.

5. Type the path name of the destination location in the **To** text box.

6. Choose OK or press Enter.

If the destination has a file with the same name as the file you are copying, you are asked to confirm that the destination file can be replaced by the copy.

T I P   You can link a file to a different document by selecting the **Copy to Clipboard** option in the Copy dialog box. Linking and embedding are covered in detail in Chapter 6.

Use the DOS wild cards * and ? in the **From** text box of the Copy dialog box to copy multiple files with similar names. Remember that the * wild card matches any group of letters; the ? wild card matches any single letter in the same location. Following are some examples:

File Name Pattern	Files Matched
PROJ*.XLS	PROJ05.XLS
PROJECT.XLS	PROJECTA.XLS

File Name Pattern	Files Matched
SM?TH.DOC	SMITH.DOC
	SMYTH.DOC but not SMITHS.DOC
*.XL?	anyname.XLS
	anyname.XLC
	anyname.XLW
.	all file names

> **T I P**
>
> Use the Windows Recorder accessory to make a macro duplicating the keystrokes and commands you use when making backup copies of files to disk. For example, if you daily want to back up any file you have created or modified that day, use the Recorder to record each of the steps in the process. Then play back the macro at the end of each day. If you use keystrokes and commands with the Recorder rather than mouse actions, you can play back the recording no matter where or how the directory window is located.

Moving Files or Directories

You can move files just as easily as you can copy them. Moving files puts them in a new location and removes the originals from the old location. You move files when you need to reorganize a disk. You can move files or directories to a new directory or disk. Moving a directory moves this directory's files and subdirectories.

> **Selecting All Files in a Directory**
> If you want to move all the files in a directory, you can select all the files in the current window by choosing the File Move command and typing *.* in the From text box. Or, you can do the following:
>
> 1. Choose the File Select Files command.
>
> 2. Type *.* in the File(s) text box.
>
> 3. Choose Select or press Enter.

To move files or directories with the mouse, follow these steps:

1. Activate the source and destination directory windows.

2. Select the files or directories you want to move.

3. To move, drag the file or directory to the destination if the destination is on the same disk. If the destination is on a different disk, press and hold down the Alt key as you drag to move a file, files, directory, or directories.

4. Release the mouse button when the icon or file is over the destination.

5. If you are asked to confirm the move, consider whether you are copying or moving and how the files will change. Then choose **Yes** to complete the action, **No** to stop a single move, or Cancel to cancel all moves.

Using the Mouse To Move or Copy Files
The following chart summarizes the mouse actions you use to move or copy files with the mouse:

Desired Action	Mouse Action
Copy to a different disk	Drag
Copy to the same disk	Ctrl+drag
Move to a different disk	Alt+drag
Move to the same disk	Drag

To move files or directories with the keyboard, follow these steps:

1. Activate the source and destination directory windows.

2. Select the files or directories you want to move.

3. Choose the **File Move** command or press F7.

4. If you did not select files in step 2, type in the **From** text box the names of the files to be moved. Use DOS wild cards if you want to move multiple files with similar names.

5. In the **To** text box, type the destination path name, drive, and directory.

6. Choose OK or press Enter.

Creating Directories

Creating directories on a disk is like adding new drawers to a filing cabinet. Creating directories is an excellent way to reorganize or restructure the disk for new categories. After you build directories and subdirectories, you can put existing files in them using the **File Move** and **File Copy** commands.

To make new directories, follow these steps:

1. Activate the directory tree area. (This step is unnecessary if you want to put the new subdirectory under the currently selected directory.)

2. Select the directory under which you want a new subdirectory.

3. Choose the **File Create Directory** command. The Create Directory dialog box appears (see fig. 5.25).

```
┌─────────────────────────────────────────┐
│ ▬           Create Directory             │
├─────────────────────────────────────────┤
│ Current Directory: C:\PM      ┌────────┐ │
│                               │   OK   │ │
│ Name: [_____]      └────────┘ │
│                               ┌────────┐ │
│                               │ Cancel │ │
│                               └────────┘ │
│                               ┌────────┐ │
│                               │  Help  │ │
│                               └────────┘ │
└─────────────────────────────────────────┘
```

FIG. 5.25

The Create Directory dialog box.

4. Type the name of the new directory. Directory names are the same as file names and can have eight letters in the file name and three letters in the extension.

5. Choose OK or press Enter.

Adding new subdirectories is like growing new branches on a tree. New subdirectories must sprout from existing directories or subdirectories. If you want to create multiple layers of subdirectories, first create the directories or subdirectories that precede the ones you want to add.

> **Create a Directory without Selecting a Directory**
> You can create a directory at any location without selecting the parent directory by typing the full path name in the Name text box of the Create Directory dialog box.

Renaming Files or Directories

Unless you do everything perfectly the first time, there will come a time when you want to rename a file or directory. To rename a file or directory, select the file or directory from a directory window and choose the File Rename command. When the Rename dialog box appears, type the new file name and choose OK or press Enter.

You can rename a group of files with a similar name or the same extension. To rename a group of files, select the files you want to rename and choose the File Rename command. Use the DOS wild cards * and ? in the From and To text boxes to indicate the parts of the names you want to change. Choose OK or press Enter to rename the files. Renaming with wild cards can save you a great deal of typing, as shown by the following example:

Original File Names	From	To	Resultant File Names
ACNTAR.XLS	ACNT*.*	ACCT*.*	ACCTAR.XLS
ACNTAP.XLS	ACNT*.*	ACCT*.*	ACCTAP.XLS
ACNTTRND.XLC	ACNT*.*	ACCT*.*	ACCTTRND.XLC

Deleting Files or Directories

Delete files or directories when you want to remove old work from the disk. Deleting files gives you more available storage on a disk. Deleting directories that don't contain any files makes very little difference in storage space.

Unless you have prepared the hard disk with special software, you cannot recover files or directories after you delete them. Be very careful to select only the files or directories you want to delete. If you aren't sure about deleting files or directories, turn on the warning messages by choosing the Options Confirmation command and selecting the warning messages you want.

T I P

Be careful that you do not accidentally select a directory when you select files to be deleted. If you select a directory and choose File Delete, all the files in the directory as well as the directory itself are deleted. Deleting entire directories can be convenient, but it also can be a real surprise if it is not what you wanted to do.

If you want to confirm each file or subdirectory being deleted, choose the Options Confirmation command and make sure that the File Delete and Directory Delete boxes are selected.

To delete files or subdirectories, follow these steps:

1. Activate the directory window that contains the files you want to delete. Activate the directory tree area if you want to delete only directories.

2. Select the files or directories you want to delete; alternatively, use wild cards in step 4.

3. Choose the **File Delete** command or press the Del key. The Delete dialog box appears.

4. If you did not select the files you want to delete, type their names in the Delete text box. Use DOS wild cards to select multiple files. For example, type *.* in the Delete text box to specify every file in the current directory.

5. Choose the OK button. If the Confirm File Delete dialog box appears, asking you to confirm deletions, choose **Yes** when appropriate or choose Yes to **All** to confirm deletion of several files.

    Use the **Options Confirmation** command to specify the types of deletions that require a confirmation. Only by selecting options in the Confirmation dialog box will you see a Confirm File Delete dialog box in step 5.

Copying Disks

Make duplicate copies of diskettes whenever you need another diskette for secure storage off-site or when you need a duplicate of original program disks. To copy an entire disk to another disk, the disks must be the same size and capacity. If the original is a 3 1/2-inch high-density diskette, the destination diskette must be the same. To duplicate a disk, follow these steps:

1. Protect the original disk by attaching a write-protect tab on 5 1/4-inch diskettes or sliding the protect notch open on 3 1/2-inch diskettes.

2. Insert the original diskette in the source disk drive.

3. Insert the diskette to receive the copy (the destination disk) in the second disk drive. If you don't have a second disk drive, don't be concerned; you can switch diskettes in a single drive.

4. Choose the **Disk Copy Disk** command. The Copy Disk dialog box appears. If you have only one disk drive, skip to step 7.

5. In the **S**ource In list, select the drive letter for the source drive.

6. In the **D**estination In list, select the drive letter for the destination drive (even if it is the same as the source drive).

7. Choose OK.

8. If you have only a single disk drive, you are instructed to switch the source disk and destination disk in and out of the single drive. Windows prompts you to exchange disks.

The **D**isk **C**opy Disk command formats the destination disk if it is not already formatted. If the destination disk contains data, the data is lost.

Formatting Diskettes

You usually cannot use new diskettes until you format them (some diskettes come already formatted). Formatting prepares diskettes for use on a computer. Formatting is similar to preparing a blank book for use by writing in page numbers and creating a blank table of contents. If a diskette contains data, formatting completely erases all existing data. Part of the process of formatting is checking for bad areas on the diskette's magnetic surface. All bad areas found are identified so that data is not recorded in these areas.

To format a diskette, follow these steps:

1. Put the diskette to be formatted in the disk drive.

2. Choose the **D**isk **F**ormat Disk command. The Format Disk dialog box appears.

3. Select the disk drive that contains the diskette to be formatted in the **D**isk In drop-down list box.

4. Select the appropriate diskette size in the **C**apacity drop-down list box.

5. If you want to assign a label to the diskette, type the label in the **L**abel text box.

6. Select **M**ake System Disk if you want to use the diskette to start the computer. Do not use this option unless it is needed because the system files use storage space on the diskette that can otherwise be used for data.

7. Select **Q**uick Format to save time if the disk has been formatted and you're reasonably sure that the diskette does not have bad areas.

8. Choose OK. A message box warns you that formatting will erase all data on the disk. If you're sure, choose **Yes**.

9. After this diskette is formatted, you are given the chance to format additional disks.

Format an entire box of diskettes at one time and put a paper label on each disk when it is formatted. This system lets you know that open boxes contain formatted diskettes; paper labels confirm that the diskettes are formatted.

If you have a diskette you want to change to a system disk (one that can start the computer), put the disk in a diskette drive and choose the **D**isk **M**ake System Diskette command. Choose the disk drive that contains the diskette. Windows copies files from the hard disk onto the diskette so that you can boot the computer from this diskette.

Labeling Disks

Although you may be accustomed to putting a paper label on diskettes, both hard disks and diskettes can have magnetically recorded labels, known as *volume labels*. Volume labels appear at the top of the directory tree area when the drive with the volume label is active. Not all disks have or need this kind of label.

You just learned how to create a volume label when you format a diskette. If you want to create or change a volume label on a previously formatted disk, select the drive icon and choose the **D**isk **L**abel Disk command. When the Label Disk dialog box appears, type a label name of up to 11 characters and choose OK or press Enter.

Printing Files

You can send text files directly to the printer from the File Manager. For example, many software applications come with last-minute corrections and additional information stored in a text file. The information usually is not in the printed manual. These text files, which usually have the extension TXT, contain information such as helpful tips, corrections to the manual, and hardware configuration settings not covered in the manual. It often is helpful to print these files.

When you print with the File Manager, you send the file to the default printer. To change the default printer, use the Control Panel as described in Chapter 7.

To print a file with the File Manager, the file must be associated with an application. To print a file using the File Manager, follow these steps:

1. Activate the directory window that contains the file or files you want to print.

2. Select the file or files you want to print.

3. Choose the File Print command.

4. Choose OK or press Enter.

You also can use File Manager's drag and drop feature to print; see the section, "Using the File Manager's Drag and Drop Feature," later in this chapter.

Starting Applications and Documents

Using the Program Manager and group windows is the best way to start frequently used applications. As described in Chapter 4, "Controlling Applications with the Program Manager," you can use the Program Manager to group together a frequently used application and an associated document to make them readily accessible.

On some occasions, however, the application you want to start may not be in a group window. When this happens, start the application directly from the File Manager. You can start any application from the File Manager.

Starting an Application

Starting an application from the File Manager is easy with the mouse: just open the directory window that contains the application and double-click on the name of the application.

Starting an application with the keyboard is almost as easy: open the directory window that contains the application, select the application name, and press Enter. Alternatively, choose the File Open or File Run command.

Application file names end with EXE or COM. You may have to start some DOS applications by double-clicking on a file with the extension BAT or PIF, as described in Chapter 23, "Running DOS Applications."

You can specify some document or data files so that they start an application. Choosing this associated document or data file starts the application and loads the document or data as well.

If an application is associated with a specific file extension, you can start an application by using the same starting procedures on a document file. Pretend the document file is the application you want to start. Windows starts the associated application and then loads the selected document file.

If you want to start an application with a document or with special arguments that modify how the application runs, choose the **F**ile **R**un command. In the **C**ommand Line text box, type the directory path and full application name. Press the space bar and type the name of the document you want the application to load. Choose OK or press Enter.

If you want the application to minimize to an icon as soon as it starts, select the Run **M**inimized check box from the Run dialog box before choosing OK.

See the section "Using the File Manager's Drag and Drop Feature" to learn how you can start an application by dragging a document icon onto an application icon.

Associating Documents with an Application

One of the convenient features of Windows is its capacity to start an application when you choose an associated document. An associated document is one that runs with a particular application. When you choose an associated document, Windows finds the application that runs the document, starts the application, and then loads the document. Many Windows applications create associations for their own files by modifying the Windows WIN.INI file when the application is installed. You also can add associations to fit your applications and work habits.

Spreadsheet files with the extension XLS, for example, are associated with Microsoft Excel. This association is made automatically because installing Excel modifies the WIN.INI file. You may be in an office with people who use Lotus 1-2-3. Because Excel can open and save Lotus 1-2-3 files, you can associate Lotus 1-2-3 files with the Excel application. Once you associate a Lotus 1-2-3 file with Excel, you can choose this 1-2-3 file to make Excel start and load the 1-2-3 worksheet and charts.

To associate a document file with a specific application, follow these steps:

1. Activate the directory window that contains the data file (document file) you want to associate with an application.

2. Select the name of the file you want associated. Windows associates document files to applications by checking the file extension of the document file.

3. Choose the File Associate command. This brings up the Associate dialog box (see fig. 5.26). The extension for the document you selected is listed in the Files with Extension text box.

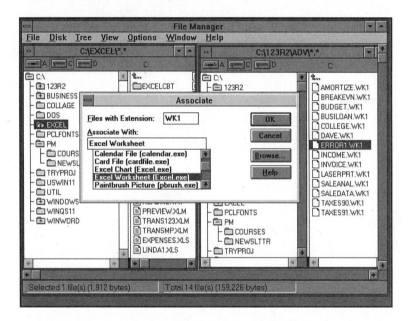

The Associate dialog box.

4. Scroll through the list box attached to the Associate With text box. Find the name of the application you want to associate with all files using the extension shown in the Files with Extension text box. Select the application name if you find it.

   If necessary, type the full path and file name of the application. If you're unsure of the correct directory path, you can search for it by choosing the Browse button.

5. Choose OK or press Enter.

Some DOS applications, such as WordPerfect, can use any file extension for data documents. In this case, you must associate each of the different file extensions you use with WordPerfect to the WordPerfect application.

Some DOS applications may not start directly from an associated file. Other applications may start but not run with optimal configuration. If either is true for the document files you are using, refer to Chapter 23 "Running DOS Applications," for information on creating a PIF.

For Related Information:

FROM HERE...

◀◀ See "Starting, Using, and Quitting Applications," p. 46.

◀◀ See "Starting an Application from the File Manager," p. 89.

◀◀ See "Starting Applications from a Group Window," p. 118.

▶▶ To learn more about macros, see "Recording and Using Macros," p. 618 and "Playing Back Macros," p. 626.

◀◀ See also, "Using Menus and Dialog Boxes," p. 35.

Using the File Manager's Drag and Drop Feature

The File Manager's drag and drop feature enables you to print files, link or embed files, create program item icons, and start applications by dragging File Manager icons or file names with a mouse. You also drag and drop icons to copy and move files, as described in other sections in this chapter.

To use the drag and drop feature, you need to be able to see two things on your screen: the File Manager, or source, displaying the file you want to drag; and the destination, displaying the icon or document where you want to drag the file. Before you drag and drop File Manager icons, arrange windows on your screen so that you can see both. In some cases, such as when you are starting an application, the File Manager is both source and destination, so you must open two File Manager windows.

To learn how to use the drag and drop feature for copying and moving, see the sections in this chapter on "Copying Files or Directories" and "Moving Files or Directories."

Using Drag and Drop To Print

To print a file using the drag and drop feature, you must be able to see the file you want to print in the File Manager, and you must be able to see the Print Manager program icon or window on your desktop. If the Print Manager is not running, start it from the Program Manager.

You also must be sure that the document you want to print is associated with its application. To learn how to do that, refer to the section in this chapter on "Associating Documents with an Application."

To use the drag and drop feature to print, follow these steps:

1. Start the File Manager, if necessary, and locate the file you want to print.

2. Start the Print Manager, if necessary.

3. In the File Manager, position the mouse pointer over the file you want to print. Click and hold down the left mouse button and drag the file onto the Print Manager window or icon.

   As you drag, you see a changing icon. When the icon appears as a page with a plus (+) sign inside it, and you are sure that you are on top of the Printer Manager window or icon, release the mouse button.

If a message box appears telling you that no association exists for the file or that the association data is incomplete, then you must complete the association or use the application to print your file.

Using Drag and Drop To Link or Embed

One of the easiest ways to link or embed a file into a document is to drag the file name from the File Manager onto the open document. Embedding a file in this way creates a package, which appears in the document as an icon. You can edit the package, or you can double-click on the icon to start the application containing the embedded file. To learn more about linking and embedding and the Object Packager, refer to Chapter 6.

To use the drag and drop feature to link or embed a file, follow these steps:

1. Start the File Manager, if necessary, and locate the file you want to link or embed.

2. Start the application containing the document into which you want to link or embed a file, if you haven't already, and open the

document. Display the location in the document where you want to insert the linked or embedded file.

3. In the File Manager, position the mouse pointer over the file you want to link or embed. Click and hold down the left mouse button and drag the file onto the document where you want the file to be linked or embedded.

    As you drag, you see a changing icon. When the icon appears as a page with a plus (+) sign inside it, and you are sure that you are on top of the document icon into which you want to link or embed the file, release the mouse button.

Using Drag and Drop To Create a Program Item Icon

You can quickly create a program item icon in the Program Manager by dragging a program file from the File Manager onto the Program Manager. Follow these steps:

1. Start the File Manager and locate the application for which you want to create a program item icon.

2. Activate the Program Manager and display the group window in which you want to add your new program item icon.

3. Arrange the File Manager and Program Manager windows so that you can see both the application for which you want to create the program item icon and the group window in which you want to create it.

4. Drag the application file name from the File Manager onto the Program Manager. Release the mouse button when the application name is over the group window where you want to create the program item icon.

Using Drag and Drop To Start an Application

You can quickly start an application by dragging a document file icon onto an application icon. The application starts, and the document opens. Follow these steps:

1. Start the File Manager and open two windows: one displaying the directory containing the document file you want to open and one

displaying the directory containing the application you want to start. Choose the **Window New Window** command to open a new window or double-click on a disk-drive icon.

2. Tile the two windows by choosing the **Window Tile** command.

3. Scroll each window so that you can see both the document and the application file names.

4. Drag the document file name onto the application file name. Release the mouse button when the document file name is over the application file name.

For Related Information:

▶▶ To learn more about printing, see "Printing a File," p. 323.

◀◀ See "Customizing Groups," p. 119.

▶▶ See "Embedding Data as Packages," p. 238.

Working with Networks in Windows for Workgroups

When you are using Windows for Workgroups on a network, you can share directories with other users in your workgroup. You can open the files in any directory that has been designated as *shared* by another user, and you can *share* any of your directories so that the files in that directory can be shared by other users. The File Manager is where you connect to directories that others have shared and where you share directories on your computer that you want others to have access to.

Connecting to Shared Directories

You can connect to any directory that has been designated as shared by any user on your network (to learn how to share a directory, see the next section, "Sharing a Directory"). You connect to a directory by using the File Manager. When you connect to a directory, File Manager creates a *network drive* for that directory and assigns a letter to that drive. You can view the files in that directory by selecting the drive icon assigned to that directory or by selecting the drive from the drive list in the toolbar. You open files in the directory in exactly the same way you open a file on your own hard disk. Whether you can modify the file depends on the level of access the owner of the directory has granted to other users.

Connecting to a Network Directory

To connect to a shared directory, follow these steps:

1. Click the Connect Network Drive button on the toolbar.

   or

   Choose the **D**isk Connect **N**etwork Drive command.

   The Connect Network Drive dialog box shown in figure 5.27 appears.

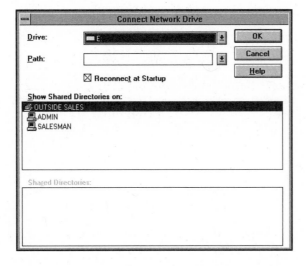

Select the directory you want to connect to in the Connect Network Drive dialog box.

2. By default, File Manager assigns the next available drive letter on your computer to the directory you select to connect to. To assign a different letter, open the **D**rive list and select a letter from the list.

3. Enter the path for the shared directory in the **P**ath box.

   The path includes the computer name where the directory is located, and the share name assigned to that directory. The computer name is preceded by double backslashes and is separated from the share name by a single backslash. For example, \\SALESMAN\SALES.

There are three methods for entering the path:

If you know the path for the directory, you can type it directly in the **P**ath text box.

or

You open the **P**ath drop-down list and select a path from a list of recently used paths.

or

Double-click on a workgroup icon in the list **S**how Shared Directories (or select the icon with the arrow keys and press Enter) to expand the workgroup. Select a name from the list of computer names listed under the workgroup to display a list of shared directories in the Shared Directories box. When you find the directory to which you want to connect, select it.

4. If you want to automatically reconnect to this shared directory at startup, select the Reconnec**t** at Startup button.

5. Choose OK or press Enter.

When you connect to a shared directory, a new window for that directory will appear if the **O**pen New Window on Connect option in the **O**ptions menu is selected. To select this option, choose the **O**ptions **O**pen New Window on Connect command. A check mark appears next to the command when it is turned on. If you do not want a new window to open each time you connect to a shared directory, turn this option off.

Disconnecting from a Network Drive

To disconnect from a network drive, follow these steps:

1. Click the Disconnect Network Drive button on the toolbar.

   or

   Choose the **D**isk **D**isconnect Network Drive command.

   The Disconnect Network Drive dialog box shown in figure 5.28 appears.

2. Select from the **D**rive list the drive you want to disconnect.

   You can select additional directories from the list if you want to disconnect from more than one directory at once. To select more than one directory, click on the first directory, hold down the Ctrl key, and click on subsequent directories. To deselect a directory, hold down the Ctrl key and click on the directory. To use the keyboard, select the first directory, press Shift+F8, use the up- and down-arrow keys to move to the next directory, and press the space bar. Move to additional directories and press the space bar. To deselect a directory and retain the other selections, move to the selected directory and press the space bar. To return to selecting a single directory at a time, press Shift+F8 again.

3. Choose OK or press Enter.

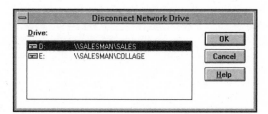

FIG. 5.28

Use the Disconnect Network Drive dialog box to disconnect from a shared directory.

Sharing Directories

You can designate any directory on your computer as shared. When you share a directory, you can assign a *share name* and *password* to that directory. You can also specify what type of access users have to the shared directory. Once you have shared a directory, other users have access to the files in that directory. You must be running in 386-enhanced mode to share a directory on your computer. The computers that have the directories you want to share must be on and logged on to the network.

Sharing a Directory

To share a directory, follow these steps:

1. Using the mouse or the keyboard, select the directory you want to share.

2. Click the Share As button on the toolbar.

   or

   Choose the **D**isk Share **A**s command.

   The Share Directory dialog box shown in figure 5.29 appears.

3. The name of the directory you selected in step 1 is the default name of the shared directory. You can type a new name in the **S**hare Name box.

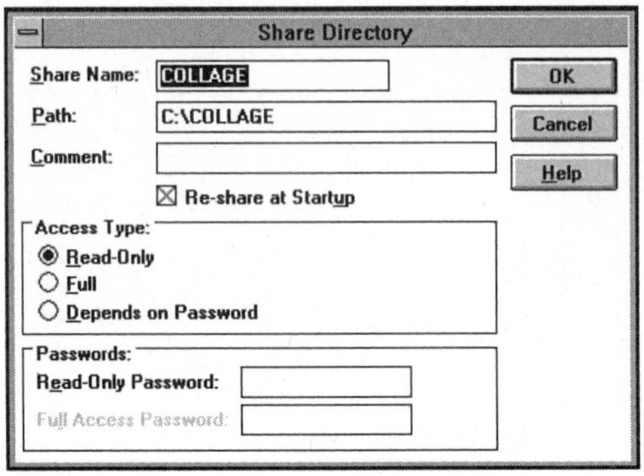

FIG. 5.29

The Share Directory dialog box is used to share a directory on your computer.

4. The path of the directory you selected in step 1 appears in the **P**ath box. If you selected the wrong directory in step 1, type in the path for the correct directory.

5. You can type a comment in the **C**omment box. This comment appears next to the share name in the Connect Network Drive dialog box and can be helpful for other users when those users are looking for a particular shared directory to connect to.

6. If you want to automatically reshare the directory at start up, select the Re-share at Start**u**p check box.

7. Select an access option in the Access Type group.

   You can grant users two levels of access of a shared directory. If you want users to be able only to read files and run programs in a directory, select the **R**ead-Only option. If you want users to be able to read, modify, rename, move, delete, or create files and run your programs, select the **F**ull option. If you want the level of access to depend on which password the user enters, select the **D**epends on Password option.

   If you want to limit access to the files in the shared directory to certain users, assign a password to the directory and only give the password to those users. If you selected the **D**epends on Password option, you need to enter two passwords, one for users who have read-only access to your files and one for users with full access. If you want all users to have access to your files, don't assign a password.

8. Type a password in one or both of the Read-Only Password or Full Access Password boxes, depending on which option you selected in step 7.

9. Choose OK or press Enter.

Unsharing a Directory

To stop sharing a directory, follow these steps:

1. Click the Stop Sharing button on the toolbar.

    or

    Choose the **D**isk St**o**p Sharing command.

    The Stop Sharing dialog box appears (see fig. 5.30).

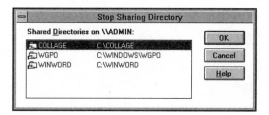

FIG. 5.30

Select the directories you want to stop sharing in the Stop Sharing dialog box.

2. Select the name of the directory you want to stop sharing in the Shared **D**irectories on list.

    You can select additional directories from the list if you want to stop sharing more than one directory at once. To select more than one directory, click the first directory, hold down the Ctrl key, and click subsequent directories. To deselect a directory, hold down the Ctrl key and click the directory. To use the keyboard, select the first directory, press Shift+F8, use the up- and down-arrow keys to move to the next directory, and press the space bar. Move to additional directories and press the space bar. To deselect a directory and retain the other selections, move to the selected directory and press the space bar. To return to selecting a single directory at a time, press Shift+F8 again.

3. Choose OK or press Enter.

Changing the Password, Share Name, or Comment for a Shared Directory

You can use the **D**isk Share **A**s command to change the password, share name, or comment for a shared directory. To change any of these properties, follow these steps:

1. Using the mouse or keyboard, select the directory you want to modify.

2. Click the Share As button on the toolbar.

    or

    Choose the **D**isk Share **A**s command.

    The Share Directory dialog box shown in figure 5.29 appears.

3. Change the entries in the **S**hare Name, **C**omment, or **P**assword, boxes, as needed.

4. Choose OK or press Enter.

Viewing Workgroup Directories

You can find out which directories are being shared in the workgroups on your network. To view the directories in the workgroups on your network, follow these steps:

1. Click the Connect Network Drive button on the toolbar.

    or

    Choose the **D**isk Connect **N**etwork Drive command.

    The Connect Network Drive dialog box shown in figure 5.27 appears.

2. Double-click the workgroup whose directories you want to view in the **S**how Shared Directories On list, or use the arrow keys to select the workgroup and press Enter.

3. Select the computer whose directories you want to view from the list of computer names under the workgroup name.

    A list of shared directories appears in the Shared Directories box.

4. In the Shared Directories box, select the shared directory to which you want to connect.

5. Choose OK or press Enter.

    As an alternative to selecting a directory and choosing OK, simply double-click on the directory to which you want to connect in the Shared Directories list.

Your computer will probably have a specified limit to the number of local or network drives to which it can be connected. If you attempt to connect to a network drive and your computer has already used all the drives it has available, then you will get a warning message. This message says that the drive letter you specified in the **D**rive pull-down list is invalid.

The number of drives your computer can be connected to is specified in the CONFIG.SYS file, which is probably located in your root (C:\) directory. Using the Windows Notepad, you can open the CONFIG.SYS file and change the LASTDRIVE command to allow additional network drives. The LASTDRIVE command will appear in the form:

LASTDRIVE=F

In this case, good drive F is the last allowable drive. Change the last letter and save the CONFIG.SYS file back to its original directory. You must exit Windows and restart your computer before you will be able to take advantage of the extra drives you can now connect.

Viewing the Users of a Shared Directory

If you are sharing directories with other users, you may want to know which of those directories are being used by other users at any time, or you may want to know which users are using specific files. For example, if someone else is using a file of yours in a directory you are sharing, you may want to find out who is using the file. You may want to know who is using one of your shared files so you can warn them if you need to turn off your computer. Some files also restrict the access or capabilities of other users while they are being shared. In that case, you may want to ask the user to stop using the file so that another user can have full access.

To view the names of users of a directory or file, follow these steps:

1. Using the mouse or keyboard, select the directory or file you want to check.

2. Choose the File Properties command or press Alt+Enter.

3. Choose the Open By button to display the Open Files dialog box (see fig. 5.31) The Open By button only appears in the Properties for dialog box when you have selected a shared directory or file in step 1.

4. Choose OK twice or press Enter twice to return to the directory window.

Closing a File in a Shared Directory

If someone is using one of your files in a directory you have shared, you cannot open that file. If you want to be able to access your file, you can close the file. Be aware that the person using the file at the time you close it may lose data. Use the procedure described in the preceding section to learn who is using the file and then ask the person to close the file.

FIG. 5.31

The Open Files dialog box displays a list of shared files that are in use by others.

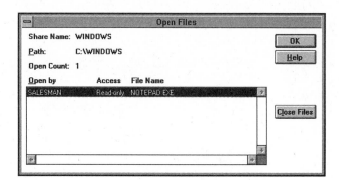

If you must forcefully close a shared file regardless of the other user, follow these steps:

1. Select the directory in which the file is located or select the file itself.

2. Choose the File Properties command (or press Alt+Enter).

3. Choose the Open By button.

4. Select the file you want to close from the Open By list.

5. Choose the Close button.

6. Choose OK twice or press Enter twice to return to the directory window.

Working with Non-Windows for Workgroups Networks

If the computer is connected to a network, you may have access to more than one hard disk drive. You can access those drives through Windows if you are logged on to the network. Each hard disk drive on the network shows up in the File Manager window as a hard disk icon different from the local drive icons. When you select a network drive icon, the path to this drive displays in the status bar at the bottom of the File Manager window. In a LAN environment, the computer is known as a *workstation*.

Drives on the network appear in the File Manager with a special network disk drive icon (see fig. 5.32).

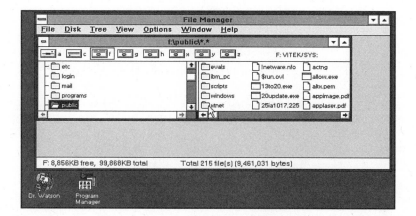

FIG. 5.32

The File Manager
showing a
network disk
drive icon.

If you want to use network drives with Windows, you must log on to the
network before you start Windows. See the network administrator for
the procedure on how to log on to the network. When you connect the
computer to a network, you have additional disk drives available. You
can use these additional drives with Windows if you know the path
name to the drive and the password.

NOTE

If you logged on to the network before starting Windows in
386-enhanced mode, you may not be able to log out from the
network while you are in Windows. To log out from the network, exit Windows and then type *Logout*, or another command, depending on your network.

If you want to use network drives with Windows, you must
connect to the network before you start Windows in order
for the Windows network commands to be available. If you
start Windows without first connecting to the network, the
network commands are gray and therefore unavailable.

NOTE

If you connect a DOS application to a network while this
application is running in Windows, disconnect from the
network before quitting the application.

Working with Network Drives

Windows 3.1 works more seamlessly with networks than did Version 3.0. If your computer is connected to a network, you can use any network drive, provided that you know which server the drive is connected to and that you have authorization to the server. Depending on the network you are using, you may be able to browse through the available drives.

Windows 3.1 remembers connections that you have established. If you established network connections in previous Windows sessions, they are reconnected. Connections made in File Manager are treated like any other drive or subdirectory on your local hard disk. You may start programs from the server or use the drag and drop feature with a file.

The next few sections enable you to manage connections to a network server. The discussion explains how to attach and detach a server, *map* a directory on a network drive to a drive letter, and delete a mapped directory.

 NOTE   Because Novell networks are widely used, this section focuses on the steps for using a Novell network. Other networks work somewhat differently.

Attaching a Network Drive

Before you can access a network drive, you must attach Windows to a network server. After you attach to the server, you can select the *path* from which to work. A path consists of the name of the server and the subdirectory on the network drive. After you select the correct path, you then assign, or *map*, the path to a drive letter. To attach to a server, follow these steps:

1. Choose the **D**isk Network Connections command. The Network Drive Connections dialog box opens.

2. Click the Browse button. The Browse Connections dialog box opens.

3. Click the Attach button. The Attach File Server dialog box opens.

4. Select the correct server from the File server drop-down list box. Type your user name in the User name text box. Type your password in the Password text box. Click OK when you are finished. The attached server appears on the Servers/Volumes list box.

5. In the Servers/Volumes list box, select the server. You see the directories that you have access to in the Directories list box.

6. Select a directory to use for your path from the Directories list box.

7. Choose OK or press Enter.

You have successfully selected a path to use from the server. To use the path with File Manager, however, you need to map the path as a drive letter.

Mapping a Network Drive

Mapping a network path using Windows is similar to mapping directories in DOS. To map a network path, follow these steps:

1. Select the path from a server on the network by typing the path in the Path text box or by Browsing for a path.

2. Select a drive letter not currently being used in the Data drives list box.

3. Click the Map button. The path from the Path text box appears in the Data drives list box, following the drive letter you selected.

You can remove a mapped drive. Select the mapped drive in the Data drives list box and then click the Map Delete button. Click OK to delete the Network device mapping or click Cancel to keep the map.

Detaching a Network Server

After you finish using a server, you can detach from the server. Be careful, however, not to detach from a server that contains the Windows environment. To detach from a server, follow these steps:

1. Click the Browse button. The Browse Connections dialog box opens.

2. Click the Detach button. The Detach File Server dialog box opens.

3. Select the server from the File server drop-down list box.

4. Click OK. Any connections that you had to the server are lost.

5. Click Cancel to return to the Network Drive Connections dialog box. Click Close.

FROM HERE...

For Related Information:

▶▶ To learn more about working with the File Manager on networks, see "NetWare Installation Issues," p. 1012; "Printing on a Network in Windows for Workgroups," p. 346; and "Adding and Configuring Printers," p. 277.

Chapter Summary

You can go in three directions from here. One option is to finish the next few chapters in this section and learn how to customize Windows with the Control Panel, how to manage fonts, how to work with object linking and embedding, and how to use the Print Manager. In Chapter 7, you learn how to use the Control Panel to change screen colors, select a new desktop background, install new printers, and control the mouse speed. Chapter 8, "Managing Fonts," teaches you about TrueType and shows you how to install new fonts. Chapter 6, "Embedding and Linking," teaches you about creating compound documents. Chapter 9, "Using the Print Manager," teaches you how to control printing, in a stand-alone mode and on a network.

The second direction you may go is toward learning how to use Windows accessory applications in Part III and learning to use Windows applets in Part IV. Accessory applications include many day-to-day desktop tools, including a word processor, a painting application, and a communications application. Windows applets are mini-applications that you use from within the primary applications.

The third option is to go to Chapters 22 and 23 and learn how to use Windows to run applications you already have. In these chapters, you learn how to copy and paste text and numeric data among Windows and DOS applications and how to link text or graphics data among Windows applications.

Sharing files is one of the first things that most workgroups do with Windows for Workgroups. But there are a couple of other features in Windows for Workgroups that can be even more valuable to you and the people you work with. The electronic mail system, Mail, that is built in to Windows for Workgroups will enable member of your group to send messages and files to each other. You can also gain personally and as a group from learning about Schedule+. Schedule+ enables you to schedule and remind yourself of important tasks. It also enables you to find time slots for meetings. It shows you when members are available or will find the next time when everyone you have specified can make the meeting. To learn more about Mail, check Chapter 10. To learn about Schedule+ see Chapter 11.

Embedding and Linking

One of the unique advantages of Windows applications is their capability to exchange and link information easily with other Windows applications. If you are accustomed to working with one application, the value of linking or embedding data is not always immediately apparent. After you begin to link and embed data, however, you will see how much it can improve your communication. The following list describes examples of how linking and embedding can work with various applications:

- Linking a mailing list in a Windows database or worksheet to a mail-merge data document in a Windows word processor

- Creating sales projections, financial analysis, inventory reports, and investment analysis with Microsoft Excel or Lotus 1-2-3 for Windows and then linking or embedding them into Windows word processing documents

- Maintaining client reminder letters and callbacks by linking PackRat, a personal information manager, to Word for Windows through the WordBASIC macros that come with PackRat

- Embedding in Word for Windows or Ami Pro, drawings or schematics that can be updated from within the word processor using Microsoft Draw

- Linking Microsoft Excel to a Windows database or SQL Server to monitor and analyze inventory

- Creating a compound document composed of pieces of text, graphics, and other data from many users on a network. Updating the shared data in the Clipbook updates the compound document.

- Posting a changing graph or worksheet table in the Clipbook so everyone on the Windows for Workgroups network can have the most current data.

Figure 6.1 shows an example of a letter that has links to a Microsoft Excel worksheet and chart.

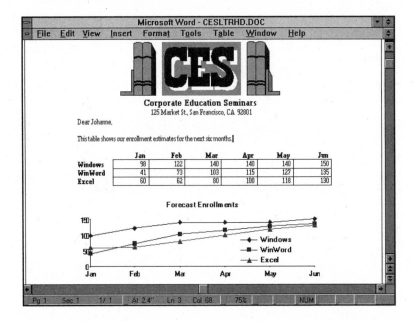

FIG. 6.1

Your documents can be linked to database, worksheet, or graphics applications.

Throughout this chapter, the *server* is the file or data in an application that is supplying data. The *client* is the application receiving information. Some applications function as both server and client. Other applications may be one or the other, but not both. Microsoft Write and Cardfile, for example, are clients—they only receive information. Windows Paintbrush however, is a server—it only can supply information.

Copying, linking, or embedding data between Windows applications may use the same or similar commands, and the results may appear the same on-screen or in the document. Each fits a different situation, however, and has unique advantages and disadvantages. The following table describes the different ways to transfer data, and the advantages and disadvantages of each method.

Table 6.1 Transferring Data

Copying   Use when you do not want to update data. Data must be replaced to be updated.

Advantages

- Data does not change when other parts of the document update.
- Less memory and storage are required to use or save the document.

Disadvantages

- Pictures may print at lower resolution if copied as a bit map.
- Updating data requires redoing each copy and paste of data.

Linking   Use when you need to update one original in the server and have the changes cascade into multiple client documents.

Advantages

- Less memory is required than for an embedded object.
- Many client documents can be updated by changing one server document.
- Older Windows applications that cannot embed objects can still link data.

Disadvantages

- Links between the server and the client may be broken if the server file names or path names are changed or deleted.
- Automatically updated links may slow down Windows operation.
- Server data must be saved, and the name and path name must be maintained.

continues

Table 6.1 Continued	
Embedding	Use when you have only a few client documents that may need updating and you want to include the server data (an *embedded object*) as part of the document.

Advantages

- Client document and server data are stored as a single file; you do not have to maintain links, path names, and server files.

- Server data is saved as part of the client document.

- You can stay within the client document and use the server application to update the embedded object.

Disadvantages

- Documents containing embedded objects are larger than other documents because they contain both client and server data.

- Updating an embedded graphic may result in a file with less printer resolution than the original.

- Each client document must be updated individually.

Two additional methods of transferring data within Windows applications are not described in this chapter. Applications such as Word for Windows and Microsoft Excel can open files created by the application, or they can use a command, such as Insert File in Word for Windows, to link to an on-disk file created by another application.

Microsoft Excel, Word for Windows, Lotus 1-2-3 for Windows, and Ami Pro can open files created by other applications. Files that are opened like this become part of the document and cannot be updated except by replacing them. To open another application's file, you must install file converters that come with the Windows application.

Applications that can link to a file on disk, such as Word for Windows, enable you to link their documents to Microsoft Excel, Lotus 1-2-3, WordPerfect, or dBASE files. When the file on disk changes, you can update the Word for Windows document to reflect the new data.

Different Windows applications sometimes use different commands to implement object linking and embedding. For example, to insert an embedded object in a Word for Windows document, you choose the Insert **O**bject command; to do the same in Windows Write, you choose **E**dit **I**nsert Object. Even when the applications use the same commands, the underlined letters in the commands (shown in **bold** in this book) may be different. To edit an embedded object in Word for Windows, the command is **E**dit O**b**ject, with the b in Object bold; in Write, the command is **E**dit Edit **O**bject, with the O bold.

The following procedures describe the commands and active letters for some of the more frequently used applications. Not all applications that have object linking and embedding capability have all the features described in this chapter.

For Related Information:

▶▶ To learn about object linking and embedding with Windows Write, see "Including Pictures in a Document," p. 515.

▶▶ To learn about object linking and embedding with Windows Paintbrush, see "Working with Other Applications," p. 580.

▶▶ To learn about object linking and embedding with other Desktop Accessories, see "Inserting Pictures in a Card," p. 672.

FROM HERE...

Viewing Data in the Clipboard

Windows 3.1 transfers copied or linked data between applications using the Clipboard. The Clipboard is a temporary storage area for data being transferred or linked. The Clipboard takes its name from an artist's clipboard, where cut items are stored until they can be pasted down in new locations. (If you are using Windows for Workgroups see the following section titled, "Viewing and Using Data in the ClipBook Viewer.")

If you need to see the information currently in the Clipboard, open the Clipboard Viewer application located in the Main program window. Inside the Clipboard Viewer window, you can see the contents or a description of the Clipboard's contents.

Use the **F**ile **S**ave command and **F**ile **O**pen command to save Clipboard contents as files that can be retrieved for later use. In the **D**isplay menu, you can see the different ways in which the current contents can be pasted. When you copy a selection into the Clipboard, Windows queries the application to see which formats it supports. Windows lists all these formats in the **D**isplay menu and selects the one that gives the best copy. Normally, the **D**isplay **A**uto command is selected. If you want to paste the Clipboard contents in a different format, you can choose a different format in the **D**isplay menu or use the **E**dit Paste **S**pecial command of the client document.

 # Viewing and Using Data in the ClipBook Viewer

When you use Windows for Workgroups, you have a Clipboard available for transferring cut or copied information between applications on your computer. But you have an additional tool at your disposal, a ClipBook.

The ClipBook serves two purposes. First, the ClipBook acts as a personal scrapbook that stores multiple *clippings*. Each different clipping can be on a *page* in the ClipBook. In the ClipBook, you can see a table of contents, thumbnail views, or full window view of each clipping. From the collection of clippings, you can choose the one you want to use. The second way to use the ClipBook is as a shared scrapbook. If you designate a page as shared, others in your workgroup can use the data on the page.

Your workgroup can use data, such as text, tables, and graphics, in shared ClipBook pages, which could reduce everyone's workload. For example, you can draw a company logo and copy that logo to a shared page in your ClipBook. Others in your workgroup can use that logo at any time by pasting or embedding the logo into their documents. You don't have to run around giving everyone a copy.

The ClipBook also enables workgroup members to link to a shared page in a ClipBook. For example, you may have created a timetable and chart using Microsoft Excel. Three different people need your timetable and chart for reports that they must update each week. The workload for your workgroup can be significantly reduced if you copy the timetable and chart into shared pages of your ClipBook. The three people in your workgroup can then paste linked copies of the timetable and chart from your ClipBook into their reports. Each week when you update your Excel timetable and chart, their reports automatically update.

Displaying the ClipBook

Windows for Workgroups displays the Clipboard and ClipBook in the same ClipBook application. The ClipBook application is located in the Main program group window of the Program Manager.

The Clipboard is where data is *temporarily* stored when it is being transferred within or between applications. This is where data is stored when you do an **E**dit Cu**t** or **E**dit **C**opy. You can view the information currently stored in your Clipboard in the Clipboard window of the ClipBook Viewer application, shown in figure 6.2.

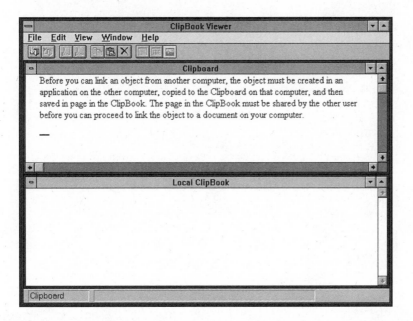

FIG. 6.2

The ClipBook Viewer has a Clipboard window and a ClipBook window.

The contents of the Clipboard remain there until you cut or copy new data into the Clipboard or until you clear the contents with the **E**dit **D**elete command. The ClipBook viewer also has a ClipBook window. If you need to store information and retain it when you cut or copy other information, you can copy the contents of the Clipboard into a page in the ClipBook. The contents of a ClipBook page can be copied back to the Clipboard at any time. You can also *share* pages in your ClipBook so that other users on your network can connect to your ClipBook and transfer the information from shared pages into documents on their computers. ClipBook pages, therefore, can be a shared resource, just like a printer or directory.

To view the contents of your Clipboard and ClipBook, choose the Main group in Program Manager, and then double-click on the ClipBook Viewer icon. You also can use the arrow keys to select the icon, and then press Enter.

T I P You can start the ClipBook or Clipboard from within some applications by selecting the application control menu and choosing the Run command. The application control menu appears as a long dash at the top-left edge of each application's title bar. Click the long dash or press Alt+space bar to open the menu. After you choose the Run command, a Run dialog box will appear. Use this dialog box to choose the Clipboard option and OK to run the ClipBook or Clipboard.

The ClipBook Viewer screen appears (see fig. 6.2), with a Local ClipBook window and a Clipboard window. One or both of these windows may be minimized to icons, which appear at the bottom of the screen. Restore icons to windows by double-clicking the icon or press Ctrl+Tab to select the icon and press Enter.

The ClipBook Viewer has a menu bar with commands for carrying out various functions. If you are using a mouse, use the toolbar, which is just under the menu bar in figure 6.2. The toolbar gives you ready access to many of the most frequently used commands. See the following table for a description of the buttons on the toolbar. The buttons in the table are listed from left to right, the order in which they appear on the toolbar. These different functions are discussed in the sections that follow.

Table 6.2 Toolbar Functions

Button	Name	Function
	Connect	Connects you to the ClipBook on another user's computer
	Disconnect	Disconnects you from the ClipBook on another user's computer
	Share	Shares the selected ClipBook page with other users
	Stop Sharing	Stops sharing the selected ClipBook page with other users

Button	Name	Function
	Copy	Copies the selected ClipBook page onto the Clipboard
	Paste	Pastes the contents of the Clipboard into a new page in the ClipBook
	Delete	Deletes the contents of the Clipboard or the selected ClipBook page
	Table of Contents	Displays a list of ClipBook page titles in the ClipBook window
	Thumbnails	Displays small graphical representations of each page in the ClipBook window
	Full Page	Displays the contents of the selected page in the ClipBook window

Saving the Information in the Clipboard

There are two ways to save information stored in the Clipboard. You can save Clipboard contents as a file on-disk or as a page in the ClipBook.

To save the contents of the Clipboard in a file, choose the **F**ile Save **A**s command from the ClipBook menu. Clipboard files are automatically given the extension .CLP. You can then use the **F**ile **O**pen command in the ClipBook application to retrieve the contents of a file and put the contents back in the Clipboard. Once in the Clipboard, you can use the information to paste, link, or embed as you would any Clipboard content.

The second way to save the contents of the Clipboard is to store the data as a *page* in the Local ClipBook. Viewing and using ClipBook pages is much easier and quicker than working with Clipboard files. You can also share ClipBook pages so that other users can use the information in those pages, which you cannot do with Clipboard files.

> **NOTE** If others in your workgroup will be linking to shared pages within your ClipBook, save the source document before you copy its data into the ClipBook. Linked data will refer back to the original source document by referencing its file name. When you change the data in the source document, all documents containing linked data will update.

To store data as a page in the ClipBook, follow these steps:

1. Save the original document if others in the workgroup will be linking to the data. Use a file name and directory that will not change.

2. Select the data (text, table, graphics, and so on), and copy it to the clipboard. Most applications use the Edit Copy command.

3. Activate the ClipBook application found in the Main group of the Program Manager.

4. Click in the Local ClipBook window or press Ctrl+Tab to activate the Local ClipBook window.

5. Click the Paste button on the toolbar or choose the **Edit Paste** command.

   The Paste dialog box appears (see fig. 6.3).

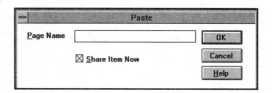

6. Type a name for the page in the **P**age Name box.

7. If you want to share the page with others in your workgroup, select the **S**hare Item Now option.

8. Choose OK or press Enter.

This pastes the data that is currently in the Clipboard into a page in the ClipBook.

If you selected the Share Item Now option, the Share ClipBook Page dialog box appears. With this dialog box, you specify how others will share the page. See "Sharing ClipBook Pages" for more information on this dialog box. When you have made the selections you want, choose OK or press Enter.

Sharing Pages in Your ClipBook

You can share pages in your ClipBook if you want other users to have access to the information in those pages. For example, you may have financial data or standard contract text that others in your workgroup could use in their own documents to save time. The ClipBook offers a simple and convenient way of sharing this common information across a network.

When you share a page in your ClipBook, the contents of that page become a shared resource, no different than a shared printer or shared directory. These contents are available to workgroup members connected to your ClipBook. You can limit the type of access to shared pages with a password. The password can determine whether users have read-only permission or permission to modify the contents.

There are two steps involved in sharing pages in your ClipBook with other users. First, you must designate the pages as shared. You can specify that a page is shared when you create the page or you can specify that a page is shared at any later time. Once a page is shared, anyone who wants to use it must *connect* to your ClipBook.

Sharing a ClipBook Page

The following steps describe how to share a page. If you selected the Share Item Now check box while creating a page in the ClipBook, begin the following process at step 3. If you want to identify an existing ClipBook page as shared, begin with step 1. To indicate that a page in your ClipBook is shared, follow these steps:

1. Using the mouse or keyboard, select the page you want to share.

2. Click on the Share button on the toolbar, or choose the **File Share** command.

   The Share ClipBook Page dialog box, shown in figure 6.4, displays.

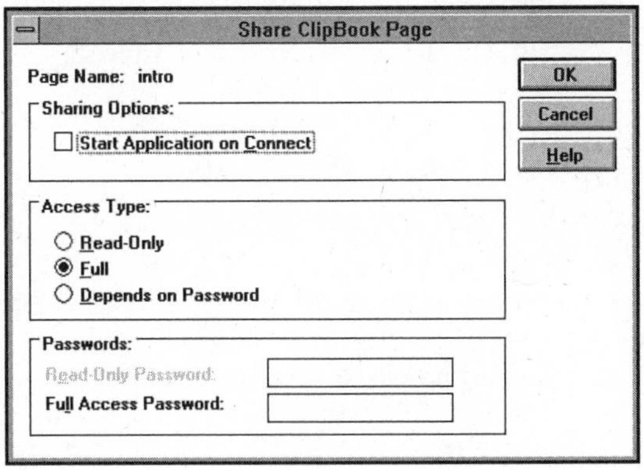

FIG. 6.4

The Share ClipBook Page dialog box.

3. Select the Start Application on Connect option if you want the application that created the data in the shared page to start up automatically when the page is transferred to another computer.

4. Select an access option in the Access Type group.

    There are two levels of access you can grant to users of a shared page. If you don't want users to be able to modify the contents of the page, select the **R**ead-Only option. Select the **F**ull option if you want users to be able to change the contents of the page. If you want the level of access to depend on which password the user types, select the **D**epends on Password option.

5. If you selected the **D**epends on Password option, type a password in one or both of the **R**ead-Only Password or **F**ull Access Password boxes, depending on the options you selected in step 4.

6. Choose OK or press Enter.

In the Table of Contents, the icon for the page you have just shared will display a hand beneath it.

Unsharing a ClipBook Page

You can stop sharing a page so that it is unavailable to others on the Windows for Workgroup network by following these steps:

1. Using the mouse or keyboard, select the page that you want to stop sharing in the Table of Contents in the ClipBook window.

2. Click the Stop Sharing button on the toolbar or choose the **F**ile Stop Sharing command.

Pages that are not shared will not display the sharing hand icon when viewed in the Table of Contents view.

Connecting to the ClipBook on Another Computer

If you want to use the information from someone else's ClipBook, you must first connect to that ClipBook. You will then have access to any shared pages in that ClipBook. Once you are connected to another's ClipBook, you can paste their shared data, link to their data, or copy their data into your ClipBook.

Before you can connect to another workgroup member's ClipBook, that person must be connected to the network. That person must specify which pages of their ClipBook he or she will share.

To connect to the ClipBook of someone in your workgroup:

1. Choose the Main group in Program Manager, and then double-click the ClipBook Viewer icon or use the arrow keys to select the icon and press Enter.

   The ClipBook Viewer window appears (see fig. 6.5). You may see the contents of your previous cut or copy in the Clipboard. Your Local ClipBook will display your pages.

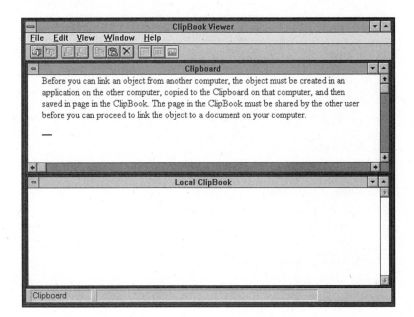

FIG. 6.5

The ClipBook
Viewer window.

2. Click the Connect button on the toolbar or choose the **File Connect** command to display the Select Computer dialog box (see fig. 6.6).

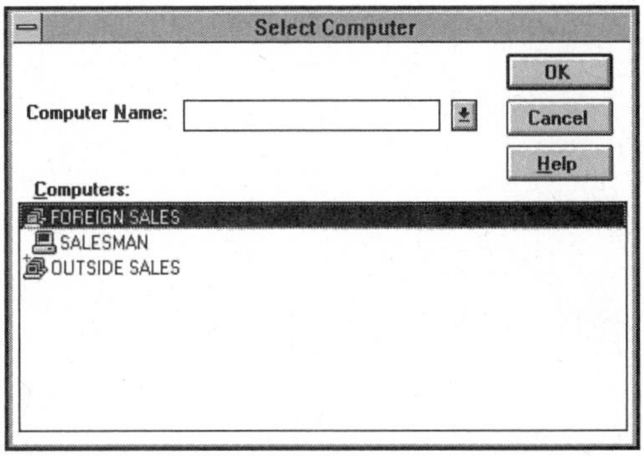

FIG. 6.6

The Select
Computer dialog
box.

3. Type or select the name of the computer you want to connect in the Computer Name box. There are three methods for entering the name of the computer:

Type the name of the computer directly in the Computer Name box if you know the name.

or

Select the name from the Computer Name list by clicking the down arrow next to the edit box or by pressing the down arrow key. Then select a computer from the list of computers you connected to recently.

or

Double-click on a workgroup icon in the Computers list (or press Alt+C, then select the icon with the arrow keys and press Enter) to expand the workgroup. Select a name from the list of computer names listed under the workgroup. The name will appear in the Computer Name box.

4. Choose OK or press Enter.

5. A ClipBook window displaying a list of pages in the ClipBook on the other computer will appear (see fig. 6.7).

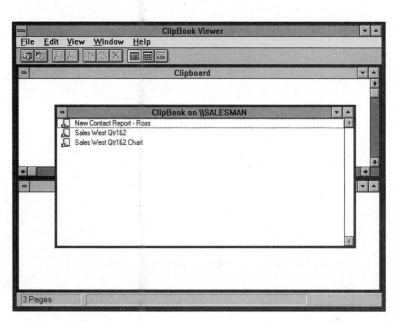

FIG. 6.7

The shared pages are listed in a ClipBook window.

Now that you can see the shared pages in the other ClipBook, you can use them just the same as you would pages from your own Local ClipBook.

> To view all the windows at once, choose the **Window Tile Horizon-tally** or **Window Tile Vertically** command.
>
> **T I P**

When you want to disconnect from the shared ClipBook, activate the window containing the shared ClipBook from which you want to disconnect, then choose the **File Disconnect** command.

Using ClipBook Pages

To use the contents of a page in your Local ClipBook or ClipBook to which you are connected, you must first copy the contents of the page to your Clipboard. To do this, select from the Local or connected ClipBook window the page whose contents you want to use. Then click the Copy button on the toolbar or choose the **Edit Copy** command (or press Ctrl+C). The contents of the page will appear in the Clipboard window. You can now paste this information into any of your windows applications using the application's **Edit Paste** or **Edit Paste Special** command.

To learn how to link or embed items from the ClipBook, see the following sections titled, "Passing Linked Documents to Other Computer Users" and "Linking Data between Computers."

Viewing ClipBook Pages

You can view ClipBook pages in one of three ways. To view a list of all the pages in the ClipBook, choose the **View Table of Contents** command. Shared pages appear with the sharing hand underneath. The Thumbnails view, shown in figure 6.8, displays a small picture for each page with the name of the page beneath the picture. Shared pages have a small hand beneath the picture. Choose the **View Thumbnails** command to see this view. To view the contents of the selected page, choose the **Full Page** command or press Enter.

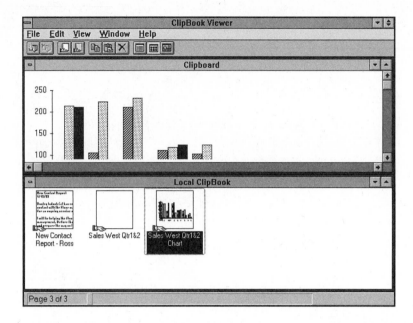

FIG. 6.8

You can view ClipBook contents as a table of contents, thumbnails, or full page.

T I P   You can use the mouse to quickly move between the Table of Contents view and the Full Page view or Thumbnail view. To toggle from the Table of Contents view to the Full Page or Thumbnail view, double-click in the Table of Contents. To toggle back, double-click in the ClipBook window. Double-clicking displays the Full Page or Thumbnail view, whichever was previously displayed.

Deleting in the Clipboard or ClipBook

You can clear the contents from the Clipboard by selecting the Clipboard window and pressing the Del key or choosing the **Edit Delete** command. Choose **Yes** when the message box asking you to confirm your choice appears.

To delete a page from the ClipBook, select the page you want to delete, and then press the Del key or choose the **Edit Delete** command. Choose **Yes** when asked to confirm your choice.

Transferring Data with Copy and Paste

Copying and pasting—the same way you move text or graphics in a document—is the simplest method of transferring small amounts of data or graphics between applications. To copy from one Windows application to another Windows application, follow these general steps:

1. Select the text, cells, or graphic in the originating document.

2. Choose the **E**dit **C**opy command.

3. Switch to the receiving document—the application in which you want to paste the data.

4. Position the insertion point where you want the data to appear in the document.

5. Choose the **E**dit **P**aste command.

Text pastes into the document as formatted text. Microsoft Excel worksheet cells or ranges paste in as a table. Graphics paste in as pictures. None of them are linked to the server document. If you double-click on the picture, however, it loads into Microsoft Draw and becomes an embedded object.

For Related Information:

◀◀ See "Starting, Using, and Quitting Applications," p. 46.

◀◀ See "Operating Applications," p. 77.

▶▶ See "Selecting and Editing Text," p. 482.

▶▶ See "Understanding the Methods of Integration," p. 848.

FROM HERE...

Linking Data between Applications

Linking documents together is another way to transfer data between Windows applications. Links in a client document create references to data in a server application or a server document from the same application. The actual data still is stored in the server document; a copy is sent through the link to the client document.

Changing a single server document can update all the client documents that depend on its data. Another major advantage to linking documents is that client documents are smaller than documents containing embedded objects because the data still resides in the server document.

The disadvantage to using links is that you must maintain the links to a server document. If the location or name of the server document changes, you must update the reference by editing the link. If you give the client document to another user, you also must provide the server documents to make updating possible.

Creating a Link

Creating a link between Windows applications capable of linking is as easy as copying and pasting. When you give the paste command, you have the option of either making the link update automatically or requiring a manual update.

The command to paste in a link may vary between applications. The client document may use a command such as Edit Paste Link or Edit Paste Special with a dialog box that contains a Paste Link button. If your client application contains a Paste Link command, you may not need to continue past step 6 in the following procedure.

T I P If your server application does not have linking capability, you will not see an **Edit Paste Link** command or **Edit Paste Special** command with a following Paste Link button.

To create a link, follow these steps:

1. Start both Windows applications—the server and the client—and open their documents. Activate the server document.

2. Save the server document using the name that it will keep during all future transactions. (You must save the server document to create a link.)

3. Select the text, range of cells, graphic, or database records that you want to link.

4. Choose the **Edit Copy** command.

5. Activate the client document that will receive the data and position the insertion point where you want the link to appear.

6. Choose the **E**dit Paste Link command to paste in the link immediately. (If your application has a Paste Link command, you do not need to continue.)

or

Choose the **E**dit Paste **S**pecial command.

A Paste Special dialog box similar to the one in figure 6.9 appears. Notice that the dialog box displays the source of the link and presents a list of different ways in which the linked data can appear.

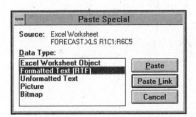

7. From the **D**ata Type list, select the form in which you want your linked data. These link types are described in table 6.3.

Selecting some data types may disable the Paste Link button because this type of data may not be able to maintain a link. If this occurs, you can paste the data or insert the data as an embedded object.

8. Choose the Paste Link button.

When you choose the Paste Link button, Windows creates an automatically updating link. To have the link update only when you manually request it, see the section "Controlling Manual versus Automatic Updates," later in this chapter.

When you create a link, the data from the server may appear in different forms in the client document. Your data may appear as tabbed text, a formatted table, a picture, or a bit map. Each server application has different forms in which it enables its data to appear. Generally, choose the type that gives graphics resolution or transfers the most text formatting. Table 6.3 describes some of the types.

T I P
Some applications enable you to reformat linked data and retain the format when the linked data is updated. In Word for Windows, for example, this is done by using switches within the {LINK} field codes. An example of a LINK field code produced by the Edit Paste Special command is as follows:

```
{LINK ExcelWorksheet C:\\FINANCIAL\\FORECAST.XLS

Result \* mergeformat \r \a}
```

In this example, a range of cells named Result within the Microsoft Excel worksheet was copied and pasted into the Word for Windows document as Formatted Text (RTF). The different arguments that specify the form for the linked data are as follows:

\r   Formatted Text (RTF)
\t   Unformatted Text
\p   Picture
\b   Bit map

Any manual changes to the format of the linked data are preserved by the following switch:

* mergeformat

You do not need to type this field code into the Word document; the code is automatically pasted in according to the selections you have made in the Paste Special dialog box.

Table 6.3 Data Types Stored in the Clipboard

Data Type	Type of Link Created
Object	Data is an embedded object. All data is stored in an object. No link is maintained with the source worksheet or chart.
Formatted Text (RTF)	Text transfers with formats. Worksheets appear formatted in tables. Data can be edited or reformatted. If Paste Link was chosen, a LINK field that links to the source document is inserted. If Paste was chosen, the data appears as unlinked text.
Unformatted Text	Text is unformatted. Worksheets appear as unformatted text with cells separated by tabs.

Data Type	Type of Link Created
Picture	Some graphics, text, database tables, and worksheet ranges appear as pictures. (A picture preserves formatting and resolution from the original application—usually resulting in a high-quality image on-screen and when printed.) They can be formatted as pictures, but text cannot be edited. Unlinking changes them to Microsoft Draw objects.
Bit map	Some graphics, text, and worksheet ranges appear as bit-map pictures. (A bit map appears at screen resolution and may be distorted if resized.) They can be formatted as pictures, but text cannot be edited in Word. Resolution is poorer than that of a picture.

Passing Linked Documents to Other Computer Users

To make changes in the linked data in a client document containing a link, you must have both the server application and the server document available. When you give a document containing links to someone else, make sure that they have access to the server document and application. If you must share a document with someone who does not own the server application, you can use embedded objects instead of linked data. You also can convert the link to simple pasted data by breaking the link.

Breaking the link changes linked word processing and worksheet information into text—as though the text were typed in the client document. Graphics become pictures or bit maps.

To break a link, follow these steps:

1. In the client document, select the linked data.

2. Choose the **Edit Links** or **File Links** command (or a similar command). The Links dialog box appears as shown in figure 6.10.

3. If you did not select in step 1 the links you want to break, select the links now from the **Links** list.

4. Choose the **Cancel Link** button.

If you want to remove linked data rather than break the link, just select the linked data and press the Del key.

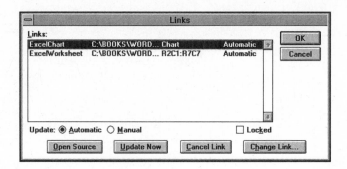

FIG. 6.10

The Links dialog box enables you to freeze linked data by breaking the link.

Editing Linked Data

To edit linked data with a mouse, double-click on the data in the client document. The server application activates and loads the file necessary to update the data. After you have made changes to the data, from within the server application, choose the **F**ile Update command or the **F**ile Exit and Return to document command to update the linked data and exit the server application. (Commands may vary somewhat, depending on the server application. If the server application does not start and load the client document, do so manually.)

Some applications can specify that linked data will not update automatically. To edit linked text or worksheet data that does not update automatically, follow these steps:

1. Select the linked data.

2. Choose the **E**dit Links or **F**ile **L**inks command.

3. If you did not select the linked data in step 1, select the links now from the **L**inks list.

4. Choose the Update Now button or its equivalent in your application.

 # Linking Data between Computers

If you are connected to a Windows for Workgroups network, you can link data between computers, just as you can link data between applications on a single computer as described in the section "Linking Data between Applications." When changes are made to the source data stored in a ClipBook, the data updates in all client documents linked to the data.

Before you can link data from another computer, the data must be created in an application on the other computer, copied to the Clipboard on that computer, and then saved in a page in that computer's ClipBook. This page in the ClipBook must be designated as a shared page so that others on the network can link to it.

Linking to the Server's Clipboard

In order to link to data stored in another computer's ClipBook, you must first connect to the other computer's ClipBook. Connecting to another ClipBook in your workgroup is described earlier in the section "Connecting to the ClipBook on Another Computer."

A ClipBook window will appear listing all the shared pages in the other computer's ClipBook. This window is shown in figure 6.7.

To link data from another computer on the Windows for Workgroups network to your computer, begin by preparing your Windows application to receive linked data. Follow these steps:

1. Activate your Windows application and document that you want to contain linked information. Press Alt+Tab until the application appears, or press Ctrl+Esc and select the application. If you need to start the application, activate the Program Manager and start your application.

2. Position the insertion point in the document where you want the linked information to appear.

3. Activate or start the ClipBook application. Press Alt+Tab until the ClipBook appears, or press Ctrl+Esc and select the ClipBook. If you need to start the ClipBook, activate the Program Manager and start your ClipBook.

Now, with your ClipBook application active, connect to another computer's ClipBook:

1. Click the Connect button or choose the **File Connect** command.

2. Select the workgroup and computer name to which you want to connect.

3. Choose OK or press Enter.

Connecting to another computer's ClipBook is described in greater detail in this chapter's section titled "Connecting to the ClipBook on Another Computer."

Finally, select the page in the other computer's ClipBook and link it into your document:

1. Select the ClipBook page to which you want to link. Click on the page or press arrow keys to select the page.

2. Click the Copy button on the toolbar or choose the **Edit Copy** command to copy the page contents into your Clipboard.

3. Activate the application and document that will receive the information. (The insertion point must be where you want the information to appear.)

4. Choose the **Edit Paste Special** or **Edit Paste Link** command. The command you use depends upon how your application creates linked data.

   A Paste Special dialog box similar to the one in figure 6.11 appears. The dialog box displays the source of the link and lists several formats in which the linked data can be displayed.

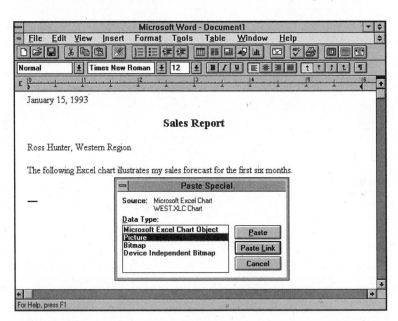

FIG. 6.11

Select from the Paste Special dialog box the type of linked data you want to paste.

5. From the **Data Type** list, select the format you want to use for your linked data. See table 6.3 for a description of the different formats.

   Selecting some data types may disable the Paste Link button because this data type may not be able to link. Some applications may not be able to link with any data type in which case the Paste Link button will be disabled for all data types. If this occurs, you may be able to paste or embed the data. Pasting or embedding across the network is described in a later section, "Embedding Data from Another Computer."

6. Choose the Paste Link button.

The data you paste in will appear in your document. For example, figure 6.12 shows a Microsoft Word for Windows document containing a chart linked to a Microsoft Excel chart.

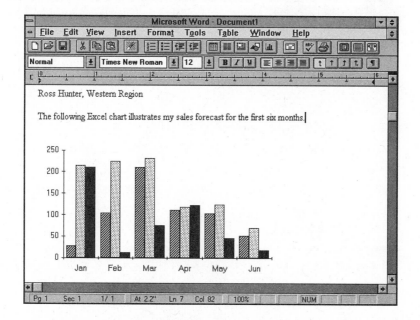

FIG. 6.12

Updating the Excel chart in another computer updates the data in this linked Word document.

Updating Linked Information

Changing the file from which the data originated, the source, will update all the links across the network. Linking data from one computer to another via the ClipBook actually creates a link to the file containing the original data. When the original file changes, any documents that contain the linked data will update. Because this link references the original file name that was the source of the data, you should not move the source file or change its name.

In some Windows applications, such as Windows Write, you are unable to see where the original data is linked to. In some applications, such as

Word for Windows, you can see the formula that creates the link. Figure 6.13 shows the same document as in figure 6.12, but the View Field Codes command has been selected to display the code that actually tells the Word document how to go across the network and find the file containing the linked data. To link an Excel chart into a Word for Windows document, Word uses a code such as the following:

```
{LINK \\\\SALESMAN\\NDDE$ "$month sales xlc.OLE" Chart \* mergeformat \p \a}
```

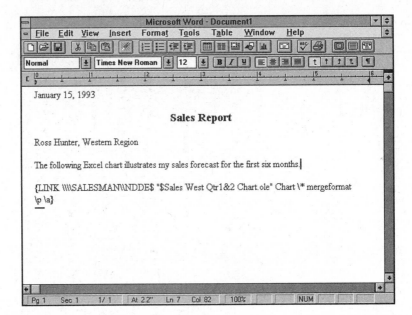

FIG. 6.13

Some applications insert a code that shows you the link between documents across the network.

If you have a document containing linked data, you can update the linked data if you can share the directory and file that created the source data. To update the linked data, start the application that created the source data, and then access the directory containing the shared file. Update the data document and resave it into the same directory with the same file name.

When you reopen a document that contains data linked across the network, you may get a dialog box asking whether you want to automatically link the document to applications outside your current application. Choose **Yes** to relink with the source document for the linked data.

You may encounter a situation in which you no longer want your client document to change when the source data changes. Some applications enable you to break a link, which then changes the linked data into pasted or embedded data. Each application has its own command or keystroke for breaking links. Once a link has been broken, you must update the data manually; it will not update when the source changes.

Embedding Data into a Document

Embedding is another method of inserting data from one application into another. Embedding enables a server document to store its data directly within a client application's document. A picture from Windows Paintbrush, for example, can be stored within a Windows Write letter.

Embedding objects gives you an alternative to pasting or linking data. It also gives applications more power because you can access one application's features from within another application. From within Word for Windows, for example, you can start Microsoft Excel and store directly within the Word document, the data from a worksheet or chart.

Linking data has some advantages, but also comes with inherent problems. Linked data requires you to keep track of where the server files are located, to make sure that the server file names do not change, and to make sure that anyone receiving your client document receives all the server files.

Embedding the linked data directly within the client document eliminates those file management problems, but creates another issue. The document becomes quite large because the client document contains both server and client data.

Windows applications became more powerful through the use of OLE-based *applets*. Applets are small applications that add functionality to larger applications. From within Windows Write, for example, you can start applets that are bundled with other Windows applications, such as Microsoft Draw and Microsoft Graph. This gives Write the power of a drawing package far more powerful than Paintbrush and a charting package with 3-D charts. Some of the applets available for Windows applications are described in Chapters 18 through 21.

In a client document, you can embed objects created by OLE-based applets or by stand-alone applications that function as OLE servers.

Creating an Embedded Object

You can create embedded objects in two ways, both of which produce the same results. In the first method, you insert an object into a client document, starting the server application so that you can create a drawing, worksheet, or chart. When you close the server application, the object is embedded in the client document. In the second method, you start the server application, copy the data, and embed it in the client document.

T I P Applets cannot run by themselves. Some applets must be started from within an OLE-capable application. If you are using an applet that cannot run by itself, use the Insert Object method of starting the applet and embedding an object.

To insert an embedded object, follow these steps:

1. Move the insertion point to where you want the object.

2. Choose the **Edit Insert O**bject or **Insert O**bject command (or a similar command in your application). A dialog box similar to the one in figure 6.14 appears, showing applications from which you can embed objects.

FIG. 6.14

The Object dialog box shows the types of objects you can embed.

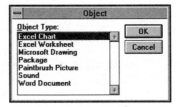

3. From the **O**bject Type list, select the type of object you want to insert and then choose OK or press Enter.

4. Create the data you want in the server application.

   You can create the server data from scratch or copy existing data into the server document from the Clipboard.

5. Embed the server data with one of the following techniques as appropriate to the application creating the object.

   Choose the **File E**xit and Return to document (or just **File E**xit) command to close the application and update the embedded object. Answer Yes if a dialog box asks you whether you want to update the object in your client document.

   or

Choose the **File Update** command to update the embedded object but keep the application and object open. (Some applications, such as Microsoft Excel, do close.)

or

If the server application supports multiple document windows, close the document window containing the object in order to update the object but keep the application open.

For an application to appear in the **O**bject Type List, the application must be registered with Windows and must be capable of producing embedded objects. Applications capable of object linking and embedding are registered when you install them in Windows.

If you already have a document that you want to embed, you need to use the second method, described in the following steps:

1. Start the server application and create the text, chart, worksheet, or database you want to embed. (Unlike linked data, you do not have to save the data you are creating because it is stored within the client document.)

2. Select the data and choose the **Edit Copy** command.

3. Switch to the client application, open the document, and position the insertion point where you want to embed the object.

4. Choose the **Edit Paste Special** command. A dialog box similar to figure 6.15 appears.

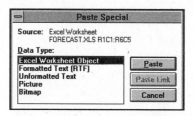

FIG. 6.15

The Paste Special dialog box lists the objects you can paste.

5. Select the *application* Object item, such as Paintbrush Picture Object, from the **D**ata Type list.

6. Choose the **P**aste button.

Editing Embedded Objects

Embedded objects are very easy to edit. Just double-click on the embedded object. With the keyboard, select the object and then choose the **Edit** *application* **O**bject command at the bottom of the Edit menu (the command may vary slightly). The server application that you used to create the object starts (or activates if it is already running) with the object in its window. You then can edit the object using the same application you used to create it—without leaving your client application.

To update the object when you are done editing or formatting it, use the same procedures used to exit when you created it.

Choose the **File Exit and Return to document** (or just **File Exit**) command to close the application and update the embedded object.

or

Close the document window containing the object to close the object but keep the application open.

or

Choose the **File Update** command to update the embedded object but keep the application and object open. (Some applications, such as Microsoft Excel, do close.)

FROM HERE...

For Related Information:

▶▶ See "Creating a Chart," p. 789.

▶▶ See "Starting and Exiting WordArt," p. 818.

▶▶ See also Chapter 21, "Using the Equation Editor," p. 827.

 # Embedding Data from Another Computer

When you are working with Windows for Workgroups, not only can you embed data from one application into another on your computer, but you can embed data from another computer on your network into an application on your computer. Embedding data, known as *objects*, from another computer is an advantage if you do not want your document to change whenever the source data changes. For example, you may want to embed a portion of an Excel cost estimate table into a Word document. By embedding the table in the Word document, changes to the original Excel worksheet will not appear in your document, but you will be able to easily change the cost estimate table with your copy of Excel as necessary.

Before you can embed an object from another computer, the object must be created in an application on the other computer, copied to the Clipboard on that computer, and then copied to a page in the ClipBook. The page in the ClipBook must be shared by the other user before you can proceed to embed the object in a document on your computer (see "Sharing the Pages in Your ClipBook"). Not all Windows applications are capable of creating objects that can be embedded. A Window application must have OLE capability for embedding to work.

To embed an object from another computer, you must first connect to the other computer's ClipBook. Connecting to another ClipBook in your workgroup is described earlier in the section "Connecting to the ClipBook on Another Computer." When you connect, a ClipBook window will appear and list all the shared pages in the other computer's ClipBook.

To embed data from another computer on the Windows for Workgroups network to your computer, begin by preparing your Windows application to receive the embedded data. Follow these steps:

1. Activate your Windows application and document that you want to contain the data.

2. Position the insertion point in the document where you want the embedded data.

3. Activate or start the ClipBook application.

Now, with your ClipBook application active, connect to another computer's ClipBook. Follow these steps:

1. Click the Connect button or choose the **File Connect** command.

2. Select the workgroup and computer name to which you want to connect.

3. Choose OK or press Enter.

Connecting to another computer's ClipBook is described in greater detail in this chapter's section, titled "Connecting to the ClipBook on Another Computer."

Finally, select the page in the other computer's ClipBook and embed its contents into your document. Follow these steps:

1. Select the ClipBook page whose contents you want to embed. Click on the page or press arrow keys to select the page.

2. Click the Copy button on the toolbar or choose the **E**dit **C**opy command to copy the page contents into your Clipboard.

3. Activate the application and document that will receive the object. (The insertion point must be where you want the embedded object to appear.)

4. Choose the **E**dit Paste **S**pecial or Insert **O**bject command. The command you use depends upon how your application creates embedded objects.

   A Paste Special dialog box similar to the one in figure 6.8 appears. The dialog box displays the source of the object and lists several formats in which the selected object embedded.

5. From the Data Type list, select the format you want to use for the embedded object. See table 6.3 for a description of the different formats.

   Some data types may not allow embedding.

6. Choose the **P**aste button.

The object you embed will appear in your document. For example, a Microsoft Excel chart embedded can be embedded as an object into a Word for Windows document. The chart still appears as it did in Excel, but it is not linked to the original file that created the chart.

An embedded object contains all the data used to create the object. If you have a copy of the application that created the object on your computer, you can edit the object. To edit the object, double-click it. This action will start the application and load the object so it can be edited. When you finish editing, use the **F**ile E**x**it or similar command to close the application. You will be asked whether you want to update the embedded object. Choose **Y**es to accept the changes. For example, if you embedded an Excel chart in a Word document, you could double-click on the chart and Excel will start and load the chart. You could then reformat the chart and close Excel to see the newly formatted chart in your Word document.

Embedding Data as Packages

In addition to linking or embedding data, you can bundle data as a package and embed in your client document an icon that represents that data. The icon, a small picture, can represent part of a document or an entire document. Only applications that support object linking and embedding can support packages of embedded data. Figure 6.16 shows a document containing packaged data.

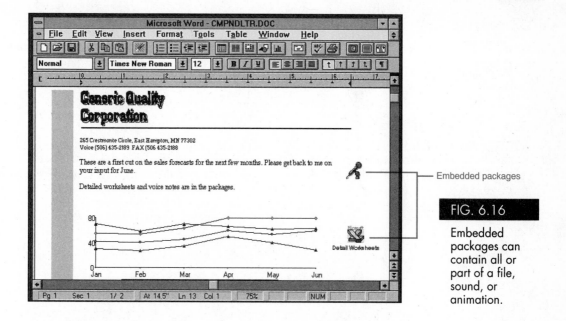

Embedded packages

FIG. 6.16

Embedded
packages can
contain all or
part of a file,
sound, or
animation.

Embedded packages act the same as embedded objects. When activated, they open the server application and display the data contained. Besides data, embedded packages can contain sound, voice, or animation, as described in Chapter 17. You also can add a label or create your own icon to represent the data.

The situations in which you may want to embed a package of data are as follows:

- A memo refers to a previous report that you want to package with the memo so that the reader can review it. Rather than inserting a lengthy report in the memo, you embed a package containing the report. Double-clicking on the package icon explodes it into the entire report.

- A new product proposal you have written gets to the point right away, but you want to make sure that all the supporting detail is included in case there are additional questions. You package the worksheets, charts, and notes and embed them in the proposal so that readers can delve into detail only if they want.

- A sales report has variances that you need to explain. Rather than break up the flow of the report, you package the variance report as notes. Each note is embedded at the proper location in the report.

To package objects, your application must support object linking and embedding. There are different methods of creating packages that depend upon when your application was written and whether you want to embed or link a package. In some applications, creating an embedded package is as easy as dragging a file from the File Manager and dropping it onto a document. For other applications, you may need to use the File Manager or the Object Packager, which is found in the Accessories group, to package embedded or linked files.

The Object Packager appears in figure 6.17. The left side of the Object Packager displays the icon that represents the data. The right side shows the name of the object, such as a filename or a picture of the object.

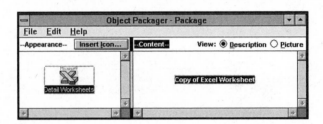

FIG. 6.17

Use the Object Packager to embed icons that represent data.

Activating Package Contents

A package may contain any form of Windows document, including multimedia files containing sound or animation. To activate the package so that it delivers its contents, double-click on the package icon. Or, select the package and then choose the **E**dit Package **O**bject command (or a similar command, such as **E**dit Package Ob**j**ect). A cascading menu may appear to the side; if it does, choose **A**ctivate Contents to start the application and load the embedded data. (In some applications, using the keyboard to edit a packaged object only enables you to edit the object using the Object Packager.)

Packaging Entire Files

Files can be packaged and embedded using the Object Packager or the File Manager. The File Manager method is easy and enables you to link a package to the server document, but the Object Packager offers you the chance to change the icon and add a custom label.

Packaging a File with the Object Packager

To include the entire contents of a file or document in the package, follow these steps:

1. Open the Object Packager found in the Accessories application window.

2. Select the Content window by clicking or pressing Tab.

3. Choose the **File I**mport command.

4. Select the file you want to package and choose OK.

Figure 6.17 shows how a package and its description appear in the Object Packager. Notice that the default icon associated with the imported file appears on the Appearance side of the Object Packager. The Content side shows a description.

At this point, you can change the appearance of the icon or the label attached to the icon. Both features are described later in this chapter.

To embed the package into a document that has object linking and embedding capability, follow these steps:

1. With the Object Packager still active, make sure that the Appearance side is active by clicking on it or pressing Tab until the title Appearance is selected.

2. Choose the **Edit C**opy Package command.

3. Activate the client application and open the document. Move the insertion point where you want the package icon to appear.

4. Choose the **Edit P**aste command.

   or

   Choose **Edit Paste S**pecial and then select Package Object as the **Data** Type and choose **Paste**.

The package appears in the document as the icon you saw in the Object Packager.

Packaging Files with the File Manager

Newer Windows applications can use the Clipboard to copy files from the File Manager and paste them as objects directly into an application that supports object linking and embedding.

Some Windows applications that have object linking and embedding enable you to drag a file from the File Manager and drop it into a client document. The file then becomes an embedded package.

To use the mouse and the File Manager to package a file, follow these steps:

1. Activate the File Manager and select the file you want to package.

2. Activate the client application to receive the package. Scroll the document so that you can see the place where you want to embed the package.

3. Arrange the application windows so that you can see both the file name and the client document.

4. To create an embedded package, drag the file name from the File Manager onto the client document and release it.

To use the keyboard to package a file with the File Manager, follow these steps:

1. Activate the File Manager and select the filename you want to package.

2. Choose the **File Copy** command.

   The Copy dialog box, shown in figure 6.18, appears.

FIG. 6.18

The Copy dialog box enables you to copy a file into the Clipboard.

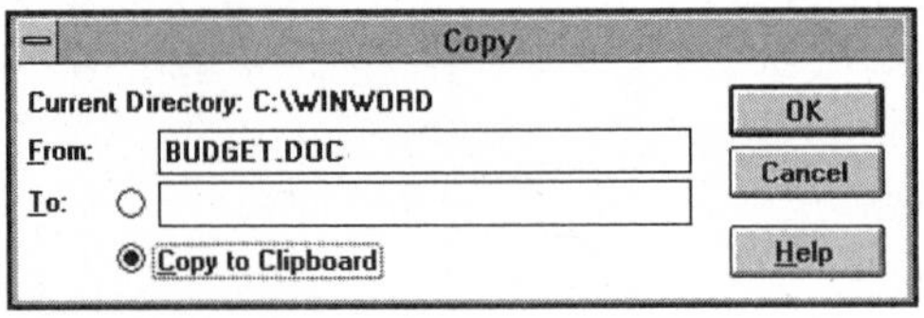

3. Select the Copy To Clipboard option and then choose OK.

4. Activate the application and open the document to receive the package. Move the insertion point to where you want the package.

5. Choose the **Edit Paste** command to embed a package or choose the Edit Paste Link (or Edit Paste Special and then Paste Link) command to create a linked package.

If your application was written before object linking and embedding were completely designed, it may not work with one of the previous methods. If one of the previous methods does not work, try the following method:

1. Activate the File Manager and select the file you want to package.

2. Choose the **File Copy** command.

3. Select the Copy To Clipboard option button and then choose OK.

Now that the file is in the Clipboard, follow these steps:

1. Activate the Object Packager.

2. Select the Content side.

3. Choose the **Edit Paste** command to create an embedded object or choose the Edit Paste Link command to create a linked object. The object icon and its contents or description appear in the Object Packager.

4. Choose the Edit Copy Package command.

5. Activate the application and open the document in which you want to paste the package. Position the insertion point where you want the icon to appear.

6. Choose the **Edit Paste** command.

Packaging Part of a Document

The procedure to package only part of a document is similar to that used with the Object Packager, except that you copy into the Object Packager only the part of the document you want packaged. As before, the applications must have object linking and embedding capability.

To package part of a document or graphic, follow these steps:

1. Open the document containing the data. Save the document if you want to create a linked package.

2. Select the data or graphic you want to package.

3. Choose the **Edit Copy** command.

4. Activate the Object Packager and select the Content side.

5. Choose the **Edit Paste** command to create an embedded package or choose the **Edit Paste Link** command to create a linked package.

6. Choose the Edit Copy Package command.

Now that the package is in the Clipboard, you can paste the package into the client document, following these steps:

1. Activate the client application and open the client document.

2. Move the insertion point to where you want the package.

3. Choose the **Edit Paste** command.

Packaging a DOS Command Line

You can create a package icon that will run a DOS batch file or DOS application. This can be useful if you have a DOS application that you want to load or run from within an application that supports object linking and embedding.

To create a package containing a DOS command line from within the Object Packager, follow these steps:

1. Choose the **E**dit Co**m**mand Line command.

2. In the **C**ommand text box, type the command line as you would enter it from a DOS prompt. Include the full path name and command or application arguments.

3. Choose OK.

   The command line you type appears in the Content window.

4. Choose the Insert **I**con button. The Insert Icon dialog box appears. Use the technique described later in this chapter to select an icon for the command line package. Choose OK after you select an icon.

   The icon appears on the Appearance side of the Object Packager.

5. Choose the **E**dit Copy Pac**k**age command.

6. Activate the client application and open the client document.

7. Move the insertion point to where you want the package to appear.

8. Choose the **E**dit **P**aste command.

Saving the Packager's Contents

If you are packaging an entire file to link or embed into your client document, you can save that file from within the Object Packager (the file must have previously been saved). After you have imported the file into the Object Packager, choose the **F**ile **S**ave Contents command. In the Save Contents dialog box, type a name for the file in the File **N**ame text box (if necessary, select a different drive in the Drives list or a different directory in the **D**irectories list). Choose OK. The file is saved in its native format.

Selecting or Creating an Icon for Your Package

Normally, when you paste or import data into the Object Packager, the icon related to the data's document appears on the Appearance side. You can change that icon or create your own icon.

To change an icon while it is in the Object Packager, follow these steps:

1. Select the Appearance side of the Object Packager.

2. Choose the Insert Icon button.

   The Insert Icon dialog box displays the current icon related to the data you are packaging.

3. Choose the **Browse** button.

4. From the Browse dialog box that appears (similar to a file open dialog box), select the name of a file containing icons. Then choose OK.

   Windows applications contain an icon; you also can buy or create files that contain a library of icons. If you do not have a file containing a library of icons, choose the PROGMAN.EXE or MORICONS.DLL file from the WINDOWS directory. Figure 6.19 shows some of the icons contained in PROGMAN.EXE.

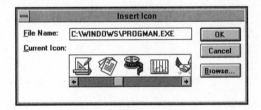

FIG. 6.19

PROGMAN.EXE contains many icons you can use for packages.

5. Select an icon from the scrolling **Current Icon** list shown in the Insert Icon dialog box. Then choose OK.

You also can create your own icons by drawing them with the Paintbrush application. One way to do that is to modify an existing icon. When you have copied data into the Object Packager and it displays an icon, follow these steps to modify an icon:

1. Select the Appearance side of the Object Packager.

2. Choose the **Edit Copy** command.

3. Activate Paintbrush.

4. Choose the **Edit P**aste command.

   The existing icon is pasted into Paintbrush, where you can modify it. If you want to create an icon, start with step 5.

5. Use the Paintbrush to modify or create an icon. Use the **File S**ave command if you want to save a copy of the icon.

6. Select the icon you have drawn and then choose the **Edit C**opy command.

7. Activate the Object Packager.

8. Select the Appearance side and choose the **Edit P**aste command.

Use the procedures described previously to paste the package with its new icon into a document.

Editing an Icon's Label

Each package is labeled by the file name if you packaged a document or by the object type if you packaged part of a file. You can create your own label or file name.

To change a label while the package is in the Object Packager, select the Appearance side of the Object Packager and choose the **Edit La**bel command. Enter a new name in the Label dialog box that appears and then choose OK.

Editing Existing Package Icons

To change the icon or label of an existing package in a client document, select the icon and then choose the **Edit Package O**bject command (or a similar command). From the cascading menu that appears, choose the **Edit P**ackage command. Object Packager loads the package, enabling you to use the preceding procedures to change the icon's appearance or label.

Sizing and Moving Package Icons

You can size and move a package within Windows Write and other applications in the same way that you size or move other graphic objects. For information on how to do this in Windows Write, refer to Chapter 12.

For Related Information:

▶▶ See "Embedding Sound and Video in Applications," p. 733.

FROM HERE...

Managing Links

Keeping track of the many links that create a complex document can be difficult. The **Edit Links** command makes the job considerably easier. When you choose **Edit Links**, the Links dialog box displays to show you a list of all the links, their types, and how they update (see fig. 6.20). From the buttons and check box, you can update linked data, lock links to prevent changes, cancel the link, and change the file names or directories where the linked data is stored.

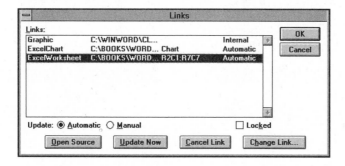

FIG. 6.20

The Links dialog box simplifies managing multiple links in a document.

> **TIP**
>
> To select multiple adjacent links, click on the first link in the Link dialog box and then Shift+click on the last. To select or clear multiple nonadjacent links, hold down the Ctrl key as you click on links.

Updating Links

To update individual links in a client document to reflect changes in the original document, select the linked data and then choose the **Edit Links** command. When the Links dialog box appears, select the links you want to update and then choose the Update Now button.

When you want to update all the links in an entire document, select either the entire document or all the links in the Link dialog box and choose the **U**pdate Now button. In some applications, shortcuts exist for updating links. For example, in Word for Windows, you can update a link by selecting it and pressing the F9 key.

Controlling Manual versus Automatic Updates

Some client/server applications enable you to specify whether a link should automatically update itself or should be updated manually only. You may want to use manual links if you have many links that change frequently because numerous automatic links can slow down Windows.

You also may want to use manual links if you want the client document to update selectively. This may occur if you have Microsoft Excel linked to a mainframe database, so inventory charts can be analyzed every ten minutes. A manually controlled link from Microsoft Excel into a Word for Windows document, however, updates an inventory report only when you request an update.

When you use the **E**dit Paste **S**pecial command to create a link, it is created as an automatic link. To change a link to a manual link, follow these steps:

1. Select the linked data or graphic.

2. Choose the **E**dit **L**inks command. The Links dialog box appears.

3. Select the Update option that specifies when you want updates.

    Manual   Link updated when you specify

    Automatic   Link updated when source data changes

4. Choose OK or press Enter.

To update a manual link, use the procedure described in "Updating Links," an earlier section of this chapter. Some applications enable you to update a link by selecting the linked data and pressing a shortcut key, such as F9. To prevent a link from updating, lock the link by using the next procedure.

Locking a Link To Prevent Accidental Changes

You may want to prevent accidental updating of a link but still want updates at your discretion. You can do this by locking or unlocking the related link. To lock or unlock a link, select the linked data and choose the Edit Links command. Select the link you want to lock or unlock and then select or clear the Locked check box.

Unlinking Inserted Files or Pictures

To unlink the server document and change the result into normal text or graphics that do not change when the server changes, select the linked data and choose the Edit Links command. Then choose the Cancel Links button. A dialog box appears, asking you to confirm that you want the link cancelled. Choose Yes to cancel the link.

Editing Links When Server File Names or Locations Change

If a server document's location, filename, or the linked range within the document changes, you need to change the link. If you do not change the link, the client document cannot find the correct server document or the correct data within the document.

To update a link, choose the Edit Links command, select the link you need to edit, and then choose the Change Link button. The Change Link dialog box shown in figure 6.21 appears. Within this dialog box, you can edit the Application, File Name, or Item text boxes to match the application, path and file name, and range name for the new server. (The Item is the range name or bookmark that describes the linked data within the document.)

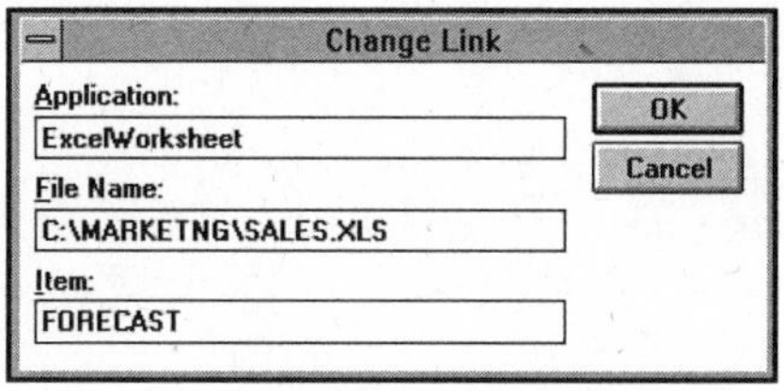

FIG. 6.21

Use the Change Link dialog box when a linked file's name or directory changes.

FROM HERE...

For Related Information:

▶▶ See "Including Pictures in a Document," p. 515.

▶▶ See "Working with Other Applications," p. 532.

▶▶ See "Integrating Windows Applications," p. 850.

▶▶ See "Copying and Linking between DOS and Windows Applications," p. 869.

Chapter Summary

This chapter gives you the techniques you need to create compound documents—documents created from many different applications and collected together. Word for Windows and the Windows applications with which it can exchange data create the most powerful document-building system available.

For information on using applets to add features to any application capable of object linking and embedding, read Chapters 18-20. If you are interested in integrating applications so that they work together, such as using PackRat's client contact database in conjunction with Word for Windows or Ami Pro, read Chapter 22.

Customizing with the Control Panel

The Control Panel gives you the power to customize Windows. You can add printers and fonts; change window colors, background patterns, or date and time formats; set Windows for different languages, keyboards, and date/time/currency formats; add a screen saver; or control how your computer interacts with a network.

Operating the Control Panel

The Control Panel icon, a program item icon within the Main group window of the Program Manager, looks like a personal computer with a clock and a mouse (see fig. 7.1).

To open the Control Panel, follow these steps:

1. Open the Program Manager.

2. Activate the Main group window.

3. Open the Control Panel by double-clicking on its icon or by pressing the arrow keys to select it and then pressing Enter.

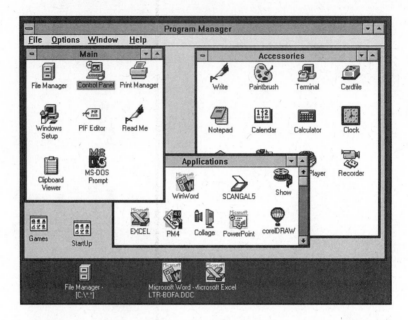

FIG. 7.1

The Control Panel icon within the Main group window.

When you start the Control Panel, its window shows the icons you see in figures 7.2 and 7.3. Each icon represents an application you can use to customize some feature of Windows. Although many of the Control Panel applications are standard with Windows, others appear only when you install certain equipment. The 386-Enhanced icon appears when Windows is running in 386-enhanced mode, for example, and a Network icon appears if you are connected to a network.

To use one of these Control Panel applications to customize Windows, choose the application that fits your needs. Double-click on its icon or press the arrow keys to select the icon and then press Enter. The following chart lists the icons in the Control Panel and describes what each application does.

Icon	Description
	Changes the colors in the desktop and other parts of the Windows environment.
	Adds or removes TrueType and other fonts; turns TrueType on or off.
	Configures the printer and communication ports (COM1 through COM$) and defines how they work. Establishes IRQ interrupt settings.
	Adjusts how fast the pointer moves when you move the mouse and the speed at which you double-click; enables or disables the mouse "trails;" and enables you to reverse the left and right mouse buttons.
	Changes the patterns or pictures used as the desktop background; specifies how icons align themselves on the desktop and icon title wordwrapping; and controls the operation of the screen saver.
	Changes the keyboard's rate of repeating.
	Controls how you interact with your network, if installed.
	Adds or removes printer drivers and defines which features they use; connects printers to the appropriate port or network queue.
	Changes display and operation between different languages, keyboards, and formats for numbers, date, time, and currency.
	Resets the computer's date and time.
	Indicates how applications run in 386-enhanced mode, which controls the default amount of processor power each application uses and how they contend with conflicts over peripherals. This icon is visible only if Windows is running in 386-enhanced mode. Also used to configure virtual memory.
	Installs and configures your system's multimedia drivers, including sound boards, CD Audio, or MIDI.
	Sets up MIDI devices (for details, refer to Chapter 17, "Multimedia").
	Sets the sounds used for different Windows events.

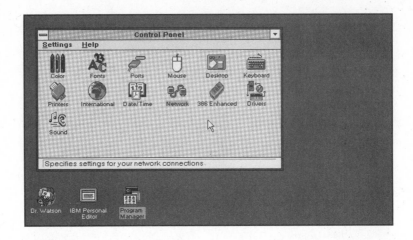

FIG. 7.2

The Control Panel showing icons representing different applications used to customize Windows, including the Network icon.

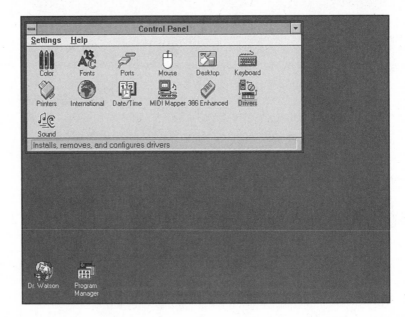

FIG. 7.3

The Control Panel showing icons, including the MIDI mapper icon.

For Related Information:

◄◄ To learn more about navigating Windows, see "Working in the Windows Environment," p. 21; "Understanding Windows Terminology," p. 26; and "Controlling the Windows in Windows," p. 30.

◄◄ See also "Using Menus and Dialog Boxes," p. 35.

Customizing Windows with Color

After working in the drab and dreary DOS computer world, one of the first changes many Windows users want to make is to customize their screens. You can pick colors for window titles, backgrounds, bars—in fact all parts of the window. Predesigned color schemes range from the brilliant Florescent and Hot Dog Stand schemes to the cool Ocean and dark Black Leather Jacket schemes. You also can design and save your own color schemes and blend your own colors.

Using Existing Color Schemes

Windows comes with a list of predefined color schemes. Each color scheme maps a different color to a different part of the screen, and you can select from existing color schemes, or you can devise your own schemes (described in the next section). Figure 7.4 shows the Color dialog box. To select one of the predefined color schemes on the list, follow these steps:

1. Choose the Color icon to display the Color dialog box shown in figure 7.4.

2. Select the Color **S**chemes drop-down list box by clicking on the down arrow.

3. Select a named color scheme from the list. The colors in the demonstration window show how Windows will appear with these colors.

4. Choose OK if you want to use the displayed color scheme.

   or

   Return to step 2 to select another color scheme.

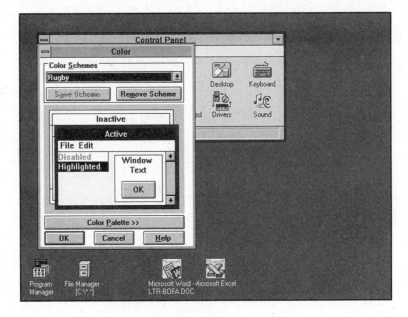

FIG. 7.4

The Color dialog box.

Using the Keyboard with a Drop-Down List Box
To use the keyboard to select from a drop-down list box, first select the list by pressing Alt+*letter*. In some dialog boxes, this automatically drops down the list. In others, you must press Alt+ the down-arrow key to drop down the list so that you can see its contents. In the Color dialog box, as in some others, you can select from a list without dropping it down—press Alt+*letter* to select the list and then press the down- and up-arrow keys to cycle through the items on the list. Each item appears in turn in the list's text box.

Creating Color Schemes

You can select all or some of the colors for different parts of your Windows desktop. For example, you can select different colors for the inactive and active title bars, for the border, for regular and highlighted text, and so on. You can use existing colors or blend your own, as described later in this chapter. To create new color schemes, follow these steps:

1. Open the Control Panel.

2. Choose the Color icon.

3. Select the Color **S**chemes list box and select the scheme that most closely matches the color combination you want.

4. Choose the Color **P**alette button to display the right side of the Color dialog box as shown in figure 7.5.

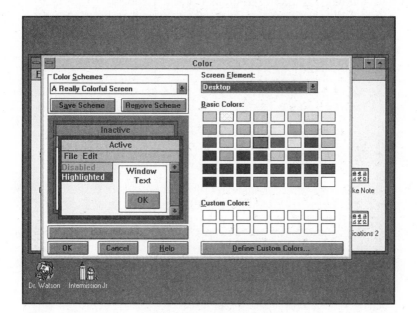

FIG. 7.5

Expanding the Color dialog box to choose your own colors.

5. Click in the demonstration window on the window element you want to change. (Some elements require that you click more than once. For example, clicking on the OK button once enables you to change the Button Shadow; clicking additional times enables you to change the Button Text, Button Face, and Button Highlight— although not necessarily in that order. To see which element you have selected, read the Screen Element text box.) Alternatively, choose the window element you want to change from the Screen Element drop-down list.

6. Select a new color for this element from the **B**asic Colors palette and click on the color you want. Alternatively, press Tab to move to the Basic Colors palette (a dotted line surrounds the current color), press the arrow keys to move between colors, and press the space bar to select a color. As soon as you select the color, the demonstration window shows the change.

7. Choose one of these alternatives for the colors you have selected:

   ■ If you want to color another window element, return to step 5.

   ■ If you want to use these colors now but not in another scheme, choose OK or press Enter.

   ■ If you want to save these colors so that you can use them now or return to them at any time, choose the Save Scheme button and type a name in the Color Schemes list box.

   ■ If you want to cancel these colors and return to the original scheme, choose Cancel.

To remove a Color Scheme, select the scheme you want to remove from the Color Schemes drop-down list box and choose the Remove Scheme button. Choose Yes to confirm.

Blending Your Own Colors

Windows lets you blend your own colors and custom design your own color schemes. In addition to the 48 colors in the Basic Colors palette, Windows can display up to 16 additional blended colors in the Custom Colors palette. You can use the colors you create for the Custom palette as you do the Basic palette. Figure 7.6 shows the Custom Color Selector box which you can use to blend your own colors.

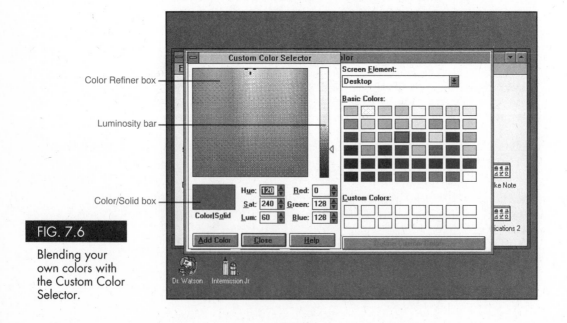

FIG. 7.6

Blending your own colors with the Custom Color Selector.

In the Custom Color Selector, you can create colors in one of two ways, described in the steps that follow. You can either use the mouse to point to the color you want and then adjust its luminosity; or you can use the keyboard or mouse to define exactly how much hue, saturation, and luminosity, or red, green, and blue goes into the color.

To blend your own colors, follow these steps:

1. Choose the Color icon from the Control Panel.

2. Choose the Color **P**alette button to open the Color dialog box shown in figure 7.5.

3. If you want the color you have created to appear in a specific box on the **C**ustom Colors palette, select the box by clicking on it. With the keyboard, press Alt+C, move to the box with the arrow keys, and press the space bar.

4. Choose the **D**efine Custom Colors button. The Custom Color Selector dialog box shown in figure 7.6 appears.

5. Select the color you want from the Custom Color Selector dialog box.

6. If you want a solid color (rather than blended), select S**o**lid by pressing Alt+O or by double-clicking on the solid side of the Color/S**o**lid box.

   Mouse: Click the pointer in the Color Refiner box to select the color you want; a crosshair appears where you clicked, and the color you selected appears in the Color/S**o**lid box. You also can drag the mouse pointer around in the Color Refiner box while holding down the mouse button; a crosshair appears when you release the mouse button. This first step selects the color's hue and saturation. Next, drag the arrowhead up or down along the side of the vertical luminosity bar to adjust the luminosity (brightness) of the color. (You can adjust the color in small increments by clicking on the up or down arrows to the right of each text box.)

   Keyboard: Select the **R**ed, **G**reen, or **B**lue box and adjust the value in the box by typing new numbers or by clicking the up or down arrow on the right side of the box to increase or decrease the number. Select the **H**ue, **S**aturation, or **L**uminosity box and adjust the value in that box by typing new numbers or by clicking the up or down arrows. The Color/S**o**lid box shows what the color appears like in a large area.

Hue, Saturation, Luminosity, and Dithering

Hue	Amount of red/green/blue components in the color
Saturation	Purity of the color; lower saturation colors have more gray
Luminosity	How bright or dull the color is
Dithering	Dot pattern of colors that can be displayed to approximate colors that cannot be displayed—in the Custom Color selector, these are the blended colors

7. Choose the **A**dd Color button to add this color to the **C**ustom Color palette. Each time you choose the **A**dd Color button, a new color is added to the next box in the **C**ustom Colors palette.

8. Return to step 5 if you want to add more colors to the **C**ustom palette.

or

Choose **C**lose to close the Custom Color Selector window.

You can assign custom colors to any part of your window by following the steps described in the preceding section, "Creating Color Schemes."

Customizing the Desktop

Changing colors is just one way you can customize the desktop. You also can change the pattern used in the desktop background, add a graphical wallpaper as a background, change the border width of windows, adjust the positioning of icons, and more.

To think of how color, pattern, and wallpaper interact on your screen, imagine the Windows desktop (screen background) as a wall. The wall can have a color selected from the Color dialog box (see fig. 7.5) and a pattern selected from the Desktop dialog box (see fig. 7.7). You also can hang wallpaper over the entire wall or just a part of the wall.

Wallpaper options you select here can include both patterns that come with Windows—including some wild and colorful ones—and designs you create or modify with Windows Paintbrush.

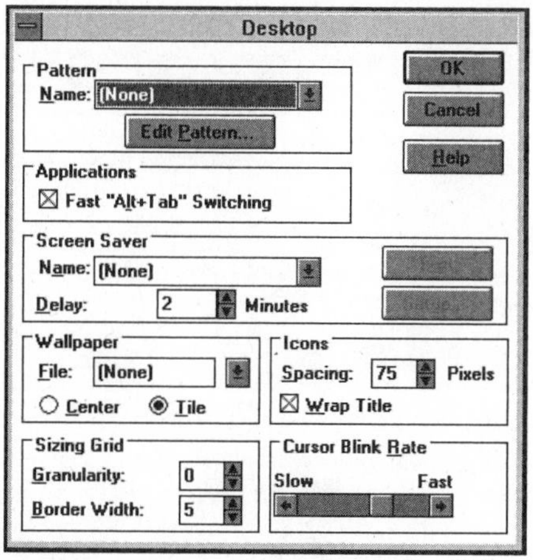

FIG. 7.7

The Desktop
dialog box.

You can put wallpaper over just the center portion of the desktop, or
you can tile the desktop with wallpaper, with the wallpaper repeating
as necessary to fill the area. Tiling wallpaper may put wallpaper pieces
edge-to-edge to fill the screen. Even when wallpaper fills the screen,
icon titles show through with the desktop's color and pattern.

Customizing the Background Pattern

Earlier in this chapter, you learned how to change the desktop's background color using the Color dialog box. In this section you learn how
to put a pattern over the desktop's color. The pattern is a small grid of
dots that repeats to fill the screen. The Sample area of figure 7.8 shows
how a background pattern appears. Windows comes with predefined
patterns you can select; you also can create your own. The color of the
pattern is the same as the color selected for Window Text in the Color
dialog box.

To choose an existing desktop pattern, follow these steps:

1. Choose the Desktop icon to display the Desktop dialog box shown
    in figure 7.7.

2. Select the Pattern Name drop-down list and press Alt+↓ to open
    the list. Select a pattern from the list. Some of the built-in repeti-
    tive patterns you can select are 50% Gray, Boxes, Diamonds,
    Weave, and Scottie.

3. Choose OK to add the pattern to the desktop. Alternatively, use
    the following procedure to edit the pattern just selected

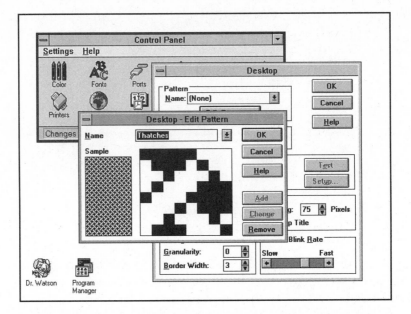

FIG. 7.8

The Desktop - Edit
Pattern dialog
box.

You can edit or create new patterns only if you have a mouse. To edit
an existing pattern or create a new pattern, follow these steps:

1. Choose the Desktop icon.

2. Choose the Edit **P**attern button to display the Desktop – Edit
   Pattern dialog box shown in figure 7.8.

3. Select an existing pattern from the **N**ame drop-down list box or
   type a new name if you want to create a new pattern.

4. Click in the editing grid in the location where you want to reverse
   a dot in the pattern. Watch the Sample area to see the overall
   effect.

5. Continue to click in the grid until the pattern is what you want.

6. When you are finished creating or editing, continue with one of
   the following options:

   ■ If you want to change an existing pattern, choose the **C**hange
   button.

   ■ If you want to add a new pattern, type a new name in the
   Name list box and choose the **A**dd button.

To remove an unwanted pattern from the list, select the pattern and
choose the **R**emove button. Confirm the deletion by choosing **Y**es. The
Remove button is available only immediately after you select a new
pattern name.

Wallpapering Your Desktop with a Graphic

Using a graphic or picture as the Windows desktop is a nice personal touch. For special business situations or for custom applications, you may want to use a color company logo or pictorial theme as the Wallpaper for your desktop.

Windows comes with a collection of graphics for the desktop. You can modify these images or draw new images for the desktop with the Windows Paintbrush application. For high-quality pictorials, use a scanner to create a digitized black-and-white or color image.

Figures 7.9 and 7.10 show two of the several wallpaper patterns that come with Windows. Most of the patterns must be tiled to fill the entire screen, which you learn how to do in the up-coming steps.

Wallpaper is created from files stored in a bit-map format. These files end with the BMP extension and, to be used as wallpaper, must be stored in the Windows directory. You can edit BMP formats with the Windows Paintbrush application. You also can read and edit files with PCX format in Paintbrush and then save them in BMP format to use as a desktop wallpaper.

Bit-map images displayed as the desktop wallpaper use more memory than a colored or patterned desktop. If you run low on memory, remove the wallpaper.

T I P

To select wallpaper, follow these steps:

1. Choose the Desktop icon.

2. Select the Wallpaper File drop-down list box.

3. Select a wallpaper from the list.

FIG. 7.9

The Arches
wallpaper as a
desktop back-
ground.

FIG. 7.10

The Tartan
wallpaper as a
desktop back-
ground.

4. Select Center to center the wallpaper in the desktop; select Tile to fill the desktop with the wallpaper. Tile uses multiple copies if necessary.

5. Choose OK or press Enter.

Creating Desktop Wallpapers

You can create your own desktop wallpapers in one of three ways:

- Buy clip art from a software vendor . If the clip art is not in PCX or BMP format, use a graphics-conversion application such as DoDot! to convert the image to one of these formats. Use Windows Paintbrush to read PCX format and resave the figure in BMP format.

- Scan a black-and-white or color picture using a digital scanner. Scanners create TIFF files with the extension TIF. Use a graphics-conversion application to convert the TIF file to a BMP file for use as a wallpaper or to a PCX file to use with Paintbrush.

- Modify an existing desktop wallpaper or create a new one with Windows Paintbrush. Use Paintbrush to read BMP or PCX files. After you edit them with Paintbrush, save the files with the BMP format.

Store your new BMP (bit-map) graphics files in the WINDOWS directory so that they appear in the Wallpaper Files drop-down list of the Desktop dialog box.

To remove a wallpaper file from the Wallpaper File drop-down list, delete or remove its BMP file from the WINDOWS directory. To remove the wallpaper from the desktop, repeat the preceding steps but select None in step 3.

Using the Screen Saver

A screen saver application prevents an image from burning into your screen by replacing a document screen with pictures or patterns. You can specify the delay before the screen saver activates, and you can set up various attributes—including a password—for most of the screen savers.

To select and set up a screen saver, follow these steps:

1. If necessary, open the Control Panel and choose Desktop.

2. Select the Screen Saver Name drop-down list and press the down or up arrow to select the screen saver you want.

    Choose Test to see what the screen saver looks like.

3. Select Delay and enter the number of minutes after you quit using your computer that the screen saver should appear.

4. Choose Setup to set various parameters for your screen saver. The parameters for each are different; figure 7.11 shows the Setup dialog box for the screen saver Mystify. Choose OK or press Enter.

5. Choose OK or press Enter to close the Desktop dialog box.

Although each screen saver has unique settings, all except Blank Screen have an area where you can specify password protection. This

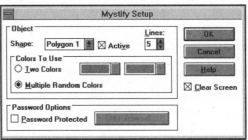

FIG. 7.11

Screen Saver
dialog box for
the Mystify
screen saver.

requires the correct entry of the password before the normal Windows desktop is restored. To set the password, first select the Password Protected check box. With the mouse, click on the box; with the keyboard, press Alt+P and then press the space bar.

To create the password, first select the Set Password button, which displays the Change Password dialog box shown in figure 7.12. In the New Password box, type your password; in the Retype New Password box, confirm your password by typing it again (both must match). Both boxes must contain the same characters. As you type in the characters for the password, an asterisk (*) is shown for each character. Passwords are not case-sensitive, can contain punctuation, but can be no longer than 20 characters. Once you have entered both passwords, choose the OK button. A dialog box will alert you if the passwords do not match. Use the Test button to test the screen saver. Then when you press a key, you can test the password before the screen is restored.

After you have set the password, you can change it with the same procedure. You first must correctly enter the existing password in the Old

Password box before you can successfully change the password. You can clear the password by leaving the password fields blank—but you need to know the old password before you can change it.

The screen saver is activated after the time-out specified in the dialog box. Any mouse movement or click, or key pressed on the keyboard—

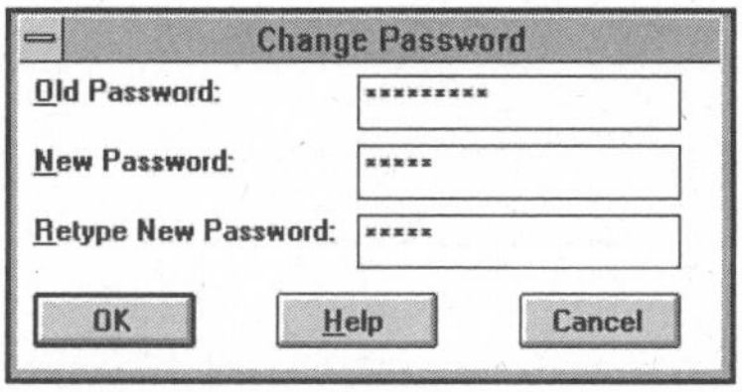

FIG. 7.12

The Change Password dialog box.

use the Shift key so that it doesn't affect any dialog box selections— restores the desktop. If you have enabled passwords, a dialog box prompts you for the password, which must be correctly entered before the desktop screen is restored.

Spacing and Aligning Icons on the Desktop

If the names of your application or program item icons overlap, you may want to change the automatic spacing of the icons. At the same time, you also can turn on a grid that helps you align icons in a neat and orderly row.

To change the space between icons, choose the Icons **S**pacing text box from the Desktop dialog box and type the desired number of pixels (screen dots) of separation between icons. The width you specify applies to both the icon and its label. The maximum number of pixels you can specify for spacing is 512.

When your icon titles are long, you can put them on multiple text lines by selecting the **W**rap Title check box; if you want the names all on one line, unselect the **W**rap Title option.

To line up icons more easily, turn on an invisible grid that icons "snap to." With the grid on, move and then release an icon close to the desired location; the icon "snaps to" the nearest grid line. Use the grid to help put all the icons on the same line. When the grid is on, it also affects window sizing so that the window edges align with the grid.

To turn on the invisible "snap to" grid system, select the **G**ranularity text box in the Desktop dialog box and type the desired number of screen dots between grid lines. If you have a mouse, you can click on the up or down arrows next to the box to change the numbers. You can enter numbers between 0 and 49; each increment of 1 moves the icons 8 pixels or screen dots apart. Enter 0 to turn off the grid.

To change the border width on most windows, select the **B**order Width option in the Desktop dialog box and type a new number or click on the up or down arrows. Widths can range from 1, the narrowest, to 50, the widest. Changing the border width to a value of 3 to 5 makes it easier to use the mouse to grab the window border for resizing.

Windows you cannot resize have a fixed border width you cannot change.

Selecting Fast Switching between Applications

The Desktop application enables you to use the Alt+Tab keys to display quickly in the center of your screen a box with the next application's name.

Select this setting—the default when Windows is installed—with the Fast "Alt+Tab" Switching check box in the Desktop dialog box. When enabled, you can select another running application by holding down the Alt key as you press the Tab key. When you see the name of the application you want to switch to, release the Alt key. The application is then restored. Press the Alt+Esc key combination to return to your original application.

Adjusting the Cursor Blink Rate

Some people are driven frantic by a rapidly blinking cursor; others fall asleep when the cursor blinks too slowly. Whichever group you happen to fall in, remember that you can control the blink rate. To change the cursor blink rate, select the Cursor Blink **R**ate option in the Desktop dialog box and press the right- or left-arrow keys. If you have a mouse, drag the box in the gray scroll bar or click on the left or right arrows. Watch the sample cursor to see the resulting blink rate.

For Related Information:

▶▶ To learn more about customizing with Windows Paintbrush,
see "Using the Paintbrush Tools," p. 543; "Typing Text in Paintbrush," p. 560; "Editing the Painting," p. 564; and "Saving Paintbrush Files," p. 579.

FROM HERE...

Customizing Date/Time

Use the Control Panel's Date/Time icon to change the date or time in
your computer system. Open the Date/Time icon from the Control
Panel to display the Date & Time dialog box shown in figure 7.13.

To change the date or time, select either the **D**ate or the **T**ime option
and press Tab to move between the month, day, and year or hour,
minute, second, and AM or PM. With the mouse, click on the up or
down arrows to scroll rapidly to the date or time you want or type the
new date or time.

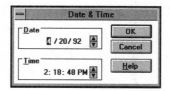

FIG. 7.13

The Date & Time
dialog box.

Choose OK or press Enter when the date or time is set correctly.

Change the formats in which Windows displays the date or time by
opening the Control Panel's International icon and selecting the **T**ime
Format Change button. Changing date and time formats is explained in
"Customizing International Settings" later in this chapter. Often you
need to select only the country to change the date and time formats
accordingly.

Creating Formats in Windows Applications
With some Windows applications, including Word for Windows
and Excel, you can create your own custom date and time formats
if you need a format different from the predefined formats.

FROM HERE...

For Related Information:

▶▶ To learn more about customizing with the Windows Desktop Accessories, see "Writing in the Notepad," p. 642; "Tracking Appointments with the Calendar," p. 655; and "Watching the Clock," p. 694.

Changing Keyboard Speed

Although changing the keyboard speed doesn't result in a miracle that makes you type faster, it does speed up the rate at which characters are repeated. You also can change the delay before the character repeats.

Change the keyboard repeat rate by choosing the Keyboard icon from the Control Panel window. The dialog box shown in figure 7.14 appears. Select the **R**epeat Rate and press the right or left arrow, or click on the arrows with the mouse, to change the repeat rate. Set the **D**elay Before First Repeat in the same manner. Test the repeat rate by selecting the **T**est box; press and hold down one letter key.

FIG. 7.14

The Keyboard dialog box.

```
┌─────────────────────────────────────────┐
│ ─│              Keyboard                 │
├─────────────────────────────────────────┤
│ ┌─Keyboard Speed──────────────┐ ┌──────┐ │
│ │ Delay Before First Repeat   │ │  OK  │ │
│ │ Long                 Short  │ └──────┘ │
│ │ [◄│        ▓        │►]      │ ┌──────┐ │
│ │                             │ │Cancel│ │
│ │ Repeat Rate                 │ └──────┘ │
│ │ Slow                  Fast  │ ┌──────┐ │
│ │ [◄│     ▓           │►]      │ │ Help │ │
│ │                             │ └──────┘ │
│ │ Test:                       │          │
│ │ ┌─────────────────────────┐ │          │
│ │ └─────────────────────────┘ │          │
│ └─────────────────────────────┘          │
└─────────────────────────────────────────┘
```

T I P   Four of the most commonly repeated keys are the arrow keys. Use the Repeat Rate option to set the repeat rate that is most comfortable for you when you press an arrow key. To test the speed of the arrows in the Test text box, you first must type text in the box.

Changing the Behavior of the Mouse

If you are left-handed or if you like a "hot-rod" mouse, you will want to know how to modify your mouse's behavior. Open the Mouse icon on the Control Panel to display the Mouse dialog box shown in figure 7.15. To change the speed at which the pointer moves as you move the mouse, select the **M**ouse Tracking Speed option. Press the left or right arrow to adjust the speed at which the pointer moves. Alternatively, click on the scroll bar with the mouse.

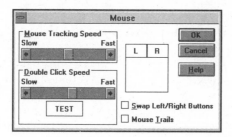

FIG. 7.15

The Mouse dialog box.

Activating the Mouse **T**rails check box causes mouse movement to leave a trail of mouse pointers on the screen. This feature is especially useful if you have an LCD screen where the mouse pointer can sometimes get lost. This option will not be shown for video display drivers that don't support it.

If you use the mouse with your left hand, you may find the mouse more comfortable to use if you reverse the left and right mouse buttons. Select the **S**wap Left/Right Buttons check box. Press the left and right mouse buttons and watch the test *L* and *R* to see the result. This option takes effect immediately, so you need to use the Right mouse button to unselect the button swapping.

Another customizable feature is the rate at which Windows recognizes double-clicks with the mouse. Some people—especially beginners— double-click the mouse slowly. As you gain experience with Windows, the speed at which you double-click increases. To change the double-click response rate, select the **D**ouble Click Speed scroll bar. Drag the square in the gray scroll bar to the left or right to change the response rate. Double-click in the TEST box to test the new rate; the TEST box will change colors when you have successfully double-clicked.

For Related Information:

▶▶ See "Getting the Mouse To Work," p. 1059.

Customizing International Settings

Another advantage with Windows applications is the ability to switch between different international character sets, time and date displays, and numeric formats. The international settings you choose in the Control Panel affect applications, such as Excel, that take advantage of these Windows features. Choose the International icon from the Control Panel window to see the International dialog box shown in figure 7.16.

FIG. 7.16

The International dialog box.

International
Country: United States
Language: English (American)
Keyboard Layout: US
Measurement: English
List Separator: ,
Date Format: 4/20/92 — Monday, April 20, 1992
Time Format: 2:19:25 PM
Currency Format: $1.22 ($1.22)
Number Format: 1,234.22
OK Cancel Help

Check with Vendors for International Software Versions
Although you can use the International dialog box to change language and country formats, doing so does not change the language used in menus or Help information. To obtain versions of Windows and Microsoft applications for countries other than the United States, check with your local Microsoft representative. Check with the corporate offices of other software vendors for international versions of their applications.

To set up Windows with a country format, language, and measurement system different from those of the United States, follow these steps:

1. Choose the International icon from the Control Panel window.

2. Select the Country drop-down list box and select a country. Watch the sample formats in the Date, Time, Currency, and Number boxes change. Changing the country also may change default paper sizes in your applications.

3. Select the Language drop-down list box and select the language you use. Changing this option enables your applications to accurately sort words that may contain non-English characters, such as accent marks.

4. Select the Keyboard Layout drop-down list box and select the international keyboard style you use. Changing this option enables you to use key-characters specific to your language.

5. Select the Measurement drop-down list box and select either English (for inches) or Metric (for centimeters).

6. Select the List Separator text box and type the character you want to use to separate lists. Applications, such as Excel, use the separator character to separate a list of arguments used in math functions.

7. Make custom changes to the Date, Time, Currency or Number Format boxes as necessary. (Details on how to make these changes follow.)

8. Choose OK or press Enter.

If the number, currency, date, and time formats do not change to what you want when you select a Country setting, you can change their formats manually. The following instructions explain how to make these manual adjustments.

To change the number format when the International dialog box is already open, follow these steps:

1. Select the Number Format box by clicking on its Change button or by pressing Alt+N. The International-Number Format dialog box appears (see fig. 7.17).

2. Select the formatting option you want:

Option	Result
1000 Separator	Changes the character separating thousands
Decimal Separator	Changes the character separating decimal and whole numbers

continues

Option	Result
Decimal Digits	Changes the number of decimal digits displayed
Leading zero	Specifies whether a leading zero displays in front of decimal numbers

3. Choose OK or press Enter.

4. Examine the sample format.

5. Return to step 2 to make additional changes or choose OK to accept the new format.

FIG. 7.17

The International-Number Format dialog box.

International - Number Format

1000 Separator:	▊	OK
Decimal Separator:	.	Cancel
Decimal Digits:	2	Help
Leading Zero:	○ .7	● 0.7

Change the currency format in the same way you changed the number format. Select the Currency Format box by choosing the Currency Format Change button or by pressing Alt+U. to display the International-Currency Format dialog box (see fig. 7.18). Then select options from the drop-down list boxes or type your entry. The following table lists the options available:

FIG. 7.18

The International-Currency Format dialog box.

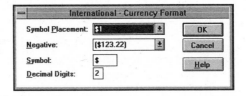

International - Currency Format

Symbol Placement:	$1 ▲▼	OK
Negative:	($123.22) ▲▼	Cancel
Symbol:	$	Help
Decimal Digits:	2	

Option	Result
Symbol Placement	Selects from a drop-down list the placement and spacing of the currency symbol.
Negative	Selects how you want negative currencies to appear.
Symbol	Specifies the currency symbol (you may have to select a different keyboard to type the character you want).
Decimal Digits	Specifies the number of decimal digits.

Changing date and time formats in the International dialog box changes the default date and time formats in most Windows applications. It also changes how they display in the Windows accessories. Choosing the country usually changes the date and time to that country's standard. To make specific changes, however, choose the **D**ate Format or **T**ime Format box from the International dialog box and select from the lists presented.

When you choose the **D**ate Format option or click on its Change button, the dialog box shown in figure 7.19 appears. Notice that the formatting group at the top of the dialog box is for short dates, such as 4/12/92, and the bottom formatting group is for long dates, such as April 12, 1992. With many Windows applications, you can format dates so that they spell out the full month or day. The following table lists date format options:

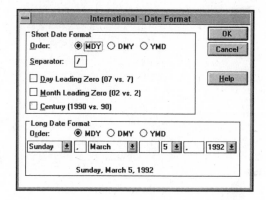

FIG. 7.19

The International-Date Format dialog box.

Short Date Format Options

Option	Result
Order	Changes the order in which month (M), day (D), and year (Y) display.

Short Date Format Options

Option	Result
Separator	Changes the character separating the month, day, and year (for example, the / in 4/12/92).
Day Leading Zero	Changes how day digits display (for example, 5/1/92 or 5/01/92).

continues

Option	Result
Month Leading Zero	Changes how month digits display (for example, 5/1/92 or 05/1/92).
Century	Changes how years display (for example, 1992 or 92).

Long Date Format Options

Option	Result

Note: When you change the long date format, watch the sample date at the bottom of the dialog box. (No sample date appears for short date formats.)

Order	Changes the order in which month (M), day (D), and year (Y) display.
Day of the week	Changes between full day name or abbreviated name.
Month	Changes from full month name, abbreviation, or numeric (with or without leading zeros).
Day	Changes between numeric day formats (with or without leading zeros).
Year	Changes between numeric year formats (the last two or all four year digits).

Be careful not to miss the Separator text boxes. These boxes contain the character that appears between segments of long dates. Type the character you prefer to use—usually a period, a slash, or a comma.

The long date format boxes are dynamic; they change order as you select different MDY orders. If you use a keyboard, move between the boxes by pressing Tab. Display a drop-down list in the selected box by pressing Alt+down arrow.

When you choose the Time Format option or click on its Change button, the dialog box shown in figure 7.20 appears. Select new time formats in the same way you did date formats. The time-format options are given in the following chart:

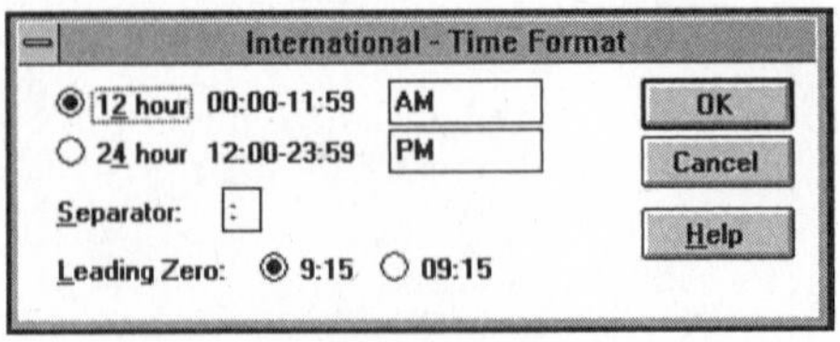

FIG. 7.20

The International-Time Format dialog box.

Option	Result
12 hour 00:00-11:59	Displays times from a 12-hour clock.
24 hour 12:00-23:59	Displays times from a 24-hour clock.
AM/PM boxes	Specifies the 12-hour time formats you want (for example, am and pm or AM and PM). If you select the 24-hour format, use the single text box to type a time zone abbreviation (such as EST for Eastern Standard Time).
Separator	Specifies the character separating time segments.
Leading Zero	Selects leading zeros for times.

Adding and Configuring Printers

When you buy a new printer and connect it to your computer, you must install and configure the printer to operate under Windows. Installing a printer adds a "printer driver" to Windows, enabling Windows to recognize your printer and access the printer's features. Configuring a printer tells Windows where and how the printer is connected to your computer.

The Control Panel gives you a way to add printer drivers and fonts not installed initially with Windows. (A *printer driver* is software that tells Windows how to work with a family of printers. You select a specific printer model from the driver.) Most printer drivers are included on your original Windows installation disks; others are available on a disk from your dealer, the printer manufacturer, or Microsoft.

Before adding a new printer to Windows, have ready your original Windows installation disks or the disk from your printer manufacturer that contains the Windows printer driver for that printer.

The Windows installation disks contain software definitions and appropriate fonts for making most printers work with Windows applications. If your printer driver is not included, call the Microsoft telephone support line or your printer's manufacturer. Microsoft maintains a library of printer and font files for additional printers.

Follow these basic steps to install a printer driver:

1. Select the printer model from the list of printers supported by the driver and add the printer driver from the printer disk to your hard disk.

2. Assign a port to the printer.

3. Change the time-out settings.

4. Select printer settings for layout and features.

5. Make the printer the default printer if you want it to be the one you use most frequently.

6. Specify the network connections for the printer if you are connected to a network.

Use the Control Panel's Printers icon to perform all these installation tasks. Not all steps are required, but you do need to install the printer driver. You also can use the Printers application to turn the Print Manager on or off, to choose the default printer, to change your existing printer's setup or connections, or to remove a printer.

Installing a Printer

To add a printer driver to Windows or to make changes to your existing printer driver, follow these steps:

1. Choose the Printers icon from the Control Panel window to display the Printers dialog box shown in figure 7.21.

The Printers
dialog box.

2. Choose the Add button. The bottom of the Printers dialog box expands to show you a list of the drivers currently available (see fig. 7.22).

3. Select the printer you want to install from the List of Printers box. The printer drivers listed in this box came with your Windows installation disks. If you press a letter, you quickly move through the list of printers to the first printer in the list starting with the letter you press.

4. Choose Install. The Install Printer dialog box appears.

5. If you are installing a new driver, Windows prompts you to insert in drive A the disk containing the printer driver. Insert either the

initial Windows installation disk or the disk you obtained from a manufacturer with a new printer driver or a new edition of the driver. If your printer files are located on another disk or directory, change the path name in the text box. Choose **B**rowse to search for the driver.

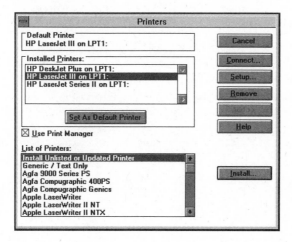

FIG. 7.22

The Printers dialog box with the available printer list.

6. If Windows needs additional disks to install the fonts for the selected driver, it prompts you for additional disks. Insert the disks as prompted and then choose OK or press Enter.

7. Windows adds the printer driver to the Installed **P**rinters list in the Printers dialog box. The printer is connected to the LPT1: port by default. To make the selected printer the printer you normally use, choose the Set As Default Printer button.

8. Complete the rest of the installation and configuration steps as described in the following sections.

Assigning a Printer Port

When you install a printer, Windows assigns that printer to the LPT1: port by default. This is sufficient for most printer installations. If your printer is connected to another port, however, you need to change that assignment before your printer can print from Windows. You also can change the Time-out settings. To select the port assignment for your printer or to change the Time-out settings, follow these steps:

1. Choose the Printers icon from the Control Panel if you are not already in the Printers dialog box.

2. Select the printer driver you want to set up from the Installed **P**rinters list box.

3. Chose the **C**onnect button. The Connect dialog box, shown in figure 7.23, appears.

4. From the **P**orts list box, select the port that is connected to your printer. Choose from LPT1: - LPT3:, COM1: - COM4, EPT, FILE, or LPT1.DOS or LPT2.DOS.

5. If your printer is connected to one of the COM ports, select the COM port and then choose the **S**ettings button to display the Settings dialog box shown in figure 7.24. Make sure that the parameters (**B**aud Rate, **D**ata Bits, **P**arity, **S**top Bits, and **F**low Control) have the same settings as your printer.

6. Choose the **A**dvanced button to change the **B**ase I/O Port Address and **I**nterrupt Request Line (IRQ) if your COM ports are not set to the standard values. The Advanced Settings for the COM1: dialog box are shown in figure 7.25. Make any required changes; then choose OK until you return to the Connect dialog box.

Printing without a Printer Driver
You have three alternatives if your printer is not included in the List of Printers box:

- Call Microsoft or your printer manufacturer to obtain a driver. Install your printer by selecting Install Unlisted or Updated Printer from the List of Printers list.

- Switch your printer into a printer-emulation mode so that it duplicates an industry-standard printer, such as the Epson FX-80 (dot matrix), HP LaserJet (laser printer), or Apple LaserWriterPlus (PostScript). You may have to change switches on your printer to put it into emulation mode. Select the driver for the printer being emulated.

- Select the Generic/Text Only driver as the last resort. This driver prints text and numbers but does not print graphics or enhanced text.

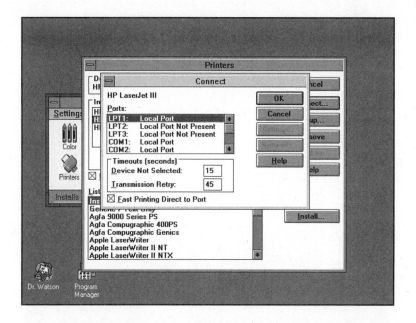

FIG. 7.23

The Connect
dialog box.

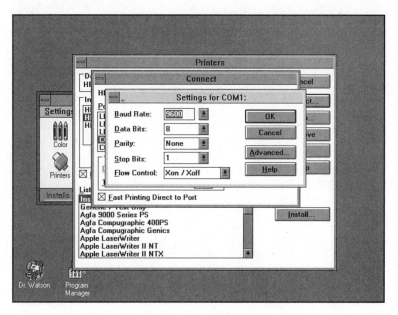

FIG. 7.24

The Settings
dialog box.

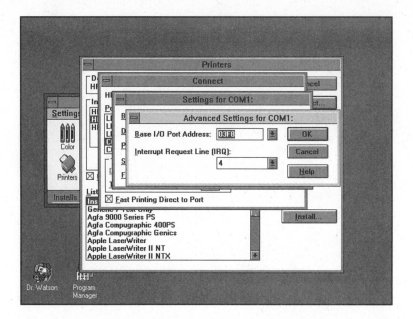

FIG. 7.25

Advanced
Settings for
COM1: dialog
box.

7. The Timeouts group of the Connect dialog box enables you to set the amount of time Windows waits before sending you a message if there are problems with the printer. Windows uses the **D**evice Not Selected time when the printer is off-line or not ready. The **T**ransmission Retry value is used when the printer is not accepting characters, such as when the printer's buffer is full.

8. The **F**ast Printing Direct to Port check box tells Windows how to send data to the printer port. When selected, it enables Windows to send data directly to the printer port, bypassing DOS printing requests. If you are using a printer spooler or "pop-up" software that controls your printer switch box, clear the check box to enable that software to recognize text sent through normal DOS interrupts. This slows down printing, however, so choose accordingly.

9. If your printer is connected to a network, choose the Network button (for details about Network options, see Chapter 28 and "Using the Network Icon" later in this chapter). Otherwise, choose the OK button to save the changes made.

Use the PRINTERS.WRI files in the Windows directory to get specific help on special settings for your printer. Use the Write application to read these files. Some printer drivers come with their own README files that also can be read with the Notepad or Write application.

If you are having trouble printing large files, try increasing the Transmission Retry value.

T I P

Changing the Default Settings for Your Printer

Selecting the **S**etup button from the Printers dialog box enables you to change many settings for your printer. These settings include paper size and source, resolution, page orientation, font cartridges, and soft fonts. You also can change other options, such as Print Quality, Intensity Control, and Dithering, depending on the printer driver. Figure 7.26 shows the dialog box for the HP LaserJet III, and figure 7.27 shows the dialog box for the Epson FX-850 printer.

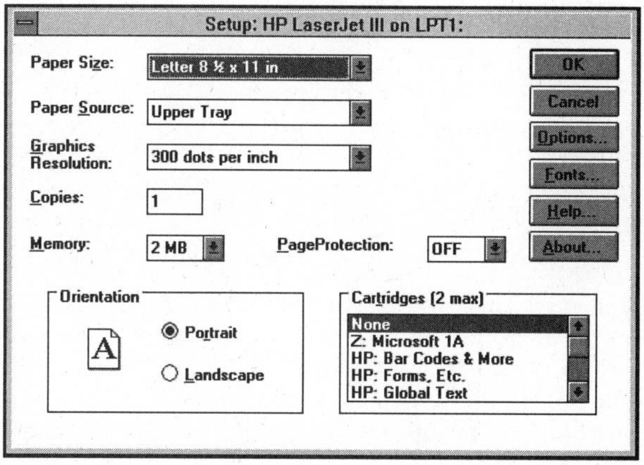

FIG. 7.26

The HP LaserJet III Setup dialog box.

In the HP LaserJet III Setup dialog box, for example, you can specify the Paper Size, how much memory the printer has, and which font cartridges are installed. You can select two font cartridges by clicking on the first and then Shift-clicking on the second. Use Ctrl+arrow and the space bar to select two cartridges with the keyboard. The Epson FX-850 Setup dialog box, however, has different choices. Since each printer is unique, use the Help button to get specific information about your printer.

Once you have made the needed selections in the printer's Option dialog box, choose the OK button to save your changes. If you need to set up additional printers, use the same procedure as above.

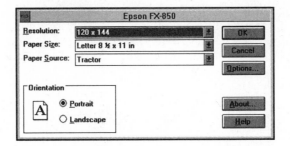

FIG. 7.27

The Epson
FX-850 setup
dialog box.

Finally, if you haven't already done it, select your default printer. Just select the printer from the Installed **P**rinters list box and then select the Set As Default Printer button. The printer name will then be shown in the Default Printer box of the Printers dialog box. Select Close (or press the Enter key) to save the changes you have made and exit the Printers application.

T   I   P   You can add memory to many laser printers. If your laser printer has more memory than is standard, be sure to increase the value in the Memory option in the Setup dialog box (see fig. 7.26).

T   I   P   Some printers do not support downloadable fonts or are not compatible with TrueType. Other printers are not perfect in their emulation and have problems with TrueType. In these cases, you can choose Print TrueType as Graphics and have the text sent as an image, rather than as text. This method, which is how ATM works, is slower and takes more memory but usually works.

Connecting to and Disconnecting from Network Printers

If you are connected to a network printer, you can print from Windows to that printer. To connect to a network printer, follow these steps:

1. Choose the Printers icon if the Printers dialog box is not open.

2. Choose the **C**onnect button.

3. Choose the **N**etwork button. This button is grayed if you are not connected to a network. See Chapter 28, "Networking Windows," for information on connecting to networks.

4. The dialog box displayed is dependent on the network you have installed. In general, you need to specify the network path, the port, and any required password. With some networks, you can use the Browse feature to get a list of available network printers; if not available, the Browse button is dimmed. If you have previously connected to a printer, choose the Previous button to reconnect to that printer.

5. Choose **C**onnect to link with the network printer.

To disconnect from the network printer, repeat the preceding steps, selecting the printer from the Network Printer Connection dialog box and choosing the **D**isconnect button.

Removing Printers from Windows

Removing a printer driver saves only a small amount of disk space, but it unclutters the printer selection and setup dialog boxes. To remove a printer driver, choose the Printers icon from the Control Panel, displaying the Printers dialog box. Select the printer from the Installed **P**rinters list and then choose the **R**emove button. Windows asks you to confirm whether you want to remove the printer driver.

Some drivers may be used by more than one printer. Do not remove a driver used by another printer from the same family.   **T I P**

Turning Print Manager On or Off

The Print Manager enables you to print multiple files as you continue to work in an application. Using the Print Manager to control the print job results in slower printing than when printing directly to the printer. If you print directly to the printer, however, you cannot continue to work as you print.

You can turn off the Print Manager so that you can print faster. To do so, open the Printers icon from the Control Panel; when the Printers dialog box appears, deselect the **U**se Print Manager check box.

If you do not use the Print Manager, you do not receive any error messages from local or network printers. If you are on a network, you probably will use the network printer queue and may not need the Print Manager.

FROM HERE...

For Related Information:

▶▶ To learn more about printing files from a network, see "Printing on a Network in Windows for Workgroups," p. 346.

▶▶ See "Installing Printers from the Print Manager," p. 344.

▶▶ See "Understanding How Computers Use Fonts," p. 307.

Working with Fonts

Fonts are families of differently shaped and sized characters. Printers that operate under Windows can use different fonts, change the font size, and enhance fonts with attributes like bold, underline, and italic.

You add or remove fonts from Windows when you add a new printer or when you purchase new fonts to give more capability to a laser printer. Normally, Windows adds fonts automatically when you install a new printer.

If you add software fonts or enhance your printer, you may need to install additional fonts after the printer is installed. For some printers, Windows needs font information to display fonts on the screen (*screen fonts*) as well as font information to print data to the printer (*printer fonts*). Some types of printers, such as dot-matrix and inkjet printers, use the screen fonts for printing.

For printers that contain their own fonts internally, Windows needs to know only how the fonts should appear on-screen. The font information for printers with internal fonts can be found on one of the original Windows installation disks, on the disk that came with the printer, or on the disk that came with the software fonts (*soft fonts*).

Adding and Removing Fonts

Windows includes a number of fonts. These fonts are used on-screen to represent a similar font that your printer uses. If you use a dot-matrix or inkjet printer, the screen fonts also are used as the printer fonts.

If you format characters for your printer with a font that is one of Windows' screen fonts, Windows uses the screen font of the appropriate size. If no screen font exists to match the font you select for your printer, Windows substitutes a font of the closest size and type. When you install a printer or add soft fonts to Windows, you also add to Windows' built-in screen fonts that match the capabilities of the printer. Windows 3.1 adds support for TrueType fonts. These fonts are scalable fonts that are printed exactly as they are seen on-screen, no matter which printer you have installed. (To learn more about TrueType, see Chapter 8.)

Fonts available in Windows may be proportional or non-proportional. Characters in *proportional* fonts vary in width so that characters can be more closely packed and appear more like typeset characters. Characters in *non-proportional* fonts are all the same width so that characters are evenly spaced and appear more like typewritten text.

Non-proportional fonts, such as Courier, are measured by their width, characters per inch (*cpi*). Such fonts can be measured this way because each character has the same width. Proportional fonts are measured by their height in *points* (72 points per inch) because each character has a different width. In Windows applications, you see character sizes specified in a **P**oints text box or scrolling list. Remember that the larger the point size, the taller the character. A 12-point character is approximately the same size as a 10-cpi character.

Fonts may also be serif or sans serif. *Serif* fonts have small marks at the ends of character strokes. *Sans serif* fonts are straighter and do not have the small strokes at the end of characters. Serif fonts, such as Times New Roman, are easier to read in body copy. Sans serif fonts, such as Arial, more often are used for headings, charts, and displays.

The following fonts are available in Windows:

Font	Description
Arial	A proportional sans serif font. Arial is a TrueType font that resembles the popular Helvetica font.
Times New Roman	A proportional serif font commonly used in newspapers and magazines. Times New Roman is a TrueType font that resembles the Times font.

continues

Font	Description
Courier New	A non-proportional serif font commonly used by typewriters. Courier New is a TrueType font.
Symbol	A proportional font containing mathematical symbols. Symbol is a TrueType font.
Wingdings	A proportional font containing desktop publishing symbols, such as arrows, boxes, circled numbers, and so on, used to draw attention to parts of a document. Wingdings is a TrueType font.
Roman	A proportional serif font.
Modern	A proportional sans serif font.
Script	A proportional font that looks like handwriting.

Adding Fonts to Windows

You can see the available font sets and their shapes in the Fonts dialog box. You also use the Fonts dialog box if you purchase additional fonts for your printer and want to add them to Windows.

To add new fonts, follow these steps:

1. Choose the Fonts icon from the Control Panel to display the dialog box shown in figure 7.28.

2. Choose the **A**dd button. The Add Fonts dialog box appears.

3. Specify the location of the font files by using the D**r**ives and **D**irectories list boxes. Then select the font files that you want to install from the List of **F**onts. To select more than one font at a time, Shift-click.

   If you want to use the fonts from their current drive or directory, rather than copying them to the Windows directory, unselect the Copy Fonts to Windows Directory option. (Windows' default is to copy the fonts.)

4. Choose OK to install the fonts.

For details about installing fonts, refer to Chapter 8.

Removing Fonts from Windows

Some fonts, especially soft fonts (stored on your hard disk) take up considerable memory. If you do not use them, you may want to remove them. Do not delete font files or change the WIN.INI file without first using the following procedure to remove the fonts from Windows.

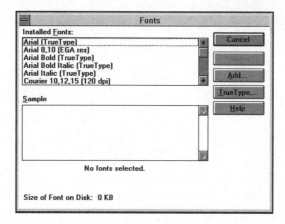

FIG. 7.28

The Fonts dialog box.

Use the Control Panel To Remove Fonts
Windows keeps track of the location of font files. Do not manually delete font references in the WIN.INI file or delete font files from the hard disk unless you have first used the Control Panel to re-move fonts from Windows. If your fonts have been "messed up," you may have to reinstall the fonts so that your system can handle the fonts correctly.

To remove a font from Windows, follow these steps:

1. Choose the Fonts icon from the Control Panel.

2. Select the font you want to remove from the Installed Fonts list.

3. Choose the **R**emove button.

4. Confirm that you want to remove the font.

This process removes the font from memory but does not remove the files from disk. If you want to add the files again later, you can leave them on the disk or copy them to diskette. Use the File Manager to remove the font files you no longer need.

Caution Do not remove the MS San Serif font. Windows uses this font for titles, menus, and dialog boxes.

TrueType Fonts

TrueType fonts are *scalable* fonts that can be sized on the screen (and to the printer) in any size, enabling the printed text to closely match the appearance of the screen text. TrueType fonts also ensure that the text will be printed at high quality on all types of supported printers.

You can choose not to use the TrueType fonts; Windows will instead use screen and printer fonts. If the exact printer font is not available, Windows substitutes a printer font similar to the screen font. Your printed output may be slightly different from the screen display of your text in the Windows application. The line lengths and page breaks when printed are the same as on the screen, though.

The Fonts dialog box enables you to set two TrueType font options when you choose the TrueType button:

Enable TrueType Fonts	Use TrueType fonts in Windows and Windows applications. You need to restart Windows for this option to take effect.
Show Only TrueType Fonts in Applications	Use only TrueType fonts in Windows applications. Non TrueType fonts will not be shown.

Enabling TrueType fonts gives your Windows application the capability to show on-screen the characters as they will be printed. It also enables the document to be portable—the text will be printed no matter which printer you use. TrueType fonts do take extra memory resources, though, so you may want to disable them if your applications need more memory.

FROM HERE...

For Related Information:

▶▶ To learn more about fonts, see "Understanding Fonts," p. 306; "Adding New Fonts," p. 316; and "Using Fonts in Windows Applications," p. 318.

▶▶ To learn more about TrueType, see "Using TrueType Fonts," p. 309.

Setting Up Communication and Printer Ports

Serial ports are hardware connections in the computer to which you connect some printers and all modems. Unlike LPT (parallel ports), serial ports (also called COM ports) must be set up so that Windows knows the speed (baud rate) of data to be sent to the port and how to package information it sends. Use the Ports icon from the Control Panel to set up COM ports. If you do not have a serial printer or a modem, you do not need to set up serial ports.

To set up a serial port, follow these steps:

1. Choose the Ports icon from the Control Panel. The Ports dialog box appears (see fig. 7.29).

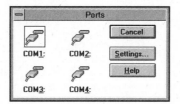

FIG. 7.29

The Ports dialog box.

2. Select the COM port you want to set up. Click on the port or use the arrow keys to select it. All ports (COM1: - COM4:) are shown, even if they are not installed on your computer.

3. Choose the Settings button to display the Settings dialog box (see fig. 7.30).

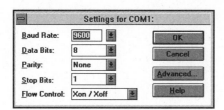

FIG. 7.30

The Ports - Settings for COM1: dialog box.

4. Select the options needed by the device you have connected to the specified COM port. Refer to your printer, plotter, or modem manual for these settings. The options you select must be compatible with the communications parameters of the device to which you are communicating. The options are as follows:

Option	Description
Baud Rate	Changes the speed at which information is sent to the port. Most modems in use are 2400 baud, although the number of 9600 baud modems is increasing. Printers generally use 9600 baud. Check your printer settings to make sure that you use the correct value.
Data Bits	Changes the amount of information sent in each package of data. The setting is usually 7 or 8.
Parity	Changes the type of error-checking performed. Most PC software uses None as the parity setting.

Option	Description
Stop Bits	Changes how data packets are marked. The setting usually is 1.
Flow Control	Changes how the computer and the device signal each other when a packet of data is received. Refer to the manual for your communication device to determine what kind of handshaking is used.

Advanced Port Settings

The Advanced Port settings enable you to specify the base Input/Output port address and Interrupt request number used by your COM ports. These settings must match those installed in your computer. The normal settings for the COM ports are as follows:

Port	I/O Address	Interrupt
COM1:	03F8	4
COM2:	02F8	3
COM3	03E8	4
COM4	02E8	3

To make changes to these settings, follow these steps:

1. Choose the Ports icon from the Control Panel. The Ports dialog box will appear.

2. Select the COM port that you want to modify. Click on the port or use the arrow keys to select it.

3. Choose the Settings button to display the Settings dialog box.

4. Choose the **Ad**vanced button, which displays the Advanced Set-tings dialog box for the port you selected (see fig. 7.31).

5. Enter the **B**ase I/O Port Address in the text box or select the down arrow to see a standard list of values. With the keyboard, press Alt-down arrow to see the list. Select the desired port address.

6. To change the Interrupt, select the Interrupt Request Line (IRQ) and change the value as in step 5.

7. Select OK to return to the Settings dialog box; then select OK to save your changes for that port.

8. Make any needed changes to the other ports with the same proce-dure; then select Close to exit the Ports setup application.

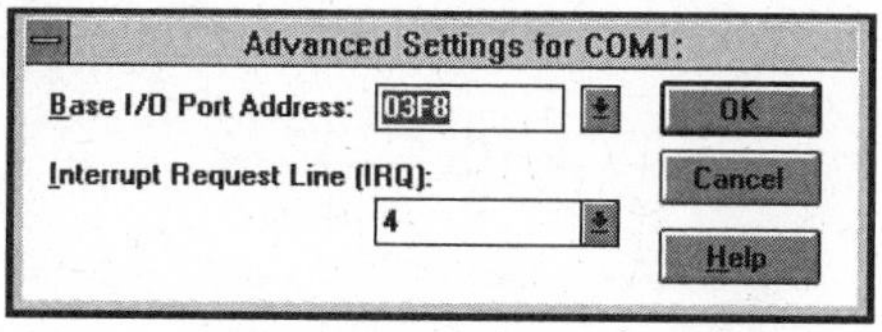

Advanced Settings for COM1:

Base I/O Port Address: 03F8

Interrupt Request Line (IRQ): 4

OK
Cancel
Help

FIG. 7.31

Advanced Settings dialog box.

Setting System Sounds

A beeping computer is one thing when you're up playing Nintendo games after the kids have gone to bed. But it's something else entirely when you are at work and each earsplitting beep tells your co-workers you have made another embarrassing computer mistake.

To turn off the warning beep, choose the Sound icon from the Control Panel, select the E**n**able System Sounds check box, and choose OK. This action disables all beeping for all applications used in Windows.

You also can use the Control Panel's Drivers application to add support for any sound devices installed on your computer. This enables you to set the sounds used for various Windows events, such as the Default Beep, Questions dialog box, or when you start or exit Windows.

To specify these settings, first use the Drivers application to install the sound drivers for your device. (See the "Configuring for Sound Devices" section later in this chapter for that procedure.) Then you can set the sounds for various Windows events by following these steps:

1. From the Control Panel, choose the Sound icon.

2. The Sound dialog box shows the available Windows **E**vents in one list box and the sound **F**iles list in another list box (see fig. 7.32).

Sound files normally have a WAV file extension. If your sound files are stored in another drive or directory, select the drive or directory from the **Files** box.

3. Select the **Event** that you want to change. The file being used for that event is selected in the **Files** box. Select another sound file if you want to change it.

4. Choose the **Test** button to see how the sound file sounds.

5. Repeat steps 3 and 4 for other Windows events.

6. When you have set sounds for the events, choose OK.

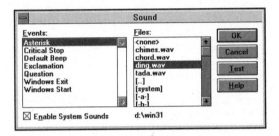

FIG. 7.32

The Sound dialog box.

Configuring for 386-Enhanced Mode

One of the two modes that Windows runs in on an 80386 computer is 386-enhanced mode. In 386-enhanced mode, you can run DOS applications in a window and continue to run applications even when they are not in the active window. In standard mode, DOS applications must run full-screen—they cannot run in a window. Also, DOS applications are suspended—they are in memory but not computing—when another application is running. Both these features could cause difficulties if it were not for the control you have with the Control Panel.

Computers with an 80386, 80386SX, 80486SX, or 80486 processor automatically run in 386-enhanced mode if they have more than 2 M of memory.

Setting Multitasking Options

If you run multiple applications simultaneously (DOS and Windows) while in 386-enhanced mode, each application uses part of the processor's calculating power and the performance of all applications degrades. Processing takes longer. By using the Control Panel, however, you can specify how much processor time is spent on each application. This becomes important if you are running an application such as a database report-generator in the *background* (an inactive window) and calculating a worksheet in the *foreground* (the active window). If these applications shared processing power equally, the worksheet would run significantly slower. If you don't need the database report quickly, you can schedule less computing power for the report-generator, leaving more calculating power for the worksheet.

To schedule different amounts of processing power for Windows and DOS applications, follow these steps:

1. Choose the 386 Enhanced icon from the Control Panel. The 386 Enhanced dialog box appears as shown in figure 7.33.

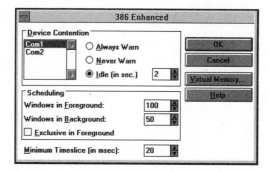

FIG. 7.33

The 386 Enhanced dialog box.

2. Select the Scheduling options you need and type a number in the text boxes. The options are as follows:

Option	Description
Windows in **F**oreground	Schedules the amount of processing time for Windows applications running in the active window relative to DOS applications running in the background. The setting can be from 1 to 10,000 for the Windows application. This setting is relative to the settings of other applications.
Windows in **B**ackground	Schedules the amount of processing time for Windows applications running in the background (inactive) window relative to DOS applications running in the foreground (active) window. The setting can be from 1 to 10,000 for the Windows application.

continues

Option	Description
Exclusive in Foreground	Ensures that Windows applications always get 100 percent of the processing time when in an active window. This setting leaves DOS applications on hold in the background.
Minimum Timeslice	Specifies the number of milliseconds each application runs before the processor gives control to the next application. All Windows applications share one time slice; each DOS application gets its own time slice. Use a number from 1 to 1000.

3. Choose OK or make changes in the **Device Contention group.** The following section provides additional information about the Device Contention group.

 NOTE   The Foreground and Background settings apply only to Windows applications; foreground and background settings for DOS applications are controlled through the PIF Editor.

Managing Device Contention

When Windows applications need a printer or modem at the same time, Windows automatically acts as a referee to prevent lost data or interference between the applications. The battle between applications for the use of a printer or modem at the same time is called *device contention*. DOS applications that want to use a printer or modem simultaneously are not so obliging. When multiple DOS applications attempt to print or use the modem at the same time, problems can result. With the Control Panel, however, you can control how Windows solves device contention for DOS applications.

To control device contention, follow these steps:

1. Choose the 386 Enhanced icon from the Control Panel.

2. Select from the **D**evice Contention list the port that may have a scheduling problem.

3. Select the way you want Windows to handle any contention problems.

Option	Description
Always Warn	Displays a message when a problem arises. You are then given the opportunity to select which application has priority over the port. In general, this is the safest and most commonly used option.
Never Warn	Allows any DOS application use of the port at any time. This can cause contention problems; use it only when you know that only one application at a time will attempt to use the port.
Idle	Specifies how long, in seconds, the port should remain idle before the next application can use it without the warning message appearing. Specify a time of 1 to 999 seconds. Use this option if you have an application that pauses between printing, such as a Lotus 1-2-3 print macro that prints multiple but separate pages or a communication application that logs on to a database, downloads information, and then logs on a second time for additional information.

Configuring 386-Enhanced Virtual Memory

When Windows is running in the 386-enhanced mode, a swap file is used to create *virtual memory*. Applications and data that are larger than what is available in RAM are stored in this area of the hard disk. Windows swaps the data or application back into memory as needed. The virtual memory functions as an extension of memory because it enables you to run more applications at once with more data than will actually fit in memory.

Several factors affect the performance of this virtual memory. The hard disk speed is an important factor, as well as the amount of space set aside for virtual memory. Other factors include the speed of your processor and the data transfer rate of the hard disk—how fast the data can be gotten from and sent to the hard disk. The amount of contiguous disk space—space that is all in the same spot rather than scattered throughout the hard disk—also is another important factor. Finally, the size of the virtual memory area on the hard disk affects the performance of virtual memory swapping.

The virtual memory, also called the *swap file*, can be either perma-nent or temporary. The TEMP DOS environment variable specifies the location of the temporary swap file. This setting, placed in your AUTOEXEC.BAT file during the installation of Windows, tells Windows where to create the temporary swap file. Use the Virtual Memory option of the 386 Enhanced dialog box to set up a permanent swap file (virtual memory area) on your hard disk. This set up enables you to look at the existing settings and configure the temporary or permanent swap file.

There are several steps that you should take before creating permanent swap files. Discussed in greater detail in Chapter 25, they include:

- Delete unnecessary files.

- Recover storage space wasted by lost file clusters.

- Compact (optimize) your hard disk so that more contiguous disk space is available.

After you have completed these preliminary steps, follow these steps to set up the virtual memory area:

1. Choose the 386-Enhanced icon from the Control Panel.

2. Choose **Virtual Memory**.

3. The Virtual Memory dialog box (fig. 7.34) shows the current swap file settings.

4. To change the settings, select **Change**. Windows will scan the current drive and then display the expanded Virtual Memory dialog box, as shown in figure 7.34. The current settings are shown on the upper portion of the dialog box.

5. Select the **Drive** you want to use for the swap file. As you select each drive, Windows recomputes the Space Available and Recommended Maximum Size values.

6. Change the **Type** of swap file you want to use; Temporary, Permanent, or None. If you select a Permanent type of swap file, the dialog box shows the Maximum Size (contiguous space) and Recommended size.

7. Enter the size of the swap file you want to create in the New **Size** box. Make this value as large as possible, but not more than the Maximum size. The use of non-contiguous disk space in your swap file slows down the swapping process. The dialog box also shows the Optimal Size for Windows, which you can use as a guide to the value to enter in the Size box.

8. Some computers have the capability of 32-bit access, which increases the performance of accessing disk drives. To use this capability, check the **Use 32-Bit Disk Access** box.

Virtual Memory

Current Settings
Drive: C:
Size: 6,804 KB
Type: Temporary (using MS-DOS)

OK
Cancel
Change>>
Help

New Settings

Drive: c:
Type: Temporary

Space Available: 58,280 KB
Recommended Maximum Size: 23,664 KB

New Size: 4905 KB

☒ Use 32-Bit Disk Access

FIG. 7.34

The Virtual
Memory dialog
box.

9. Choose OK to create the swap file with the parameters specified.
   You are returned to the 386-Enhanced dialog box. Choose OK to
   exit back to the Control Panel.

For Related Information:

◀◀ To learn more about the differences between Windows' operating modes, see "Choosing an Operating Mode," p. 20.

FROM HERE...

▶▶ To learn about the advantages and disadvantages of 386-
enhanced mode, see "Understanding How Windows Uses
Memory," p. 965.

▶▶ See also, "Using Memory Efficiently," p. 962 and "Optimizing
Hard Disk Performance," p. 969.

Using the Network Icon

A Network icon appears in your Control Panel if your computer is attached to a network. You can use this icon to enable or disable network
messages, to control drive mapping, and to set printing option and
network warnings. For more details about using Windows on a network,
refer to Chapter 28, "Networking Windows."

Enabling or Disabling Messages

Users can send each other messages through Netware using the Netware Windows Workstation Toolkit or the DOS Send command. This feature is similar to electronic mail. Such messages are not stored. Only users who are logged into the network receive these messages. In Windows, the NWPOPUP utility enables users to see the messages that have been sent. A small window pops up, even in the middle of an application, with the message text. The sending user is identified by login name. Messages sent are not stacked up past two messages. The system does keep a user from being bombarded with a flurry of messages.

To enable this feature, select the network icon from the Control Panel and select the Messages enabled option. To disable this feature, select the Messages disabled option. These options emulate the DOS commands CASTON and CASTOFF. Figure 7.35 shows the Network dialog box.

Using the 386-Enhanced Options

Certain network features are available only when you are running Windows in 386-enhanced mode. If you are, two options in the 386-enhanced group are available.

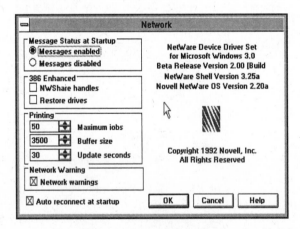

Setting Global Drive Mappings

Usually, each window you open in Windows is independent of the other. Any drive letters you create or reassign in one window are not reflected in any other window. If the NWShare Handles option is selected, however, drive mappings are global. Any changes made in one window affect all other applications in other windows.

How To Keep Drive Maps When Exiting Windows

When you exit Windows, all drive assignments made are generally lost. To keep these drive letters active, however, deselect the Restore Drives option (so that no X appears in the check box). In this way, your original drives are restored each time you start Windows. To keep your new drive assignments for the next time you start Windows, select the Restore Drives option (so that an X appears in the check box).

Using the Printing Options

The following options are effective if you choose to use the Print Manager. When printing through the network, the file server queues your print jobs for you. Generally, when you are on a network, you do not need to use the Print Manager, which queues print jobs locally, duplicating the queuing done by the network.

Configuring the Maximum Number of Jobs

This option sets the maximum number of jobs you can see in the Print Manager queue. The default is 50, and the range is from 1 to 250.

Setting the Buffer Size

This option represents the maximum size of a print job in bytes. The default is 3,500. The maximum is 30,000.

Setting the Update Interval

This parameter sets the time, in seconds, that Print Manager takes to update the Print Manager queue. The default is 30. The possible range of values is from 1 to 65.

Setting the Network Warnings Option

This option should always be set. When a check mark is placed next to this box, network warnings about things such as the File Server going down, the wrong version of the shell, and so on, are sent to your workstation.

How To Set Auto Reconnect at Startup

To automatically reconnect to your network when you start Windows, select the Auto Reconnect at Startup option.

Accessing Other Netware Utilities

Netware utilities such as SYSCON and FILER can be accessed through the Control Panel by installing them in the NETWARE.INI file. You can create and place this ASCII text file in the Windows directory along with other Windows INI files. You can list the utilities you want to have appear in the Control Panel.

FROM HERE...

For Related Information:

▶▶ To learn about using Windows on a Network, see Chapter 28. Specifically, see "NetWare Installation Issues," p. 1012.

Configuring for Sound Devices

Windows 3.1 adds the ability to install *drivers* for multimedia devices, such as sound boards or CD-ROM drives. Windows comes with some sound drivers; other drivers are part of the added device. If you add a sound board, for instance, it may come with its own custom drivers but also can use the included Windows sound drivers.

Using sounds have their limitations. If you are running a communications application in the background, a sound "task" in the foreground may cause data loss.

To install a driver, follow these steps:

1. From the Control Panel, select Drivers.

2. The Drivers dialog box shows a list of drivers that are standard with Windows (see fig. 7.36).

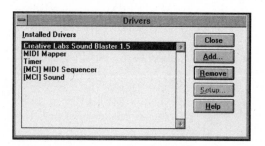

3. If you have one of the listed devices, select from the Installed Drivers list, choose **S**etup, and skip to step 5.

4. To see additional drivers, choose **A**dd. The Add dialog box includes the **L**ist of Drivers. Select yours from the list. To use a driver installed in another drive or directory other than your Windows directory, select Unlisted or Updated Driver and then select OK. The Install Driver dialog box asks you for the disk with the driver file. Or use the **B**rowse button to select the drive or directory that contains the driver file. Select OK to return to the Drivers dialog box.

5. Each driver installed has different settings you can select with the **S**etup button. You can select the Port and Interrupt, for example, for the Creative Labs Sound Blaster board.

6. Some driver settings dialog boxes have a **T**est button for testing your settings. Some also may have Help available for additional information.

7. To complete the driver installation, select OK until you exit back to the Control Panel. As you exit, a dialog box advises that you need to restart Windows to enable most drivers. Select the Restart Now button to exit and restart Windows so that the installed drivers are available to Windows.

If you remove a device from your computer, you should remove its driver also. The file itself is not deleted. Do not delete any required device driver's files—Windows will not work properly.

To remove a device driver, follow these steps:

1. From the Control Panel, select Drivers.

2. Select the driver you need to remove.

3. Choose the **R**emove button. A dialog box will ask for confirmation. Choose OK until you are returned to the Control Panel.

4. Since Windows has to be restarted for the change to take effect, choose the Restart Now button. That exits and restarts Windows so that your changes can take effect.

The documentation or Help files for your device should have additional information about using the device in Windows.

FROM HERE...

For Related Information:

▶▶ To learn more about using multimedia, see "Installing Multimedia Equipment and Drivers," p. 716 and "Using the MIDI Mapper," p. 737.

▶▶ To learn more about improving system performance, see "Optimizing Hard Disk Performance," p. 969.

▶▶ To learn how to create your own desktop backgrounds, see "Getting To Know the Paintbrush Window and Tools," p. 539.

Chapter Summary

Working with the Control Panel is something you need to do only to get your system working better, to customize your system, or to add fonts, printers, or drivers to your system.

Managing Fonts

T he days of limited font selections—when the one or two fonts that came with the printer were the only fonts you had—are long gone. Fortunately, with Windows 3.1 and TrueType, the days of complex solutions to the problem of limited font selections also are gone. TrueType brings you easily accessible, built-in, scalable fonts that don't care what kind of printer or display monitor you have.

Windows comes equipped with only a few TrueType fonts, but you can easily add more fonts to your system. Many font manufacturers offer TrueType fonts, so you aren't limited to using only TrueType fonts with Windows. You still can use any downloadable fonts that you may have purchased previously. You also can use, if you want, the fonts built into the printer along with the TrueType fonts.

Understanding Fonts

Loosely defined, a *font* is a style of type, or the way the letters and numbers look—whether straight-sided *sans serif* fonts or *serif* fonts with strokes (serifs) that extend from the ends of each line (see fig. 8.1). Fonts can appear wide and rounded, or thin and condensed. Fonts can have an old-fashioned appearance or look contemporary. Type design is an art form hundreds of years old, and thousands of type styles are available.

Despite the many type styles in existence, only a few basic categories of type styles exist: serif, sans serif, script, symbol, and decorative fonts are the most common styles. Serif type styles are characterized by thick and thin lines with tiny strokes (or serifs) at the ends of each line. Because these fonts are considered more readable than other fonts, you see serif type styles used in most books, magazines, and newspapers. Sans serif type styles have lines of uniform thickness and have no strokes (or serifs) at the end of each line. Because these fonts are easier to read from a distance, sans serif type styles are frequently used in signs and bold headlines. Script type styles resemble handwriting; symbol type styles replace characters with mathematical or *dingbat* symbols. Finally, decorative type styles each have a specialized appearance.

FIG. 8.1

Times Roman is one of the most popular serif fonts; Helvetica is a common sans serif font.

> Times Roman is one of the most commonly used serif fonts.
>
> Helvetica is a popular sans serif font.

The terminology used to describe fonts and type styles can be confusing. Windows defines a font as a type and the style: Times regular is a font; Times New Roman italic is a font; Arial bold is a font. Each font may appear in a wide range of sizes. Fonts are grouped in type families: the Times New Roman family includes Times New Roman regular, Times New Roman bold, Times New Roman italic, and Times New Roman bold italic. Most serif and sans serif type families come in four font styles: regular, bold, italic, and bold italic. Symbol and decorative type styles usually include only a single font style.

Type is measured in *points*, and an inch contains 72 points. A typical type size for a newspaper may be 9 or 10 points. Books frequently are printed in 10- or 11-point fonts. Subheadings are larger: 12, 14, or even 18 points. Titles range from 18 points up to about 36 points. Screaming headlines in a newspaper may measure more than 100 points.

Early computers used *monospace* type, which resembled an old type-writer with each character occupying the same horizontal width on a page. A narrow *i* occupied the same space as a wide *w*. The fonts on many computers today, however, are *proportional* rather than mono-space: each character's width is appropriate to the character. An *i* oc-cupies much less horizontal space than a *w*. Although you are going to use proportional fonts for most work, Windows also provides a monospace font (Courier New).

Type does more than deliver words to a reader. Type makes the text easier or harder to read, determines how much text fits on a page, cre-ates a mood, and sets a tone. Don't use type carelessly; pick the font best suited to the job.

Understanding How Computers Use Fonts

With so many fonts available, you may find it comforting to know that most computers have access to only a select group of fonts. This knowledge greatly simplifies the job of selecting the right font for the task. (And you can always add more fonts to the system as you grow more discriminating about the fonts you use.)

Computers gain access to fonts in several ways. Fonts may be built into the operating system, such as Windows TrueType fonts. Fonts may be built into the printer, as in many PostScript printers, some HP LaserJet models, and most dot-matrix printers. Fonts also may be added to the printer with a cartridge or added to the computer hard disk as soft fonts, which are downloaded to the printer either before or as the fonts are needed.

The fonts that reside in the computer or on the printer are stored in one of two ways, either as bit-map representations or as scalable outlines.

Bit-map fonts store a unique bit-map (or graphic) image for each font in each size (see fig. 8.2).

FIG. 8.2

Bits are the
on-screen pixels,
or the dots,
that make up a
printed
character.

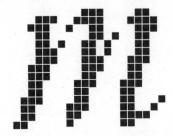

When you want to print a 10-point Helvetica bold capital E, the computer searches for that specific bit map. Bit-map fonts can quickly consume a large amount of storage space on the computer, in the printer, or in both. Many downloadable and cartridge fonts use bit-map technology.

Scalable outline fonts store an outline of each character in a font and, when needed, scale the outline to size (see fig. 8.3).

FIG. 8.3

Scalable fonts
are stored as
outlines, rather
than as bit maps.

Because only one outline is scaled to create all sizes, scalable fonts usually consume far less disk storage space than do bit-map fonts. PostScript fonts, TrueType fonts, and fonts built into the HP LaserJet III are scalable fonts.

No matter how you store fonts in your system, each font must fulfill two roles: it must appear on-screen and print on the printer. Before TrueType, computers needed separate screen and printer fonts because monitors have a different resolution than printers. Even scalable fonts depended on bit-map fonts for on-screen display because these fonts could be scaled only to printer resolution.

With the introduction of TrueType, however, a single font outline fulfills both roles. The TrueType outline scales to any resolution—screen resolution, dot-matrix printer resolution, laser printer resolution, or high-quality typesetting resolution.

TrueType fonts, therefore, have two space-saving advantages over other fonts: these fonts are scalable, so only one picture of each character is needed (rather than an image for each character in each size) and these fonts are *device-independent*, so only one version of the font must reside in the system.

Windows offers another advantage over DOS in using fonts. Some DOS applications each require separate font files, which means that you must reinstall the same font for each separate application (these duplicated font files can quickly consume a large amount of disk space). Windows, however, shares resources among applications. After you install a font in Windows, the font is available to all Windows applications that support multiple font usage.

Using TrueType Fonts

Windows comes with TrueType font technology built in, along with 14 TrueType fonts in five families. These scalable fonts are installed in Windows and are ready to use immediately.

Three of the TrueType families are Times New Roman, Arial, and Courier New (see fig. 8.4). Each family includes regular, bold, italic, and bold italic fonts. The Symbol font is made up of only a single font. The Wingdings font also is a single-font family. Times New Roman, a serif font, is similar to the popular Times Roman font. Arial, a sans serif font, is similar to Helvetica.

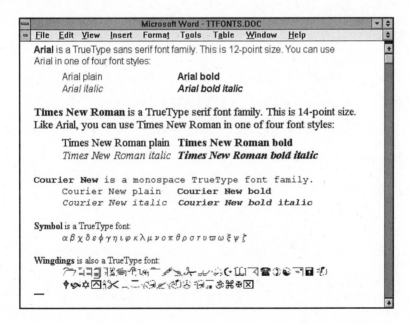

FIG. 8.4

The Windows TrueType fonts.

TrueType offers the following advantages over other alternatives for producing fonts on-screen and on the printer:

■ TrueType is a scalable font, so only a single version of each font is stored in the computer. A single outline can produce a font of any size. In contrast, bit-map fonts store a different picture for each font in each size and either consume massive amounts of storage or severely limit the number of sizes available.

■ TrueType fonts adapt to both the screen and the printer. A single outline suffices for both and produces equally high quality on both screen and printer. Most other fonts, however, require separate screen and printer fonts. To save disk space, many fonts come in limited screen sizes only, rendering blocky representations of a size you request that is not stored as a screen font.

■ Whether you use a laser printer or a dot-matrix printer, TrueType fonts print on all printers that Windows supports. Many other fonts are printer specific, so you're tied to using a single printer or, if you switch printers, you may switch to a different set of fonts, which results in different line breaks and page breaks. With TrueType, you can print the same fonts on all printers.

A final advantage of TrueType over many downloadable fonts is that TrueType fonts are immediately available to all Windows applications; many downloadable fonts first must be installed for each application you use.

Because of the benefits, TrueType is a Windows default. When you start using Windows, TrueType is on. You can turn off TrueType, however.

Turning TrueType On and Off

By default, TrueType is always turned on in Windows. TrueType fonts, however, consume memory on a computer and may slow the display on-screen. They also may print somewhat slower than other fonts because the first time you use a TrueType font, Windows must create the screen image by scaling the outline. This process takes longer than using a bit-map font. Windows, however, remembers this font and, when next used, the font is as quick to use as a pre-built bit-map screen font. Downloading a TrueType font to the printer also takes longer than printing with a printer-resident font, so TrueType may print more slowly than fonts built into the printer.

If the computer has limited memory or runs slowly, you may want to turn off TrueType. With TrueType turned off, you have access to all other fonts installed in the computer or on the printer. You can turn TrueType back on for printing, if necessary.

To use TrueType fonts exclusively, you can turn off all other fonts so that these fonts don't appear in font lists in applications.

To turn TrueType off or on or to turn other fonts off or on, take the following steps:

1. Display the Windows Program Manager and open the Main Window.

2. Choose the Control Panel by double-clicking the Control Panel icon or by pressing arrow keys to select the Control Panel icon. Press Enter. The Control Panel window appears.

3. Choose the Fonts icon by double-clicking it or by pressing arrow keys to select the Fonts icon and then pressing Enter. As shown in figure 8.5, the Fonts window appears.

    Fonts currently installed are listed in the Installed Fonts list box.

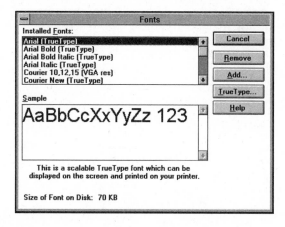

FIG. 8.5

The Fonts window shows currently installed fonts.

4. Choose the TrueType button. The TrueType dialog box appears (see fig. 8.6).

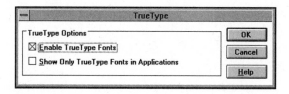

FIG. 8.6

This TrueType dialog box shows TrueType turned on.

5. To turn off TrueType, deselect the Enable TrueType Fonts option so that no X appears in the check box.

   To display only TrueType fonts in applications, select the **S**how Only TrueType Fonts in Applications option. (This option is unavailable if you previously deselected the Enable TrueType Fonts option.)

6. Choose OK.

7. A dialog box advises that you must restart Windows so that the changes can take effect. To restart Windows, choose the **R**estart Now button. Otherwise, choose the **D**on't Restart Now button.

8. Choose Close if you did not restart Windows.

Using Non-TrueType Fonts

Though TrueType offers significant advantages, for some people TrueType also has a big disadvantage: Windows ships with only a few TrueType fonts. You may need more fonts and as a result, you may have already invested in non-TrueType fonts.

Fortunately, you can continue to use the existing fonts and also the new TrueType fonts.

Non-TrueType fonts come in various styles and may be *built-in fonts*, which are built into the printer (as are PostScript fonts, LaserJet III fonts, and many dot-matrix fonts). Fonts may come as *cartridge fonts*, which are contained in a cartridge that you plug into a printer and which act like printer fonts. Another way to add non-TrueType fonts to the system is with *soft fonts*, also known as downloadable fonts. Built-in and cartridge fonts reside in the printer. Soft fonts reside in the computer and are downloaded to the printer as needed (this process may happen by default, or you may need to use a command to download the fonts).

Although the fonts you add may have scalable outlines to use on the printer, these fonts usually display bit-map screen fonts. This may be true of both printer and soft fonts. Screen fonts come from one of two sources. For printer fonts with no corresponding screen fonts, Windows includes a set of generic bit-map screen fonts in serif, sans serif, and symbol models, available in 8-, 10-, 12-, 14-, 18-, and 24-point sizes;

a Courier screen font is available in 10-, 12-, and 15-point sizes. Some printer fonts have corresponding screen fonts that match the printer fonts, and when you install them, you decide the sizes to include. Because a bit-map font file can be quite large—especially the larger font sizes—the number of bit-map screen font sizes is limited.

Bit-map screen fonts have long presented a problem to people concerned with making a screen display closely match the printed output. Bit-map screen fonts fail to match printer output in two ways. First, if you don't have screen fonts to specifically match the printer fonts, Windows substitutes the closest generic screen font and spaces the on-screen characters as closely as possible to the actual font's print requirements. The line and page breaks may be correct but don't count on accurate letter and word spacing. Second, if you specify a size that doesn't match an available screen font size, Windows scales the nearest bit-map size to the size you want, which often results in a jagged-looking letter. (At large point sizes, Windows may substitute a vector font, designed for use on plotters. *Vector fonts* appear on-screen as outlines.)

You can turn TrueType on or off when using non-TrueType fonts, but leaving TrueType on can solve at least part of the problem of mismatched screen appearance and printer output. With TrueType off, Windows always uses bit-map screen fonts—either the generic Windows bit maps or bit maps specific to the font. With TrueType on, Windows creates display fonts in one of two ways. If no screen font specific to the font exists, Windows substitutes the nearest TrueType font, accurately scaling the font to size. If, for example, you choose the Bookman font (which is installed in your PostScript printer but for which you have no corresponding screen font), Windows substitutes the serif TrueType font Times New Roman for the screen display. Therefore, with TrueType turned on, fonts look better than if Windows scales a bit-map screen font to size. However, even with TrueType turned on, if Windows detects a screen font specifically designed to match the printer font, then the screen font is used for display, rather than the TrueType font (see a following section, "Using Non-TrueType Fonts with TrueType," for more information).

Another solution to the problem of mismatched screen and printer fonts is a type management application (such as Adobe Type Manager, which scales screen fonts, or Agfa Type Director, which creates bit-map screen fonts from scalable printer fonts).

Working with Mismatched Screen and Printer Fonts

If the printer font doesn't have a matching set of screen fonts, Windows uses its own screen fonts to try to match the printer fonts. These screen fonts may not be as accurate as custom screen fonts, however, and you may see discrepancies between the text on-screen and the text as printed.

This difference between screen and printer fonts can cause the following problems:

- Words wrap at a different place on-screen than they do in print.
- Titles or sidebars extend further than expected.
- On-screen text extends past the margin set in the ruler.
- On-screen text in tables overfills cells in tables.
- Bold or italic formatting causes lines to appear longer on-screen than the lines look when printed.

Another cause of mismatched screen fonts and printer fonts arises when fonts unavailable in the printer are used on-screen. This problem can occur because selecting a font—even a font unavailable on the current printer—is possible in many applications. (Understanding this quirk can be useful if you want to create a document for printing on another printer.) If you use a font not available in the printer in the document, Windows substitutes a font close in style and size to the unavailable font. Windows tries to find a similar typeface and size. If the requested size isn't found, Windows substitutes the next smaller size.

You can remedy these issues in one of two ways. First, if you are using soft fonts or a font manager, make sure that you generate and install the screen fonts that go with the printer's soft fonts. Second, use fonts available in the printer. You can tell if a font is in the current printer because a small printer icon appears to the left of the font name in your application's Font list.

Using Non-TrueType Fonts with TrueType

TrueType fonts work side by side with non-TrueType fonts. As discussed previously in this chapter, you can turn off TrueType so that you use only non-TrueType fonts, or you can turn off non-TrueType fonts so that you use only TrueType fonts. But an advantage exists to working with both TrueType and non-TrueType fonts.

Many printer fonts don't include corresponding bit-map screen fonts. In previous versions of Windows, applications depended on the generic Windows screen fonts to supply screen fonts for these printer fonts. Windows' *font metrics* files provided information to help the application in spacing characters and words more accurately and increasing the similarity between screen display and printed output. TrueType, however, takes over the job of supplying screen fonts for printer fonts that don't have screen fonts. One advantage of using TrueType scalable screen fonts is that you can scale these fonts to any size. Bit-map screen fonts, however, are not scalable and when you request a size not included on the disk (such as 11 or 13 points), Windows fashions a rather jagged-looking font from the nearest available font size.

One disadvantage, however, exists when using TrueType screen fonts. TrueType substitutes the nearest TrueType font for the font you request so that the on-screen representation of a PostScript font, such as Palatino (for which you may not have a specific screen font), looks exactly the same as the TrueType font Times New Roman, as shown in figure 8.7. You see the difference between the two fonts when you print. Although line and page breaks remain accurate, character and word spacing are inaccurate when Windows substitutes a TrueType screen font for the printer font you request.

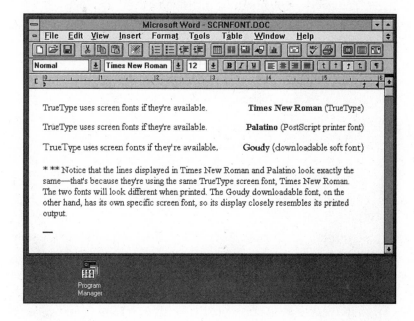

FIG. 8.7

TrueType displays non-TrueType printer fonts with a TrueType scalable font if no corresponding screen font exists.

To get an accurate screen display, you must either use TrueType fonts only, which look the same on-screen and on the printed page, or you must provide a screen font that matches the printer font. If you have a screen font that matches the printer font, TrueType uses this screen font rather than scaling the closest TrueType font. Therefore, you see a screen display that closely matches the printed page. In figure 8.7, you can see that the font Goudy, which has a screen font, is not displayed in the TrueType font, as is the Palatino font, which lacks a screen font. The tradeoff is that bit-map screen fonts take up extra disk space, but the screen display is more accurate.

Adding New Fonts

You can easily add fonts to a computer, whether they are TrueType fonts or another kind of font.

To install TrueType fonts, you can use the Fonts program you see in the Windows Control Panel. To install some downloadable or cartridge fonts, you may need to use special installation software that comes with the fonts. Printer-resident fonts are usually installed by default when you install a printer.

Before you add a new font, be sure that the original font diskettes are available. You need these disks during the installation process.

To add a new font to the system by using the Fonts application, follow these steps:

1. Display the Windows Program Manager and open the Main Window.

2. Choose the Control Panel.

3. Choose the Fonts icon. The Fonts window appears. Fonts currently installed are listed in the Installed Fonts list box.

4. Choose the Add button. The Add Fonts dialog box, shown in figure 8.8, appears.

5. In the Drives list, select the drive that contains the font you want to add.

6. In the Directories list, select the directory that contains the font you want to add.

   The fonts in the directory and drive you selected appear in the List of Fonts box.

7. From the List of Fonts box, select the font or fonts you want to add.

   If you want to add all the fonts, choose the Select All button.

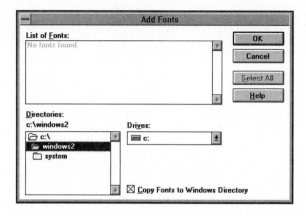

FIG. 8.8

The Add Fonts
dialog box.

8. If you decide not to add the fonts to the system, but rather, to use the fonts from the current drive and directory, deselect the **Copy Fonts to Windows Directory** so that no X appears in the check box.

   Use this option only if you want to use the fonts occasionally and don't want to use up disk space by storing these fonts permanently.

9. Choose OK to add the font or fonts to the system.

10. Choose Close to close the Fonts window.

When you install fonts by using the Font Installer, you install both the screen fonts and printer fonts at the same time.

If you are adding fonts by installing a new font cartridge, then you must set up the printer to recognize the new cartridge. If the fonts are built into the print driver, then you need do nothing more. If, however, you don't have access to the fonts after you installed the printer and set up the cartridge, then you need to install the fonts. Use the Font Installer or check the font documentation to see if you must use a special font installation application.

To set up a new font cartridge, take the following steps:

1. Turn off the printer and insert the cartridge. Turn the printer back on.

2. From the Main group in the Program Manager, choose Control Panel.

3. From the Control Panel, choose Printers.

4. From the Installed **P**rinters list, select the printer into which, in step 1, you inserted the new font cartridge.

5. Choose **S**etup.

6. From the Cartridges list, select the name of the cartridge you inserted.

7. Choose OK to close the Setup dialog box. Then choose Close to close the Printer dialog box. Close the Control Panel.

FROM HERE...

For Related Information:

◀◀ To learn more about printers and fonts, see "Installing a Printer," p. 278.

Using Fonts in Windows Applications

After installation, fonts become available for use in all Windows applications. Because you may have several kinds of fonts installed in Windows, special icons identify each font. By looking at these icons, which appear to the left of the font names in font list boxes, you can tell whether a font is a TrueType font, a printer font, or a Windows system font.

In the font list (from Word for Windows, a word processing application) shown in figure 8.9, you can see that TrueType fonts display a TT icon to the left of the TrueType font, and printer fonts display a printer icon.

Removing Old Fonts

You can remove from Windows a font that you no longer need. Removing fonts saves memory on a computer with limited memory or a computer running memory-hungry applications. If you remove the disk file, you also save disk space (but you must reinstall this font to be able to use the font again in future work sessions).

To remove a font, follow these steps:

1. Display the Windows Program Manager and open the Main Window.

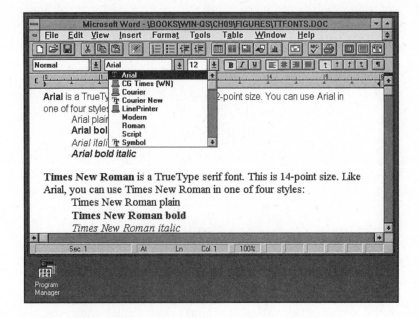

FIG. 8.9

In most Font lists, you can identify fonts by the icons that appear to the left of the font name.

2. Choose the Control Panel.

3. Choose the Fonts icon. The Fonts window appears. Currently installed fonts are listed in the Installed **Fonts** list box.

4. In the Installed **Fonts** list box, select the font you want to remove.

5. Choose the **R**emove button.

   A dialog box confirms that you want to remove the font. To proceed with removing the font, choose **Yes**.

6. If you also want to remove the font files from the disk, select the **D**elete Font File From Disk check box.

   DO NOT delete font files from the disk if you unselected the **Copy** Fonts to Window Directory option when you installed the fonts (in other words, if you were using fonts from the original disks rather than copying the fonts to Windows). Doing so deletes the font files from the original font disk, and you cannot reinstall these fonts.

7. Choose Yes or choose Yes to All to remove several fonts at once.

   You return to the Fonts dialog box.

8. Choose Close.

Don't remove the MS Sans Serif font, which is used in Windows dialog boxes.

FROM HERE...

For Related Information:

▶▶ To learn more about using fonts with Windows Write, see "Formatting Characters," p. 491.

▶▶ To learn more about using fonts with Windows Paintbrush, see "Typing Text in Paintbrush," p. 560.

◀◀ See "Adding and Removing Fonts," p. 287.

▶▶ See "Using Microsoft Draw Drawing Tools," p. 761.

Chapter Summary

Without doing anything special, you have access to Windows TrueType fonts, scalable fonts that look the same on-screen and on the printer. TrueType fonts offer many advantages over other kinds of fonts and work with any printer Windows supports. TrueType fonts consume less disk space than bit-map fonts and provide a more accurate screen display than other fonts. Three TrueType font families come free with Windows: Times New Roman, Arial, and Courier—each font is available in plain, bold, italic, and bold italic styles. Windows also includes the TrueType font Symbol, available only in plain style.

You also can use soft, or downloadable, fonts with Windows, as well as printer-resident fonts and cartridge fonts. If the fonts that come with Windows and the printer don't give you enough variety, you can purchase and easily install additional fonts.

Nearly every stand-alone Windows application takes advantage of the fonts in Windows. To learn more about using applications, refer to Chapter 1, which covers basic Windows operations. To learn more about specific applications, turn to other Que books, such as *Look Your Best With Word for Windows*, by Susan Plumley; *Using Word for Windows 2*, Special Edition, by Ron Person and Karen Rose; *Using PowerPoint* by James G. Meade; *Using Microsoft Publisher*, by Kathy Murray; and *Using Excel 4 for Windows*, Special Edition, by Ron Person.

Using the Print Manager

Windows applications share more than a common graphical interface; they also share printing resources. In regular DOS applications, such as Lotus 1-2-3 and WordPerfect, printer "drivers" are built into each application. These drivers—a driver for each different printer—translate the text or data that you want to print into commands understood by the printer. But Windows applications are different. Windows applications, such as Excel and Word for Windows, have no printer drivers. Instead, these applications use the printer drivers built into Windows. (Some applications, such as WordPerfect for Windows, can use both their own printer drivers and the Windows drivers.) Windows has a special application, the Print Manager, that manages printing for all Windows applications. The Print Manager is initially located in the Main group window.

Print Manager springs into action when you issue the command to print a file, causing two things to happen. First, Print Manager intercepts text or graphics output and sends it not to the printer, but to a *buffer*, or *queue*, where files waiting to be printed are lined up (or *queued*) for printing. Second, these output files are routed, in the order received, to the printer. If the application isn't maximized (that is, if you can see the Windows background), you can see the Print Manager icon at the bottom of the screen while the file or files are printing (see fig. 9.1). The icon disappears after printing is complete.

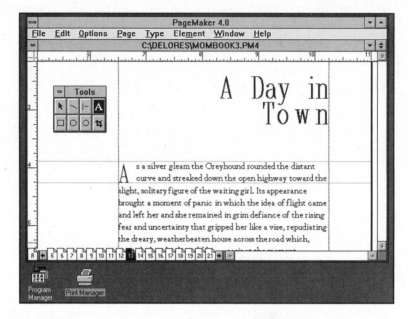

FIG. 9.1

Print Manager icon shown on the lower-left corner of the desktop when files are printing.

Windows gives Print Manager control over the printing rather than letting the application control printing (as happens with DOS applications) because you can continue using the application or switch to another application while Print Manager handles the print job. You don't have to wait for the document to print before you can start working on something else.

T I P   To print a Windows file, you must install the correct printer drivers when you install Windows or use the Windows Control Panel to install the printer drivers after you install Windows. You can set up or change the printer from the Print Manager by choosing the **O**ptions **P**rinter Setup command.

For Related Information:

◀◀ To learn how to install printers in Windows, see "Adding and Configuring Printers," p. 277.

Printing a File

The procedure for printing may vary slightly from application to application, but the basic steps remain the same when you print from a Windows application. Usually, two steps are required. First, you set up the printer you plan to use by choosing the File Print Setup command. This step includes selecting the correct printer from a list of the printers previously installed in Windows and selecting printer setup characteristics, such as paper source, size, and orientation. These selections remain in effect until changed again, so you usually make this change only when you change printers or setup options.

The second step in printing from a Windows application is to print the file by choosing the File Print command. Depending on the application, in this step, you identify the number of copies to print, the range of pages to print, and other choices. (For details about printing with Windows applications, refer to the application documentation or to a Que book, such as *Using Excel 4 for Windows*, Special Edition or *Using Word for Windows 2*, Special Edition.)

After you have issued the print command from the Windows application, Print Manager takes over, transferring information and instructions to the printer as you work.

Although the Print Manager manages the task of printing, you manage the Print Manager. You can open the Print Manager window to see which files are in queue to print on which printer, and you can make changes. You can, for example, pause the printing, cancel a print job, or reorder the print queue. These procedures and more are explained in following sections of this chapter.

You Cannot Use an Application Until the File Reaches the Print Manager
While the Print Manager is printing a file, you can continue working with the application. If you print a large file, however, you may wait a while for the file to reach the Print Manager. You can't use the application while the application sends the file to the Print Manager. Be patient; the file reaches the Print Manager much quicker than it takes to print!

Despite the Print Manager's advantages, you may find times when you don't want to use it. Printing on a network printer often goes faster with Print Manager turned off. Printing large files to printers with limited memory also occasionally causes problems that you can solve by turning off the Print Manager.

To turn off the Print Manager, follow these steps:

1. In the Main window, choose the Control Panel.

2. Choose Printers. The Printers dialog box appears.

3. If the Use Print Manager option is selected—if an X appears in the Use Print Manager check box—then Print Manager is turned on. Turn off Print Manager by selecting the option so that no X appears in the box.

4. Choose Close.

With the Print Manager turned off, you print from the application in the usual way.

> **Different Printers Produce Different Results**
> Printers have different characteristics and capabilities. Some laser printers print at a resolution of 300 dots per inch; some dot matrix printers print at a much coarser resolution. Some printers have built-in fonts that you may want to use; with others, you rely on Windows' TrueType technology to supply fonts. Some printers have enough memory to print a full page of graphics; others have limited memory. Before you print a document, become familiar with your printer's capabilities, possibilities, and limitations.

FROM HERE...

For Related Information:

◄◄ See "Managing Files and Disks," p. 177.

◄◄ See "Using the File Manager's Drag and Drop Feature," p. 191.

◄◄ See "Starting, Using, and Quitting Applications," p. 46.

Using the Print Manager Window

While a file is printing from a Windows application, the Print Manager application is running. If the application isn't *maximized* (if the application doesn't occupy the entire computer screen), you can see the Print

Manager icon at the bottom of the screen (see fig. 9.1). The icon represents the Print Manager application.

Activate the Print Manager in the same way you activate other applications: double-click on the program icon or hold down the Alt key, press Tab to highlight the Print Manager icon or display its name, and release both keys. When you activate Print Manager, the Print Manager window opens on-screen, shows the status of current print jobs, and enables you to change several things about the print job.

The Print Manager window shows the status of the *print queue*. The window shows you which printer is active, which printer is printing, which file is being printed, and which other files are in queue for printing. The window also can show you the time and date you sent the file to the printer and the size of the file. Figure 9.2 shows a sample Print Manager window.

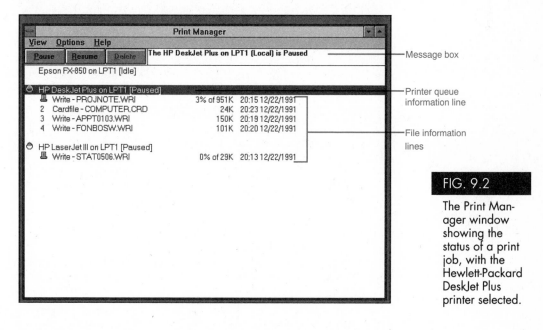

FIG. 9.2

The Print Manager window showing the status of a print job, with the Hewlett-Packard DeskJet Plus printer selected.

The Print Manager window contains several buttons and areas that you use to control the print job. The following chart lists these areas and uses.

Window Area	Use
Pause button	Stops printing temporarily for the selected printer

continues

Window Area	Use
Resume button	Restarts the selected printer after pausing
Delete button	Removes the selected file from the print queue
Message box	Provides information about the currently selected printer or print job
Printer queue information line	Lists the printer name, printer port, and printer status (if you have more than one printer connected to the computer, you have more than one printer queue information line)
File information lines	Lists a file's position in the queue, the title of the print job, the file size, the percent of the file already printed, and the time and date you sent the file to the printer (if you have more than one printer, you may see more than one list of files in queue for printing)

To use the **P**ause, **R**esume, and **D**elete buttons, you must indicate the printer that you want to pause or resume or the file that you want to delete from the print queue. You perform these actions by selecting the appropriate printer or file. The selected printer or file is highlighted (in fig. 9.2, the HP DeskJet Plus printer is selected). To select a printer or file, click on the printer or file with the mouse or press the up or down arrows to move the selection bar.

The file information line for each print job disappears after printing completes.

Start Print Manager from the Program Manager
Print Manager starts by default when you print a document. You can run Print Manager, however, even if you aren't printing. In the Program Manager, activate the Main window. Then double-click on the Print Manager icon or press arrow keys to select the Print Manager icon and press Enter. To close the Print Manager, choose the **V**iew Exit command.

Changing the Print Order

The number to the left of each file listed in the print queue tells you the order in which the files print. Print Manager, however, makes changing your mind about this order easy. (Notice that the first file listed in the print queue isn't numbered but shows a printer icon to the left.

Because this file is already printing, you cannot change its print order. You can change only the print order of the numbered files.)

To use the mouse to change the order of the files to be printed, follow these steps:

1. Point to the file you want to reorder.

2. Press and hold down the mouse button. The pointer changes to an arrow.

3. Drag the file to a new position in the queue.

4. Release the mouse button.

To use the keyboard to change the order of the files to be printed, follow these steps:

1. Press the down-arrow key to select the file you want to reorder.

2. Press and hold down the Ctrl key.

3. Press the up-arrow or down-arrow key to move the file to the new position in the queue.

4. Release the Ctrl key.

Pausing and Resuming Printing

You can interrupt a print job temporarily by pausing the printer, and you can resume the print job when you're ready. While a printer is paused, the word Paused appears in parentheses at the end of the printer queue information line. Note that although you Paused the printer, the printer continues to print all text in the printer's buffer, so printing may not stop immediately.

To pause printing, follow these steps:

1. Select the printer queue information line. Select the line for the *printer* you want to pause; do not select the line for the file.

2. Select the **P**ause button or press Alt+P.

To resume printing, follow these steps:

1. Select the printer queue information line. Select the line for the *printer* you want to resume; do not select the line for the file.

2. Select the **R**esume button or press Alt+R.

Deleting a File from the Queue

To cancel a specific print job, you can delete a file from the print queue. To cancel all printing, you can exit the Print Manager. (If you want to close the Print Manager window without canceling printing, minimize the window.)

To delete a file from the print queue, follow these steps:

1. Select the file information line. Select the line for the *file* you want to delete; do not select the printer queue information line.

2. Select the **D**elete button or press Alt+D. A dialog box appears on-screen, asking you to confirm that you want to delete the print job for this file.

3. Choose OK or press Enter.

To cancel all printing, follow these steps:

1. Choose the **V**iew E**x**it command. A dialog box appears on-screen, asking for confirmation.

2. Choose OK or press Enter.

You May Have To Reset the Printer
If you delete a file currently being printed, especially if the file contains graphics, you may have to reset the printer to clear the print buffer. The printer may print *buffered* information long after you delete the file currently printing. Resetting the printer stops the printer from continuing to print a file. You can reset the printer by turning it off and back on again (or, if the printer has a reset option, by selecting this option). Performing a reset is some-times necessary for laser printers because of these printers' un-usually large memories.

Changing the Printer's Priority

Because Windows can print in the background as you work in the fore-ground, the PC must divide resources between these two tasks. You can, however, choose which task has priority. If given the high priority, the printer prints more quickly but the application in which you are working may slow down. If given low priority, the printer prints more slowly but doesn't interrupt the application in which you're working. If the printer is given medium priority (Windows' default choice), the PC shares resources equally between the printer and application.

The printer priority you select appears with a check mark to its left in the **O**ptions Background Printing menu. The selection remains in effect—for all printing in the current Windows session and for all future sessions—until you change it again (see fig. 9.3).

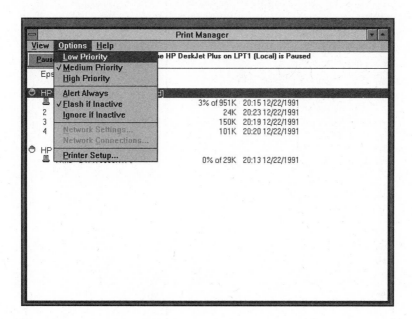

To change the printer priority, follow these steps:

1. Choose the **O**ptions Background menu.

2. Select one of the following options:

Option	Result
Low Priority	Printer runs slower; application runs faster
Medium Priority	Printer and application have the same priority
High Priority	Printer runs faster; application may slow down

Displaying Print Manager Alerts

Occasionally, the printer needs attention. If you're printing envelopes and you need to insert the next envelope, some printers alert you to do this. You can control whether Print Manager always alerts you with a message, whether the Print Manager icon or inactive title bar flashes to let you know a message is waiting, or whether Print Manager ignores the printer's request if Print Manager is an icon or the window is inactive.

To control printer alert messages, follow these steps:

1. Choose the **O**ptions menu.

2. Select one of the following options:

Option	Result
Alert Always	Always alerts you with a message box when the printer needs attention
Flash if Inactive	Beeps and flashes if the Print Manager is an icon or if the window is inactive; you must activate the Print Manager window to see the message (this is Print Manager's default setting)
Ignore if Inactive	Ignores the printer's request if the Print Manager is an icon or if the window is inactive (you might not know that the printer needs attention)

Displaying Print Time, Date, and File Size

You have the option to display (or not display) in the Print Manager window each file's size and the time and date you sent the file to the printer. Make these selections from the View menu (see fig. 9.4).

To display (or not display) the file size and the print time and date, follow these steps:

1. Choose the View command.

2. Select one of the following options:

Option	Result
Time/Date Sent	Displays the time and date you sent a file to the printer
Print File Size	Displays the size of the files in the Print Manager print queue

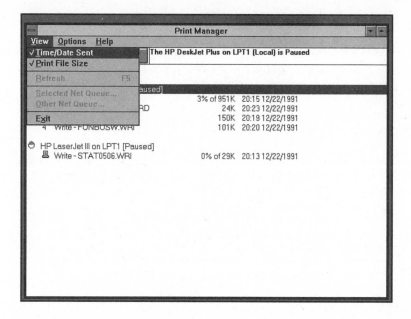

FIG. 9.4

Choosing whether to display the file size and the time and date sent to printer.

For Related Information:

◄◄ See "Controlling the Windows in Windows," p. 30.

◄◄ See "Operating in Windows," p. 67.

FROM HERE...

Using the Print Manager Window in Windows for Workgroups

The Print Manager window in Windows for Workgroups is shown in figure 9.5. The window displays a list of all the printers that are available for your use, including the following:

■ Printers that are connected to your computer

■ Printers that are connected to your computer and designated as shared so that others on your network can use them

■ Printers that are connected to other computers on your network and designated as shared and available for your use

The *default printer*, which is the printer that is used automatically when you issue the Print command in Windows applications, is listed in bold type. Listed under each printer are the files that are currently in the *print queue* for that printer. To the left of each printer and file name are icons indicating the status of that printer or file. Table 9.1 explains the meaning of each of these icons.

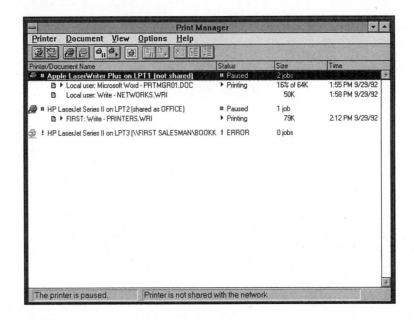

FIG. 9.5

The Print Manager window in Windows for Workgroups.

Table 9.1 Status Icons Used in the Print Manager Window

Icon	Description
🖨	A printer connected to your computer not shared with others on your network.
🖨	A printer connected to your computer shared with others on your network.
🖨	A printer on your network shared and available for you to use.
▶	A printer or document currently printing.

Icon	Description
II	A printer or document paused.
!	A printer or document stopped printing because of an error. (See status bar for message explaining the error.)

The log-on name of the person who sent a file to the printer is listed next to each file name. To the right of each printer and file name are three columns listing additional information. The first column indicates the status of the printer or file—for example, whether a printer or file is printing, paused, or stopped because of an error. The second column lists the number of jobs sent to the printer or the size of the file and what percentage of the file has been sent to the printer. The third column lists the time and date you sent a file to a printer.

At the top of the Print Manager window, just below the menu bar, is the toolbar containing several buttons that you can use to control your print jobs. Table 9.2 describes the function of each of these buttons on the toolbar. A corresponding menu command exists for each of these buttons.

Table 9.2 Toolbar Functions in Print Manager

Icon	Button Name	Function
	Connect Network Printer	Connects to any shared printer on your network.
	Disconnect Network Printer	Disconnects from a network printer.
	Share Printer As	Shares your printer with others on your network. (Available only if you are working in 386-enhanced mode.)
	Stop Sharing Printer	Stops the sharing of your printer with others on your network. (Available only if you are working in 386-enhanced mode.)
	Pause Printer	Temporarily stops the selected printer from printing.
	Resume	Printer Resumes printing for the selected printer.

continues

Table 9.2 Continued

Icon	Button Name	Function
	Set Default Printer	Designates the selected printer as the *default printer*, which is the printer that is used automatically when you issue the Print command from Windows applications.
	Pause Printing Document	Temporarily stops the selected document from printing.
	Resume Printing Document	Resumes printing of the selected document.
	Delete Document	Removes the selected document from the print queue.
	Move Document Up	Moves the selected document towards the top of the printer queue.
	Move Document Down	Moves the selected document towards the bottom of the printer queue.

To use the toolbar buttons, you first must select the printer or file on which you want to carry out an action. Select the printer or file by clicking on the file or printer with the mouse or by using the arrow keys to move the selection bar. Then click on the appropriate button.

Changing the Print Order in Windows for Workgroups

Print Manager enables you to control the order in which documents print. You can change the print order of any document on printers that are connected to your computer. On printers that are on your network but not connected to your computer, you can change only the printing order of your own documents, and you can only move documents down the print queue. You cannot move a document while it is printing.

To move a document in the print queue using the mouse, follow these steps:

1. Move the mouse pointer to the document name you want to move.

2. Press and hold down the mouse button. The pointer changes to an arrow.

3. Drag the document to a new position in the queue.

4. Release the mouse button.

   or

1. Select the document you want to move.

2. Click the Move Document Up or Move Document Down button on the toolbar.

To move a document by using the keyboard, follow these steps:

1. Use the up- and down-arrow keys to select the document you want to reorder.

2. Press and hold down the Ctrl key.

3. Press the up- or down-arrow key to move the document to the new position in the queue.

4. Release the Ctrl key.

Pausing and Resuming Printing in Windows for Workgroups

When working with Windows for Workgroups, you can pause printing for any printer connected to your computer or for any of the files listed under a printer connected to your computer, regardless of whether the printer is shared. When working with a printer that is on your network but not connected to your computer, you can pause only your own documents. While a printer or document is paused, the word *Paused* appears in parentheses in the Status column. Although you paused the printer or document, the printer continues to print all text in the printer's buffer; therefore, printing may not stop immediately.

To pause printing, follow these steps:

1. Select the printer or document you want to pause in the Print Manager window.

2. Click the Pause Printer or Pause Printing Document button on the toolbar.

   or

   Choose the Printer Pause Printer or Document Pause Printing Document command.

To resume printing, follow these steps:

1. Select the printer or document you want to pause in the Print Manager window.

2. Click the Resume Printer or Resume Printing Document button on the toolbar.

   or

   Choose the Printer Resume Printer or Document Resume Printing Document command.

Deleting a Document from the Queue in Windows for Workgroups

When working with Windows for Workgroups, you can delete any of the documents on your printer even if they came from another user to be printed on your shared printer. If you are printing on a shared printer that is not connected to your computer, you can delete only documents that you created.

To delete a document from the print queue, follow these steps:

1. Select the document you want to remove from the queue.

2. Click the Delete Document button on the toolbar.

   or

   Choose the Document Delete Document command or press Del.

3. Choose OK or press Enter when the confirmation message box appears.

 NOTE   If you exit Print Manager by using the Printer Exit command, a message box appears and warns you that all pending print jobs will be cancelled. Choose OK if your intention is to cancel all print jobs, including those sent to your printer by others on your network.

Changing the Printer's Priority in Windows for Workgroups

Windows has the capability to perform more than one task at a time. Therefore, you can print while you are working in one or more applications. Each task, however, consumes some of the computer's computational power. You have the ability to balance how much of the computer's power is spent on applications and how much on printing. If you want your applications to run faster while a document is printing, then you can give a low priority to printing. If you want printing to run faster, then you can give a high priority to printing.

To change the printer priority in Windows for Workgroups, follow these steps:

1. Choose the Options Background Printing command. The Background Printing dialog box appears (see fig. 9.6).

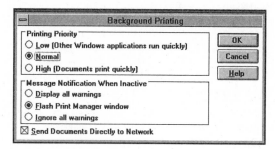

Change the priority that your printer has in the Background Printing dialog box.

2. Select one of the following options:

Option	Result
Low	Printer runs slower; application runs faster.
Normal	Printer and application have the same priority.
High	Printer runs faster; application may run slower.

Displaying Print Manager Alerts in Windows for Workgroups

Your printer will send you a message if it runs out of paper, has a paper jam, or a technical problem. You can decide how to receive those printer messages.

To control printer alert messages in Windows for Workgroups, follow these steps:

1. Choose the Options Background Printing command to display the Background Printing dialog box (see fig. 9.6).

2. Select one of the following options:

Option	Result
Display all warnings	Always alerts you with a message box when the printer needs attention.
Flash Print Manager window	Beeps and flashes if the Print Manager is an icon or if the window is inactive when the printer needs attention. You must activate the Print Manager window to see the message; this is Print Manager's default setting.
Ignore all warnings	Ignores the printer's request if the Print Manager is an icon or if the window is inactive; you may not know that the printer needs attention.

Changing the Display in Print Manager in Windows for Workgroups

You can use several options for changing the look of Print Manager in Windows for Workgroups. You can decide how much information is displayed in the Print Manager window and you can modify the format of several of the displayed items.

You can choose whether to display the Status, Size, and Time columns in the Print Manager window. To display or not display any of these items, follow these steps:

1. Choose the View menu (see fig. 9.7).

2. Select one of the following options.

   A check mark appears next to each selected option in the View menu.

Option	Result
Time/Date Sent	Displays the time and date you sent a file to the printer.
Print File Size	Displays the size of the files in the Print Manager print queue.
Status Text	Displays the status of printers and files.

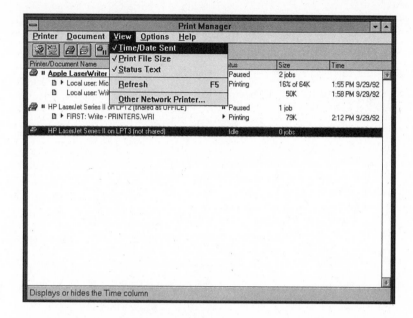

FIG. 9.7

The View menu.

You also can decide whether to display the status bar and toolbar. To display or not display the status bar and toolbar, follow these steps:

1. Choose the Options menu (see fig. 9.8).

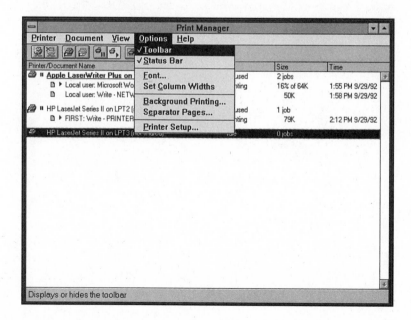

FIG. 9.8

The Options menu.

2. Select Toolbar to remove the toolbar from the display, or select Status Bar to remove the status bar from the display.

A check mark appears next to these options when they are selected.

To change the font, font style, and font size of displayed text, follow these steps:

1. Choose the Options Font command to display the Font dialog box (see fig. 9.9).

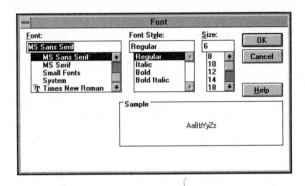

FIG. 9.9

Modify the display font using the Font dialog box.

2. Select a font from the Font drop-down list.

3. Select a style from the Font Style list.

4. Select a font size from the Size list.

5. Choose OK or press Enter.

You can change the widths of the Status, Size, and Time columns. To resize these columns, follow these steps:

1. Point to one of the column borders located just below the toolbar and above the Status, Size, and Time columns. The mouse pointer will change to a two-headed pointer when it is correctly positioned over a column border.

2. Drag the border until the column is the desired width.

or

1. Choose the Options Set Column Widths command, and use the arrow keys to change the width of the columns. Press the Tab key to move between columns.

2. Press Esc when you have finished setting the column widths.

Using Separator Pages

In Windows for Workgroups, you have the option of inserting separator pages between printed documents. This process can help you to identify the owner of documents on shared printers or to simply separate your documents on your own printer. You can use a simple standard separator page, or you can create a custom separator page that can include custom fonts and graphics.

To print a separator page, follow these steps:

1. Choose the Options Separator Pages command. The Separator Pages dialog box appears (see fig. 9.10).

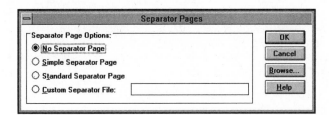

2. Choose one of the following options:

Option	Result
No Separator Page	Prints documents without pages between them.
Simple Separator Page	Prints a page using courier font.
Standard Separator Page	Prints a separator page using a larger font.
Custom Separator Page	Prints a separator page containing a .WMF (Windows Metafile) or .CLP (Clipboard file) that you have specified. Specify the file and path to the .WMF or .CLP file in the edit box. CLP files are created by copying to the Clipboard and then saving from the Clipboard. WMF files are created by some Windows applications.

3. Choose OK or press Enter.

Closing the Print Manager Window

Print Manager may shut down when printing is complete. If Print Manager started when you selected to print from an application, the Print Manager shuts down when printing is complete. However, if you started Print Manager from the Main program group, you must exit the Print Manager manually after printing ends. You also can have Print Manager minimized so that you can drag and drop files from the File Manager.

Be careful; if you exit Print Manager while print jobs still are outstanding in the queue, the print jobs are canceled. To close the Print Manager window without canceling print jobs, minimize the window by clicking on the minimize button (the down arrow at the top right of the window). If you use the keyboard, choose the Minimize command from the Control menu. After the window is minimized to an icon, Print Manager shuts down after printing is completed.

To exit the Print Manager, choose the View Exit command.

NOTE   When you exit Print Manager while print jobs are still pending, not only will your print jobs be canceled, but any jobs sent by other users sharing your printer also will be canceled. *Be careful!* You may want to use the Chat available on Mail or send a Mail message to the person who is printing before you attempt to shut down.

For Related Information:

FROM HERE...   ◄◄ See "Understanding Windows Terminology," p. 26.

◄◄ See "Controlling the Windows in Windows," p. 30.

Printing to a File

On occasion, you may want to print to a file rather than to the printer. If you want to print a desktop-published document on a high-resolution typesetter owned by a service bureau, for example, you can more easily print from an EPS (Encapsulated PostScript) file. You create an EPS file by selecting a PostScript printer and then printing to an EPS file (by selecting a PostScript printer, you instruct Windows to create a file that is PostScript-compatible). As another example, suppose that you share a laser printer with someone down the hall. You can print the document to a file, walk down the hall with a floppy disk, and copy the file to the laser printer. In both cases, you can create the document even if you don't have the printer, and the person who prints the file can print the file even if he or she doesn't have the application you used to create the file.

To print to a file, you must direct the printer's output to a file (rather than to the port to which the printer is connected). When you are done printing to a file, remember to redirect the printer to the correct port.

To print to a file, follow these steps:

1. If the Print Manager isn't running, choose the Print Manager icon in the Main group in the Program Manager.

2. Choose the **O**ptions **P**rinter Setup command. The Printers dialog box appears.

3. From the Installed **P**rinters box, select the printer on which you (or a service bureau) eventually will print the file. The printer you select doesn't have to be connected to your computer. To create an EPS file, select a PostScript printer.

4. If the desired printer isn't the current default printer, select the printer and choose the "Set As Default Printer" button (or press E).

5. Choose the **C**onnect button. The Connect dialog box appears.

6. From the **P**orts list, select FILE. You may need to use the scroll button to select FILE. Then choose OK to return to the Printers dialog box.

7. Choose the **S**etup button and set up the print options. For example, select the Paper **S**ource, Paper Size, and Orientation (Portrait or **L**andscape). To create an EPS file, you also must choose the **O**ptions button, select En**c**apsulated PostScript File, and enter a file name.

8. Choose OK enough times to return to the Printers window; then select Close to return to the Control Panel window.

9. Return to the application and print as usual. Choose the **F**ile **P**rint command to print the file. The Print to File dialog box asks you to name the file to which the file is going to print.

You also can access the Printers dialog box by choosing the Control Panel from the Main window in the Program Manager. Then choose the Printers application.

Set Up a Bogus Printer for Printing to a File
If you plan to print to a file frequently, set up a bogus printer. For example, set up a second PostScript printer to create EPS files. Use the **O**ptions **P**rinter Setup command (or the Printers application in the Control Panel) to install a new printer; accept the current driver if you already have a PostScript printer installed or to add the PostScript driver if you don't have one installed. Follow the preceding procedures to direct this printer's output to an EPS file. When you're ready to print from the application, choose the **F**ile **P**rint Setup command to select the bogus printer and print.

Installing Printers from the Print Manager

You can use the Print Manager to add, configure, and remove a printer on your system—just as you can use the Printers application in the Control Panel. Before you add a printer, be sure to have your original Windows diskettes on hand—they contain the printer driver you will need.

To add, configure, or remove a printer by using the Print Manager, follow these steps:

1. Choose Print Manager from the Main window in the Program Manager.

2. Choose the **O**ptions **P**rinter Setup command. The Printers dialog box appears.

3. To add a printer, choose the **A**dd button. The Printers dialog box expands to show a list of available printers, as shown in figure 9.11.

4. Select the printer you want to add and then choose the **I**nstall button. Follow instructions for inserting the Windows diskette containing the driver for the printer you want to install and choose OK.

5. Select your newly installed printer from the Installed **P**rinters list and choose **C**onnect to link your printer to a port or to a network. Choose OK when you are finished.

6. With your printer still selected in the Installed **P**rinters list, choose **S**etup to change the paper size and orientation. Choose OK when you are finished.

7. If you want to use your printer as the default printer, while your printer is still selected, select the Set as Default Printer option.

8. Choose Close.

FIG. 9.11

The Printers dialog box showing a list of available printers.

NOTE You can set the default printer without using the Printer Setup command in the Print Manager in Windows for Workgroups. To set the default printer, select the printer in the Print Manager window that you want to be the default printer, and choose the Printer Set Default Printer command.

If you want to remove a printer, select it in the Installed **P**rinters list and choose **R**emove.

For Related Information:

◄◄ To learn more about installing printers, see "Adding and Configuring Printers" p. 277.

◄◄ See "Managing Files and Disks," p. 177.

FROM HERE...

Printing on a Network in Windows for Workgroups

If you are using Windows for Workgroups and are connected to a network, you can print on *network printers*, which are printers connected to other computers on the network, and other users on the network can use printers connected to your computer. Before you can print on a network printer, that printer must be designated as *shared* by the person using the computer the printer is connected to. In the same way, you must *share* a printer connected to your computer before other users can print on it.

Connecting to a Network Printer

Before you can connect to a network printer, you need to install the *printer driver* for that printer on your computer. See the section "Installing Printers from the Print Manager" for instructions on how to install a printer from the Print Manager. When you have installed the printer on your computer, follow these steps to connect to a network printer from within the Print Manager:

1. Click the Connect Network Printer button on the toolbar.

   or

   Choose the Printer Connect Network Printer command.

   The Connect Network Printer dialog box is displayed (see fig. 9.12).

2. Select from the Device Name list the port that corresponds to the port you assigned to the network printer.

3. Type in the Path box the path for the shared printer.

   The path includes the computer name for the computer the printer is connected to and the share name assigned to that printer. The computer name is preceded by double backslashes and is separated from the share name by a single backslash. For example, *\\ADMIN\OFFICE*.

   You can use three methods for entering the path:

   - If you know the path for the printer, you can type it directly in the Path box.

   - You can display the Path drop-down list and select a path from a list of recently used paths.

■ Double-click on a workgroup icon in the Show Shared Printers on list—or select the icon with the arrow keys and press Enter—to expand the workgroup. Select a name from the list of computer names listed under the workgroup to display a list of shared printers in the Shared Printers box. When you find the printer you want to connect to, select it.

FIG. 9.12

The Connect
Network Printer
dialog box.

4. If you want to automatically reconnect to this shared printer at startup, check the Reconnect at Startup button.

5. Choose OK or press Enter.

Disconnecting from a Network Printer

To disconnect from a network printer, follow these steps:

1. Click the Disconnect Network Printer button on the toolbar.

   or

   Choose the Printer Disconnect Network Printer command.

   The Disconnect Network Printer dialog box shown in figure 9.13 appears.

2. Select the printers in the Printer list from which you want to disconnect.

3. Choose OK or press Enter.

FIG. 9.13

Use the Disconnect Network Printer dialog box to disconnect from other printers.

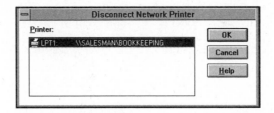

You can select additional printers from the list if you want to disconnect from more than one printer at the same time. To select more than one printer, click on the first printer, hold down the Ctrl key, and click on subsequent printers. To deselect a printer, hold down the Ctrl key and click on the printer. To use the keyboard, select the first printer, press Shift+F8, use the up- and down-arrow keys to move to the next printer, and press the space bar. Move to additional printers and press the space bar. To deselect a printer and retain the other selections, move to the selected printer and press the space bar. To return to selecting a single printer at a time, press Shift+F8 again.

Sharing Your Printer

If you want others on your network to be able to use your printer, you must first *share* your printer. You must be running in 386-enhanced mode to share a printer with other users. To share your printer, follow these steps:

1. Using the mouse or keyboard, select the printer you want to share in the Print Manager window.

2. Click the Share Printer button on the toolbar.

   or

   Choose the Printer Share Printer As command.

   The Share Printer dialog box displays as shown in figure 9.14.

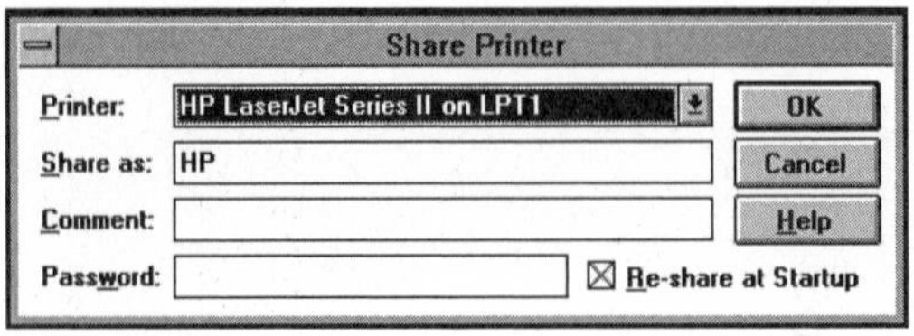

FIG. 9.14

The Share Printer dialog box.

3. The name of the printer you select in step 1 appears in the Printer drop-down list. You can select another printer from the drop-down list if you want.

4. Type a new share name in the Share as box if you do not like the default suggestion.

5. Type a comment in the Comment box if you choose. This comment appears next to the share name in the Connect Network Printer dialog box and can be helpful for other users when they are looking for a particular shared printer to connect.

6. If you want to limit access to the shared printer to certain users, assign a password to the printer and only give the password to those users. Type the password in the Password edit box.

7. If you want to automatically reshare the printer at start up, select the Re-share at Startup option.

8. Choose OK or press Enter.

To stop sharing a printer, follow these steps:

1. Click the Stop Sharing Printer button on the toolbar.

   or

   Choose the Printer Stop Sharing Printer command.

   The Stop Sharing Printer dialog box appears (see fig. 9.15).

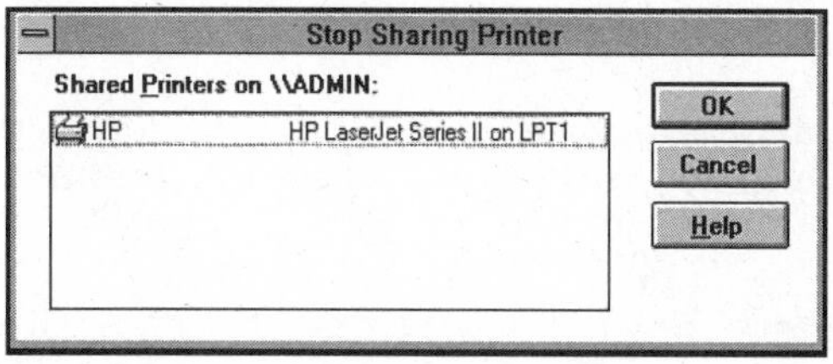

FIG. 9.15

Select printers you want to stop sharing in the Stop Sharing Printer dialog box.

2. Select the printer you want to stop sharing from the Shared Printers On list.

   You can select additional printers from the list if you want to stop sharing more than one printer at the same time. To select more than one printer, click on the first printer, hold down the Ctrl key, and click on subsequent printers. To deselect a printer, hold down the Ctrl key and click on the printer. To use the keyboard, select the first printer, press Shift+F8, use the up- and down-arrow keys to move to the next printer, and press the space bar. Move to additional printers and press the space bar. To deselect a printer and retain the other selections, move to the selected printer and press the space bar. To return to selecting a single printer at a time, press Shift+F8 again.

3. Choose OK or press Enter.

Changing the Password, Share Name, or Comment of a Shared Printer

You can change the password, share name, or comment for any printer you are sharing with others on your network. To change the password for a shared printer, follow these steps:

1. Using the mouse or keyboard, select the printer you want to change in the Print Manager window.

2. Click the Share Printer As button on the toolbar.

   or

   Choose the Printer Share Printer As command.

3. Change the Share As, Comment, or Password entries.

4. Choose OK or press Enter.

Viewing Other Network Print Queues

The names and information for every file that is currently printing or waiting to be printed on your printers and any other printers you are connected to are listed in the Print Manager window. You can use the Other Network Printer command if you also want to view the activity on network printers you are not connected to—to decide, for example, whether you can speed up the printing of a file by connecting to another network printer. To view the queue for a printer you are not connected to, follow these steps:

1. Choose the View Other Network Printer command to display the Other Network Printer dialog box (see fig. 9.16).

2. Type the network path name for the other network printer you want to view in the Network Printer box.

3. Choose the View button or press Enter.

   A list of files in the queue for the designated printer is displayed in the box.

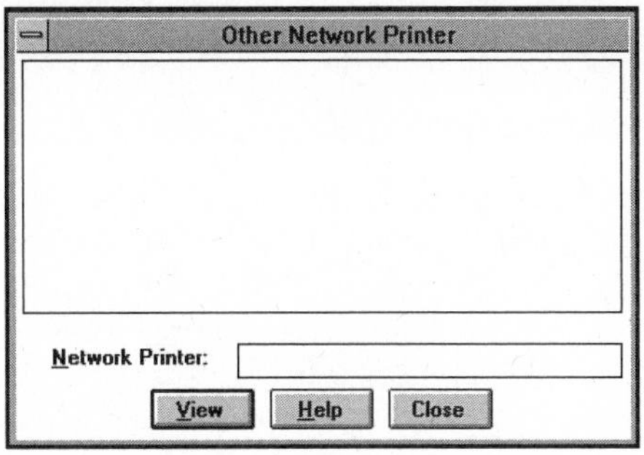

FIG. 9.16

The Other Net-
work Printer
dialog box.

4. When you have finished viewing the files, choose Close or press
   Esc.

Updating Network Queue Status

Print Manager regularly updates the status of network printer queues
displayed in the Print Manager window. However, you can manually
update the status if you want to be sure that you have an up-to-the-
minute status report. To manually update the status of network printer
queues, choose the View Refresh command or press F5.

Printing Directly to a Network in Windows for Workgroups

When you are using Print Manager, all files that you send to print, including those you send to another printer, are managed by the Print
Manager on your computer. Often, you can speed up the printing of
files you are sending to a network printer by sending these files directly
to the network printer, bypassing Print Manager. If you choose to do
this, you can still use Print Manager to view the print queues on network printers and to control the printing of files on your printers.

To send files directly to network printers, follow these steps:

1. Choose the Options Background Printing command.

2. Select the Send Documents Directly to Network check box.

3. Choose OK or press Enter.

Printing on a Non-Windows for Workgroup Network

If you share printers with others on a local area network, printing with the Print Manager is a little different. Additional Print Manager options, such as **Network Settings** and **Network Connections**, become available in the **Options** menu. You also have the option to bypass the Print Manager altogether, which is sometimes a faster way to print on a network.

When you print on a network, no Print Manager icon appears at the bottom of the screen.

Connecting to a Network Printer

If Windows is installed for a network and is connected to the network, you can print on a network printer. First, however, you must be sure that you are connected to the network printer you want to use—while you are installing a printer or by using the Print Manager window.

To connect to a network printer from the Print Manager window, follow these steps:

1. From the Main group, choose the Print Manager. The Print Manager dialog box appears.

2. Choose the **O**ptions Network **C**onnections command. The Network Connections dialog box appears, which lists all network printers to which you are already connected (see fig. 9.17).

3. In the **Network Path** box, type the name of the network.

4. Select the port you want to use from the Por**t** list.

   A network printer may already be connected to the port you want to use. Disconnect this printer before connecting a new printer (see the following section, "Disconnecting from a Network Printer").

5. If necessary, type a password in the Pass**w**ord text box.

6. Choose the **C**onnect button.

7. Choose Close.

Windows remembers the network path and port settings for network printers to which you connected in the past. To quickly reconnect to a network printer you used before, choose the Options menu and select the Network **C**onnections command. Choose the **P**revious button. From the list, select the network path for the printer to which you want to reconnect. Choose **S**elect. Select the port you want to use, type a password if necessary, choose Connect, and then choose Close.

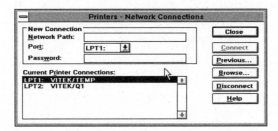

FIG. 9.17

Use the Network Connections dialog box to connect to a network printer.

Viewing a Network Print Queue

When you print to a network printer, Print Manager lists the files you previously sent to a printer. By choosing the **S**elected Net Queue command, you can see all the files everyone on the network has sent to the same printer. Seeing this list can give you an idea of how much time will pass before the printer prints your job.

To view a network print queue, follow these steps:

1. Print the file and open the Print Manager window.

2. Select the printer queue information line.

3. Choose the **View S**elected Net Queue command. Print Manager displays a list of all the files in queue for the printer.

4. Select Close or press Enter to close the dialog box.

Viewing Other Network Print Queues

If you have access to a number of printers on a network, you can view queues for all the printers before deciding which printer to use—even if this printer isn't installed or activated. (Before you can print to a printer, you must install it by using the **O**ptions **P**rinter Setup command in the Print Manager or by choosing the Printers application in the Control Panel. See Chapter 7, "Customizing with the Control Panel," for details about installing printers.)

To view network queues for uninstalled printers, follow these steps:

1. Open the Print Manager window.

2. Choose the **View O**ther Net Queue command. A dialog box asks you for the location and name of the network queue you want to view.

3. Type the network path name for the network queue you want to view in the **Network Queue** box.

4. Choose the **V**iew button. Information about the other print queues appears in the dialog box.

5. Type the name of another queue or choose the Close button.

Updating Network Queue Status

By default, Print Manager tracks and periodically updates the status of a network queue. If you want, you can turn off automatic network queue updating so that you can update the network queue from the keyboard. By updating the network queue manually, you can make sure that you have an up-to-the-minute status report.

To turn off automatic network status updating, follow these steps:

1. Open the Print Manager window.

2. Choose the **O**ptions Network Settings command. The Network Options dialog box, shown in figure 9.18, appears.

3. Select the **U**pdate Network Display box so that no check mark appears in the box.

4. Choose OK or press Enter.

To update the network queue status, choose the **View R**efresh command or press F5.

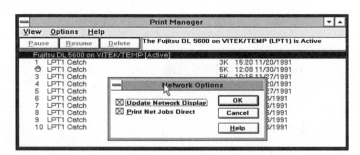

FIG. 9.18

You can use the Network Options dialog box to manage network queue updating.

Printing Directly to a Network

Usually printing is faster when you print files on a network directly, bypassing the Print Manager. Because this is true, the **P**rint Net Jobs Direct option is Print Manager's default choice. Networks differ, however, so experiment with printing times on network to determine whether printing directly or with the Print Manager is faster.

When you bypass the Print Manager, the information lines aren't updated to show the current status of the printers or the jobs currently printing. When you print directly to a network, the network completely controls the print job.

To print directly to a network printer, follow these steps:

1. Open the Print Manager window.

2. Choose the **O**ptions **N**etwork Settings command.

3. Select the **P**rint Net Jobs Direct box so that an X appears in the box. To print by using the Print Manager, select this box so that no X appears in the box.

4. Choose OK or press Enter.

> When you print directly to a network, no Print Manager icon appears at the bottom of the screen. To use the Print Manager, you must start the Print Manager as an application from the Main group in the Program Manager.
>
> **T I P**

Disconnecting from a Network Printer

After you are finished using a network printer, you can disconnect from the printer. Do this when you need to connect a different network printer to the same port.

To disconnect from a network printer, follow these steps:

1. Open the Print Manager window.

2. Choose the **O**ptions **N**etwork **C**onnections command.

3. In the Current Printer Connections list, select the printer you want to disconnect.

4. Choose the **D**isconnect button.

5. Choose Close.

FROM HERE...

For Related Information:

◀◀ See "Adding and Configuring Printers," p. 277.

◀◀ See "Setting Up Communication and Printer Ports," p. 291.

◀◀ See "Configuring for 386-Enhanced Mode," p. 294.

Correcting Printing Problems

Occasionally, problems arise when you try to print. If you run into trouble, read through the following checklist. Sometimes, the solution to printing problems is simpler than you expect. Many printer difficulties arise from installation and setup errors that you can correct by using the **O**ptions **P**rinter Setup command. (You also can use the Printers application in the Control Panel to do the same thing. See Chapter 7.)

■ *Is the printer plugged in and turned on?*

■ *Are you out of paper?*

■ *Do you have the right printer cable, and is it correctly connected to the printer and the computer?*

■ *Is the printer driver installed in Windows?*

To install printers for Windows, use the **O**ptions **P**rinter Setup command in the Print Manager, or the Printers application in the Control Panel, and then choose the **A**dd button.

■ *Did you select the correct printer name when you installed the printer?*

Choose the **O**ptions **P**rinter Setup command in the Print Manager. Then choose **A**dd and check which printer is selected in the List of Printers. Make sure that you select the right printer.

■ *Is the correct printer selected as the default printer?*

Choose the **O**ptions **P**rinter Setup command in the Print Manager or choose the Printers application in the Control Panel to set the default printer. Select the printer you want to be the default in the Installed **P**rinters list; then choose Se**t** as Default Printer.

■ *Is the printer connected to the correct port?*

Choose the **O**ptions **P**rinter Setup command in the Print Manager or the Printers application in the Control Panel and then choose the **C**onnect button to set the printer port.

■ *Are the port settings correct?*

Use the Ports application in the Control Panel to select port settings. If the serial printer loses text, try reducing the baud rate.

■ *Are the paper source, size, and orientation correct?*

Check the **F**ile **P**rint Setup command in the application. You also can choose the **O**ptions **P**rinter Setup command in the Print Manager or the Printers application in the Control Panel and select **S**etup.

■ *Is TrueType enabled?*

Choose the Fonts application in the Control Panel; then choose the TrueType button and select the Enable TrueType fonts option.

■ *Is the font cartridge all the way in the slot?*

Push the cartridge in firmly.

■ *Are the soft fonts properly installed?*

Check the installation manual that came with the font package or choose the Fonts application in the Control Panel and then choose the **A**dd button to add fonts.

■ *Was the printer turned off after you downloaded fonts?*

Download the fonts again.

■ *Is the printer short on memory?*

A printer that lacks enough memory may not print all the fonts or graphics you expect; printers like the HP LaserJet with 512K of memory may not have enough memory to print multiple fonts or large graphics. You must either print smaller graphics or buy more memory for the printer.

FROM HERE...

For Related Information:

▶▶ See "Solving Font and Printing Problems," p. 1075.

▶▶ See "Solving Communication and Port Difficulties," p. 1084.

▶▶ To learn more about printing with Windows Write, see "Printing," p. 526.

▶▶ To learn more about printing with Windows Paintbrush, see "Printing Paintbrush Files," p. 585.

▶▶ To learn more about printing with other Windows accessories, see "Setting Up the Page for Printing," p. 651; "Saving and Printing Notepad Files," p. 652; "Saving and Printing Calendar Files," p. 666; and "Saving and Printing Cardfile Documents," p. 687.

Chapter Summary

The Print Manager really can speed up work because you can print *in the background* as you work *in the foreground*. Now that you know how to use the Print Manager, you may want to learn more about preparing printers to work with Windows applications. Part III, "Using Windows Accessories," discusses each of the various applications.

Using Windows Accessories

PART

III

OUTLINE

Using Mail with Windows for Workgroups

A workgroup can accomplish far more when everyone can communicate easily. *Mail* is a program that enables you and others in your workgroup to send and store *messages*, which are text notes that you send to or receive from other users on your network. You also have the option of attaching files to a message, for example, a word processing document or spreadsheet file. Mail is a stripped-down version of Microsoft's full-featured mail application. Although it lacks some of the more high-powered electronic mail features, Mail's design meets the needs of small groups of users who work together.

In some ways, Mail offers features more powerful than mail applications not designed specifically for use on a Windows network. You can accomplish the following tasks (among others) with Mail:

- Send messages to coworkers
- Receive messages
- Attach files to messages

■ Work with messages and files away from the office

■ Create linked files across the network

■ Embed objects in messages and files

Starting Mail

Mail is a message system built around a Postoffice. The Mail Postoffice can be set up on any workgroup member's computer. The workgroup member whose computer stores the Postoffice directory administers the mail system. See "Administering the Postoffice" for details on creating and maintaining Postoffice.

Before any workgroup member can begin to send and receive mail, the member must set up a user account with the Postoffice (see "Creating Your User Account"). The administrator can set up the account or the user can do it. After the member has a user account, the Postoffice acts as a collective *mail* drop with an Inbox folder and an Outbox folder for the member, as well as a Sent Mail folder that holds copies of the messages the user sends.

You don't need to be logged on to the network (*on-line*) to work with your messages and their attached files. If you work *off-line*, you don't have to deal with mail interruptions; you can even work with messages off-site. The "Using Mail Off-Line" section, later in this chapter, describes how to work with your messages off-line.

To start Mail, you first must start Windows. You normally start Windows by typing *WIN* at the DOS prompt. Your system may start Windows automatically, or you may have some other arrangement. For more information on starting and setting up Windows and Windows applications, see Chapter 1, "Operating Windows," Chapter 4, "Controlling Applications with the Program Manager," and Chapter 25, "Enhancing Windows Performance."

T   I   P   A Postoffice must be created before the first person in a workgroup can use Mail. If no one has set up a Postoffice, then refer to the section "Administering the Postoffice" near the end of this chapter for information on how to set up a Postoffice.

If you have already created a user account and only need to sign-in and check your mail, refer to the following section, "Signing In to Mail."

T I P

The first time you start Mail, you must connect to an existing Postoffice, and you must create a user account if the Postoffice administrator hasn't already created one for you. See "Creating Your User Account" for details on how to set up a user account. To start mail and connect to a Postoffice, follow these steps:

1. Select and open the Main group window within the Program Manager.

2. Find the Mail icon in the Main window of the Program Manager. It looks like a gold-plated mail slot (see fig. 10.1). Select this icon and press Enter, or double-click the icon.

   The first time you execute this step, Mail displays the Welcome to Mail dialog box (see fig. 10.2).

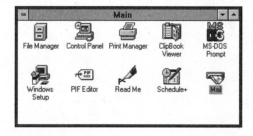

FIG. 10.1

The Mail Icon in the Main program group.

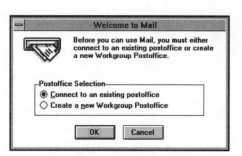

FIG. 10.2

Windows for Workgroups greets new users and invites them to connect to an existing Postoffice.

3. Select the Connect to an Existing Postoffice option. Then choose OK or press Enter. The Network Disk Resources dialog box opens (see fig. 10.3).

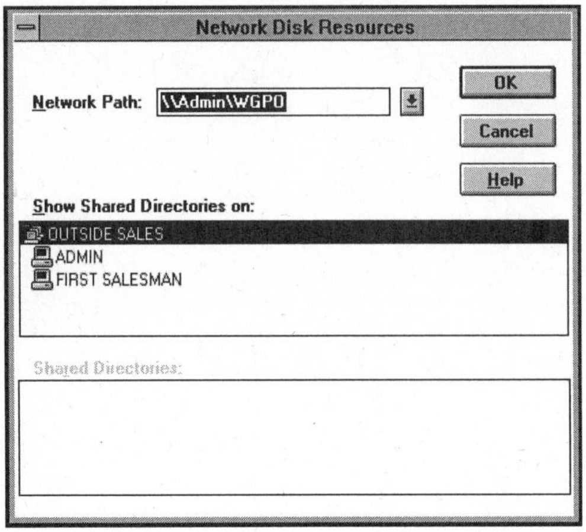

FIG. 10.3

The Network Disk
Resources dialog
box.

4. If you know the location of your workgroup's Postoffice,
   type the path in the **Network Path** text box. Use the format
   *computername**sharename*. (The term *computername* refers
   to the name of the computer and the drive on that computer
   where the Windows for Workgroups software is installed. The
   term *sharename* refers to the directory on *computername*
   containing your workgroup's Postoffice.)

   If you are unsure of the path of the Postoffice, select the name of
   the computer containing the Postoffice in the **S**how Shared Directories On list box. The Shared Directories list box displays the
   shared directories contained on the selected computer. Select
   the shared directory containing your workgroup's Postoffice. The
   selected directory name appears in the Network Path text box.

5. Choose OK or press Enter.

6. If the Postoffice directory is password-protected, Mail displays the
   Enter Shared Directory Password dialog box (see fig. 10.4). Type
   the password in the text box (the characters appear as asterisks);
   then press Enter.

   If the Postoffice directory isn't password-protected, this dialog
   box doesn't appear.

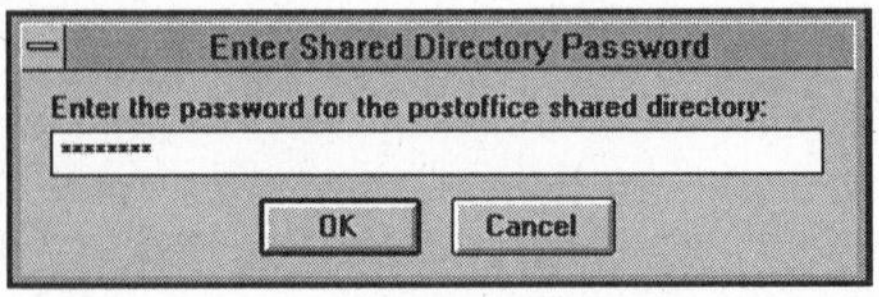

FIG. 10.4

The Enter Shared
Directory Pass-
word dialog box.

7. Mail displays a dialog box that asks whether you have an account (see fig. 10.5).

   Choose **Yes** if the administrator has created an account for you; then skip the rest of these steps.

   Choose **No** if you need to set up your account. See the following section for details on how to set up an account.

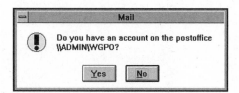

FIG. 10.5

The dialog box that asks whether you have an account.

Creating Your User Account

If you do not already have a user account set up for you when you connect to a Postoffice, as described in the previous section, and you select No when you are asked whether you have an account on the postoffice, you are presented with the Enter Your Account Details dialog box, as displayed in figure 10.6.

FIG. 10.6

The Enter Your Account Details dialog box.

To set up a user account, follow these steps:

1. In the Enter Your Account Details dialog box, enter your name in the **N**ame text box, a name for your mailbox in the **M**ailbox text box, and a password in the **P**assword text box. All other details are optional. (The details are described following these steps.) After you complete the information in the dialog box, choose OK or press Enter.

In the Enter Your Account Details dialog box, you must enter the following information:

- *Name.* Enter a name of up to 30 characters.

- *Mailbox.* Enter a mailbox name not longer than 10 characters.

- *Password.* If you don't want to use the default password (*PASS-WORD*), type a unique password of up to 8 characters.

T I P   Because Postoffice is indifferent to case, you can use any combination of upper- and lowercase letters for your name, mailbox name, and password. Be sure to use words that are simple and easy to remember.

The following details in the dialog box are optional:

- *Phone #1 and Phone #2.* Enter one or two phone numbers (for example, enter your office phone number and your fax number). You can use up to 32 characters for each number.

- *Office.* Enter up to 32 characters describing your office location (for example, *fourth floor, room 12*).

- *Department.* Enter up to 32 characters identifying your department name (for example, *Packaging* or *New Sales*).

- *Notes.* Enter a note of up to 128 characters.

NOTE   After you establish your user account, Mail creates the MSMAIL.INI file and the MSMAIL.MMF message file in your Windows directory. The MMF file records all your messages and addresses (MSMAIL.MMF is the default file name). Every user should have a uniquely named MMF file.

Signing In to Mail

You need to connect to the Postoffice and create your user account only once. Subsequently, you can sign in to Mail each time you start Windows, using one of the following methods:

- Go through the normal sign-in and password procedures

- Set up the Mail icon's properties to bypass the normal sign-in procedure

To use the normal Mail start-up and sign-in procedures, follow these steps:

1. Choose the Mail icon in Program Manager's Main group window to start Mail. The Mail Sign In dialog box appears (see fig. 10.7).

FIG. 10.7

The Mail Sign In dialog box.

2. Check your Mailbox **Name** to be sure that it is correct.

3. In the **Password** text box, type your password (Mail displays asterisks in place of the characters you type) and then press Enter. The Mail Inbox window opens (see fig. 10.8).

NOTE If security is a concern in your business or organization, be sure to create a password. Don't use the default password (*Password*).

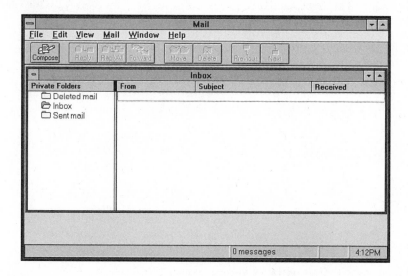

FIG. 10.8

The Mail application window and Inbox window at start-up.

To skip the sign-in procedures when you start Mail, follow these steps:

1. Select the Mail icon in the Main group window in Program Manager.

2. Choose **F**ile **P**roperties or press Alt+Enter to display the Program Item Properties dialog box.

3. In the **C**ommand Line text box, at the end of the path statement, type a space, your mailbox name, another space, and then your password. Choose OK and start Mail.

 If you are concerned about the security of your data, don't type your password in the command line.

T   I   P   You can automatically start Mail when Windows starts by dragging a copy of the Mail icon to the Program Manager Startup group window (for details on using Program Manager, see Chapter 4, "Controlling Applications with the Program Manager").

Using Help

Like most Windows applications, Mail comes with its own Help file and on-line Help system. To access Help, you can press F1, choose **H**elp **C**ontents, or choose **H**elp Index. If you access Help from a dialog box or while a command in the menu is selected, Mail displays Help for that dialog box or command. If you choose **H**elp **C**ontents, the Mail Help Contents window opens. In this window, expansion buttons reveal topic lists (see fig. 10.9). See Chapter 3, "Getting Help" for a detailed explanation on how to use the help facility.

Quitting Mail

Quitting Mail is slightly different from quitting other applications. You can exit and sign out of Mail or you can exit without signing out. If you exit and sign out, applications that require the Postoffice (such as the Scheduler+) close when Mail closes, and you must sign in again if you restart Mail. To quit and sign out of Mail, choose **F**ile Exit and Sign Out.

If you exit without signing out, other applications dependent on the Postoffice can run, and you don't have to sign in again when you restart Mail. To quit without signing out of Mail, choose **F**ile Exit, press Alt+F4, or open the Control menu of the Mail window and choose the **C**lose command.

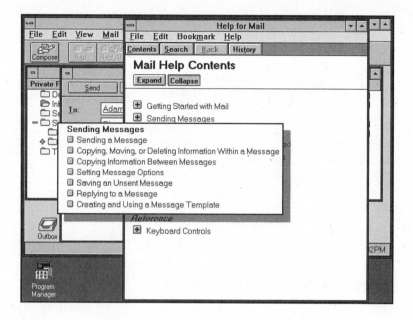

FIG. 10.9

The Mail Help Contents window with a topic selected.

NOTE If no applications dependent on the Postoffice are running when you exit Mail, choosing File Exit signs you out of Mail.

Sending Messages with Mail

Sending messages to group members is a two-step operation. First you compose and address your message; then you send the message. Mail gives you some options to consider, but sending a message can be as simple as making a phone call.

Composing the Message

To prepare a message, you first must display the Send Note window (see fig. 10.10). You display the window in one of three ways: by choosing the Compose button on the toolbar (refer to fig. 10.8), by choosing the Mail Compose Note command, or by pressing Ctrl+N.

When composing your message, you first address the message by specifying the recipient in the To text box. If you want to copy the message to other recipients, use the Cc text box. You can type the address of the recipient or choose the address from a list of addresses. The next two sections describe manual and automatic addressing of messages.

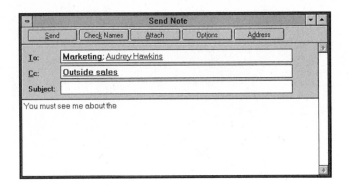

FIG. 10.10

The Mail Send Note window.

Manual Addressing

If you decide to address your message by typing addresses in the **To** and **Cc** text boxes, you need to type only the first few characters of an address; then press Alt+K. Mail completes the entry from its address list.

To address the message manually, follow these steps:

1. In the **To** text box, enter the name of the person(s) or group(s) to receive the message. To include multiple names, type a semicolon and a space between the names.

2. To send a copy of the message to another person or group, type the name(s) in the **Cc** text box. To include multiple names, type a semicolon and a space between the names.

3. If you want to check your entries in the **To** and **Cc** text boxes, choose the Chec**k** Names button in the Send Note dialog box.

   If the entries don't match names in the Mail address list of users, an information box appears, instructing you to check the names you have typed.

   If the entries match the Mail address list, the names appear underlined in the **To** and **Cc** text boxes.

Automatic Addressing

Mail contains an address list. New addresses are automatically added to the address list when you send a message to an address you have not sent to previously. The address list enables you to keep a list of people or groups to which you frequently send messages. It reduces typing and incorrect addresses. To address your message by using the address list, follow these steps:

1. Choose the **Ad**dress button in the Send Note dialog box or choose the **M**ail Ad**d**ress command. The Address dialog box appears (see fig. 10.11).

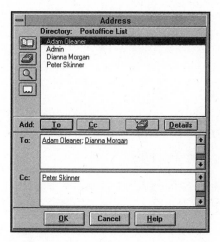

FIG. 10.11

Use the Address dialog box to select addresses for your messages.

2. In the Postoffice List, select the names of people or groups to whom you want to send the message. Then choose the **To** button in the Address dialog box. The names appear in the To text box.

3. In the Postoffice List, select the names of people or groups to whom you want to send copies of the message. Then choose the **Cc** button in the Address dialog box. The names appear in the Cc text box.

4. Choose **OK** or press Enter.

A later section of this chapter, "Sending the Message," describes other features of the Address dialog box.

The selected names appear in the **To** and **Cc** text boxes of the Send Note dialog box. Mail underlines the names that match names in its records.

Completing the Message

After you have addressed the message, press Tab to move to the Subject text box, or click the box. Then type the subject, using up to 480 characters (a brief subject is more considerate than a lengthy one). You don't need to list a subject, but a subject listing helps workgroup members to sort and prioritize incoming mail. After you finish typing the subject, press Tab to move to the text editing area. Your subject text appears in place of "Send Note" in the title bar of the Send Note window.

In the text editing area, you can type and edit text as you do in many Windows text editing or word processing programs, such as Write or Notepad. You can do any of the following tasks:

■ Type letters, numbers, and symbols from the keyboard.

■ Select and delete text by pressing Del or by choosing **Edit Delete**.

■ Change fonts. You have only two choices: the Windows default (Times New Roman) or a nonproportional typewriter typeface. Choose **View Change Font** to toggle between these fonts.

■ Select and copy text to the Windows Clipboard by choosing **Edit Cut** or **Edit Copy**.

■ Insert text copied from other Windows applications or other messages, that is, any text stored in the Clipboard, by placing the insertion point where you want to insert the text and choosing the **Edit Paste** command. To copy between messages, you must close the message you copied from and open the message you are copying to. You cannot have two Send Note windows open at one time.

■ Insert special characters from the Windows Character Map.

T I P You can cancel a message in the Send Note window at any time by pressing the Esc key.

Saving or Storing the Message

After you finish entering the message, you can send the message immediately (as described in the next section). Occasionally, you may want to save the message as a text file, for example, if you want to use the text in the message in another application, or you may want to store it in a folder for sending later.

To save a message as a text file, choose the File **S**ave As command to display the Save Message dialog box. A truncated version of the text you entered in the Subject box is used for the default file name that appears in the File **N**ame text box. The extension TXT is added to the file name.

You can store your message to send later by moving or copying it to a folder. Mail comes with three default folders: Deleted Mail, Inbox, and Sent Mail. You can also create your own folders. (See "Creating and Using Folders" later in this chapter). You can store your message temporarily in a folder and open and send the message later. To store a message in a folder follow these steps:

1. To copy the message, choose **File Copy**. The Copy Message dialog box appears.

   To move the message, choose **File Move** or click the Move button on the toolbar. The Move Message dialog box appears.

   The Copy Message and Move Message dialog boxes are identical except for the name on the title bar (see fig. 10.12).

The Move Message and Copy Message dialog boxes are identical except for name and function.

2. Select a folder in the Move **T**o or Copy **T**o list box.

   As in any list, you can scroll the list to find a name that does not show in the box. You cannot scroll horizontally to see beyond the right side of the box.

3. Choose OK or press Enter.

Mail moves or copies the message to the new folder and displays your Inbox window. When you select the folder that the message was moved or copied to, the listing of the message appears with a gray envelope and note icon next to it.

T I P If you frequently send a message to the same addresses, copy a version to a new folder called Templates. (For a description of how to create a new folder, see "Creating and Using Folders" later in this chapter.) When you need to send that message, drag its template to the Outbox, adjust the text and address information as necessary, and send the message. Mail sends the message, but the template copy remains intact in the Template folder.

Sending the Message

You can send a Mail message immediately after you compose it, or you can retrieve and send messages from any folder available to you. The Inbox window displays folder icons (Deleted Mail, Inbox, Sent Mail, and any folders you have created) to the left of the message listing. (To learn how to create a folder, see "Creating and Using Folders," later in this chapter.)

To send a message immediately, choose the **S**end button in the message's Send Note window after you finish addressing and composing the message. Mail delivers the message to the Inbox of the addressee(s).

To send a stored message from the Inbox window, select and open the folder in which you stored the message. You can use either of these two methods to select and open the folder: double-click the folder; or press Tab to move to the folder list, use the direction keys to select the desired folder, and then press Enter. The title bar displays the name of the new folder, and Mail lists the stored messages by priority, addressee, subject, and date and time sent.

From the folder, you can send a message in the following ways:

■ Select a message and open it by double-clicking the message name or pressing Enter. You can change the addresses if necessary.

■ Click the message name and drag it to the Outbox (see fig. 10.13). Mail opens the Send Note window with the message title in the title bar. You can change the addresses if necessary.

Finding Addresses

Remembering all the names of all the users on the network and the many different groupings may be difficult; however, Mail gives you a way to remember all the names and find them easily.

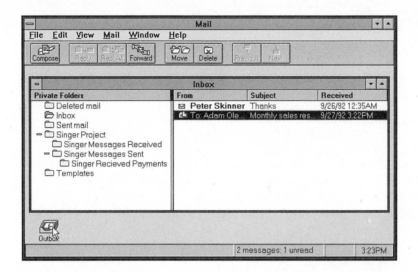

FIG. 10.13

To send the
selected mes-
sage, drag it to
the Outbox.

If you are familiar with the name, you will want to use the first method. In the **To** text box of the Send Note window, begin typing a name; then press Alt+K. Mail completes the name if it finds a matching name in the address list (for a description of this process, see "Composing the Message," earlier in this chapter).

Four other methods of entering addresses use the Address dialog box. With the Send Note window or any message open, choose the **Ad**dress button or choose the **M**ail **Ad**dress command. Mail displays the Address dialog box (refer to fig. 10.11). Then use one of the following methods:

■ Type the first letter of the name you want to find. The displayed list of users scrolls to the names beginning with that letter. Typing *S*, for example, may scroll the list to Sales Group, which may be followed by Sam Taylor, Scot, and any other names that fit in the list box. Select the desired name in the list box.

■ Click the Search button in the Address dialog box (it shows a magnifying glass icon) or press Ctrl+F. The Name Finder dialog box appears, as shown in figure 10.14. In the text box, type as much of the name as you remember; then choose **F**ind. Name Finder searches for all instances of the specified characters. When the search is complete, Mail lists the matching names in the address list box; select the name you want. If the address you want doesn't appear, modify what you typed in the Name Finder box and try again.

FIG. 10.14

Use the Name
Finder to find
and select users.

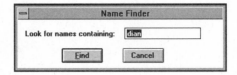

■ Click the Directory button in the Address dialog box (it shows an address book icon) or press Ctrl+L. The Open Directory dialog box appears, listing two directories—your Personal Address Book and the Postoffice list. Select the directory you want to use and choose OK. The list of users in the selected directory appears in the Address dialog box.

■ Click the Personal Address Book button in the Address dialog box (it shows an index card file icon) or press Ctrl+P. This address book records all users to whom you have sent a message and all personal groups you have created. Search for names alphabetically, select the users, and choose the **To** or **Cc** button in the Address dialog box to add these names to the To or Cc text box.

T I P   You can select more than one user from the list in the Personal Address Book. To select more than one user, click on the first user, hold down the Ctrl key, and click on subsequent users. To deselect a user, hold down the Ctrl key and click on the user. To use the keyboard, select the first user, press Shift+F8, use the up- and down-arrow keys to move to the next user, and press the space bar. Move to additional users and press the space bar. To deselect a user and retain the other selections, move to the selected user and press the space bar. To return to selecting a single user at a time, press Shift+F8 again.

Getting Details on a User

Even if Mail finds a name that matches your search criteria, you may not be sure that you have found the right address. If you are unsure, you can look at the information provided by the user when he or she first set up the account. To display the detail information, follow these steps:

1. Open the Address dialog box by clicking the Address button on the toolbar or choosing the Mail Address command.

2. Find a potential addressee by using any of the methods described in the preceding "Finding Addresses" section.

3. Choose the **D**etails button in the Address dialog box. An information dialog box appears, with the addressee's name in the title bar.

Reading and Working with Messages

All of your incoming messages are stored in your Inbox folder. At your convenience, you can read your messages and then you have several options for processing your messages. You can store them in a folder of your choice, forward them to other users, reply to them, print them, or delete them. Each of these tasks can be accomplished very easily in Mail, which enables you to use your electronic mail system to stream-line communications with your co-workers.

Reading Messages

Mail notifies you in a couple of different ways when you receive an incoming message. If you are working in another Windows application you may hear your computer beep to indicate that new messages have come in. You can control how Mail notifies you and how frequently it checks for new mail by using the Mail Options command as described later in this chapter.

If you are viewing your Inbox in Mail when a message from another user arrives, your computer will beep, your mouse pointer will briefly change to an envelope icon, and the new message will be listed in the Inbox folder's list of messages. An icon of a closed envelope appears next to the listing, indicating that the message has not been read.

If Mail is reduced to an icon on your desktop when a message arrives, your computer will beep and the icon will change to show an envelope popping out of the mail slot. If you want to know when a message has arrived when you are working in another application, you can minimize Mail, that is, reduce it to an icon on your desktop, and arrange your application windows so that you can see the Mail icon on your desktop. That way, when a message arrives, you will see the Mail icon change (as well as hear a beep) and you can quickly restore Mail to a window and read the message.

378

To read a message, follow these steps:

1. Switch to Mail and open the Inbox folder by double-clicking on the Inbox folder icon or pressing the Tab key to move to the Private Folders window, using the arrow keys to select the Inbox folder, and pressing Enter.

2. Double-click on the listing of the message you want to read in the right side of the Inbox window or press the Tab key to move to the right side of the Inbox window, select the message you want to read with the arrow keys, and press Enter.

The selected message is displayed in a window, as shown in figure 10.15.

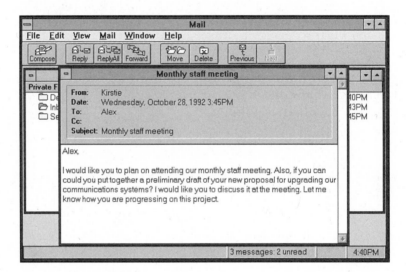

FIG. 10.15

When you open a message, it appears in its own window.

After you read a message, you can reply to the message, forward the message to another address, print the message, store the message in a folder, save the message as a text file, or delete the message.

Replying to Messages

Replying to a letter is cordial, but not always expedient. In the electronic mail environment, replying to a message may lead to problems in disk storage space and may slow down the network. Replying to every message received also may prove too great a task or one of low priority. If you need confirmation that an addressee has received your message, Mail offers a Return Receipt option (see "Setting Message Options" later in this chapter).

Nevertheless, you may need to send a reply message to workgroup members. You can reply to just the sender of a message or to every recipient of the message. To reply to a message, follow these steps:

1. If you are already viewing the message you want to reply to, click the Reply or ReplyAll button on the toolbar or choose the Mail Reply or Mail Reply to All command

   or

   Double-click on the folder in the left side of the Mail window that contains the message you want to reply to or press the Tab key to move to the left side of the window, use the arrow keys to select the folder containing the message, and press Enter. Select the message you want to reply to from the list and click the Reply or ReplyAll button on the toolbar or choose the Mail Reply or Mail Reply to All command.

   A Reply Note window appears (see fig. 10.16). The addressee(s) are listed in the To and Cc text boxes and RE appears at the beginning of the Subject text box, indicating that this message is a reply to another message. RE also appears in the title bar, followed by the text from the Subject box, The text editing area contains a copy of the original message text.

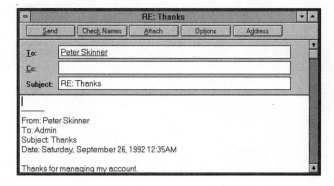

FIG. 10.16

The addressee and subject fields in a reply are automatically inserted.

2. Using the usual editing techniques, compose your reply in the text area of the reply window.

3. Add or delete names in the To and Cc text boxes as necessary. Separate the names with semicolons.

4. Choose the Send button in the reply window. Mail sends the reply message to all the addressees.

Forwarding Messages

In this information-driven age, the ability to pass information to others quickly is a great advantage. Because your workgroup may depend on this shared information, you can easily forward to any name or group in your address list any message that you can access.

To forward a Mail message, follow these steps:

1. With the message displayed in its Send Note window or selected in the folder's list of messages, choose the Forward button on the toolbar, or choose the Mail Forward command.

   Mail displays the message in a Send Note window and FW appears at the beginning of the Subject text box.

2. Change addresses, change the subject, or modify the text as necessary.

3. Choose the Send button in the Send Note window; Mail sends the message.

Deleting Messages

If you have no reason to save a message, you should delete it to conserve disk space and reduce the clutter in your Mail folders. You can move files to the Deleted Mail folder at any time. When you quit Mail, the program deletes these messages. To delete a message or messages, use one of the following techniques:

1. While viewing the message (or with the message selected in a folder), choose the Delete button on the toolbar, press the Del key, or choose the File Delete command. Mail moves the message to the Deleted Mail folder.

   or

   Double-click on the folder in the left side of the Mail window that contains the message you want to delete or press the Tab key to move to the left side of the window, use the arrow keys to select the folder containing the message, and press Enter. Select the message you want to delete from the list and click the Delete button on the toolbar, drag the message to the Deleted Mail folder, or choose the File Delete command.

T I P

You can select several messages at once and delete them with one command. To select more than one message, click on the first message, hold down the Ctrl key, and click on subsequent messages. To deselect a message, hold down the Ctrl key and click on the message. To use the keyboard, select the first message, press Shift+F8, use the up- and down-arrow keys to move to the next message, and press the space bar. Move to additional messages and press the space bar. To deselect a message and retain the other selections, move to the selected message and press the space bar. To return to selecting a single message at a time, press Shift+F8 again. When you have selected all the messages you want to delete, click the Delete button on the tool bar, drag the message to the Deleted Mail folder, or choose the File Delete command.

If you mistakenly delete a message, you can open the Deleted Mail folder and move the message back to its former folder or to any other folder. When you exit Mail, the program deletes the messages in the Deleted Mail folder; at that point, you cannot retrieve them.

Printing Messages

You can easily print a message, either as you view it or by selecting from the list of messages in a folder. To print a message, follow these steps:

1. If you are already viewing the message, choose the File Print command (or press Ctrl+P).

   or

   Double-click on the folder in the left side of the Mail window that contains the message you want to print or press the Tab key to move to the left side of the window, use the arrow keys to select the folder containing the message, and press Enter. Select the message you want to print from the list and choose the File Print command (or press Ctrl+P).

> **T I P**   You can select two or more messages at once from the list of mes-
> sages in a folder and print them with one command. To select mul-
> tiple messages, click on the first message, hold down the Ctrl key,
> and click on subsequent messages. To deselect a message, hold
> down the Ctrl key and click on the message. To use the keyboard,
> select the first message, press Shift+F8, use the up- and down-arrow
> keys to move to the next message, and press the space bar. Move to
> additional messages and press the space bar. To deselect a message
> and retain the other selections, move to the selected message and
> press the space bar. To return to selecting a single message at a
> time, press Shift+F8 again.

The Print Dialog box appears (see fig. 10.17).

FIG. 10.17

Mail's Print
dialog box.

2. If you have selected more than one message to print, select the
   Print Multiple Notes on a Page option if you want the messages to
   print continuously, one after another. Deselect this option if you
   want a new page for each message.

3. Choose the desired print quality from the Print Quality drop-down
   list.

4. Choose OK or press Enter.

> **NOTE**   Embedded objects in a message will print, but you can print
> attached files only from their original application (see "At-
> taching and Embedding in Mail," later in this chapter). You
> must use Excel, for example, to print an Excel spreadsheet—
> even if you received it as part of a message.

Finding Messages

Mail provides a convenient way to find messages you need to reference, forward, copy, or otherwise use in your work. Using the Message

Finder, you can specify the criteria that are used for finding messages, based on the text in the To, From, Subject, and Text fields of the message. For example, you can search for all messages sent to a specific person or for messages containing a particular word or phrase. You can search all folders for a message or limit the search to a particular folder. When the search is completed, the headings for all of the messages that meet the criteria you specified are listed in the Message Finder window. From this list, you can select messages to read, reply to, forward, print, or delete. You can run the Message Finder as many times as you want, specifying different search criteria each time, and you can reduce a Message Finder window to an icon on your Mail desktop so that you can rerun a search at a later time using the original criteria that you specified in that Message Finder window.

To search for a message, follow these steps:

1. Choose the File Message Finder command. The Message Finder window opens (see fig. 10.18).

   When you first open a Message Finder window, the title bar will display the words Message Finder and a number indicating what instance of the Message Finder this window is.

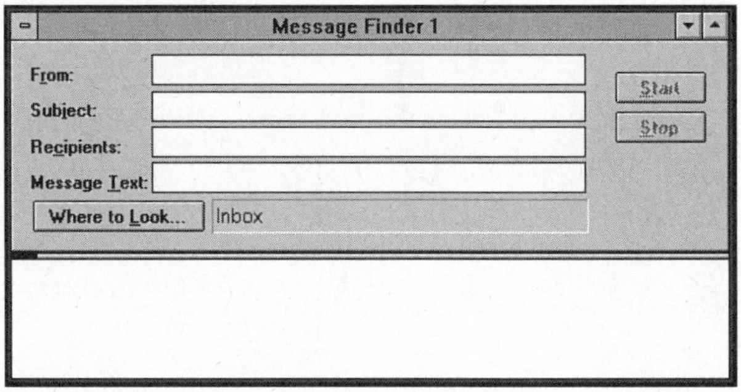

FIG. 10.18

The Message Finder locates messages by using search criteria that you specify.

2. In each text box, enter as much information about the message as you know: in the From text box, type the name of the sender; in the Subject text box, type the subject; and in the Recipients text box, type the names of the To and Cc workgroup members.

   If you type criteria into more than one of the text boxes, Message Finder will only find messages that meet each and every one of the conditions specified. For example, if you type *Peter* in the From text box and *Budget Reports* in the Subject text box, Message Finder will only locate messages that are from Peter and about budget reports.

3. If you know which folder may hold the message, choose the Where To Look button in the Message Finder window. The Where To Look dialog box opens; select the Look in All Folders option, or select a specific folder in which you want to search. Then choose OK or press Enter to close the Where To Look dialog box.

4. Choose the Start button in the Message Finder window. The Message Finder searches all the folders or the folder you specified for any match to the specified criteria.

   Mail lists the titles of the matching messages in the Message Finder window. If you see the message you are looking for before the search is completed, you can choose the Stop button to end the search.

You can select any message from the list of message titles in the Message Finder window and read, reply to, forward, print, move (to any folder), or delete it, using the methods described in the previous sections.

NOTE When you delete a message from the Message Finder, Mail also deletes the message from its folder.

T I P If you often search for messages using the same criteria, you only need to set up a Message Finder window for those particular criteria once. When you have finished searching for messages using these criteria, minimize the Message Finder window to an icon on your Mail desktop. When you need to repeat a search using these criteria, double-click on the icon or press Ctrl+Tab until the icon is selected, press Enter to restore the Message Finder window, and select the Start button. Message Finder icons on the Mail desktop are saved when you exit Mail, so that they will be available whenever you use Mail. You can set up as many Message Finder windows, each with different search criteria, as you want.

Attaching Files to a Message

Mail allows you to easily attach a file to a message, so that the recipient of the message receives an actual copy of the file along with the message. For example, if you want to distribute a copy of a document you have been working on to several co-workers, you can address a message to those co-workers explaining what the document is about and attach the document file to the message. Each of the addressees will receive the message and a copy of the file. Think how much quicker and easier this is than hand-delivering a diskette with the file on it to each of your co-workers.

There are three methods for attaching a file to a message. The first method works well if you are already working in Mail and working on a message. With this method, you can quickly select the file or files you want to attach to the message as you compose the text for the message. The second two methods use File Manager. If File Manager is already opened, it may be to your advantage to use one of these methods. For example, if you need the facilities in File Manager for finding a file that you want to attach to a message (see Chapter 5, "Managing Files with the File Manager"), you can find the file and then attach a message to it all from within File Manager.

Attaching Files to Messages in Mail

If you are working in Mail and know what file you want to attach to a message and where it is located, it is easiest to attach the file from Mail. To attach a file to a message as you compose the message in Mail, follow these steps:

1. While composing the text in the Send Note window, position the insertion point at the point in the text where you want to insert a file or files.

2. Choose the **A**ttach button in the Send Note window. The Attach File dialog box appears (see fig. 10.19).

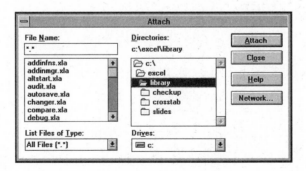

FIG. 10.19

You can select a file to attach to a message in the Attach dialog box.

3. Use the Attach File dialog box (as you do any Open dialog box) to locate and select the file you want to attach to your message.

4. Choose the **A**ttach button or double-click the file name. The Attach File dialog box remains on-screen and a file icon corresponding to the type of file you selected, for example, the Paintbrush icon for BMP files or the WinWord icon for Word DOC files, appears at the insertion point in the text.

5. Repeat steps 3 and 4 for as many files as you need to attach and then choose the Close button in the Attach File dialog box.

6. When you have finished composing the message, send it as you would any message.

Attaching Files to Messages with File Manager

There are two methods for using the File Manager to attach files to a message. If you are already working on a message in Mail and want to use the File Manager to locate and attach a file to the message, use the first method. On the other hand, if you are working in File Manager and decide you want to send a file to another user with a message attached to it, use the second method. In the end, the results of any of the methods described here or in the previous section for attaching a file to a message (or a message to a file) are the same; the recipient will receive a message in his or her Inbox with the attached file or files. Attached files can be opened by the recipient using the application that originally created the file.

To attach a file to a Mail message that you are already working on using File Manager, follow these steps:

1. Switch to Program Manager and open the File Manager in the Main program group (see Chapter 5, "Managing Files with the File Manager," for details on how to open File Manager).

2. Arrange your File Manager and Mail windows so that you can see both at the same time (see Chapter 1, "Operating Windows").

3. In File Manager, locate and select the file or files you want to attach to the message.

4. Drag the files from the File Manager to the locations in the text in the Mail message where you want them to appear. A file icon appears in the text to mark the location of the embedded file or files.

5. Finish composing the message and send it as you would send any message.

T I P

Drag a file or group of files from File Manager directly to your Outbox. A Send Note window appears with the files attached in the text box. Then just add explanatory text, addresses, and a subject.

You also can attach a message to a file while you are working in File Manager, without switching over to Mail. To attach a message to a file from within File Manager, follow these steps:

1. In File Manager, select the file or files you want to send.

2. Click the Attach Message button (it has a picture of an open envelope with a note paper clipped to it) or choose the **M**ail **S**end Mail command. The Attached Files window opens (see fig. 10.20).

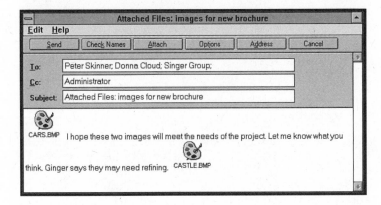

FIG. 10.20

The Attached Files window.

3. Compose the text, indicate the address or addresses, set the message options, and change the Subject text as necessary to complete the message.

4. Choose the **S**end button in the Attached Files window. Mail delivers your message.

Viewing and Saving Attached Files

When you receive a message with attachments, you probably want to view the attached files. Mail cannot display these files; you must have an application that can display the attachment's contents. To display a picture created in Paintbrush, for example, you must have the Paintbrush application installed on your computer. You can open a text file in most text editing, word processing, or desktop publishing applications, however.

To view an attached file, you use one of two methods. The first technique is to double-click the attachment icon or select it and choose **File Open**. If the file's extension is associated with its application, Windows starts the application and the application loads the attached file. If the file is not associated with an application, you can create an association (see Chapter 5, "Managing Files with the File Manager") or you can use the following method for viewing the file:

1. Select the attachment's icon and choose **File Save Attachments**. Mail displays the Save Attachment dialog box. The message attachments are listed in the Attached Files list box (see fig. 10.21).

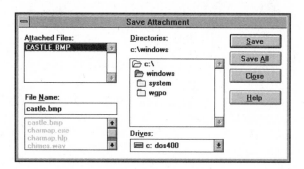

FIG. 10.21

Saving attachments from Mail.

2. Select the attached file or files you want to save. If desired, change the drive, directory, and/or file name with the **Drives** and **Directories** list boxes and File **Name** text box. Then choose the **Save** button in the Save Attachment dialog box. Alternatively, you can choose the Save **All** button to save all attachments.

   Mail changes the Cl**ose** button to a **D**one button and saves the file or files in the current directory.

3. Choose the **D**one button. The Save Attachment dialog box closes.

4. Open the file by using File Manager or by loading the file into an application that can display it.

T I P   Create a file-naming scheme for your workgroup that indicates what iteration each modification represents and who was the last worker to modify the file. The file name FBUDGT17.XLS, for example, may indicate that Fred was the last to modify the spreadsheet for a project called Budget, and that this is the seventeenth version of the spreadsheet.

Embedding an Object in a Message

To embed an object in a message, follow these steps:

1. In the application containing the data you want to embed, select the data and copy it to the Clipboard. (The usual command for this step is **Edit Copy**.)

2. Switch to the Send Note window and place the insertion point where you want to embed the object.

3. Choose **Edit Paste Special**. The Paste Special dialog box appears (see fig. 10.22).

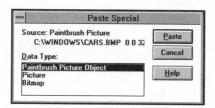

Use the Paste Special dialog box to embed an object in a message.

4. In the **Data Type** list box, select the form in which you want your linked data. (See Chapter 6, "Embedding and Linking" for more information on data types.)

5. Choose the **Paste** button in the Paste Special dialog box. Mail returns to the Send Note window and displays an object (a replica of the original object) in the text at the insertion point.

Embedding a File in a Message

When you need to embed an entire file from an application that has Object Linking and Embedding capability, follow these steps:

1. Save the file you want to embed.

2. In the Send Note window, place the insertion point where you want to insert the object and choose **Edit Insert from File**. The Insert from File dialog box appears (see fig. 10.23).

3. Select the file.

4. Choose OK.

The object (that is, its icon) appears at the insertion point.

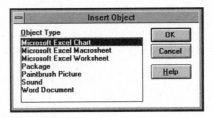

FIG. 10.23

The Insert from
File dialog box.

Creating an Object for Embedding

Occasionally, you may need to create objects to illustrate a point.
When you need a quick chart, picture, or other object, you can use Mail
to create it. Follow these steps:

1. In the Send Note window's text area, place the insertion point
   where you want to insert the object; then choose **Edit Insert**. The
   Insert Object dialog box appears, listing the available Windows
   OLE applications (see fig. 10.24).

FIG. 10.24

The Insert Object
dialog box.

2. Select the application you want to use to create the new object.

3. Choose OK. The application opens.

4. Create the object. Then choose the originating application's **File
   Update** command or simply close the application. The object
   appears at the insertion point in the Send Note window.

Managing Messages with Mail

Just as you manage the files on your hard disk with the File Manager,
you can manage the messages you send and receive with the facilities

provided in Mail. Mail provides several options that can help you keep track of your messages.

Setting Message Options

Mail can reduce the number of interruptions and the time you spend on the phone or in conference with individuals. To reduce the interruptions to work and help focus time effectively, you can put a priority on mail messages; this lets the receiver know how important the message is and whether it should be handled immediately. (When setting the priority on a message, don't forget the tale about the boy who cried wolf too many times.)

If you just need a quick acknowledgment that someone has received your message, don't force them to write a note back to you. Instead, send your message with a return receipt requested. As soon as they open your message a postcard is sent back to you telling you that your message was opened.

To set these message options while in the Send Note window, choose the Options button. Mail displays the Options dialog box (see fig. 10.25).

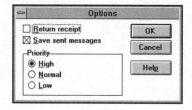

FIG. 10.25

Message options can save time and effort.

In this dialog box, you can set the following options:

- *Priority.* Choose the name of an addressee in the Send Note dialog box; then specify a priority of **High**, **Medium**, or **Low** in the Options dialog box. The priority rating will appear in the addressee's Inbox message list. Repeat this action for each addressee.

- *Return Receipt.* If you choose this option, the message displays a yellow sealed envelope icon and a red exclamation point to the right of the folder's From column. When the addressee opens the message, Mail sends you a postcard message, confirming delivery (see fig. 10.26).

- *Save Sent Messages.* Choose this option to retain (in your Sent Mail folder) a copy of the messages you send.

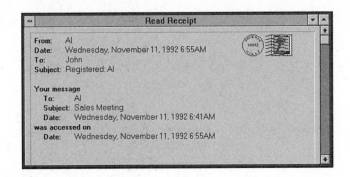

FIG. 10.26

You get a post-
card when an
addressee has
read a return
receipt message.

Creating and Using Folders

A workgroup may exchange hundreds of messages per week and thousands in a month. Keeping track of this electronic paper can be a night-
mare without an orderly filing system. Mail provides folders as the
means for storing and organizing messages sent and received, as described in the next sections.

Adding Folders

When you first open your account, Mail includes three folders: Deleted
Mail, Inbox, and Sent Mail. The Inbox and Sent Mail folders may overflow, because Mail brings into the Inbox folder every message you receive, and stores in the Sent Mail folder a copy of every message you
send. You can add folders to handle this overflow. The folders can be
private folders for your exclusive use or shared folders used by any
workgroup member with shared folder access privileges. For example,
use shared folders for messages concerning a shared project.

Mail displays folders as yellow folder icons with names below each icon
in the left side of the Mail window. To add a folder, follow these steps:

1. Choose File New Folder. The New Folder dialog box appears (see
   fig. 10.27).

FIG. 10.27

The New Folder
dialog box.

2. In the **Name** text box, type a name for the folder. The name can use any combination of characters, including spaces. For efficiency, keep the names of your folders brief.

3. In the Type section, choose the **P**rivate or **S**hared option:

Private   Messages stored in a private folder can only be viewed by you.

Shared   Messages stored in a shared folder are accessible to other users in your Postoffice. To set the access level other users have to messages in a shared folder, choose the Options button in the New Folder dialog box, and select or deselect the Read, Write, and Delete options in the Other Users Can group.

4. Choose OK or press Enter.

An icon of a folder will appear next to the name of the folder in the folders section in the left side of the Mail window. Folders are listed alphabetically by name. By default, the folder will be a top level folder, that is, it will not be subordinate to any other folders. The following section shows you how to add subfolders.

Adding Subfolders

A single-level filing system may not handle all your messages. Mail enables you to create multiple levels of subfolders. You can gather messages from general to specific categories. For example, you may have a folder named Projects that contains messages sent by all project managers. You can then have subfolders subordinate to the Project folder for each of the specific projects.

To create a subfolder, you normally select the folder to contain the subfolder; then follow the steps to create a new folder. The new folder is created as a subfolder of the selected folder (the *parent folder*). To create a subfolder with no parent folder selected, however, follow these steps:

1. In the New Folder dialog box, choose the **O**ptions button to expand the dialog box.

2. Type the name of the subfolder in the **N**ame text box.

3. In the Level section, select the Su**b**folder Of option. (The **T**op Level Folder option creates a folder independent of all other folders.)

4. In the Subfolder Of file list, select the name of the parent folder.

5. Choose OK or press Enter.

   An indented listing for the new folder appears beneath the listing for the parent folder. You have the option of displaying or not displaying the subfolders of a parent folder. When the subfolders are not displayed, a plus sign appears next to the parent folder. To expand the listing to show the subfolders, click the plus sign or press the Tab key to move to the folders list, use the arrow keys to select the parent folder you want to expand, and press the plus sign on the keyboard. To collapse a listing, click the minus sign next to the parent folder or select the parent folder with the keyboard and press the minus sign.

Moving, Renaming, and Deleting Folders

Essentially, anything you can do with a message, you can do with a folder. This section describes how to manage your folders.

To move a folder or subfolder to another folder, drag the folder from its existing location to the location where you want it. Alternatively, with the folder selected, choose File Folder Properties or press Alt+Enter. The Folder Properties dialog box appears, displaying the settings for that folder (see fig. 10.28). Select the Subfolder Of option and specify the folder that you want to use as the parent of the selected folder.

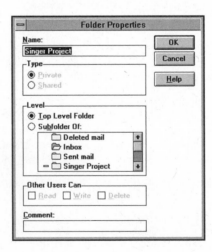

FIG. 10.28

Use the Folder Properties dialog box to change the properties of a folder.

To rename a folder, type the folder's new name in the **N**ame text box of the Folder Properties dialog box. Choose OK or press Enter, and the folder's new name appears under the selected folder.

NOTE   You cannot change the name of the Inbox, Sent Mail, or Deleted Mail folders.

To delete a folder, select the folder and then press Del, choose **F**ile **D**elete, or press Ctrl+D. A message box appears to warn you that deleting a folder also deletes the folder's contents, including messages, attachments, embedded objects, and subfolders. If you still want to delete the folder, choose the **Y**es button in the warning box; if you don't want to delete the folder, choose the **N**o button or press Enter.

Backing Up Message Files

Electronic messaging eliminates the excessive use of paper, but it increases the number and kind of messages sent. Mail keeps all your messages in folders, and keeps all the folders in the MSMAIL.MMF file. (As mentioned earlier, you can rename your MMF file; MSMAIL.MMF is the default name.) Your Personal Address Book, generated as you add addressees to your messages, is also part of the MMF file. You should back up, make a copy of, your MMF file regularly to protect the data stored in it.

To back up, make a copy of, your MSMAIL.MMF file (the message file), follow these steps:

1. Choose **M**ail **B**ackup. Mail displays the Backup dialog box (see fig. 10.29).

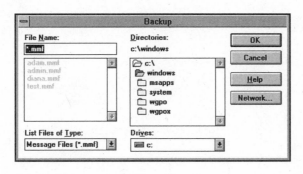

FIG. 10.29

The Backup dialog box.

2. In the File **N**ame text box, type the name you want to use for the back up, duplicate copy, of the current MMF file you are using.

3. Specify the drive and directory in which you want to save the backup file.

4. Choose OK.

If the mail file you normally use becomes corrupted, Mail displays a dialog box asking you to locate your backup file. When you select your back up file, Mail recreates your mail contents as it existed when you created that back up file.

Controlling the Mail System

Most people keep their mail and telephone systems at home organized with an address book; in the office, many people used index card files and Rolodex thumb files until computers came along. These methods have one thing in common: you must establish a *protocol* for using the system, especially with a group of people dependent on the information's accessibility and integrity. The protocol is a set of procedures for using your Personal Address Book and common rules for your workgroup. This section explains what you can do to modify and organize your Mail options to enhance your personal productivity.

Setting Up Your Personal Groups

Mail enables you to define groups of addresses for easy message addressing. This makes it convenient to send a message to a task team or to all the people working for you. To set up groups, follow these steps:

1. Choose Mail Personal Groups. The Personal Groups dialog box appears (see fig. 10.30).

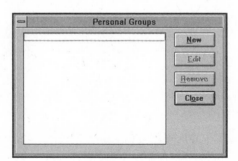

The Personal Groups dialog box.

2. Choose the **New** button in the dialog box. The New Group dialog box appears (see fig 10.31).

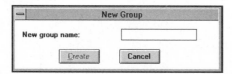

FIG. 10.31

The New Group dialog box.

3. Type the name of the new group in the New Group Name text box. Then choose the **Create** button in the dialog box or press Enter.

   The Personal Groups dialog box appears (see fig. 10.32). The name of the dialog box changes to reflect the name of the group you typed at the beginning of this step. This dialog box resembles the Address dialog box that you can access when you are composing a message. You can search for group member names, get details, and select names one at a time or in sets.

FIG. 10.32

Selecting groups of users.

4. Choose the **Add** button for each member or group selected. The group member names appear in the Group Members list box. (If you prefer, you can type the names you want to add in the Group Members text box.)

5. Choose OK or press Enter.

To edit an existing personal group, follow these steps:

1. Choose the Mail Personal Groups command.

2. In the Personal Groups dialog box, select the group you want to edit.

3. Choose the Edit button.

4. Add and remove members from the group using the Add and Remove buttons.

5. Choose OK and then choose Close.

To delete a personal group, follow these steps:

1. Choose the Mail Personal Groups command.

2. Select the group you want to remove from the list of groups.

3. Choose the Remove command.

4. Choose the Close button.

Building Your Personal Address Book

Each time you send a message, Mail adds the addressees of the message to your Personal Address Book. Mail saves this address book in your MMF file. You can also add addresses to your Personal Address Book even if you are not sending a message to these addresses.

Adding an Address

To add a name to your Personal Address Book, follow these steps:

1. Choose Mail Address Book. The Address Book dialog box appears (see fig. 10.33).

The Address dialog box is used for maintaining your Personal Address book.

2. Choose the Open Directory icon, which looks like an open address book, to display the Open Directory dialog box.

3. Select Postoffice List from and choose OK.

   The Address Book directory will now list all of the users in your Postoffice. You can select one or more names from the list and add them to your Personal Address book.

4. Select the names from the list that you want to add to your Personal Address book.

   To select more than one name from the list at one time, click on the first name, hold down the Ctrl key, and click on subsequent names. To deselect a name, hold down the Ctrl key and click on the name. To use the keyboard, select the first name, press Shift+F8, use the up- and down-arrow keys to move to the next name, and press the space bar. Move to additional names and press the space bar. To deselect a name and retain the other selections, move to the selected name and press the space bar. To return to selecting a single name at a time, press Shift+F8 again.

   To search for a name in the Postoffice list, click on the Search button, which looks like a magnifying glass, or press Tab until the Search button is selected and press Enter. Type the name or part of the name in the Name Finder dialog box that appears and choose Find. Every name that contains the text string that you typed in the dialog box will be listed in the Address Book dialog box. You can then select the name or names you want to add to your Address Book.

5. Click on the Add Names button at the bottom of the dialog box, which looks like a Rolodex file with an arrow pointing into it, or press the Tab key until the Add Names button is selected and press Enter.

   If you need to find out more about a name that you have selected before you add it to your Personal Address Book, choose the Details button to display the detailed information associated with that name. If you decide you want to add the name, you can choose the Add Names button at the bottom of the dialog box. Then choose the Close button to return to the Address Book dialog box.

6. When you have finished adding names, choose the Personal Address Book button, which looks like a Rolodex file (without an arrow pointing into it). You will see the names you added to your Personal Address book in the list of names.

7. Choose Close.

Several shortcut keys make maintaining your Personal Address Book easier and faster. These shortcuts are described in the following table:

Action	Keys
Open a new directory	Ctrl+L
Open your Personal Address Book	Ctrl+P
Find a name	Ctrl+F
Enter a new address	Ctrl+N
Add a name to your Personal Address Book	Ctrl+A
Close the Address Book	Esc

Creating a Custom Address

If your Windows for Workgroups network has a gateway connecting your workgroup to electronic mail systems on other computers or networks you can add to your address book the addresses of the people on those other mail systems. Follow these steps:

1. Choose the New Address button in the Address Book dialog box (it looks like a single index card). The New dialog box appears (see fig. 10.34).

FIG. 10.34

The New dialog box is used for creating custom addresses.

2. Select Custom Address in the Create What Kind of Entry list and choose OK or press Enter. The New User dialog box appears (see fig. 10.35).

3. Type the new user's name in the Name text box (the dialog box title bar adopts the name of the new user). Type the E-mail address and E-mail type in the appropriate text boxes; then choose

the Add User button, which shows an index file with an arrow pointing to it. Mail adds the new user to your Personal Address Book.

FIG. 10.35

Adding a user from another network.

4. Choose Cancel or press Esc to return to the Address Book dialog box and then choose Close.

Setting Mail Options

You can set Mail options for sending, receiving, and deleting messages.

To access these global settings, choose **Mail O**ptions to access the Options dialog box (see fig. 10.36). All options in the dialog box are selected by default; the user in figure 10.36 has specified that he or she wants to receive mail only once a day.

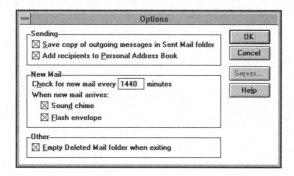

FIG. 10.36

The Options dialog box.

The following list describes the options in the dialog box:

Option	Function
Save Copy of Outgoing Messages in Sent Mail Folder	Saves a copy of each message you send in Sent Mail folder.

continues

Option	Function
Add Recipients to Personal Address Book	Adds all the addressees to whom you send a message to your Personal Address Book.
Check for New Mail Every *XXXX* minutes	Specifies how frequently Mail should check for new messages. Type the number of minutes in the text box.
When New Mail Arrives	Controls how Mail notifies you of new message arrivals. Choose Soun**d** Chime if you want Mail to sound a chime or beep from the computer's sound system. Choose **F**lash Envelope if you want Mail to change its desktop icon from a plain mail slot to a mail slot with letters sticking through it.
Empty Deleted Mail Folder When Exiting	Mail automatically empties the Deleted Mail folder when you exit the program.

Controlling How You View Folders

Mail gives you several options for controlling how you view folders and sort their contents. Many of these options are available on the **View** menu (see fig. 10.37) or by using the buttons along the top of the folder window (see fig. 10.38). Some viewing options are available only by using the mouse.

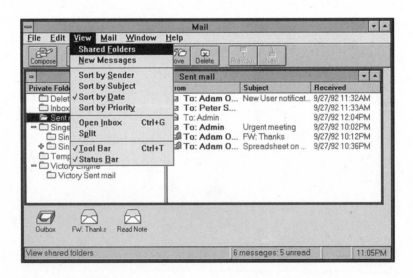

FIG. 10.37

The View menu.

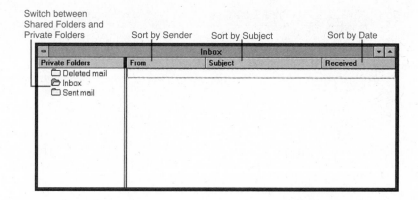

FIG. 10.38

The folder window showing buttons used to change views.

The following table summarizes Mail's folder-viewing options.

Action	View Menu	On-Screen Option
Choose private or shared folders	View Shared **F**olders or View Private **F**olders	Click the Shared Folders or Private Folders button bar to toggle between these two views
Open a folder	no equivalent	Select a folder and press Enter or double-click a folder
Search for new messages	View **N**ew Messages or View Open **I**nbox	Open the Inbox folder (Ctrl+G)
Sort messages by sender	View Sort by **S**ender	Click the From button bar
Sort messages by subject	View Sort by Sub**j**ect	Click the Subject button bar
Sort messages by date and time	View Sort by **D**ate	Click the Received button bar
Sort messages by priority	View Sort by Priority	no equivalent
Redistribute window space for folder and message lists	View S**p**lit selects the vertical line between the folder list and the Messages list, which you control with arrow keys or the mouse.	Place mouse arrow on the black line between the Folders button bar and the From button bar; when the arrow changes to a white line with black arrows pointing left and right, click and drag the line.

continues

Action	View Menu	On-Screen Option
Redistribute window space among messages	no equivalent	Place mouse arrow on the black line between the From and Subject or the Subject and Received button bars; click and drag the line
Display or remove the toolbar from beneath the menu	View **T**ool Bar	no equivalent (Ctrl+T)
Display or remove the status bar* from the bottom of the window	View Status **B**ar	no equivalent

The status bar displays an explanation of a menu command, the number of messages in a selected folder (and how many are unread), the time of day, and a disconnected net-work icon if you are working off-line or the incoming message icon if you are working on-line when a message arrives.

Changing Your Password

You can change your Mail password. Changing your password on a regular basis is advised because security systems depend on limited access to your data and passwords may be spread around.

To change your password, follow these steps:

1. Choose **Mail Change** Password. The Change Password dialog box appears (see fig. 10.39).

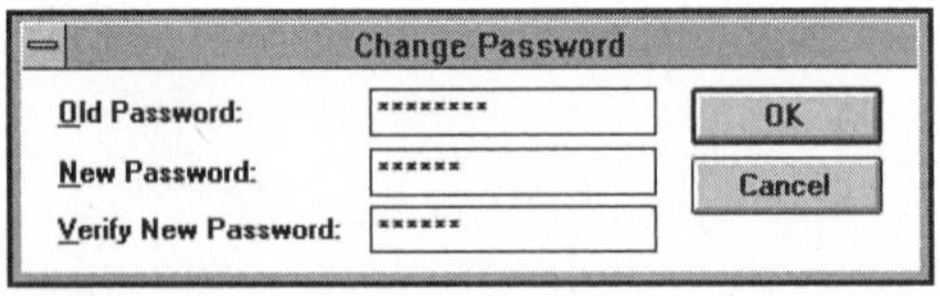

FIG. 10.39

The Change Password dialog box.

2. Type your old password in the **O**ld Password text box. Mail displays asterisks in place of the characters you type.

3. Type your new password in the **N**ew Password text box and then type the new password again in the **V**erify New Password text box.

If the characters typed in the Verify New Password text box match
the password typed in the New Password text box, the OK button
becomes available for selection. Retype your new password in the
Verify New Password text box if the OK button remains gray.

4. Choose OK or press Enter. Write your password down and keep it
   somewhere safe in case you forget it.

If you forget your password, see your Postoffice Administrator. The
Administrator can change your password (see "Controlling User Accounts," later in this chapter).

Using Mail Off-Line

Mail assumes that you do all your work at a single computer and on the
network, but sometimes you may need to work when the Postoffice
server computer isn't available (for example, on weekends, holidays,
and after work hours). You also may use a portable computer, with
which you want to work away from the network. In these cases, Mail
enables you to work off-line.

By default, Mail stores your MSMAIL.MMF (or other MMF) file in your
computer's WINDOWS directory. The MSMAIL.INI file also must be in
the WINDOWS directory. In some situations (for example, to conserve
local disk space), you may choose to rename and store your MMF file
on the Postoffice server computer. Before you can work off-line, however, you must move your MMF file to a directory on your local
computer.

Be prepared to work off-line by having your MMF file stored locally.   **T I P**

To move your MMF file to your local drive, use Windows File Manager.
You cannot use the Mail Backup command in Mail because it leaves a
copy of your MMF file intact and other users may send messages to this
MMF file while you are off-line. For information on moving files, see
Chapter 5, "Managing Files with the File Manager."

To work off-line, follow these steps:

1. With your computer disconnected from the network, start Mail. A
   message box appears, telling you that Mail didn't find your network files. Choose OK.

2. Another message box asks whether you want to work off-line.
   Choose OK again. The Mail Sign In dialog box appears.

3. Type your password and choose OK or press Enter. If Mail cannot find your MSMAIL.MMF file, it displays a dialog box asking you to type the path and name of your message file.

4. Type or otherwise designate the path (usually, C:\WINDOWS) and file name for your MMF file and then choose OK or press Enter. Mail displays your Inbox folder as usual and you can begin working with messages.

You may face the situation of working on both a desktop computer and a laptop and wanting to maintain the same message files on both. If both computers have Windows for Workgroups installed, you can maintain your Mail files on your laptop while you travel and update your desktop when you return. To use this method of working off-line with Mail:

1. Delete or move the MSMAIL.MMF file (or your MMF file with a personalized name) from your laptop's Windows directory. This will later force the laptop to ask you for the directory of your MMF file.

2. Copy the MSMAIL.INI file from your desktop computer to the Windows directory of your laptop.

3. Copy your MSMAIL.MMF file (or your MMF file with a personalized name) from your desktop computer to a diskette. This diskette file will be used as your postoffice while you are on the road.

4. Do not run Mail on your desktop computer while you are using Mail on your laptop. Doing so will cause you to lose messages when you return and copy the laptop's MMF file back to the desktop computer.

5. When you are ready to work with mail on your laptop, start Mail on your stand-alone system with the diskette containing the MSMAIL.MMF file in the diskette drive.

6. When Mail asks for the path to your MSMAIL.MMF file, specify the diskette drive.

7. Work with Mail on the laptop as usual.

8. When you return to your networked desktop computer, copy the current version of your MSMAIL.MMF file from the diskette you used with the laptop back into your Windows directory on your desktop computer. Do this before you start Mail on your desktop or you will lose messages that people have sent to you while you were gone.

While working off-line, as you send, reply to, or forward messages, Mail places these messages in your Outbox, where they become part of your MSMAIL.MMF file. When you next start Mail on-line, Mail sends these messages immediately.

Importing and Exporting Folders

Workgroups by definition must share information—sometimes, whole folders of information. When creating a folder, if you choose to share it, the whole workgroup has access privileges to that folder. You control the access by giving users read, write, or delete capabilities for the folder (see "Creating and Using Folders," earlier in this chapter), but sometimes you may need to give all the messages you have in a folder to another workgroup member. In this case, you can export the folder to another member's MMF file or that member can import the folder from your MMF file.

To import or export a folder, follow these steps:

1. To import a folder, choose File Import Folder; the Import Folder dialog box appears (see fig 10.40).

   or

   To export a folder, choose File Export Folder; the Export Folder dialog box appears (similar to fig. 10.40).

2. Specify the drive, directory, and MMF file name for the target folder (when importing a folder) or the destination folder (when exporting a folder).

3. Choose OK or press Enter. Mail displays a modified version of the Import Folders dialog box (see fig. 10.41) or the Export Folders dialog box (similar to fig. 10.41). This version of the dialog box lists the folders for the MMF file that you selected in step 2.

4. In the Folders To Import or Folders To Export list, choose All Folders or Selected Folders. If you choose Selected Folders, specify the folder or folders you want to import or export (to select multiple folders, click on the first name, press the Shift key, and click on the last name to select a sequential range or Ctrl-click individual names).

5. Choose the Options button. The Options dialog box appears (see fig. 10.42); select All Messages or Messages Received or Modified. If you choose the latter option, specify beginning and ending dates in the From and To text boxes.

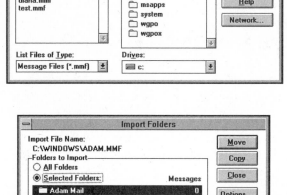

FIG. 10.40

Select the MMF file name from which you want to import folders in the Import Folders dialog box.

FIG. 10.41

After choosing an MMF file, you can select which folders you want to import.

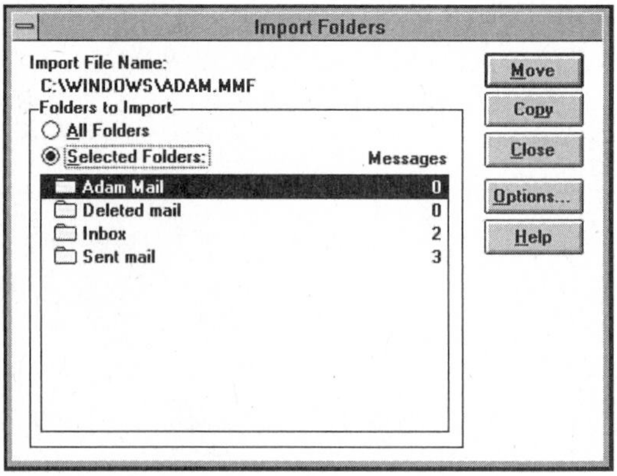

FIG. 10.42

You can import all messages or only those for a range of dates.

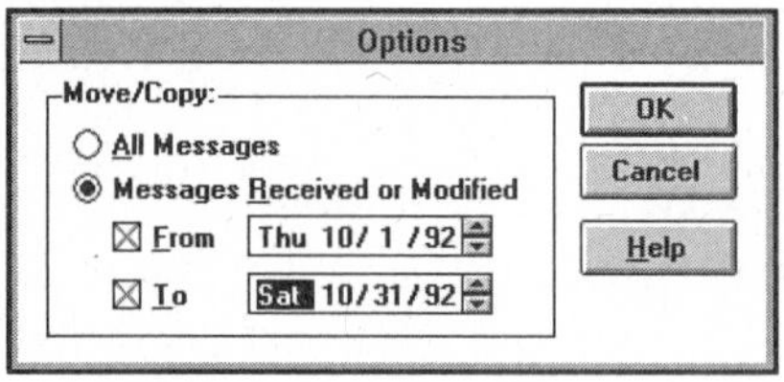

6. Choose OK or press Enter to close the Options dialog box.

7. Choose the **M**ove or Co**p**y button. Mail moves or copies the folder and files to the appropriate MMF file. If you are importing the folder, it appears in your list of folders.

Administering the Postoffice

Any member of the workgroup can be the Postoffice administrator, but these responsibilities usually go to a member whose computer system offers the most storage space and the fastest performance features. The administrator must have this computer turned on for the workgroup to use Mail on-line. More minor administrative tasks are covered in the Microsoft Windows for Workgroups manual, but this section presents the basic administrator skills.

Creating the Postoffice

The first task of the Postoffice administrator is to create the Workgroup Postoffice (WGPO). You may recognize this task as a variation of the directions for creating a user account. To create a Postoffice, follow these steps:

1. Check the hard disk storage space available for applications and tools. You need 360K disk space for an empty Postoffice and 16K disk space for each user account. In addition, each user must have enough disk space to hold the size and number of messages he or she expects to send and receive. Remember that a large Postoffice could require tens of megabytes of storage.

2. Start Mail. This must be the first time you start Mail anywhere on the network. Mail displays the Welcome to Mail dialog box; in this version of the dialog box, you specify whether you want to connect to an existing Postoffice or create a new one (see fig. 10.43).

FIG. 10.43

The Welcome to Mail dialog box.

3. Choose the Create a New Workgroup Postoffice option.

4. Choose OK or press Enter. A message box appears, reminding you of your responsibilities as a Postoffice administrator and advising that only one Postoffice per workgroup should exist.

5. The message then asks if you want to create a new Postoffice. Choose Yes or press Enter. The Enter Your Administrator Account Details dialog box appears (see fig. 10.44). Notice that the details for the administrator are the same as those for the user accounts.

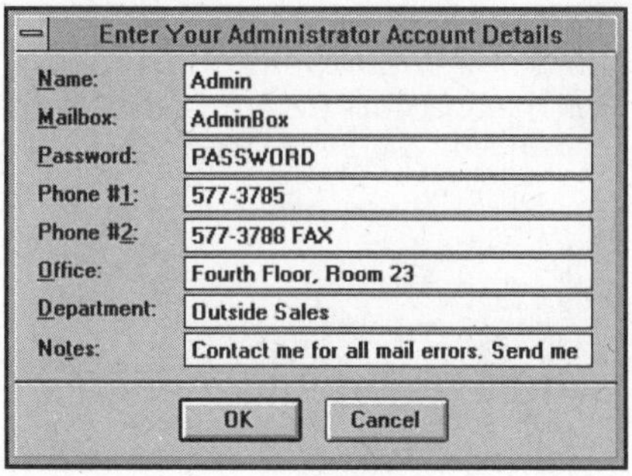

Enter Your Administrator Account Details	
Name:	Admin
Mailbox:	AdminBox
Password:	PASSWORD
Phone #1:	577-3785
Phone #2:	577-3788 FAX
Office:	Fourth Floor, Room 23
Department:	Outside Sales
Notes:	Contact me for all mail errors. Send me

OK   Cancel

FIG. 10.44

The administrator is the first user defined on the system.

6. In the dialog box, enter your name in the **N**ame text box, a name for your mailbox in the **M**ailbox text box, and a password in the **P**assword text box. All other details are optional. Choose OK or press Enter.

Mail displays a reminder to share the WGPO directory. Other users must have full access to the WGPO directory that Mail creates on the Postoffice Administrator's computer. The procedure for sharing the WGPO directory is explained in the next section.

7. Choose OK or press Enter. Mail creates the new Postoffice as the subdirectory \WGPO in the directory C:\WINDOWS (WGPO is the default directory name).

Sharing the WGPO

Immediately after creating the WGPO directory, you must share this directory so that other users have full access to it. Until you do so, other users will be unable to create an account on the Postoffice. To share the WGPO directory, follow these steps:

1. In File Manager, select the Postoffice directory (the default directory is C:\WINDOWS\WGPO).

2. Choose **D**isk Share **A**s. The Share Directory dialog box appears (see fig. 10.45).

3. Type a different name for the Postoffice or keep the default WGPO in the **S**harename text box.

The Sharename is the name Windows assigns to a directory that you share with other users. It does not have to be the same name as the directory itself.

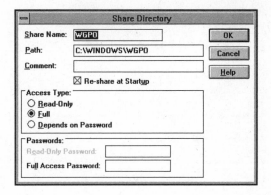

FIG. 10.45

The Share Direc-
tory dialog box
in File Manager.

4. Select the Re-Share at Startup option.

   Selecting this options instructs Windows for Workgroups to automatically share this directory each time you startup your computer.

5. Select the Full Access option.

   Selecting the Full Access option allows other users to open, read, and write to files in the WGPO directory. This level of access to the files stored in the WGPO directory is necessary for other users to connect to and use the Postoffice.

6. Type a full access password in the Full Access Password text box if you choose to have one (notify users of this password).

7. Choose OK or press Enter.

Controlling User Accounts

The Postoffice Administrator should control the creation and removal of user accounts. To remove a user account, follow these steps:

1. Choose the **M**ail **P**ostoffice Manager command. Mail displays the Postoffice Manager dialog box (see fig. 10.46). The dialog box lists the users by drive and path (specified above the list box).

2. Select the name of the user you want to delete and choose the **D**etails button. A user details dialog box appears, with the user's name on its title bar. The dialog box shows the information that the user or administrator provided when creating the account (refer to fig. 10.6). Look over the information to be sure this is the account you want to delete and then choose OK.

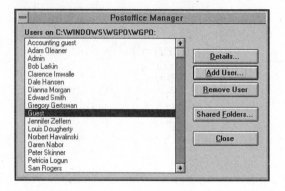

FIG. 10.46

You can add or
delete users with
the Postoffice
Manager dialog
box.

3. In the Postoffice Manager dialog box, choose the **R**emove User
   button. A confirmation box appears. Choose **Yes** if you are sure
   you want to remove this user; choose **No** or press Enter if you
   don't want to remove this user from the mail system.

To add a user, follow these steps:

1. In the Postoffice Manager dialog box, choose the **A**dd User button.
   An Add User dialog box appears (the dialog box shows the details
   for the user—refer to fig. 10.6).

2. Specify the user's name, mailbox name, and password in the
   Name, **M**ailbox, and **P**assword text boxes. The rest of the information in the dialog box is optional.

3. Choose OK or press Enter. The new user's name appears in the
   user list in the Postoffice Manager dialog box.

 This procedure doesn't create an MMF file for the new
user. Mail creates the MMF file when the user first signs
in to Mail.

To modify user account information, follow these steps:

1. In the Postoffice Manager dialog box, select the name of the user
   whose information needs to change; then choose the **D**etails button. The user's details dialog box appears.

2. In the details dialog box (the user's name appears on the title bar
   of the dialog box), change any or all of the information fields (for
   example, change the password if the user needs a new one).

3. Choose OK or press Enter. Be sure to inform the user of the
   changes you made.

Compressing the Size of the Postoffice

The Postoffice Administrator can recover hard disk storage space on the administrator's computer by monitoring shared folders and compressing them when additional storage space is needed. Shared folders can be created by any user (see "Creating and Using Folders"); any user can access the messages in a shared folder. To monitor and compress shared folders, follow these steps:

1. Choose **M**ail **P**ostoffice Manager. Mail displays the Postoffice Manager dialog box.

2. Select a user account name and choose the Shared **F**olders button. Mail displays the Shared Folders dialog box, which shows the current status of shared folders. This information includes the number of shared folders, the total number of messages in the shared folders, the collective byte count of the shared folders, and the number of bytes you can recover by compressing the shared folders.

3. If desired, choose the Compress button. Mail compresses the files.

 NOTE Be absolutely certain that no users are using the shared folder before you compress it. Warn all users before you attempt to compress the folder.

4. Choose Close to return to the Shared Folders dialog box.

Renaming, Moving, or Removing the Postoffice

Occasionally, you may need to recreate, relocate, or remove the Postoffice. Other workgroups may need to network with yours, which means that the two Postoffices must share information and folders; if both Postoffices have the same name, one name must change. Sometimes when disk space becomes sparse, relocating the Postoffice can be a temporary solution. If you forget your administrator password, you must remove the old Postoffice, create a new one, and reestablish user accounts in the renamed Postoffice system. For all of these tasks, you use File Manager.

To rename a Postoffice, select the Postoffice directory (WGPO by default) and then choose **D**isk Share **A**s. Type a new name in the Share Name text box. Share the directory with the new name as described in the section "Sharing the WGPO," earlier in this chapter.

If you need to move the Postoffice, for example, to a new computer, or to a different drive on your current computer, there are several steps you need to complete. To move a Postoffice, follow these steps:

1. Inform all users that they must Exit and sign out of Mail.

2. Open File Manager and select the WGPO directory.

3. Choose the File Move command.

4. Type the new path name for the WGPO directory in the To text box.

5. Choose OK or press Enter.

6. Share the new directory as described earlier in Sharing the WGPO.

7. Using Notepad or another text editor, modify the following line in the Postoffice administrator's MSMAIL.INI file:

       ServerPath=DRIVE:\DIRECTORY

   where DRIVE is the letter designator for the drive the directory is on, for example, D:\, and DIRECTORY is the path name for the relocated WGPO, for example, \WINDOW\WGPO.

8. Instruct all users to modify the following line in the [Microsoft Mail] section of their MSMAIL.INI file, using Notepad or another text editor:

       ServerPath=\\COMPUTERNAME\SHARENAME

   where COMPUTERNAME is the name of the computer on which the WGPO directory is located, and SHARENAME is the share name that you assigned to the WGPO directory in step 6.

 NOTE   Do not attempt to move your Postoffice unless you feel comfortable with each of the steps outlined above. Seek help from a more experienced user if necessary. Also, you may want to assist other users with step 8 if they are not familiar with working with text files.

To remove a Postoffice, select the Postoffice directory and then choose File Delete or press Del.

Chapter Summary

Mail can be a valuable tool to reduce wasted time while increasing communication within your workgroup. The key to making it work is to keep information succinct. This saves you time in composing the message and saves the recipient time in reading it. And studies have shown that the shorter the message, the more likely it is to be understood. Don't obfuscate the obvious!

While Mail can help your workgroup, electronic mail can also hurt companies that have a poor or bureaucratic culture. Companies like this soon get swamped by electronic mail. They get mired down in the morass of "for your information" and "this is what I did, was it OK?" so that soon no one reads their messages. In fact, one manager confided to us that on returning from vacation and seeing all the electronic mail waiting, the manager just erased all of it. His response was, "If it's really important they'll call me on the phone."

One advantage to Mail is that it enables you to use Schedule+. This scheduling program makes it easy for you to schedule conference rooms or quickly confirm that three decision-makers are available at the same time for an important meeting. No longer do you need to spend so much time on the phone that you get calluses on your ear. To learn more about Scheduler+, see Chapter 11.

Using Schedule+ with Windows for Workgroups

Schedule+ is a tool for keeping track of your appointments, meetings, and tasks. Schedule+ serves as a personal scheduling tool and as a tool for scheduling others in your workgroup, if you are working with Windows for Workgroups.

The *Appointment Book* is your place in Schedule+ for assigning time-specific events, such as your appointments and meetings (see fig. 11.1). You can schedule in the Appointment Book one-time-only events or events that occur at regular intervals—for example, a weekly staff meeting. For recurring events, you need to enter the event into your appointment book only once and specify the time interval for its recurrence. Schedule+ then fills in the appropriate slots in your appointment book for all subsequent occurrences of the event.

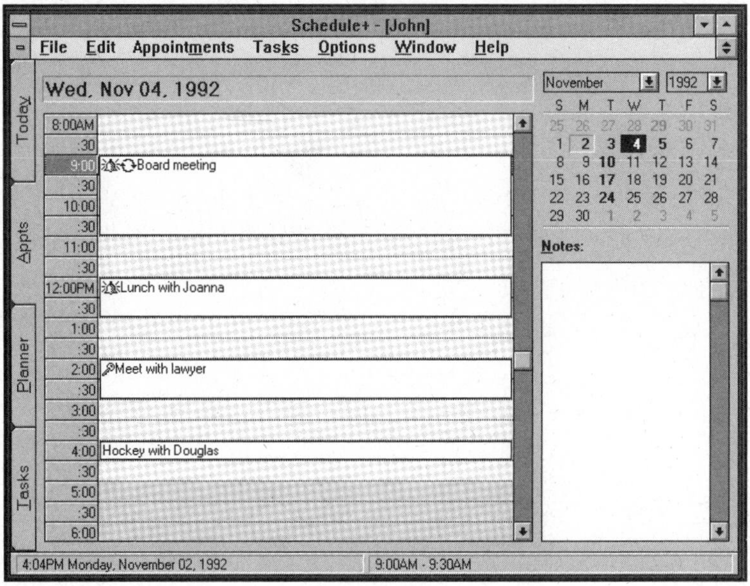

FIG. 11.1

The Schedule+
window,
showing the
Appointment
Book.

Schedule+ also acts as a group scheduling tool that enables you to see when others in your workgroup have slots open in their calendars so that you can schedule meetings during these times. After you schedule these meetings, Schedule+ sends a message to those people you have requested to attend. Potential attendees can, in return, accept or decline your proposed time. Schedule+ then communicates back to you the responses to your request.

The *Task List* is the place in Schedule+ to list anything you must accomplish that is not necessarily assigned to a specific time period, as is an appointment (see fig. 11.2). The Task List is, essentially, a to-do list of all the tasks you need to complete, either by a specific date or whenever you can.

Items in the task list remain listed until you complete the task and delete the item from the list. You also can specify the starting and due dates for each task on the list. After you specify its starting and due dates, the task appears on your to-do list on a specific date; overdue tasks—those tasks you fail to complete by the due date—appear in red in the Task List. You can also assign a priority to each task and sort your tasks by those priorities.

The Schedule+ *Planner* displays the busy and free times in your schedule in a day-by-time grid, which enables you to view several days at a time (see fig. 11.3). If you are working *on-line*—that is, you are connected to the mail server on your network—you can view the busy and free times of others in your workgroup as well. The mail server is the computer on which the Postoffice is located; through the mail server, communication among computers collected together in a workgroup occurs. (See Chapter 10, "Using Mail with Windows for Workgroups.") The primary function of the Planner is to help you schedule meetings with others in your workgroup at times that do not conflict, a topic that is covered in detail in this chapter (see "Scheduling a Meeting" for detailed discussion of how to use the Planner). You can also use the Planner to get an overview of your time committments over a period of several days.

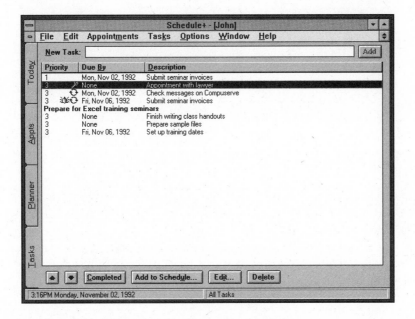

FIG. 11.2

The Schedule+ window, showing the Task List, with the last item in the list selected.

Starting Schedule+ from the Program Manager

Schedule+ is started from the Main group in the Windows Program Manager. Unless you are already signed in to Mail, you must sign in to Schedule+. To sign in, you must have a user account with Mail and know your mail box name and password. (See Chapter 10, "Using Mail with Windows for Workgroups," for information on Mail.)

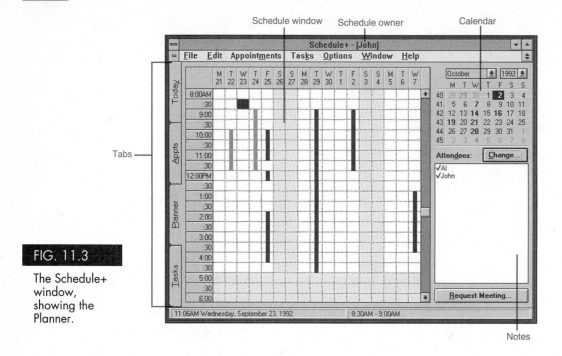

Schedule window   Schedule owner   Calendar

Tabs

Notes

The Schedule+
window,
showing the
Planner.

To start and sign in to Schedule+, follow these steps:

1. Open the Program Manager, and choose the Main group (see fig. 11.4)

2. Choose the Schedule+ icon by double-clicking on the icon or selecting the icon with the arrow keys and pressing Enter. The Mail Sign In dialog box appears (see fig. 11.5).

3. Type your mailbox name in the **N**ame text box of the Mail Sign In dialog box, as shown in figure 11.5.

4. Press the Tab key or click the **P**assword text box, and type your mailbox password in the **P**assword box. (Asterisks rather than alphabetical characters appear in the text box as you type to prevent someone else from reading your password.)

5. Choose OK, or press Enter.

After Schedule+ opens, the Appointment Book is displayed in the Schedule+ window, with the current date displayed, as shown in figure 11.1. You perform most of your work with Schedule+ within the Schedule+ window. The title bar of the window displays your name, and tabs along the left side of the window list the Appointment Book (**A**ppts), the **P**lanner, and the Task List (**T**asks). Clicking on a tab or pressing Alt+*letter* takes you to the appropriate feature. A Today tab enables you to return immediately to your Appointment Book schedule for the current day. When you are viewing or responding to meeting requests, you are working in a different window and you will not see your name in the title bar or tabs along the side of the window. Also, if you are viewing someone else's schedule, which you will learn how to do in this chapter, you will see that person's name in the title bar.

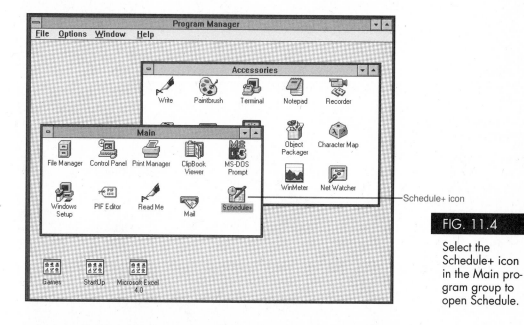

FIG. 11.4

Select the Schedule+ icon in the Main program group to open Schedule.

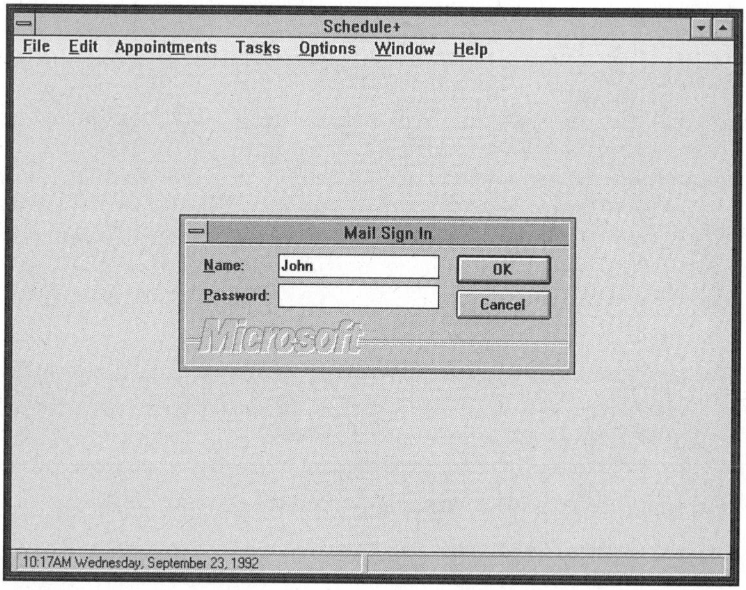

FIG. 11.5

The Mail Sign In dialog box.

After you sign in to Schedule+, you are working with Schedule+ *on-line*. Working on-line with Schedule+ means you are connected to your network's mail server and can use the features of Schedule+ that take advantage of your network. You can view the schedules of others in your workgroup, for example, and schedule meetings based on your coworkers' available time (see the sections, "Working with Another User's Appointment Book and Task List" and "Scheduling a Meeting," later in this chapter).

Working with Schedule+ Off-Line

You also can work *off-line*, which simply means working with Schedule+ without being connected to your Postoffice. Normally, when you are working on-line, your scheduling information is saved in a *local file,* located on your computer and in a *network file*, located on the computer where the Postoffice is located. If the computer serving as the network's mail server is temporarily off-line, for example, or you want to work on your portable or home computer, working off-line is your only option.

If you want to work on another computer that is not connected to your network, for example, your portable computer, you need to copy the file with your scheduling information to that computer. And then, when you return to your office, you need to copy the file back onto your computer (the one connected to the network) so that the information on the *network file,* the file located on the computer with the Postoffice, can be updated.

If you neglect to copy the file back to your networked computer, then when others view your schedule—for example, to schedule a meeting—they will not see any appointments you made while using Schedule+ away from your office. Keep in mind, that when you work with Schedule+ off-line, whether it is on your networked computer or on another computer, you will not have access to anyone else's schedule and will not be able to use the workgroup scheduling features.

If you are already working on-line with Schedule+ on your networked computer, choose the File Work Offline command. You may want to do this if you receive a lot of messages, and want to be able to work uninterrupted for a period of time.

If you want to work with Schedule+ on a standalone computer, that is, on a computer that is not connected to your network, follow these steps:

1. Copy the file named SCHDPLUS.INI from the C:\WINDOWS subdirectory on your networked computer to the C:\WINDOWS directory on your standalone computer. (See Chapter 5, "Managing Files with File Manager" for instructions on how to copy a file.)

   The SCHDPLUS.INI file contains information on your setup of Schedule+. Unless you make changes in how Schedule+ is set up on your networked computer, for example, if you make changes in the General Options dialog box, you only need to copy this file once to your standalone computer.

2. Log on to Schedule+ on your networked computer.

3. Insert a diskette into your floppy drive.

4. Choose the File Move Local File command.

5. Select the correct drive designation from the Drives drop-down list and, if necessary, change the directory in the Directories list.

6. Choose OK or press Enter.

   Your Schedule+ file, containing all the information from your Appointment Book, Task List, and Planner, is moved onto the floppy diskette. The name of the file is your mailbox name with the extension CAL.

7. Log on to Schedule+ on your standalone computer with the floppy diskette inserted in the floppy drive.

8. When you are prompted for the location of your local file, specify the floppy drive.

9. Work with your schedule as usual, with the exception that you cannot do group scheduling.

10. When you next log on to Schedule+ on your networked computer, use the File Move Local File command to move your scheduling file back to the WINDOWS directory in your networked computer.

    or

    Use File Manager to copy the file from the diskette to the WINDOWS subdirectory on your networked computer.

When you open Schedule+ on your networked computer, your Schedule+ file will automatically be updated on the mail server (assuming you are working on-line).

To work off-line when your computer is connected to a network, choose the File Work Offline command. To return to working on-line, choose File Work Online. You may want to work off-line while using your networked computer to prevent interruptions from Mail or Chat or to prevent others from using files on your drives.

If you are connected to your mail server, as described in Chapter 10, you can display a Messages window (see fig. 11.6). This window is where you receive and view replies to your requests for meetings or requests from others in your workgroup for meetings. See "Reading Responses to a Meeting Request" and "Responding to a Meeting Request" later in this chapter for details on how to use the message window.

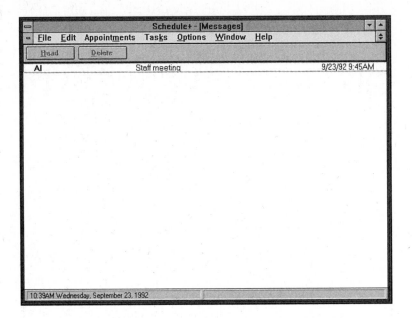

FIG. 11.6

The Messages
window in
Schedule+.

Using the Appointment Book

The Schedule+ Appointment Book is where you assign your appointments and meetings to specific time slots. A time slot can contain up to six appointments or tentative appointments. Each appointment is listed in its own section of the time slot. When you fill in a time slot in the Appointment Book, that time period is blocked out on the Planner as busy time so that you or others viewing your Planner know not to schedule anything else during that time. Tentative appointments do not show up on your Planner as busy time, however, so when others look at your schedule, they see that time as open.

If you need to schedule an appointment that recurs at regular time intervals, you can enter the appointment once in your Appointment Book and specify at what intervals and for how long a period you want that event to appear on your schedule. You also can attach a reminder to any or all appointments so that a pop-up message box appears on-screen to remind you of an appointment.

Adding an Appointment

Adding appointments to your Appointment Book involves several steps. You must designate the date on which the appointment takes place. You also must indicate on the appropriate page of your Appointment Book the starting and ending times of the appointment. Finally, you must include a description of the appointment. You also may want to designate the appointment as tentative or private and set up a reminder of the appointment to appear at a specified time beforehand.

There are two methods for adding an appointment to your Appointment Book. The first method is the quickest and works well if you do not need to designate options, such as making the appointment private or tentative or setting a reminder for the appointment. With this method, you select the time slot and enter a text description of the appointment directly on the page of your Appointment Book. The second method uses the New Appointment command in the Appointments menu. This method is slower but more powerful, because you have several options that are not available with the first method. You can select a time slot for your appointment from a display showing several days of your schedule at a glance, and you can designate the appointment as private or tentative and set a reminder from the Appointment dialog box.

To add an appointment to your schedule, your Appointment Book must be on-screen in the Schedule+ window that displays your name in the title bar. If you are not in that Schedule+ window, choose the **W**indow menu from the menu bar, select your name from the **W**indows menu by clicking with the mouse or using the arrow keys and pressing Enter; or type the number that appears next to your name on the menu. Your personalized Schedule+ window appears. If your Appointment Book is not currently displayed in your personalized Schedule+ window, click on the **A**ppts tab along the left side of the window or press Alt+A.

Adding an Appointment Directly in Your Appointment Book

To add an appointment in your Appointment Book, you must first display the page for the date of the appointment. You can use the small *calendar* located in the upper-right corner of the Appointment Book (refer to fig. 11.1) to select the appointment date by following these steps:

1. Click the arrow to the right of the month box in the calendar. A drop-down list of months appears; click the desired month. The name of the month you chose from the drop-down list appears in the month box, and the calendar changes to show the dates of that month in the year that appears in the year box. The Appointment Book also changes to display whatever date is selected in the calendar.

2. If you need to change the year, click the arrow to the right of the year box to display a drop-down list of years. Click the year in which the appointment is to take place. The year you selected appears in the year box and the dates in the calendar change to those of the chosen month in that year.

3. To set the exact day of the appointment, click that date in the month calendar. The date you have chosen appears at the top of your appointment book, including the exact day of the week on which the appointment is to take place.

You also can use the calendar to set the date of your appointment by pressing Alt and then using the arrow keys to select the desired day in the calendar. The date you select in the calendar appears in color and the schedule changes to that date. To select a different month, press Shift+Alt and use the arrow keys to select the desired month. As you press Shift+Alt+*arrow key,* the month shown in the drop-down list and the month in the schedule change.

Another method of setting the date for your appointment uses the Go To Date dialog box. To set an appointment date with the Go To Date dialog box, follow these steps:

1. Choose **Edit Go** To Date or press Ctrl+G; the Go To Date dialog box appears (see fig. 11.7)

FIG. 11.7

The Go To Date dialog box.

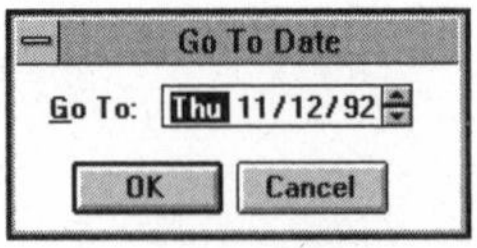

2. Type the desired date in the Go To Date dialog box.

   or

   Use the right- and left-arrow keys to move to different parts of the date and type the numbers of the new date. (You also can click on the up or down scroll arrows to the right of the date box until the correct date appears.)

3. After you have finished entering the correct date, choose OK or press Enter. The correct day and date appears at the top of the page in your Appointment Book.

If you are working in the Planner, you can quickly move to a date and time in the Appointment book by double-clicking on the square of the date and time to which you want to move. The Appointment book will display with the date and time you clicked on selected.

After you set the date for your appointment, you must set the beginning and ending times of the appointment and enter a description of the appointment. (After these times are set, the total time of the appointment is blocked off in your Planner.) Enter the time and description for the appointment by following these steps:

1. Click the time the appointment begins in the column of half hour time periods that lies along the left side of the Appointment Book and drag the mouse pointer down to the ending time for the appointment and release the mouse button. The entire time for the appointment is highlighted.

   or

   Press Shift+Tab to move to the time column of the appointment list. Use the up- or down-arrow keys to move to the beginning time of the appointment, press the Shift key and use the down arrow to move to the end time, and release the Shift key. The time period for the appointment is highlighted.

2. Type a description for the appointment.

   As soon as you start typing, the highlighted time slot is displayed with a white background, with green lines before and after the time. The text description for the appointment appears inside the box. If you type beyond the limits of the box, the box will scroll to allow you to continue adding text. When you select another time slot or appointment, the green borders will disappear from this time slot. You do not have to press Enter when you have finished typing the description.

Adding an Appointment by Using the New Appointment Command

To designate any appointment as tentative or private (or both) and to set up a reminder for an upcoming appointment, you must use the Appointment dialog box. Just as when you add an appointment directly to your Appointment Book, you can select the time for your appointment and enter a description for it. You can also view the time slots for several days at a glance by using the Choose Time option in the Appointment dialog box, and then selecting the time for your appointment from this display of time slots. To set an appointment using the Appointment dialog box, follow these steps:

1. Choose Appointment New Appointment, or press Ctrl+N. The Appointment dialog box appears, as shown in figure 11.8.

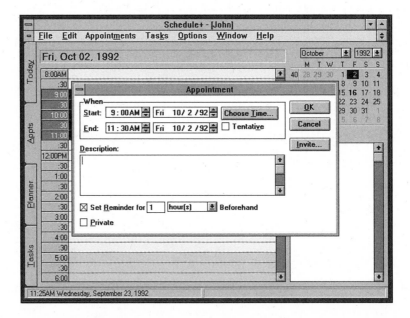

FIG. 11.8

The Appointment dialog box.

2. Set the start and end times and dates for the appointment in the Start and End boxes.

   To set the times and dates using the mouse, click in the part of the time or date that you want to change to select it and then type in a new number, or click on the up or down arrows on the right side of the time and date boxes to change the entry in the selected slot.

To set the times and dates using the keyboard, press the Tab key to move to the starting or ending time or date you want to change, and then use the right and left arrow keys to select the part of the time or date you want to change. Then type in a new entry or use the up and down arrows on the keyboard to select a new entry.

If you chose the date and the time slot for a new appointment as described at the beginning of the previous section, using the small calendar in the upper-right corner of the Appointment Book, the date and the beginning and ending times for the appointment appear in the **S**tart and **E**nd boxes of the Appointment dialog box. If the dates and times that appear in the **S**tart and **E**nd boxes are correct, you can skip this step.

To view the time slots for several days of your schedule at a glance, choose the Choose **T**ime button. The Choose Time dialog box, shown in figure 11.9, appears. You can select a time slot for the new appointment with the mouse by clicking on the starting time on the day you want to schedule the appointment and dragging to the ending time. To use the keyboard to select a time, use the right and left arrow keys to select the day for the appointment, and then use the up and down arrow keys to select the starting time, press the Shift key, and use the down arrow key to select the ending time. If you want to schedule the appointment for a date that is not displayed in the dialog box, follow steps 1-3 at the beginning of the previous section to select the date from the small calendar in the upper-right corner of the dialog box. When you have finished selecting a time, choose OK to return to the Appointments dialog box.

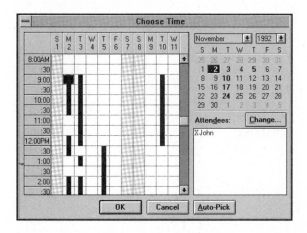

FIG. 11.9

The Choose Time dialog box displays several days of your schedule at a glance.

3. Enter a description of the appointment in the **D**escription text box.

4. You can select the Tentati**v**e option.

   When you designate an appointment as tentative, it appears against a gray, rather than white, background in your Appointment Book, and the appointment is not blocked out in your Planner. When you or others in your workgroup view your schedule in the Planner, this time slot appears open. Designate an appointment as tentative if you want to get the appointment down in your Appointment Book so you won't forget it, but are not ready to make a final committment to the time for the appointment and don't want to eliminate that time slot for others who are trying to schedule meetings.

5. To set a reminder for the appointment, select the Set **R**eminder check box and enter the amount of time you want to be reminded before the appointment. (See "Setting Appointment Reminders," later in this chapter, for details on how to set reminders for appointments.)

   After you set a reminder for an appointment, a bell icon appears next to that appointment in your Appointment Book (see fig. 11.1).

6. To designate an appointment as private, select the **P**rivate check box.

   When you designate an appointment as private, others in your workgroup cannot view the appointment in your schedule (see "Viewing or Modifying Another User's Appointment Book or Task List"). After you make an appointment private, a key icon appears next to the appointment in your Appointment Book (see fig. 11.1)

7. Choose OK, or press Enter.

The appointment now appears in your Appointment Book on the scheduled date, as well as in the Planner if it is not a tentative appointment, just as you described it in the Appointment dialog box.

After you have entered an appointment in your Appointment Book, you can edit that appointment or you can designate the appointment as a recurring appointment.

Editing an Appointment

As often happens, you may need to change the details of an appointment after you have recorded the appointment in your Appointment Book. Schedule+ enables you to make such changes with a few easy edits, whether the changes involve the appointment's description, a complete change in day or time, or selecting one of the options described earlier, such as a reminder or making the appointment private.

To change the description of an appointment, follow these steps:

1. Display the page in your Appointment Book for the date of the appointment you want to edit. Follow steps 1-3 at the beginning of the previous section to select the date from the small calendar in the upper-right corner of the Appointment Book.

2. Double-click the time slot containing the appointment you want to edit or press the Tab key to select the appointment then choose the **Edit Edit** Appt command (or press Ctrl+E).

   The Appointment dialog box appears (refer to fig. 11.8).

3. Edit the text that appears in the **D**escription text box of the Appointment dialog box as you would edit the text in any dialog box, using the Backspace, Delete, and arrow keys.

4. If necessary, change the time for the appointment. See the previous section for details on how to change the time.

5. Choose OK, or press Enter.

   You can also select or deselect the Tentative, **P**rivate, or Set **R**eminder For options in the Appointment dialog box by marking or unmarking the appropriate check boxes. (See "Adding an Appointment Using the New Appointment Command," earlier in this chapter, and "Setting Appointment Reminders," later in this chapter, for information on these options.)

T I P

You can change the description and time slot for an appointment without using the Appointment dialog box. To change the description, select the appointment, and edit the text in the time slot, as you edit any text. To change the beginning time for the appointment, click on the top edge of the time slot and drag the appointment to the new starting time. The duration of the appointment will stay the same; only the start time changes. To extend the time slot for the appointment, click on the bottom edge of the appointment and drag the edge to the new ending time.

Moving an Appointment

Moving an appointment to a new date and time is easy. To move an appointment, follow these steps:

1. Display the page in your Appointment Book for the date of the appointment you want to move. Follow steps 1-3 at the beginning of the section "Adding an Appointment Directly in Your Appointment Book" to select the date from the small calendar in the upper-right corner of the Appointment Book.

2. Click on the time slot for the appointment you want to move or press the Tab key to select the appointment.

3. Choose the **E**dit Move Appt command (or press Ctrl+O). The Move Appointment dialog box appears (see fig. 11.10).

FIG. 11.10

The Move
Appointment
dialog box.

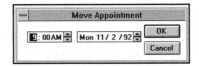

4. Set the new time and date for the appointment.

To set the times and dates using the mouse, click in the part of the time or date that you want to change to select it and then type in a new number or click on the up or down arrows on the left side of the time and date boxes to change the entry in the selected slot.

To set the times and dates using the keyboard, press the Tab key to move to the starting or ending time or date you want to change, and then use the right or left arrow keys to select the part of the time or date you want to change. Type in a new entry or use the up and down arrows on the keyboard to select a new entry.

5. Choose OK or press Enter.

Schedule+ moves the appointment to the new day and time in your Appointment Book.

Copying an Appointment

You may be able to save time by copying an existing appointment to another time slot in your Appointment Book rather than having to reenter the appointment. To copy an appointment, follow these steps:

1. Display the page in your Appointment Book for the date of the appointment you want to copy. Follow steps 1-3 at the beginning of the section "Adding an Appointment Directly in Your Appointment Book" to select the date from the small calendar in the upper-right corner of the Appointment Book.

2. Click on the time slot for the appointment you want to move or press the Tab key to select the appointment.

3. Choose the **E**dit **C**opy Appt command (or press Ctrl+Y).

4. Select the new date and time for the appointment, as described at the beginning of the section "Adding an Appointment Directly in Your Appointment Book."

5. Choose the **E**dit **P**aste command (or press Ctrl+V).

A copy of the original appointment appears at the new day and time in your Appointment Book.

If you have a recurring appointment, use the Recurring Appointment feature in Schedule+ to set an appointment that repeats at a consistent interval. To learn how to work with repetitive appointments, see the following section titled "Creating a Recurring Appointment."

T I P

Deleting an Appointment

If you want to delete an appointment from your Appointment Book, follow these steps:

1. Display the page in your Appointment Book for the date of the appointment you want to delete. Follow steps 1-3 at the beginning of the section "Adding an Appointment Directly in Your Appointment Book" to select the date from the small calendar in the upper-right corner of the Appointment Book.

2. Click on the time slot for the appointment you want to delete or press the Tab key to select the appointment.

3. Choose the **E**dit **D**elete command or press Ctrl+D.

Schedule+ removes the appointment from your Appointment Book and from your Planner.

Setting Appointment Reminders

You can tell Schedule+ to notify you in advance of any or all appointments listed in your Appointment Book by setting up a *reminder*. After you set a reminder, a pop-up message box appears on-screen at a designated time interval before the specified appointment. You can set a reminder when you are creating a new appointment, or you can add a reminder to an existing appointment. You also can choose an option that sets reminders for all new appointments as you add those appointments to your Appointment Book.

To set a reminder for an existing appointment, follow these steps:

1. Display the page in your Appointment Book for the date of the appointment on which you want a reminder. Follow steps 1-3 at the beginning of the section "Adding an Appointment Directly in Your Appointment Book" to select the date from the small calendar in the upper-right corner of the Appointment Book.

2. Double-click the appointment or press the Tab key to select the appointment and choose the **E**dit **E**dit Appt command (or press Ctrl+E).The Appointment dialog box appears (refer to fig. 11.8).

3. Select the Set **R**eminder For option by placing a mark in the check box.

   The text box and the Beforehand field to the right of the Set **R**eminder For check box list the amount of time and the time interval before the reminder appears.

4. To set a different time interval for the length of time before the appointment reminder appears on-screen, type a new number in the text box immediately to the right of the Set **R**eminder For check box. Then select the appropriate time interval—minutes, hours, days, weeks, or months—by clicking the down-arrow box to the right of the second text box and selecting the interval from the Beforehand drop-down list that appears.

5. Choose OK or press Enter.

To set a reminder for a new appointment, use the method described in "Adding an Appointment by Using the New Appointment Command" to add the new appointment. Follow steps 3 and 4 while you are in the Appointment dialog box to set the reminder.

After you set a reminder for an appointment, a bell icon appears next to the appointment in your Appointment Book.

T I P

To set reminders for all new appointments, choose the Options General Options command and select Set Reminders Automatically in the General Options dialog box. Specify the length of time before the appointment you want reminders to appear and choose OK or press Enter. With this option set, every new appointment will automatically have a reminder set for it. To turn off all reminders, choose the File Turn Off Reminders command. When you do this, the command toggles and changes to File Turn On Reminders command. Choose this command to turn all reminders back on. You can toggle back and forth between these two options by successively selecting these commands.

Creating a Recurring Appointment

If a certain appointment recurs on a regular basis, you can save time by entering the appointment once in your Appointment Book and designating that appointment as a *recurring appointment*. Schedule+ enters the recurring appointment in your Appointment Book at the designated times for as long a time period as you specify.

To create a recurring appointment, follow these steps:

1. If the appointment you want to make recurring already exists, select that appointment using the techniques described in previous sections. If you have not already entered the appointment in your Appointment Book, select the time slot for the appointment using the techniques outlined in the section "Adding an Appointment."

2. Choose the Appointments New Recurring Appt command or press Ctrl+R. The Recurring Appointment dialog box appears, as shown in figure 11.11.

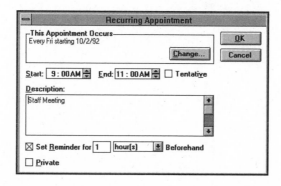

FIG. 11.11

The Recurring Appointment dialog box.

3. Choose the **C**hange button to display the Change Recurrence dialog box (see fig. 11.12).

4. Select one of the options in the This Occurs group.

When you select a frequency option, such as **W**eekly from the This Occurs group, the check boxes immediately to the right change. In figure 11.12, these check boxes appear as days of the week because the **W**eekly option button has been selected. The different collections of check boxes that appear for each This Occurs option are listed in the following table:

Occurs option	Frequency that check boxes appear
Daily	Every day or Every weekday
Weekly	Every Week On (specify which days of the week)
Bi-Weekly	Every Other Week On (specify which days of the week)
Monthly	Specify which day of every month; for example, first Monday or day seven of every month
Yearly	Specify a date, for example, March 1 of every year, or a particular day, for example, the first Monday of March

5. Select from the check boxes to the right of the This Occurs group to specify the frequency of the recurring appointment.

6. To specify starting and ending dates for the recurring event (that is, the first date the event occurs and the last date it occurs), select the **S**tarts and E**n**ds options in the Duration box and edit the date entries in the two fields.

To set the times and dates using the mouse, click in the part of the time or date that you want to change to select it and then type in a new entry or click on the up or down arrows on the right side of the date boxes to change the entry in the selected slot.

To set the times and dates using the keyboard, press the Tab key to move to either the Starts or Ends date, and then use the right or left arrow keys to select the part of the date you want to change. Type in a new entry or use the up and down arrows on the keyboard to select a new entry.

If you select the Ends option but do not change the end date, the appointment is automatically set to recur for one year from the date of the page currently displayed in the Appointment Book. Alternatively, you can select the No End Date option, in which case the appointment is set to recur indefinitely (until you change the end date or delete the recurring appointment).

7. Choose OK or press Enter to return to the Recurring Appointment dialog box.

8. If necessary, change the starting and ending times for the appointment using the Start and End boxes.

   To set the times using the mouse, click in the part of the time that you want to change to select it and then type in a new entry or, click on the up or down arrows on the right side of the time boxes to change the entry in the selected slot.

   To set the times using the keyboard, press the Tab key to move to the starting or ending time you want to change, and then use the right or left arrow keys to select the part of the time you want to change. Type in a new entry or use the up and down arrows on the keyboard to select a new entry.

9. If you are working with an appointment not already entered, type a description of the appointment in the Description text box. If the appointment is already described, skip to the next step.

10. Select any or all Tentative, Private, or Set Reminder For options, as described in detail in the "Adding an Appointment" and "Setting Appointment Reminders" sections earlier in this chapter.

11. Choose OK or press Enter.

The appoinment is now entered in your Appointment Book for every date that falls within the criteria designated in the Change Recurrence dialog box. A circular arrow icon is displayed next to recurring appointments in your Appointment. The circular arrow can be seen in figure 11.1.

Editing or Deleting a Recurring Appointment

You can edit or delete any particular occurrence of a recurring appointment in your Appointment Book by using the same method as for editing or deleting a regular appointment. (See the section "Editing an Appointment," earlier in this chapter, for details.) You also can edit or delete *all* occurrences of a recurring appointment.

To delete all occurrences of a recurring appointment, follow these steps:

1. Choose the Appointments Edit Recurring Appts command to display the Edit Recurring Appointments dialog box (see fig. 11.13). The dialog box lists all the recurring appointments currently entered in your Appointment Book.

FIG. 11.13

The Edit Recurring Appointments dialog box.

2. Select the recurring appointment you want to delete by clicking it or press the up or down arrow keys on the keyboard until the item is selected.

3. Choose the **D**elete button; the selected recurring appointment is removed from the appointment list in the dialog box.

4. Choose the **C**lose button. Schedule+ removes the recurring appointment from your Appointment Book and your Planner.

To edit all occurrences of a recurring appointment, follow these steps:

1. Choose the Appointments Edit Recurring Appts command to display the Edit Recurring Appointments dialog box (refer to fig. 11.13).

2. Select the recurring appointment you want to change by double-clicking the appointment in the dialog box list or by using the arrow keys to select the item and choosing the **E**dit button.

3. Choose the **E**dit button. The Recurring Appointment dialog box is displayed (refer to fig. 11.11).

4. Make the desired changes in the Recurring Appointment dialog box, as described in the preceding section "Creating a Recurring Appointment." To change the time interval for the recurring appointment, choose the **C**hange button, make the desired interval changes in the Change Recurrence dialog box (refer to fig. 11.12), and choose OK or press Enter to return to the Recurring Appointment dialog box.

5. Choose OK or press Enter to return to the Edit Recurring Appointments dialog box.

6. Select another appointment to edit or choose **C**lose. Schedule+ makes the appropriate changes in all the occurrences of the recurring appointment in your Appointment Book and Planner.

Adding Notes to Your Appointment Book

Sometimes you may want to make a note for a particular day that is not associated with an appointment in the Appointment Book. To accommodate such a need, Schedule+ enables you to add notes to the pages of your Appointment Book. These notes are displayed in the **N**otes box in the lower right corner of the Appointment Book. Notes apply to a specific day but need not be associated with a particular time slot.

To add a note to your Appointment Book, follow these steps:

1. Change to the date in your Appointment Book to which you want to add your note, if not the current date. See the steps outlined at the beginning of the section "Adding an Appointment Directly in Your Appointment Book" for details on how to select the date in your Appointment Book.

2. Click inside the **N**otes text box, or press Alt+N.

    The Notes text box is in the lower-right corner of the Appointment book as shown in figure 11.1. An insertion point appears inside the Notes box where you can start entering text.

3. Type the text for the note into the **N**otes box.

    If you need more room for notes than appears in the box, just keep typing. The text scrolls up as you continue to type, just as with any text you type. You can use the scroll bar to the right of the **N**otes box to move up and down within the box, just as with other Windows programs.

Just as you can add notes to your Appointment Book, you can edit your notes or delete them altogether, as with any text. To edit or delete a note, click inside the **N**otes box or press Alt+N and edit or delete the text of your notes as you would edit text in any Windows application, using the Del, Backspace, and arrow keys.

You can set an option to display a pop-up reminder message on days that have notes. The reminder message appears on-screen when you first open up Schedule+ on a day that has notes associated with it. Although you would be able to see the notes in your Appointment Book when you open Schedule anyway, adding a reminder to your notes serves to bring your attention immediately to those notes as soon as you open Schedule+. When you select this option, it applies to all days that have notes associated with them. Choose the **O**ptions **G**eneral Options command, select the Set **R**eminders for Notes option, and choose OK or press Enter.

If you need to locate any particular appointment or note within your Appointment Book, you can use the **F**ind command in the **E**dit menu to search for strings of text. This command is especially helpful if you know you have scheduled an appointment regarding a specific topic or with a person you remember, but you cannot remember on what day.

To find text in your Appointment Book, follow these steps:

1. Choose the **E**dit **F**ind command or press Ctrl+F to display the Find dialog box (see fig. 11.14).

2. Type the text string you want to locate in the Search For text box.

3. Choose one of the three search options: **F**orward from Today, **B**ackward from Today, or **W**hole Schedule.

   The first two search options search through your Appointment Book in the stated direction from the current date only. The last searches the entire Appointment Book.

4. Choose the **S**tart Search button.

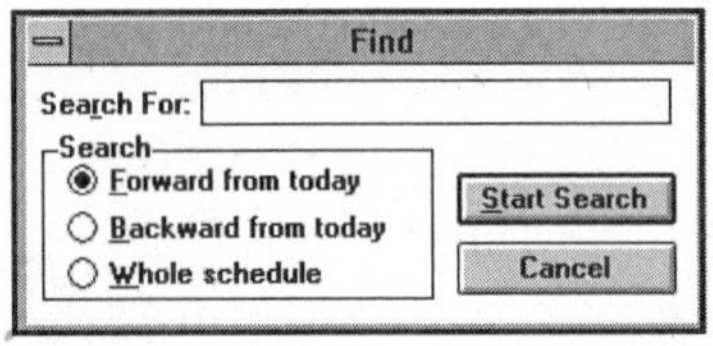

FIG. 11.14

The Find dialog box.

If the text you specified is found, the Appointment Book page for the day in which the text occurs is displayed and the text is highlighted. The Find dialog box stays open and the **S**tart Search button changes to the Find Next button so you can continue your search using the same text string by choosing the Find Next button. After you have located the appointment or note you want, choose the Cancel button or press Esc. If the Find dialog box covers text that you need to see, you can move it by clicking on the title bar and dragging the dialog box to a new location, or by pressing Alt+space bar, choosing Move from the control menu, using the arrow keys to move the dialog box, and pressing Enter.

Using the Task List

The Task List in Schedule+ is where you can list tasks you need to accomplish but that are not necessarily associated with a specific block of time, as is an appointment. You can keep in this list a running collection of what you want to accomplish, removing items as each task is completed. You can designate a *starting time* and *due date* for a task. The starting time determines when the task becomes *active* in your Task List. If you have the Show Active Tasks options selected (see "Sorting Projects and Tasks" later in this chapter), only those tasks that are active are displayed. The due date is when the task is noted as *overdue*. When a task becomes overdue, it will continue to be listed in your task list but will be displayed in red typeface.

You can create recurring tasks that are added to your Task List at specific time intervals. You can even attach a reminder to a task so that a pop-up message box appears on-screen to remind you to start the task. You can assign a priority to a task, according to the importance of the task's completion. You then can sort tasks by priority, due date, or description.

You also can create a *project* and add tasks to that project. You can then view all the tasks associated with a particular project. A project is simply a grouping of all tasks associated with a particular job, for example, all the tasks associated with creating a budget or opening a new office.

Adding a Task to Your Task List

As you work with your Task List, you are certain to discover that, as you finish certain tasks, you need to add others to the list. To add a new task to your Task List, therefore, follow these steps:

1. If you are not already in the Schedule+ window that bears your name, choose the Window menu, and select your name (or type the number listed next to your name) from the menu.

2. If your Task List is not displayed in the Schedule+ window, click the **Tasks** tab along the left side of the window or press Alt+T. The Task List appears on-screen (refer to fig. 11.2).

3. Choose the **Tasks New Task** command, or press Ctrl+T, to display the Task dialog box (see fig. 11.15).

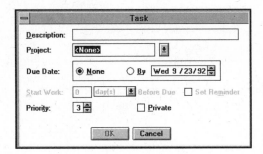

FIG. 11.15

The Task dialog box.

4. Type a description of the task in the **D**escription text box.

5. To add the task to a specific project you have created, select the project from the Project drop-down list by clicking the arrow to the right of the Project field. (See "Adding a Project" later in this chapter.) Select *None* from the list if you do not want to add the task to a project.

6. To specify a due date for the task, select the **By** option in the Due Date box. Select **N**one if you do not want to specify a due date. (If you select **N**one, skip to step 10.)

   If you select the **By** option, you must change the date in the date field to the desired due date. (If the correct due date already appears in the date field, skip to step 8.)

7. To change the date, click in the date field and edit the date by using the arrow, Del, and Backspace keys. Alternatively, you can click the up and down arrows to the right of the date field until the desired date is selected.

   After you specify a due date for a task, the **S**tart Work and Set Reminder options are enabled. You may use these options to designate a starting date for your work on the task and to set a reminder for yourself to start the task on the designated starting date.

8. To specify a starting time for the task in the **S**tart Work box, type a number in the text box and then click on the arrow to the right of the Before Due field. Select a unit of time—days, weeks, or

months—from the Before Due drop-down list. (If you do not want to specify a starting time, type 0 in the text box; the unit of time becomes unimportant if 0 is entered into the Start Work box.)

The time interval you specify in the **S**tart Work box and Before Due field determines how long before the due date the task becomes active in your Task List—that is, before the task is actually displayed in your Task List.

9. Select the Set Re**m**inder check box if you want Schedule+ to display a pop-up message box reminding you of the task on the starting date. (You must set a starting date before you can select this option.) The pop-up message box will appear on-screen in whatever Windows application you happen to be working.

   After you set a reminder for a task, a bell icon appears next to the task in the Task List (see fig. 11.2).

10. If you do not want the default priority assigned to a new task, select a new priority level from the Priority box by clicking the up and down arrows to the right of the box.

    Priority levels range from 1 to 9 or from A to Z (if you prefer to use letters).The highest priority level is 1, or A if you are using letters. If you use a both numbers and letters to prioritize your tasks, numbers have a higher priority than letters, That is, 9 has a higher priority than A. The default level is 3, or C.

    For the best time management in your day, you should have one to three A or 1 level tasks. These are tasks that must get done. They are necessary to achieving your most important goals. You might have three to five B or 2 level tasks. These are supporting tasks or daily work type of tasks. Frequently, they are the mundane but necessary tasks to keep your job functioning, but they may not advance your career.

    Finally, there are the C or 3 level tasks or tasks at an even lower level. These tasks are the ever present administrivia that can clutter your day and keep you from advancing your career, spending time with your family, or meeting personal goals. They are such tasks as returning non-mandatory phone calls, attending meetings where you are not a contributor, cleaning out filing cabinets, and so on. Everyone needs an occassional level Cor 3 task to give their brain or body a moment to unwind, but try to stay away from them until you are forced to move them into the level Bor 2 priority.

11. To prevent other users from viewing this task, select the **P**rivate check box.

After you designate a task as private, a key icon appears next to the task in the Task List (see fig. 11.2)

12. Choose OK, or press Enter. The new task now appears in your Task List.

Adding a Project

Just as you can create and add new tasks to your Task List, you can create projects and add to them those tasks associated with each project. After tasks are added to projects, you can choose to view the tasks grouped by project in the Task List.

To add a project to your Task List, follow these steps:

1. With the Task List displayed, choose the Tasks New **P**roject command. The Project dialog box appears, as shown in figure 11.16.

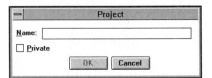

FIG. 11.16

The Project dialog box.

2. Type a name for the project in the **N**ame text box.

3. To make the project private, select the **P**rivate check box.

   After you make a project private, that project cannot be viewed by other users. A key icon is displayed in the Task List next to projects that have been designated as private.

4. Choose OK or press Enter.

The new project appears in your Task List. The title for a project appears in bold in the Task List (refer to fig. 11.2). If tasks are grouped by project (see below), all of the tasks for a given project will be listed under the title for the project.

Tasks are assigned to a project by selecting the project's name from the Project list in the Task dialog box for that task, as described in the section, "Adding a Task," earlier in this chapter. Existing tasks also may be added to a new project by clicking the task name on the Task List and dragging and dropping the task under the new project's name on the list, as discussed in the following section, "Editing Tasks and Projects," which concerns moving tasks from a project.

Tasks assigned to a project are listed under the project name on the Task List only after the View by Project option in the Tasks menu is turned on. To turn on the View by Project option, choose the Tasks View by Project command. A check mark appears next to this command if it is selected. To turn off the View by Project command, choose the command again. If View by Project is not turned on, all tasks are listed together on the Task List and project names do not appear in the Task List.

Editing Tasks and Projects

Sometimes you must change the description of a task or project or alter other aspects of a task in your Task List. You may even need to delete a task or project altogether—especially if you have completed it. Schedule+ enables you to edit or delete any existing tasks or projects in your list.

To edit or change a task, follow these steps:

1. With the Task List displayed, double-click the task you want to edit, or select the task by clicking it (or using the arrow keys to highlight it) and pressing Enter. The Task dialog box appears.

2. Edit the task **D**escription in the Task dialog box by using the arrow, Del, and Backspace keys and adding any new text necessary.

   You also can change the task's due date and starting date, set a reminder for the task, change the priority level, or designate the task as private in this dialog box, as discussed in the section "Adding a Task," earlier in this chapter.

3. Choose OK or press Enter.

Changes you make in the Task dialog box are reflected in the task's listing in the Task List after you choose OK or press Enter.

To change the priority level of a task without using the Task dialog box, select the task in the Task List and click the up or down arrow at the bottom of the Task List.	**T I P**

You can edit a project name the same way you edit a task name. To edit a project name, follow these steps:

1. Double-click the project name in the Task List, or select the project by clicking it (or using the arrow keys to highlight it) and pressing Enter. The Project dialog box appears.

2. Edit the text in the Name text box of the Project dialog box.

3. Choose OK or press Enter to transfer the changes to the project name from the dialog box to the Task List.

To delete a task, follow these steps:

1. With the Task List displayed, select the task you want to delete.

2. Click the Delete button at the bottom of the Task List, or press Alt+L. The task is removed from the Task List.

After you complete a task, you may want to keep a reminder that the task is finished. Schedule+ enables you to insert a note about the completed task in your Appointment Book at the same time you remove the task from your Task List.

To remove a completed task from the Task List and insert a note in your Appointment Book about the completed task, select the task and choose the Completed button at the bottom of the Task List. Schedule+ inserts the description of the task in the notes section of your Appointment Book for the day on which the Task was completed

You can delete a project and all its associated tasks simultaneously. To delete a project and its tasks, follow these steps:

1. Select the project in the Task List, and choose the Delete button. A message box appears informing you that the project and all its tasks will be deleted.

2. Choose OK.

The project and all its tasks are removed from your Task List.

To delete a project without deleting its tasks, you must first move all the tasks from that project on the Task List. You can perform this operation by clicking on each task and dragging and dropping the task in an area of the Task List where tasks not associated with the project are listed. You also can double-click on the task, or select the task and press Enter, to display the Task dialog box. Select *None* from the Project drop-down list, and choose OK or press Enter. After all the tasks have been moved from the project, select the project name and choose the Delete button to remove it from the Task List.

To copy a task from one project to another, first select the task you want to copy in the Task List. Holding down the Ctrl key, drag and drop the task on or under the name of the project to which you want the task copied.

Adding a Task to Your Appointment

Some tasks may need to be completed at specific times or on specific dates. To ensure you don't forget this type of task, you can add a task to a time slot in your Appointment Book. To add a task to your Appointment Book:

1. Click on the Tasks tab or press Alt+T to select the Task List.

2. Select the task you want to schedule by clicking on it or pressing the up or down arrow keys.

3. Choose the Add To Schedule button. This displays the Choose Time dialog box.

4. Select the date from the calendar and the time slot to which you want to assign the task.

5. Choose OK or press Enter.

The tasks will still appear in your Task List but they will also be shown in the Appointment Book.

Adding a Recurring Task

If you must complete a certain task on a regular basis, you can save yourself time by entering the task once in your Task List and then designating the task as a recurring task. Schedule+ then enters the task at the designated times for as long a time period as you specify.

To create a recurring task, follow these steps:

1. Choose the Task New Recurring Task command to display the Recurring Task box (see fig. 11.17.)

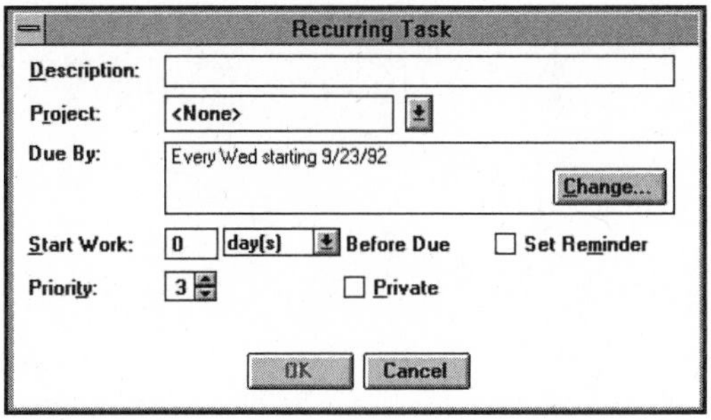

FIG. 11.17

The Recurring Task dialog box.

2. Type a description of the task in the **D**escription text box of the Recurring Task dialog box.

3. To add the recurring task to a specific project you have created, select the project to which you want to assign the task from the **P**roject drop-down list. Select *None* from the list if you do not want to add the task to any project.

4. Choose the **C**hange button to display the Change Recurrence dialog box (refer to fig 11.8).

5. Refer to "Creating a Recurring Appointment" section for details on how to set up the recurring task.

6. Choose OK or press Enter to return to the Recurring Task dialog box.

7. Follow the steps outlined in "Adding a Task to Your Task List" to finish creating the recurring task.

8. Choose OK or press Enter.

The recurring task now appears in your Task List for every day that falls within the criteria designated in the Change Recurrence dialog box. A circular arrow icon is displayed next to each listing of a recurring task in the Task List (refer to fig. 11.2).

Editing a Recurring Task

You can edit or delete any occurrence of a recurring task in your Task List by using the same method as for editing or deleting a regular task. (See the section "Editing a Task," earlier in this chapter, for details.) You also can edit or delete *all* occurrences of a recurring task.

To delete or edit all occurrences of a recurring task, follow these steps:

1. Choose the Ta**s**ks Edit Re**c**urring Tasks command to display the Edit Recurring Tasks dialog box (see fig. 11.18). The dialog box lists all the recurring tasks currently entered in your Task List.

2. Follow the steps outlined in "Editing a Recurring Appointment" to select, delete or edit the task.

3. Choose **C**lose. Schedule+ makes the appropriate changes in all occurrences of the recurring task in your Task List.

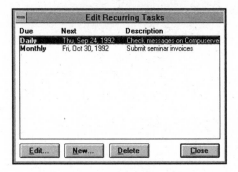

FIG. 11.18

The Edit Recurring Tasks dialog box.

Sorting Projects and Tasks

Tasks can be arranged in several ways on your Task List. You can display your tasks arranged by project, for example, and you can sort tasks by priority, due date, or description. You also can restrict your Task List to displaying only *active* tasks—that is, tasks with no starting or due dates, or tasks with a starting date that has arrived, or you can display all tasks, including tasks that have not yet become active.

To view your tasks organized by project on the Task List, choose the Tasks View By Project command (or press Ctrl+Shift+V). Return to viewing your tasks ungrouped by project by choosing the Tasks View By Project command (or pressing Ctrl+Shift+V) again.

You can sort your tasks by priority, due date or description. If your tasks are grouped by project, your tasks will be sorted within each project. Tasks that are not part of a project are grouped and sorted together, separate from tasks assigned to projects.

To sort your tasks by priority, click the Priority button at the top of the Task List, or choose the Tasks Sort By Priority command.

To sort your tasks by due date, click the Due By button at the top of the Task List, or choose the Tasks Sort by Due Date command.

To sort your tasks by description, click the Description button at the top of the Task List, or choose the Tasks Sort By Description command.

To view only your active tasks on the Task List, choose the Tasks Show Active Tasks command. To return to viewing all your tasks, choose the Tasks Show Active Tasks command again.

Scheduling a Meeting

One of the most powerful and useful features of Schedule+, when you are connected to the mail server in Windows for Workgroups (or working *on-line*), is that Schedule+ enables you to schedule meetings with others in your workgroup without ever leaving your desk or making a phone call. When you work on-line with Schedule+, everyone in a workgroup can access the schedules of the others in that workgroup. This accessibility enables anyone in the workgroup to schedule a meeting at a time that does not conflict with the appointment times for the others who are to attend the meeting.

When you schedule a meeting, you can select who you want to attend the meeting and suggest a date and time for the meeting, based on times that appear to be open in the schedules of the people you want to attend. After you have scheduled a meeting, a request is sent to each of the people you have asked to attend. You have the option of attaching a message to this request, for example, to explain more about the agenda for the meeting. This request appears in the form of a message in the message window in Schedule+, as well as in the Inbox in Mail. Each potential attendee can then reply to your request by declining, accepting, or tentatively accepting the proposed meeting time. Those people responding have the option of attaching a text message to their reply. Responses to meeting requests appear in your message window in Schedule+ and in your Inbox in Mail.

Schedule+ gives you several options for designating how much other users can access your schedule. You can designate any of the following levels of access:

- Users have no access to your schedule.

- Users can view your free and busy time slots without actually viewing your appointments.

- Users can actually read your appointments and tasks.

- Users can create or modify your appointments and tasks.

You can also assign an assistant, who has complete access to your schedule, act for you in scheduling meetings and responding to meeting requests.

You can schedule a meeting from your Appointment Book or from your Planner. The Planner (refer to fig. 11.2) displays blocks of time for several days at a glance in a day-by-time grid. When you—or others in your workgroup whose schedules you are viewing—have an appointment, that appointment is represented in the Planner by a vertical line running through the time slot allotted for the appointment. Your appointments are represented by a blue line and the appointments of others in your workgroup are represented by a gray line. A calendar in the upper right corner of the Planner window, similar to the one in the Appointment Book, enables you to change the days displayed in the Planner.

Not only can you view the schedules for everyone in your workgroup, including your own, but you can also mark out a block of time when you want to schedule a meeting, select the people you want to attend the meeting, and send meeting requests (along with an optional message) to each person you want to attend the meeting. If the people you have asked to attend a meeting reply positively, the meeting time is marked in the Planners of all attendees.

Just as you can schedule a meeting, so can you schedule a resource, for example, a meeting room or slide projector. In order to schedule a resource, the Postoffice Administrator has to set up a Mail account on the Postoffice for that resourse (see Chapter 10, "Using Windows for Workgroups Mail"). If you then grant full access privileges to other users for that account, anyone can view the schedule for that resource and book the resource during any open time slot. Or, someone can be designated as the assistant for the resource, so that all requests for the resource must be confirmed by the assistant.

Scheduling a Meeting by Using the Planner

To schedule a meeting using your Planner, follow these steps:

1. If you are not already in your schedule window, choose the **W**indow menu and select your name (or type the number next to your name).

2. If your Planner is not already displayed, click on the *Planner* tab along the left side of the window or press Alt+P.

3. Notice who is already listed in the Attendees list in the lower-right corner of the Planner window. Choose the **C**hange button to select the additional attendees. The Select Attendees dialog box appears (see fig. 11.19).

4. Select the people you want to attend the meeting from the Directory box at the top of the dialog box.

   Select the people you want to attend the meeting from the list of names at the top of the dialog box. If the list does not include the names of the people you want to send a request to, click on the Directory button (the icon of the open book) or press Ctrl+L and select a new directory in the Open Directory dialog box. To make the directory you have selected the default directory, choose the Set **D**efault button. Choose OK or press Enter.

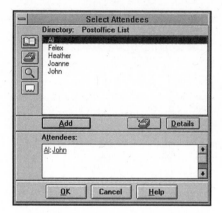

FIG. 11.19

The Select
Attendees dialog
box.

5. Choose the **A**dd button; the names of the people you selected appear in the Attendees box.

6. After you finish selecting the attendees, choose OK.

   If the Attendees list in Planner includes people you don't want to attend, you can click on their names in the Attendees box. The schedules for these people are not shown in the Planner, and these people are not sent a meeting request.

7. Click on the beginning time for the proposed meeting in the Planner and drag to the ending time for the meeting.

   or

   Use the arrow keys to select the beginning time, hold down the Shift key, and use the arrow keys to move to the end time.

   Be sure to select a time when everyone you want to attend is available.

T   I   P   To quickly find a time when everyone in your attendees list is available, select a time slot in the grid equal to the length of time the meeting is scheduled for and choose the Appointments Auto-Pick (or press Ctrl+A).

8. Choose the **R**equest Meeting button to display the Send Request dialog box (see fig. 11.20).

9. Type the subject of the meeting in the Subject box.

   What you type in the subject box is also used as the description of the appointment in everyone's Appointment Book.

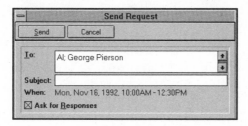

FIG. 11.20

The Send Request
dialog box.

10. By default, the recipients of your request are asked for a response. If you don't want a response, deselect the Ask For **Re**sponses check box.

11. Press the Tab key or click in the message area, and type a message to accompany the request. You do not have to include a message.

12. Choose the **S**end button.

A messsage box informing you that the meeting was successfully booked appears. Click on OK or press Enter to return to the Planner. A hand-shaking icon is displayed next to meetings in your Appointment Book.

T I P

The following are some tips for selecting from the Personal Address Book:

■ To view the names in your Personal Address Book, click on the Personal Address button (the index file icon) or press Ctrl+P.

■ To search for a name in the names list, click on the Find button (the magnifying glass icon) or press Ctrl+F, type the name in the Name Finder dialog box, and choose the **F**ind button.

■ To select two or more names listed consecutively in the names list, click the first name (or use the arrow keys to select the first name), hold down the Shift key, and click on the last name (or use the arrow keys to select the last name).

■ To select two or more names *not* listed consecutively, click on the first name (or use the arrow keys to select the first name), hold down the Ctrl key, and click on the other names you want to select (or use the arrow keys to select a name and press the space bar). To deselect a name in the list, hold down the Ctrl key and click on the name (or hold down the Ctrl key, use the arrow keys to select the name, and press the space bar).

For additional information about the Personal Address book, for example, if you want to add names to your address book, see Chapter 10, "Using Mail with Windows for Workgroups."

Scheduling a Meeting by Using the Appointment Book

To set up a meeting using your Appointment Book, follow these steps:

1. If you are not already in your schedule window, choose the **W**indow menu and select your name (or type the number next to your name).

2. If your Appointment Book is not already displayed, click on the *Appts* tab along the left side of the window or press Alt+A.

3. Select a proposed time for the meeting. This time can be changed after you view the schedules of the other people you want to attend the meeting.

4. Choose the Appointments **N**ew Appointment command (or press Ctrl+N) to display the Appointment dialog box (refer to fig. 11.8).

5. To view the free and busy times of the people you want to invite to the meeting, choose the Choose **T**ime button to display the Choose Time dialog box (see fig. 11.21).

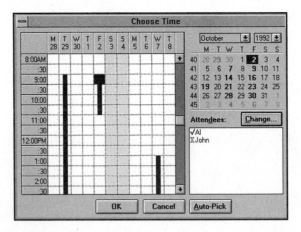

FIG. 11.21

The Choose Time dialog box.

6. Choose the **C**hange button to display the Select Attendees dialog box (refer to fig. 11.19).

7. Complete steps 4-6 described in the "Scheduling a Meeting by Using the Planner" section, earlier in this chapter.

8. If conflicts arise with the time you originally selected in your Appointment Book, select a new time in the Choose Time dialog box.

> **T I P**
>
> To quickly find a time when everyone in your attendees list is available, select a time slot in the grid equal to the length of time the meeting is scheduled for and choose the **Auto-Pick** button. If you do not like the scheduled time choosen by Auto-Pick, continue to choose the **Auto-Pick** button to see other times that meet everyone's schedule.

> **T I P**
>
> If you do not need to view the busy and free times of the proposed attendees, you can choose the Invite button in the Appointment dialog box to go directly to the Select Attendees dialog box.

9. Type a description of the meeting in the **D**escription box.

10. Choose OK or press Enter.

     The Send Request dialog box is displayed (refer to fig. 11.20)

11. Complete steps 9-12 described in the "Scheduling a Meeting by Using the Planner" section, earlier in this chapter.

Scheduling a Resource

You can use Schedule+ to schedule a resource, just as you would schedule a meeting. For example, you may need to schedule a meeting room, a portable computer, or an overhead transparency projector. Before you can schedule a resource, the Postoffice Administrator must create a mail account for that resource and someone has to open up Schedule+ and set up the resource so that it is either accessible to all users or has an assistant assigned to it who will handle the scheduling for that resource.

To add a resource, follow these steps:

1. Ask your Postoffice Administrator to create a Mail account for the resource (see Chapter 10, "Using Mail with Windows for Workgroups").

2. Sign into Schedule+ by using the name and password for the resource.

3. Choose the **O**ptions **G**eneral Options command.

4. Select the This **A**ccount is for a Resource option.

5. Choose OK or press Enter.

6. Choose the **O**ptions Set **A**ccess Privileges command.

7. Either select the **C**reate Appointments & Tasks to give all users the ability to schedule the resource themselves.

   If this option is selected, any user can schedule a resource using the methods outlined in the section "Working with Another User's Appointment Book and Task List" later in this chapter.

   or

   Select the Assistant option and assign an assistant to manage the resource.

   If you assign an assistant to the resource, only that person can actually schedule the resource; all requests for the resource go to the assistant. See "Assigning an Assistant for Your Schedule" later in this chapter for details on how to designate an assistant.

Reading Responses to a Meeting Request

After others respond to your meeting requests, their responses appear in the message window of Schedule+, as well as in your Inbox in Mail.

To read these responses, follow these steps:

1. Choose **W**indow Messages to display the message window (see fig. 11.22).

2. Double-click on the response you want to read.

   or

   Select the response you want to read using the mouse or arrow keys and choose the **R**ead button (press Alt+R).

3. To delete a response, select the response using the mouse or keyboard and choose **D**elete.

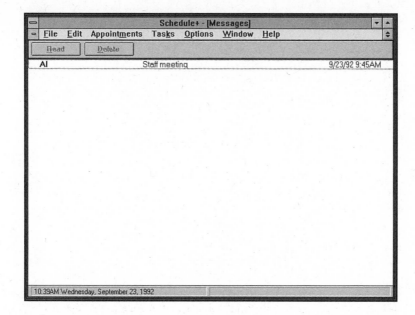

FIG. 11.22

The message
window.

Rescheduling a Meeting

To reschedule a meeting, follow these steps:

1. If you are not already in your schedule window, choose the
    Window menu and select your name (or type the number next
    to your name).

2. If your Appointment Book is not already displayed, click on the
    Appts tab along the left side of the window or press Alt+A.

3. Find the meeting in your Appointment Book and move the meeting
    to the new proposed time. (See the section "Editing an Appoint-
    ment," earlier in this chapter.)

    At this point, Schedule+ asks whether you want to notify the at-
    tendees of the meeting of the change.

4. Choose **Yes** to display the Meeting Request window.

5. If you choose, you can add a message to the request, and choose
    the **S**end button.

Attendees receive a new meeting request with the new time, to which
they can respond as with any meeting request.

Canceling a Meeting

To cancel a meeting, follow these steps:

1. If you are not already in your schedule window, choose the **W**indow menu and select your name (or type the number next to your name).

2. If your Appointment Book is not already displayed, click on the *Appts* tab along the left side of the window or press Alt+A.

3. Select the meeting in your Appointment Book.

4. Choose **E**dit **D**elete Appt (or press Ctrl+D).

   A message box appears asking if you want to notify the meeting attendees of the cancellation.

5. Choose **Y**es to display the Cancel Meeting window.

6. Type a message in the message area, and choose **S**end.

All attendees of the meeting receive a message notifying them of the cancellation and the meeting is removed from everyone's Appointment Books and Planners.

Responding to a Meeting Request

If someone else in your workgroup sends a request to you to attend a meeting, you receive the request in your message window in Schedule+ as well as in your Inbox in Mail. You can read and respond to such requests in the message window.

To read and respond to meeting requests, follow these steps:

1. Choose **W**indow Messages.

2. Double-click the request you want to respond to.

   or

   Select the request using the mouse or keyboard and choose **R**ead (or press Alt+R).

   The Meeting Request window appears, as shown in figure 11.23.

3. Choose the View **S**chedule button to view your schedule.

   To return to the Meeting Request window, choose **W**indow Meeting Request.

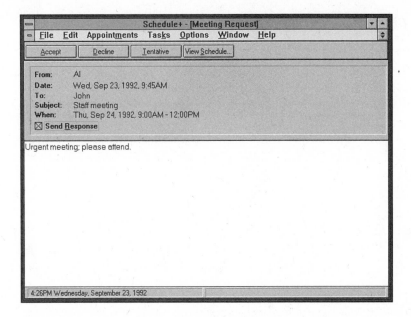

FIG. 11.23

The Meeting
Request window.

4. Choose the **A**ccept button, the **D**ecline button, or the **T**entative
   button.

   If you choose to accept or tentatively accept the request,
   Schedule+ enters the meeting into your Appointment Book.

   The Send Response window appears, as shown in figure 11.24.

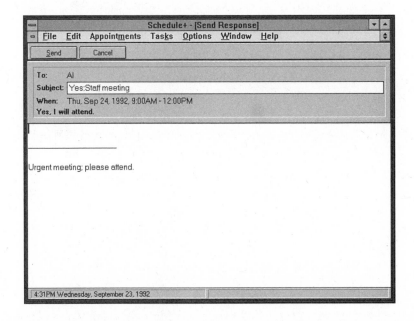

FIG. 11.24

The Send
Response
window.

460

5. You can add a message to your response by typing the message in the upper portion of the message area.

6. Choose the **S**end button.

Assigning an Assistant for Your Schedule

Schedule+ gives you the option of designating another user on your network as an assistant. That person can then view and change your Appointment Book as if the book were his own. The assistant also receives meeting requests and responses to meeting requests for the *owner* of the Appointment Book. Responses to meeting requests are logged in the owner's appointment book.

You have the option to have meeting messages sent only to your assistant. Choose **O**ptions **G**eneral Options, select the Send **M**eeting Messages Only to My Assistant check box, and choose OK or press Enter.

Designating an Assistant

To designate another user as your assistant, follow these steps:

1. Choose the **O**ptions Set **A**ccess Privileges command to display the Set Access Privileges dialog box (see fig. 11.25).

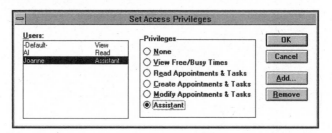

FIG. 11.25

The Set Access Privileges dialog box.

2. Select the user's name from the **U**ser's box if the name is listed.

or

Choose the **A**dd button and select the user's name from the names list.

If the list does not include the name of the person you want to designate as your assistant, click on the Directory button (the icon of the open book) or press Ctrl+L and select a new directory in the Open Directory dialog box.

Choose the **A**dd button and choose OK or press Enter.

You are limited to designating one assistant for your schedule at a time.

3. Choose the Assistant option from the Privileges group of options.

4. Choose OK or press Enter.

Removing or Changing your Assistant

To change your assistant, you must first remove your current assistant and then designate a new assistant, since you can only have one assistant.

To remove an assistant, follow these steps:

1. Choose the **O**ptions Set **A**ccess Privileges command.

2. Choose the assistant's name from the **U**ser's box.

3. Select a new access privilege for your assistant.

T I P

You can remove the assistant status and assign the default access privilege to your assistant in one step by selecting the assistant's name from the **U**ser's list and choosing the **R**emove button. The default access privilege is applied to all users except those who have specifically been assigned another access privilege. (See the section "Designating Specific Privileges to a User," later in this chapter.)

Working as an Assistant for Another User

If you are acting as the assistant for someone else's schedule, you must open up that person's Appointment Book before you can work with his schedule.

To open up the owner's Appointment Book, follow these steps:

1. Choose the **F**ile **O**pen Other's Appt. Book command. The Open Other's Appt. Book is displayed (see fig. 11.26).

FIG. 11.26

The Open
Other's Appt.
Book dialog box.

2. Choose the name of the owner from the names listed at the top of the dialog box.

   If the list does not include the name of the person whose Appointment Book you want to open, click on the Directory button (the icon of the open book) or press Ctrl+L and select a new directory in the Open Directory dialog box.

3. Choose the **A**dd button.

4. Choose OK or press Enter.

After you open the owner's Appointment Book, you can schedule meetings and respond to meeting requests just as you do with your own Appointment Book. You receive responses to meeting requests sent by you, and Schedule+ logs the responses in the owner's Appointment Book.

You can act as an assistant for a resource in the same way you assist another user. If you are in charge of scheduling for a conference room, for example, you must be assigned assistant privileges for that resource. You then receive all requests for the resource. After you receive a request, you check for the availability of the resource at the time requested and respond to the request, just as with a meeting request.

Working with Another User's Appointment Book and Task List

In Schedule+, you can view another user's Appointment Book or Task List if the user has granted you that privilege. Several levels of access privileges can be assigned to a user. These levels range from no access to the ability to view and modify another user's Appointment Book or Task List. Each user can designate the level of access any other user has to his Appointment Book and Task List.

Designating Default Access Privileges

If you fail to assign specific access privileges to a user, that user is granted the default access privilege. You can change the default access privilege, which is the privilege granted to all users except those specifically granted another access privilege.

To set the default access privilege, follow these steps:

1. Choose the Options Set Access Privileges command to display the Set Access Privileges dialog box (refer to fig. 11.25).

2. In the Users box, select *default* if that option is not already selected.

3. Select one of the access privilege options from the Privileges group.

   The access privilege options are described in table 11.1.

Table 11.1 User Access Privileges

Option	Description
None	No access
View Free/Busy Times	User can view the times when you are free or busy but cannot view the descriptions of your appointments.
Read Appointments & Tasks	User can read your appointments and tasks but cannot modify them.
Create Appointments & Tasks	User can add new appointments and tasks to your Appointment Book and Task List.

continues

Table 11.1 Continued

Option	Description
Modify Appointments & Tasks	User can modify your appointments and tasks.
Assistant	User can act as your assistant, so as to view and modify your schedule, schedule meetings, and reply to meeting requests.

4. Choose OK or press Enter.

Designating Specific Privileges to a User

To designate a specific privilege other than the default privilege to a user, follow these steps:

1. Choose the **O**ptions Set **A**ccess Privileges command.

2. Select the user's name from the **U**sers box if the name appears there.

    or

    Choose the **A**dd button and select the user's name from the names list.

    If the list does not include the name of the person whose access privilege you want to set, click on the Directory button (the icon of the open book) or press Ctrl+L and select a new directory in the Open Directory dialog box.

3. Choose the **A**dd button, and click OK or press Enter. Then select the user's name from the **U**sers box.

4. Select from among the options in the Privileges group. Table 11.1 describes each option.

5. Choose OK or press Enter.

You can determine what access privileges a user has to your schedule by choosing **O**ptions Set **A**ccess Privileges, selecting the user whose access privileges you want to view, and looking in the Privileges group to see which privilege is selected. Choose Cancel to close the dialog box.

Viewing or Modifying Another User's Appointment Book or Task List

If other users grant you access privileges to their schedules, you can work with their schedules. You may be restricted to viewing other users' schedules, but even this privilege can help you schedule a meeting at a time available to everyone you want to invite. If your access level is more extensive, you may have the privilege not only of viewing another user's appointments or tasks but even of adding to or modifying that user's appointments or tasks. Your level of access to another user's schedule depends on what access privilege the user has granted you. (See "Designating Specific Privileges to a User," earlier in this chapter, for details on how access privileges are assigned to a user.)

To work with another user's schedule you must open that user's Appointment Book. To open another user's Appointment Book, follow these steps:

1. Choose the **F**ile **O**pen Other's Appt Book command. The Open Other's Appt. Book dialog box appears, as shown in figure 11.26.

2. Select the user's name from the Directory box if the name is listed, and choose **A**dd.

   If the list does not include the name of the person whose Appointment Book you want to open, click on the Directory button (the icon of the open book) or press Ctrl+L and select a new directory in the Open Directory dialog box.

3. Choose OK or press Enter.

The user's Appointment Book appears in your Schedule window. If you do not have access to that user's Appointment Book, you are informed of that restriction. After you have opened a user's Appointment Book, you can work with it in the same way as you work with your own Appointment Book, except that you can perform only those operations for which you have been granted access. To access the user's Task List, click the Task tab on the left side of the Appointment Book or press Alt+T.

Taking Your Appointments, Tasks, and Notes with You

You would be very limited if you were restricted to viewing your Appointment Book, Task List, and notes only on-screen. Schedule+ enables you to print your appointments, tasks, and notes in various formats to carry in your briefcase, insert in your personal scheduling notebook, or post on your wall.

Printing Your Appointments and Notes

To print your appointments and daily notes, follow these steps:

1. If you are not already in your schedule window, choose the **W**indow menu and select your name (or type the number next to your name).

2. If your Appointment Book is not already displayed, click on the *Appts* tab along the left side of the window or press Alt+A.

3. Choose the **F**ile **P**rint command (or press Ctrl+P) to display the Print dialog box (see fig. 11.27).

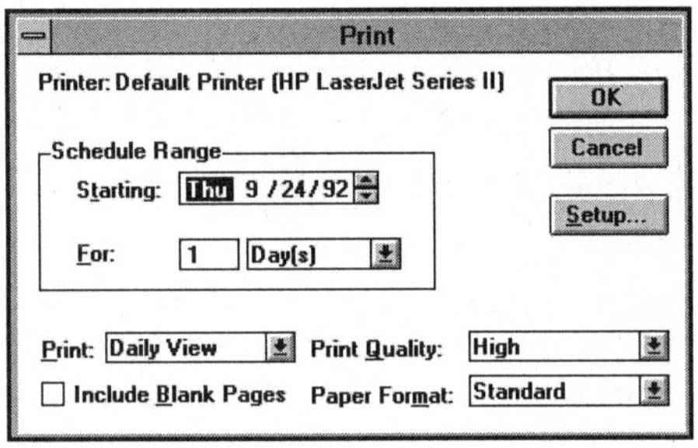

FIG. 11.27

The Print dialog box.

4. Select a starting date for the printout in the **S**tarting box, and how many days you want the printout to include in the **F**or box.

5. Select how you want your printout organized in the **P**rint drop-down list.

6. Select the print quality you want from the Print **Q**uality drop-down list.

7. Select the size of your printout from the Paper For**m**at drop-down list. These paper formats are designed to fit many personal and desktop scheduling or time-management systems.

   To change the margins of your printout, choose the **S**etup button to display the Print Setup dialog box (see fig. 11.28). Change the settings in the Ma**r**gins edit boxes and choose OK or press Enter. You can also make other changes related to your printer in this dialog box.

8. Choose OK or press Enter.

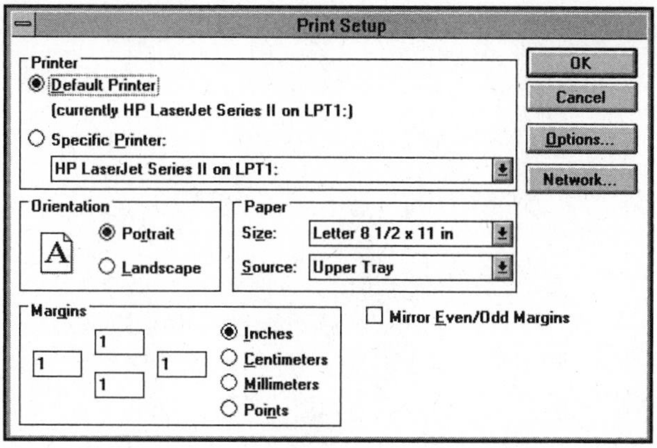

FIG. 11.28

The Print Setup
dialog box.

Printing Your Tasks

To print your tasks, follow these steps:

1. If you are not already in your schedule window, choose the **W**indow menu and select your name (or type the number next to your name).

2. If your Task List is not already displayed, click on the *Tasks* tab along the left side of the window or press Alt+T.

3. Choose to display all your tasks or just your active tasks. (See the section "Sorting Projects and Tasks," earlier in this chapter.)

4. Choose whether to display your tasks by project (see "Sorting Projects and Tasks").

5. Sort your tasks by priority, due date, or description (see "Sorting Projects and Tasks").

6. Choose the **File Print** command.

7. Choose Tasks from the **Print** drop-down list.

8. Choose OK or press Enter.

Customizing Schedule+

Several options are available for customizing the way Schedule+ looks and behaves. You can change the colors used in displaying Schedule+ with the **O**ptions **D**isplay command. You can change the password you

use to log into Schedule+ with the **O**ptions **C**hange Password command. Several other options can be controlled by using the **O**ptions
General Options command.

Changing Schedule+ Colors

To change the colors used in Schedule+:

1. Choose the **O**ptions **D**isplay command to display the Display
   dialog box (see fig. 11.29).

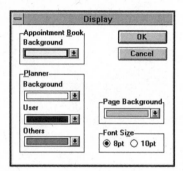

The Display
dialog box.

2. Select the colors you want to use for the different elements of
   Schedule+ and change the font size for the display, if necessary.

3. Choose OK or press Enter.

Changing Your Password

You must be working on-line when you change your password, since
passwords are maintained on the mail server. See beginning of chapter
for details on how to work on-line. To change your password, follow
these steps:

1. Choose the **O**ptions **C**hange Password command.

2. Type your current password in the Change Password dialog box.

3. Choose OK or press Enter.

4. Type the new password.

5. Choose OK or press Enter.

6. Type the new password again, to verify your new password.

7. Choose OK or press Enter.

 NOTE This password is the same password you use to sign into Mail, so after you change your password in Schedule+, you must use this new password when you sign into Mail.

Changing Other Schedule+ Options

To select other options that affect how Schedule+ works:

1. Choose the **O**ptions General Options command to display the General Options dialog box (see fig. 11.30.)

General Options

- ☐ Startup **O**ffline
- Reminders
  - ☒ Set **R**eminders for Notes
  - ☒ Set Reminders Automatically
  - **f**or [1] [hour(s) ▣] before appointments
  - ☒ Sound A**u**dible Alarm

Day **S**tarts at: [8 : 00 AM ▣]

Day **E**nds at: [5 : 00 PM ▣]

Week Starts on: [Monday ▣]

- ☒ Show Week Numbers in the **C**alendar
- ☐ Send **M**eeting Messages Only to my Assistant
- ☐ This **A**ccount is for a Resource

[OK] [Cancel]

FIG. 11.30

The General Options dialog box.

2. Change whatever options you want. See table 11.2 for a description of each of the options.

Table 11.2 Description of General Options

Option	Description
Startup Offline	After selected, Schedule+ starts up in the off-line mode and creates a *local file* for your schedule. This option is useful when working with Schedule+ installed on a portable or home computer.

continues

Table 11.2 Continued

Option	Description
Set Reminders for Notes	After selected, a reminder pops up on days with a note attached.
Set Reminders Automatically	After this option is selected, a reminder is set for all new appointments, using the default reminder settings.
Sound Audible Alarm	After selected, an audible alarm sounds when a reminder message pops up.
Day Starts at	Determines the starting hour for your workday.
Day Ends at	Determines the ending hour for your workday.
Week Starts On	Determines what day your working week starts on.
Show Week Numbers in the Calendar	After selected, the number for each week is displayed along the left side of the calendar in your Appointment Book.
Send Meeting Messages Only to My Assistant	After selected, only the user you have designated as your assistant receives meeting requests and responses to meeting requests.
This Account is for a Resource	Designates an account as a resource. See "Scheduling a Resource."

Exiting Schedule+

You can exit Schedule+ in one of two ways: You can quit Schedule+ but stay logged onto Mail, or you can exit Schedule+ and Mail with one command.

To exit Schedule+ only:

Choose the **F**ile E**x**it command.

To exit Schedule+ and Mail:

Choose the **F**ile E**x**it command and Sign Out.

Chapter Summary

Schedule+ can improve how you and the people around you work. You can use Schedule+ to manage your own time, making sure you get back to people on time and don't miss appointments or deadlines. You can even use its Task List to set priorities for all the things you have to do. If you are the type of person who is on the go and can't be tied to a scheduler in your desktop computer, then you can copy Schedule+ to your portable or laptop computer or even print pages that fit in most standard personal time management books or schedulers.

Everyone in your workgroup can take advantage of Schedule+ and stop wasting time doing the meeting room shuffle. Schedule+, combined with Mail's capability to send and acknowledge messages, enables you to check when key people are available for meetings and see which meeting rooms and other facilities are available. Schedule+ uses Mail to notify attendees when the meeting will be. You can even request a return receipt that acknowledges the meeting.

Windows for Workgroups can really help you build a team to solve business problems. Use Mail to send and receive messages and pass files and documents to others. It's quick and you don't have to get tied up in conversations about the weekend, traffic, and the spouse and kids. Mail is described in Chapter 10. Don't forget to read Chapter 5 about the File Manager. It's one of the first features most workgroups use. With the File Manager, you can share selected directories between members of the workgroup. No more of the "Nike network" using the running shoes to carry the latest file around to workgroup members. Now, everyone can stay up-to-date with the most current files, templates, and documents.

Using Windows Write

W rite is a simple but powerful word processor for Windows. Although it is one of the easiest word processors to use, Write can handle the majority of general business typing needs and produces high-quality results. It offers many of the editing and formatting capabilities commonly found in more advanced applications, including the following:

■ Moving and copying text

■ Finding and replacing text

■ Undoing the last edit

■ Setting tabs, indentations, and margins

■ Enhancing text with boldface, italic, and underline

■ Changing text font and size

■ Centering and justifying text

■ Adding headers, footers, and page numbers

Write offers an advantage that many applications don't provide: the capability of sharing information with other applications and files. You easily can cut, copy, and paste text and graphics between Write documents. Because Write also is a Windows application, you can move text and graphics between Write and other applications, including Windows accessories (such as Notepad and Paintbrush), Windows applications (such as Excel and Word for Windows), and standard DOS applications (such as Lotus 1-2-3). Write handles one document at a time, but you can have many copies of the Write application open at once, each in a separate on-screen window.

Another advantage to Write is that it uses the same structure of menus, commands, icons, and dialog boxes that all Windows applications use. Therefore, what you learn about managing text in Write applies to most of the Windows applications involving text. The consistency of the Windows environment makes learning new applications quick and easy.

Write files are fully compatible with files created by Word and Word for Windows, Microsoft's full-featured Windows word processors. Word and Word for Windows offer features, such as mail merge, spell checking, and automatic indexes and footnotes, and are ideal for long documents or complex editing tasks. Write is a simpler application, and is ideal for many day-to-day word processing needs.

Creating Write Documents

Creating a Write document is as simple as starting the application and typing the text. Because margins, a font, and tabs are already set, you can begin using Write as soon as you start the application.

Write is similar in operation to other Windows applications, and its screen contains many of the same elements that you see in other Windows applications. Write is a simple application that opens only a single document at a time, but, in this chapter, you learn how to start Write a second time if you want to work on more than one Write document at a time.

Starting Write

Because Write is a Windows accessory, you must start Windows before you can start Write. In general, you can start Windows by typing *WIN* at the DOS prompt. The computer, however, may be set up differently; to learn more about starting and setting up Windows, refer to Chapter 1, "Operating Windows," Chapter 4, "Controlling Applications with the Program Manager," and Chapter 25, "Enhancing Windows Performance."

After you start Windows, follow these steps to start Write:

1. Open the Accessories group window from within the Program Manager.

2. With the mouse, double-click the Write icon. With the keyboard, select the Write icon by pressing the direction keys and then press Enter.

Starting Write opens a new Write file (see fig. 12.1).

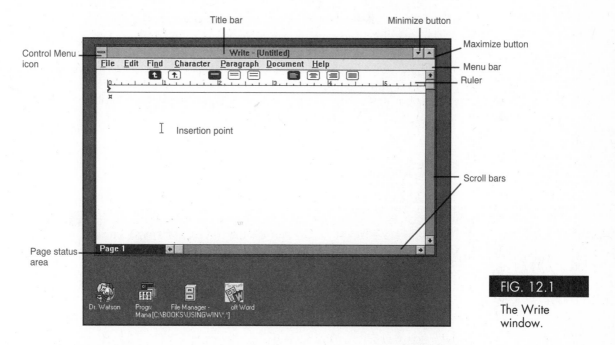

FIG. 12.1

The Write window.

The Write window includes a title bar at the top, which shows the name of the document (a new document is known as *Untitled*). Below the title bar is the menu bar. A maximize and minimize button at the top right of Write's window enable you to shrink the window to an icon or expand the window to fill the screen. Scroll bars, along the bottom and right sides, show the relative position in the document and let you move around in the document. A status box at the bottom left tells you the page number.

As with all Windows applications, Write windows are manipulated by a Control menu located at the top left of the window. The Control menu icon looks like a space bar; you open the menu by pressing Alt and the space bar. The remaining menus control Write and are unique to Write (although the **F**ile and **E**dit menus work the same way in Write as they do in most Windows applications). Write's menu operations are covered in following sections of this chapter.

Using Menus and Dialog Boxes

To better work with Write, you may want to review Windows' operation. You can choose from a menu by one of these methods:

Mouse: Click the menu heading; then click the command.

Keyboard: Press Alt, press the underlined letter in the menu heading, and then press the underlined letter in the command. Alternatively, press Alt, press the left- or right-arrow key to move to the menu heading, press the up- or down-arrow key to move to the command, and then press Enter.

You can move between areas in a dialog box using one of these methods:

Mouse: Click the text box or option.

Keyboard: Press Tab to move forward or Shift+Tab to move backward to another option area. Alternatively, press Alt plus the underlined letter of the option you want to set.

After you select an area of a dialog box, turn selections on or off by using one of these methods:

Mouse: Click the selection.

Keyboard: To turn on square check boxes or round option buttons, press Alt plus the underlined letter. To turn off a square check box, press Alt plus the underlined letter a second time. To turn off a round option button, press Alt plus the underlined letter of a different option or press the left- or right-arrow key to move to a different option button. Another way to turn on and off a selected check box is to press the space bar.

After you make the dialog box selections, carry out the command using one of these methods:

Mouse: Click the command button (such as OK or Cancel).

Keyboard: Select the command button (such as OK or Cancel) and press the Enter key.

In the top left of the text area is a flashing insertion point followed by an end mark. The insertion point (sometimes known as a *cursor* in other word processors) is where text appears when you start typing; the end mark shows where the file ends. Move the insertion point by typing text, pressing the arrow keys, or by moving the mouse pointer (an I-beam) to a different location and clicking the mouse button. Remember that you can never move the insertion point beyond the end mark (if you want to move the end mark further down, position the insertion point before the end mark and press Enter as many times as you want).

The ruler, used for quick formatting, is an optional element in the Write window and doesn't appear when you first start Write, but remains on throughout a Write session after you display it in any one document. To learn about the ruler, refer to the sections on formatting text, paragraphs, and the document later in the chapter.

Starting Write and an Existing Document Together

You can open an existing Write document directly from the File Manager if the file ends with the extension WRI. Simply open the document as though you were starting the Write application: double-click the Write document (a WRI file) with the mouse or select the document from the keyboard and press Enter. Another way to open Write and an existing document together is to select the WRI file and choose the File Open command.

You also can open Write and a Write document together by associating Write and the document together in a program item icon in the Program Manager. To learn how, refer to Chapter 4, "Controlling Applications with the Program Manager."

Creating a Write Document

The easiest way to create a new Write document is to start Write, which opens a new file. A blank Write window (the document) appears.

In Write, you can work on only one document at a time. You can start a new document (or open a different document) while you are working on an existing Write document, but the existing document closes. If you haven't saved changes to the existing document, you see the dialog box shown in figure 12.2, asking whether you want to save the changes. Choose Yes to save the changes, No to discard the changes, or Cancel to return to the existing document. When you save the existing file, the window clears, and a new, blank document appears. (For details about saving, read the section "Saving and Naming a Write File.")

478

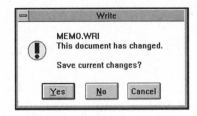

Typing in Write

A new Write window is empty except for the blinking insertion point
and the end mark. You can begin typing as soon as you open a file. If
you make a mistake, press Backspace to back up and erase one character at a time. You also can ignore the mistakes and edit them later.
(Editing techniques are explained later in this chapter.)

When you reach the end of a line, continue typing. Write by default
wraps the text to the next line. Press Enter to begin a new paragraph.
Press Enter twice to leave a space between paragraphs. As you fill the
page, the screen scrolls down (or left and right), keeping the insertion
point in view.

Keep Margins Narrower Than the Screen
If the text is wider than the screen, the Write window scrolls left
and right as you type. Some people find this annoying. To prevent
left-to-right scrolling, set the margins so that the text is narrower
than the width of the screen. (Do this by making the margins
wider.) If you want, you can return the margins to their original
settings before you print the document.

Opening an Existing Write Document

To view, edit, or print a file already created and saved, you must open
the file.

To open an existing file from within Write, follow these steps:

1. Choose the **File O**pen command. The Open dialog box appears
   (see fig. 12.3), which contains the items listed in table 12.1.

2. From the **D**rives list, select the drive containing the file you want to open (do this only to open a file on a drive different from the drive currently displayed in the **D**irectories list).

3. From the **D**irectories list, select the directory containing the file you want to open.

4. From the File **N**ame list, select the file you want to open.

5. Choose OK or press Enter.

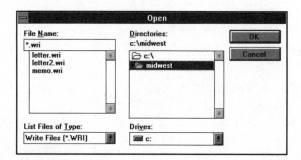

FIG. 12.3

The Open dialog box.

Table 12.1 Parts of the Open Dialog Box

Item	Description
Drives	From the list, select the drive containing the file you want to open.
Directories	Select the directory containing the file you want to open.
List Files of **T**ype	Select the file type you want to list in the File **N**ame list.
File **N**ame	From the list, select the file you want to open. Or, in the text box, type the name of the file you want to open. (If you want to open a file in a different directory than the one listed in the **D**irectories list, type the full path name.)
OK	Opens the file or directory selected in the list box.
Cancel	Returns to the current document.

Working with Multiple Write Documents

There is a way to work with multiple Write documents: open the Write application multiple times. Follow the instructions in "Starting Write," earlier in this chapter to start Write the first time from the Windows Program Manager. Follow the same procedure to start Write again. You can have a separate document in each Write window, and you can copy or move text (and pictures) between documents using the Edit Cut, Edit Copy, and Edit Paste commands.

The number of times you can open Write is limited only by the amount of memory in the computer. Because the different copies of Write share parts of their program code, you can open more copies than seems possible for a given amount of memory.

Working with Multiple Copies of Write Is Easy
Working with multiple copies of Write makes comparing different documents, or copying or moving information between documents, easy. There are two ways to work with multiple copies of Write. One is to maximize the Write application you're currently working with, minimize it when you're finished, and then maximize the next Write application. Another is to keep all the Write windows open and overlapping on-screen and to switch between the windows by clicking the one you want with the mouse button or by pressing Alt+Tab.

FROM HERE...

For Related Information:

◄◄ To learn more about associating applications and documents in the Program Manager, see "Customizing Groups," p. 119.

◄◄ See "Controlling the Windows in Windows," p. 30.

◄◄ See "Starting an Application from the Program Manager," p. 75.

►► See "Responding to an Application Failure," p. 1071.

Moving through the Document

Before you can edit the text, you must be able to move the insertion point through the document. You can use either the keyboard or the mouse to move the insertion point.

To use the mouse to move the insertion point to a different location on-screen, move the I-beam where you want the insertion point and click the mouse button. To scroll to a different area of the document, use the scroll bars at the right and bottom edges of the window. To scroll vertically with a mouse, click the arrows at the top or bottom of the scroll bar at the right edge of the window. Scroll left or right over the document by clicking the arrow at the left or right end of the horizontal scroll bar at the bottom of the screen. Click in the gray area in either scroll bar to jump up or down, or left or right, one screen at a time. Drag the scroll box in either scroll bar to make a large jump to another position in the document. (The scroll box in the scroll bar indicates your relative position in the document. If, for example, the box is in the middle of the scroll bar, then you are near the middle of the document.)

To move with the keyboard, use the techniques listed in table 12.2.

Table 12.2 Keystrokes for Moving the Insertion Point

Movement	Press
Single character	Left-arrow or right-arrow key
Single line	Up-arrow or down-arrow key
Next or previous word	Ctrl+left-arrow key or Ctrl+right-arrow key
Beginning of the line	Home
End of the line	End
Next or previous sentence	Goto (5 on the keypad)+left-arrow or right-arrow key
Next or previous paragraph	Goto (5 on the keypad)+up-arrow or down-arrow key
Top or bottom of window	Ctrl+PgUp or Ctrl+PgDn
Next or previous page	Goto (5 on the keypad)+PgUp or PgDn
Continuous movement	Hold any of the above keys or key combinations
One screen	PgUp or PgDn
Beginning of document	Ctrl+Home
End of document	Ctrl+End

To jump to a specific page, follow these instructions:

1. Choose the Find Go To Page command (or press F4).

2. Type the page number in the Go To dialog box.

3. Choose OK or press Enter.

> **You Cannot Go Where There Is No Text**
> Remember, the insertion point cannot travel past the end mark in a document. If you want to move the insertion point farther down, press Enter to add more blank lines to the end of a document.

Selecting and Editing Text

Editing the text you type is one of a word processor's most important capabilities. Write gives you the power to add to, delete from, change, move, copy, or replace text. You even can change your mind and undo the last edit.

You can make simple edits by moving the insertion point and deleting or inserting text. But more complex editing requires that you first *select* the text you want to edit. In fact, the rule "select, then do" applies in Write just as it does in many other Windows applications: you must *select* text before you can *do* something to it.

Inserting and Deleting One Character at a Time

To make simple insertions, place the insertion point where you want to add text and begin typing. The new text is "threaded" into existing text. Simple deletions also are easy. To erase one character at a time, position the insertion point next to the character and press Backspace (to delete characters to the left) or Del (to delete characters to the right). By default, Write reformats the paragraph.

Undoing an Edit

Write lets you change your mind about an edit you just made or a sentence you just typed. To undo, select **E**dit **U**ndo or press Alt+Backspace or Ctrl+Z. You can restore text you just deleted, delete text you just added, or remove formatting. You can even undo an undo.

When you undo typing, the text is removed back to the location of the last nontyping insertion-point movement or the last file save. The Undo Typing command has no character limit. If you find that **E**dit **U**ndo removes too much typing, choose **E**dit **U**ndo a second time to undo the undo.

Notice that the **E**dit **U**ndo command changes depending on the kind of edit you have made. For example, the command may appear as **U**ndo Typing, **U**ndo Formatting, or **U**ndo Editing.

Selecting Text

Many edits you need to make are more complex than simply entering or deleting one character at a time. You may want to change a word, delete a sentence, or move a whole paragraph. Or you may want to change the appearance of text or format a paragraph. To do these things, you must identify the text you want to edit or format by *selecting* it. Selected text appears in reverse video on-screen, as shown in figure 12.4. You can select the text using either the mouse or the keyboard, or a combination of the two.

To select text with the mouse, position the I-beam at the beginning of the text, hold down the mouse button, drag to the end of the text, and release the mouse button. Write also offers time-saving selection shortcuts, such as double-clicking to select a word. The selection bar also is convenient. The *selection bar* is the white space between the left edge of the screen and the left margin of the text. (For example, in fig. 12.4, the selection bar is the blank area between the left edge of the Write window and the left edge of the text in the letter.) When you move the I-beam to the selection bar, the I-beam turns into a right-pointing arrow. You can select a line of text by pointing at the line and clicking the mouse button. Dragging the mouse pointer down the selection bar selects entire lines and paragraphs at a time.

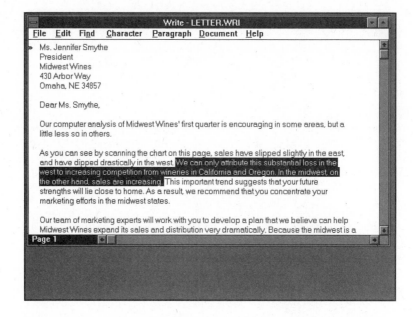

FIG. 12.4

Two sentences
selected for
editing.

Techniques for selecting with the mouse are shown in table 12.3.

Table 12.3 Techniques for Selecting with the Mouse

Selection	Action
One word	Double-click the word.
Several words	Double-click the first word and drag to the end of the last word.
Any amount of text	Press the mouse button and drag from the beginning to the end of the text.
Between two points	Move the insertion point to the beginning, click, move to the second point, press and hold down Shift, and click at the second point.
One line	Click the selection bar (white space) to the left of the line.
Several lines	Press the mouse button and drag up or down in the selection bar.
Paragraph	Double-click in the selection bar to the left of the paragraph.
Entire document	Press Ctrl and click in the selection bar.

To select text with the keyboard, press and hold down Shift while moving the insertion point with the arrow keys. To select a word at a time, press Shift+Ctrl+left-arrow key or right-arrow key. In fact, by holding down Shift, you can select text while you move the insertion point using any of the techniques described in table 12.2.

To deselect text with the mouse, click once anywhere in the text portion of the window. To deselect text with the keyboard, press any arrow key. Deselected text returns to its normal appearance.

Deleting Text

To delete a block of text, select it and press Delete or Backspace or choose the **Edit Cut** command. You also can replace text by selecting it and then typing; Write deletes the selected block and inserts the new words.

When you delete text by pressing Delete or Backspace, the text is erased for good, and you can only get it back by selecting the **Edit Undo** command. But if you delete text by choosing **Edit Cut**, you can retrieve it by choosing **Edit Paste** (see the next section on "Moving Text").

Moving Text

Any amount of text—a letter, a word, part of a sentence, or several pages—can be moved from one place in a document to another. The process is like "cutting" and "pasting" the text with glue and scissors. Start by selecting the text. Text you cut is stored in the *Clipboard*, a temporary memory space that holds one (and only one) selection at a time.

When you move text, remember that the text is stored in the Clipboard and that the Clipboard holds only one selection at a time. The next text you cut replaces what was in the Clipboard. When you move text, paste the text immediately after cutting so that you do not lose the information.

To move text, follow these steps:

1. Select the text to be moved.

2. Choose the **Edit Cut** command or press Shift+Del or Ctrl+X to cut the text to the Clipboard.

3. Move the insertion point to the new location for the text you cut.

4. Choose the **Edit Paste** command or press Shift+Ins or Ctrl+V to paste the text in its new location.

> **An Easy Way To Remember the Cut and Paste Keys**
> Remembering two of the shortcut keys for cutting and pasting is easy. Just think that you want to *shift* text to a new location, so you Shift+Del (Delete) it from one location and Shift+Ins (Insert) it to a new location.

You can use the mouse and these steps as another method for moving text:

1. Select the text to be moved.

2. Using the scroll bars, scroll the screen until you can see the point where you want to relocate the text. (Do not move the insertion point, which deselects the text selected in step 1.)

3. Press and hold down Shift+Alt; click the mouse button where you want the text to appear. The selected text is cut and pasted where you clicked.

Copying Text

You can copy text from one place to another or to several other places in a document. The process is similar to moving, but the original text is left in place.

Copied text is stored in the Clipboard (as is cut text) and can be pasted as often as you like. Remember that cutting or copying another block of text replaces the existing contents of the Clipboard.

To copy text, follow these steps:

1. Select the text to be copied.

2. Choose the **Edit Copy** command or press F2, Ctrl+Ins, or Ctrl+C.

3. Move the insertion point to the place in the document where you want to copy the text.

4. Choose the **Edit Paste** command or press Shift+Ins or Ctrl+V.

You can paste additional copies of the text in the Clipboard by moving the insertion point and choosing **Edit Paste** again.

You can use the mouse and these steps as a shortcut for copying text:

1. Select the text to be copied.

2. Scroll the screen to display where you want the copied text. (Make sure that the text remains selected.)

3. Press and hold down Alt; click the mouse button where you want the text to be copied.

Finding and Replacing Text

You can use Write to help search a document to find or change text— for example, to change a misspelled name or correct an old date. The **Find** menu includes three commands that help you find text and make changes quickly: **Find**, Repeat **L**ast Find, and **R**eplace.

The **Find Find** and **Find Replace** commands operate through dialog boxes. After you enter the text you want to find or change, Write starts at the insertion point and searches forward through the document. It finds and selects the first occurrence of the text. At this point, you have three choices: you can move the insertion point into the document and edit the text while the dialog box remains on-screen; you can close the dialog box; or you can continue searching for the next occurrence of the text. Close the dialog box when the search is complete. (To move the insertion point between the document and the dialog box, click the document with the mouse or press Alt+F6 on the keyboard.)

If Write cannot match the text you indicated, Write shows a dialog box with the message Text not found.

If this happens, choose the OK button and try a different search word.

Undoing 12 Years of Bad Habits Taught in School

Twelve years of schooling has conditioned most people to write perfect sentences, with perfect structure, and without spelling or grammar errors. The problem is that we are conditioned to try to do all this on the first try. However, people don't work in this way. As a result, many people say "I can't write" and others say "I've got writer's block."

One of the greatest benefits of writing with a word processor is that you need not get it right the first time. Just be concerned with getting the ideas down. You can reorganize and correct them later. You should type your ideas as fast as you can, one idea to a paragraph. Don't worry about spelling or grammar. Never stop writing. When you come across a number, name, date, or fact you don't know, enter a "missing-information" marker and keep typing. If you stop writing to look up a fact or get a book, you can lose ideas and may have to warm up to writing all over again.

Following are some markers you can leave in the text to flag incomplete thoughts:

Marker	Meaning
???	Unknown text
###	Unknown numbers and dates
***	Note to yourself or someone sharing the document

After you have the ideas listed, go back and use the Edit commands to reorganize the good material, delete the bad material, and filter out the unnecessary material. Expand the ideas into sentences and paragraphs. Brutally slash out unneeded words, sentences, and paragraphs. Cut and cut until the writing is clear and concise. Use Find Find to locate the markers in the document. Then, go back and check grammar and spelling.

To find text, follow these steps:

1. Choose the Find Find command. Figure 12.5 shows the Find dialog box. Move the dialog box if it obstructs your view of the document.

2. Type the text you want to find in the Find What text box.

3. Select the Match Whole Word Only check box to match only whole words. Select the Match Case check box to match capitalization.

4. Choose the **F**ind Next button or press the Enter key.

5. When Write is finished finding, you see a dialog box that reads `Find Complete`. Choose OK or press Enter.

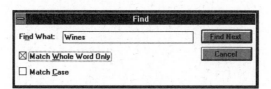

To close the Find dialog box, press Esc or choose Cancel. To repeat the last find, choose Fi**nd** Repeat **L**ast Find or press F3.

Finding Close Matches

You can use Fi**nd** **F**ind and Fi**nd** **R**eplace to find words even when you are not certain which words you want. Do this by using a wild card in the words. For example, the question mark wild card represents unknown characters. If you want to look for *Smith* or *Smythe*, but are unsure whether the name is spelled with a *y* or an *i*, you can search for *Sm?th?*. Write finds occurrences of both *Smith* and *Smythe*.

The following chart lists the wild cards you can use with Fi**nd** **F**ind and Fi**nd** **R**eplace. The caret mark (^) is Shift+6 on the keyboard.

Wild Card	Item Selected
?	Any character
^w	Any empty (white) space
^t	Tab
^p	Paragraph end mark
^d	Manual page break

You can find text in only part of your document by selecting that part before choosing the Fi**nd** **F**ind command.

T I P

Write also enables you to make repetitive changes rapidly throughout the document with the Find Replace command. Some word processors call this a search-and-replace feature.

To change text, follow these steps:

1. Choose the Find Replace command. The dialog box shown in figure 12.6 appears.

2. Type the text you want to find in the Find What text box.

3. Type the text you want to replace the selected text with in the Replace With text box.

4. Check the Match Whole Word Only check box to match only whole words. Check the Match Case box to match capitalization.

5. Choose the Find Next button to select the next occurrence of the text.

6. Select the type of change you want. Following are the selections you can make and a description of the change made:

Find Next	The first time used, it finds the first occurrence of the text. Used subsequently, it finds the next occurrence of the text without replacing the current occurrence.
Replace	Makes the change on the found text and then finds the next occurrence.
Replace All	Changes the specified text throughout the document.

7. When Write is finished replacing, you see a dialog box that reads Find Complete. Choose OK and then choose the Close button.

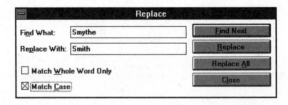

FIG. 12.6

The Replace dialog box.

T I P   You can replace text in only part of your document by selecting that part before choosing the Find Replace command. The Replace All button changes to read Replace Selection.

Formatting Characters

Formatting or enhancing letters and words—by changing the size and style of the letters, or adding boldfacing, underlining, and so on—can improve the appearance of almost any document. Using Write, you have the capacity of enhancing and emphasizing text much like a typesetter.

The **C**haracter menu controls the appearance of characters. If you already have typed the characters, you can change their appearance by selecting the text and choosing commands from the **C**haracter menu. (If you're not sure how to select text, refer to the earlier section in this chapter, "Selecting Text.") If you have not yet typed the text, position the insertion point where you want the enhanced text to begin, choose the enhancement, and type the text. Choose the enhancement a second time to turn off the enhancement (alternatively, choose **C**haracter Regular or press F5 to turn off all enhancements).

Enhancing Text with Boldface, Italic, and Underline

Boldface, italic, and underline are character enhancements you can use to signify something special in the text: a level of meaning, a pause in the thought process, a change of topic. **Boldface** is useful for calling attention to important text or for creating subheadings in a long document. *Italic* identifies titles and can be used for calling attention to text. Underlining works well for list headings and section breaks. Using these devices consistently helps make reading the document easy and pleasurable.

Many of the character enhancement options, shown in the **C**haracter menu in figure 12.7, "toggle" on and off like a light switch—you turn them on the same way you turn them off: by choosing the command. To make plain text bold, for example, you select the text and choose the **B**old command; to make bold text plain, you do the same thing. The **C**haracter menu shows a check mark next to selected enhancements. Some enhancements, such as bold and italic, can be used together, so you see two check marks. (Shortcuts for choosing enhancements include Ctrl+*key* combinations, as shown in the **C**haracter menu, and function keys listed in the following steps.)

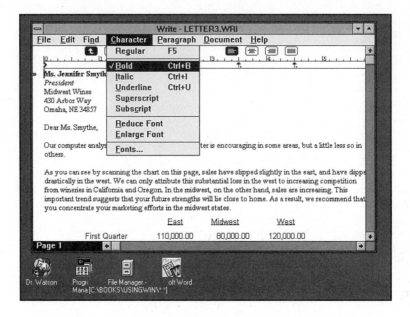

FIG. 12.7

The **C**haracter menu and examples of enhanced text.

You can enhance existing text, or you can enhance new text as you type.

To enhance text, follow these steps:

1. Select the existing text or position the insertion point where you want the enhancement to begin.

2. Choose the **C**haracter menu.

3. Choose one or more of the following commands: **B**old, **I**talic, **U**nderline.

4. Move the insertion point to deselect the text or type the enhanced text and choose the enhancement command a second time to toggle it off.

Several shortcuts exist for quickly enhancing text:

Enhancement	Function Key	Ctrl+Key Combination
Boldface	F6	Ctrl+B
Italic	F7	Ctrl+I
Underline	F8	Ctrl+U

Most fonts (including TrueType fonts) come in four styles: regular, italic, bold, and bold italic. You can add these enhancements through the **C**haracter menu or by using shortcuts, but you can also add them through the Font dialog box. To learn how, refer to the section "Changing the Font." Using the Font dialog box is handy when you want to make several changes to the same text because it enables you to change the font, font style, and font size all at once.

Removing enhancements is easy. If text has more than one enhancement, you can remove just the enhancement you don't want.

To remove an enhancement, follow these steps:

1. Select the enhanced text.

2. Choose the enhancement from the **C**haracter menu or press the appropriate function or Ctrl+key combination.

To remove all enhancements, follow these steps:

1. Select the enhanced text.

2. Choose the **C**haracter Re**g**ular command or press F5.

Because character enhancements toggle on and off, be careful how you select text when you want to remove an enhancement. If, for example, you select a boldfaced word and choose the **B**old command, the boldface is removed. But if you select a bold word along with a plain word or character and then choose the **B**old command, boldface is applied to both words.

T I P

Creating Superscripts and Subscripts

Superscripts (raised text) and *subscripts* (lowered text) are useful in science, math, and footnoting: for example, H_2O or "So proclaimed the King."[4] These features raise or lower the selected text and shrink it slightly so that the changed text fits easily between lines.

To create a superscript or a subscript, select the text to be raised or lowered. Then choose the **C**haracter Su**p**erscript command to raise the selected text or the **C**haracter Subscript command to lower the text.

Unavailable Enhancements

If you try to enhance text but the enhancement doesn't change on-screen or when printed, either the printer isn't capable of printing this enhancement, or you are using a printer driver that doesn't take advantage of the printer's capabilities. Chapter 7, "Customizing with the Control Panel," describes how to get a printer driver to match the printer.

Reducing and Enlarging Text

Another use for **C**haracter menu commands is to enhance a passage by changing the size of the type. You can enlarge type to the next larger size or reduce it to the next smaller size. (Write displays only the sizes the printer can print.)

Type sizes are measured in *points* (72 points per inch). A common size for text is 10 points, which produces about six lines of text per vertical inch. Many books and newspapers use 10-point type.

To change the size of characters you are about to type, choose **C**haracter **E**nlarge Font or **C**haracter **R**educe Font and then type the characters.

To enlarge or reduce text you have already typed, follow these steps:

1. Select the text.

2. Choose the **C**haracter **E**nlarge Font or the **C**haracter **R**educe Font command.

You can repeat this step, enlarging or reducing the text as large or small as you want.

Another way to change the font size is to use the **C**haracter **F**onts command, as follows:

1. Select the text to change.

2. Choose the **C**haracter **F**onts command.

3. Select the size you want from the **S**ize list or type the size you want in the **S**ize text box.

4. Choose OK or press Enter.

A sample of the font and font size appear in the Sample box.

Changing the Font

With Write, you are not limited to using a single *font* (the style or type-face of characters). Instead, you can choose from several fonts and sizes; with Windows and TrueType, the only restriction is the number of fonts that you own (to learn more about TrueType, refer to Chapter 8).

The Font dialog box also enables you to change the font style and size (see fig. 12.8). Table 12.4 lists the parts of the Font dialog box.

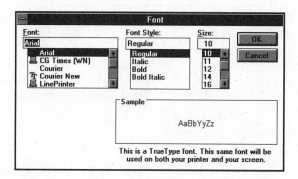

FIG. 12.8

The Font dialog box.

Table 12.4 Parts of the Font Dialog Box

Item	Description
Font	The Font text box displays the font selected in the Font list. You can select a font by choosing it from the list or by typing its name in the text box.
Font Style	Lists font styles for the selected font.
Size	Lists font sizes available for the selected font.
Sample	Shows a sample of the selected font, along with a message describing the nature of the font.

To choose a font, follow these steps:

1. Select the text to change.

2. Choose the **Character Fonts** command.

3. Select the font you want from the **Font** list or type the font you want in the **Font** box.

4. Select the style you want from the Font Style list.

5. Select the size you want from the **S**ize list or type the size in the **S**ize box.

6. Choose OK or press Enter.

In the **F**ont list, an icon to the left of each font describes the nature of the font. TrueType fonts have a "TT" icon; printer fonts have a printer icon (screen fonts have no icon).

The font you choose is displayed in the Sample box, along with a message describing the nature of the font. For example, the message accompanying the TrueType fonts shown in the figure explains that the same font will be used both on the screen and by the printer. If you choose a non-TrueType font, a message says, This is a printer font. The closest matching Windows font will be used on your screen. Using TrueType fonts give you a more accurate screen representation of the final output. To learn more about TrueType, refer to Chapter 8, "Managing Fonts."

Avoid Using Too Many Fonts on a Page
Graphic designers warn against cluttering a page with too many fonts. Although the temptation is great when you have such a wide selection, resist using more than two fonts in a document. Instead, choose one font and vary it with other enhancements. Make titles large, boldface, and centered. Italicize book titles. Make subheads boldface and perhaps one size larger than the text.

How do you choose a font? It depends on the purpose of the document. If a document has a lot of text, most publishers recommend a serif type. *Serifs* are the end strokes on characters that you see in most books and newspapers. Common serif types are Times New Roman and Palatino.

If, however, you are creating a document meant to be easily read from a distance, such as a foil (transparency), poster, or sign, choose a *sans serif* type (type with plain, straight letters). Common sans serif types include Arial and Helvetica.

Determining Fonts and Sizes
To find out what font or size a section of text is, select the text and choose **Character Fonts**. The current font and size are shown selected in the Font dialog box. If you selected text containing more than one font or size, the text boxes are empty; you should select a smaller amount of text.

Linking Text and Data

Through the Windows technology called object linking and embedding, or OLE, you can embed or link objects into a Write document. In "Including Pictures in a Document," later in this chapter, you learn how to embed and link pictures.

You also can link text and other data, such as a portion of an Excel spreadsheet, into your Write document. Linked objects retain their connection to the original file, and when you change the original, the linked copy in Write updates to reflect your changes. You can link the same object into many different Write documents—sharing information between documents.

OLE requires two types of applications: a server application, used to create the objects that are linked in a document; and a client application in which objects are linked. Write is an OLE client application. OLE servers include Word for Windows and Excel.

To link text or an object into a Write document, follow these steps:

1. Start the server application (such as Excel) and create the data you want to link into your Write document or open the file containing the data.

2. Save the original data file.

3. Select the data you want to link into Write and choose the Edit Copy command.

4. Switch to your Write document and position the insertion point where you want the linked data to appear.

5. Choose the Edit Paste Link command.

One of two things appears in your Write document, depending on the server application. Either you see an icon representing the data in your Write document, or you see the data itself. When you link text from Word for Windows, for example, you see an icon; when you link data from an Excel spreadsheet, you see a spreadsheet.

If you edit the original data file, the linked data in your Write document updates, by default, to reflect the changes. You can edit the data from within Write or in the server application. Editing links and linked data from within Write is the same as editing a link or a linked picture; to learn how, refer to the sections "Editing a Link" and "Editing Pictures" later in this chapter.

To learn more about object linking and embedding, refer to Chapter 6.

Formatting Paragraphs

Write (like all word processors) defines a *paragraph* as a block of text that ends with a return character (entered when you press the Enter or Return key on the keyboard). A paragraph may be two letters long, two lines long, or two pages long. You can create a new paragraph by pressing Enter at the end of any string of text. Press Enter twice to leave a blank line between paragraphs. Paragraph formatting is preserved when you move or copy text.

Paragraph formatting describes the appearance of a paragraph (or of a single line that stands by itself as a paragraph). Formatting includes characteristics such as centering, line justification, indentation, and line spacing. In Write, some formatting choices were made for you already: text is left-aligned, and no paragraphs are indented. You can change the paragraph format by using the **P**aragraph menu (see fig. 12.9) or the ruler.

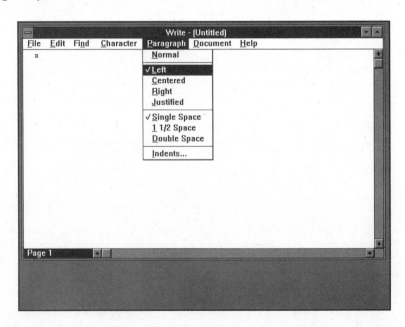

FIG. 12.9

The **P**aragraph menu lists commands for formatting paragraphs.

The optional ruler, shown in figure 12.10, provides a quick way to apply paragraph formatting if you have a mouse. You can use the ruler as a handy alternative to choosing commands from the **Paragraph** menu. (The ruler also is used as an alternative to the **Document Tabs** command for setting tabs.)

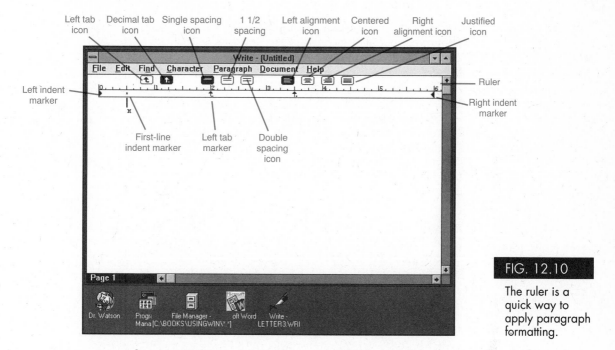

Choosing the **Document Ruler** On command displays the ruler at the top of the screen. The ruler reflects formatting exactly as it occurs in Write's menus; the ruler includes as icons any format settings you have made through menu commands. Therefore, if the insertion point is in a centered paragraph, the centering icon in the ruler is selected (reversed). If you move the insertion point to a left-aligned paragraph, the left-align icon is selected.

The ruler contains the following paragraph formatting features:

- A ruler with inch (or centimeter) markings

- Black triangles that set paragraph indents (within the page margins set with **Document Page Layout**)

- A white square inside the left indent triangle or a black square outside the left indent triangle that indicates a first-line indentation (or a hanging indent if it is to the left of the left indent marker)

■ Tab icons for left and decimal tabs

■ Three line-spacing icons for single spacing, one-and-a-half spacing, and double spacing

■ Four paragraph-alignment icons for left aligned, centered, right aligned, and justified paragraphs

To turn on the ruler, choose **D**ocument **R**uler On. To hide the ruler (without losing its settings), choose **D**ocument **R**uler Off. The ruler's zero point begins at the left margin set by the **D**ocument **P**age Layout command, not at the left edge of the page.

The End of Paragraph Mark Holds the Formatting Code
A paragraph's formatting is stored in the paragraph mark that defines the paragraph. This paragraph mark doesn't appear on-screen, but you can delete or select it. If you accidentally delete the paragraph mark, the paragraph merges with the paragraph below it, assuming the lower paragraph's formatting.

You may want to use the paragraph mark to copy a paragraph's formatting. To copy paragraph formatting, select the paragraph mark that belongs to the paragraph with the formatting you want to copy and choose the **E**dit **C**opy command (a quick way to select the paragraph mark is to double-click after the last character in the paragraph). Then select the paragraph mark for the paragraph you want to change and choose the **E**dit **P**aste command. The paragraph formatting is copied from the first paragraph to the second.

Aligning Paragraphs

In Write, paragraphs can be aligned with the left margin, the right margin, both the left and the right margins, or in the center between the margins. The alignment for the paragraph containing the insertion point is identified with a check mark in the **P**aragraph menu. The four different kinds of paragraph alignment are shown in figure 12.11.

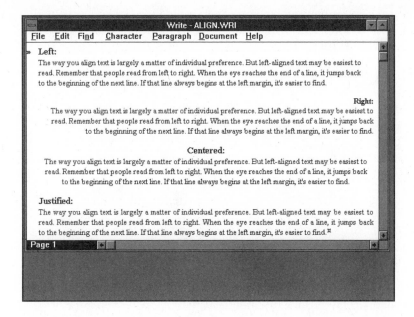

FIG. 12.11

Four ways to
align para-
graphs.

How you align text is largely a matter of individual preference, but following a couple of guidelines can improve readability. Left-aligned text
tends to be the easiest to read. When you reach the end of a line, your
eyes move back to the left margin. If you know exactly where this left
margin is, you find it more quickly. Justified text (aligned on both margins) also can be easy to read. The only drawback is that to make both
margins even, Write increases the spaces between words. If words are
separated by too much space, reading is slower. To help, you can hyphenate long words that appear at the beginning of lines by pressing
the hyphen (-) key or the optional hyphen key (Shift+Ctrl+hyphen).
Centered and right-aligned text is difficult to read and should be reserved for special effects, such as for headings or short blocks of text.

To change paragraph alignment, follow these steps:

1. Select the paragraphs to be aligned. (To align only one paragraph,
   position the insertion point anywhere inside the paragraph.)

2. Choose the **P**aragraph menu and select **L**eft, **C**entered, **R**ight, or
   Justified.

You can restore a paragraph to Write's default format choices—left-
aligned, single-spaced, and unjustified with no indentations—by choosing the **P**aragraph **N**ormal command.

To change paragraph alignment with the ruler, follow these steps:

1. Position the insertion point inside the paragraph you want to change.

2. Click the left, center, right, or justify alignment icon.

Using Hyphens To Smooth Justified Text

To justify text (make the margins even on both sides), the computer adds spaces between the words on a line. Doing so sometimes creates large gaps between words, which can make reading difficult. To help avoid wide spaces, hyphenate long words that fall at the beginning of lines. The portion of the word in front of the hyphen moves up to the preceding line, if there's room for it.

Write uses two kinds of hyphens: the normal hyphen, used to join two words (such as *built-in* or *first-rate*), and the optional hyphen, which you insert where a word should break if the word falls at the end of a line.

To insert an optional hyphen between the syllables of a word, press Shift+Ctrl+hyphen. Write doesn't use the optional hyphen unless needed. You can use a dictionary to check the hyphenation of a word.

Suppose that the word *hyphenation* occurs at the beginning of a line of text, but the line above this word has large spaces between the words. Insert optional hyphens by pressing Shift+Ctrl+hyphen in the word like this: *hy-phen-a-tion* (see fig. 12.12). If the line above has room for any portion of the word, these syllables move up, and only the needed hyphen appears.

Spacing Lines in Paragraphs

Lines in paragraphs can be single, one-and-a-half, or double-spaced. You may want to type a document in single space so that you can see the maximum number of lines on-screen; you may want to print a rough draft in one-and-a-half or double space, to leave room for notes when you edit it. The spacing for the paragraph with the insertion point is shown with a check mark in the **P**aragraph menu.

To change paragraph spacing, follow these steps:

1. Select the paragraphs to be spaced. (To change the spacing of only one paragraph, position the insertion point anywhere inside the paragraph.)

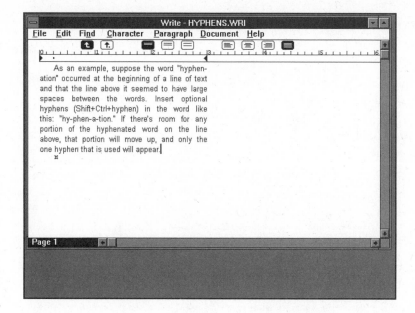

As an example, suppose the word "hyphen-ation" occurred at the beginning of a line of text and that the line above it seemed to have large spaces between the words. Insert optional hyphens (Shift+Ctrl+hyphen) in the word like this: "hy-phen-a-tion." If there's room for any portion of the hyphenated word on the line above, that portion will move up, and only the one hyphen that is used will appear.

FIG. 12.12

Using optional hyphens to prevent excess space between words in justified text.

2. Choose the **P**aragraph menu and select **S**ingle Space, **1** 1/2 Space, or **D**ouble Space.

To change line spacing with the ruler, follow these steps:

1. Position the insertion point inside the paragraph you want to change.

2. Click the single, one-and-a-half, or double-spacing icon.

Selecting What You Want To Reformat with the Ruler
When no text is selected, the ruler changes margins, spacing, or alignment for only the paragraph with the insertion point. To change several paragraphs, select all the paragraphs you want to change. To select the entire document, press Ctrl and click the selection bar between the left margin of the text and the left edge of the screen.

Indenting Paragraphs

Paragraphs can be indented to set them off from the main body of text—for example, for long quotations. Also, the first lines of paragraphs can be indented so that you do not have to press Tab at the beginning of each paragraph.

Indentations, like all measurements in Write, are measured in inches rather than characters, because Write supports different font sizes and proportional spacing.

Understanding Character Spacing

In *proportional* spacing, the widths of letters are proportional; for example, the letter *i* is narrower than the letter *m*. If margins and indentations were measured in characters, Write would not know how large to make an indentation: an inch might contain 16 *i*'s but only 12 *m*'s. Similarly, varying font sizes means that Write cannot measure the length of a page by lines.

Measurements are calculated in inches and are typed in decimals (rather than in fractions). Half an inch is typed as *.5* rather than *1/2*. Use a negative number for a hanging indent (a *hanging indent* makes the first line start to the left of the left margin or indent).

The **P**aragraph **I**ndents command works through a dialog box, shown in figure 12.13. The settings shown in the figure indent a selected paragraph one-half inch from the left and right margins, and the first line one-quarter inch from the indented margin.

FIG. 12.13

The Indents dialog box.

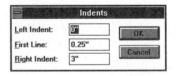

To indent a paragraph using a command, follow these steps:

1. Select the paragraphs to be indented. (To change the indentation of only one paragraph, position the insertion point anywhere inside the paragraph.)

2. Choose the **P**aragraph **I**ndents command.

3. Type the left indentation value in the **L**eft Indent box. Always enter indentation values in inches, using decimals for fractions of inches (one-half inch is .5).

4. In the **F**irst Line box, type the amount of space to indent the first line. Type a negative value to create a hanging indent.

5. In the **R**ight Indent box, type the value of the right indentation.

6. Choose OK or press Enter.

To indent a paragraph with the ruler, use the following steps:

1. Position the insertion point inside the paragraph you want to change.

2. Drag either of the indent markers to the left or right. This method is good for creating paragraphs with double indentations.

To set a first-line indentation, follow these steps:

1. Position the insertion point inside the paragraph you want to indent.

2. Drag the first-line indentation marker (the white box inside the left indentation marker) to the right. The box turns black when it moves away from the left indentation marker.

Hanging Indents Are Useful for Creating Lists
When you want to create a bulleted or numbered list, create a hanging indent, in which the first-line indent is to the left of the left indent. Using the Indents dialog box, you can do this by setting a positive left indent and a negative first-line indent. For example, for bullets to appear at one-quarter inch from the margin and the text of the list at one-half inch from the margin, enter these indentation values:

Left Indent: .5"

First Line: −.25"

To create the same hanging indent with the ruler, drag the left indentation marker (the black triangle at the ruler's left edge) to the .5-inch position on the ruler and drag the first-line indentation marker (the white square inside the left indentation marker) to the .25-inch position on the ruler.

Removing Paragraph Formatting

You can add many different kinds of paragraph formatting to a paragraph, and you can change or remove each one individually. If, for example, the paragraph is centered, but you want it to be left aligned, you simply select the paragraph and select the left alignment command from the **P**aragraph menu or the ruler.

If you want to remove all paragraph formatting at once, select the paragraph (or paragraphs) and choose the **P**aragraph **N**ormal command. The selected paragraphs return to Write's default settings: left-aligned, no tabs or indents, and single spaced.

Formatting a Document

Document formatting affects an entire document and its appearance: headers, footers, and tab and margin settings. The **D**ocument menu controls document formatting; the ruler offers an additional way to set tabs.

In a new Write document, many document formatting choices are made for you already. Margins, for example, are set to 1.25 inches on the left and right, and 1 inch on the top and bottom. Default tab settings are every .5 inch. You can change all these settings and many more.

Adding Headers, Footers, and Page Numbers

You can add one header and one footer to each Write document; headers appear at the top of every page of the printed document; footers at the bottom (you can exclude headers and footers from the first page, if you prefer). You can include automatic page numbers as part of a header or footer.

You create headers and footers using a special screen and dialog box (see fig. 12.14). The screen, where you type the header or footer text, works like any other Write screen: you can format the header or footer just as you format any Write text. Use the dialog box to specify where on the page to place the header or footer, and whether to include a page number. Headers and footers appear wherever you position them on the page, regardless of the top and bottom margins.

The parts of the Page Header and Page Footer dialog boxes are described in table 12.5.

FIG. 12.14

The Page Footer
screen and
dialog box.

Table 12.5 Parts of the Page Header and Page Footer Dialog Boxes

Item	Description
Distance from Top text box	Where you type, in decimal inches, the distance from the top of the page to the header. (This box appears only when you are creating a header.)
Distance from Bottom text box	Where you type, in decimal inches, the distance from the bottom of the page to the footer. (This box appears only when you are creating a footer.)
Print on First Page check box	Select if you want the header (or footer) to appear on the first page (leave unselected to leave the header or footer off the first page).
Insert Page # button	Inserts the (page) page-number symbol in the header or footer at the insertion point. The page number is printed in this spot.
Clear button	Removes the header or footer.
Return to Document button	Closes the header (or footer) window and returns to the document, saving the settings.

To create a header or footer, follow these steps:

1. Choose the **D**ocument **H**eader or the **D**ocument **F**ooter command.

2. Type the header or footer text. Format the header or footer as you would any document.

3. Activate the Header or Footer dialog box by clicking it with the mouse button, or by pressing Alt+F6.

4. Select the **D**istance from Top or **D**istance from Bottom box and type the distance in decimal inches (1/2 of an inch is .5) for the header or footer to appear from the top or bottom of the page.

5. Select the **I**nsert Page # button to include automatic page numbering. The (page) page-number symbol appears at the insertion point, marking where page numbers will print.

6. Select the **P**rint on First Page box if you want the header or footer to print on the first page of the document. Leave the box deselected if you don't want the header or footer to appear on the first page.

7. Choose the **R**eturn to Document button.

To remove a header or footer, choose the **C**lear button in the Page Header or Page Footer dialog box and choose the **R**eturn to Document button. Pressing Esc in the header or footer dialog box acts the same as choosing the **R**eturn to Document button. If you want to undo a mistake, use the **E**dit **U**ndo command.

Note that a selection in the Page Layout dialog box controls the starting page number in headers and footers. To change the starting page number, choose the **D**ocument **P**age Layout command and type the starting page number in the **S**tart Page Numbers At text box.

Headers and footers do not appear in the document on-screen—you do not see them until you print the document.

Positioning a Header or Footer
Make sure that the position of the header or footer agrees with the top and bottom margins set for the text. Write has default top and bottom margins of 1 inch. Make sure that the headers and footers stay within the margins. Also keep in mind that your printer may have limitations on how close to the edge of a page it can print. Most laser printers, for example, cannot print within one-quarter of an inch from the edge of a page.

Setting Tabs

Write's tab settings apply to the entire document. Write includes preset tabs at every half inch, but you can override these tab settings using the **D**ocument **T**abs command or using the ruler. The tab settings tell the insertion point where to go when you press the Tab key in the document.

You can choose from two kinds of tabs: left-aligned and decimal. A left-aligned tab lines up text from the left; decimal tabs align numbers by a decimal (which is useful for columns of dollar amounts). You also can use the decimal tab as a right-aligned tab, aligning entries that do not contain a decimal point so that the right edge is on the tab setting.

You can have up to 12 tabs in the document.

Setting Tabs with a Menu Command

The Tabs dialog box is shown in figure 12.15 and described in table 12.6. Set tabs in inches from the left margin (as shown in the figure), not from another tab setting. Press Tab to move between boxes in the dialog box. Remember that tab settings apply to the entire document.

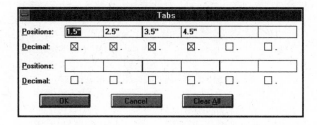

FIG. 12.15

Entering tab measurements in the Tabs dialog box.

Table 12.6 Parts of the Tabs Dialog Box

Item	Description
Positions	Where you type how far from the left margin to set each tab (type tab settings in decimal inches; for example, a tab one-quarter inch from the left margin is typed as *.25*).
Decimal check boxes	Specifies that the tab above the box is a decimal tab. Click the box or tab to the box and press the space bar to select or deselect this box.
Clear **A**ll button	Clears the tabs you have typed and restores the default 1/2-inch tabs.

To set tabs using the keyboard, follow these steps:

1. Choose the **D**ocument **T**abs command.

2. Type tab positions in decimal inches from the left margin in the **P**ositions text boxes. (Press Tab to move between the boxes.)

3. Select the **D**ecimal boxes to specify decimal tabs.

4. Choose OK or press Enter.

To change or remove a tab setting with the keyboard, follow these steps:

1. Choose the **D**ocument **T**abs command.

2. Select the tab setting you want to change. (Press Tab to move between the boxes.)

3. Type a new tab setting (or press Del to remove the current tab setting).

4. Choose the OK button.

To restore the default tabs at every half inch, follow these steps:

1. Choose **D**ocument **T**abs.

2. Choose the Clear **A**ll button.

3. Choose the OK button.

Change tab locations in a document by changing the tab settings. Suppose that you use tabs to create a table with three columns and then discover you need more space between the columns. You can move the columns by choosing **D**ocument **T**abs and entering the new tab settings. Because the tabs are in the text, the columns move to align on the new settings. If you have a mouse, use the ruler to experiment with spacing (see "Setting Tabs with the Ruler," later in this chapter).

Using the Decimal Tab

Use a decimal tab to line up columns of numbers that include decimals, such as dollar amounts. The decimal positions itself on the tab setting, and the numbers extend before and after the decimal.

You also can use the decimal tab to right-align columns of text or numbers that contain no decimal points. A right-aligned column is useful in an index, a table of contents, or a menu. Figure 12.16 shows a table created entirely with decimal tabs. Notice that the first column in this chart is right-aligned; this effect is created using the decimal tabs.

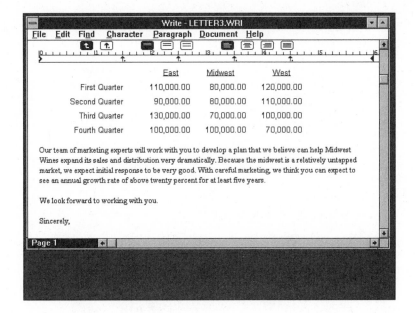

FIG. 12.16

Using decimal
tabs.

Setting Tabs with the Ruler

If you use a mouse, the ruler may be the easiest way to set tabs in the
document. The ruler (shown in fig. 12.16) contains two kinds of tab
icons: left and decimal. Set tabs by selecting the icon for the kind of tab
you want and then clicking the ruler where you want the tab setting.
You easily can move tab settings by dragging the tab arrows left or
right. Remove tabs by dragging them down off the ruler. When you
move tab settings, any tabbed text in the document moves with them.

To set tabs with a mouse and the ruler, follow these steps:

1. Choose the **D**ocument **R**uler On command to display the ruler.

2. Click either the left-align tab icon or the decimal tab icon to identify the kind of tab you want.

3. Click the blank bar below the numbers on the ruler to set a tab at
   this point.

By default, the ruler uses inches as a measurement system; if you select
centimeters (cm) in the Page Layout dialog box, the ruler displays centimeters instead. To access the Page Layout dialog box, choose the
Document **P**age Layout command.

Setting Margins

Write's margins are preset to 1 inch on the top and bottom, and 1.25 inches on the left and right. With the **D**ocument **P**age Layout command, you can change the margins. You also can specify a starting page number other than 1 for automatic page numbering in headers and footers and can change the measurement system from inches to centimeters.

To set margins, follow these steps:

1. Choose the **D**ocument **P**age Layout command.

2. Select the **L**eft, **R**ight, **T**op, and **B**ottom boxes in turn and type a decimal measurement for each margin.

3. Choose OK or press Enter.

Choosing **D**ocument **P**age Layout displays the Page Layout dialog box, which you use to change margins (see fig. 12.17). Table 12.7 lists the parts of the dialog box.

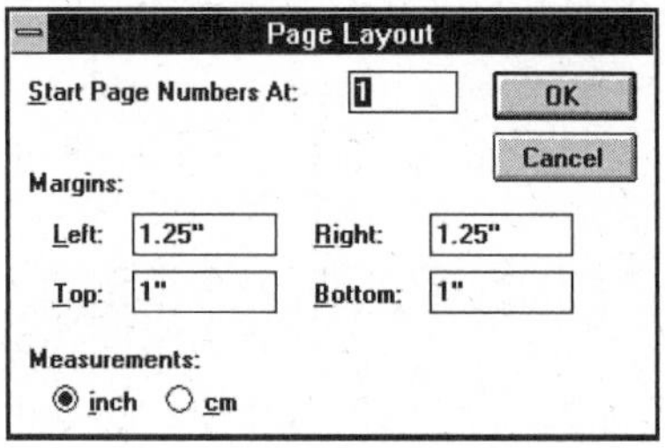

FIG. 12.17

The Page Layout dialog box.

Table 12.7 Parts of the Page Layout Dialog Box

Item	Description
Start Page Numbers At	Where you type the page number at which automatic page numbering is to start (useful for documents that extend across several files)
Left	Where you type the left margin in decimal inches
Top	Where you type the top margin in decimal inches
Right	Where you type the right margin in decimal inches

Item	Description
Bottom	Where you type the bottom margin in decimal inches
inch and **c**m Measurements	Select either **i**nch or **c**m for the type of measurement you want to use—inches or centimeters

Your Printer May Have Margin Limits
The printer may have mechanical limits that prevent you from using no margins or very wide margins. Most laser printers, for example, must have at least a .25-inch margin on all sides. If you set margins that the printer doesn't allow, you see a dialog box telling you that the printer cannot print with these margins. Enter new margins and try printing again.

Controlling Page Breaks

When you print, Write determines by default where to end one page and begin the next. Write inserts page breaks to start each new page. The number of lines per page depends on line spacing, margin settings, and font size.

If you want precise control over where page breaks occur (or if you simply want to see where page breaks will occur) you can repaginate the document before you print, inserting page breaks where you want them.

Choosing the **F**ile **R**epaginate command displays the Repaginate Document dialog box, shown in figure 12.18.

FIG. 12.18

The Repaginate Document dialog box.

To repaginate with page breaks, follow these steps:

1. Choose the **F**ile **R**epaginate command.

2. Select Confirm Page **B**reaks if you want to confirm each page break.

3. Choose OK or press Enter.

If you didn't select Confirm Page **B**reaks in step 2, Write inserts page breaks and then returns to the document. Page breaks appear as double arrows (>>) in the left margin.

If you selected Confirm Page **B**reaks in step 2, Write displays a page break mark (>>) at the first proposed page break and displays a dialog box you can use to move or confirm page breaks (see fig. 12.19). You can move the page break up or move it back, but you cannot move a page break further down than Write originally positioned it. After you confirm a page break, Write advances to the next proposed page break.

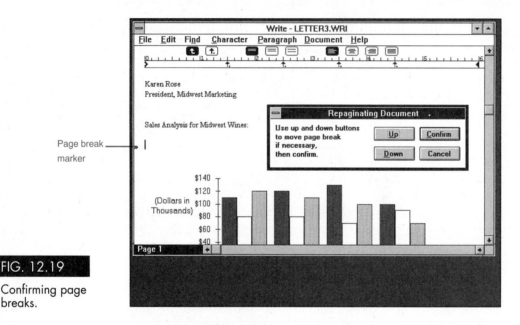

FIG. 12.19

Confirming page breaks.

To move or confirm proposed page breaks, follow these steps:

1. Choose the **U**p button to move the proposed page break up. Choose the **D**own button to move down a page break you previously moved up. Select neither button to accept the proposed page break.

2. Choose **C**onfirm.

Another way to force a page break is to move the insertion point to the spot where you want to start a new page and press Ctrl+Enter. The forced page break appears on-screen as a dotted line. To delete a forced page break, move the insertion point just below the line and press Backspace enough times to erase the dotted line.

You also can confirm or delete a forced page break as part of the repagination process. If you're confirming page breaks, when Write encounters a forced page break in the document, it highlights the page break and displays a dialog box asking whether you want to keep it or remove it. Choose **K**eep to keep the break or choose **R**emove to remove it.

After you repaginate or print a document, you see two changes in the document. Page breaks you entered by repaginating appear as double arrows (>>) in the left margin; page breaks you entered by pressing Ctrl+Enter appear as dotted lines that extend the full width of the page. Additionally, the current page number appears at the bottom left of the window in a status box.

If you made any editing changes, the page numbers shown before repaginating may be incorrect. Repaginate before trusting page numbers or page breaks.

T I P

Including Pictures in a Document

Pictures of all kinds—graphs from Excel or 1-2-3, sketches from Windows Paintbrush, clip art from files of graphics, and even scanned images of photographs—can be pasted into Write files, lending a professional effect and increasing communication in finished documents.

There are three ways you can include a picture in a Write document. The first, and simplest, is to copy a picture from a graphics application and paste it into the Write document. The second way is to embed a picture created by a graphics application that supports object linking and embedding (such as Microsoft Paintbrush). You can edit an embedded graphic in Write. The third way to include a picture is to link it from an application that supports object linking and embedding. By default, Write updates linked graphics when you change the original.

Object linking and embedding, or OLE, requires two types of applications: a server application, used to create the objects (such as pictures) embedded or linked in a document; and a client application, in which objects are embedded or linked. Write is an OLE client application.

To learn more about object linking and embedding, read Chapter 6. For details about transferring data between DOS and Windows applications, refer to Chapter 22.

Write does its best to accurately represent the picture on-screen. However, the picture is displayed in printer—rather than screen—resolution. If the printer resolution doesn't match the screen resolution (and it probably doesn't), then the screen image may appear slightly distorted. But because the picture prints at printer resolution, the graphic will look fine when you print it.

Whether it's copied, embedded, or linked, you can move or size the graphic after you have added it to the Write document.

Copying a Picture

The **E**dit commands enable you to copy a picture from another application into a Write document. Figure 12.20 shows a chart copied from Excel and pasted into a Write document.

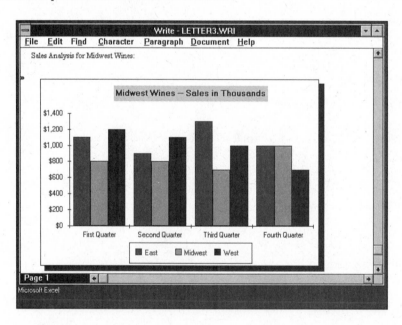

FIG. 12.20

A spreadsheet chart copied into a Write document.

To copy a picture from one application into another, follow these steps:

1. Open the application containing the picture or chart.

2. Select and copy the picture to the Clipboard. For Windows applications, select the portion of the picture you want copied and choose a command such as **E**dit **C**opy. For standard DOS applications, such as 1-2-3, display the picture on-screen and press Alt+PrtSc.

3. Close or Minimize the application.

4. Open or activate the Write file.

5. Position the insertion point where you want the picture.

6. Choose the **E**dit **P**aste command.

To learn more about using applications together, refer to Chapters 22 and 23.

The result you get when you paste in a copied picture depends on the graphics application you used to create the picture. If the graphics application does not support object linking and embedding, the pasted picture is a static object that retains no connection to the graphics application. To edit the picture, you must create a picture and replace the existing one in your Write document. However, if the application supports object linking and embedding (as does Windows Paintbrush, an OLE server), the copied picture is automatically embedded in your Write document when you choose the Edit Paste command. You can edit the embedded picture—using the original graphics application—from within your Write document (see the later sections in this chapter, "Embedding Pictures" and "Editing Pictures").

If you want to copy in a picture from an application that supports object linking and embedding, but you do not want the picture to be embedded, follow these steps:

1. Start the sever application, such as Paintbrush, and create the picture or open the file containing the picture.

2. Select the picture and choose the **E**dit **C**opy command.

3. Switch to your Write document and position the insertion point where you want the picture to appear.

4. Choose the **E**dit Paste Sp**e**cial command. The Paste Special dialog box appears.

5. From the Data Type list, select Bitmap or Picture.

6. Choose Paste or press Enter.

Embedding Pictures

To embed a picture, you can open a graphics application from within the Write document. On the computer, Write opens any application compatible with object linking and embedding technology. You use the graphics application to create the picture and when you update the file or exit the application, the picture is added to the Write document.

Figure 12.21 shows a Windows Paintbrush picture being embedded into a Write file. You also edit the picture in Write.

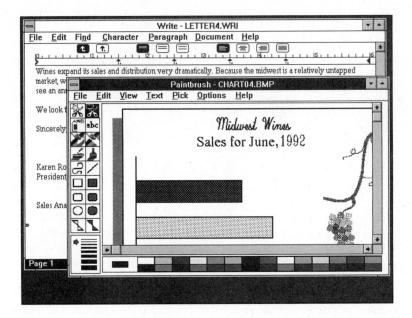

FIG. 12.21

You can embed
a Windows
Paintbrush
picture in a Write
document.

To embed a picture in a Write file, follow these steps:

1. Position the insertion point where you want the picture to appear in the Write document.

2. Choose the **E**dit **I**nsert Object command. The Insert Object dialog box appears, listing all applications that support object linking and embedding (see fig. 12.22).

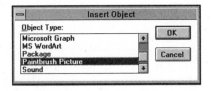

FIG. 12.22

The Insert Object
dialog box.

3. Select the application you want to use to create an embedded picture. For example, select Paintbrush Picture.

4. Choose OK or press Enter. Paintbrush opens.

5. Use Paintbrush to create the picture or choose the **Edit Paste** command to paste in a picture from the Clipboard.

6. When you're finished with the picture, choose the **File Update** command to include a copy of the picture in the Write document.

7. Choose the **File Exit** and Return to document command from the Paintbrush menu.

If you get an error telling you of a memory shortage when you choose the **File Update** command, resize the picture to make it smaller and then try again.

When you choose the **Edit Insert Object** command, the Insert Object dialog box lists all the applications on your computer that support object linking and embedding. Because Paintbrush comes free with Windows, you always see Paintbrush on the list (unless you have deleted it), but you also see applets like MS WordArt and Microsoft Draw if you have installed an application such as Word for Windows, which includes these applications for free. See Part IV, "Using Windows Applets," to learn more about these applets.

T I P

When you use the **Edit Insert Object** command to embed a Paintbrush picture in the Write document, the picture comes in at the full size of the Paintbrush screen. Write doesn't provide a way to crop away unneeded portions of the picture. If you want to embed a small Paintbrush picture, start Paintbrush from the Program Manager (rather than activating it by choosing **Edit Insert Object**). Select the picture in Paintbrush, then copy the picture, switch back to Write, and paste in the picture. The picture comes in at the size you selected, and you can edit the picture in the same way you edit an embedded Paintbrush picture.

Linking Pictures

Linking a picture is similar to embedding a picture—the picture remains connected to the application used to create it. But a linked picture goes a step further: you can update the original, and any Write documents that contain linked copies are updated by default to reflect the changes. Like an embedded picture, you can edit a linked file in Write.

To link a picture to a Write file, follow these steps:

1. Position the insertion point where you want the linked picture to appear.

2. Open the application containing the picture you want to link. For example, open Microsoft Excel to link a chart.

3. Open the file containing the chart or picture you want to link or create a new chart or picture.

4. Save the chart or picture.

5. Select the chart or picture.

6. Choose the **Edit Copy** command.

7. Switch back to the Write document (Alt+Tab switches between running applications).

8. Choose the **Edit Paste Link** command.

9. Save the Write file.

Editing a Link

If you have linked a picture or chart in Write, the picture or chart remains connected to the original file. If the original changes, the image in the Write file changes. But there are several ways you can edit the link between the original file and the Write file, using the Links dialog box shown in figure 12.23. Table 12.8 describes the selections in the Links dialog box.

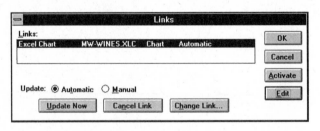

FIG. 12.23

The Links dialog box.

Table 12.8 Parts of the Links Dialog Box

Item	Description
Links	Lists all the linked files in a Write document. The link you select is the one that the commands in this dialog box will act on.
Update Automatic	Select this option if you want the link in a Write document to update by default any time the original file changes. (This option is Write's default.)
Update Manual	Select this option if you want to update the link manually.
Update Now	Choose this command to update the link (use this command for manually updated links).
Cancel Link	Choose this command to cancel the link between the object in Write and the original file. The formerly linked object in Write will no longer update when the original file changes.
Change Link	Choose this command to change the original file to which the linked object is linked or to update the location of the original file if it has moved to a different drive or directory. You see a dialog box similar to the Open dialog box. Choose the new original file.
Activate	Choose this command to activate the server application.
Edit	Choose this command to edit the linked object, using the server application.

To edit a link, follow these steps:

1. Choose the Edit Links command. The Links dialog box appears.

2. From the Links list, select the link you want to edit.

3. Choose the options you want (see table 12.8).

4. Choose OK or press Enter.

Editing Pictures

From within Write, you can edit pictures that are embedded from, or linked to, Windows Paintbrush or another graphics application that supports object linking and embedding. Editing the picture causes the graphics application to open, with the picture displayed in its window. Though you can start the graphics application using either a mouse or the keyboard, you need a mouse to operate Paintbrush and most other graphics applications.

To edit an embedded drawing using the mouse, follow these steps:

1. Double-click the drawing to open Paintbrush and display the picture.

2. Edit the picture.

3. Choose the **File Update** command.

4. Choose the **File Exit and Return to document** command. Or, you can just exit the application, and a message asks whether you want to update the picture in the Write document. Choose **Yes** to update.

To edit an embedded drawing using the keyboard, follow these steps:

1. Select the picture. Click on the picture or with the keyboard, position the insertion point above the picture you want to edit and press the down-arrow key to select the picture.

2. Choose the **Edit Edit Paintbrush Picture O**bject command. Paintbrush opens, with the picture in its drawing window.

   If you are editing an object created by an application other than Paintbrush, you see its name in the command instead of Paintbrush.

3. Edit the picture.

4. Choose the **File Update** command to update the picture in Write.

5. Choose the **File Exit and Return to document** command.

   You also can select the embedded object and start the graphics application by double-clicking on the object.

You can edit a linked picture in Write the same way that you edit an embedded drawing. Because you're using the original graphics application to edit the picture, any changes you make are reflected in any other file containing a link to the original picture.

To edit a linked drawing using the mouse, follow these steps:

1. Double-click the drawing to open the graphics application and display the picture.

2. Edit the picture.

3. Choose the **File S**ave command. The picture in the Write document is updated by default.

4. Choose the **File E**xit command in Paintbrush.

To edit a linked drawing using the keyboard, follow these steps:

1. In Write, choose the **Edit Lin**k**s** command.

2. When the Links dialog box appears, select the file containing the picture you want to edit.

3. Choose **E**dit to display the graphics application, with the picture in its drawing window.

4. Edit the picture.

5. Choose the **File S**ave command. The picture in the Write document updates to reflect the changes you made.

6. Choose the **File E**xit command.

You also can edit a linked picture by selecting the picture, choosing the Edit Edit...**O**bject command, editing and saving the picture, and exiting the graphics application.

If you have set links to update manually, then the Write document will not reflect the changes to the linked picture until you update the link using this process:

1. In Write, choose the **Edit Lin**k**s** command.

2. When the Links dialog box appears, select the linked picture you want to update and choose the **U**pdate Now button.

3. Choose OK or press Enter.

Moving a Picture

A picture is included in a Write document at the insertion point, but you can move it to another location. A menu command enables you to position the picture wherever you want it relative to the left and right margins; in addition, if the picture exists as a separate paragraph, you can use paragraph formatting commands to align the picture to the left, right, or center of a page. You also can move a picture by selecting and cutting it from one location (or document) and pasting it into another location (or document).

To move a picture to the right or left in a Write document, follow these steps:

1. Select the picture by clicking it or by using the same techniques you use to select a word (position the insertion point before or after the picture, press and hold down the Shift key, and press the left- or right-arrow key).

2. Choose the **Edit M**ove Picture command. A square cursor appears at the center of the picture.

3. Move the picture left or right, using the following techniques for the mouse and the keyboard:

   Mouse: Without clicking the mouse button, drag the square insertion point left or right.

   Keyboard: Press the left- and right-arrow keys.

   As you move the picture, a dotted frame moves to show the picture's new position.

4. Click the mouse button or press Enter when the picture is where you want it.

To move a picture up or down on the page, insert or delete lines above the picture using Enter or Backspace. To move a picture to a different place on the page, select it, cut it with **E**dit Cut, and paste it with **E**dit **P**aste.

If you change your mind about moving the picture after selecting it, press the Esc key to remove the selection. Choose **E**dit Undo to undo a move.

Use Paragraph-Formatting Commands To Move a Picture
You can center a picture on the page or align it to the right margin by using paragraph-formatting commands. Select the picture and then choose the **P**aragraph Centered or **P**aragraph **R**ight command or use the ruler to select the centered or right-aligned icon. You can, of course, align the picture to the left margin by choosing the **P**aragraph **L**eft command or selecting the left-aligned icon on the ruler.

Sizing a Picture

You can change the size of a picture using a process similar to the one you use when you move a picture.

To change the size of a picture, follow these steps:

1. Select the picture by clicking it or by using the same techniques you use to select a word (position the insertion point before or after the picture, press and hold down the Shift key, and press the left- or right-arrow key).

2. Choose the **E**dit **S**ize Picture command. A square cursor appears at the center of the picture, and a dotted line appears on all sides.

3. Size the picture, using the appropriate techniques for the mouse or keyboard:

   Mouse: Without clicking the mouse button, drag the square insertion point to the left, right, or bottom side or corner from which you want to resize the picture and then drag that side or corner to resize the picture.

   Keyboard: Press the left-, right-, or down-arrow key to select the side from which you want to resize the picture (or press the two arrows to select a corner). Press the arrow keys to move the selected side or corner to resize the picture.

   As you size the picture, a dotted frame around it moves, indicating the size to which the picture will grow or shrink.

4. Click the mouse button or press Enter. The picture is redrawn at the new size.

As you resize a picture, its measurements appear in the status box at the bottom left corner of the window. The measurements appear as X and Y coordinates; the X coordinate refers to the picture's horizontal width; the Y coordinate refers to the vertical height. You usually should make the measurements the same (3X wide by 3Y high, for example) to keep the picture in proportion; try to use whole numbers to prevent distortion.

For Related Information:

FROM HERE...

◄◄ See "Transferring Data with Copy and Paste," p. 223.

◄◄ See "Linking Data between Applications," p. 223.

◄◄ See "Embedding Data into a Document," p. 233.

◄◄ See "Embedding Data as Packages," p. 238.

◄◄ See "Managing Links," p. 247.

Printing

Printing with Write involves three steps: installing a printer in Windows, selecting the printer you use in Write, and printing the current document.

To install the printer, you must tell Windows during installation which printer (or printers) you want to use; alternatively, you can add printers after installation by using the Control Panel. (The Control Panel also is used to set printer connections and default settings for printers. To learn more about using the Control Panel, refer to Chapter 7, "Customizing with the Control Panel.")

Selecting a Printer

To select a printer, you must access the Print Setup dialog box. You can do this by choosing the File Print Setup command or by choosing the Setup button in the Print dialog box. Once a printer is selected, it remains selected for all documents—you won't have to select a printer again unless you want to change to a different printer.

The Print Setup dialog box lists all the printers installed for Windows on the computer, as well as options for selecting paper orientation, size, and source. When you select a printer, page orientation, paper size, and paper source, the choices remain in effect until you change them—even after you start a new document. The dialog box also includes an Options button; choose it to select additional information, such as gray scale image type on an HP LaserJet printer, or scaling on a PostScript printer. The Print Setup and Options dialog boxes are shown in figure 12.24.

To identify and set up the default printer, follow these steps:

1. Choose the File Print Setup command or choose the File Print command and choose the Setup button.

2. Select either the Default Printer or another printer from the Specific Printer list.

3. Select the paper orientation: Portrait (vertical pages) or Landscape (horizontal pages).

4. Select a Paper Size and Source from the lists provided.

5. Choose Options to make additional choices, depending on the printer.

6. Choose OK to close the Options dialog box; then choose OK or press Enter to close the Print Setup dialog box.

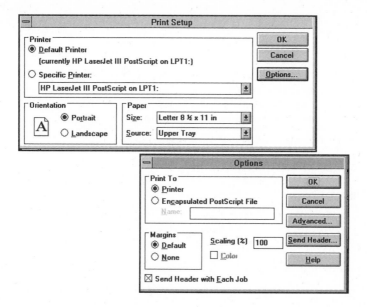

FIG. 12.24

The Print Setup
and Options
dialog boxes.

Figure 12.24 shows the Print Setup and Options dialog boxes for an HP
LaserJet III printer (the Options dialog box you see depends on the
printer you select). Table 12.9 describes the contents of the Print Setup
dialog box.

Table 12.9 Parts of the Print Setup Dialog Box

Item	Description
Default Printer	Select this option to print on the default printer (you choose the default printer in the Control Panel).
Specific **Printer**	Select a printer from this list if you want to print on any of the other printers installed in Windows.
Orientation **Portrait**	Prints text vertically on the page
Orientation **Landscape**	Prints text horizontally on the page
Paper **Size**	Select from a list of available paper sizes.
Paper **Source**	Selects a different paper source, if the printer has more than a single paper tray or bin

Printing a Document

When you print a document, you have several choices to make. You can select a range of pages to print (by default, Write prints the entire document); you can select the print quality (on some printers you can save time by printing in draft quality); you can print to a file rather than to the printer; and you can select the number of copies and whether they are collated.

To print a document, follow these steps:

1. Choose the File Print command. The Print dialog box appears (see fig. 12.25).

2. Select the Print Range All button to print all the pages; select Print Range Selection to print only the selected text; or select the Pages From and Pages To text boxes and type a range of pages to print.

3. From the Print Quality list, select the print resolution you want.

4. Select the Print to File option to print to a file rather than to the printer.

5. In the Copies box, type the number of copies you want to print.

6. To collate multiple copies of the document, select Collate Copies (available if your printer supports collating).

7. Choose OK or press Enter.

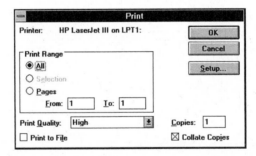

FIG. 12.25

The Print dialog box.

Table 12.10 lists the parts of the Print dialog box shown in figure 12.25.

Table 12.10 Parts of the Print Dialog Box

Item	Description
Print Range **All**	Prints all the pages in a file
Print Range **S**election	Prints the selected text
Print Range **P**ages From	Begins printing with this page
Print Range **P**ages To	Ends printing with this page
Print **Q**uality	Selects from a list of optional print qualities—draft printing is at a lower resolution and can save printing time
Print to File	Prints to a text file rather than to the printer (Write prompts you for a file name if you select this option.)
Copies	Where you type the number of copies you want to print
Collate Copies	Collates copies of multiple documents
Cancel	Returns you to the document without printing

When you send a document to be printed, Write presents a dialog box that tells you the file is being printed and offers a Cancel button. (Notice that the currently selected printer is named at the top of the dialog box.)

For Related Information:

◀◀ To learn more about using the Control Panel, see "Adding and Configuring Printers," p. 277.

◀◀ See "Printing a File," p. 323.

◀◀ See "Using the Print Manager Window," p. 324.

Saving and Naming a Write Document

When you open a new file, you are working in the computer's random-access memory (RAM). If the electricity goes off, or even blinks for a split second, you lose what you wrote if you haven't saved the file.

Therefore, save your work often. A good guideline is to save work every 15 minutes. When you save a file, the information from memory transfers to permanent storage on a hard or floppy disk.

Write includes two commands for saving: **File Save** and **File Save As**. **File Save** quickly saves a previously saved document using its current name. **File Save As** allows you to save an unnamed file or to rename a file you already saved.

The first time you save a document, both **File Save** and **File Save As** call up the File Save As dialog box, enabling you to enter the new file name (see fig. 12.26). Using the same dialog box, you can change the directory in which you save the file, and you can select a different file format in which to save the file. Table 12.11 lists the contents of the Save As dialog box.

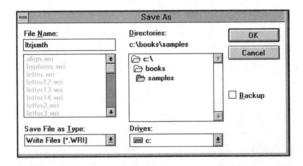

FIG. 12.26

The Save As dialog box.

Table 12.11 Parts of the Save File Name As Dialog Box

Item	Description
File Name	Where you type the file name (if you already saved the file, the file name appears in this text box)
Directories	Lists available directories; select the directory into which you want to save the file.
Save File as **Type:**	Enables you to save a file in a format other than Write
Write Files (*.WRI)	Standard Write format
Word for DOS (*.DOC)	Microsoft Word format (not Word for Windows). Saving in Word format doesn't preserve pictures.
Word for DOS/TXT only	Unformatted Microsoft Word text file

Item	Description
Text files (*.TXT)	Windows ANSI text format—useful when you send a file via a modem
Drives	Selects the drive on which you want to save the file
Backup	Makes a backup copy of the file along with the primary file (the backup copy has the same name as the current file but with the extension BKP for Write files and BAK for Word files)
OK button	Saves the file with the name in the text box. You can press Enter at any time to choose OK.
Cancel button	Returns to the document without saving

The next time you save the same file, you can choose either File **S**ave (keeping the current file name and replacing the old file) or F**i**le Save **As** (giving the file a different name and, therefore, creating a new version of the file). Unlike Save **As**, **S**ave isn't followed by a dialog box if the document was saved previously.

Before saving a file, the name `Write-(Untitled)` appears in the document's title bar. After saving, the file name you assigned appears there.

To save and name a file, follow these steps:

1. Choose the **F**ile Save **As** command.

2. Select the drive where you want to save the file in the **D**rives list.

3. In the **D**irectories list, select the directory in which to save the file. By default, Write saves files in the current directory.

4. In the File **N**ame text box, type the file name.

5. If you want to save the file in some format other than Write, select a format from the Save File as **T**ype list.

6. To make a backup copy of the file (besides the saved WRI file), select **B**ackup. Note that backup Write files use the extension BKP rather than WRI. Backup Word files use the extension BAK.

7. Choose OK or press Enter.

To resave a file with its current name, choose the **F**ile **S**ave command.

> **Rules for File Names**
>
> A file name identifies the file so that you can retrieve it later. A file name has two parts: the *root name* (up to eight characters) and the *extension* (up to three characters). Unless you type a different extension, Write assigns the extension WRI to all Write files. Usually, just type the first eight characters and let Write add the WRI default extension.
>
> Characters in file names can be letters, numbers, or certain characters. Never use a period or a space. Allowable characters include ! @ # $ % ^ & ( ) _ but not the asterisk or plus sign. These characters work well as replacements for spaces between names.
>
> If you want to track different versions of a document, use File Save As to assign a different name each time you save the file. Including version numbers in the name, such as BUDGT_05, helps you identify the most recent version quickly. Saving versions enables you to go back to earlier work. You can delete old, unneeded versions by choosing **File Delete** from the Windows File Manager.

Exiting Write

After you finish writing or are ready to stop for the day, exit Write and return to the Windows desktop by choosing File Exit from the Write menu.

If you have not saved the most recent changes, Write reminds you that the document has changed and asks whether you want to save the changes. Select Yes if you want to save the changes, No to discard the changes, or Cancel to cancel the Exit command and return to the document.

Working with Other Applications

Like other Windows applications, Write can share information—not only between Write files, but also between applications. Information you can add to Write files includes graphics created in Windows applications (such as Paintbrush) and worksheet data from applications such as Excel. Write also is highly compatible with another Microsoft word processing application—Word for Windows.

You move or copy information between Windows applications by using the Clipboard and Edit commands, which work in all Windows applications. Cut, copy, and paste text or graphics between documents by using the Edit commands and pressing Alt+Tab to switch between application windows. You can move text between Write files in the same way.

You do not have to have both Windows applications open at the same time to transfer text or pictures. If, for example, the computer's memory is limited, you may not have room for many large applications. If so, cut or copy from one application, close the application, start the other application, and paste the selection. Be sure that you do not delete, cut, or copy another selection before you paste the first selection. If you do, the second cut or copy replaces what is in the Clipboard.

To move or copy a selection between Windows applications or Write files, follow these steps:

1. Open the application that contains the text or picture you want to move or copy.

2. Select the text or picture you want to move or copy.

3. Choose the Edit Cut command (to move the selection) or the Edit Copy command (to duplicate it).

4. Open or activate the Write document to receive the selection.

5. Position the insertion point where you want the selection to appear.

6. Choose the Edit Paste command.

Starting a Library of Standard Text
Write offers a way to save time if you work on documents that have repetitive or standard parts: create a *library* of standardized pieces (also known as *boilerplate* text), such as paragraphs for a sales proposal or a legal contract. Save this library as a Write document.

When you need a paragraph contained in the library, just start a new Write application and open this library document. You can copy the paragraph from the library and paste it into the work document (Alt+Tab switches between open applications).

Do not close the Write application holding the library. Instead, keep it as an icon at the bottom of the screen so that you can get to the next standard paragraph quickly. See Chapters 1 and 4 for information on using icons.

You can open several file formats in Write. You can, for example, open a Word for Windows file or an ANSI text file. (To list files with any extension in the File Open dialog box, type *.* in the File **N**ame box to list files in all formats or select the file format you want to open from the List Files of **T**ype list.) When you open these files, you see a dialog box asking whether you want to convert the files to Write format. Sometimes you do, but sometimes you don't. Most Windows applications, for example, save text files in ANSI format, and you must *not* convert these files when you open them in Write. Select the **N**o Conversion option in the dialog box. (If you accidentally convert a Windows ANSI format file, close it without saving to return the file to its original format.) If a text file comes from a DOS application such as Word for DOS, select the **C**onvert option in the dialog box to convert the file to Write format.

Copying and Pasting from Standard DOS Applications
Commands to operate standard DOS applications vary. However, copying text or graphics from a standard DOS application and pasting the copy into a Write document is easy. Chapter 23, "Running DOS Applications," describes how to transfer selections between DOS and Windows applications.

Word for Windows and Microsoft Word for DOS are advanced word processing applications used by writers who need features such as mail merge, footnotes, style sheets, a spelling checker, and automatic hyphenation. Word for Windows works in Windows like Write but has far more powerful features. Write, Microsoft Word for DOS, and Word for Windows files are compatible, although some features not available in Write are lost in translation between the two applications.

To use a Write file in Word for DOS, follow these steps:

1. Choose the **F**ile Save **A**s command.

2. Type a file name in the File **N**ame box.

3. In the Save File as **T**ype list, select the Word for DOS option.

4. Choose OK. If the file contains pictures, you see a dialog box advising you that the pictures will be deleted. Choose OK to delete the pictures or choose Cancel to return to the document without saving.

5. Open the file in Word for DOS.

If you open the file in Word for Windows, you must be sure that the Windows Write filter is installed, which by default translates files. Installing this filter in Word for Windows is described in depth in *Using Word for Windows 2*, Special Edition, published by Que Corporation.

For Related Information:

▶▶ To use Write in combination with the Windows desktop accessories, see "Tracking Appointments with the Calendar," p. 655 and "Storing and Retrieving Information in the Cardfile," p. 669.

◀◀ To learn more about embedding and linking pictures in Write, see "Embedding Data into a Document," p. 233 and "Embedding Data as Packages," p. 238.

▶▶ See "Understanding the Methods of Integration," p. 848.

▶▶ See "Integrating Windows Applications," p. 850.

◀◀ See "Using Menus and Dialog Boxes," p. 35.

◀◀ See "Starting, Using, and Quitting Applications," p. 46.

◀◀ See "Operating Applications," p. 77.

FROM HERE...

Chapter Summary

The Write word processor is an excellent personal word processor that meets most personal and business needs. The Copy, Cut, and Paste commands make it easy to brainstorm ideas and reorganize thoughts into finished prose. With Write's three levels of formatting (character, paragraph, and document), you easily can format and print impressive-looking letters and reports. When you feel comfortable with the menus, read through this chapter again and look for the time-saving shortcut keys and tips.

If you use simple graphics in business documents, such as organizational charts or floor plans, you may find the Paintbrush application helpful. Chapter 13 explains Paintbrush. Although Paintbrush is only a fundamental drawing application, it incorporates many of the principles used in more comprehensive, professional drawing applications.

Using Windows Paintbrush

A computer is a business tool—everyone knows that. Sometimes when you sneak up on someone who has Windows on their PC, however, you find that they are not working—they are playing Solitaire, or creating a masterpiece with Windows' fun and colorful painting application, Paintbrush.

Even though Paintbrush is a simple, easy-to-use graphics application, it may be as powerful a graphics application as you will ever need. Paintbrush is fun, but it also is a serious business tool. With Paintbrush, you can create everything from free-flowing drawings to precise mathematical charts, and you can use your creations in other Windows applications, such as Windows Write, Windows Notepad, Windows Cardfile, or Word for Windows. You can use your computer "paintings" to illustrate a story, to emphasize an important point in a report, or to clarify instructions.

The following are some of the graphic effects you can create using Paintbrush:

- Lines in many widths, shades, and colors

- Brush strokes in a variety of styles, widths, shades, and colors

- Unfilled or filled shapes with shades or color

■ Text in many sizes, styles, and colors

■ Special effects like rotating, tilting, and inverting

Windows Paintbrush is fun, but it also is a tool you can use in your work. People are attracted to pictures. They understand pictures better than they understand text alone. Whatever type of work you do, think about how you can communicate more effectively by using illustrations you create with Windows Paintbrush.

Starting Windows Paintbrush

Because Paintbrush is a Windows accessory, you must start Windows before you can start Paintbrush. You usually can start Windows by typing *WIN* at the DOS prompt, but your computer may be set up differently. (Your AUTOEXEC.BAT file, for example, may include a command that starts Windows when you turn on your computer.) To learn more about starting Windows, refer to Chapter 1, "Operating Windows."

The Paintbrush program item icon is located inside the Accessories group, which may be open as a window or closed as a group icon. Follow these steps to start Paintbrush:

1. If the Accessories group appears as an icon, select the icon and press Enter or double-click on the Accessories group icon. Either method opens the Accessories window.

2. Select the Paintbrush icon and press Enter or double-click on the Paintbrush icon.

Starting Paintbrush opens a new, empty Paintbrush file. You can customize a program item icon, however, so that when you start the application, an existing file opens automatically (see Chapter 4).

FROM HERE...

For Related Information:

◀◀ To learn more about starting Windows applications, see "Starting, Using, and Quitting Applications," p. 46 and "Starting an Application from the Program Manager," p. 75.

▶▶ See also "Responding to an Application Failure," p. 1071.

Getting To Know the Paintbrush Window and Tools

The Paintbrush window, like other windows, has a *title bar* across the top, a *menu bar* below the title bar, *scroll bars* on the right and bottom, and a *drawing area* in the middle. Unique to Paintbrush are its three tool areas: the *toolbox* on the left side; the *line-width box* in the bottom left corner; and the color and shades *palette* along the bottom. Figure 13.1 shows a labeled Paintbrush screen.

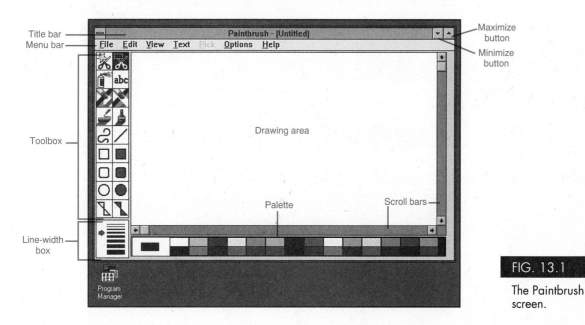

FIG. 13.1

The Paintbrush screen.

To paint, draw, fill, color, shade, write, and edit in Paintbrush, you first must select the appropriate tool, line width, and shade or color. Figure 13.2 labels the individual tools in the toolbox on the left side of the screen.

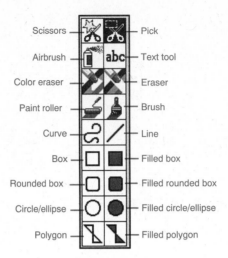

Scissors	Pick
Airbrush	Text tool
Color eraser	Eraser
Paint roller	Brush
Curve	Line
Box	Filled box
Rounded box	Filled rounded box
Circle/ellipse	Filled circle/ellipse
Polygon	Filled polygon

FIG. 13.2

The Paintbrush
Toolbox.

On a color system, the palette appears in color. If your system is mono-
chrome, shades of gray are in your palette.

To select a tool, line width, or shade or color, follow the appropriate
instructions:

Mouse: Position the pointer on the tool, line, or shade or color
you want and click the left mouse button.

Keyboard: Press Tab to move between areas in the window; press
the arrow keys to move between selections in the toolbox, line-
width box, or palette; press the Ins key to select a tool, line, or
shade or color.

The general procedure for using Paintbrush is as follows:

1. Select the tool with which you want to draw from the toolbox.

2. Select the line width you want from the line-width box.

3. Select the color you want from the palette.

4. Move the pointer into the drawing area and draw a shape. (The
   pointer changes into a different shape in the drawing area, depending on which tool you select.)

To draw an unfilled red box with a wide line, for example, select the
unfilled box tool; select a wide line; select red; move the pointer into
the drawing area, where the pointer turns into a crosshair; and drag the
crosshair while holding down the mouse button. Release the mouse
button when the box is the size and shape you want.

Because Paintbrush is a bit-map graphics application (rather than
an object-oriented application) the shapes you create are painted

on-screen in one layer. You cannot reshape a box or move an object behind another object, but you can select a box and move it some- where else, select a picture of a house and tilt it, select a pattern and flip it, or change the colors of your painting. You also can erase your painting (or part of it) and paint something new.

For Related Information:

▶▶ See "Understanding the Microsoft Draw Screen," p. 757.

FROM HERE...

Using the Keyboard with Paintbrush

Paintbrush is easiest to use if you have a mouse. The instructions in this chapter assume that you have a mouse; if you're using a keyboard, use the following keystrokes in place of the equivalent mouse action:

Mouse Action	Keyboard Equivalent
Click left mouse button	Press Ins
Click right mouse button	Press Del
Double-click left mouse button	Press F9+Ins
Double-click right mouse button	Press F9+Del
Drag	Press Insert+arrow keys

You also can use the keyboard to move around the Paintbrush screen. You may find that some of these techniques work as shortcuts, even if you have a mouse:

Press	To Move
Tab	Among drawing area, toolbox, line-width box, and palette
Arrow	In the direction of arrow
Home	To top of drawing area
End	To bottom of drawing area

continues

Press	To Move
PgUp	Up one screen
PgDn	Down one screen
Shift+up arrow	Up one line on the screen
Shift+down arrow	Down one line on the screen
Shift+Home	To left edge of drawing area
Shift+End	To right edge of drawing area
Shift+PgUp	Left one screen
Shift+PgDn	Right one screen
Shift+left arrow	Left one space on the screen
Shift+right arrow	Right one space on the screen

Selecting Tools, Line Widths, and Shades or Colors

When you draw a picture with Paintbrush, you draw it with the tool you select, in the line width you select, and in the shade or color you select. Before you start drawing, select a tool, line width, and shade or color.

To move the pointer from the toolbox to the line-width box and then to the palette with the keyboard, press the Tab key. To move the pointer among the selections in each area, press the arrow keys.

To select a tool or line width with the keyboard, press Insert (Ins). To select a tool or line width with the mouse, position the pointer on the tool or line width you want and press the left mouse button.

The palette offers two choices: foreground and background shade or color. At the left end of the palette, shown in figure 13.3, is a box within a box. The *inner* box is the *foreground* shade or color; the *outer* box is the *background* shade or color. You use the foreground shade or color to create lines, brush strokes, shapes, and text. The background shade or color has three functions: it borders a filled shape; it shadows the edges of text typed with the **S**hadow style; and it becomes the background of the next *new* Paintbrush file you start (but not the current file).

Foreground shade or color (left mouse button)

Background shade or color (right mouse button)

FIG. 13.3

The Paintbrush
palette.

To select a shade or color from the palette, follow these steps:

1. Move the pointer over the shade or color you want to select.

2. Press the *left* mouse button to select the *foreground* color; press the *right* mouse button to select the *background* color.

If you are selecting colors with the keyboard, press Insert (Ins) to select the foreground color and press Delete (Del) to select the background color.

Using the Paintbrush Tools

The toolbox includes tools for cutting out, airbrushing, typing text, erasing, filling, brushing, drawing curves or straight lines, and drawing filled or unfilled shapes. Most of the tools operate using a similar process: press and hold down the left mouse button, drag the mouse, and release the mouse button. (Three exceptions are the text tool, which works by clicking and typing; the paint-roller tool, which works by pointing and clicking; and the curve tool, which works by clicking, dragging, and clicking.)

Whichever tool you use, the **Edit Undo** command is a useful ally. Use it to undo your most recent action. Keep one rule in mind when you use Undo: *it undoes everything back to when you selected the tool you're using, used a scroll bar, opened another application, or resized the window.* When you select Undo, you may undo one line or ten. To keep Undo useful, reselect the tool each time you draw a successful line or shape.

Several Tools Use the Right Mouse Button To Undo
Several tools, including the selection tools, the line tools, and the shape tools, use the right mouse button to undo. To cancel the line or shape you're currently drawing, click the right mouse *before* you release the left mouse button.

Using the Cutout Tools

 With the cutout tools, you can draw an enclosure around any part of your Paintbrush drawing. Whatever is inside the enclosure is selected and can be moved, cut or copied (and then pasted), resized, tilted, flipped, or inverted. "Editing the Painting" and "Creating Special Effects," later in this chapter, explain the things you can do with a selected object or area of the painting.

The toolbox has two cutout tools: the *Scissors* is the icon on the left side of the toolbox, and the *Pick* is the icon on the right side of the toolbox. The Scissors cutout tool draws a free-form enclosure. The Pick cutout tool draws a rectangular enclosure. Both tools select everything inside the enclosure—the object and the space around it.

To use the scissors tool, follow these steps:

1. Select the scissors tool from the top *left* of the toolbox.

2. Position the mouse pointer where you want to begin the enclosure; press and hold down the left mouse button.

3. Drag the mouse to draw a line that encloses the area you want to select.

4. Release the mouse button at the same place you started drawing the line.

Press the Mouse Button To Cancel a Cutout
If you make a mistake while using either of the cutout tools, click the left mouse button outside the cutout area to cancel the cutout and try again.

To use the pick tool, follow these steps:

1. Select the pick tool from the top *right* of the toolbox.

2. Position the mouse pointer where you want to begin the enclosure; press and hold down the left mouse button.

3. Drag the mouse to draw a rectangle around the area you want to select.

4. Release the mouse button.

Figure 13.4 shows an image selected with the pick tool. Notice that the selection box—the box that surrounds the image—is formed of dashed lines.

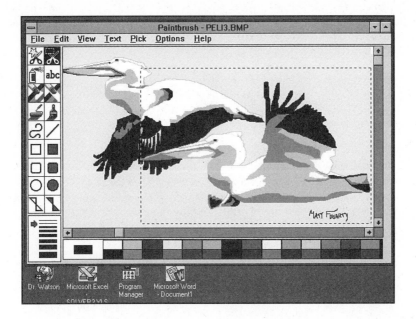

FIG. 13.4

Using the Pick
cutout tool to
select an object
or area.

Expanding the Paintbrush Screen
To blow up the Paintbrush screen to the full size of the monitor,
double-click the Pick cutout tool in the toolbox. You cannot edit
the painting in this view, but you can see more of it. To return the
screen to the normal editing size, click the mouse button or press
the Esc key.

Using the Airbrush Tool

The Airbrush tool works like a can of spray paint, spraying a
mist of color. When selected, the Airbrush tool turns into a
crosshair that produces a circular pattern of dots when you
click it on-screen (to produce an airbrushed dot) or drag it across the
screen (to produce an airbrushed line). The line width you select determines the diameter of the circle of dots; the palette foreground color
determines the shade or color that the Airbrush tool sprays. The speed
you drag determines the density of dots—if you drag the crosshair
slowly, you get a dense pattern of dots; if you drag it quickly, the spray
is lighter.

Unlike other tools, the Airbrush draws transparently. Any image under the airbrush spray may remain visible, depending on how densely you spray over the image (see fig. 13.5).

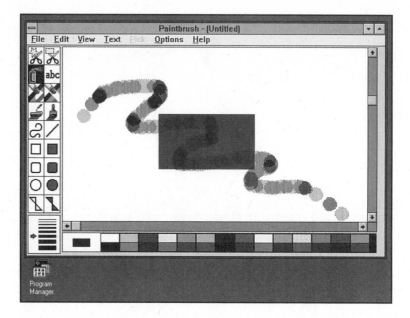

FIG. 13.5

Using the Airbrush tool to draw a circular, transparent mist of dots in the foreground shade or color.

To use the Airbrush, follow these steps:

1. Select the Airbrush tool from the toolbox.

2. Select a line width and foreground color.

3. Position the pointer where you want to begin the airbrush stroke; press and hold down the left mouse button.

4. Drag the crosshair to paint the airbrush stroke.

5. Release the mouse button.

Using the Text Tool

abc With the Text tool, you can add words to your computer painting. Paintbrush has limited typing capabilities: text does not wrap from line to line; you must press Enter to begin the next line of text. You can press the Backspace key to erase a letter when you type, but after you click the mouse button, you cannot return to the text to edit it.

The following steps briefly explain how to use the text tool; refer to "Typing Text in Paintbrush," later in this chapter for details about changing the font, style, and size of the text.

To type text, follow these steps:

1. Select the Text tool from the toolbox.

2. Select the color you want your text to be from the palette.

3. Position the I-beam where you want to start typing and click to display the insertion point.

4. Type the text. Press Backspace to erase characters; choose any command from the Text menu to change the appearance of the text.

5. Press Enter to begin the next line of text.

Using the Eraser Tools

 Paintbrush has two eraser tools: the *Color Eraser* on the left side of the toolbox and the *Eraser* on the right side of the toolbox.

The Color Eraser tool is really a color switcher. It works two ways, and both ways depend on the foreground and background color choices you make in the palette. (The foreground color is the color in the center box at the left end of the palette; you select the foreground color by clicking on the color you want with the *left* mouse button. The background color is the border color in the palette box; you select the background color by clicking on the color you want with the *right* mouse button.)

Dragging the Color Eraser tool across an area in your painting changes every occurrence of the selected foreground color to the selected background color. Double-clicking on the Color Eraser tool in the toolbox changes every occurrence of the selected foreground color in the visible area of your painting to the selected background color. (The Color Eraser changes only the *selected* foreground color; the Eraser tool, described next, changes *all* foreground color.) Be aware that the Color Eraser tool also erases or alters custom colors blended from the foreground color.

Suppose that you have on-screen a red square with a wide black border. Red is the selected foreground color, and yellow is the selected background color. If you drag across the square with the Color Eraser, the red foreground color turns to yellow, but the black stays black (see fig. 13.6). (If you use the Eraser tool instead of the color-eraser, the black also turns yellow, as does any area outside the square you drag the eraser across.)

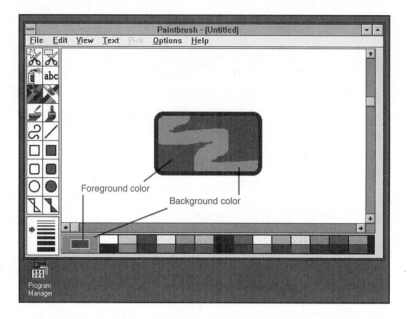

FIG. 13.6

Using the Color Eraser tool to change the selected foreground color to the selected background color.

To use the Color Eraser tool on part of your painting, follow these steps:

1. Select the Color Eraser tool.

2. Select a line width—the width of the area this tool erases depends on the line width you select.

3. Select a foreground color from the palette. When you drag the Color Eraser over your painting, you change this color.

4. Select a background color from the palette. When you drag the Color Eraser over your painting, the foreground color changes to this color.

5. Press and hold down the left mouse button.

6. Drag the Color Eraser tool across the part of your drawing you want to change.

7. Release the mouse button.

> **The Color Eraser Tool Doesn't Work with Shades**
> You can paint with shades or colors, but the color-eraser tool
> works only with colors. If you work on a monochrome monitor,
> the Color Eraser tool works the same as the Eraser tool.

The Color Eraser tool makes it easy for you to change a color throughout your painting. Suppose that you used green in your painting and
now think that the painting would look better if the green were blue. In
the palette, select green as the foreground color and blue as the background color. Double-click the color-eraser tool to change all the green
to blue. (Be sure to select as the foreground color the same shade of
green you used in the original painting.)

Double-clicking on the Color Eraser changes the *displayed* portion of
the painting. If the painting is larger than the screen and you want to
change all the painting, scroll to display each portion and then double-
click to change each displayed portion.

To change a color throughout your painting, follow these steps:

1. Display the portion of your painting you want to change.

2. Select a foreground color from the palette. This is the color in
   your painting that you want to change.

3. Select a background color from the palette. You want the selected
   foreground color in your painting to change to this color.

4. Double-click the Color Eraser tool in the toolbox. If you don't have
   a mouse, move the pointer over the Color Eraser tool and press
   F9+Ins.

The Eraser tool (the tool on the *right* side of the toolbox) "erases" by
changing every part of the painting it touches to the background color
(see fig. 13.7). It erases everything in the foreground.

To use the Eraser tool, follow these steps:

1. Select the Eraser tool from the toolbox. The width of the area it
   erases depends on the line width you select.

2. If necessary, select a background color from the palette. Everything in your painting changes to this background color when you
   pass the Eraser over it.

3. Press and hold down the left mouse button.

4. Drag the Eraser tool across the part of your drawing you want to
   erase.

5. Release the mouse button.

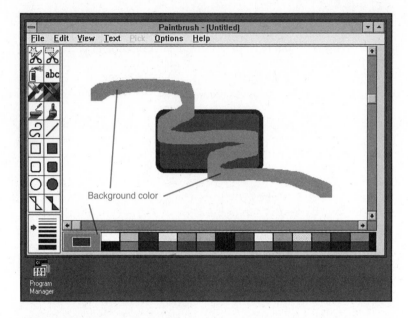

Background color

Using the Eraser tool to change all foreground color to the selected background color.

Use the Eraser as a Brush
Because the eraser tool works by converting foreground shades or colors into the background shade or color, you can turn the eraser tool into a giant paintbrush. Select the shade or color you want to paint with as the *background* shade or color; select a wide line width (the wider the line width, the bigger the eraser); and then click and drag the Eraser to draw a wide line of the background color.

Use the Eraser Tool To Erase the Entire Painting
To erase an entire painting, double-click the Eraser tool in the toolbox. Paintbrush asks whether you want to save changes (choose **Yes** if you do, **No** if you do not), closes the current file, and opens a new file. The new file has the same background color as the file you close. (If you want a white background, be sure that white is the selected background color before you use this method.)

Using the Paint Roller

The Paint Roller fills a closed shape with the selected foreground shade or color (see fig. 13.8). You can use it to fill a solid shape (if the shape is filled with a solid color or black or white) or an empty shape enclosed by a border.

The Paint Roller tool looks like a paint roller with paint flowing out of its end. The tip of this flowing paint is the *active* part of the tool—where the selected foreground shade or color flows out from. Because the tip is sharply pointed, you can fill very small shapes with the Paint Roller tool.

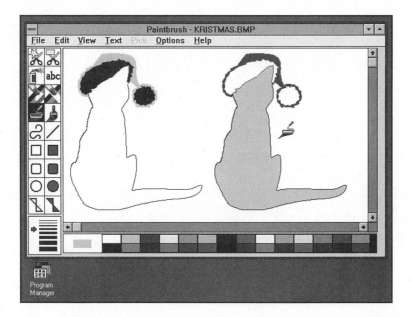

FIG. 13.8

Using the Paint Roller tool to fill a shape with a shade or color.

If you fill a shape that has a gap in its border, the paint leaks out onto the entire painting. Choose the Edit Undo command, fix the leak, and try again. You can use the View Zoom In command to help patch a leak.

Be Careful When You Use the Undo Command
The Edit Undo command undoes all edits up to the last time you selected a tool, saved the file, used a scroll bar, or resized the window. If you're filling many areas in a painting with the Paint Roller tool, *set* each successful fill by saving the file or reselecting the Paint Roller tool. If you issue Undo incorrectly, however, you can undo the undo.

To fill a shape using the Paint Roller tool, follow these steps:

1. Select the Paint Roller tool from the toolbox.

2. Select a foreground color from the palette. This color will fill the shape.

3. Position the pointed tip of the Paint Roller tool inside the shape you want to fill. The pointed tip of the Paint Roller tool is where the paint comes out; because the tool is very precise, you can use it to fill even a small shape.

4. Click the left mouse button. The shape fills with the selected foreground color.

T I P   The Paint Roller tool is one of the two tools that you can use when you zoom in to edit a portion of a painting in detail (see "Getting Different Views of the Painting," later in this chapter). The other tool that you can use when you zoom in is the Brush tool.

Using the Brush Tool

 The Brush tool brushes an opaque stroke of the selected foreground shade or color onto your painting (see fig. 13.9). The brush stroke appears in the line width selected in the line-width box.

To use the Brush tool, follow these steps:

1. Select the Brush tool from the toolbox.

2. Select a foreground shade or color from the palette.

3. Position the pointer where you want the brush stroke to begin; press and hold down the left mouse button.

4. Drag the brush to paint a brush stroke.

5. Release the mouse button.

You can use the Brush tool in any of six shapes you choose from the Brush Shapes dialog box (see fig. 13.10). The default square shape paints with a square brush; the round shape paints with a round brush. The straight-line and diagonal-line brushes paint with a thin line and can paint a variable-width brush stroke, as shown in figure 13.9 (fig. 13.9 was painted with the diagonal-line brush shape shown selected in fig. 13.10). No matter what the brush shape, its width is determined by the selected line width.

FIG. 13.9

An opaque brush
stroke painted
with the brush
tool.

To select a brush shape, follow these steps:

1. Choose the **O**ptions **B**rush Shapes command. Alternatively,
   double-click on the Brush tool in the toolbox.

2. Select the brush shape you want to use from the Brush Shapes
   dialog box (see fig. 13.10).

3. Choose OK or press Enter. Alternatively, double-click on the
   brush shape you want in the dialog box.

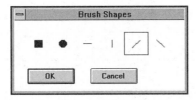

FIG. 13.10

The Brush Shapes
dialog box.

Using the Curve Tool

The curve tool is probably the most unusual tool in the Paintbrush toolbox. Unlike the brush, you cannot use the curve tool
to draw freehand shapes. Instead, you use the tool to draw very
accurate curves.

To use the curve tool, you use a series of three click-and-drag movements. Follow these steps:

1. Select the curve tool from the toolbox.

2. If necessary, select a line width and foreground color.

3. Press, drag, and release the mouse button to draw a straight line. Notice that the line appears thin and black.

4. Move the crosshair to one side of the line you drew.

5. Press the left mouse button and drag the pointer away from the line to pull the line into a curve. If this is the shape you want, click the mouse button to complete the line. If you want an s-shaped curve, go on to step 6.

6. Move the crosshair to the other side of the line, press and hold down the left mouse button, and drag the pointer away from the line to pull the line in the opposite direction. You now have an s-shaped curve, as shown in the flower stem in figure 13.11.

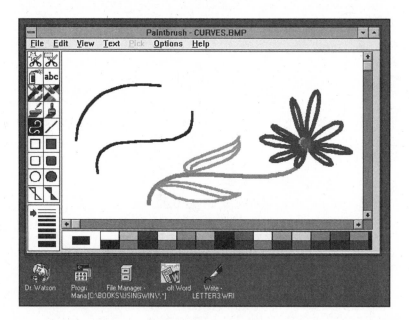

FIG. 13.11

Using the curve tool to help draw accurate curves.

You can use a special type of undo with the curve tool: any time before you complete the line, you can click the right mouse button to undo the line and start over.

Draw a Petal Shape with the Curve Tool
To draw a petal shape with the curve tool, click the mouse one time to anchor the base of the petal, click a second time at the wide end of the petal, and then click and drag away from the wide end of the petal to form the petal shape. The petal appears as a thin black line until you release the mouse button.

Using the Line Tool

With the line tool, you can draw a straight line in the foreground shade or color and in the selected line width. When you draw the line, it appears as a thin, black line. When you release the mouse button to complete the line, however, the line appears with the width and color you selected.

Like with the curve tool, you can use the right mouse button to undo an action. To undo the line you're drawing, click the right mouse button before you release the left mouse button.

To draw a line that is perfectly vertical, perfectly horizontal, or at a 45-degree angle, press and hold down the Shift key as you draw (see fig. 13.12).

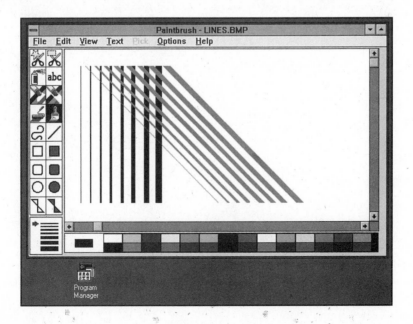

FIG. 13.12

Using the Shift key and the line tool to draw perfectly horizontal lines.

To use the line tool, follow these steps:

1. Select the line tool from the toolbox.

2. Select a line width and foreground color.

3. Position the pointer where you want to start the line; press and hold down the left mouse button. To draw a vertical, horizontal, or 45-degree line, press and hold down the Shift key as you press and hold down the left mouse button.

4. Continue holding down the mouse button and drag the crosshair in any direction to draw a line. If you're holding down the Shift key, keep pressing it, too.

5. Release the mouse button to complete the line. Release the Shift key.

Using the Box and Rounded Box Tools

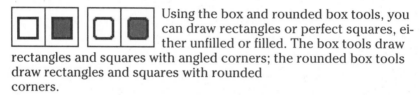 Using the box and rounded box tools, you can draw rectangles or perfect squares, either unfilled or filled. The box tools draw rectangles and squares with angled corners; the rounded box tools draw rectangles and squares with rounded corners.

An unfilled box line is the selected foreground shade or color. A filled box line is the selected background color, and its fill is the selected foreground color. The border of any box is the selected line width. (If you don't want a border, select the same foreground and background shade or color, or make sure that the selected background color is the same as your painting's background.)

To draw a perfectly square box or rounded box, hold down the Shift key as you draw.

Figure 13.13 shows a selection of rectangles drawn with the various box tools.

To use the box tools, follow these steps:

1. Select the box, filled box, rounded box, or filled rounded box tool from the toolbox. The box tool appears on-screen as a crosshair.

2. Select a line width, foreground color, and background color.

3. Press and hold down the left mouse button to anchor one corner of the rectangle. To draw a square, press and hold down the Shift key as you draw.

4. Continue holding down the mouse button and drag the crosshair in any direction to draw the rectangle. The rectangle appears as a thin, black line.

5. Release the mouse button when the rectangle is the shape you want. The rectangle takes on the selected line width and shade or color.

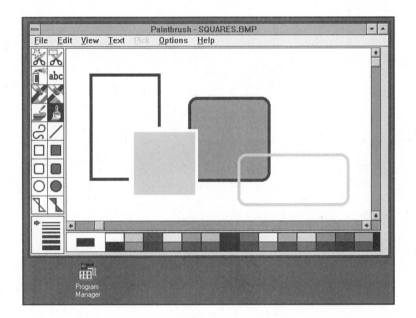

FIG. 13.13

Using the box and rounded box tools to draw unfilled or filled rectangles or squares.

Using the Circle/Ellipse Tools

You can use the circle/ellipse tools to draw ovals and circles. If you use the unfilled circle/ellipse tool, Paintbrush draws the resulting shape in the selected foreground color and leaves the center empty. If you use the filled circle/ellipse tool, Paintbrush draws the border in the selected background color and fills the shape with the selected foreground color. (If you don't want a border, select the same foreground and background shade or color.) With either tool, the border is the selected line width.

The circle tools draw an oval (ellipse) shape by default; if you want a perfect circle, press and hold down the Shift key as you draw.

Figure 13.14 shows a selection of circles and ellipses drawn with the circle tools.

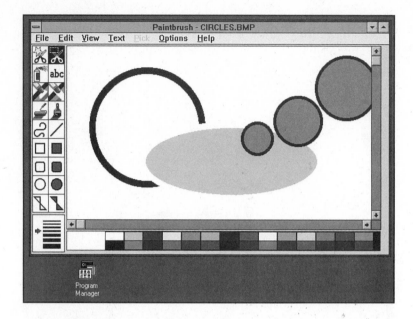

FIG. 13.14

Using the circle
tools to draw
ovals or circles.

To draw an ellipse or circle, follow these steps:

1. Select the circle/ellipse or filled circle/ellipse tool from the toolbox. The circle/ellipse tool appears on-screen as a crosshair.

2. Position the pointer where you want to start the ellipse or circle; press and hold down the left mouse button. To draw a perfect circle, press and hold down the Shift key as you draw.

3. Drag the crosshair away from the starting point in any direction. The ellipse or circle appears as a thin black line.

4. Release the mouse button to complete the circle or ellipse. Release the Shift key if you're drawing a circle. The border and fill take on the characteristics you selected.

Using the Polygon Tools

You can use the polygon tools to draw closed multisided shapes (unfilled or filled). If you use the unfilled polygon tool, Paintbrush draws the polygon in the selected foreground color and leaves the center empty. If you use the filled polygon tool, Paintbrush draws the border in the selected background color and fills the polygon with the selected foreground color. (If you don't want a border, select the same foreground and background shade or color.) With either tool, the border is the selected line width.

Drawing a shape with a polygon tool requires three steps: click-drag-release to draw the first side of the polygon; click to define each of the polygon's remaining corners; and double-click to close the polygon.

Figure 13.15 shows a filled polygon.

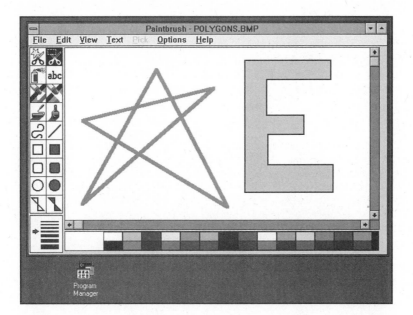

FIG. 13.15

Using the polygon tool to draw a multi-sided shape.

To draw an unfilled or filled polygon, follow these steps:

1. Select the polygon or filled polygon tool from the toolbox. The polygon-drawing tool appears on-screen as a crosshair.

2. Position the crosshair where you want to start the polygon and press and hold down the left mouse button.

3. Drag the crosshair to draw the first side of the polygon; release the mouse button when the line is finished. Press and hold down the Shift key to draw a perfectly horizontal, vertical, or diagonal line.

4. Click the left mouse button to define each of the polygon's remaining corner points. The border appears as a thin black line.

5. Double-click the left mouse button to complete the polygon. The end point joins the starting point to close the polygon, and the border and fill take on the characteristics you selected.

Typing Text in Paintbrush

A picture may be worth a thousand words, but sometimes words can help clarify your message. You can use the text tool to add text to your painting in any of several fonts, sizes, styles, and shades or colors.

As explained in the section titled "Using the Text Tool," typing in Paintbrush has some limitations. You can edit the text you type only until you complete the typing by clicking the mouse button. The text becomes part of the picture, and the only way you can edit the text is to erase it or paint over it. Paintbrush doesn't have a word-wrap feature; when you reach the edge of the screen, you must press Enter to move the insertion point to the next line.

When you type text, it appears in the selected font, the selected style, the selected size, and the selected foreground color. You can change any of these selections *while* you are typing to change the *current* block of text. Alternatively, you can change any of these selections *before* you start typing to set the style for the *next* block of text you type. Each block of text, however, can have only one font, style, size, or color. The fonts available in Paintbrush are the same as those fonts installed in Windows. Figure 13.16 shows some examples of text you can use in your drawings.

To change the font or type style before you begin typing, refer to the upcoming sections on "Enhancing Text" and "Selecting a Font, Style, and Size."

To type text, follow these steps:

1. Select the Text tool from the toolbox.

2. Move the pointer into the drawing area, where it becomes an I-beam.

3. Position the I-beam where you want to start typing and then click the left mouse button. (The I-beam turns into a flashing cursor or insertion point.)

4. Type the text (press Enter when you want to start a new line). If you make a mistake, press Backspace to erase it.

5. Click the mouse button to *set* the text into your painting—after you click the mouse button, you cannot edit the text.

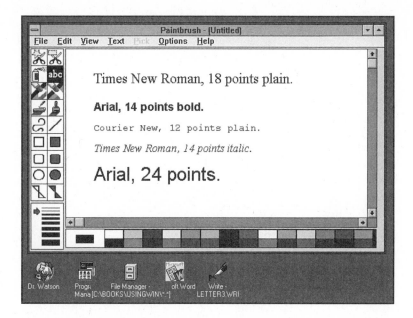

FIG. 13.16

Examples of
Paintbrush fonts
and styles.

Enhancing Text

A text enhancement is a variation of the selected font. Paintbrush offers
several text enhancements: **R**egular, **B**old, **I**talic, **U**nderline, **O**utline,
and **S**hadow. You can use as many enhancements as you like at the
same time. For example, you can type a bold and underlined title. Select **R**egular to delete all text enhancements. All of these choices and
the font, style, and size choices described in the next section are available from the **Text** menu shown in figure 13.17.

Typed text appears in the selected foreground color, with one exception: shadow text adds a shadow in the selected background color.

If you choose enhancements while the insertion point is flashing inside
a block of text, the enhancements apply to the current block of text and
to future blocks of text that you type. If you choose enhancements before you click the I-beam on the painting to begin a block of text or after
you click the mouse button to end a block of text, enhancements apply
to the next block of text that you type.

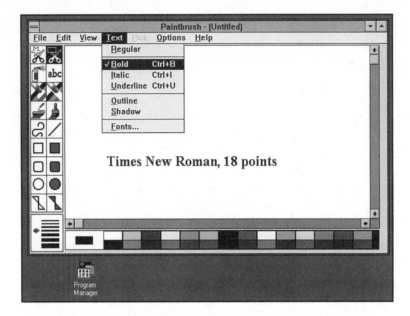

FIG. 13.17

You can select
text enhance-
ments from the
Text menu.

To select a text enhancement, follow these steps:

1. Choose the **T**ext menu.

2. Select one of the following enhancements:

    Regular

    Bold

    Italic

    Underline

    Outline

    Shadow

3. Repeat the process to select additional enhancements for the
    same text.

You can select a text enhancement before you begin typing or while
you are typing, but after you click the mouse button to set your text
into the painting, you cannot change the text enhancement. (For information on how to erase the text and type new text, see the upcoming
section, "Editing a Painting.")

Selecting a Font, Style, and Size

A font is an alphabet of characters that have the same appearance. Fonts that come with Windows (if you are using TrueType) include Times New Roman, Arial, and Courier New. You may have additional fonts supplied by your printer or by font software. Using a dialog box, you can change the font, font style, and font size all at once (font styles are the same as the font enhancements listed in the **T**ext menu). You also can add strikeout and underlining.

If you are not using TrueType, the fonts you have available to use are those fonts installed in your printer or those fonts that you download from your computer. In the Font dialog box (shown in fig. 13.18) you can tell whether a font is a TrueType font, a printer font, or a system font by the icon that appears to the left of the font name in the Font list. TrueType fonts have a "TT" icon; printer fonts have a printer icon; and system fonts have no icon. A sample box shows you how your font, style, and size will look on-screen and when you print. To learn more about TrueType, refer to Chapter 8.

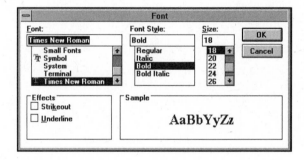

FIG. 13.18

The Font dialog box.

To select a font, style, and size, follow these steps:

1. Choose the **T**ext menu and select the **F**onts command.

   The Font dialog box appears, which enables you to change font, style, and size all at once.

2. From the Font list, select the font you want to use.

3. From the Font Style list, select the style you want.

4. From the Size list, select the size you want your text to be.

5. In the Effects group, select Stri**k**eout if you want a line through your text or select **U**nderline if you want text underlined.

6. Choose OK or press Enter.

When you select a font, that font applies to any new text you type and to any text you are currently typing, if you haven't clicked the mouse button.

FROM HERE...

For Related Information:

◄◄ See "Starting, Using, and Quitting Applications," p. 46 and "Operating Applications," p. 77.

►► To learn more about Microsoft Draw, see "Understanding the Microsoft Draw Screen," p. 757 and "Using Microsoft Draw Drawing Tools," p. 761.

Editing the Painting

With Paintbrush, you can edit a painting by using the eraser tools (described earlier in this chapter); the **U**ndo command; the **E**dit Cut, **C**opy, and **P**aste commands; the **P**ick commands; the Backspace key; and the right mouse button.

As you are editing, be aware that objects in a Paintbrush painting are always completed or uncompleted. Anything uncompleted is subject to edits. You can cancel an uncompleted line or curve, for example, by clicking the right mouse button; you can change the appearance of uncompleted text by making a selection from the **T**ext menu. The method you use to complete an object depends on the object. To complete a straight line, for example, you release the mouse button; to complete text, you click the mouse button.

Using the Undo Command

Use the **U**ndo command to cancel all the work you did up until when you saved the file, selected the tool you're currently using, resized the window, or scrolled the page. For example, if you select a box tool, draw five rectangles, and choose **U**ndo, you erase all five rectangles.

(To undo the Undo, select Undo again.) If you draw four rectangles, select the rectangle tool, draw one more rectangle, and *then* choose Undo, however, you remove only the most recent rectangle.

Be careful when you use Undo. Save the file or reselect the tool you are using to prevent what you are doing from being undone.

To undo your most recent work, choose the Edit Undo command. Alternatively, press Ctrl+Z.

Using Backspace as an Eraser

While you are working with any drawing tool, you can press the Backspace key to display a temporary eraser that looks like a square with an *X* through it. You can use this eraser to erase the work done with the current tool, but you can erase work done only from the point at which you selected the tool. When you're finished erasing, the eraser turns back into the tool you were using before you pressed the Backspace key.

To use the Backspace eraser, follow these steps:

1. Press the Backspace key. The tool turns into an eraser that looks like a box with an *X* in it; the size of the box depends on the selected line width.

2. Press and hold down the mouse button and drag over the part of your drawing you want to erase.

   Remember that the Backspace eraser removes only what you just drew; you cannot erase a completed painting.

3. Release the mouse button. The Backspace eraser changes back to a drawing tool.

Cutting, Copying, and Pasting

In Paintbrush, you cut, copy, and paste objects just as you do in any other Windows application. You start by *selecting* the object with one of the two cutout tools. Techniques for using the cutout tools are described in "Using the Cutout Tools" earlier in this chapter.

To cut or copy a portion of your painting, follow these steps:

1. Use the scissors or the pick cutout tool to select the area you want to cut or copy. A dashed line appears around the selected area.

2. To cut, choose the **Edit Cut** command (Ctrl+X); to copy, choose the **Edit Copy** command (Ctrl+C). The selection is cut or copied into the Clipboard.

To paste the portion of the painting you cut or copied, follow these steps:

1. Display the area of the painting where you want to paste the contents of the Clipboard.

2. Choose the **Edit Paste** command (Ctrl+V).

The pasted object appears at the top left of the screen and is enclosed by a dotted line to show that the object still is selected. You can move the selection by clicking on it and dragging. For additional information, see "Moving a Selection" later in this chapter.

Copying a Selection to a File

You can save a portion of your painting to a file by using the **Edit Copy To** command. When you use this command, name the file and choose a file format. If you don't choose a file format, Paintbrush saves the file in its native format, which ends with the extension BMP. Files that have the extension BMP can be opened in Paintbrush.

To copy part of a painting to a file, follow these steps:

1. Use the scissors or the pick cutout tool to select the portion of the painting you want to save to a file.

2. Choose the **Edit Copy To** command. The Copy To dialog box appears.

3. Type a file name in the File **Name** text box and select from the list in the **Directories** box the directory in which you want to save the file.

4. In the List Files of **Type** list, select one of the following file formats:

Format	File Extension Assigned
PCX	PCX
Monochrome bitmap	BMP
16 Color bitmap	BMP
256 Color bitmap	BMP
24-bit bitmap	BMP

If you don't select one of these formats, Paintbrush saves the file in Paintbrush bit-map format with the extension BMP.

5. Choose the **I**nfo button to see a dialog box describing the width, height, number of colors, and number of planes in your painting. Choose OK.

6. Choose OK or press Enter.

Pasting from a File

The **E**dit Paste **F**rom command enables you to merge the contents of two or more Paintbrush files. When you choose the command, a dialog box appears, listing all the Paintbrush files (those files with the extension BMP). You also can list and open files with the extensions PCX and MSP. When you select one of the listed files, Paintbrush pastes it into the top left corner of the file currently open. Because the pasted picture arrives selected (as if it were selected with a cutout tool), you easily can move it where you want it on the page.

To paste from a file, follow these steps:

1. Choose the **E**dit Paste **F**rom command.

2. If necessary, select the file format of the files you want to list and open. The available selections are as follows:

   BMP

   MSP

   PCX

   All Files

3. From the File **N**ame list, select the file you want to open. (If necessary, first select a different directory from the **D**irectories box.) Alternatively, type the name of the file you want to open in the File Name box.

4. Choose OK or press Enter. The file is pasted in the top-left corner of the screen.

Moving a Selection

You can move an object or area on-screen after you select it with the scissors or pick cutout tool. (The object already is selected if you just pasted it.) Paintbrush has several tricks for moving selections. You can move a selection and make it transparent or opaque. You can move a selection and leave a copy of the selection behind. You can *sweep* a selection across the screen and leave a trail of copies of the selected image behind.

To move a selection, follow these steps:

1. Use the scissors or pick cutout tool to select an object or area of the drawing. A dashed line encloses the selection.

2. Move the crosshair over the selection (so that the crosshair is inside the dashed line that defines the edges of the selection). The crosshair turns into an arrow.

3. Press and hold down the left mouse button to drag the selection to its new location and make it a *transparent* object. Press and hold down the right mouse button to drag the selection to its new location and make it an *opaque* object.

4. Release the mouse button.

5. Click the mouse button outside the selection to fix the selection in its new location.

If you move a selection transparently, the space between the object and the dashed selection line—usually a white border around the outside edge of the object you want to move—is transparent. If you move opaquely, the white space between the object and the selection line is also opaque and erases whatever is underneath it when you release the mouse button.

To copy a selection, follow the preceding steps for moving a selection, but press and hold down the Ctrl key as you drag the object to its new location. You can copy the selection and make it a transparent object (by holding down Ctrl and dragging with the left mouse button) or an opaque object (by holding down Ctrl and dragging with the right mouse button).

To sweep an image, follow the preceding steps for moving a selection, but press and hold down the Shift key as you sweep the image to its new location and leave a trail of images behind. You can sweep the selection and make it a transparent or opaque image. The faster you sweep the selection, the fewer copies of the image it leaves behind. Figure 13.19 shows an example of sweeping a transparent object.

Getting Different Views of the Painting

You can zoom in to get a closer look at your painting or zoom out to see the whole page. Zoom In mode shows you the pixels, or tiny

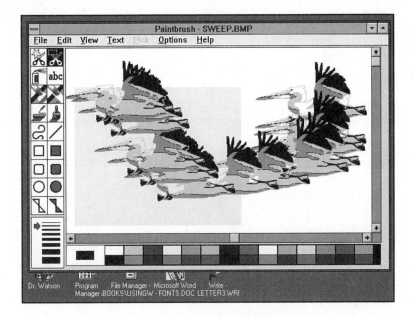

FIG. 13.19

Sweeping an
object by holding
down the Ctrl key
as you drag.

squares of color, that make up your painting. You can paint *pixels* in
the selected foreground color by clicking the dots with the left mouse
button and in the background color by clicking the right mouse button.
You can use the paint roller tool in Zoom In mode, or you can click and
drag the mouse to change all the pixels in a selected area. (Click with
the left mouse button to change all selected pixels to the foreground
color; click with the right mouse button to change all selected pixels to
the background color.) The upper-left corner of the Zoom In view will
show a normal view of the Zoom area.

To zoom in for a close-up view of your painting, follow these steps:

1. Choose the **View Zoom In** command (or press Ctrl+N). A zoom
   box appears to help you define where you want to zoom in.

2. Position the zoom box over the spot on which you want to
   zoom in.

3. Click the mouse button to zoom in. Paintbrush displays a close-up
   view of your painting on-screen (see fig. 13.20).

To zoom back out to regular editing view, choose the **View Zoom Out**
command (or press Ctrl+O). You also can choose **View Zoom Out** when
you are in the regular view to display a reduced picture of the entire
page. Choose **View Zoom In** to return to normal size.

> **You Can Do Some Editing in the Zoom Out View**
> When you zoom out to see your whole painting, you can cut, copy, and paste selections. You can rearrange a painting that is larger than your screen. You only can paste, move, or sweep the selection as an opaque object, however. To paste, move, or sweep transparently, zoom in to the regular editing view.

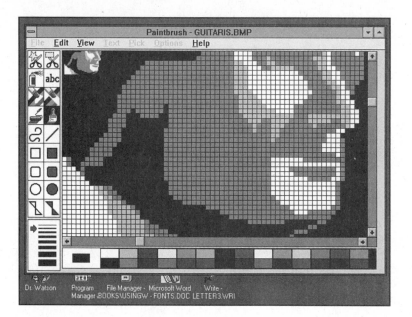

FIG. 13.20

Zooming in to get a closer look of your work.

If your painting is larger than your computer screen, you can see more of it by using the **V**iew **P**icture command. When you choose View Picture, all toolboxes, menus, and scroll bars disappear, and your picture expands to fill the window. You only can view in this mode; you cannot edit your painting in Picture mode.

To view more of your painting, follow these steps:

1. Choose the **V**iew **V**iew Picture command or press Ctrl+P.

2. Return to the normal editing view by clicking the mouse button or by pressing the Esc key.

When you're drawing lines or shapes that must line up accurately on-screen, you will find the **V**iew **C**ursor Position command helpful. **V**iew **C**ursor Position displays a small window at the top-right corner of the screen. In the window are two numbers that tell you the position of the insertion point or drawing tool on-screen. The position is given in XY coordinates, measured in pixels, from the top left corner of the painting. The left number is the X-coordinate (the position relative to the left edge of the painting); the right number is the Y-coordinate (the position relative to the top of the painting). If the numbers in the Cursor Position window read *42, 100,* for example, the cursor is 42 pixels from the left edge of the painting and 100 pixels down from the top of the painting.

To display the Cursor Position window, follow these steps:

1. Choose the **View Cursor** Position command. The window appears as shown in figure 13.21.

2. Hide the Cursor Position window by choosing the **View Cursor** Position command again. Alternatively, double-click the control bar at the top left of the Cursor Position window.

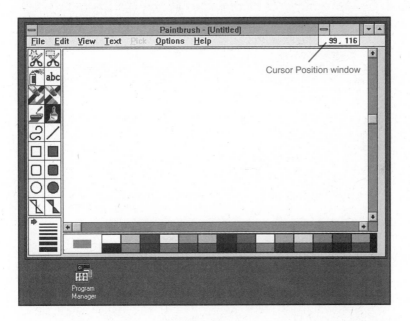

FIG. 13.21

The Cursor Position window appears at the right end of the title bar.

If the Cursor Position window is not conveniently located, you can move it to another place on-screen. With the mouse, drag the window by its title bar to a new location. With the keyboard, press Alt+F6 to activate the window; press Alt+space bar to open that window's Control menu; and then choose the **M**ove command to display the four-cornered move arrow. Press the arrow keys to move the window; press Enter to anchor the window in its new position.

Creating Special Effects

Using the **Pick** menu, you can flip, invert, shrink, enlarge, or tilt objects you selected with the scissors or pick cutout tool. These special effects can help you refine your Paintbrush painting by altering selected objects in subtle or not-so-subtle ways.

Flipping a Selection

You can flip a selection in two ways: horizontally (left to right) or vertically (top to bottom). Flipping horizontally reverses an image from left to right; you can use this technique to create mirror images by copying the selection and then flipping the pasted copy as shown in figure 13.22. Flipping vertically flips an image from top to bottom, making it upside-down.

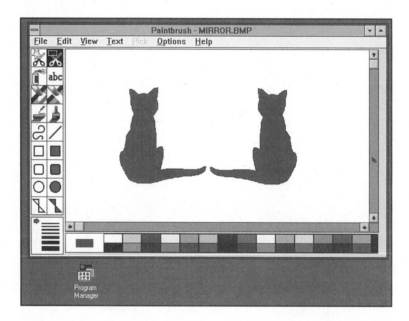

FIG. 13.22

You can create mirror images by flipping a copy of your selection horizontally.

To flip a selection, follow these steps:

1. Use the scissors or pick cutout tool to select the object or area you want to flip.

2. Choose the **P**ick Flip **H**orizontal command to flip horizontally; choose **P**ick Flip **V**ertical to flip vertically.

Inverting Colors

You can invert the colors in your painting, changing them to their opposite on the red/green/blue color wheel. In an inverted black-and-white painting, for example, black becomes white, and white becomes black; in an inverted green-and-yellow painting, green becomes purple, and yellow becomes blue (any white border area turns black). Use this technique to *reverse* a selected object.

To invert colors, follow these steps:

1. Use the scissors or pick cutout tool to select the object or area you want to invert.

2. Choose the **P**ick **I**nverse command.

Shrinking and Growing a Selection

You can use the **P**ick **S**hrink + Grow command to reduce or enlarge a selection. After you select the object and choose the command, you drag the mouse to draw a box the size in which you want the resized image to fit. When you release the mouse button, the object fills the box you drew, and the box disappears.

If you choose the **P**ick **C**lear command before you choose the **P**ick **S**hrink + Grow command, Paintbrush erases the original selection after resizing the image. (If you choose Clear, make sure that the selected background color in your palette matches the background color in your painting—the area you select will be filled with the background color when you shrink or grow the selection.) If you don't choose **P**ick **C**lear, you create a resized duplicate of the original.

To shrink or grow a selection, follow these steps:

1. Use the scissors or pick cutout tool to select the object or area you want to shrink or grow.

2. Choose the **P**ick **S**hrink + Grow command.

3. Position the crosshair where you want the new resized image.

4. Press and hold down the mouse button; drag the mouse to draw a box the same size as you want the new, duplicated image. To keep the new image proportional to the original, hold down the Shift key while you press and hold down the mouse button, drag the mouse, and release the mouse button.

5. Release the mouse button. Release the Shift key if you used it.

When you finish shrinking or growing your selection, select a tool to cancel the Shrink & Grow command—otherwise, you can shrink or grow your image again and again.

Tilting a Selection

Drawing an angled polygon is a precise science. Fortunately, Paintbrush makes it easy with the Pick Tilt command. The Tilt command works a little like the Shrink + Grow command: after you select the object and choose the command, drag the mouse to draw a box at the angle at which you want the tilted image to appear. When you release the mouse button, the object appears—tilted—in the box you drew, and the box disappears.

If you choose the Pick Clear command before you choose Pick Tilt, Paintbrush erases the original selection after tilting the image. If you don't choose Pick Clear, you create a duplicate of the original. If you choose Pick Clear, make sure that the background color in your painting matches the background color selected in your palette.

To tilt a selection, follow these steps:

1. Use the scissors or pick cutout tool to select the object or area you want to tilt.

2. Choose the Pick Tilt command.

3. Position the crosshair where you want the tilted object to appear.

4. Press and hold down the mouse button; drag left or right to create a tilted box that is the same shape you want your tilted object to be. Notice that the box you're drawing has a dashed-line border.

5. Release the mouse button. The selected object fills the tilted box you drew, and the box disappears.

Figure 13.23 shows an image before and after it was tilted.

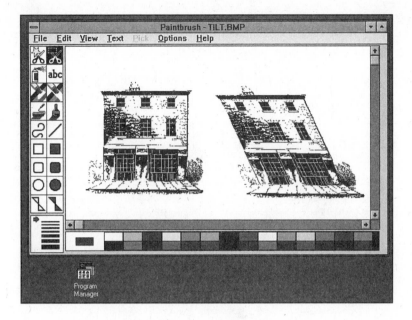

FIG. 13.23

Tilting an image.

Working with Color

Color is a tremendously important component in daily life, giving meaning to what you see. Psychologists have studied color's effects on people; advertisers use color carefully to attract attention; artists use color as one of their most important tools. If you have a color monitor, you can use color in your Paintbrush paintings, and you can use your colorful paintings in applications such as Windows Write, Word for Windows, and Aldus PageMaker. If you are lucky enough to have a color printer, you can print your painting in color.

Computer color is different from pigment color because computer color is made of light. In Paintbrush, colors are blended from three primary colors—red, green, and blue—each of which has 255 degrees of shading. Black is no light: zero red, zero green, and zero blue. White is pure light: 255 red, 255 green, and 255 blue.

Paintbrush has 28 colors in its palette, including black and white. All these colors are blended from the three primary colors. You can customize the Paintbrush palette by blending your own colors. If you create a palette of colors you like, you can save it and retrieve it to use in another Paintbrush painting. (You can retrieve palettes from Microsoft Draw if they have no more than 28 colors and end with the extension PAL.)

To customize colors in Paintbrush, start with an existing foreground color and modify it by adding or subtracting amounts of the three primary colors. A sample box at the right side of the Edit Colors dialog box shows you the color you are creating.

To create a custom color, follow these steps:

1. Select from the palette the foreground color you want to alter.

2. Choose the **O**ptions **E**dit Colors command. Alternatively, double-click on the color in the palette you want to customize. The Edit Colors dialog box appears (see fig. 13.24).

3. Increase or decrease the amount of each color (**R**ed, **G**reen, and **B**lue) by clicking the left or right arrows in the scroll bars. Watch the color in the sample box on the right side of the dialog box change when you alter the amount of each color.

4. Choose OK or press Enter to add your custom color to the palette, replacing the color that was there before. Alternatively, choose **R**eset to reset the color to what it was originally.

FIG. 13.24

The Edit Colors dialog box.

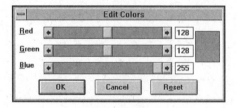

The colors you customize don't change the current painting, but they make different colors available on the palette. Your custom palette remains in effect when you start a new Paintbrush painting; unless you save the custom palette, the colors are gone when you close the Paintbrush application. If you save a custom palette, you can retrieve it into any Paintbrush file.

To save a custom palette, follow these steps:

1. Choose the **O**ptions **S**ave Colors command. The Save Colors As dialog box appears.

2. Type a name in the File **N**ame box. If necessary, select a different directory in the **D**irectories box or a different drive in the Drives list.

3. Choose OK or press Enter.

When you save a palette, Paintbrush assigns the extension PAL, but you can specify a different extension if you want.

To retrieve a custom palette, follow these steps:

1. Choose the **O**ptions **G**et Colors command.

2. Select a palette file from the File **N**ame list box. (If necessary, first select a directory from the **D**irectories box.) If you know the file name of the palette you want to retrieve, you can type its name in the File **N**ame box.

3. Choose OK or press Enter.

Remember that you can reset a custom color to its original palette shade by selecting the color and choosing the **R**eset button in the Edit Colors dialog box. You can reset a color to its original color even if you have changed it more than once or have saved the palette.

If you customize your palette, the customized version appears in any new document you create until you restart Paintbrush—at which time, you revert to the default 28-color palette.

For Related Information:

▶▶ To learn more about using colors with Microsoft Draw, see "Working with Colors," p. 772.

FROM HERE...

Setting Up the Page

Page-setup choices affect your printed paintings. Margins, for example, determine where your painting is positioned on the page. You add headers and footers to the top and bottom of your printed pages. (See table 13.1 for a list of the commands you can use in headers and footers.)

To set up your page for printing, follow these steps:

1. Choose the **F**ile Page Se**t**up command. The Page Setup dialog box appears.

2. Select the **H**eader box and type a header to appear at the top of your printed page. Headers appear inside the top margin.

3. Select the **F**ooter box and type a footer to appear at the bottom of your printed page. Footers appear inside the bottom margin.

4. In the Margins box, select the **T**op, **L**eft, **B**ottom, and **R**ight boxes and type the margins you want. Paintbrush warns you if your margins are too large for your painting.

5. Choose OK or press Enter.

When you type the text of the headers and footers, you can include any or all of the commands listed in table 13.1.

Table 13.1 Commands for Headers and Footers	
Command	**Function**
&d	Includes the current date
&p	Numbers the pages
&f	Includes the file name
&t	Includes the current time
&l	Aligns the header/footer to the left margin
&r	Aligns the header/footer to the right margin
&c	Centers the header/footer between the margins (This command is the default choice.)

Controlling Screen Size and Appearance

Paintbrush determines the capabilities of your computer monitor and the amount of memory your computer has available for printing graphics. With this information, Paintbrush creates an appropriately sized drawing area. You can override the *default* image area by resizing the image area to make it smaller or larger.

To resize the Paintbrush image area, follow these steps:

1. Choose the **O**ptions **I**mage Attributes command.

2. In the **W**idth box, type the width you want for the image area.

3. In the **H**eight box, type the height you want for the image area.

4. In the **U**nits group, select in (inches), cm (centimeters), or pels (pixels).

5. Choose OK or press Enter.

If you plan to expand the size of your painting, keep in mind that a larger painting (or one with colors) uses more of your computer's memory and takes more memory to print. If you expect to print at printer resolution rather than screen resolution (see "Printing Paintbrush Files" later in this chapter), enter the height and width dimensions in pels (pixels, or picture elements) in proportion to the current screen dimensions.

To return to the default image area size, select the **D**efault button. In the same dialog box, you can select whether the palette appears in black and white or color (and hence whether your drawing is in black and white or color). The changes you make in this dialog box don't affect the current Paintbrush document; they take effect when you open a *new* Paintbrush document and remain in effect for all new documents until you change them again.

Saving Paintbrush Files

When you save a Paintbrush file, Paintbrush assigns the extension BMP to the file name and saves the file in Windows bit-map format. If you prefer, you can save the painting in a different format so that you can use it in another application. For example, you can save a file in PCX format to use with several PC painting applications.

To save a Paintbrush file, follow these steps:

1. Choose the File Save **A**s command. The File Save As dialog box appears.

2. Type a file name in the File**n**ame text box; select from the **D**irectories box the directory where you want to save the file.

3. Select the **O**ptions box to select one of the following file formats:

Format	File Extension Assigned
PCX	PCX
Monochrome bit map	BMP
16 Color bit map	BMP
256 Color bit map	BMP
24-bit bit map	BMP

If you don't select one of these formats, Paintbrush saves the file in Paintbrush bit-map format with the extension BMP.

4. Select the Info box to see a dialog box describing the width, height, number of colors, and number of planes in your painting.

5. Choose OK or press Enter.

To resave your file later without changing the name, select the Edit Save command.

Working with Other Applications

The paintings you create in Paintbrush make wonderful illustrations that you can use with many other applications. If the other application does not support object linking and embedding, you can include a Paintbrush painting by copying the painting. (Such a painting remains static in your other application—you cannot change it.) You also can link or embed it in an application that supports object linking and embedding. Linked and embedded paintings can be edited from within the other application.

To copy a Paintbrush painting into another application, follow these steps:

1. Select the painting, or portion of the painting, that you want to copy to another application.

2. Choose the Edit Copy command.

3. Start the other application, open the document where you want to copy the painting, and position the insertion point where you want the painting to appear.

4. Choose the Edit Paste command.

With some applications, you can insert a Paintbrush file without opening Paintbrush. In PageMaker, you can choose the File Place command. In Word for Windows, you can choose Insert Picture.

Applications such as Windows Write, Word for Windows, and Page-Maker include commands you can use to move and resize illustrations that you paste into your documents.

When you copy a Paintbrush painting onto the Clipboard (or copy part of a painting), the painting is stored in various formats so that you can paste the painting into documents in other applications. Some applications, however, cannot paste those formats. For those applications, you must remove the formatting before you copy the painting or selection onto the Clipboard.

To remove formatting, follow these steps:

1. Choose the **O**ptions **O**mit Picture Format command.

   A check mark appears next to the command.

2. Select the portion of the painting you want to copy.

3. Choose the **E**dit **C**opy command.

Remember to choose the **O**ptions **O**mit Picture Format command a second time to turn it off for future copies, if necessary.

Embedding and Linking Paintbrush Paintings

Besides being a stand-alone painting application, Paintbrush also is an OLE *server* application. OLE stands for object linking and embedding. A server is an application that can create objects that can be embedded inside or linked to documents created in other applications. Paintbrush can create objects that can be embedded or linked to documents created by applications such as Windows Write and Word for Windows.

For example, you can embed or link a Paintbrush painting (or part of one) inside a letter created in Windows Write or a report created in Word for Windows. When you embed or link objects inside a document, the application used to create that document is functioning as an OLE client. Applications besides Write and Word for Windows also can function as OLE clients.

When a Paintbrush object is embedded or linked in a document, you can start Paintbrush—with the object displayed in its drawing window—from within that document. For example, if a bar chart that you created in Paintbrush is embedded or linked in a letter you created in Write, you can start Paintbrush and edit the bar chart from within your Write document.

Embedding and linking differ in three ways: in the way you get the embedded or linked object from the server document into the client document; in the way the client application stores the object; and in the way you update the object.

Embedding a Paintbrush Object

You can use two different methods to embed a Paintbrush painting inside a document created by a application that supports OLE. You can either copy the painting into the client application's document, or you can use a command in the client program to insert the object. Each way has advantages. If you copy the painting, you can use an existing painting; if you create a painting, you can save it to a separate file that you can embed in other documents. If you embed a painting from within the client document, you cannot use an existing painting, and you cannot save the painting as a standalone file, but you can create the painting without leaving the client document.

When you embed an object inside a document, the client application stores the entire object with the client document. For example, you can give someone a disk containing a Write file with an embedded Paintbrush picture, and as long as they have Paintbrush on their computer, they can view, edit, and update the picture. Similarly, if someone gives you a Word for Windows file containing an embedded object created by a graphics application that you do not own, you still may be able to view, edit, and update the picture—because Windows has all the information about the picture, it will use another graphics applications (such as Paintbrush) to display, edit, and update it.

To embed a Paintbrush painting by copying, follow these steps:

1. Start the client application (into which you want to embed your Paintbrush painting) and Paintbrush.

2. In the client application, open the document into which you want to embed the Paintbrush painting. Scroll to display the exact place where you want to embed the painting.

3. In Paintbrush, open the document containing the painting you want to embed in the client document. Or, you can create the painting (save the painting if you want to use it again later).

4. Select the Paintbrush painting (or part of it) that you want to embed.

5. Choose the **E**dit menu and select the **C**opy command.

6. Switch to the client application and position the insertion point in the document where you want to embed the painting.

7. Choose the **E**dit **P**aste command.

The commands for embedding a Paintbrush painting from within a client application vary. In the following example, you see the command for embedding a painting into a Windows Write document. Using this technique, you must create the painting from within your Write document, and you cannot save the painting to use in any other document. (You also can use the same technique to embed many other types of objects besides Paintbrush paintings.)

To embed a Paintbrush painting from within Windows Write, follow these steps:

1. Start Windows Write and open the document into which you want to embed a painting. Position the insertion point where you want the painting.

2. Choose the **E**dit menu and select the **I**nsert Object command. The Insert Object dialog box appears.

3. From the **O**bject Type list, select Paintbrush Painting. Choose OK or press Enter.

   Paintbrush appears on your screen with a new, blank painting window.

4. Create your painting.

5. To add your painting to your Write document without closing Paintbrush, choose the **F**ile menu and select the **U**pdate command. Choose the **F**ile menu and select the E**x**it & Return command when you are ready to close Paintbrush and return to your document.

   Or, to add your painting to your Write document and at the same time, close Paintbrush, choose the **F**ile menu and select the E**x**it & Return command. When a dialog box appears asking whether you want to update your Write document, choose **Y**es.

To embed a Paintbrush painting into a Word for Windows document, choose the **I**nsert menu and select the **O**bject command. From there, the steps are the same as for Write. If you have a different application, check the menus to see which command will work; although the command may not be exactly the same as the commands in Write or Word for Windows, it is likely to be similar.

Be sure to save your Write or Word for Windows file in order to save your Paintbrush painting.

After a Paintbrush object is embedded inside a client application's document, you can edit the object from within that document. In almost any application, you can do that by double-clicking on the object to start Paintbrush. You also can use keyboard commands to edit embedded objects in most applications, but the commands vary. In Write, select the object, choose the **E**dit menu, and select the Edit Paintbrush Picture **O**bject command. In Word for Windows, select the object, choose the **E**dit menu, and select the Paintbrush Picture **O**bject command. Look for a similar command if your application is different.

To update an embedded Paintbrush object, follow these steps:

1. Start Paintbrush from within the client document by double-clicking on the Paintbrush picture or by choosing the appropriate command from the client application's menu.

2. Change the Paintbrush object.

3. Choose the File menu and select the Update command.

4. Choose the File menu and select the Exit & Return command to exit Paintbrush and return to your document.

To learn more about object linking and embedding, read Chapter 6.

Linking a Paintbrush Object

Linking an object from Paintbrush into a client document is similar to embedding. There is only one way to do it, however: you must copy a saved picture into the client document using a special command.

A linked picture is not stored as a complete file inside the client document, as is an embedded picture. Instead, the client document stores a link to the original file. If you give someone a disk with a Write file containing a linked Paintbrush picture, therefore, you also should include the Paintbrush picture on disk.

The advantage to linking is that when you change the original picture, the picture in the client document updates to reflect your changes. Because the client document stores a link to the original, rather than storing the original, you can create a single original picture and link it to many client documents (even if they are created by different applications). All the client documents update to reflect changes to the original.

To link a Paintbrush picture to a client document, follow these steps:

1. In Paintbrush, create or open the picture you want to link to the client document. If you make any changes, you must save the file.

2. Select the portion of the picture you want to link and choose the Edit Copy command.

3. Start the client application and open the document where you want to link the picture. Position the insertion point where you want the picture.

4. Choose the Edit Paste Link command.

Most client documents link objects so that they update automatically when the original object changes. However, you can edit the link in many ways: you can set it for manual update; you can update the link to reflect a new location for an original file that you have moved; or you can link the picture to a different original file.

Like an embedded object, you can edit a linked object from within the client document. The technique for starting the server application is the same as for embedding: you can double-click on the linked picture, or you can select the picture and choose an editing command. The application starts, and you edit and save the picture.

To learn more about linking, read Chapter 6.

Printing Paintbrush Files

Paintbrush gives you great flexibility in printing paintings. You can print all or part of a painting, in draft or final quality, scaled smaller or larger. Before you print, be sure that you have the correct printer selected and set up.

To select and set up a printer, follow these steps:

1. Choose the File Print Setup command.

    The Printer Setup dialog box appears.

2. Select a printer from the Printer group. You can select the Default printer or any other printer from the Specific Printer list.

3. Select an option from the Orientation group: Portrait prints your painting vertically on the page; Landscape prints it horizontally.

4. If necessary, choose options from the Paper group: to change the paper size, select an option from the Size list; to change paper source on your printer, select an option from the Source list.

5. Choose OK or press Enter.

Setting up a printer in Paintbrush is the same as in any application. Remember that printer setup choices you make in one Windows application apply to *all* Windows applications. For details about printer setup, refer to Chapter 7, "Customizing with the Control Panel."

To print the Paintbrush painting on the selected printer, follow these steps:

1. Choose the File Print command. The Print dialog box appears (see fig. 13.25).

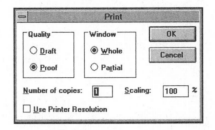

FIG. 13.25

The Print dialog
box.

2. In the Quality box, select **D**raft or **P**roof. **D**raft prints an
   unenhanced version of the painting quickly; **P**roof prints an accurate version of the painting. (On some printers, such as laser
   printers, there is no difference between Draft and Proof printing.)

3. In the Window box, select **W**hole or **P**artial. **W**hole prints the entire painting; **P**artial displays the painting on-screen and enables
   you to drag a crosshair to enclose the part of the painting you
   want to print.

4. In the **N**umber of copies box, type the number of copies of the
   painting you want to print.

5. In the **S**caling box, type a percent at which you want to print the
   painting. *100%* is actual size; *50%* is half size; *200%* is double size,
   and so on.

6. Select the **U**se Printer Resolution option to print the painting at
   printer resolution rather than Paintbrush screen resolution.
   Printer and screen resolution may be different; Paintbrush
   stretches a painting to make it print the same as it appears on-
   screen if you do not select Use Printer Resolution.

7. Choose OK or press Enter.

FROM HERE...

For Related Information:

◄◄ To learn how to use Paintbrush paintings inside Write word processing documents, see Chapter 12, "Using Windows Write," p. 473.

►► To learn how to add paintings to a Cardfile or a Notepad file, see
Chapter 16, "Using Desktop Accessories," p. 639.

►► To learn how to integrate Paintbrush paintings with other Windows applications, see Chapter 22, "Using Windows Applications
Together," p. 847.

Chapter Summary

This chapter presented the information you need to use Paintbrush to paint useful illustrations. Now that you know how to create with Paintbrush, use your paintings to enliven the documents you create in other applications. If you find Paintbrush useful but want to do more, you may be ready for a more powerful graphics application.

Using Windows Terminal

Webster's defines communication as the giving or exchanging of information. This definition provides a good start toward explaining what a communications application does. It enables a user to give information to or get information from a variety of sources—a mainframe, a public bulletin board, or another PC. The information may be as varied as corporate manufacturing data, medical or literary information, on-line airline information, budget worksheets, or messages sent to other users of a bulletin board.

Personal computers provide a wonderful quick way to create letters, track business data, and generate financial information. But users need to share the information created. Information from a mainframe may help create a management report. To transfer the information from place to place—from an office computer to a home computer, for example—you need communications software, such as the Terminal application.

Communications applications use software and hardware components to link computers. The software component translates computer information into a signal that can be transmitted quickly and accurately over telephone lines. The hardware component may be a modem that converts computer signals into telephone signals and connects the computer to the telephone line. The hardware and software components of both your PC and the other computer must use the same methods of communication and the same *protocol* (communication language).

For computers to communicate, they must use the same communication settings, including type of communications port, memory parity (a checking method), stop bits (end of a word), and baud rate (the transmission rate). If you are dialing through a modem, you also may need a telephone number. Once the settings are in place, you can start the communications process.

Normally, to communicate with another computer, you follow this procedure:

1. Start the Terminal application.

2. Use the **S**ettings menu to change settings, if necessary, or use **F**ile **O**pen to open and load settings you saved previously.

3. Use the **P**hone menu to dial the phone line of the other computer.

4. Enter log-on information and then either interact with an on-line computer service or receive or send files in text or binary format and save them to disk.

5. Disconnect from the other computer.

6. Hang up the phone line, using the **P**hone menu.

7. Save the settings using the **F**ile menu if settings have changed or if you want to use them again.

8. Exit the Terminal application.

Terminal Cannot Connect to Another Terminal Application
Designed to send or receive information to and from a host communication program, the terminal cannot act as a host itself. For this reason, you can connect Terminal to a corporate database system, to a public service such as CompuServe, or to another personal computer that uses a communication program that can act as a host.

Starting Terminal from the Program Manager

To start Terminal, choose the Accessories group in the Program Manager and then open the Terminal application. Open this application by double-clicking on it with a mouse or by pressing an arrow key until the icon is selected and then pressing Enter.

Creating and Using Settings Files

If you frequently use Terminal to connect to the same source of information, you may want to save the settings for this communication. This makes reconnecting quick and easy. Settings files contain the information selected in the Settings menu. All commands in the Settings menu are saved except the last three menu items: Printer Echo, Timer Mode, and Show Function Keys.

Creating a Settings File

Choose the File New command to reset Terminal settings back to their default, or normal, state. Choosing File New deletes any phone number entered, clears the Terminal scroll buffer, and resets the communications port to 1200 baud, 8 bits, 0 stop bits, and no parity. If you made changes before choosing New, Terminal asks whether you want to save the existing settings before it resets all options to their default states.

Saving a Settings File

To save any changes made to the currently loaded settings file, choose the File Save command. Save automatically overwrites the existing settings file and saves all currently selected settings options. If the current file is untitled, Save automatically defaults to the Save As command so you can name the settings file.

To save the current settings under a new file name, choose the File Save As command. The previous settings file remains unchanged. Save As displays the dialog box shown in figure 14.1.

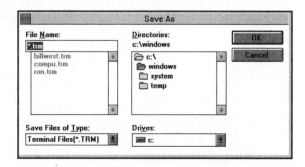

FIG. 14.1

The File Save As dialog box.

If you enter the name of an existing file, Terminal displays a dialog box asking whether you want to replace the selected file with a Terminal settings file.

T I P   If you save a settings file with the name TERMINAL.TRM, Terminal loads this file as the default when you start the application.

Opening a Settings File

Use the **F**ile **O**pen command to load a previously saved settings file. If you have made changes to the currently loaded settings file, Terminal asks whether you want to save any current settings before loading the new settings file. When you choose **F**ile **O**pen, the dialog box shown in figure 14.2 appears.

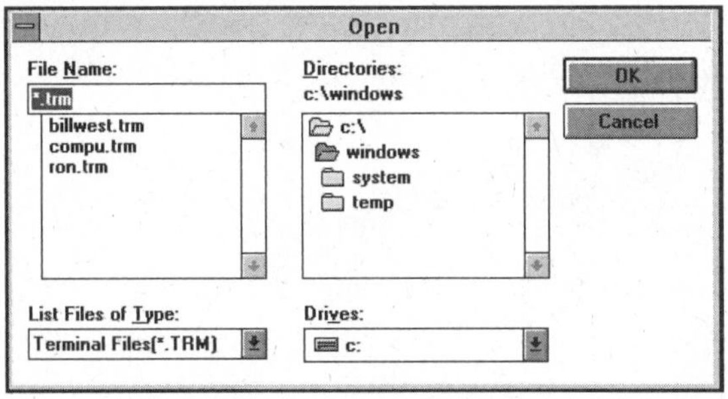

FIG. 14.2

The File Open dialog box.

As shown in figure 14.2, Terminal defaults to the file extension TRM. You can change this extension to anything you want. You can use the Windows Program Manager to create a Terminal program item icon that appears in a group window of the Program Manager. You can associate a particular settings file with this icon so that when you start Terminal, it automatically loads with all the options saved in the settings file.

FROM HERE...

For Related Information:

◀◀ To learn how to associate files with applications so that you can start them together from the Program Manager, see "Operating the Program Manager," p. 116; "Customizing Groups," p. 119; and "Operating in Windows," p. 67.

▶▶ See also "Responding to an Application Failure," p. 1071.

Leaving Terminal

Choose the File Exit command to leave the Terminal application. If you have made any changes to the settings, you are asked whether you want to save the changes before exiting Terminal.

Remember to Hang Up!
If you are currently connected with a modem, Terminal asks whether you want to hang up. Failing to hang up the phone when you exit can leave you connected to a remote computer system, causing you to be billed for unused connect time. Do not worry about being billed for days of use, however; most systems automatically hang up if you have not made an entry in the last few minutes.

Using the Edit Menu

The Edit menu enables you to copy information from an application and paste the information into the Terminal window. You then can send what you paste to the computer to which you are connected.

Suppose that you have written a note in Windows Notepad and want to send it as though you were typing directly into the Terminal program.

Make the Notepad window active, select a block of text, and copy it to the Clipboard. Next, activate Terminal, and when the computer you are connected to requests that you type your message, select Edit Paste. Although you are pasting information into Terminal, the computer you are connected to assumes that you are typing the message from the keyboard. The following sections explain how to use the Terminal Edit menu to manipulate text from other applications.

Copying Text to the Clipboard

Use normal copying procedures for Windows or non-Windows applications to copy text or numbers into the Clipboard. Terminal purges all blanks at the end of each selected line and ends each line with a carriage return and line feed.

If you want to send graphics through Terminal, you need to send them as a binary file. Sending a binary file is described later in this chapter.

Using the Send Command To Save Steps

To send text directly to another computer, without copying and pasting, wait until the computer you are connected to requests your message. Then select the text, choose the Edit Send command, or press Ctrl+Shift+Ins. Terminal copies the text you pasted to the Clipboard and sends it to the remote computer. This option is particularly useful when you are replying to electronic mail and want to forward part of a message you have received.

Selecting All the Text in Terminal's Buffer

Terminal stores information it has received in an area of memory called a *buffer*. To select the entire contents of Terminal's buffer, choose the Edit Select All command. This option is equivalent to selecting all of Terminal's received messages with the mouse or keyboard.

Clearing Terminal's Buffer

To clear the contents of Terminal's scroll buffer and window, choose the Edit Clear Buffer command. This command clears the data that has scrolled through Terminal's window.

Tailoring Terminal to Your Needs

You can tailor most of Terminal's options to your needs through the Settings menu, where you configure Terminal to match the communication requirements of other computers. The Settings menu enables you to select the default phone number, terminal emulation, terminal preferences, function keys, text transfers, binary transfers, communications parameters, and modem commands. Each operation is described in the following sections.

Using CompuServe

CompuServe is one of the most widely used public databases. Anyone can join CompuServe for a low membership fee. You then can connect to many different types of information services at rates of $12 per hour and up. The information services you can connect to cover a wide-range of topics:

Help for Windows and Windows applications

Libraries of free programs and sample files

On-line airline guides that help you find and schedule the lowest air fares

Dow-Jones stock quotes

Wall Street Journal articles and analyses

News reports that have been filed but not yet published

Medical and legal databases

Engineering and technical databases

Games

The settings to connect to CompuServe are as follows:

Settings **P**hone Number	Local CompuServe phone number (call CompuServe for this number)
Settings **B**inary Transfers	**X**Modem/CRC (remember this setting; every time you download files, CompuServe will ask you for this information)
Settings **C**ommunications	
Baud Rate	1200
Data Bits	8
Stop Bits	1
Parity	None
Flow Control	Xon/Xoff
Connector	(choose the COM port your modem is connected to)

Chapter 30 lists some of the CompuServe forums related to Windows and Windows applications. These forums are an excellent source of software updates, shareware and freeware programs, access to technical support from Microsoft engineers, and more.

Entering a Phone Number

From the **S**ettings menu, choose Phone **N**umber to specify the phone number you want Terminal to dial. The dialog box shown in figure 14.3 appears when you select this option.

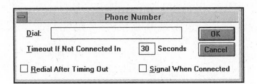

In the **D**ial text box, type the phone number you want to use. The phone number can contain parentheses and dashes. A comma placed anywhere in the text field causes the modem to pause for two seconds before dialing any remaining digits. Use this option when you need to dial 9 to get an outside line and must pause briefly.

In the **T**imeout If Not Connected In text box, type the time (in seconds) you want Terminal to wait before assuming that the remote computer is not answering the phone. The minimum time allowed is 30 seconds.

Select **R**edial After Timing Out to make Terminal automatically redial the phone number after the time limit has been reached.

Select **S**ignal When Connected to have the computer beep to indicate that the connection has been made. This feature can be very useful when you are working on several tasks and want Terminal to signal you when it connects with the remote computer.

Selecting a Terminal Emulation

Choose the **S**ettings Terminal Emulation command to specify which type of terminal you want to emulate. Terminal emulation makes the Terminal program act like one of three industry standard hardware terminals used with most computers. The dialog box shown in figure 14.4 appears.

Terminal supports three terminal emulations: TTY, VT 52, and VT 100. The TTY emulation recognizes only ASCII text and responds to carriage returns and line feeds. The VT 100 and VT 52 emulations are based on the popular DEC VT 100 and DEC VT 52 terminals. When you select either of these terminal emulations, Terminal responds to all the display requests these terminals have, such as bold, underline, and the DEC line-drawing character set.

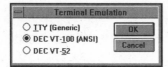

FIG. 14.4

The Terminal
Emulation dialog
box.

Using Arrow and Function Keys During Terminal Emulation
When Terminal emulates VT 52 or VT 100 terminals, your PC keyboard can emulate the VT 52 or VT 100 keyboard. Press the Scroll
Lock key to switch from the Windows keyboard to the terminal
keyboard. When emulating a terminal, the arrow keys work the
same, the F1 through F4 function keys become the PF1 through
PF4 keys, and the numeric and punctuation keys are the same.
Press the + key on your keyboard for the VT 52 or VT 100 Enter
key.

Choosing Terminal Preferences

To modify local terminal parameters, choose the **S**ettings Terminal
Preferences command. This specifies how your personal computer
accepts the characters it receives—for example, how it wraps lines of
text and whether it double-spaces lines. When you choose this command, the Terminal Preferences dialog box appears (see fig. 14.5).

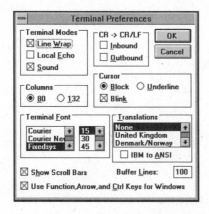

FIG. 14.5

The Terminal
Preferences
dialog box.

Select the Line **W**rap check box if you want Terminal to wrap characters that pass the last character column displayed in Terminal. Do
not check this option if you want Terminal to lose and not display

characters that exceed the width of the Terminal display. Select this option if Terminal is set to display 80 columns, but the computer you are connected to sends 132 columns. Selecting Line Wrap ensures that data is not lost.

Select the Local Echo check box if you want Terminal to echo (repeat on your screen) keystrokes you're sending. Otherwise, Terminal displays outgoing keystrokes on the remote system only. You cannot see them.

In some hardware, the remote system echoes the transmitted keystrokes back to you (a condition called *remote echo*). In this instance, deselect Local Echo to avoid displaying each keystroke twice on your screen. If the remote system is not configured for remote echo or if you are not currently connected, select Local Echo to display the outgoing keystrokes as you type them. By default, the Local Echo setting is deselected.

Select the Sound check box to direct Terminal to sound warning bells (^G characters) coming from the remote system. Disable the bell by deselecting the Sound check box. By default, this setting is selected.

Select the Inbound check box to display incoming carriage returns as carriage returns followed by line feeds. Deselect the Inbound check box to display incoming carriage returns as carriage returns only. By default, the Inbound setting is deselected. If your computer receives the transmission with double-spacing, change this setting.

Select the Outbound check box to display outgoing carriage returns as carriage returns followed by line feeds. Deselect the Outbound check box to display outgoing carriage returns as carriage returns only. By default, the Outbound setting is deselected. If the other computer receives the transmission with double-spacing, change this setting.

Select the width of the scrolling region for your window by specifying in the Columns group the desired number of columns (one character per column). You can select a width of either 80 or 132 characters. If the width you specify is too wide to display in the Terminal window, you may have to scroll right to view the entire document. The default number of columns is 80.

Depending on the type of display monitor you have, you may find that one type of insertion point or cursor is more visible than another. Portable computers especially may require some experimentation to find the best cursor type. Select Block to display the cursor as a block; select Underline to display the cursor as an underscore character. If you want the cursor to blink, select the Blink check box. Deselect the Blink check box if you want the cursor to display without blinking. By default, the Blink setting is selected.

As is true of any good Windows application, you can select the font and point size used for the characters on-screen. Select fonts and sizes for the Terminal window from the scrolling-list boxes in the Terminal Font group. All Windows display fonts are available for use in the Terminal window.

If you use Terminal in an international environment, you may need to use international-character sets. Select the desired character translation from the Translations scrolling list. By default, Terminal selects the country specified in Country Settings in the WIN.INI file. You can see and change these settings through the International option in the Control Panel window. Modifying the Translations setting in this dialog box does not permanently alter the WIN.INI file.

If your message is long or its characters exceed the screen width, you need to scroll the window. You use the scroll bars to scroll with the mouse. If you work strictly with the keyboard, you may want to remove the scroll bars so that you can see more of the screen. Select the Show Scroll Bars check box to direct Terminal to display the scroll boxes in the Terminal window. Deselect the Show Scroll Bars check box to remove the scroll-bar display. This choice is valid whether or not the Terminal window is maximized.

Terminal keeps the information you send and receive in an area of memory called the *buffer*. You can control the size of the buffer. Enter in the Buffer Lines text box the desired size of the buffer in numbers of lines. If you type a number smaller than 25, Terminal allocates a scroll buffer containing 25 lines. The default number of buffer lines is 100. With the mouse, use the scroll bars at the sides of the Terminal window to determine the size of the buffer you need. Scroll backward and forward through the buffer to display the text you typed and received.

If you know that you want to save all the lines you send and receive, use the techniques described in "Receiving Text Files," later in this chapter.

If you want to use the function, arrow, and Ctrl keys to carry out Windows tasks—for example, using Ctrl+Esc to open the Task List—select the Use Function, Arrow, and Ctrl Keys for Windows options. If you want to use these keys to control the software on the remote computer, deselect this option.

After you specify the Terminal Preferences settings, you can use them, discard them, or save them to a settings file.

Creating On-Screen Function Keys

Using function keys is an easy way to automate the communications process. Instead of using the menu items, for example, you can program a function key to dial a number, send your user ID, or hang up. You can display function keys as buttons at the bottom of Terminal's screen, as shown in figure 14.6. Display or hide function keys with the Settings Show Function Keys or Hide Function Keys command.

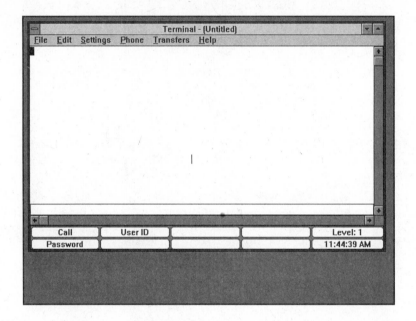

FIG. 14.6

Function keys display at bottom of Terminal's screen.

You can create up to 32 function keys. Because the function keys have other purposes in Windows, you must press Ctrl+Alt+*function key* to activate the custom keys.

The 32 possible function keys appear in four *levels* of 8 keys, as you can see at the bottom of figure 14.6. For convenience, put the keys you use most often in level 1. You can access level 1 function keys without additional mouse clicks or key presses.

Switch between levels with the mouse by clicking on the level-indicator button at the far right of the banks of buttons. (This indicator reads Level:1 in figure 14.6.) Switch between levels with the keyboard by creating a function key in each level that takes you to the next level. The code you use to define such a key is described later in this chapter.

As you can see in figure 14.7, a function key definition has two parts: the function key name and the function key command.

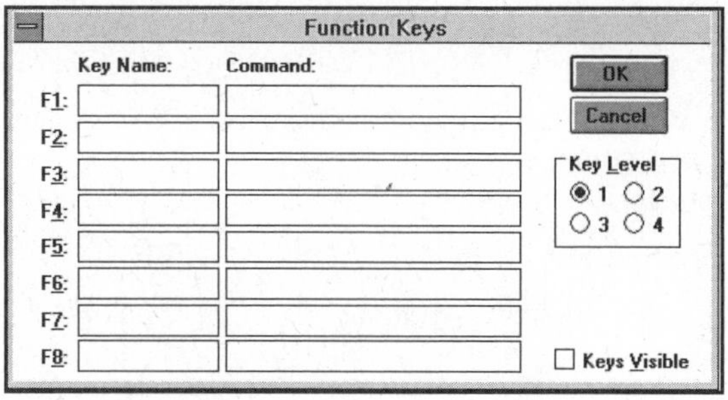

FIG. 14.7

The Function
Keys dialog box.

To customize function keys, follow these steps:

1. Choose the **S**ettings Function **K**eys command. The dialog box shown in figure 14.7 appears.

2. Select a Key **L**evel of 1 through 4 to specify the group of function keys you want to create. Usually, you start with level 1.

3. Select the Key Name of the function key you want to customize and type the text you want to appear in the button (the label of the button). Press Tab to move to the Command text box for that key.

4. In the Command text box, type the text or commands you want the key to perform. A chart later in this section describes those commands.

5. Repeat steps 3 and 4 to customize any other function keys in this level.

6. Select the Keys Visible check box to display the function keys.

7. Choose OK or press Enter.

The Command text boxes can contain any combination of text and codes from the following chart. The chart lists the actions you may want a function key to perform and provides the appropriate commands to achieve those actions.

Action	What To Type in the Command Text Box
Send Control-A through Control-Z (note that these commands do not include a $)	^A through ^Z
Send a Break code (each number is a unit equal to 117 milliseconds)	^$B*number*
Choose the **P**hone **D**ial command	^$C

continues

Action	What To Type in the Command Text Box
Delay Terminal for *number* of seconds (use this command while waiting for password or log-on response)	^$D*number*
Choose the **Phone Hangup** command	^$H
Change to the level of key group indicated by number (1 through 4); enables you to use the four groups of eight function keys	^$L*number*
Send a caret (^) to the remote computer	^^
Send a NULL character to the remote computer	^@
Send *number* escape code sequences to remote computer	^[*number*

Those codes preceded by ^ are typed with the Shift+6 key and not the Ctrl key.

You can assign the key name *MyLogin* to F1, for example, and type the following commands in the Command text box:

    ^$C^$D10LOGIN^M^$D10PASSWORD^M

When you press F1 or click the on-screen button containing this command, Terminal executes the ^$C command and calls the number specified in the active settings file. Terminal waits 10 seconds as specified by ^$D10, sends the string LOGIN and a carriage return (^M), waits 10 more seconds, sends the string PASSWORD, and sends another carriage return (^M).

If you want a key that changes between function-key levels, use a code like the following in that key's Command box:

    ^$L3

When you press Ctrl+Alt+*function key* (where *function key* is the key to which this command is assigned), the display changes to show the function keys on level 3.

Displaying Function Keys On-Screen
To display the function keys on-screen when you open a settings file, check the Key Visible check box in the Function Keys dialog box and save the settings file. If you want to toggle between displaying and hiding the on-screen function keys, choose the **Set**tings **Show Function Keys** command. This command toggles between Show Function Keys and Hide Function Keys.

Changing How Terminal Sends Text

You use text transfers to transmit text files. Text files are usually word processing or mainframe files that do not contain formatting. (To transfer other types of files, see the following section on binary transfers.) Choose the **S**ettings Text Transfers command to set the text-transfer protocol and the text margins. The dialog box shown in figure 14.8 appears.

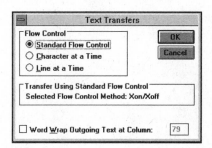

FIG. 14.8

The Text Transfers dialog box.

To transfer text in XON/XOFF mode, select **S**tandard Flow Control. In this mode, the receiving system sends an XOFF message to the transmitting system when the receiving system's input buffer is nearly full. The transmitting system then halts transmission until it receives an XON message from the receiving system, indicating that the input buffer has been cleared.

Select **C**haracter at a Time to transfer text one character at a time. Notice that when you select this option, the dialog box changes, as shown in figure 14.9.

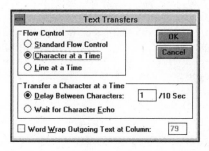

FIG. 14.9

The Character at a Time option in the Text Transfers dialog box.

Select **D**elay Between Characters to specify the delay between characters. Enter the desired delay in tenths of a second in the text box. Changes are sent at even intervals without regard to whether they have been received correctly.

Select Wait for Character **E**cho to instruct Terminal to wait until the receiving computer echoes back its response. In this mode, the transmitting system waits for the transmitted character to be returned by the receiving system before it sends the next character. The transmitting system compares the two characters to verify that the correct character was received.

To transfer one line at a time, select **L**ine at a Time from the Flow Control group. The dialog box options change, as shown in figure 14.10. Select Delay **B**etween Lines to specify the delay between lines. Enter the desired delay in tenths of a second in the text box. Lines are sent at even intervals without regard to whether they have been received correctly.

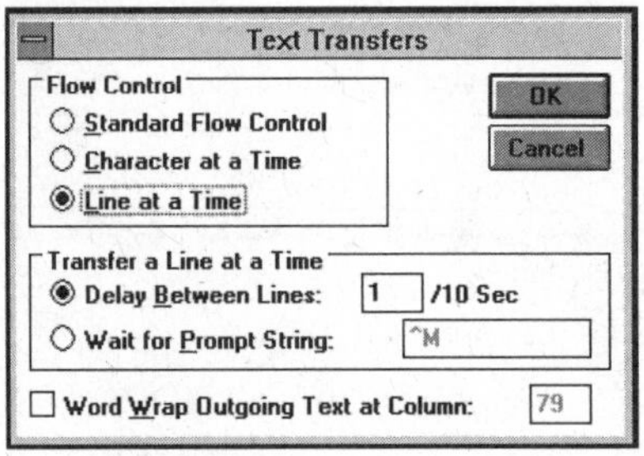

FIG. 14.10

The Line at a Time option in the Text Transfers dialog box.

Select Wait for **P**rompt String to prompt Terminal to wait to receive a line from the remote system before sending the next line. ^M is the suggested end-of-line character. Use this method when you have difficulty with character transmission.

If the text you are sending may be formatted wider than the width of the receiving screen, select Word **W**rap Outgoing Text at Column. (This option frequently is needed when you send text files from a word processor.) You then can specify the column number at which you want the text to wrap. For example, if the receiving terminal has a 132-column screen, set the Word **W**rap option to 131 columns. This setting leaves one character position for the ^M end-of-line code. If you do not select this option, text is sent as it is formatted.

Selecting Binary Transfers Options

Use a binary transfer when you want to transfer a file in its native format—for example, an Excel XLS or XLC file, a Lotus WK1 file, a formatted Word for Windows file, a graphics file, or a compressed PKZIP or archived file.

Choose the **S**ettings **B**inary Transfers command to specify the binary transfer protocol. The dialog box in figure 14.11 appears. You can choose either **X**Modem/CRC or **K**ermit protocol; the default binary transfer protocol is XModem/CRC. Make sure that the sending and receiving communications applications are using the same protocol. Some computers or services to which you connect, such as Compu-Serve, ask you which method of transmission you want to use.

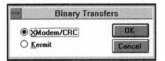

FIG. 14.11

The Binary Transfers dialog box.

Transmitting Application Files

If you want to use Terminal to send a Microsoft Excel, Word for Windows, or 1-2-3 file from one PC to another, make sure that both computers are transmitting at the same baud rate and with the same file-transfer protocol—either XModem or Kermit. After you connect with the other PC, test the connection by typing some text in your Terminal window. The text you type should appear on the other PC's screen. When text is typed on the other PC, that same text should appear on your screen.

When you know that you have established the connection, choose the **T**ransfers Send **B**inary File command, select the file you want to send from the scrolling list, and then choose OK.

If the user of the other PC selects the **T**ransfers Receive Binary File command, you can see the progress of the transfer in the status bar. You also can make Terminal an icon and watch the background color of the icon change as the transfer progresses. You may work in other applications while the transfer is proceeding. When the transfer is complete, the icon flashes.

Selecting Communications Parameters

An important aspect of using your computer to exchange information is setting the communications *parameters*. These communications characteristics ensure that two computers "talk" at the same rate, use the same bundles of information, and use the same dialect. If you are connecting to a commercial database service, such as CompuServe, or with a local bulletin board system, call the service to find out what settings you should use. (Settings for CompuServe are listed in a tip in this chapter.) To change or set parameters, choose the **S**ettings **C**ommunications command (see fig. 14.12).

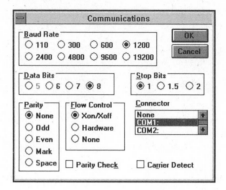

FIG. 14.12

The Communications dialog box.

Select the speed at which you want data to be sent and received by specifying the **B**aud Rate. The maximum baud rate at which you can communicate is a function of many factors, such as the type of modem and the quality and length of the communications line. The default baud-rate setting is 1200. Most telephone communication is done at 1200 or 2400 baud.

Select the number of **D**ata Bits to be transmitted in each character packet. The default **D**ata Bits setting is 8.

Select the number of **S**top Bits to be transmitted. The default **S**top Bits setting is 1.

Select the **P**arity type. Parity is used for detecting errors during transmission. If you selected 8 for the Data Bits setting, then select None for the Parity setting. If you select Mark parity, the eighth bit is set to on. If you select Space parity, the eighth bit is set to off. Odd and Even parities calculate the total of the first seven bits; the eighth bit is then set by Terminal to make the total of the eight bits either always odd or always even.

Select the **F**low Control. If XON/XOFF is selected, the receiving system sends an XOFF message to the transmitting system when its input buffer is nearly full. The transmitting system halts transmission until it receives an XON message from the receiving system, indicating that the input buffer has been cleared. If you select Hardware, flow control is handled through the pins on the RS-232 serial cable. If you select None, no flow-control method is used.

Your modem connects your computer to another computer's telephone line or directly to a minicomputer or mainframe computer. For Terminal to send information to the modem, Terminal must know which communication port the modem is connected to. If the serial ports in the back of your computer are not labeled, check with your dealer or support representative to find out which one the modem is connected to. Select the desired communications port from the **C**onnector scrolling list. In Windows 3.1, you can use COM1 through COM4. Select None when the modem is disconnected because you're using its serial port for a printer or other device.

Select the Parity Chec**k** check box to direct Terminal to replace with a question mark (?) characters that do not match the specified parity. Characters may not match because of transmission errors or noise in the telephone line. Deselect the Parity Chec**k** check box to ignore parity errors. The default Parity Chec**k** setting is deselected.

Hayes-compatible modems have a hardware-connect signal that is set to TRUE when a communications connection is made. Select the Ca**r**rier Detect check box to enable Terminal to use this signal to determine whether the Receive Line Signal Detect (RLSD) is set. If you select this check box, Terminal automatically hangs up if the carrier is lost, preventing you from having to select **H**angup from the **P**hone menu before dialing. Deselect the Ca**r**rier Detect check box if you do not want Terminal to hang up automatically or if your modem's RLSD is unreliable. The default Ca**r**rier Detect setting is deselected.

Changing Modem Options

Change the **S**ettings **M**odem Commands command to modify the commands Terminal sends to your modem (see fig. 14.13). The correct modem commands for the modem type selected (Hayes is the default) are displayed in the text boxes. You can use these commands "as-is" or modify them to accommodate the codes used by nonstandard modems. Be sure to check your modem manual for the appropriate commands. In most cases, you only need to select the type of modem you are using from the **M**odem Defaults group; you need not enter your own commands.

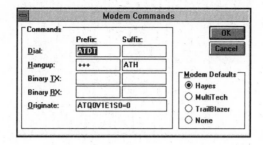

FIG. 14.13

The Modem
Commands
dialog box
showing Hayes
commands.

The following chart lists the various text boxes in the Modem Commands dialog box and the kind of information expected by each.

Text Box	Description
Dial	The prefix and suffix appended to the phone number that direct the modem to dial
Hangup	The prefix and suffix that direct the modem to hang up
Binary **T**X	The prefix and suffix necessary for initiating a binary file transfer
Binary **R**X	The prefix and suffix necessary for receiving a binary file transfer
Originate	How Terminal directs the modem to exit answer mode

Consult your modem manual before you modify these commands. If you make a mistake, choose one of the **M**odem Defaults options to reset the settings.

FROM HERE...

For Related Information:

◄◄ See "Using Menus and Dialog Boxes," p. 35.

◄◄ See "Operating in Windows," p. 67.

Viewing Text Files from Disk

Before you send a text file you may want to view its contents. Choose the **T**ransfers View Text File to see in the Terminal window the file you request. The dialog box shown in figure 14.14 appears. The *.TXT in the

File **Name** text box appears by default, listing all text files with the extension TXT. Select the file you want to view. Display a file in this fashion when you want to review a file before sending it or when you want to add to the file or replace it with an incoming text file.

To view the file, enter the desired file name in the File **Name** text box and choose OK or press Enter.

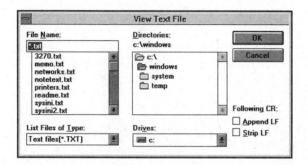

FIG. 14.14

The View Text File dialog box.

Select **Append LF** to add a line feed after each carriage return in the file, producing a new line after each paragraph. Deselect the **Append LF** check box to leave carriage returns as they appear in the file. The default **Append LF** status is deselected.

Select the **Strip LF** check box to strip line-feed characters after carriage returns. Deselect the **Strip LF** check box to leave carriage returns and line feeds as they appear in the file. The default **Strip LF** status is deselected.

After specifying the options in the View Text File dialog box, choose OK or press Enter. The file you specified is displayed on-screen (see fig. 14.15).

A status bar displays in the lower portion of the Terminal window as you view the text file. To stop the **View** Text File from scrolling past, choose either the Stop button or the **Transfers St**o**p** command. To pause the scrolling text temporarily, choose either the Pause button or the **Transfers P**ause command. After you click on the Pause button, it changes to a Resume button. To restart the suspended file display, choose either the Resume button or the **Transfers Resume** command. Terminal displays the name of the file being viewed, and the scale at the bottom changes to indicate the portion of the text that has been displayed.

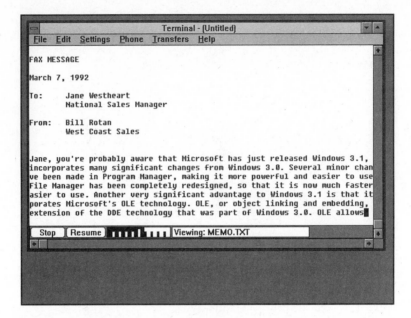

FIG. 14.15

A text file before
it is replaced or
sent.

Printing Incoming Text from Terminal

Choose the **S**ettings Printer **E**cho command to print all data received in the Terminal window. When active, this option is preceded by a check mark in the **S**etting menu. To exit Printer **E**cho mode, choose the Printer **E**cho command again. When you exit Printer **E**cho mode, Terminal sends the printer a form feed to eject the current sheet of paper.

You also can paste information from the Terminal window into a word processing application or the Notepad, where you can edit, save, or print copy. If you receive a large amount of text data, a much more efficient method of printing is to save incoming text to a file. Read "Receiving Text Files" later in this chapter to learn how to save received text directly to a file. Open this file into a word processing application when you want to edit or print it.

Keeping Track of Time with Timer Mode

If you connect with a commercial database, you are charged by the amount of time you are connected, by which database you access, and by your transmission rate (baud rate). Dawdling while you are connected to one of these databases can cost you money, so watch the time. You can have Terminal's clock function as a timer. Just choose the **S**ettings **T**imer Mode command, and the digital timer is displayed at the lower right when the function keys are visible. To reset the timer to zero, deselect and reselect the Timer Mode command from the **S**ettings menu.

Displaying and Hiding On-Screen Function Keys

To see the function keys as buttons at the bottom of your screen, choose the **S**ettings Show Function Keys command. Once the function keys are displayed, the menu option changes to Hide Function Keys. Select this option to remove the function-key display.

Figure 14.6 showed you how the function keys appear when they are displayed. To program your own function keys, refer to "Creating On-Screen Function Keys," earlier in this chapter.

Making a Call with Terminal

Once you have set all the settings necessary to connect to another computer, choose the **P**hone **D**ial command to dial the other computer's modem and make a connection. The **P**hone menu commands dial a telephone number or hang up from the current connection. The **D**ial option directs Terminal to dial a phone number. By default, Terminal dials the phone number specified in the settings file. If no phone number is in the active settings file, enter the number in the **D**ial option dialog box.

Choose the **P**hone **H**angup command to send the hang-up prefix and hang-up suffix specified in the **M**odem Commands dialog box.

Sending Text Files

To send a text file, choose the **Transfers Send** Text File command. This command sends the text file you select, whether created by Notepad or a word processor. When you choose the **Transfers Send** Text File command, the dialog box shown in figure 14.16 appears.

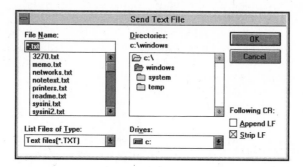

FIG. 14.16

The Send Text File dialog box.

You may choose one of the Following CR check boxes if you want to remove line feeds from the end of each line sent. If the information you receive has overlapping lines (no line feed was sent), select **A**ppend LF. If the information you receive has double-spaced lines, select **S**trip LF. If you are in doubt about how the receiving terminal handles lines, transmit with these boxes cleared. Check the message received by the receiving terminal and then select one of these check boxes so the text is received the way you want it.

A status bar appears in the lower portion of the terminal window as you send a text file. Click on the Stop button or choose **Transfers St**op to cancel the Send Text File option. Click on the Pause button or choose **Transfers P**ause to suspend the file transfer temporarily. When you click on the Pause button, it changes to a Resume button. This procedure is equivalent to using the **Transfers Resume** command to restart the suspended file transfer.

Terminal also displays the name of the file being sent. The scale changes to display the portion of the text file that has been sent.

Receiving Text Files

To receive a text file, choose the **Transfers Receive** Text File command (see fig. 14.17). This command can be used either to receive a text file from the remote system or to capture text coming into the Terminal window and save it to a file.

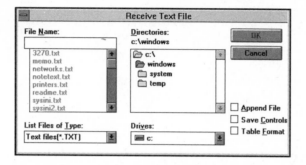

FIG. 14.17

The Receive Text
File dialog box.

Use the **Directories** list box to specify the directory where you want the incoming file saved. In the File **N**ame text box, enter the file name under which you want the text stored.

Select the **A**ppend File check box to save incoming text to the end of the file you specify without clearing the current contents of the file. To replace the current file contents with the incoming text, deselect the **A**ppend File check box. The default **A**ppend File status is deselected.

To save incoming control characters, select the Save **C**ontrols check box. Some applications use control characters to format text, set options, and so on. If you are unfamiliar with control characters, try both settings and then open the files with a word processing application and check the results. To strip incoming control characters, deselect the Save **C**ontrols check box. The default Save **C**ontrols status is deselected.

To save incoming text in tabular format, select the Table **F**ormat check box. Terminal puts tab characters between incoming text fields separated by two or more consecutive spaces. Use this setting when you want to receive a Lotus 1-2-3 print file (which contains only characters and spaces) or a Microsoft Excel TXT file (which uses tabs to separate cell values). Clear the Table **F**ormat check box to save the file in its current format. The default Table **F**ormat status is cleared.

Control buttons appear in the lower portion of the Terminal window as you receive a text file. Click on the Stop button or choose **T**ransfers St**o**p to cancel the **R**eceive Text File option. Click on the Pause button to stop temporarily storing the incoming text to the specified file. After you click on the Pause button, it changes to a Resume button, and the **T**ransfer **R**esume command becomes available. Choose the Resume button or the **T**ransfer **R**esume command to resume storing the incoming text to the specified file.

Caution   Choosing the Pause button or the **Transfer Pause** command to stop temporarily storing incoming text does not prevent the remote system from sending text. The incoming text is not saved while the Receive Text File option is paused. This option is useful for saving (or not saving) parts of a file, but it can cause you to miss data if you select it at the wrong time.

Terminal displays at the bottom of the screen the name of the file in which the incoming text is stored (see fig. 14.17). The Bytes indicator changes to reflect the number of bytes received.

Sending Binary Files

If you are sending formatted word processing files, database files, worksheets, programs, graphics, or compressed files of any type, you probably want to send them as binary files. Choosing the **Transfers Send Binary File** command enables you to send a file in binary format (see fig. 14.18). The *.* in the File **Name** text box appears by default to list all the files in the current directory. The file is sent according to the binary transfer protocol established by the **Settings Binary Transfer** command.

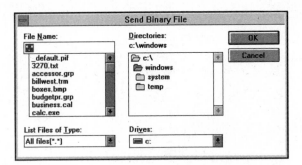

FIG. 14.18

The Send Binary File dialog box.

To send a binary file, use the **Directories** list box to select the directory containing the file. Select the file from the **Files** list or type the file name in the File **Name** text box.

A status bar displays in the lower portion of the Terminal window while you send a binary file. Click on the Stop button to cancel the Send **Binary** File command.

Occasionally, a communications error occurs, preventing the transfer of a packet of data in the binary file. When an error occurs, Terminal tries to send the data packet again. After making the maximum number of unsuccessful retries, Terminal cancels the file transfer. The Retries indicator displays the number of times Terminal tried to resend the data packet.

If an error occurs, check with the receiving party to ensure that you are using the same settings. Line noise or static also may cause the problem. If the problem is telephone noise, try sending the file later.

Terminal displays the name of the binary file being sent. The scale at the bottom of the screen shows the portion of the file that has been sent.

Receiving Binary Files

Choose the **T**ransfer Receive Binary **F**ile option to receive a file in binary file format. The file is received according to the binary-transfer protocol established by the **S**ettings **B**inary Transfer command.

To receive a binary file, check to make sure that you are using the same settings as the computer sending the information. Prepare the file you want to receive and choose the **T**ransfer Receive Binary **F**ile command. The dialog box in figure 14.19 appears. Enter the name of the file you want to receive. To receive the file, click on the OK button or press Enter.

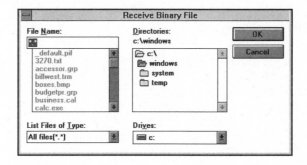

FIG. 14.19

The Receive Binary File dialog box.

A status bar displays in the lower portion of the Terminal window as you receive a binary file. Clicking on the Stop button or choosing the **T**erminal St**o**p command instructs Terminal to cancel the Receive Binary **F**ile option.

Occasionally, a communications error occurs, preventing the transfer of a packet of binary data. When an error occurs, the remote system tries to send the data again. After the remote system makes the maximum number of unsuccessful retries, Terminal cancels the file transfer. The Retries indicator at the bottom of the screen displays the number of times the remote system tried to resend data packets. With XModem/CRC protocol, the maximum number of retries is 20; with Kermit protocol, the maximum number of retries is 5.

Terminal also displays the name of the binary file being received. The scale changes to display the portion of the file that has been received.

FROM HERE...

For Related Information:

◄◄ See "Starting, Quitting, and Using Applications," p. 46.

◄◄ See "Operating Applications," p. 77.

Chapter Summary

You and a co-worker in the same office—or across the country—may want to use Terminal to send and receive files. Although you cannot communicate directly from Terminal to Terminal, you can leave messages for each other in a public database such as CompuServe or upload and download information from your company's computer.

Many people enjoy using on-line databases and mail services. Companies such as CompuServe offer business information, access to buying services, discussions on many topics, and even games.

Using Windows Recorder

The Windows Recorder enables you to automate many repetitious tasks you now perform manually. The Recorder tracks the keystrokes you type, the shortcut keys you press, and the mouse actions you make and saves them in a macro you can later replay. When you replay the macro, Windows repeats the keystrokes and mouse actions exactly.

The Recorder can be used with any Windows application. Even with powerful applications such as Excel and Word for Windows, which have built-in macro recorders, you may find the Windows Recorder useful. The Windows Recorder can make your work easier in many ways:

- Automates any long procedure that you perform frequently or that takes multiple keystrokes

- Types repetitive words, phrases, titles, or boilerplate text in Windows word processing or other applications

- Creates macros that produce the same actions even when they run in applications that have macro recorders

- Automates data exchanges between Windows applications that do not support object linking and embedding

- Opens multiple applications and loads multiple documents with one command

You create macros by getting the applications and documents ready on-screen, turning on the Recorder, and then performing the actions you want the Recorder to remember. When you are finished, turn off the Recorder. The recorded macro is placed in a file with other macros.

Macros are stored in Recorder files—you can store as many macros as you want in one file. When you want to replay a macro, you start the Recorder, open the file that contains the macro you want to replay, and run the macro. In most cases, all your frequently used macros are in one Recorder file; when the file is open, you need only press a shortcut key to replay the macro you want.

Recording and Using Macros

Recording a macro with the Recorder is no more difficult than recording sound with a simple portable tape recorder. When you create a macro, all your keystrokes, shortcut keys, and mouse actions are recorded and given the name and shortcut key you assign. The recording is called a *macro*. Unlike macros in applications such as Excel and Word for Windows, macros in the Windows Recorder cannot be edited. To change a macro, you must record the macro again.

The macro you record is stored in a Recorder file. Each Recorder file can contain more than one macro. When you display the Recorder and open a file, you see all the macros in the file in a scrolling list, like the list shown in figure 15.1.

Recorder - BASIC.REC	
File Macro Options Help	
ctrl+shift+Scroll Lock	My Signature Block
ctrl+shift+B	List all BAK files in current drive
ctrl+F7	Resume the current Printer
alt+F7	Pause the Current Printer

FIG. 15.1

A Recorder file's list of macros.

Although macros can be very simple, you can make them longer to handle complex tasks. When you make complex macros, the best procedure is to make and test smaller macros and then link them in one master macro.

Setting Up and Recording Macros

Before you begin recording a macro, you should have a good idea of what you want to do. In fact, practicing the procedure you want to record is a good idea. You may find that each time you practice a procedure, you think of a shorter or better way to do it.

If the process you want to record is very long, you may want to divide the process into segments and record the segments as separate macros. After you confirm that each of the separate, smaller macros works correctly, you can create a master macro that runs all the smaller ones in the correct sequence. In programming languages, the smaller macros are known as *subroutines*.

To prepare your applications for a recording, follow these steps:

1. Open the applications and documents you need for the recording.

2. Practice the task you want to record, if necessary.

3. Position the applications and documents where you want them to be when the macro starts.

To prepare the Recorder, follow these steps:

1. Open the Program Manager and the Accessories group window, as shown in figure 15.2.

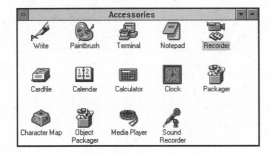

FIG. 15.2

The Recorder icon in the Accessories group window.

2. Start the Recorder application.

3. Minimize the Program Manager, if necessary, to get it out of the way of the applications and documents with which you want to work.

4. Position the insertion point in the application's document or select the text or graphics you want the macro to work on.

5. Activate the Recorder window (make the Recorder window the current window), shown in figure 15.1. If you have not recorded other macros, the Recorder window is blank.

For example, if your macro copies an address block from a Cardfile document into Write, the following conditions are required before you create or play back the macro:

■ You must start the Write and Cardfile applications.

■ You must open the Write and Cardfile files.

■ The format of the address block must be consistent: the macro should take into account the possibility that an address can contain three or more lines.

■ The cursor should be placed at the beginning of the Cardfile document's address block.

■ Cardfile must be the current (active) window.

Each of these conditions is important for the macro to perform properly. The key to creating a successful macro is to ensure that the macro actions are repeatable. This advance planning is important when you create a macro, because you cannot edit a macro after you have created it.

Selecting Options That Do Not Have Active Letters
Some dialog boxes—for example, the one shown in figure 15.3—have options you cannot select directly with an Alt+key combination because they do not have underlined letters. To select options in these cases, press Alt+*letter* to select the group. Watch for the enclosing dashed line that indicates which option is the *focus*. Move the focus by pressing Tab or Shift+Tab. Select or deselect the option by pressing the space bar. Open a drop-down list box by moving the focus to the list and then pressing Alt+the down-arrow key.

To record a macro, follow these steps:

1. To add the macro you are going to record to an existing file of macros, choose the Recorder **F**ile **O**pen command to open the file.

2. Choose the **M**acro Re**c**ord command. The dialog box shown in figure 15.3 appears.

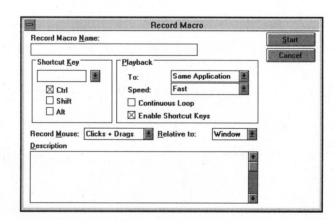

FIG. 15.3

The Record Macro dialog box.

3. Enter a macro name of up to 40 characters in the Record Macro Name text box.

4. Select options to control the playback:

Option	Description
Shortcut **Key**	Specifies the key or key combination you press to activate the macro. Type a letter in the text box or choose a special key from the drop-down list. Select Ctrl, Shift, or Alt to use in combination with the shortcut key.
Playback To	Determines what applications the macro runs in. Select Same Application to run the macro in only the application in which it was recorded. Select Any Application to run the macro in any application.
Playback Speed	Determines the speed of the macro. Select Fast to play back the macro at maximum speed. Select Recorded Speed to play back the macro at the speed at which you recorded it. The Fast playback can cause problems if the macro operation has to wait for the keystrokes to be processed. For example, use Recorded Speed when creating a macro that looks for a group of files in the File Manager. This option ensures that the Search operation is completed before the macro does the next step.
Playback Continuous Loop	Repeats the macro continuously. Press Ctrl+Break to stop the macro.
Playback Enable Shortcut Keys	Enables you to press shortcut keys that run other macros while you record a new macro. This procedure enables you to nest one macro inside another.
Record **M**ouse	Determines the type of mouse actions that are recorded, as described later in this chapter.
Relative To	Determines how mouse movements appear in the macro. Select Screen to make mouse movements relative to the screen position. Select Window to make mouse movements relative to the active window.
Description	Provides room for you to type a description of what the macro does and what applications the macro works with.

5. Choose the **S**tart button.

6. Perform the procedure you want to record.

7. Stop the Recorder by clicking on the blinking Recorder icon or pressing Ctrl+Break. The dialog box in figure 15.4 appears.

8. Choose one of the options in the dialog box.

Option	Description
Save Macro	Saves the macro you have recorded (you also must save the file to keep your macro)
Resume Recording	Continues recording from where you stopped
Cancel Recording	Cancels the recording; does not record what you have done

9. Choose OK or press Enter.

While you are recording, notice that the Recorder application has minimized itself into an icon at the bottom of the screen. While you are recording, the icon flashes.

If you want your macro to work on text or graphics that you select, select a representative piece of text or graphics before you start the Recorder. This procedure enables you to use the macro with any text or graphics you select. If you wait to select text or graphics until after the Recorder is on, the Recorder always tries to select the same text or graphics you selected in the original recording.

T I P   In the **Description** text box, include the names of the applications that must be open in order to use the macro, along with any necessary conditions (for example, that text must be selected). Therefore, if you have trouble running the macro, you can check this box to see whether you have missed any of these necessary pre-conditions. (You can read the **Description** box by selecting the macro and choosing the **Macro Properties** command.)

> **Record Macros with Keystroke Commands and Shortcut Keys**
> The Recorder can record mouse actions and keystrokes. Recording mouse actions, however, can cause problems if you run the macro in an application when the windows are in different locations than when you originally recorded the macro, or if you run the macro on a computer with screen resolution (number of dots) different from that of the original screen. Mouse actions are recorded in units of the current screen. A mouse movement on an EGA screen is a different distance than one on a Super-VGA screen.
>
> When the Recorder records mouse actions, it actually records the mouse pointer's position on-screen at the time you click, drag, select, and so on. If application or document windows are in different locations when the macro runs (which is likely), the macro may miss the command, option, or object on which the mouse was supposed to work. If you run the macro on a computer with a different screen resolution, the relative location of the pointer is different. Therefore, use keystrokes and shortcut keys if you want a macro to run in different situations.

In many cases, if you make a mistake during a recording, you can correct the mistake and continue; the macro records the correction. For example, if you choose an italic font instead of bold, return to the normal font and then choose bold. When you play back the macro, it may operate so quickly that you do not see the correction taking place. You cannot correct some mistakes, such as deleting files. Careful planning of the macro can save time. After you record a macro, you cannot edit it.

Pausing during Recording

You can pause during a recording and continue when you are ready. To pause the Recorder, click on the Recorder icon or press Ctrl+Break. When the Recorder stops, you see the dialog box shown in figure 15.4. Move the Recorder window out of the way, if necessary, and go on to another task. When you are ready to continue, select the Recorder window, select the **R**esume Recording option in this dialog box, and choose OK to continue recording.

Recording with Mouse Actions

Recording macros of mouse movements can cause difficulty if windows are in different positions when you play back the macro than they were when you recorded the macro. One way to reduce this problem is to record the mouse pointer's position relative to the *application window* and not relative to the *entire screen*. To record relative to the window, choose the **R**elative To drop-down list box from the Record Macro dialog box. Select Window (the other option is Screen).

You can choose the mouse actions you record. If you select the Record **M**ouse drop-down list box from the Record Macro dialog box, you see the following choices:

Mouse Option	Description
Ignore Mouse	Records only keystrokes. Use this option if the macro is to be used in multiple applications with windows in varying positions or if the macro will be copied to computers with different graphics resolutions.
Everything	Records keystrokes and mouse actions even if you don't press the mouse button. Press Ctrl+Break to stop the recording if you use this option.
Clicks + Drags	Records keystrokes and mouse actions that result in a command choice.

Using Macros To Run Other Macros

If you need to create large macros or macros that perform similar tasks, you can make your job easier by creating macros that run other macros. Smaller macros that act as building blocks for other macros are known as *subroutines*. Creating macros from subroutines makes sense and can save you time. Subroutine macros have several advantages:

■ Small subroutines are easier to troubleshoot than large, complex macros.

■ Subroutines can be used by more than one macro.

■ Subroutines can be replaced (not edited) without damaging the larger macro they run within.

Before creating a macro that runs other macros, decide how you can divide tasks so that the subroutine macro you create can be used by many other macros. For example, you may want a macro that changes the printer setup to landscape mode for sideways printing. That macro can be used within many other macros that print reports or charts.

Macros to be run by other macros *must* be activated by a shortcut key. You use the shortcut key to activate the subroutine macro during re-cording.

You can *nest* macros inside other macros up to five layers deep.

To use an existing macro within the macro you are recording, follow these steps:

1. Ensure that the **O**ptions **S**hortcut Keys command is selected. (A check mark appears next to the command when selected.)

2. Choose the **M**acro Record command.

3. In the **P**layback group of options, select the **E**nable Shortcut Keys check box.

4. Record the macro up to the point where you want to use a sub-routine macro.

5. Press the shortcut key that activates the subroutine macro.

6. Continue recording the macro, adding other shortcut keys for subroutine macros if needed.

7. Stop and save the recording when you are finished.

The subroutine macro can be used as a normal macro even though you nest it within another macro. If you record over the subroutine macro and use the same shortcut key name, the new subroutine macro runs as the nested macro.

To record a macro that cannot use subroutine macros, deselect the **E**nable Shortcut Keys check box in the Record Macros dialog box.

Changing the Recorder Preferences

You can change the default settings in the Record Macro dialog box by choosing the **O**ptions **P**references command. The dialog box shown in figure 15.5 appears, enabling you to change the default settings for the **P**layback To, **P**layback Speed, Record **M**ouse, and **R**elative To options. The choices and their meanings are the same as those described for the Record Macro dialog box earlier in this chapter.

FIG. 15.5

The Default
Preferences
dialog box

Saving Macros

When you record a macro, the recording is placed in the current Recorder file along with other macros. If you do not save this file, you lose the macros you have made since the last time you saved the file. Files containing macros normally use the extension REC, although you can specify any extension to *hide* your macro files.

To save your new macros, follow these steps:

1. Choose the File Save As command.

2. Select the drive where you want to save your macro file from the Drives list and select the directory from the Directories list.

3. Type a one-to-eight-character name in the File Name box. Recorder adds the extension REC.

4. Choose OK or press Enter.

If you have added macros to an existing file and want to save the file without changing its name, choose the File Save command.

Related Information:

◄◄ See "Controlling the Windows in Windows, " p. 30.

◄◄ See "Using Menus and Dialog Boxes, " p. 35.

◄◄ See "Starting, Using, and Quitting Applications," p. 46.

▶▶ See "Responding to an Application Failure," p. 1071.

Playing Back Macros

You can play back any of the macros in the file currently open in the Recorder. The Recorder must be running, and the file containing the macro you want to run must be open. To replay a macro, press the shortcut key or choose the macro's name from the list in the Recorder file.

Opening Macro Files

After you save a file containing macros, you can retrieve the file and use the macros. You can have only one file at a time open in the Recorder, so you can use only the macros in the open file.

To open a file, follow these steps:

1. Activate the Recorder.

2. Choose the **File O**pen command. (If a file is already open, the file closes, and you are prompted to save the file if you haven't already.)

3. If necessary, select the drive containing your macro file from the Drives list and select the directory from the **D**irectories list.

4. To see a list of all file types, select All Files (*.*) from the List File of **T**ype list. Otherwise, select Recorder Files (*.REC) to list just the files that end with the extension REC.

5. Select the file you want to open from the File **N**ame list.

6. Choose OK or press Enter.

If all the macros you use are combined in a single Recorder file, associate that file with the Recorder program item icon in the Program Manager. When you start Recorder, therefore, you automatically will open your macro file. (To learn how to associate a file and application, refer to Chapter 7.)

T I P

Replaying Macros from a File

You can replay a macro in two ways: by pressing its shortcut key or by choosing its name from a list in the Recorder. When you replay a macro, the Recorder window minimizes (if you have selected the **O**ptions **M**inimize on Use command) or moves behind the window that is just below the Recorder window. The Recorder reacts in one of two ways with the currently loaded applications in Windows:

■ If the macro is the type that runs with any application, the macro replays in the current window. If more than one window is open, the macro replays in the topmost window.

■ If the macro is the type that replays only in a specific application, the Recorder activates that application's window when the macro replays. If the application has not been started or is an icon, the macro does not replay, and an error dialog box is displayed.

To use a shortcut key to replay a macro, follow these steps:

1. Choose the **File Open** command to open the file containing the macro, if necessary.

2. Activate the application in which you want the macro to play; position the insertion point or select text or graphics, whichever the macro expects.

3. Press the shortcut key assigned to the macro you want to play back.

You can assign a new shortcut key to a macro if the current shortcut key interferes with the shortcut keys in an application. "Editing and Changing Macros," later in this chapter, explains how to change the properties of a recorded macro.

T I P   If one of your Recorder macros uses a shortcut key that conflicts with an application's shortcut key, you can turn off the Recorder's shortcut key by choosing the **O**ptions command and selecting the **S**hortcut keys command so that no check mark appears next to it. You can run the Recorder macro by selecting its name and choosing the **M**acro **R**un command.

> **Reduce the Recorder to an Icon During Playback**
> If you want the Recorder to reduce to an icon during playback, choose the Recorder **O**ptions **M**inimize on Use command before replaying the macro.

Macros that operate when you choose their names are useful if you have too many macros to conveniently assign to shortcut keys or if your macros are complex and you need a reminder about their actions. To choose a macro's name to replay the macro, follow these steps:

1. Choose the **File Open** command to open the file containing the macro, if necessary.

2. Activate the application in which you want the macro to play; position the insertion point or select text or graphics, whichever the macro expects.

3. Activate the Recorder.

4. Choose the name of the macro you want to play back by double-clicking on the name or by selecting the name with the arrow keys and choosing the **M**acro **R**un command.

Troubleshooting Macros

If you run a macro that cannot properly carry out its recorded instructions, the macro stops and Windows displays the Recorder Playback Aborted! dialog box shown in figure 15.6.

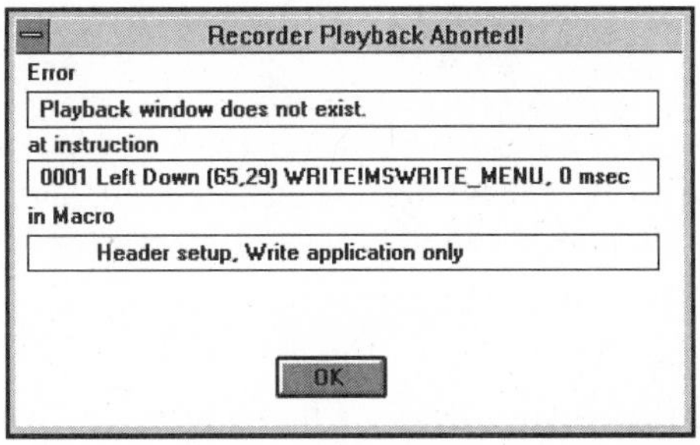

FIG. 15.6

The Recorder
Playback
Aborted! dialog
box.

In the dialog box, the Error text box indicates the probable reason that the macro stopped. In figure 15.6, the macro was recorded specifically for the Write application, using mouse movements and mouse actions. When the macro was run, however, the Write application wasn't running. The Error box message, therefore, says Playback window does not exist. The instruction that the Recorder was trying to execute (at instruction) was the first instruction in the macro, which was trying to access the Write menu. The in Macro text box shows you the name of the macro being executed.

To correct this macro error, you need to start the Write application. If a macro fails, check to see whether it runs when you correctly position the windows. If the macro continues to fail, re-record the macro using keystrokes. Note which applications are used by the macro. When you play back the macro, make sure that these applications are in active or inactive windows. The first application used by the macro does not have to be in the active window, because the macro activates windows as it needs them. The applications, however, have to be running.

Use keystrokes when possible when you record your macros. Mouse actions depend on screen resolution and expect window positions to be the same each time you run the macro.

If a long macro fails, consider re-recording it as subroutine macros—smaller reusable macros that run under the control of a larger macro. You can troubleshoot each subroutine macro and then link them together under the control of the large macro. If a subroutine macro later has trouble or must be changed, you need to change only that subroutine, not the entire large macro. Subroutine macros are described earlier in this chapter in "Using Macros To Run Other Macros."

Do not use a Recorder macro with DOS applications. When you record a macro for use with the Terminal application, the macro should control the application only up to the point that Terminal connects to the other computer.

Looking at the Contents of a Macro

Although you cannot edit a macro, you can look at the keystrokes, mouse clicks, and movements that are part of the macro. Looking at the contents of an improperly working macro may help you create a macro that *will* work.

To look at a macro's contents, follow these steps:

1. Activate the Recorder and load the macro file with the **File Open** command.

2. Select the macro with the mouse or by using the arrow keys.

3. Hold down the Shift key and choose the **Macro Properties** command.

The Macro Events dialog box appears, as shown in figure 15.7. Each mouse or keystroke is shown, along with the window application name and the amount of time used by the keystroke or mouse clicks and movements. You can use the scroll bars to see additional commands. For example, figure 15.7 shows that the Ctrl+F7 macro that pauses the printer consists of the following keystrokes:

■ Pressing the Alt key

■ Pressing the P key

■ Releasing the P key

■ Releasing the Alt key

Choose OK to close the Macro Events dialog box.

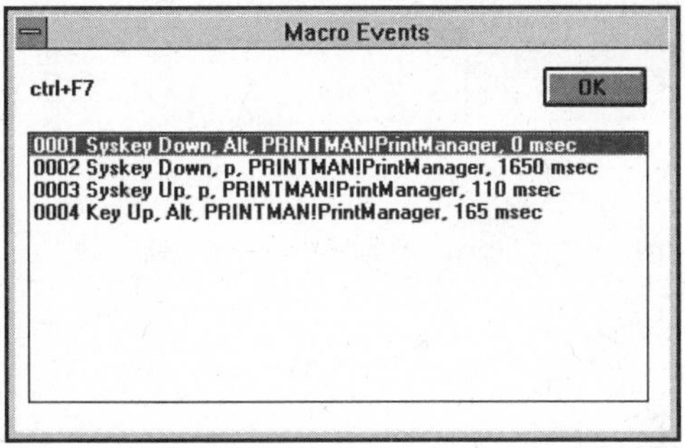

FIG. 15.7

The Macro Events dialog box showing the contents of a macro that pauses the current printer in Print Manager.

Stopping Macros

To stop most macros from running, press Ctrl+Break. You can specify that your macros not be stopped with Ctrl+Break by choosing the **O**ptions **C**trl+Break Checking command. If no check mark appears next to the command, you cannot turn off a macro by pressing Ctrl+Break; you must wait for the macro to finish. If you turn off Ctrl+Break checking for a continuously running macro, you must restart the computer to stop the macro. To do this without turning off the electricity, press Ctrl+Alt+Del; press Enter to close only the current application. Stopping a macro this way can be dangerous, because data in other open applications may be lost if Windows cannot successfully close the current window that is running the macro. Make sure that the macro is working correctly before you disable the Ctrl+Break checking option.

Creating Continuously Playing Macros

To create a demonstration, a tutorial, or an action that replays over and over, you need to know how to make macros repeat continuously. To make a macro repeat continuously, select the **P**layback Continuous Loop check box in the Record Macro dialog box before you record the macro.

If you already have recorded the macro, you can use the **M**acro **P**roperties command to change a normal macro to one that loops by enabling the **P**layback Continuous Loop option.

Stop a continuously playing macro by pressing Ctrl+Break. If Ctrl+Break checking has been turned off, you have to restart the computer to stop the macro.

Caution   Beware of creating continuously playing macros that you cannot turn off by pressing Ctrl+Break. If Ctrl+Break checking is turned off, you must restart the computer to stop a continuously playing macro. Turning off the computer causes you to lose unsaved data in other currently running applications.

For Related Information:

◄◄ To learn more about associating files and applications with macros, see "Customizing Groups," p. 119.

Editing and Changing Macros

You cannot change the steps that a recorded macro performs (although you can look at the macro commands as described in the preceding section). You can change some properties of a recorded macro, such as its shortcut keys, whether it works with only one application or with any application, whether it plays back continuously, and so on.

Figure 15.8 shows the Macro Properties dialog box, which enables you to change settings for a macro you already have recorded.

```
┌──────────────────────────── Macro Properties ─────────────────────────┐
│ Macro Name:                                              ┌────────┐     │
│ [My Signature Block                        ]             │   OK   │     │
│                                                          └────────┘     │
│ ┌─Shortcut Key──────┐  ┌─Playback────────────────────┐  ┌────────┐     │
│ │ [Scroll Lock  ]▼  │  │ To:    [Any Application   ]▼ │  │ Cancel │     │
│ │   ☒ Ctrl          │  │ Speed: [Fast              ]▼ │  └────────┘     │
│ │   ☒ Shift         │  │   ☐ Continuous Loop          │                 │
│ │   ☐ Alt           │  │   ☒ Enable Shortcut Keys     │                 │
│ └───────────────────┘  └──────────────────────────────┘                 │
│ Mouse Coordinates Relative To:        Window                            │
│ Contains no mouse messages.                                             │
│ Description                                                             │
│ ┌────────────────────────────────────────────────────────────┐ ▲       │
│ │ Types in my Signature text at current cursor location.     │ ▒       │
│ │                                                            │ ▒       │
│ │                                                            │ ▼       │
│ └────────────────────────────────────────────────────────────┘         │
└────────────────────────────────────────────────────────────────────────┘
```

FIG. 15.8

The Macro Properties dialog box.

To change a macro's properties, follow these steps:

1. Activate the Recorder.

2. Select the name of the macro you want to change.

3. Choose the **M**acro **P**roperties command.

4. Select and change a property.

5. Choose OK or press Enter.

6. Save the changed macro into its Recorder file with the **F**ile **S**ave or **F**ile Save **A**s command.

The properties of macros are described in "Setting Up and Recording Macros," earlier in this chapter. Notice that you cannot change the Mouse Coordinates Relative To property. If you didn't record any mouse actions, then you also see a message saying `Contains no mouse messages`. If you did record mouse actions, you see a message telling you what type of monitor the actions were recorded on. (This information helps you tell whether the macro is compatible with a different display).

Managing Macros

Macros are like files; they seem to expand and grow on their own. One moment, you have only 2 on your disk; the next time you look, you have 176. Before incalculable volumes of macros swamp your sea of serenity, learn to manage them.

Deleting a Macro from a File

To delete a macro from its file in the Recorder, load the file containing the macro, select the macro name, and choose the **M**acro **D**elete command. When you are asked to confirm that you want to delete the macro, choose OK. Then save the Recorder file.

Merging Files

To use one macro in multiple files, you can merge Recorder files. Merging files brings the macros from a file on disk into the active file in the Recorder. If the macros have duplicate shortcut keys, the duplicate key is removed, but the macro remains. The shortcut keys assigned to macros in the active file in the Recorder are retained.

To merge the macros in two files, follow these steps:

1. Open an existing Recorder file by choosing the File **O**pen command or create a file by choosing the File **N**ew command.

2. Delete unwanted or duplicate macros from the file.

3. Choose the File **M**erge command.

4. In the File **N**ame list, select the name of the file you want to merge into the existing file (change the drive and directory to locate the file, if necessary).

5. Choose OK or press Enter.

The file in the Recorder now contains the combined set of macros. You can save this file under the same name as the original active file by choosing the File **S**ave command, or you can save the file under a new file name by choosing the File Save **A**s command.

Creating Some Useful Macros

After you work with a few common macros, you probably will think of different macros to create that can help save you time. To get you started, the following list contains a few useful macros that you can create. You may find that a few extra commands in a macro will give you even more flexibility.

When you start creating macros, you may find it hard to stop. Many of the following macro ideas take advantage of the fact that most Windows applications use the same keystrokes for the same types of commands.

■ *To print the current document:* This simple macro contains only the Alt+F, P, and Enter keys. Because most Windows applications use this standard for printing the entire document, you may want to set the Playback to Any Application. Also, assign a shortcut key to this macro for quick printing. Place the macro in your default macro file.

■ *To create a common header or footer:* If you always want the page number to appear at the bottom of each page, this macro sets up the footer for you. You may have to make a customized one for each type of word processing application (Write, Notepad, or other Windows applications) or generalize the macro enough so that you are placed in the Header or Footer editing screen.

■ *To pause/resume the Print Manager:* One macro can pause the printer (through the Print Manager) and one can restart the printer. To use these macros, you need to make sure that the Print Manager is running; one way you can do that is by placing a Print Manager program item icon in the Start-up group.

■ *To start bulletin board systems (BBSs):* If you regularly log onto several different BBSs, create a macro that does this for you. The steps required in the macro depend on your communications application. With Terminal, for example, you want the macro to load the configuration file name, dial, and log on. You can create a group of macros that have start-up commands for different BBSs. Then place this macro group in a Recorder file containing communications macros. You may want to store this group of macros in a file with an extension other than REC, if you share your computer with others, or if your Recorder files are stored in a common directory on your network.

■ *To start your fax board application or to print faxes:* If you have a fax board in your computer, a macro to print the current faxes would be useful. Enter the commands that the application requires to print any unread faxes. You also can create a macro that starts up your fax board application.

■ *To perform start-up tasks:* This complex macro may use several subroutine macros. For example, create a macro to check your electronic mail, another macro to print your calendar page for the current day, and other macros to do other start-up functions. Then combine these macros into a master macro that performs each macro subroutine.

■ *To perform address book maintenance:* If you write many letters to people, you can store their addresses in a Cardfile or similar application. Create a macro that copies the current card into your word processing application. For new people, create another macro that copies the address block into a new entry in your Cardfile application. This one may require a bit of advance planning, because you need to have the Cardfile application running. You also need to select the address block before you start the macro.

■ *To print an envelope:* Set up a Write document that contains the proper formatting commands to print an envelope. Then create a macro that takes the address block from your word processing application, copies the block to the Clipboard, and pastes the block into the Write document. Then continue the macro with a Print command. You also can use your Print macro as a macro subroutine by assigning it a shortcut key and using the shortcut key in your envelope macro. This macro takes a bit of advance planning so that you can specify the exact Write commands required to properly set up the envelope document. After you have set that document up, select the address block and then record the macro. When you have built the macro, select the address block in any application and then start it. Make sure that the Write window is open.

You can see that there are many uses for the Recorder. A little advance planning is important when you create the macros. Try to make your macros as general as possible so that they can be shared among applications.

Setting Up a Windows Start-Up Macro

You can set up your Windows environment so that your own Recorder file is loaded when you start Windows. Then your standard macros are available to you as needed.

Follow these steps:

1. Open the Start-up group from the Program Manager window.

2. Choose the **F**ile **N**ew command and select the Program **I**tem Icon option. Choose OK. The Program Item Properties dialog box appears.

3. In the **D**escription box, type a name for your new icon.

4. In the **C**ommand Line box, type the Recorder's full path and name, followed by a space, followed by the path and name of the Recorder file you want to open on start-up. (Use the **B**rowse button if you are not sure of a path or name.)

5. If you want, assign a **W**orking Directory and a **S**hortcut Key. Choose Change **I**con to select an icon. Select **R**un Minimized to start Recorder and to minimize Recorder to an icon every time you start your computer.

6. Choose OK to save the Program Item.

The next time you start Windows, Recorder opens; your macro file automatically is loaded. If you selected the **R**un Minimized option, the Recorder icon is minimized at the bottom of the screen. All the macros in the macro file that loads on start-up are available for you to use.

For Related Information:

◀◀ See "Customizing Groups," p. 119.

FROM HERE...

Chapter Summary

Your computer is best used when it automates repetitious procedures for you. The Windows Recorder can help you automate those common, everyday actions. If you find yourself starting the same group of applications each day, let a macro do that for you. Build simple macros and then combine them into more complex macros by running macro subroutines. The possibilities are almost endless.

As you work with Windows, keep an eye out for those routine actions. Then take a few moments to create a macro that performs that action. You then make the computer work for you, rather than you working for the computer.

When you are working with Windows applications like Excel and Word for Windows, be on the watch for tasks specific to those applications that you can automate with their own macro applications. These macro applications are even more powerful than the Recorder and enable you to not only record macros but to program and edit macros as well.

Using Desktop Accessories

The desktop accessories that come with Windows can help you perform special tasks related to a current project without leaving the application. You may be working in Excel, for example, and need to make a quick note; the Windows Notepad is the perfect companion. When working in Word for Windows, you may need to make a quick calculation; the Windows Calculator can do the job. You may want to make a telephone call but can't remember the phone number; use the Cardfile to find, and even dial, the number. If you need to insert a special character or symbol in a Windows application; you can select the desired symbol from the Character Map.

If you are using Windows for Workgroups, then you will be interested in the WinMeter and NetWatcher accessories. They help you manage your computer while it is on the network.

These desktop accessories take advantage of one of Windows' most powerful features: the capability of running several applications simultaneously. As you work in the main application, you can keep the Windows desktop applications running at the same time. You get quick access to these useful tools—without closing the application in which you're currently working. Because so little of the computer's memory is used, the desktop accessories don't slow you down.

The Write, Paintbrush, Terminal, and Recorder applications are discussed in previous chapters. The PIF Editor, which helps you specify how DOS applications run, is discussed in Chapter 24, "Customizing PIFs." The Media Player and Sound Recorder are described in Chapter 17. The Object Packager is discussed in Chapter 6, "Embedding and Linking." This chapter covers the smaller desktop applications listed in the following chart.

Application	Description
Notepad	A text editor for medium size (up to 64K) text files.
Character Map	A table of symbols and characters for each of the character sets you have available. Copy one or more characters or symbols from the map and paste them in any Windows document that supports multiple fonts.
Cardfile	A computerized stack of cards that stores and retrieves text or graphics. You can quickly find cards that contain a specified word or phrase and use Cardfile's dialer feature to dial telephone numbers.
Calendar	An application that shows you daily or monthly views of a schedule. You can specify times, make notes, and set alarms to track appointments.
Clock	A clock that enables you to be a clock watcher as you stare at the screen. Even as an icon, Clock shows the time.
Calculator	An application that works just like a normal or scientific calculator, except that you don't need batteries and someone won't borrow it off your desk.
WinMeter	This chart shows you how your computer's power is being used by your applications and its network administrative duties.
NetWatcher	Before you shut off your computer you will want to see who is using your shared directories or printer. Let NetWatcher tell you who you are sharing your computer with.
Solitaire	The classic card game that makes you wonder how 1:00 a.m. arrived so quickly.
Minesweeper	An analysis game to help you get tense about something other than work.
Hearts	Now everyone on the network can become addicted to the same card game. If you can't find three friends to play it with over the network, let the computer take up the other card hands.

In this chapter, you learn the features of the Notepad, including how to copy and move text, create a time-log file, and save and print Notepad files. You also learn how to use the Calendar to track appointments and organize your time. You learn how the Cardfile works as a handy database of names and phone numbers, which even can dial phone numbers for you. You see how you can quickly start up a computer Calculator to do math and how you can copy results from the Calculator in the current application. You see how the Clock helps you keep track of time. Finally, for recreation, you learn how to play Minesweeper or Solitaire at the end of the day.

All the Windows accessories are located in the Accessories group window, which you can find in the Program Manager window (see fig. 16.1). Open the Program Manager window by double-clicking the Program Manager icon or by pressing Alt+Tab until the Program Manager title appears and then releasing the keys. Within the Program Manager, you see different icons and windows. Open the Accessories window by double-clicking on the Accessories icon or by pressing Ctrl+Tab to select the icon and pressing Enter. If the Accessories window is open but underneath another window, click on the window to bring it to the top or press Ctrl+Tab until it appears on the top of the on-screen stack of windows.

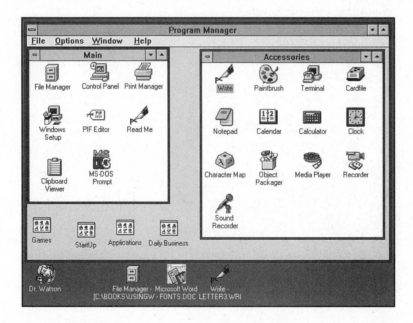

FIG. 16.1

The Program Manager window.

Writing in the Notepad

Notepad is a miniature text editor. Although with limited functions when compared to an application like Windows Write or a professional word processor like Word for Windows or Ami Pro, Notepad is an ideal tool for many purposes. Just as you use a notepad on the desk, you can use Notepad to take notes on-screen while working in other Windows applications. Notepad uses little memory and is useful for editing text that you want to copy in a Windows or DOS application that lacks an editing capability.

The Notepad retrieves and saves files in text format. This feature makes Notepad a convenient editor for creating and altering the Windows WIN.INI file, MS-DOS batch files, CONFIG.SYS files, and other text-based files. (Chapters 25, 26, and 28 describe how to customize Windows by changing configuration files, start-up files, and networking files.) Because Notepad stores files in text format, almost all word processors can retrieve Notepad's files.

Another handy use for the Notepad is to hold text you want to move to another application. The Clipboard can hold only one selection at a time, but the Notepad can serve as a text *scrapbook* when you are moving several items as a group.

As a bonus, Notepad also includes a feature for logging time, so you can use Notepad as a time clock, which enables you to know when you opened a file or to monitor the time you spend on a project. Notepad files cannot hold graphics.

Opening and Closing the Notepad and Notepad Files

Open the Notepad application by double-clicking the Notepad icon in the Accessories window or by pressing arrow keys to select the icon and then pressing Enter. A blank Notepad appears (see fig. 16.2).

You can open a new or existing file from within the Notepad application by choosing the File New or File Open command. To open the file, choose the File Open command to display the Open dialog box, select the directory and file you want to open, and choose OK.

As an alternative, you can open an existing text file that has the extension TXT in Notepad directly from the Windows File Manager. To perform this step, double-click the filename in the File Manager or select the file name and press Enter. Notepad opens and loads the TXT file.

Notepad can open files with the extensions BAT, SYS, INI, and files with the extension TXT. To open files with an INI or BAT extension, choose the **F**ile **O**pen command, change the *.TXT in the Filename text box to *.*BAT*, *.*SYS*, or *.*INI*, and press Enter. A list of files with this extension appears. To see a list of all files with all extensions, in the List Files of **T**ype list, select All Files(*.*).

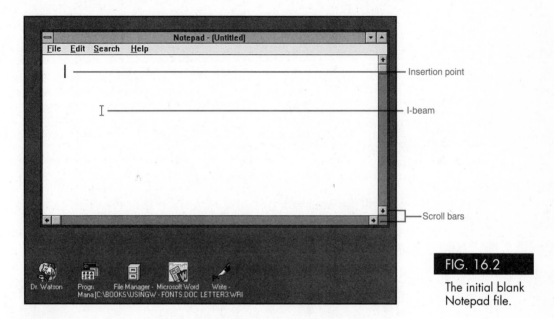

Insertion point

I-beam

Scroll bars

FIG. 16.2

The initial blank Notepad file.

Caution	Be careful when you edit with Notepad. Because Notepad creates text files, you can open and edit important system, application, and data files. To avoid loss of data or applications, make sure that you open only files with which you are familiar or that have the file extensions TXT, BAT, or INI.

Incorrectly editing a batch file (BAT), a system file (SYS), or a Windows initialization file (INI) file can cause problems with computer or application operation. Before making changes, use the **F**ile **C**opy command in the Windows File Manager to create a backup copy of the file with a different name (for example, WIN.BAK). If the system doesn't restart after you make the changes, use a start-up, or *system*, diskette to start the computer and then, using the original file name, copy the backup file back on.

When you open a new file from Notepad, the currently open file closes. If your file has changed, a dialog box asks whether you want to save the current changes. Choose **Yes** to save or **No** to discard the changes. Choose Cancel to return to the original file.

You can close a Notepad file in two ways: open a new file or close the Notepad application. To close the Notepad application, choose **F**ile E**x**it.

Typing Text in the Notepad

Immediately after you open a new Notepad file, you can begin typing. Each character you type appears to the left of a blinking vertical line known as the *insertion point*.

Unlike most word processing applications, Notepad doesn't by default wrap text to the following line. You must either choose the **E**dit **W**ord Wrap command or press Enter at the end of each line. With Word Wrap turned on, text wraps to fit the width of the Notepad window, no matter how wide the window is. If you change the size of the window, the text rewraps to fit (see fig. 16.3). You can activate Word Wrap at any time. When Word Wrap is active, a check mark appears beside the command on the menu.

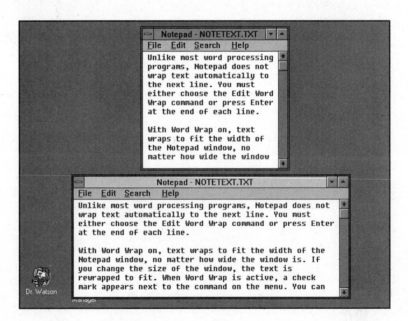

Two examples of text wrapping to fit the Notepad window.

If you choose the Edit Word Wrap command again, the word-wrap feature turns off, and text stretches out until it reaches a hard return. Without automatic word wrap, lines can reach up to 160 characters long (if you type beyond the right edge of the window, the page scrolls to the left). When Word Wrap is turned off, no check mark appears beside the command on the menu.

> **T I P**
>
> If you want to edit in Notepad a file from another application, first open the file in the other application and then save the file in text format. Most word processors, spreadsheets, and databases have this option. Some spreadsheets or databases come with a translator utility that converts the applications files to or from text. Open the text file in Notepad by using the Notepad File Open command.

Moving and Scrolling on the Page

To edit existing text or to add new text in Notepad, you must learn to scroll the page and move the insertion point. Although Notepad pages scroll through the Window, the best way to think of this action is as a Notepad window that moves down a long strip of document. The horizontal and vertical scroll bars along the left and bottom edge of the Notepad window move the window around on this strip of paper. The length and width of the scroll bars represent the entire Notepad document and the scroll box represents the Notepad window's current position on the document. To scroll by line, click on the arrows in the scroll bars. To move one full screen at a time, click in the gray area of the scroll bar. For larger moves, drag the scroll box to a new vertical or horizontal location. With the keyboard, press the page up key to scroll up one screen at a time; press the page down key to scroll down one screen at a time.

> **NOTE** The horizontal scroll bar appears only when the Word Wrap command is selected (has a check mark to its left) in the Edit menu.

You can move the insertion point by using either the mouse or the keyboard. To move the insertion point with the mouse, position the *I-beam*, (the text-screen mouse pointer) where you want the insertion point and click the mouse button. With the keyboard, use the arrow keys to move the insertion point. As in any word processing application, the insertion point in Notepad travels only where typed characters appear, even if these characters are spaces or Enter characters. You cannot move the insertion point beyond where you already typed.

Keyboard shortcuts for moving the insertion point and scrolling are listed in table 16.1.

Table 16.1 Keyboard Commands To Move the Insertion Point and To Scroll the Screen

Keyboard Command	Action
End	Move to end of line
Home	Move to beginning of line
Ctrl+Home	Move to beginning of document
Ctrl+End	Move to end of document
PgUp	Scroll one screen up
PgDn	Scroll one screen down

T I P   Experienced typists know how to save time by using a combination of techniques for moving around the screen and for selecting and editing text. The quickest way to select text, for example, may be to drag the mouse across the text, but the fastest way to scroll down the page may be to press the PgDn key. If you have both a mouse and the keyboard, you aren't limited to using only one method or the other.

Selecting, Editing, and Formatting Text

You select and edit text in the Notepad the same way you select and edit text in Write.

To add text, move the insertion point to the new text location and start typing (if you use a mouse, position the I-beam where you want the insertion point and click). Delete a single character by moving the insertion point to the left of the character and pressing Del or by moving the insertion point to the right of the character and pressing Backspace.

To delete or replace more extensive amounts of text, you first must select the text. To select with the mouse, press and hold down the mouse button and drag the I-beam across the text you want to select.

To select text by using the keyboard, hold down the Shift key and press any arrow key. Select all text in the Notepad document at one time by choosing the Edit Select All command.

To replace selected text, just type new text. To delete text, select the text to delete and choose the Edit Delete command or press the Del key.

You can correct editing mistakes by choosing the Edit Undo command or by holding down Ctrl and pressing Z. Remember that you can undo only the most recent edit.

The Notepad enables you to perform limited formatting by using the File Page Setup command. When you select this command, the Page Setup dialog box appears (see fig. 16.4), where you can change the margins and add a header or footer to the note. In Notepad, you cannot format characters or paragraphs in any way. You can use Tab, the space bar, and Backspace to align text. Tab stops are preset at every eight characters.

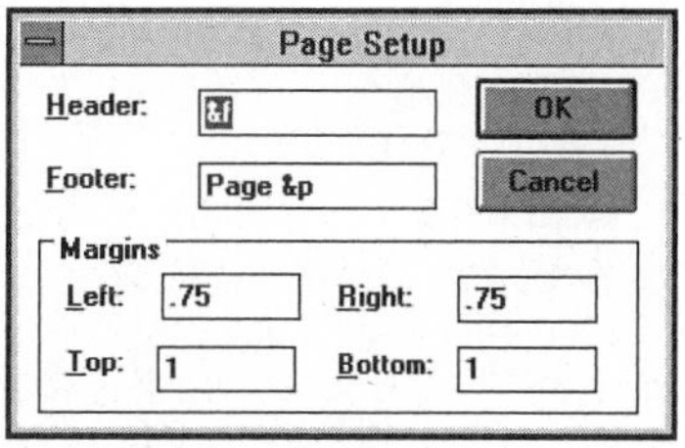

```
┌──────────────────────────────────────┐
│ ▬          Page Setup                 │
├──────────────────────────────────────┤
│  Header:  [&f]          ┌─────────┐   │
│                         │   OK    │   │
│  Footer:  [Page &p]     └─────────┘   │
│                         ┌─────────┐   │
│                         │ Cancel  │   │
│  ┌Margins───────────────└─────────┘─┐ │
│  │ Left:  [.75]    Right:  [.75]    │ │
│  │ Top:   [1]      Bottom: [1]      │ │
│  └──────────────────────────────────┘ │
└──────────────────────────────────────┘
```

FIG. 16.4

Set margins and insert header/ footers in the Page Setup dialog box.

A handy shortcut for selecting a single word is to double-click on the word. To select a large block of text, click at the beginning of the selection, use the scroll bars to scroll to the end of the selection, and then hold down the Shift key as you click at the end of the selection. All text between the original insertion point and the Shift click is selected.

To select with the keyboard, move the insertion point to the beginning of the selection, press and hold down Shift, and scroll to the end of the selection. Holding down Shift as you scroll or move the insertion point selects all text between the starting and ending points.

Copying and Moving Text

With Notepad's Edit commands, you can cut, copy, and move selected text from one place in a file to another. As in any Windows application, text you cut or copy is stored in the Clipboard, a temporary file that holds only one selection at a time. When you paste text, this text is copied from the Clipboard to the document at the insertion point.

To cut, copy, and paste text, follow these steps:

1. Select the text you want to cut, copy, or move (see fig. 16.5).

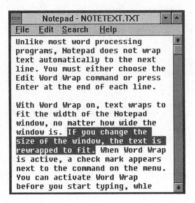

FIG. 16.5

Selected text in
reverse type.

2. To move text, choose the **E**dit **Cu**t command; to make a duplicate
    of the text and leave the original in place, choose **E**dit **C**opy. The
    selected text is stored in the Clipboard.

3. Move the insertion point where you want to paste the text.

4. Choose the **E**dit **P**aste command. The text is copied from the Clip-
    board in the document at the location of the insertion point.

Remember that you can use keyboard shortcuts: cut using Ctrl+X; copy
using Ctrl+C; paste using Ctrl+V. (If you select text and press Del, text is
deleted without being copied to the Clipboard. The only way to retrieve
this kind of deletion is to immediately choose the **E**dit **U**ndo command.)

Cut or copied text is saved in the Clipboard and stays there until you
cut or copy something else. You can paste text from the Clipboard as
many times as you like. The Clipboard holds only one item at a time,
however; so be sure that you paste things as soon as you cut or copy
them.

Searching through Notepad

Notepad's Search command finds and selects any word or phrase. You
can search forward or backward through a document, beginning at the
insertion point. You can specify whether to search for an exact uppercase or lowercase match or whether to search for any match.

To search for text, follow these steps:

1. Choose the **S**earch **F**ind command. The Find dialog box appears (see fig. 16.6).

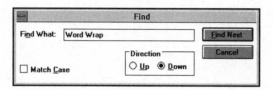

FIG. 16.6

The Find dialog box.

2. In the Fi**n**d What text box, type the text you want to find.

3. To find text that exactly matches the text you typed in uppercase and lowercase letters, select the Match **C**ase check box.

4. Select **D**own to search forward from the insertion point; select **U**p to select backward from the insertion point.

5. Choose **F**ind Next or press F3.

The application selects the first occurrence of the word or phrase. The dialog box remains open so that you can continue the search by choosing Find Next again. To return to the document, choose Cancel. If Notepad cannot find the word or phrase, a message box appears and tells you that it cannot find the text. Choose OK to acknowledge the message and then choose Cancel to return to the document. To continue the search after you close the dialog box, choose **S**earch Find Next (or press F3).

NOTE You can find whole, partial, or embedded words or characters. If you want to find a string of characters—even characters located inside another word—type the string of characters in the Fi**n**d What text box. To find the "search" in researches, for example, type *search* in the text box.

To find only the occurrences of a whole word, enter a space at the beginning and at the end of the word in the Fi**n**d What text box. To find only the word "search," for example, type <space>*search*<space>. Be aware that this kind of entry, however, doesn't find the word when "search" is followed by a comma or a period.

Creating a Time-Log File with Notepad

By using a simple command, .LOG, you can have Notepad enter the time and date at the end of a document each time you open the file. This feature is convenient for taking phone messages or for calculating the time spent on a project. An example of the Notepad with a time log is shown in figure 16.7. As an alternative to the .LOG command, you can choose the **E**dit Time/**D**ate command to insert the current time and date at the insertion point.

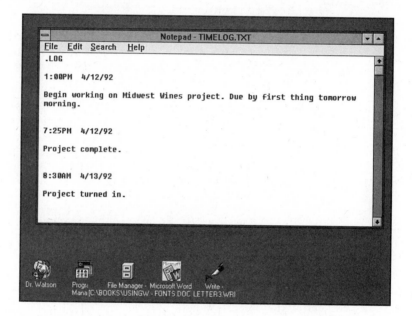

FIG. 16.7

You can track times in a Note-pad document in two ways.

To create a time log by default in a document, follow these steps:

1. Move the insertion point to the left margin of the first line in the Notepad document.

2. In capital letters, type the command *.LOG*.

3. Save the file.

4. Reopen the file.

    When you reopen the Notepad file, the time and date are inserted by default. You now can type a note that describes the project. By entering notes that describe your work between the times, you keep an accurate log of how much time is spent on a project.

5. Save the file again.

6. After you finish the project, reopen the file.

    Again, the time and date are entered by default. Type a log entry that states the project is finished.

To insert the time and date from the keyboard, follow these steps:

1. Move the insertion point where you want to enter the time and date.

2. Choose the **E**dit Time/**D**ate command or press F5.

Notepad takes the time and date information from the computer's internal clock. To make sure that the inserted time and date is accurate, you must set the computer's clock correctly. Use the Control Panel to change the time and date, as described in Chapter 7, "Customizing with the Control Panel."

The format of the time and date are determined by the International application in the Control Panel.

T I P

Setting Up the Page for Printing

You can use the **F**ile Page Setup command to set the margins for a document and to add a header or footer to a document. Headers and footers print at the top and bottom of each page of a document. Several codes are available to enhance headers and footers.

To set the margins for a document, follow these steps:

1. Choose the **F**ile Page Setup command.

2. Set the margins as desired in the **L**eft, **R**ight, **T**op, and **B**ottom boxes.

3. Choose OK or press Enter.

To add a header or footer to a document, follow these steps:

1. Choose File Page Setup.

2. In the **H**eader or **F**ooter text box, type the text you want to appear in the header or footer.

You can use any of the following codes in headers or footers:

Code	Result
&d	Inserts current date
&p	Inserts page number
&f	Inserts file name
&l	Left justifies text following code
&r	Right justifies text following code
&c	Centers text following code
&t	Inserts the current time

Saving and Printing Notepad Files

To save and name a Notepad document, follow these steps:

1. Choose the **File** Save **As** command.

2. From the **Directories** list box, select the directory in which you want to save the file.

    By default, Notepad saves the file in the current directory.

3. In the File **Name** text box, enter a name.

4. Choose OK or press Enter.

If you previously saved a file but want to save it again with the same file name, choose **File Save**. The current file replaces the original version.

If you don't enter a file extension, Notepad adds the extension TXT. To save a different kind of file, such as a batch or the WIN.INI file, enter the file name and add the desired extension.

You can print a Notepad file on the currently selected printer. If you want to select a different printer, follow these steps:

1. Choose the **File P**rint Setup command.

2. From the Specific **P**rinter list, select the printer you want to use.

3. Make the selections that pertain to the printer you use: the paper size, orientation, source, and so on. Depending on the printer you select, these selections vary.

4. Choose the Options button to display a dialog box containing additional Print Setup options, depending on what type of printer you selected. Select the options you want.

5. Choose OK or press Enter.

6. Choose OK or press Enter a second time to close the Print Setup dialog box.

To print a Notepad file on the selected printer, follow these steps:

1. Open the file to be printed.

2. Choose the **File Print** command.

Although you don't see a dialog box when you issue the **File Print** command, a message box appears that tells you the document is printing. To cancel the print job, select the Cancel button in the dialog box.

For Related Information:

◄◄ To learn more about the Clipboard, see "Viewing Data in the Clipboard," p. 211.

►► See "Integrating Windows Applications," see p. 850.

FROM HERE...

Inserting Symbols with Character Map

The Character Map accessory gives you access to symbol fonts and ANSI characters. One symbol font, Symbol, is included with most Windows applications. Other symbol fonts may be built into the printer. Most PostScript printers, for example, include Zapf Dingbats. When you setup and indicate the model of the printer, font cartridges, and so on, the printer tells Windows what symbol fonts are available. (Printer fonts appear in character map only when they include a matching screen font.)

ANSI characters are the regular character set that you see on the keyboard and more than a hundred other characters, including a copyright symbol, a registered trademark symbol, and many foreign language characters.

To use the Character Map accessory, you first must start the application from Program Manager. You then can select any characters or symbols from the Character Map dialog box and, by using the Clipboard, insert these items in any Windows application.

Open Character Map by double-clicking the Character Map icon in the Accessories window or by pressing arrow keys to select the icon and then pressing Enter. You are presented with the Character Map dialog box (see fig. 16.8). The dialog box includes a drop-down list box, from which you can select any of the available fonts on the system. After you select a font, the characters and symbols for this font appear in the Character Map table.

FIG. 16.8

Select characters from the Charac-ter Map dialog box for use in Windows documents.

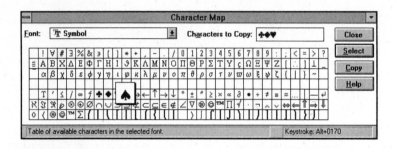

To insert characters and symbols in a Windows application, you copy the characters you selected from the Character Map dialog box to the Clipboard and then paste the characters in the application by using standard Windows copy-and-paste procedures.

To insert a character in a Windows application from the Character Map, follow these steps:

1. From Program Manager, open the Character Map accessory.

2. Select the font you want to use from the **F**ont list.

   The Character Map displays on-screen the characters for the se-lected font. Each set of fonts may have different symbols. Some fonts, such as Symbol and Zapf Dingbats, contain nothing but sym-bols and special characters.

3. You view characters by clicking on them and holding down the mouse button or by using arrow keys to move to the character.

4. Double-click on the character you want to insert or choose the **S**elect button to place the current character in the Characters text box.

5. Repeat steps 2 through 4 to select as many characters as desired.

6. Choose the **C**opy button to copy the characters that appear in the **C**haracters to Copy text box in the Clipboard.

7. Open or switch to the application in which you want to copy the character(s).

8. Place the insertion point where you want to insert the character(s) and choose the **Edit Paste** command.

If the characters don't appear as they did in Character Map, you may need to reselect the characters and change the font to the same font in which the character originally appeared in the Character Map.

> If you plan to use the Character Map frequently, you may want to add this application to the StartUp program group in the Program Manager so that Character Map opens when you start Windows.
>
> **T I P**

For Related Information:

◄◄ See "Understanding Fonts," p. 306.

FROM HERE...

Tracking Appointments with the Calendar

The Windows Calendar is a computerized appointment book that records appointments, marks special dates, and even sets an alarm to remind you of important events. Calendar operates in two views: daily and monthly. When you open the Calendar for the first time, you see the daily view (see fig. 16.9). This calendar is marked in hourly intervals; you can scroll through the times and type appointments for each hour. To view an entire month, switch to the monthly view. In this view, you can scroll through the months and add notes to any date. The notes you type in the monthly view also appear in the daily view for this date.

Calendar creates and stores files like any other application. After you open the Calendar, you see a new, blank calendar. You can save as many different calendar files as you want. For example, you may want to create a separate calendar file for each of several projects.

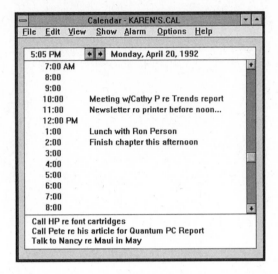

FIG. 16.9

The Calendar
daily view.

T I P

The date formats shown in the Calendar are those selected by using the International application in the Control Panel. If you don't like the way the dates are formatted in the Calendar, change the **Date** format in the International dialog box.

T I P

If you are using Windows for Workgroups, you may want to use the Schedule+ application. Schedule+ comes with Windows for Workgroups. It is more functional as both a personal scheduling system and for scheduling meetings that involve other people in your workgroup.

Opening and Closing the Calendar

Open the Calendar application by double-clicking the Calendar icon in the Accessories window or by pressing the arrow keys to select the icon and then pressing Enter. You also can open a new or existing file from within the Calendar application by choosing the File **N**ew or File **O**pen command. In the Open dialog box, select the directory and file you want to open. If you want to open a file without being able to edit it (when you're opening someone else's Calendar file, for example) select the **R**ead Only option in the Open dialog box. Choose OK to open the file. Alternatively, you can open an existing Calendar file directly from the Windows File Manager by double-clicking on the file name or selecting the file name and pressing Enter. Calendar files have the extension CAL.

When you open a new file from within the Calendar, the currently open file is closed. A dialog box asks whether you want to save the current changes (this dialog box appears only if changes were made). Choose **Y**es to save the changes, choose **N**o to discard them, or choose Cancel to return to the original file.

You can close a Calendar file in only two ways: open a new file or close the Calendar application. To close the Calendar application, choose **F**ile E**x**it.

Looking at the Calendar's Two Views

At the top of the Calendar window are a title bar and a menu bar listing all the Calendar's commands. Below the menu bar is a status bar that shows the current time and date (if they're wrong, reset them using the Windows Control Panel). The title, menu, and status bars appear in both the daily and monthly views of the Calendar.

At the bottom of the Calendar window is a scratch-pad area where you can enter up to three lines of notes for each day. Like the status bars, the scratch pad appears in both the monthly and daily views. Figure 16.10 shows the Calendar in monthly view.

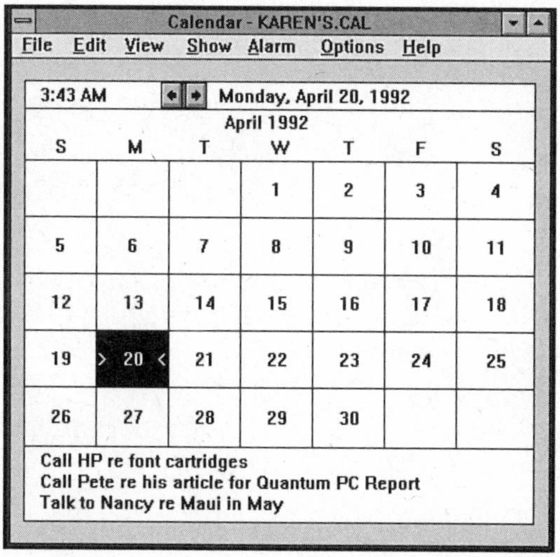

FIG. 16.10

The Calendar monthly view.

Switching between the two views is easy. Just choose the **View M**onth command or press F9 to switch to the monthly view. Choose the **View D**ay command or press F8 to switch to the daily view. If you have a mouse, double-click on the date in the status bar to switch between monthly and daily views (in the monthly view, double-click on any day to switch back to this date in the daily view).

Typing Appointments in the Daily View

After you open the Calendar, you see the daily view for the current time and date. On the left of the calendar are listed times; to the right of the times is room to enter appointments. To enter an appointment, position the insertion point at the desired time and type the text. You can type about 80 characters on each line; if you type beyond the right margin, the Calendar window scrolls to the right so that you can see all the text.

To move the insertion point to a time with the mouse, click the I-beam where you want to type. To move the insertion point with the keyboard, press the arrow keys.

Although only part of the day is displayed in the Calendar window, all 24 hours are available. To enter an appointment at a time not displayed, use the scroll bar on the right side of the calendar to scroll up or down to the time you want. From the keyboard, use the up and down arrows and PgUp and PgDn to scroll up and down. Take a shortcut to the original starting time by pressing Ctrl+Home; go to the time 12 hours after the starting time by pressing Ctrl+End.

To enter an appointment, follow these steps:

1. Scroll to display the time you want.

2. Move the insertion point to the time of the appointment.

3. Type the appointment.

4. Press Enter to move the insertion point to the next line.

At the bottom of each day and month calendar is a three-line scratch pad in which you can type notes (see the bottom of fig. 16.9 or 16.10). A note stays attached to its date; whenever you turn to this date, the note appears in the scratch pad.

To move between the scratch-pad area and the appointment area, click in the area you want or press Tab. Once in the scratch-pad area, type and edit using normal Windows procedures.

If you want to enter an appointment at a time not displayed on the Calendar (for example, 1:45), you must insert this "special" time. Refer to

"Changing the Starting Time and Intervals" later in this chapter, for more information.

Editing and Moving Calendar Appointments

You can edit Calendar appointments and scratch-pad notes in the same way you edit text in other Windows applications. You can insert and delete text for any date, and you can select, cut, copy, or paste appointments from one location to another between days, months, and even years. Using the Clipboard, you can move text not only between times and days, but also between applications. Moving an appointment in this way is a convenient way to update the schedule.

To move appointments or notes to other dates, follow these steps:

1. Select the text you want to move.

2. Choose the **Edit Copy** (Ctrl+C) or **Edit Cut** (Ctrl+X) command.

3. Move the insertion point to the new date.

4. Choose the **Edit Paste** (Ctrl+V) command.

Removing Appointments from the Calendar

Because old appointments use disk space, you probably don't need these notations on the calendar. Fortunately, you can remove appointments for an individual day or for a range of days. You can remove appointments only from the active Calendar file. To remove appointments from other Calendar files, you first must open the files.

To remove appointments from the current Calendar file, follow these steps:

1. Choose the **Edit Remove** command. The Remove dialog box shown in figure 16.11 appears.

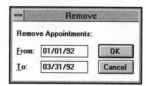

FIG. 16.11

The Remove dialog box.

2. In the From and To boxes in the dialog box, enter the range of dates you want to remove. To remove a single date, type the date in the From text box.

3. Choose OK or press Enter.

Displaying Different Dates, Times, and Views

After you open a new or existing Calendar file, you always see the current date in the daily view, but you can move between dates, between times, and between views by using the techniques listed in table 16.2.

Table 16.2 Moving in the Calendar

Location To Move To	Actions
Previous day (daily view) Previous month (monthly view)	Choose **S**how **P**revious Press Ctrl+PgUp Click on left arrow in status bar
Next day (daily view) Next month (monthly view)	Choose **S**how **N**ext Press Ctrl+PgDn Click on right arrow in status bar
Today's date	Choose **S**how **T**oday
A specific date	Choose **S**how **D**ate or press F4; then type desired date in mm/dd/yy format and press Enter
A different time (daily view)	Press up or down arrow Press PgUp or PgDn Click on scroll-bar arrows
Scratch pad	Tab
Appointment area	Tab
Monthly view	Choose **V**iew **M**onth Press F9 Doubleclick on date in status bar
Daily view	Choose **V**iew **D**ay Press F8 Double click on date in status bar Double click on day in monthly view

Setting an Alarm

To be reminded of an important appointment, you can set an alarm in the Calendar's daily view, with or without sound. You can set alarms for as many appointments as you like in the daily view of the Calendar.

To turn on the alarm, move the insertion point to the time you want the alarm to sound and choose **A**larm **S**et or press F5. (To remove the alarm, repeat this procedure.) After you set the alarm, a small bell appears to the left of the appropriate time on the calendar (see fig. 16.12). When this time arrives, the computer beeps (unless you inactivate the sound), and a dialog box flashes on-screen to remind you of the appointment (see fig. 16.13).

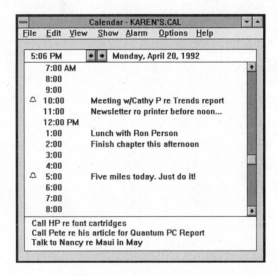

FIG. 16.12

An alarm bell to the left of an appointment time.

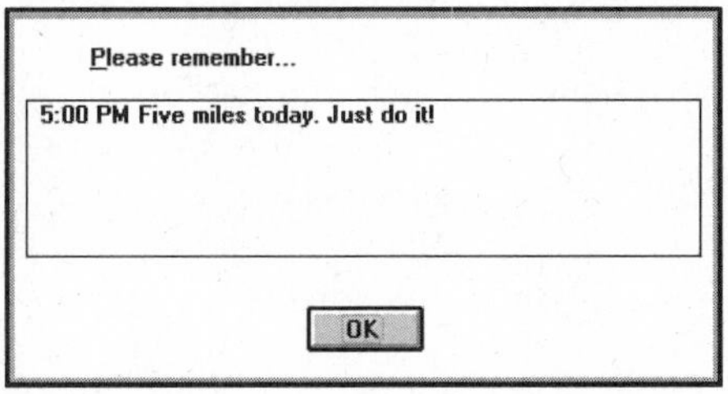

FIG. 16.13

The dialog box that reminds you of appointments.

To continue working, you must respond to the Alarm dialog box. To turn off the Alarm dialog box, choose the OK button. If the Calendar is minimized to an icon when the alarm goes off, the title bar or icon flashes. You must activate the Calendar window to display and respond to the Alarm dialog box. If you plan to use the Calendar alarm feature, keep the Calendar running so that the alarm can sound to warn you of imminent appointments and deadlines.

T I P If you use alarms, start the Calendar each time you start Windows. The Calendar can notify you of appointments only if loaded in the computer's memory. Because the Calendar uses only a small amount of memory, you may want to copy the Calendar icon to the StartUp group in the Program Manager so that the Calendar starts when you start Windows. To copy the icon, open the Accessories and StartUp groups in side-by-side windows. Hold down the Ctrl key and drag a copy of the Calendar icon from the Accessories group to the StartUp group.

You can control the alarm in two ways: by setting the alarm to ring from 1 to 10 minutes early and by turning off the alarm sound so that you get a silent alarm (the on-screen reminder) rather than a beep.

To control the alarm options, follow these steps:

1. Choose the **Alarm Controls** command. The Alarm Controls dialog box, shown in figure 16.14, appears.

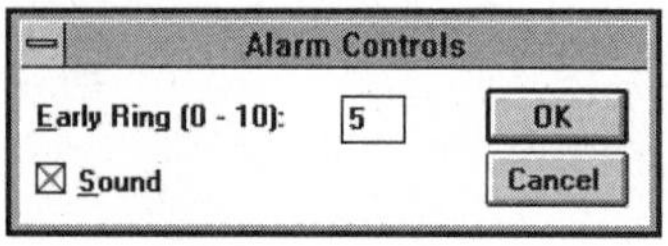

FIG. 16.14

The Alarm Controls dialog box.

2. If you want the alarm to sound before the scheduled time on the Calendar, select **Early Ring** and enter a number from 1 to 10.

3. To turn off the alarm beep (for a silent alarm), select the **Sound** option box so that no X appears in the option box. Leave this option on (so that an X appears in the box) if you want the alarm to beep.

4. Choose OK or press Enter.

Changing the Starting Time and Intervals

When you open a new Calendar file, the times are set at one-hour intervals; the day begins at 7:00 a.m. You can change these intervals, and you can set the calendar to display a different first hour if your day typically starts at a different time than 7:00. You also can change the hour format to a 24-hour clock rather than the conventional 12-hour clock. You always have a full 24 hours for appointments, no matter what changes you make to the Calendar's appearance.

To change the day settings, follow these steps:

1. Choose the **O**ptions **D**ay Settings command. The Day Settings dialog box appears (see fig. 16.15).

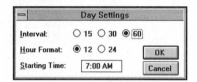

FIG. 16.15

The Day Settings dialog box.

2. Select **I**nterval and select a 15-, 30-, or 60-minute time interval for the display of the appointment calendar.

3. Select **H**our Format and select a 12- or 24-hour format.

4. In the **S**tarting Time text box, enter a different time to change the Calendar's first displayed hour.

5. Choose OK or press Enter.

Occasionally, appointments don't fall exactly on a Calendar's preset time interval. For this kind of appointment, you can insert special times in the Calendar. In figure 16.16, the time intervals were changed to 30 minutes, and a special time was inserted at 2:40 p.m.

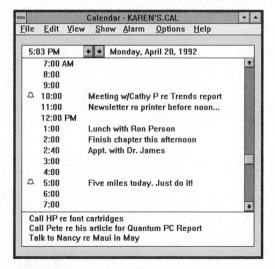

FIG. 16.16

Adding a special time to the calendar.

To add a special time, follow these steps:

1. Choose the **O**ptions **S**pecial Time command or press F7. The Special Time dialog box appears (see fig. 16.17).

FIG. 16.17

The Special Time dialog box.

2. Select **S**pecial Time and enter the special time you want to insert in the Calendar.

3. Select **AM** or **PM**. (If the Calendar is set to the 12-hour format, the Calendar assumes a.m. unless you specify p.m.)

4. Choose the **I**nsert button.

To delete a special time, follow these steps:

1. Move the insertion point to the special time you want to delete.

2. Choose **O**ptions **S**pecial Time or press F7.

3. Choose the **D**elete button.

Viewing the Calendar by Month

After you start the Calendar, you see the daily view; you can switch to a monthly view (see fig. 16.10). As in the daily view, the current time and date in the monthly view always appears in a status bar below the menus. The day selected in the monthly view is the same day you were on when you switched from the daily view. The current date (today's date) appears on the monthly calendar enclosed in angle brackets (> <).

Notice that the scratch pad for the selected day in the monthly calendar is the same as the scratch pad for the current day in the daily view. You can move to the scratch pad to type or edit text by pressing Tab or by clicking the mouse button in the scratch-pad area.

To select a different day in the monthly view, press the arrow keys to move the highlight or click on the day you want to highlight. Table 16.2, which appears in a previous section of this chapter, summarizes the other moves you can make in the monthly calendar. You can jump, for example, as far forward as December 31, 2099.

One of the quickest ways to jump between appointment lists on different dates is to use the mouse. Switch from daily to monthly view by clicking the status bar at the top of the window. After the monthly view appears, double-click on the day that contains the appointment list you want to see.

Marking Important Days

In the monthly view, you can mark a date to remind you of a special event, such as a report due, a project-completion date, or a sister's birthday. (Making a note in the scratch-pad area to remind you why the occasion is marked is a good idea.) In figure 16.18, dates are marked with Calendar's different marker symbols.

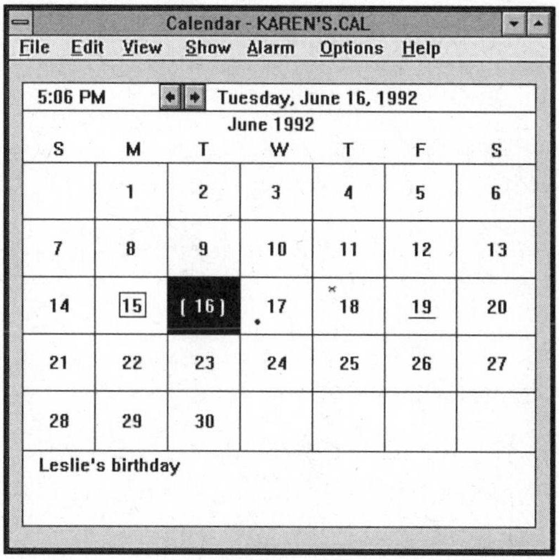

FIG. 16.18

Using five different symbols to mark dates in the monthly view.

To mark a date in the Calendar's monthly view, follow these steps:

1. Select the date you want to mark by clicking on it or by pressing the arrow keys until it is highlighted.

2. Choose the **Options Mark** command or press F6. The Day Markings dialog box shown in figure 16.19 appears.

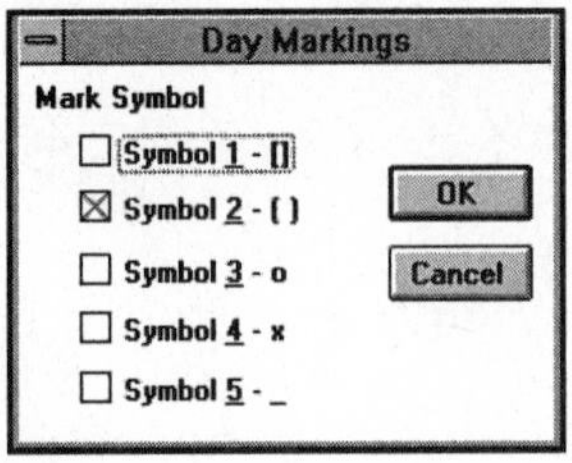

FIG. 16.19

The Day Markings dialog box.

3. Select the desired mark symbol from the following list. Figure 16.18 shows dates marked.

Symbol **1**	[ ]
Symbol **2**	( )
Symbol **3**	o
Symbol **4**	x
Symbol **5**	_

4. Choose OK or press Enter.

Saving and Printing Calendar Files

You can save as many different Calendar files as you like so that you can have separate files for different projects, different resources, different clients, and so on. The first time you save a file, you must assign the file a name.

To save a new Calendar file, follow these steps:

1. Choose the File Save **As** command.

2. In the File **Name** text box, enter a file name.

3. From the **Directories** box, select the directory in which you want to save the file. By default, Windows saves the file in the current directory.

4. Choose OK or press Enter.

To save an existing Calendar file without changing the name, choose the File **Save** command.

The new version of the file replaces the existing version on the disk.

You can print appointments for a day or for a range of days from the current calendar by using the Print dialog box (see fig. 16.20).

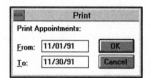

FIG. 16.20

The Print dialog box.

To print a range of appointments, follow these steps:

1. Choose the **File Print** command.

2. In the **From** text box, enter the first appointment date you want to print; in the **To** text box, enter the last date you want to print. If you want to print a single date, type the date in the **From** text box.

3. Choose OK or press Enter.

On the printed calendar, you can include headers and footers, and you can print within specified margins. You specify headers, footers, and margins in the Page Setup dialog box shown in figure 16.21.

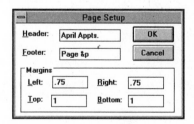

FIG. 16.21

The Page Setup dialog box.

Before you print the Calendar file with the preceding steps, follow these steps to create headers and footers and set margins for the printed Calendar:

1. Choose the **File Page Setup** command.

2. Select the **Header** text box and type the text of the header you want to print.

3. Select the **F**ooter text box and type the text of the footer you want to print.

4. Select the **L**eft, **R**ight, **T**op, and **B**ottom Margins boxes and type, in decimal numbers, the margins you want. Remember that Windows uses a default measurement of inches.

5. Choose OK or press Enter.

The Calendar provides several special codes you can use in headers and footers. The codes center the header or footer, add the current date or time, and number the pages. The codes you can use are listed in table 16.3.

Table 16.3 Special Codes To Use in Headers and Footers

Code	Result
&d	Current date
&p	Page numbers
&f	Current file name
&l	Header or footer text follows the code and is justified at left margin
&r	Header or footer text follows the code and is justified at right margin
&c	Header or footer text follows the code and is centered between margins
&t	Current time

The Calendar prints on the currently selected printer. To select a printer, choose the File **P**rint Setup command and select the printer you want, **D**efault Printer or Specific **P**rinter, as well as the paper Orientation (select Po**r**trait or **L**andscape), the Paper Si**z**e, and the Paper **S**ource. Choose the **O**ptions button to make additional selections specific to your printer. Choose OK to close the Options dialog box; choose OK again to close the Print Setup box.

Storing and Retrieving Information in the Cardfile

The Cardfile is like a computerized stack of three-by-five index cards that gives you quick reference to names, addresses, phone numbers, and all other information stored—even graphics—in the cardfile. The Cardfile is an excellent way to store free-form information that you may need to retrieve quickly. You even can store *embedded* information, such as a map that you drew in Windows Paint, in the Cardfile. Double-clicking on the map brings up Windows Paint so that you can edit the map.

Each *card* in a Cardfile has two parts: a single index line at the top and an area for text or graphics below. Cards always are arranged alphabetically by the index line (see fig. 16.22). The active card is the top card on the stack.

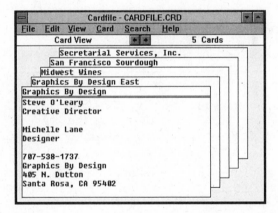

FIG. 16.22

Cards in a Cardfile store information you can get at quickly.

You can have as many cards in a Cardfile file as the computer's memory can hold, and you can use as many Cardfile files as the disk can hold.

Accessing the information in a Cardfile file is easy. Display the card you need and read, copy, or print the information the card contains. If the computer is connected to a modem or a phone, you can use Cardfile to dial a phone number.

T I P   Cardfile is convenient for handling small amounts of simple information. While it can function to keep track of clients or mailing lists you
will be more efficient and less frustrated if you use a true mailing list
manager, personal information manager (PIM), or database to handle
large or related lists of information. Many of these programs are
available on Windows and share information with the major Windows word processors.

Opening and Closing the Cardfile

You open the Cardfile application from the Accessories window by
double-clicking on the Cardfile icon or by selecting the icon by using
the arrow keys and pressing Enter. After you open the application, a
new, untitled Cardfile appears on-screen.

You also can open new or existing Cardfile files from within Cardfile
by choosing the File Open or File New command. When you open a
new file from within Cardfile, the currently open file closes. If you
made changes to this file, a dialog box asks whether you want to save
the changes. Choose Yes to save current changes, No to discard the
changes, or Cancel to return to the file.

You also can simultaneously open a Cardfile file and the Cardfile application by double-clicking on a data file from the Windows File Manager
or by selecting a cardfile and pressing Enter. Cardfile data files have the
extension CRD.

You can close a Cardfile file only by opening a new file or by closing the
Cardfile application. To close the Cardfile application, choose Control
Close or File Exit.

Entering Information in the Cardfile

After opening a new Cardfile file, you see a single blank card (see
fig. 16.23). The insertion point flashes in the top left corner of the card,
just below the double line. This location is where you type information,
such as names, addresses, and phone numbers, in the body of the card.
To enter information in the card, just begin typing. Use Tab, Backspace,
and the space bar to arrange the text. If you reach the right edge of the
card, the text wraps to the next line.

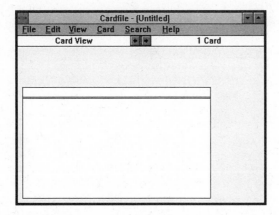

FIG. 16.23

A new Cardfile, displaying only a blank card.

The index line at the top of the card is important: Cardfile arranges cards alphabetically by index lines. After you type the body of the first card, you are ready to enter an index line.

To type text in the index line, follow these steps:

1. Choose the **Edit I**ndex command or press F6. The Index dialog box appears (see fig. 16.24).

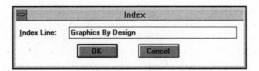

FIG. 16.24

The Index dialog box.

2. In the Index Line text box, type the text that identifies the contents of the card. Remember that cards are arranged alphabetically by index lines.

3. Choose OK or press Enter. The insertion point returns to the body of the card.

Like the cards in a rotary card file, Cardfile cards always stay alphabetized—even when a card in the middle of the stack is on top. If you want to arrange the Cardfile alphabetically by last name, type the last name first in the index line. You can begin an index line with a number; numbers are listed before letters in alphabetical order.

To edit existing index lines, select the card and choose the Edit Index command or press the F6 key.

Inserting Pictures in a Card

You can paste pictures of all kinds in Cardfile cards: graphs from Microsoft Excel or 1-2-3, sketches from Windows Paintbrush or Windows Draw, clip art from files of graphics, and even scanned images of photographs.

Three ways are available to insert a picture in a card:

- The simplest way is to copy and paste into the card a picture from a graphics application to the card that does not support object linking and embedding. After pasting, you cannot edit this picture; you must replace it with another picture.

- You can insert by choosing to *embed* a picture. The picture must be created by a graphics application that supports object embedding, such as Microsoft Paintbrush or Microsoft Draw. Object linking and embedding is known as OLE. You can edit an embedded graphic from within Cardfile. The advantage of embedded pictures is that these images contain all the information needed to recreate and edit the picture. Embed a picture when you don't need to update many copies of the picture and when you want the data in the picture to go with the cardfile so that the receiver of the cardfile can make changes.

- You can insert a picture by choosing to *link* the image. The picture must come from an application that supports object linking. By default, Cardfile updates linked graphics when you change the original picture in the original file. Linking is useful when you have one original picture or chart that feeds into multiple documents. By updating the single original, all the documents that use this picture also are updated. A disadvantage of linking is that if you want to send the cardfile to another user, you should send copies of all the linked pictures used in the cardfile.

To learn more about object linking and embedding, read Chapter 6.

Cardfile tries to accurately represent the picture on-screen. The picture, however, is displayed in screen—rather than printer—resolution. If the printer resolution doesn't match the screen resolution (usually the case), the screen image may appear slightly distorted. Because the picture prints at printer resolution, the picture looks fine when printed.

You can include only one picture in a card.

Copying a Picture in a Card

With the **E**dit commands, you can copy a picture from another application to a Cardfile card. Figure 16.25 shows a map that was copied from Microsoft Paintbrush and pasted in a Cardfile card. Some applications can create pictures that you can use as a pasted picture, as a linked picture, or as an embedded object.

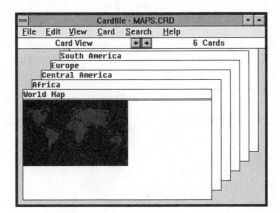

FIG. 16.25

Applications like Paintbrush can create unlinked pictures, embedded objects, or linked pictures.

To copy a picture from one application to another, follow these steps:

1. Open the application that contains the picture or chart.

2. Select and copy the picture.

   For Windows applications, select the portion of the picture you want copied and choose a command such as **E**dit **C**opy. For standard DOS applications, such as 1-2-3, display the picture on-screen and press Alt+PrtSc.

3. Open or activate the Cardfile application and the card in which you want to paste the picture.

4. Position the insertion point where you want the picture to appear.

5. Choose the **E**dit **P**icture command.

6. Choose the **E**dit Paste **S**pecial command. The Paste Special dialog box appears (see fig. 16.26).

7. From the **D**ata Type list, select an unlinked or nonembedded format for the picture. Selecting a Bitmap or Picture type will paste the image in unlinked and nonembedded format.

8. Choose the **P**aste button.

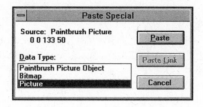

FIG. 16.26

The Paste Special dialog box enables you to paste pictures in different ways.

To learn more about using applications together, refer to Chapters 22 and 23.

If you attempt to edit a picture that isn't linked or embedded, an alert box appears with the message, `Cannot activate static object`.

> **T I P** Some applications, such as Microsoft Excel, may have more than one way to copy a graphic. **Edit Copy**, for example, copies a graphic that you can link or embed, while holding down the Shift key and repeating the same procedure copies a bit map picture that you can paste and that is neither linked nor embedded. (Pasted bit maps have the poorest quality print resolution.)

Embedding Pictures in a Card

Pictures embedded in a card contain the actual data that created the picture. Windows tracks the location of the original application that created the picture so that you can activate and edit an embedded picture, using the application that created the picture. Embedding a picture is useful when sending a Cardfile file to another user and making sure that all the picture information is included so that they can edit pictures used in the cards.

Embedded pictures must be created with drawing or charting applications capable of object linking and embedding, such as Windows Paintbrush, Microsoft Draw, or Microsoft Excel. You can embed a picture in two ways. You can open a drawing or charting application from within Cardfile and embed the resulting picture or you can create a drawing or chart in the other application and then copy and embed by pasting the graphic in a card.

If you already drew a picture or created a chart in a Windows application capable of object linking and embedding, then you can embed the graphic in a card by following the previously listed steps for pasting. However, when you reach step 7, select from the **D**ata Type list the type for an object, such as *Paintbrush Picture Object*.

If you are in the Cardfile application and want to embed a new object, follow these steps:

1. Position the insertion point where you want the picture to appear in the Cardfile card.

2. Choose the **Edit Picture** command to enable picture editing features. (The **Edit Picture** command is selected when a check mark appears to its left.)

3. Choose the **Edit Insert Object** command. The Insert New Object dialog box appears, shown in figure 16.27, listing all Windows applications that support object linking and embedding.

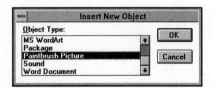

FIG. 16.27

The Insert New Object dialog box enables you to start an OLE application and embed an OLE document.

4. Select the application you want to use from the **O**bject Type list. For example, select Paintbrush Picture.

5. Choose OK or press Enter. The application opens.

6. In the application, create a drawing.

7. After you finish the picture, choose the **File Update File Exit** and **Return** command (this command may vary between applications) to embed a copy of the picture in the Cardfile card and close the application.

To preserve the embedded picture, save the Cardfile. You can edit this picture by using techniques described in following sections of this chapter.

Linking Pictures in a Card

Although linking a picture is similar to embedding a picture, the picture is in a file separate from the Cardfile file. A link is created between the Cardfile card and the application document that contains the picture. The advantage of using linked pictures is that you can update the picture in the original application, and any Cardfile card linked to the application is updated. Use linked pictures when you link multiple cards to a single picture and you want only to update the picture one time. The disadvantage to linked pictures is that if you send another user a copy of the Cardfile file, you also should send copies of the picture files to which the picture is linked.

> **NOTE** Do not rename or move the picture or chart file to which a card is linked, or the card will lose the picture the next time you update the card. If the link is lost in this way, use the techniques in Chapter 6 to reestablish the link. If a picture or chart is to be used in only one card, embedding is probably preferable. If you want one original picture or chart to update many cards at the same time, use linking. With linking, a single original picture can be linked to many cards.

To link a picture in a Cardfile file, follow these steps:

1. Position the insertion point where you want the linked picture to appear.

2. Open the application that contains the picture you want to link. Open Microsoft Excel, for example, to link in a chart.

3. Open the file that contains the picture you want to link or create a new chart.

4. Save the chart or picture by using the file name that the file will keep.

5. Select the chart or picture. (Applications may use different commands to select all or part of a picture or document.)

6. Choose the **E**dit **C**opy command.

7. Switch back to the Cardfile card.

8. Choose the **E**dit Pictu**r**e command to enable picture editing in cards.

9. Choose the Paste **L**ink command.

Managing the Links between Original Pictures and Cards

If you linked a picture or chart in Cardfile, the picture or chart remains connected to the original file. If the source picture or chart changes, the image in the Cardfile file changes. Renaming, deleting, or moving the file that contains the original picture or chart, however, can destroy the link. As a result, the card loses the picture or chart.

To learn how to re-create or change links between a card and the linked picture or chart, read the sections on managing links in Chapter 6, "Embedding and Linking."

Editing Embedded and Linked Pictures

From within Cardfile, you can edit pictures embedded from—or linked to—Windows Paintbrush or another application that supports object linking and embedding. Editing the picture causes the application to open, with the picture or chart appearing in the window. To learn how to activate and edit embedded or linked pictures that were previously pasted in a card, read the sections on editing pictures and linked data in Chapter 6. Usually, the procedures for most embedded or linked pictures are similar to the following procedures for Paintbrush.

To edit an embedded Paintbrush drawing by using the mouse, follow these steps:

1. To open Paintbrush and display the picture, double-click on the drawing.

2. Edit the picture.

3. In Paintbrush, choose the File Update command.

4. In Paintbrush, choose the File Exit and Return to Document command.

You also can just exit Paintbrush, and a message asks whether you want to update the picture in the Cardfile card. To update the card, choose **Yes**.

To edit an embedded drawing by using the keyboard, follow these steps:

1. Choose the Edit Edit Paintbrush Picture Object command. Paintbrush opens, with the picture in the drawing window.

2. Edit the picture.

3. In Paintbrush, choose File Update to update the picture in Cardfile.

4. In Paintbrush, choose File Exit and Return to Document.

You can edit a linked picture in Cardfile the same way that you edit an embedded drawing. One major difference is that you must save changes to the original picture or chart. Use standard file saving techniques. Because you're using the original graphics application to edit the picture, all changes you make are reflected in all other files that contain a link to the original picture.

To edit a linked drawing using the mouse:

1. To open Paintbrush and display the picture, double-click on the drawing.

2. Edit the picture.

3. In Paintbrush, choose the File Save command. By default, the picture in the Cardfile card is updated.

4. In Paintbrush, choose the File Exit command.

To edit a linked drawing using the keyboard:

1. In Cardfile, choose the Edit Link command.

2. After the Links dialog box appears, choose the Edit button to display Paintbrush, with the picture in the drawing window.

   Cardfile can accept only one picture. In applications that may have multiple links, you need to first select the link you want to edit before you choose the Edit button.

3. In Paintbrush, edit the picture.

4. Choose the Paintbrush File Save command. The picture in the Cardfile card updates to reflect the changes you made.

5. Choose the File Exit command in Paintbrush.

If you previously set links to update upon command, the Cardfile card won't reflect the changes to the linked picture until you update the link by using the following process:

1. In Cardfile, choose the Edit Link command.

2. After the Links dialog box appears, choose Update Now (see fig. 16.28).

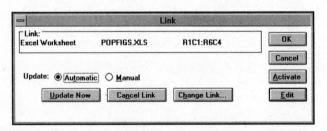

FIG. 16.28

The Link dialog box.

3. Choose OK or press Enter.

If you want a picture to update on command, rather than automatically, choose the Edit Link command and select the Update Manual option.

You also can change a link command when the location of the original picture changes (or when you want to link to a different original picture). Choose the **E**dit Lin**k** command, choose the C**h**ange Link button, and in the Change Link dialog box that appears, select the new file you want to link to or select the new location for the existing original file. Choose OK or press enter. Finally, you can cancel a link by choosing the **E**dit Lin**k** command and choosing the Cancel Link button. The picture then is no longer linked. To close the Link dialog box, choose OK or press Enter.

Adding Cards

Adding new cards to an existing card file is easy. After you add a new card, the Add dialog box appears, which prompts you to type the index line. When you finish entering the index line, the new card, complete with index line, appears in front of the other cards in the file.

To add a new card, follow these steps:

1. Choose the **C**ard **A**dd command or press F7. The Add dialog box appears.

2. In the **A**dd text box, type an index line for the new card.

3. Choose OK or press Enter.

The new card with the index line you just typed is displayed on top of the stack. The insertion point is at the top left of the card, ready for you to type the contents of the card.

Scrolling through the Cards

Cardfile provides several ways to search through the stack of cards and bring the card you want to the front of the stack. You can scroll through the cards, as described in this section, or you can search through the cards to find a card with specific information, as described in the following section.

In the status bar of the Cardfile window, you see a pair of arrows. You can scroll through the cards, one card at a time, by clicking on these arrows. To scroll backward one card, click left; to scroll forward one card, click right. The PgUp and PgDn keys on the keyboard perform the same tasks. These and other ways of scrolling in the Cardfile are summarized in table 16.4.

Table 16.4 Scrolling the Cardfile

Direction To Scroll	Action
Backward one card	PgUp Click on left arrow
Forward one card	PgDn Click on right arrow
To a specific card	Click on card's index line
To first card	Ctrl+Home
To last card	Ctrl+End
To card with index, beginning with *letter*	Shift+Ctrl+letter

Searching through Information in the Cards

You can search through the cards in a Cardfile by the index line or by the information in the body of the card. Both searches use a menu command and a dialog box to locate the card that contains the word or phrase you want to find. A third menu command enables you to quickly repeat the most recent search.

To search through index lines in the Cardfile, follow these steps:

1. Choose the **S**earch **G**o To command or press F4. The Go To dialog box appears.

2. In the **G**o To text box, type any portion of the index line you want to find (even a partial word works), as shown in figure 16.29. Because the search isn't case-sensitive, you can type either upper- or lowercase letters.

FIG. 16.29

Using the Search Go To command to search through index lines.

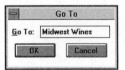

3. Choose OK or press Enter.

After you select OK, the first card with *Midwest Wines* in the index line is brought to the top of the stack.

Moving Quickly to a Card by Using the Index Line
To quickly bring up the first card with a specific beginning letter in the index line, press Shift+Ctrl+*letter*. Press Shift+Ctrl+M, for example, to bring to the top of the stack the first card that has *M* as the first letter of the card's index line.

To search through information in the body of the cards, follow these steps:

1. Choose **Search Find**. The Find dialog box, shown in figure 16.30, appears.

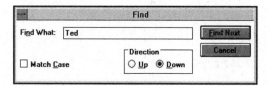

FIG. 16.30

Using Search Find to search through text in the cards themselves.

2. In the **Fin**d What text box, type any portion of the information for which you want to search (a partial word also works with this search).

3. From the direction options, select **U**p or **D**own and the Match **C**ase option if you want to make the search sensitive to upper- and lowercase.

4. Choose the **F**ind Next button.

Cardfile finds and selects the first occurrence of the word. To continue the search, choose **F**ind Next again. To close the dialog box, choose Cancel. To repeat the most recent search after closing the dialog box, choose the **S**earch Find **N**ext command (or press F3).

T I P   In the Find dialog box shown in figure 16.30, choosing OK or pressing Enter brings to the top of the stack the next card that contains the letters *ted* anywhere in the body of the card. The search may bring up a card that contains the word *interested*. If you are looking for the name Ted and want the search to ignore the letters ted within words, use the space bar to enter a space before and after the search word: <space>*ted*<space>.

Duplicating and Deleting Cards

Often, the information on two cards is so similar that duplicating the current card and making minor changes to the duplicate is faster than typing a new card. You may want, for example, two separate cards for two people in the same company—the names and phone numbers are different but the company name and address are the same.

To duplicate a card, follow these steps:

1. Bring the card you want to duplicate to the top of the stack.

2. Choose the **C**ard Du**p**licate command.

Using normal Windows text-editing procedures, edit the duplicated card text. (Choose the **E**dit **I**ndex command or double-click the index line to edit the index line.)

You can delete from the Cardfile all cards you no longer need. To delete a card, follow these steps:

1. Bring the card you want to delete to the top of the stack.

2. Choose the **C**ard **D**elete command. A message box appears, asking for confirmation.

3. Choose OK or press Enter.

> **Once It's Gone, It's Gone**
> After you delete a card, you cannot use the Edit Undo command to undo the deletion. Be absolutely certain that you no longer need the information on a card before you delete it.

You can retrieve an important card that you deleted, provided you have not saved the Cardfile to disk after deleting the card. Open a new

Cardfile application from the Accessories window and reopen the same file on which you are currently working. A copy of the unedited Cardfile on the disk loads into memory. From the unedited file, copy the card you accidentally deleted and paste it in the file where the card is missing.

Another way to recover from an accidental deletion is to choose the **File Open** command and reopen the current file. This method closes the current file. Do not save the changes. Use care when performing this procedure and use this method only when you don't mind losing all changes made since the last time you saved the file.

Editing and Moving Text

You can change, add, or delete text from a card or the index line, move text or graphics from one card to another, transfer data from the Cardfile to another application (such as the Notepad or Windows Write), or transfer text or graphics in Cardfile from another application (such as Windows Write or Paintbrush).

To edit the text on a Cardfile card, display on-screen the card you want to change. The insertion point flashes at the top left of the card. Use normal editing techniques to edit the text: move the insertion point where you want to make a change by positioning the I-beam and clicking the mouse button or by pressing the arrow keys. Then press Backspace or Delete to delete text or just type to insert text. Select longer blocks of text to edit by dragging the mouse across the text or by holding down the Shift key and pressing the arrow keys. Just type to replace selected text or press Del or Backspace to remove the text.

If you want to edit an index line, you must display the card and choose the **Edit Index** command. If you have a mouse, double-click on the index line of the top card. The Index Line dialog box appears, in which you make the changes.

To move text between cards or to other applications, follow these steps:

1. Bring the card that contains the text you want to move to the top of the stack.

2. Select the text you want to move.

3. Choose the **Edit Copy** (Ctrl+C) or **Edit Cut** (Ctrl+X) command.

4. Position the insertion point in another card or application.

5. Choose the **Edit Paste** (Ctrl+V) command.

> **Use the Edit Text Command To Work with Text**
> If you worked with pictures and graphics, you chose the Edit Picture command. While the Edit Picture command is selected, you can't edit text. To edit text again, choose the Edit Text command.

Two more useful editing commands are Undo and Restore. Cardfile *remembers*, and can undo, the most-recent edit—if you use Undo before you make another change. Cardfile also remembers the information on the card before editing began and can restore the card to original condition if you do not turn to another card after editing the first card.

To undo the most recent edit, choose the Edit Undo command or press Ctrl+Z. To restore a card to original condition, choose the Edit Restore command.

Moving Pictures in a Card

You can move the single picture in a card anywhere in the lower area. To move a picture with a mouse, choose the Edit Picture command and then drag the picture to the new location. To move a picture with the keyboard, choose the Edit Picture command and then press arrow keys to move the picture.

Viewing a List of Index Lines

After you first open Cardfile, you view the entire first card. You can see all the information on the top card but cannot see more than a few cards at a time. For a quick review of a file's contents, you can look at only the index lines (see fig. 16.31).

To view a list of the index lines, choose the View List command. To restore the full view of the cards, choose the View Card command.

As a shortcut, you can double-click on any index line listed in the List View window. The Index dialog box appears with the selected index line highlighted and ready for changes.

Dialing a Phone with Cardfile

If your computer is connected to a Hayes or Hayes-compatible modem, you can use Cardfile to dial a phone number that appears on a card. You must be in the Card view.

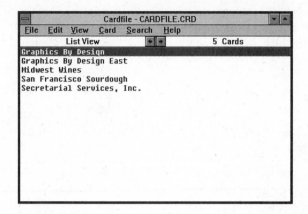

FIG. 16.31

A list of the index
lines in the
Cardfile.

When you choose the **C**ard Autodial command or press F5, Cardfile
dials the first number that appears on the top card. Figure 16.32 shows
Cardfile just after the **C**ard Autodial command has been chosen. Notice
that the phone number in the dialog box is the same as the phone number on the top card. To dial another number on the card, select this
number before you choose the **C**ard Autodial command. To change the
number after choosing Autodial, type the new number in the **N**umber
text box in the Autodial dialog box.

FIG. 16.32

Dialing numbers
with Cardfile's
Autodial
command.

If you select the **U**se Prefix box, Autodial dials the number in the Prefix
box before dialing the phone number on the card, which is helpful for
long-distance dialing. After you type a prefix in the Prefix box, the prefix remains until you enter a new prefix.

When you type a phone number on a card, be sure that you include the
area code (if different from your area code). Leave no spaces between
numbers; spaces cause some or all of the phone number to be ignored.
Remove parentheses from around the area code; numbers between
parentheses are ignored. Hyphens don't interfere with autodialing, so a
good format for phone numbers is 707-555-4247.

The first time you use Autodial to dial a number, check the dial settings
(choose **S**etup in the Autodial dialog box). All settings, the dial type,
port, and baud rate, stay set and don't have to be changed. After you

select Setup, a dialog box appears, from which you make the following choices:

1. Depending on the kind of phone line you have, from the Dial Type box, select Tone or Pulse.

2. From the Port box, select COM1, COM2, COM3, or COM4, depending on the port to which the modem is connected.

3. From the Baud Rate box, select 110, 300, 1200, 2400, 4800, 9600, or 19200, depending on the modem's baud rate.

Tone or Pulse Phone?
If you don't know what kind of phone line you have, try the following experiment. Pick up the phone and dial a few numbers. If you hear different tones when you dial, you have a touch-tone phone. If you hear clicks, you have a pulse phone.

To dial a phone number with Autodial, follow these steps:

1. Display the card with the phone number you want to dial. If the number you want to dial is not the first number listed on the card, select the number you want to dial.

2. Choose the Card Autodial command or press F5.

3. Select Prefix and type a dialing prefix, if necessary.

4. Select Use Prefix if you want Autodial to begin dialing with the prefix (usually not needed for local calls).

5. If necessary, choose Setup and make the appropriate dialog-box selections.

6. Choose OK or press Enter. The computer dials and displays a message box with instructions.

7. Pick up the phone receiver when instructed to do so by the dialog box.

8. Choose OK or press Enter to complete the connection.

To make Autodial pause or wait during dialing, insert a comma. For example, type a comma after a prefix to add a 5-second delay after the prefix.

Merging Cardfile Data Files and Counting the Cards

You can have as many different Cardfile files as you want. You can have one file for business contacts, one file for personal friends, a file for pictures you use frequently, and so on. On certain occasions, however, you may want to merge multiple Cardfile files into a single file.

A special command appends the contents of an unopened Cardfile to the open Cardfile. The application then alphabetizes all the cards. The unopened file is preserved in original form, and the open file includes both files.

To merge two Cardfile files, follow these steps:

1. Open the Cardfile you want to contain both files.

2. Choose the **File Merge** command.

3. From the **File Name** list, select the file you want to merge in the open file.

4. Choose OK or press Enter.

5. If you want to preserve both original files, save the resulting Cardfile file under a new name.

Saving and Printing Cardfile Documents

To print the top card in the stack, choose the **File Print** command. To print all the cards in a Cardfile, choose the **File Print All** command. No dialog boxes appear after you select the command; the cards just print on the selected printer. You can cancel printing by selecting the Cancel button that appears in the on-screen status box during printing. The cards are printed as actual card representations, which you can cut out and tape to cards on a rotary file.

To select a printer, choose the **File Print Setup** command. In the Print Setup dialog box, select **D**efault Printer or Specific **P**rinter and then select the printer you want from the list of installed printers.

When Cardfile documents are saved, they receive the default extension, CRD. You can use a different extension, but if you do, Cardfile doesn't list the file in the Open dialog box, and you can't open the file directly from the Windows File Manager.

To save and name a Cardfile, follow these steps:

1. Choose the **File** Save **As** command.

2. Type a name in the File **Name** box.

3. From the **Directories** list box, select the directory in which you want to save the file. By default, Cardfile saves files in the current directory.

4. Choose OK or press Enter.

To save an existing Cardfile with the same name, choose the **File S**ave command. The new version of the file replaces the existing version on disk.

If, when you save a file, you assign a file name already in use, Cardfile asks whether you want to replace the original file with the new file. If you do, choose Yes; if not, choose No and type a different name.

FROM HERE...

For Related Information:

◄◄ To learn more about object linking and embedding, see "Embedding Data into a Document," p. 233; "Embedding Data as Packages," p. 238; and "Linking Data between Applications," p. 223.

Performing Desktop Calculations with the Calculator

Like a calculator you keep in a desk drawer, the Windows Calculator is small but saves you time (and mistakes) by performing all the calculations common to a standard calculator. The Windows Calculator, however, has added advantages: you can keep this calculator on-screen alongside other applications, and you can copy numbers between the Calculator and other applications.

The standard Windows Calculator, shown in figure 16.33, works so much like a pocket calculator that you need little help getting started. The Calculator's *keypad*, the on-screen representation, contains familiar number *keys*, along with memory and simple math keys. A display window just above the keypad shows the numbers you enter and the results of calculations. If your computational needs are more advanced, you can choose a different view of the calculator, the Scientific view (see fig. 16.34).

FIG. 16.33

The Standard Calculator.

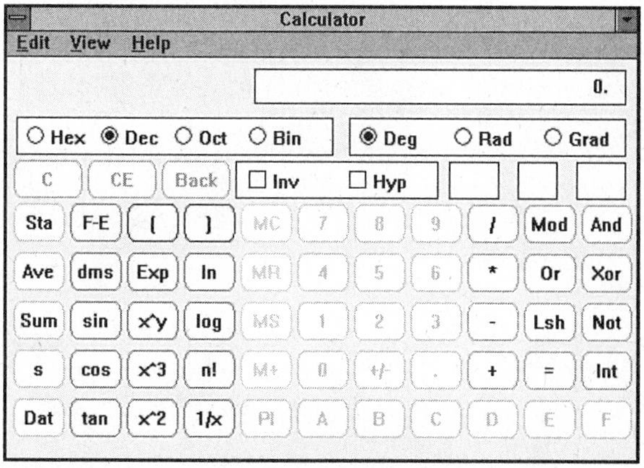

FIG. 16.34

The Scientific Calculator.

The Calculator has only three menus: **Edit**, **View**, and **Help**. The **Edit** menu contains two simple commands for copying and pasting, the **View** menu switches between the Standard and Scientific views, and the **Help** menu is the same as in all Windows accessories.

Although you cannot change the size of the Calculator (as you can other Windows applications), you can shrink the Calculator to an icon for easy availability when working in another application.

Opening, Closing, and Operating the Calculator

You open the Calculator application by double-clicking on the Calculator icon in the Accessories window or by pressing the arrow keys to select the icon and then pressing Enter. The Calculator opens in the same view (Standard or Scientific) as was displayed the last time the Calculator was used.

You close the Calculator by choosing Close from the Control menu (or pressing Alt+F4). If you use the Calculator frequently, however, don't close it; minimize the Calculator to an icon. As an icon, you can access the Calculator quickly when needed.

To use the Calculator with the mouse, just click on the appropriate number and sign keys, like you press buttons on a desk calculator. Numbers appear in the display window as you select them, and the results appear after the calculations are performed.

Operating the Calculator with the keyboard also is easy. To enter numbers, use either the numbers across the top of the keyboard, or you can use the numeric keypad (although you first must press the NumLock key). To calculate, press the keys on the keyboard that match the Calculator keys. If the Calculator button reads +, for example, press the + key on the keyboard (press either the + key near the Backspace key or the + key on the numeric keypad). Table 16.5 shows the Calculator keys for the keyboard.

Table 16.5 Calculator Keys

Calculator Key	Function	Keyboard Key
MC	Clear memory	Ctrl+L
MR	Display memory	Ctrl+R
M+	Add to memory	Ctrl+P
MS	Store value in memory	Ctrl+M
CE	Delete displayed value	Del
Back	Delete last digit in displayed value	Backspace
+/_	Change sign	F9
/	Divide	/
*	Multiply	*

Calculator Key	Function	Keyboard Key
–	Subtract	–
+	Add	+
sqrt	Square root	@
%	Percent	%
1/x	Calculate reciprocal	R
C	Clear	Esc
=	Equals	= or Enter

Calculating Percents

To calculate a percentage, treat the % key like an equal sign. For example, to calculate 15% of 80, type 80*15%. After you press the % key, the Calculator displays the result 12.

Working with the Calculator's Memory

You can use the Calculator's memory to total the results of several calculations. The memory holds a single number, which starts as zero; you can add to, display, or clear this number, or you can store another number in memory. After the number in memory appears in the display window, you can perform calculations on the number, just as you can on any other number. When a number is stored in memory, the letter M appears in the box above the sqrt key on the Calculator.

Buttons and keystrokes for using the Calculator's memory are described in the preceding table in this chapter.

Use the Calculator's Memory To Sum Subtotals

You can use the Calculator's memory to sum a series of subtotals. Sum the first series of numbers, for example, and add this sum to memory by clicking the M+ button or pressing Ctrl+P on the keyboard; then clear the display and calculate the second subtotal. Add the second subtotal to memory. Continue until you add all the subtotals to memory; then display the value in memory by clicking the MR button or by pressing Ctrl+R.

Copying a Number from the Calculator in Another Application

When working with many numbers or complex numbers, you make fewer mistakes if you copy the Calculator results in other applications rather than retyping the result. To copy a number from the Calculator in another application, follow these steps:

1. In the Calculator display window, perform the math calculations required to display the number.

2. Choose the Edit Copy (Ctrl+C) command.

3. Activate the application you want to receive the calculated number.

4. Position the insertion point in the newly opened application where you want the number copied.

5. From the newly opened application, choose Edit Paste (or its equivalent).

Keeping the Calculator Handy
If you are working on a Windows application that needs several calculations, reduce the Calculator to an icon so that you can activate it quickly. To minimize Calculator to an icon, click the minimize button in the top right corner or press Alt+space bar and choose the Minimize command. To restore Calculator to a window, double-click the Calculator icon or press Alt+Tab until you see its name and then release the keys.

Copying a Number from Another Application in the Calculator

You can copy and paste a number from another application into the Calculator. After the number is in the calculator, you can perform calculations with the number and then copy the result back in the application.

A number pasted in the calculator erases the number currently shown in the display window.

To copy a number from another application in the Calculator, follow these steps:

1. In the other application, select the number.

2. Choose **Edit Copy** (or its equivalent) from the application.

3. Activate the Calculator and choose the **Edit Paste** command or press Ctrl+V.

If you paste a formula in the Calculator, the result appears in the display window. If you copy *5+5* from Windows Write and paste the calculation in the Calculator, the resulting number 10 appears. If you paste a function, such as @ for square root, Calculator performs the function on the number displayed. If, for example, you copy @ from a letter in Windows Write and paste in a Calculator displaying the number 25, the result 5 appears.

Numbers and most operators (such as + and -) work fine when pasted in the Calculator display, but the Calculator interprets some characters as commands. The following chart lists the characters that the Calculator interprets as commands:

Character	Interpreted As
C	Ctrl+L (clears memory)
E	Scientific notation in decimal mode; the number E in hexadecimal mode
M	Ctrl+M (stores current value in memory)
P	Ctrl+P (adds value to memory)
Q	C button or Esc key (clears current calculation)
R	Ctrl+R (displays value in memory)
:	Ctrl if before a letter (:m is Ctrl+M); function-key letter if before a number (:2 is F2)
\	Data key

Using the Scientific Calculator

If you have ever written an equation wider than a sheet of paper, you're a good candidate for using the Scientific Calculator. The Scientific Calculator is a special view of the Calculator.

To display the Scientific Calculator, follow these steps:

1. Activate the Calculator.

2. Choose the **View Scientific** command.

The Scientific Calculator works the same as the Standard Calculator, but adds many advanced functions. You can work in one of four number systems: hexadecimal, decimal, octal, or binary. You can perform statistical calculations, such as averages and statistical deviations. You can calculate sines, cosines, tangents, powers, logarithms, squares, and cubes. These specialized functions aren't described here but are well documented in the Calculator's Help command. To learn more about using Help, refer to Chapter 3, "Getting Help."

Watching the Clock

Windows comes equipped with a standard clock, which you can display on-screen in different sizes (see figs. 16.35 and 16.36). Even after you shrink the clock to an icon at the bottom of the screen, the hands still are readable in Analog view.

Start the Clock application by double-clicking the Clock icon in the Accessories window or by pressing the arrow keys to select the icon and then pressing Enter. Close the Clock by choosing Close from the Control menu or pressing Alt+F4. By minimizing, rather than closing the Clock to an icon, you can keep the clock visible on-screen; even as a small icon at the bottom of the screen, you can read the time.

The Clock application has one menu—the Settings menu. From this menu you choose whether to display the clock in Analog or Digital view. The Analog view shows a round clock face with ticking hands; the Digital view shows a numeric readout of the time. You also can change the font used in the Digital view, remove the title bar, and choose whether or not to display seconds and the date (in the title bar). Windows remembers the settings you choose and uses these settings every time you start the Clock application.

The time displayed by the Clock is based on either the computer's internal clock (if the computer has an internal clock) or on the time you type when you start the computer. If the time on the clock is inaccurate, use the Control Panel application to reset the clock as described in Chapter 7, "Customizing with the Control Panel."

T I P   To display just the clock—with no title or menu bar—double-click the clock face or choose the Settings No Title command. (Repeat the procedure to redisplay the title and menu bars.) This technique works in either Analog or Digital view.

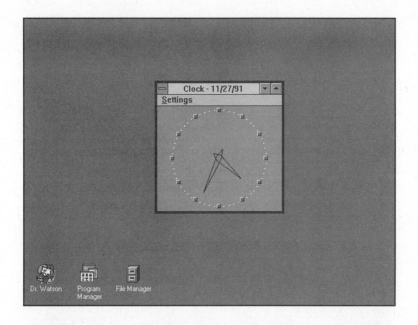

FIG. 16.35

The Clock in
Analog view.

FIG. 16.36

The Clock in
Digital view.

Monitoring Network Activity

When you work with Windows for Workgroups, you can *share* directories, printers, and ClipBook pages with other users. When you share resources like directories, printers, and your ClipBook with others, you will want a way to see which resources you share are being used and who is using them. NetWatcher, an accessory located in the Accessories group window, enables you to do exactly that. Not only can you learn who is using which resource, but you can also disconnect other users from your computer or close a file that another user has opened.

Monitoring Network Activity on Your Computer

To monitor the activity of users connected to your computer, choose the Accessory group in Program Manager and then double-click on the NetWatcher icon or use the arrow keys to select the NetWatcher icon and press Enter. The NetWatcher icon is shown in figure 16.37.

The NetWatcher window shown in figure 16.38 appears when you start NetWatcher. The left side of the window lists the *computer names* of every user connected to your computer. When you select a user from the list, the directories, printers, and ClipBook pages the selected user is using are listed in the right window. Any files the user has opened are listed under the directories for those files. Directories and files with read-only access are designated with an eyeglasses icon, while those with full access are designated with a pencil icon (see "Sharing a Directory" in Chapter 5 for a detailed explanation of the different levels of access for files and directories).

The information in the NetWatcher window updates every 20 seconds. If you want to update the information manually, choose the **O**ptions **R**efresh command or press F5.

The toolbar, located below the menu bar, gives you ready access to three of the NetWatcher commands you use most frequently. The functions of the three buttons on the toolbar are described in the following table. See the following sections to find out how to use each of these commands.

Button	Function
Properties	Display additional information for the selected user

Button	Function
Disconnect	Disconnect the selected user from your computer
Close File	Close the selected file

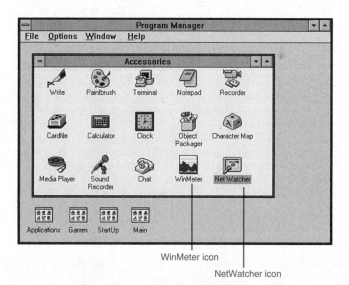

FIG. 16.37

See how your resources are shared on the network by starting NetWatcher.

WinMeter icon

NetWatcher icon

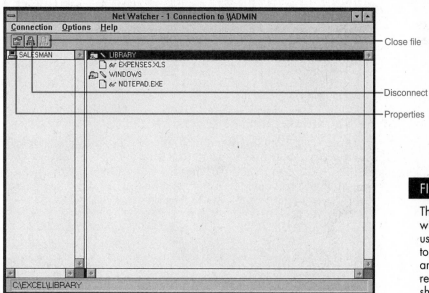

FIG. 16.38

The NetWatcher window lists the users connected to your computer and shows the resources being shared.

If you don't use the toolbar or need to make more room for displaying users, you can hide the toolbar. Choose the **O**ptions **T**oolbar command to turn off the display of the toolbar. To display the toolbar, choose the **O**ptions **T**oolbar command again. A check mark appears next to the command in the Options menu when the toolbar option is selected.

You can also display or not display the status bar that runs along the bottom of the NetWatcher window. Additional information about the selected item in the NetWatcher window appears in the status bar. To remove the status bar, choose the **O**ptions **S**tatus Bar command. To display the status bar, choose the **O**ptions **S**tatus Bar command again. A check mark appears next to the command in the Options menu when the status bar option is selected.

If you need to make more room on one side or the other of the NetWatcher window, you can move the split bar that divides the window. Use the mouse to drag the split bar to the right or left, or choose the **O**ptions Split **W**indow command, use the arrow keys to move the split bar, and press Enter when the split bar is located where you want it.

Displaying Information about a User

You can display additional information about any user connected to your computer. To find out more about a user, follow these steps:

1. Click the name of the user in the left window. If you are using a keyboard, use the Tab key to move the selection to the left window if it isn't already there, and then use the arrow keys to select the user.

2. Click the Properties button on the toolbar. If you are using a keyboard, choose the **C**onnection **P**roperties command (or press Alt+Enter).

The Properties dialog box will appear, as shown in figure 16.39.

The properties dialog box lists the name of the computer you selected, the name of the user logged on to that computer, the name of the network the user is connected to, what time and how long the user has been connected to your computer, and how much time has passed since the user last accessed resources on your computer.

Disconnecting a User

You can disconnect any user who is connected to your computer. To disconnect a user, follow these steps:

1. Click the user in the list on the left side of the NetWatcher window. If you are using the keyboard, press the Tab key to move the cursor to the left side of the window if it is not already there, and then use the arrow keys to select the user.

2. Click the Disconnect button on the toolbar. Or choose the **Con**nection **D**isconnect command.

   A message box warning you that the user may lose data appears. Choose **Y**es to disconnect the user or choose **N**o if you change your mind.

 NOTE Be aware that when you disconnect someone from your computer, the user may lose data in files that they are using on your computer. For this reason, you should notify a user and give that person time to disconnect or save files before you disconnect him or her.

Properties	
Computer Name:	SALESMAN
User Logged on:	SALESMAN
Network:	Microsoft Workgroup Client
Connected Since:	10/7/92 9:55:04AM (2:58:02)
Idle Time:	2:57:52

OK

FIG. 16.39

The Properties dialog box shows information about connected users.

Closing a File

You can close a file that another user has opened on your computer. When you close a file that another user is working with, the user may lose file information. To close a file, follow these steps:

1. Click the file in the right side of the NetWatcher window. If you are using a keyboard, press the Tab key to move the selection to the right side of the window if it is not already there, and then use the arrow keys to select the file.

2. Click the Close File button on the toolbar or choose the **Connec**tion **C**lose File command.

   A message box warning you that the user may lose data appears. Choose Yes to disconnect the user or choose No if you change your mind.

NOTE You should always notify the user before you close a shared file that someone else is working with.

Monitoring the Network's Share of Your Computer

Located in the Accessories group window, WinMeter is an application that uses a graph to show you how your computer is sharing its power between your work and the network's work. You can change how much of your computer's time is shared so that your computer applications run faster, or so that the network applications, like fiie sharing and Mail, run faster.

T I P If you don't like the way your computer is sharing its time with the network, you can change the sharing percentage by dragging the Performance Priority slide bar to a new percentage. The Performance Priority slide bar is located within the Network option in the Control Panel. The Network option is discussed in Chapter 27.

To use WinMeter, choose the Accessory group in Program Manager, and then double-click the WinMeter icon or use the arrow keys to select the icon and press Enter. The WinMeter window appears as shown in figure 16.40.

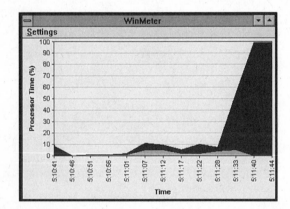

FIG. 16.40

The WinMeter accessory shows how your computer's time is shared with the network.

The percentage of CPU time allocated to your applications and to the shared resources on your computer are represented by two different colors. You can change the colors used with the **S**ettings **A**pplication Color and the **S**ettings **S**erver Color commands. You can also control how frequently the readings are updated by opening the Settings menu and selecting the time interval you want to use. To hide the title bar, choose the Settings **H**ide Title Bar command. Press the Esc key to redisplay the title bar. To see a larger WinMeter graph, drag a corner of the WinMeter window so the window is larger.

Chatting with Others in Your Workgroup

When you use Windows for Workgroups, you can send Mail to a single person or a group. An organization that uses Mail correctly can cut down on unnecessary meetings and phone tag. But there are occasions when you may not want to use Mail. You want to chat with someone immediately and directly. For example, you can ask questions of anyone else on the network—questions like the following:

"Susan, can you save this shared file to your local drive so we can shut down the computer the shared file is on?"

Or one of those dreaded messages like:

"Alrich, where are you! Everyone else is already in the boardroom waiting for your presentation."

When you need to *chat* with someone in your workgroup, use Chat. Chat is an application in the Accessory group. Its icon looks like a telephone and works almost exactly like a telephone.

With Chat, you talk by typing with anyone in your workgroup who is logged on. When you *call* someone, that person is notified of an incoming call. When the person activates his or her Chat application, you can *talk* back and forth with that person by typing in separate portions of the Chat screen. Figure 16.41 shows the Chat screen. The top portion shows what the sender is typing—the bottom portion shows what the receiver is typing. And both people can type and receive messages at the same time. It's as interactive as a telephone.

Making a Call

Remember how to use a telephone and you'll remember how to use Chat. You can chat with anyone in your workgroup who is logged on. To call someone, follow these steps:

1. Click the Dial button on the toolbar or choose the **C**onversation **D**ial command.

   The Select Computer dialog box shown in figure 16.42 will appear. Notice that the Dial button, first button on the left of the toolbar, looks like a rotary dial from an old phone.

2. Select the computer name of the person you want to chat with.

The status bar at the bottom of the Chat window will show you when the other person is connected. As soon as the status bar shows you are connected, you can begin typing in the top window. As you type, your message appears in the receiver's bottom window.

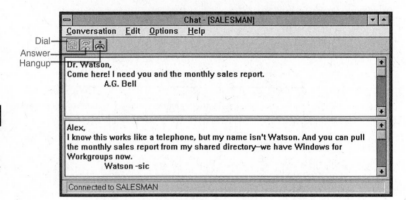

FIG. 16.41

You can chat with someone else in your work-group using the Chat accessory.

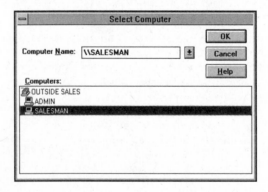

FIG. 16.42

Select the computer of the person with whom you want to chat.

Answering a Call

The person receiving a call is alerted to an incoming call in one of two ways. If Chat is not running, the incoming call starts as a telephone icon at the bottom of the desktop of the person receiving the call. You see the handset on the telephone bounce as the telephone rings. If you have sound turned on, you hear the ring sound you have designated. If Chat is active in a window, you see a message that someone is calling in the status bar at the bottom of the screen. You see the computer name of the person calling you.

To answer a call, click the Answer button in the toolbar or choose the Conversation Answer command. If Chat is an icon, you need to activate the application before you can answer the call. Activate Chat by double-clicking the Chat icon, or by selecting it and pressing Enter. You can begin typing as soon as you answer the call.

Editing, Copying, and Saving Conversations

Chat uses all the Windows editing conventions to which you are accustomed. Use the editing keys with which you are familiar from Windows Write or most word processors. The receiver sees corrections as you make them. You also have the Edit Cut, Edit Copy, and Edit Paste commands available so that you can transfer text and numbers into Chat.

The Edit Undo command is not available because your conversational partner watches everything you type and correct, so there is no reason for after-the-fact editing.

To save a Chat message for later reference, choose the Edit Select All command, and then choose the Edit Copy command. This puts the entire message in the Clipboard. You can then paste the message into Windows Write or a word processor, where it can be saved. Your portion of the window and the receiver's portion must be selected and copied separately. To switch between the two portions of the screen, click in the portion you want or press the F6 key.

> **T I P**
>
> Chat works with text and numbers. If you need to transmit a formatted word processing file, a spreadsheet, a chart, or graphic, attach the file to a Mail message. Because Windows enables you to run more than one application at a time, you can send the files attached to a Mail message as you talk over Chat.

Ending Your Conversation

As with the telephone, a conversation in Chat ends by hanging up. To hang up, click the Hangup button or choose the Conversation Hangup command. The Hangup button looks like a phone receiver coming down onto the phone cradle.

Changing Chat's Appearance and Sound

Like most Windows applications, Chat offers numerous features that you can customize so that Chat is more to your personal taste. For example, you can change the background color, change or turn the sound on or off, or change the font.

To change the background color on your typing portion (the upper half) of the screen, follow these steps:

1. Choose the Options Background Color command.

2. Select the color you want from the Basic Colors.

3. Choose OK or press Enter.

T I P   You may select a patterned color from the Basic Color group, but the closest solid color will be used. In some cases, you may see no change or a totally black screen.

The Custom Colors option is not available in Chat even though it appears in the Color dialog box, because the Color dialog box is shared between different applications, some of which do have custom color capability.

To change the font your Chat screen uses, follow these steps:

1. Choose the Options Font command.

2. Select or type the font name in the Font edit or list box.

3. Select a style in the Font Style list.

4. Select a size from the Size scrolling list.

5. Select the Strikeout or Underline check box for these effects.

6. Select a character color from the **C**olor combo list.

7. Choose OK or press Enter.

You can use the same font that the person on the other end of the conversation is using by choosing the **O**ptions **P**references command, and then selecting the Use **P**artner's Font or Use **O**wn Font selection.

You may want to display your screen in the side-by-side display shown in figure 16.43. To toggle your chatting windows between vertical and horizontal, choose the **O**ptions **P**references command, and then select either the **T**op and Bottom option or the **S**ide by Side option.

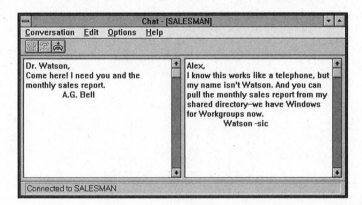

FIG. 16.43

Using Options Preferences, you can change window orientation.

Chat rings at both the caller's and receiver's personal computers. The sound of the ring depends upon whether you have a sound board, and which sound you have selected to act as the ring. If you do not have a sound board, you hear a beep. If you are a very popular person, you may want to turn the sound off so your office mate isn't disturbed during his or her afternoon nap. To toggle the sound between on and off, choose the **O**ptions **S**ound command. Each time you select the command, it changes the sound status.

Like most Windows applications with toolbars and status bars, you can turn those options on or off if you need more screen area or do not use them. To toggle the toolbar on and off, choose the **O**ptions **T**oolbar command. To toggle the status bar at the bottom of the screen on or off, choose the **O**ptions Status **B**ar command. If you want to reverse the current condition of the toolbar or status bar, just choose the **O**ption **T**oolbar or **O**ption Status **B**ar command again.

Developing Strategic Skills with Minesweeper, Solitaire, and Networked Hearts

A good reason exists to include Minesweeper and Solitaire at the end of this chapter: many Windows users stay up until the late hours of the evening, trying to beat the computer at a challenging game of Minesweeper or Solitaire! Now you have a good excuse for playing these games: you can claim that you're developing strategic skills and honing your hand-eye coordination. And if you use Windows for Workgroups' you can develop a closer working relation with members of your workgroup while learning about workgroup applications by playing Hearts against people on other computers.

Opening and Closing Minesweeper and Solitaire

To open the game applications, double-click icons in the Games window (they are not located in the Accessories window), or press the arrow keys to select an icon, and then press Enter. Close either game by choosing Exit from the **G**ame menu.

Playing Solitaire

After you start Solitaire, you see a screen like the one shown in figure 16.44. The screen has three active areas: the deck in the upper left corner of the playing area; the four suit stacks in the upper right corner of the playing area (which start out empty); and the seven row stacks in the bottom half of the screen. The number of cards in each row stack increases from one to seven, from left to right. The top card in each row stack is face up; all other cards in each stack are face down.

The object of the game is to move all the cards from the row stacks into the suit stacks at the top right of the screen. You must build the stack upwards, in sequential order, from Ace to King, one suit per stack. To start the stack, you need an Ace.

To get an Ace, you must either display this card in the lower stacks or turn over an Ace from the deck. The lower stacks build from high cards downward, in suits of alternating colors. You can build a lower stack, for example, starting with the King of Diamonds, the Queen of Spades, the Jack of Hearts, the Ten of Clubs, and so on. When you get an Ace, you can move the card to an upper suit stack and start building the suit stack there.

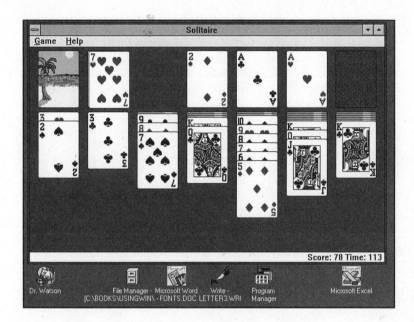

FIG. 16.44

Playing Solitaire.

In the lower stacks, you can move cards between the stacks, or from the deck to the stacks. You can move a single card at a time, or a group of cards. After all the upturned cards are moved from a lower stack, you can turn over the top card on the stack. To turn a card, click it with the mouse button or move the arrow to the card (by using the arrow keys) and press the space bar.

To deal from the deck, select the deck (by clicking the deck or by pressing the arrow keys to move to the deck and pressing the space bar). The dealt card appears to the right of the deck. If you can, move this card to a stack. You can move, for example, a King onto a blank space in the lower stack area.

To move a card (or cards), click and drag with the mouse. (You can move a card quickly from the lower stacks to the upper suit stacks by double-clicking on the card you want to move.) You can use the left and right arrow keys to move the selection arrow to the card you want to move: press Enter, use the arrow keys to move the card where you want, and press Enter to complete the move. If you want to move more than one card in a stack, press the up-arrow key to select a card higher up in the stack before you press Enter. If you make an illegal move, Solitaire moves the card to its original location.

Solitaire offers several options. Choose the **G**ame De**ck** command to choose a different deck illustration. Choose the **G**ame **O**ptions command to select the number of cards in each draw (one or three cards) and scoring options. Solitaire even has a **G**ame **U**ndo command to undo the last action.

When you finish playing and want to start a new game, choose the **G**ame **D**eal command.

To learn the rules of Solitaire, browse through the **H**elp command.

Watch the Dealer's Hand!
If you're playing with the deck that shows a hand full of aces, watch what the dealer has up his sleeve! Give it time and you may see amazing things.

Playing Minesweeper

Minesweeper is a game of analysis and tension. It requires a totally different flair than Solitaire.

When you open Minesweeper, you are faced with a grid of squares that represent a mine field. The goal of this game is to mark all the mines; if you step on a mine, the game is over. When you step on a square, three outcomes are possible: the square contains a mine that "blows up," and the game ends; the square contains no mine, and the minesweeper indicates that no mines exist in the surrounding eight squares; or the square contains no mine, and the minesweeper indicates that a certain number of mines exist in the surrounding eight squares (the number that appears in the square).

As you successfully uncover squares without stepping on a mine, the information provided by your minesweeper helps you deduce which squares contain mines. When you know a square contains a mine, you can mark this square, which effectively deactivates this mine. The object of the game is to mark all mines *before* stepping on one.

To uncover a square, click it. If the square contains no mine, either a number appears in the square, indicating the number of mines in the surrounding eight squares, or a blank space appears. If the square contains a number, you can try to deduce and mark which of the surrounding squares contains a mine or mines. To mark a mine, click the square with the right mouse button.

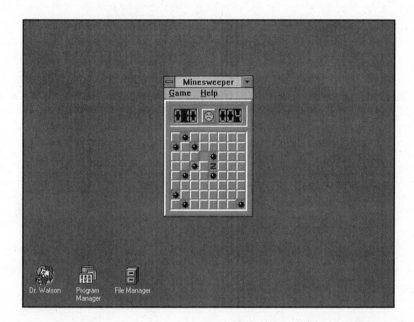

FIG. 16.45

Minesweeper is a game of analysis and tension.

Watch for patterns in the numbers. Once you play a few games, you will begin to see repeating patterns of numbers on the mine field. From those numbers, and the mines you can see, you can deduce where it is safe to take your next step.

Three predefined skill levels, which you select from the **G**ame menu, are available in Minesweeper: **B**eginner, **I**ntermediate, and **E**xpert. The levels differ in the size of the minefield and in the total number of mines per minefield. You also can define custom minefields with the **G**ame **C**ustom command. For more information on the rules of Minesweeper and some strategic hints on playing the game, choose the **H**elp command.

Starting and Playing Networked Hearts

Hearts is a card game that many people know. Many college grades have been marked down due to the affect of late night games of hearts and poker. Now you can bring the same productivity and late nights to your group at work by playing hearts over the network. Hearts is available only in Windows for Workgroups.

To start or join an open game of Hearts:

1. Double-click on the Hearts icon in the Game group window in the Program Manager.

   The Microsoft Hearts Network dialog box shown in figure 16.46 appears.

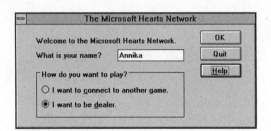

FIG. 16.46

You can start a game as a dealer or join a game as a player.

2. Type the name you want to be identified with to the group in the What is your name? edit box.

3. Select the hand that you want to play from the How do you want to play? group. If you want to start the game and be dealer select the I want to be **d**ealer option. If you want to join a game as a player select the I want to **c**onnect to another game option.

4. Choose OK or press Enter.

The Hearts card table and dealt hands will appear as shown in figure 16.47. It takes four card hands to play Hearts, but if you don't have enough players to play, the computer will play for the absent players. If you play by yourself against the computer, you must play the dealer's hand. If someone quits during the game, the computer will continue to play their hand.

As you play Hearts, the appropriate card hands will display on each player's screen. To learn how to play Hearts and learn about the options available in the game, choose the **Help** **C**ontents command and select from such topics as Keep Score, Play the Game, Start the Game, Understand the Rules, or Use Strategy.

FROM HERE...

For Related Information:

▶▶ To learn how to use Windows Write to integrate applications, see "Integrating Windows Applications," p. 850.

▶▶ To learn how to run DOS applications with Windows applications, see "Understanding How Windows Handles DOS Applications," p. 879 and "Loading and Running DOS Applications," p. 886.

◀◀ To learn more about object linking and embedding, see Chapter 6, p. 207.

◀◀ See "Using Menus and Dialog Boxes," p. 35.

◀◀ See "Starting, Using, and Quitting Applications," p. 46.

◀◀ See "Starting an Application from the Program Manager," p. 75.

◀◀ See "Operating Applications," p. 77.

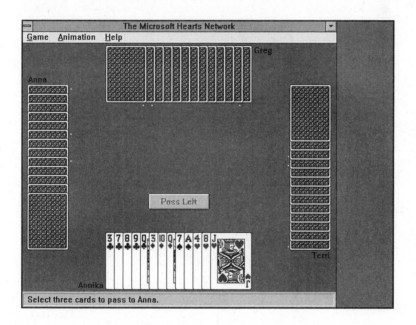

FIG. 16.47

You can play hearts against others in your workgroup or against the computer.

Chapter Summary

Because Windows' desktop accessories are so convenient to use, they quickly become part of your daily business tools. The Cardfile and Calendar are two applications you may want to load by default when you start Windows. Copy the appropriate program item icons to the StartUp group window in the Program Manager.

After checking appointments and a *To Do* list, you can minimize these accessories to icons, or close the desk accessories if you need maximum memory. The Notepad is a great way to track telephone conversations, ideas about a project in progress, lengthy notes while you work in a spreadsheet, and so on. When needed, you can transfer these notes easily to Windows Write or retrieve the TXT file with another word processor.

Multimedia

A s computers edge into more and more aspects of everyday life, they take on new roles. Consider these roles: computer as musician, as storyteller, as business presentation tool, as educational tool, and as research assistant.

Multimedia plays a part in each of these roles because it combines two familiar communications media—sound and sight—in a single package and gives you control over producing and delivering sound and visual effects.

You can use multimedia in several ways. With the right equipment, you can play all of the many multimedia packages available commercially. Included are games, stories, full encyclopedias, complete reference texts, and more. You can record simple messages, tunes, or motion pictures and embed them in documents you create in Windows applications. If you are adventurous, you can move beyond the simple applications that come with Windows to a multimedia authoring application and create original multimedia presentations and applications.

Using multimedia requires that you have the right equipment. You need a CD-ROM player, speakers, and a sound board. All hardware must be compliant to the MPC standard developed by Microsoft and the Multimedia PC Marketing Council. You can supply the equipment you need in one of two ways: by upgrading a present PC or by buying a special multimedia PC equipped with all you need.

Upgrading Your Equipment to Multimedia Standards

To take advantage of multimedia, you need the right equipment. Basically, you need a powerful PC, VGA graphics, a sound board, speakers, and a CD-ROM drive. You can add many optional pieces of equipment, including VCRs, microphones, joysticks, MIDI synthesizers, and music keyboards.

To ensure compatibility among all multimedia software and equipment, the Multimedia PC Marketing Council has established standards for multimedia PC hardware (listed in table 17.1). You can get the right equipment in one of two ways. You can purchase an MPC-compliant computer, ready to play. Several manufacturers sell these MPCs, which include all the hardware (and, often, the software) you need. The second way to get the proper equipment is to upgrade your current system by adding a sound board, a CD-ROM drive, and (if necessary) VGA graphics. Make sure that the equipment you choose conforms to this standard. The best way to accomplish this task is to look for the MPC logo, which ensures compliance; another way is to understand the hardware requirements and purchase equipment that conforms to these standards.

You already may have some of the equipment you need. Your stereo system can serve as the amplifier and speakers, and an MPC-compliant CD-ROM player that you use for music also may play multimedia disks.

Table 17.1 Multimedia Equipment Requirements

System Element	Minimum Requirements	Recommended
Computer		
CPU	80386SX, 16 MHz	80386, 25 MHz
RAM	2 M	4 M
Diskette	3 1/2-inch, 1.44 M capacity	Same
Fixed disk	30 M	80 M
User input	101-key keyboard, mouse	Same
I/O	1 serial, 1 parallel, 1 joystick*	Same

System Element	Minimum Requirements	Recommended
Graphics		
Display	VGA, 640 × 480, 16 colors	Same, 256 colors
Audio		
Sampling type	Linear PCM	Same
Resolution	8-bit	16-bit
Sampling rate, DAC**	11.025 and 22.05 kHz	44.1 kHz
Sampling rate, ADC**	11.025 kHz, microphone input	22.05 and 44.1 kHz
Melody notes/timbres	6/3 simultaneous	16/9 simultaneous
Percussive notes/timbres	2/2 simultaneous with melody	16/8 simultaneous
External audio input	Microphone	Added stereo input
Internal mixing	CD, synthesizer, and DAC	Added aux. input
Audio Output	Line level, –10 db, stereo***	Same
MIDI I/O	In, Out, Thru, interrupt-driven	Same
CD-ROM Drives		
Transfer Rate	150 kB/second, 16 kB blocks	64 kB (with buffers)
Seek time	1 second	Same
MTBF	10,000 hours	Same
Mode	1	2, form 1 and 2
Subchannels	Q	P and R-W
Driver	Microsoft MSCDEX 2.2	Same

Joystick input usually is provided by the audio adapter card.

****DAC is an abbreviation for digital-to-analog converter, a device that converts digital data to audio signals. ADC stands for analog-to-digital converter, which converts audio input signals to digital data.*

***** Referenced to standard consumer audio line level –0 db = 1 milliwatt into 600 ohms.*

Installing Multimedia Equipment and Drivers

Before you can use a multimedia device, such as a sound board or a CD-ROM player, you first must physically plug the device into the computer; then you must install the device driver in Windows; and finally you must set up the hardware. The process is similar to installing a new printer on the system: plugging in the hardware establishes the physical connection; installing the driver tells Windows the device exists; setting up the device tells Windows how to communicate with the device.

Installing Equipment

Plugging in a device—whether a sound board or a CD-ROM player—isn't difficult. If the device is internal, such as a sound board, turn off the power, remove a few screws from the sides of the *system unit* (the computer box that holds the CPU), and slide off the cover. (You also may have to remove a port cover from the back of the PC to provide external access to the new board's ports.) Boards plug into an area of the PC reserved for boards.

Look at the boards already installed in the PC to see how these circuit boards are attached. Then look at the new board; you can see that the board has ports at one end that must point toward the back of the PC for external access and a wide *tab* on one side of the board that pushes into any of the available slots in the PC. Although you need firm pressure to push the tab into the slot, the process is neither complex nor dangerous. When you are finished, slide the cover back on the PC and replace the screws. (Just think how impressed your colleagues will be when you casually mention that you installed a new board in your PC today.)

CD-ROM players may be internal or external, but either way, these players usually connect to a PC via a cable. If you have the space, you can install an internal CD-ROM player inside the PC (you need an available drive bay). To install an internal CD-ROM, you have to take off the cover of the PC, as you do to install a board. Follow the manufacturer's instructions for connecting the cables inside the PC. If you don't have space inside the PC, add an external CD-ROM player; this installation is a simple matter of connecting cables. Read the documentation that comes with the device for details about attaching multimedia equipment to your PC.

You also may need to attach the multimedia device to other equipment. A sound board, for example, requires speakers (if you have a stereo system, you can connect the sound board to the amplifier and use the stereo's speakers). The documentation tells you how to make this connection. Sound boards often include connectors that make adding a microphone or joystick or connecting to your CD-ROM player simple. Sound boards also usually include a connector for a MIDI musical synthesizer or keyboard, but you may need an additional converter box to operate the MIDI equipment. Check with the sound board documentation or manufacturer.

After attaching the device to the PC, you may need to run a test to check that the device is successfully attached. After you plug in a Sound Blaster board, for example, you run a test to determine whether the board is successfully connected to both the PC and the speakers. If the test is successful, you hear music you never thought could come from a computer. From the test, you learn that the speakers are correctly attached and that the PC and the board are communicating. If the test is unsuccessful, you may have to change the setup. For more information about changing the setup, see "Setting Up a Device Driver" later in this chapter.

Write down all information the test application gives you about the installation. The Sound Blaster test, for example, may tell you that the board is currently using I/O address #220 and Interrupt #7. You may need this information when you install the driver in Windows.

Adding Multimedia Drivers

For Windows to recognize and communicate with the multimedia equipment you install, you must install the correct device driver in Windows. Windows comes with many multimedia equipment drivers, which you find listed in Windows but which are not yet installed. You know whether Windows includes a driver for the equipment when you display a list of existing drivers (step 4 in the following instructions). If the driver you need isn't included, you may be able to use the generic driver that comes with Windows. If you learn that the generic driver doesn't work for the equipment, check the documentation for the new equipment to find out whether a Windows driver is available (or call the manufacturer).

To install the driver, you must have the original Windows installation diskettes (or the disks that came with your device, if you are using the manufacturer's driver). The Windows diskettes contain the driver you need for the device.

After the multimedia device is successfully attached, follow these steps to install the driver and set up the device in Windows:

1. In the Windows Program Manager, open the Main window and then choose the Control Panel. The Control Panel window appears (see fig.17.1).

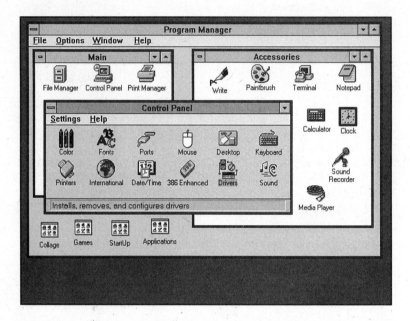

The Control Panel contains the Drivers icon.

2. Choose the Drivers application by double-clicking the Drivers icon with the mouse or by pressing the arrow keys to select the icon and then pressing Enter. The Drivers dialog box appears (see fig.17.2).

3. Choose the **A**dd button. The Add dialog box appears (see fig. 17.3).

4. Select the equipment's name in the List of Drivers list and choose OK. If the equipment isn't listed, select Unlisted or Updated Driver. A dialog box appears, prompting you to insert the diskette that contains the device driver (see fig. 17.4).

5. Insert the diskette that contains the driver into drive A. If the driver is located on a different drive or directory in the PC, type the drive and directory names (but not the driver's file name).

   If you don't know where the driver is located, choose **B**rowse (see fig. 17.5). Then select the drive and directory that contains the device driver and choose OK.

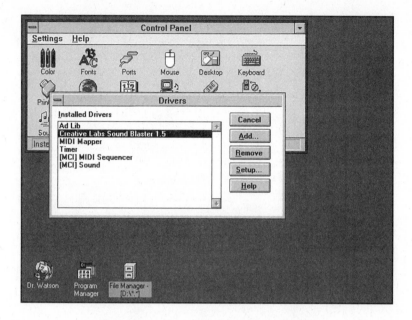

The Drivers dialog box shows a list of the drivers already installed in Windows.

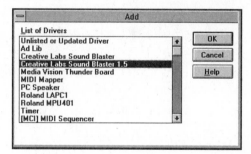

The Add dialog box shows all the drivers that Windows supplies.

The message tells you exactly which disk to insert.

6. When you return to the Add dialog box, choose OK. A Setup dialog box may appear, requesting configuration information (see fig. 17.6).

FIG. 17.5

To locate the driver, you can browse through drives and directories.

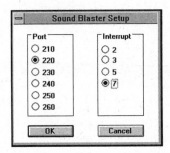

FIG. 17.6

The Setup dialog box already may show the correct setup information.

7. After referring to the notes you took when you tested the device, select the necessary setup information and choose OK.

8. If Windows requires more drivers to go with the driver you installed, Window installs them by default and may ask you for more setup information. Respond to any dialog box that appears and choose OK.

   If, however, the installation is complete, a dialog box advises you that you must restart Windows for the installation to take effect.

9. Choose **R**estart Now to restart Windows so that you can use the driver. (If you don't restart, you can use the driver the next time you use Windows.)

Setting Up a Device Driver

Windows communicates with devices, such as sound boards and CD-ROM players, through only a limited number of channels. When you install and set up the new device, you must make sure that the settings you choose don't conflict with settings already in use by other devices.

Testing after you connect the equipment to your PC is the best way to ensure that no conflict exists. If, however, you have trouble using the device after connecting, installing, and setting up the system, a conflict may exist. To determine where the conflict lies, refer to the device's documentation. You also can call the manufacturer or the Microsoft support line (this number is included in Chapter 30).

Finally, you can check the setup for other equipment installed on the PC to see if a port or IRQ interrupt is in conflict. (If you suspect a printer, check by choosing the Printers application in the Control Panel and choosing the **C**onnect Button. Choose OK and then Close after you change the connection. If you need to change an IRQ interrupt, choose the Ports application in the Control Panel, select the COM port to change, choose **S**ettings, choose **A**dvanced, and select a different IRQ number from the **I**nterrupt Request Line list. Finally, choose OK twice and then choose Close.)

To make changes to the driver setup, follow these steps:

1. Choose the Drivers icon in the Control Panel. The Drivers dialog box appears.

2. From the **I**nstalled Drivers list, select the driver you want to set up.

3. Choose the **S**etup button. (If the driver requires no settings, the **S**etup button is dimmed.) The Setup dialog box appears.

4. Select the setup options you need, referring to the device's documentation.

5. Choose OK.

6. When the System Setting Change dialog box appears, choose **R**estart Now to force the changes to take effect immediately or choose **D**on't Restart Now and choose Close to close the Drivers dialog box.

Removing a Driver

You can remove a driver you no longer use from the Installed Drivers list. Removing a driver doesn't remove the file from the hard disk, so you can easily re-connect if you subsequently find that you need the driver. Do not remove drivers that Windows installed (just to be safe, don't remove any drivers you don't recognize).

To remove a driver, follow these steps:

1. In the Control Panel, choose the Drivers icon. The Drivers dialog box appears.

2. Select the driver you want to remove from the **I**nstalled Drivers list.

3. Choose the **R**emove button. A dialog box appears, asking you to confirm removal of the driver.

4. Choose **Y**es.

5. Choose **R**estart Now to force the removal to take effect immediately.

FROM HERE...

For Related Information:

▶▶ See "Providing a Good Environment for Windows," p. 957.

▶▶ See "Using Memory Efficiently," p. 962.

▶▶ See "Optimizing Hard Disk Performance," p. 969.

◀◀ See "Configuring for Sound Devices," p. 302.

Operating the Sound Recorder

To use sound on a PC, you must add a sound board that conforms to the Multimedia Personal Computer specifications for the PC. You must install the board after adding it, as described in the previous section "Adding Multimedia Drivers." If you use high-level MIDI sound or a synthesizer, you also must install the drivers for these devices.

To record sound, you also need a microphone; the sound board probably has a microphone jack (or port), but you should check the documentation to find out the connector you need. You also need to be sure that the microphone is powerful enough to replicate your voice adequately; check documentation for specifications.

Using the Sound Recorder application, you can play, record, and edit sounds that have the WAVE format (designated by the file extension WAV). You can play these sounds on the speakers, assign sound to events, or embed sounds in applications that support object linking and embedding. You can embed a spoken message, for example, inside an Excel spreadsheet file or a Word for Windows document. (To learn more about object linking and embedding, refer to Chapter 6.)

The Sound Recorder application appears as a small window on-screen that shows a menu across the top, buttons on the bottom, and an oscilloscope-like display in the center. You use the menus to open, edit, and save sound files. You watch the wave-like display to monitor the sound file's progress. You use the buttons to start and stop the Recorder, just like a tape recorder.

Starting the Sound Recorder

To start the Sound Recorder, follow these steps:

1. In the Program Manager, open the Accessories window (see fig. 17.7).

2. Choose the Sound Recorder. (Double-click on the Sound Recorder icon with the mouse or press the arrow keys to select the icon and then press Enter.) The Sound Recorder window appears (see fig. 17.8).

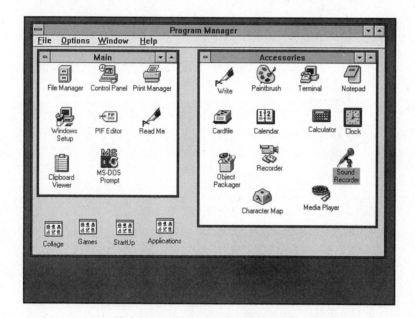

FIG. 17.7

The Sound Recorder icon is among the accessories.

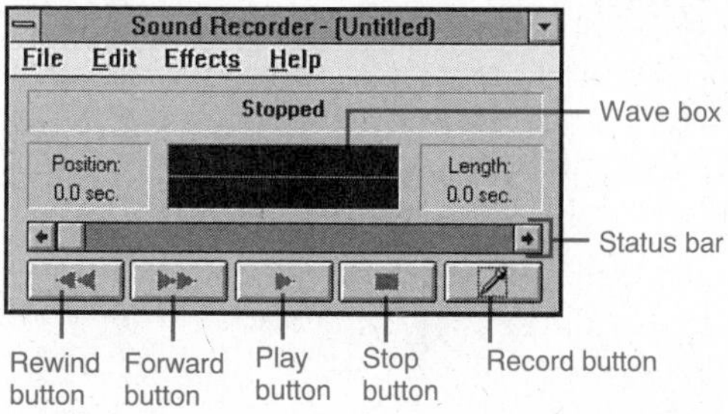

FIG. 17.8

The Sound Recorder window gives you a visual display of sound wave forms.

Opening and Playing Sounds

On a PC, sound is stored as a file, just like other documents. To play a sound, you first must start the Sound Recorder (see the preceding section) and open a sound file recorded in the WAVE format (a file with the extension WAV). Windows includes several sound files that use the WAVE format, and you can use Sound Recorder to record, edit, or mix sounds that you create.

To open and play a sound file, follow these steps:

1. Choose the **File** menu and select the **O**pen command. The Open dialog box appears (see fig. 17.9).

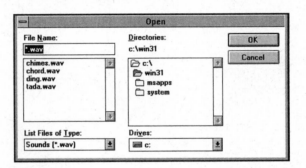

FIG. 17.9

Use the Open dialog box to locate the WAV file you want to open and play.

2. In the Drives list (if necessary), choose the drive that contains the file and, in the **D**irectories list, select the directory. In the File Name list, select the file you want to open.

3. Choose OK to open the sound file.

   The Length message on the right side of the Sound Recorder dialog box tells you the playing length, in seconds, of the file you opened.

4. Choose the Play button.

   The Position message on the left side of the Sound Recorder dialog box tells you the current position, in seconds, of the sound you are playing.

The status bar reads Playing, and you see a visual representation of the sound waves in the Wave box (see fig. 17.10). You also see the scroll box move to the right as the file progresses.

Each time you choose the Play button, the sound plays from beginning to end. When the file ends (or when you choose the Stop button), Stopped appears in the Status bar.

You can stop the file manually by choosing the Stop button, and you can resume by choosing Play again. You also can move around in a sound file. To move forward by one tenth of a second, click on the right arrow of the scroll bar (to move backward, click the left arrow of the scroll bar). To move one second at a time, click on the shaded part of the scroll bar in the direction you want to move. With a keyboard, press the Tab key to select the scroll bar and press the left- or right-arrow keys to move forward or backward by tenths of a second.

You can move quickly to the end of a sound file by choosing the Forward button or pressing the End key; you can move to the beginning by choosing the Rewind button or pressing Home.

Creating a Sound File

You can create a sound file by recording the sound, by adding to an existing sound file, by inserting one sound file into another, or by mixing together two sound files. To record a voice, you need to attach a microphone. Check the device documentation to learn how.

You can record up to one minute of speech. To record a voice, follow these steps:

1. Choose the File menu and select the New command.

2. Choose the Record button.

3. To record the message, speak into the microphone.

4. Choose the Stop button when you finish.

To record from a stereo, plug the stereo's output attachment into the microphone input port on the sound board (this procedure may require a special connector; check with an electronics store). If you find that recording exactly what you need is difficult, record a little more than you need and delete the extra (described in the following paragraphs of this section).

To record into an existing file, open the file and use the Play and Stop buttons (or the scroll bar) to move to the position where you want to add the new sound. Choose the Record button and speak into the microphone. Choose Stop when you finish and save the file.

You also can merge two sound files. Open the sound file into which you want to add another sound file and use the Play and Stop buttons to move to the place where you want to add another sound file. Choose the **E**dit menu and select the **I**nsert File command. Select the file you want to insert and choose OK. Save the new file.

Another option is to mix two files so that the sounds of both files play simultaneously. One file may be music and the other file a voice. Open one of the files and use Play and Stop (or the scroll bar) to move to the place where you want to mix in another file. Choose the **E**dit menu and select the **M**ix With File command. Select the file you want to mix in and choose OK. Save the new file.

To delete part of a sound file, move to either immediately before or after the point at which you want to delete the sound and choose the **E**dit menu and select either the Delete **B**efore Current Position or the Delete **A**fter Current Position command.

Before you save the sound file, you can *undo* changes at any time by choosing the **F**ile menu and selecting the **R**evert command.

Editing a Sound File

You can edit a sound file after you create it by adding special effects, changing the volume, speeding up or slowing down, adding an echo, or reversing the sound. (If you reverse the file, be sure that you don't include offensive subliminal messages.)

To edit a sound file, follow these steps:

1. Choose the **F**ile menu and select the **O**pen command.

2. Select the file you want to edit and choose OK.

3. Choose the Effect**s** menu and select one of the following commands:

Command	Effect
Increase Volume (by 25%)	Make the sound file 25% louder
Decrease Volume	Make the sound file 25% softer

Command	Effect
Increase speed (by 100%)	Double the speed of the sound file
Decrease Speed	Halve the speed of the sound file
Add Echo	Add an echo to the sound
Reverse	Play the sound file backwards

By choosing the **F**ile menu and selecting the **R**evert command, you can *undo* changes at any time before you save the sound file.

Saving a Sound File

Be sure to save after you create or edit a sound file.

To save a sound file, follow these steps:

1. Choose the **F**ile menu and select the Save **As** command.
2. Select the drive where you want to save the file in the Dri**v**es list.
3. Select the directory where you want to save the file in the **D**irectories list.
4. Type a file name in the File **N**ame box. Include the file extension WAV to make the file easier to open at a later time.
5. Choose OK.

If you decide not to rename a file, instead of **F**ile Save **As**, choose **F**ile **S**ave.

Exiting Sound Recorder

When you finish using Sound Recorder, choose the **F**ile menu and select the E**x**it command.

Assigning Sounds to Events

The simplest form of sound on a computer is the sound you can assign to computer-related events, such as pressing the asterisk key or question mark or starting or stopping Windows. Windows comes equipped with several sound files you can assign to these events (and you can use the Sound Recorder to create custom sounds). You also can turn off system sounds so that the PC operates more discreetly.

To assign sounds to computer events, follow these steps:

1. From the Control Panel, choose the Sound icon. The Sound dialog box appears, showing the available Windows Events in one list box and the sound Files in another list box (see fig. 17.11). Sound files usually have the WAV file extension.

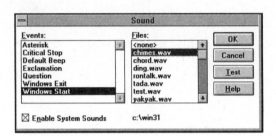

2. If the sound files are stored in another drive or directory, select the drive or directory from the Files text box.

3. Select the Event that you want to change. The sound file currently assigned to this event is selected in the Files text box. Select another sound file to assign a different sound to the event.

4. Choose the Test button to see how the sound file sounds.

5. Repeat steps 3 and 4 to assign sounds to other Windows events.

6. After you set the desired sounds for the events, choose OK.

To turn off the PC's warning beep, select the Enable System Sounds check box and choose OK. This action disables all beeping for all applications used in Windows.

FROM HERE...

For Related Information:

◄◄ To learn more about embedding sound in applications that support OLE, see "Embedding Data as Packages," p. 238.

◄◄ See "Using Menus and Dialog Boxes," p. 35.

◄◄ See "Starting, Using, and Quitting Applications," p. 46.

◄◄ See "Operating Applications," p. 77.

Operating the Media Player

Using the Media Player application, you can play Windows-compatible multimedia voice, animation, and music files. Where Sound Recorder only plays WAVE-format sound, Media Player can play animated video files and MIDI-based music files.

Before you use the Media Player, you must connect the multimedia device (usually a CD-ROM player, VCR, or MIDI synthesizer) to the PC, and you must install the device in Windows and set up the driver to run with Windows. For more information, refer to the earlier section on "Installing Multimedia Equipment and Drivers."

The Media Player is a small window that contains menus, a scroll bar, and buttons. The menus enable you to open files, select the device to play on, and switch between time and tracks. The scroll bar follows the progress of the file you play. The buttons play, pause, stop, and eject the media, just like a VCR or CD-ROM player.

Unlike the Sound Recorder, you cannot use the Media Player to create custom files. To create multimedia files, you must purchase a multi-media authoring kit, such as Multimedia ToolBook from Asymetrix or Guide Media Extensions from Owl International.

Starting the Media Player

The Media Player is a Windows accessory, and, therefore, is located in the Accessories window.

To start the Media Player, follow these steps:

1. Activate the Accessories window in the Program Manager. You see the Media Player icon (see fig. 17.12).

2. Choose the Media Player. (Double-click on the Media Player icon with the mouse or press the arrow keys to select the icon and press Enter.) The Media Player window appears (see fig. 17.13).

Choosing a Media Device

Before you can play a multimedia game, movie, or story, you must specify the device on which you plan to play the game, movie, or story. Two kinds of devices exist: simple and compound. *Simple* devices play whatever is physically loaded into the device. To play a *compound* device, you must choose the device and then open the file you want to play. The listed devices reflect the equipment and drivers you previously installed.

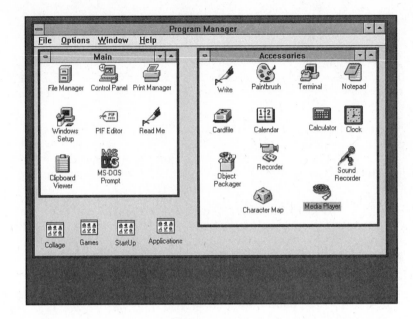

FIG. 17.12

Use the Media
Player icon
to start the
Media Player
application.

To choose a media device, follow these steps:

1. Choose the **D**evice menu (see fig. 17.14).

2. Select the device that you want to play. Simple devices are not followed by a dialog box.

   Compound devices (like **S**ound and **M**idi Sequencer in fig. 17.14) are followed by a dialog box.

FIG. 17.13

The Media Player
window enables
you to open and
play multimedia
files.

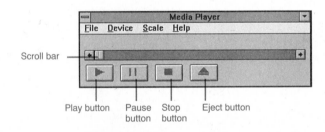

FIG. 17.14

The devices listed
in the Device
menu depend on
what is installed
on the system.

3. If you selected a compound device, select the file that you want to play and choose OK.

If you installed a sound board and attached speakers, you can open and play one of two 2-minute music files included in the Windows directory: CANYON.MID and PASSPORT.MID.

Opening a File

After you specify a compound device and open a file, you can open a different file to play on the same device, without choosing the device again (unless you want to switch to a different device).

To open a file, follow these steps:

1. Choose the File menu and select the Open command. The Open dialog box appears.

2. Select in the Drives list the drive where the file is located.

3. Select the kind of file you want to list in the List Files of Type list. (Select MIDI Sequencer, for example, to list files with the extensions MID and RMI.)

4. In the Directories list, select the directory that contains the file.

5. In the File Name list, select the file that you want to open.

6. Choose OK.

Playing a Media File

After you selected a device and either inserted the media (if you selected a simple device) or opened a file (if you selected a compound device), Media Player is ready to play. The buttons in the Media Player window enable you to play, pause, stop, and eject the media (if the device supports ejecting).

Choose the following buttons to operate the Media Player:

Button	Action
Play	Begin playing the media in the simple device or begin playing the file in the compound device
Pause	Pause the media (choose either Pause or Play to restart)
Stop	Stop the media (choose Play to restart)
Eject	Eject the media (if the device supports this action)

The scroll box in the scroll bar moves to the right as the media or file plays.

Changing the Scale and Moving to a Different Position

By default, no scale appears above the scroll bar in Media Player, but two scales—Time and Tracks—are available. The Time scale shows your progress through the media or file by time. The Track scale counts the tracks as the media or file plays. Because these scales appear above the scroll bar, you can move to a specific position in the file by watching the scale as you move the scroll box in the scroll bar.

To change the scale, follow these steps:

1. Choose the Scale menu.

2. Select the Time command. The Time scale appears (see fig. 17.15).

FIG. 17.15

The Time scale enables you to watch the progress, by time, of the file you are playing.

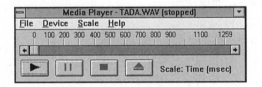

You also can select the Tracks command. The Tracks scale appears (see fig. 17.16).

You can move to a different spot in the file by clicking on the left or right arrow in the scroll bar; dragging the scroll box; clicking in the scroll bar; or pressing the left-arrow, right-arrow, PgUp, or PgDn keys.

FIG. 17.16

The Tracks scale enables you to watch the progress of the file you are playing by tracks.

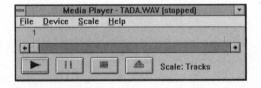

Exiting Media Player

After you finish playing the multimedia file or device, choose the File menu and select the Exit command. If the multimedia file or device is not finished playing when you exit, a simple device continues playing, and you must turn off the actual device.

For Related Information:

◄◄ See "Using Menus and Dialog Boxes," p. 35.

◄◄ See "Starting, Using, and Quitting Applications," p. 46.

◄◄ See "Operating Applications," p. 77.

FROM HERE...

Embedding Sound and Video in Applications

One of the promises of multimedia is that you can integrate pieces from different applications into a unified presentation. In its simplest form, a multimedia presentation may consist of a file that contains embedded sound or video.

You can embed sound and video into a file by using one of two methods. The first—and preferable—way is to use the Object Packager accessory to package a sound or video object together with the related application and embed the object in a file, which causes a microphone icon to appear in the file. This method is preferable because you can quickly play the embedded sound or video. The other way to embed sound is to choose an *insert* command to embed a sound object within the file (using this technique, you cannot embed a Media Player object—only a Sound Recorder object). This method also shows a microphone icon in the file but, rather than playing the sound, starts the Sound Recorder window with no file loaded. To play a sound, you first must load the sound file. Because this method for embedding sound seems less useful than using the Object Packager, this method isn't discussed in this chapter. To learn how to use this method, refer to Chapter 6.

To embed sound or video in a file, all the applications involved must support object linking and embedding, or OLE. Sound Recorder and Media Player are OLE servers; the application in which you want to embed a sound or video object must be an OLE client.

After a sound or video file is embedded in a document by using the Packager, an icon appears in the document. The icon for a Sound Recorder object is a microphone; the icon for a Media Player object is a reel of film. If the embedded object is a WAVE-format sound file, you can double-click the microphone icon to either play the sound or display the Sound Recorder with the sound file loaded. (Whether you play the sound or display the Sound Recorder depends on how you packaged the object—here, you learn both ways.) If the embedded object needs the Media Player (as do MIDI files), when you double-click the film-reel icon, the Media Player appears on-screen with the file loaded, and you must select the Play button to play the file.

To embed a multimedia object so that the Sound Recorder or Media Player window appears on-screen when you double-click the icon, the file already should be created and saved. (This technique is the only one that works with Media Player files; a second technique, described in a following part of this section, is available for Sound Recorder files.)

To package and embed a multimedia object in a file so that double-clicking the icon shows either the Sound Recorder window or the Media Player window, follow these steps:

1. In the Accessories Window, choose the Object Packager. (Double-click the Object Packager icon or select the icon by using the arrow keys and press Enter.) The Object Packager window appears, as shown in figure 17.17.

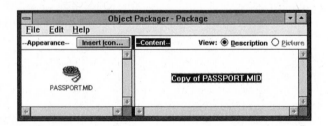

FIG. 17.17

Use the Object Packager to embed sound and video objects in a file.

2. Select the Content window (on the right side) and choose the File Import command. After the Import dialog box appears, select the multimedia file you want to embed and choose OK. A copy of the file is added to the Object Packager.

   To change the text below the icon before you copy the package and paste the icon in the document, choose the Edit Label command and type new text. You may want to include a call to action, such as double-click here, so that whoever uses the file knows exactly what to do to play the sound or video file.

3. Choose the **Edit** Copy Package command.

4. Position the insertion point in the document where you want to embed the package.

5. Choose the **Edit P**aste command. An icon appears in the document, as shown in figure 17.18.

6. Save the document.

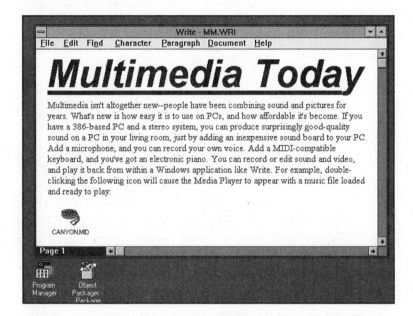

When you double-click the icon in the document, the Sound Recorder or Media Player window appears (depending on the kind of file you embedded). The sound or video file loads, and all you have to do is select the Play button.

To package a sound to embed in a file so that when you double-click the icon, the sound plays, follow these steps:

1. Open the Sound Recorder.

2. Create the sound that you want to embed or open the file that contains the sound.

3. Choose the **Edit C**opy command, which copies the sound to the Clipboard.

4. Activate the Object Packager and select the Content window (right side).

5. Choose the **Edit Paste** command. The sound is copied from the Clipboard to the Object Packager.

   To change the text below the icon before you copy and paste the package in the document, choose the **Edit Label** command and type the new text.

6. Choose the **Edit Copy Package** command. The package is copied.

7. Activate the application, open the file, and position the insertion point in the document where you want to embed the package.

8. Choose the **Edit Paste** command. A microphone icon appears, as shown in figure 17.19.

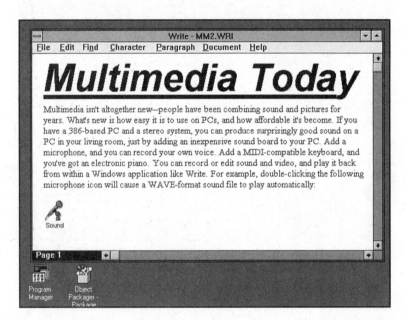

FIG. 17.19

A microphone icon indicates that a Sound Recorder object is embedded.

If you use this second technique—copying the sound directly from the Sound Recorder and pasting the sound in the Object Packager, rather than using the **File Import** command in the Object Packager—when you double-click the icon in the file, the sound plays without displaying the Sound Recorder.

In many applications, you can play an embedded multimedia object by double-clicking or by selecting the object and choosing a command such as **Edit Package Object, Activate Contents** in Write.

For Related Information:

◀◀ To learn more about embedding sound in applications that support OLE, see "Embedding Data into a Document," p. 233 and "Embedding Data as Packages," p. 238.

◀◀ See "Using the File Manager's Drag and Drop Feature," p. 191.

FROM HERE...

Using the MIDI Mapper

When you install a device that supports MIDI, such as the Sound Blaster sound card, an application for controlling MIDI devices is added by default. The application, MIDI Mapper, appears as a new icon in the Control Panel. You can use MIDI Mapper to choose a preconfigured MIDI setup for the MIDI device or to create custom setup specifications.

Choosing a MIDI Setup

When installing Windows, some predefined MIDI settings designed to work with common MIDI devices are included. A new device probably will conform to one of these settings and, therefore, work flawlessly with Windows. However, you can change the settings by using the MIDI Mapper application in the Control Panel. You may need to change these settings if you use a nonstandard MIDI setup or if the device doesn't include a MIDI setup.

To alter a MIDI setting, follow these steps:

1. In the Program Manager, select the Main window and choose the Control Panel. You can see the MIDI Mapper icon if you installed a MIDI device (see fig. 17.20).

2. Choose the MIDI Mapper icon. The MIDI Mapper dialog box appears (see fig. 17.21).

3. Make sure that the Show Setups option is selected. Then from the Name list, select the setup you want to use.

4. Choose Close.

If no setting for the device is listed, first call the manufacturer to see whether an updated MIDIMAP.CFG setup file, which includes a setup for this device, is available. If an updated file is available, make a backup of the existing MIDIMAP.CFG file and copy the new file to the Setup subdirectory in the Windows directory. If no setup file is available, you may need to create a custom file.

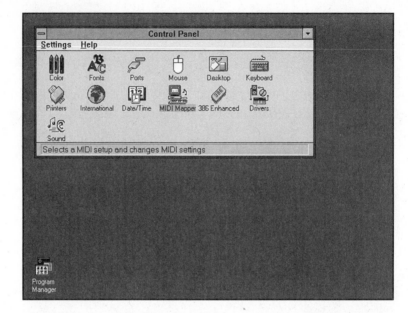

FIG. 17.20

The MIDI Mapper enables you to map the MIDI device to Windows.

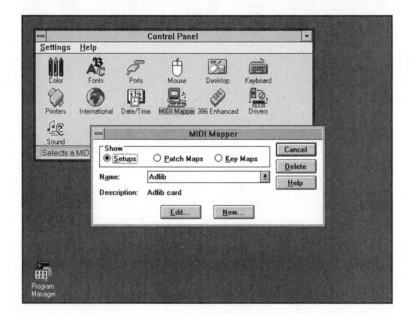

FIG. 17.21

Use the MIDI Mapper dialog box to choose a different MIDI setup.

Creating a Custom MIDI Setup

All MIDI devices conform to certain musical specifications. However, the output is not mapped in a standard way, which is why different MIDI setups are available for different pieces of equipment. Choosing the correct mapping is like using computer keyboards from different manufacturers, each of which uses a proprietary key layout—to get a K on-screen, you have to know where the K key is, and the PC also has to know.

Similarly, Windows must know which key and which channel the MIDI device uses for each sound. The process is known as *mapping*, which means that you map the PC keys and channels to the corresponding keys and channels in the device. This way, when you press a key that is supposed to play a middle-octave C from an acoustic grand piano, you get a middle-octave C that sounds like an acoustic grand piano, rather than a high D that sounds as though the note was played by an oboe.

This procedure is complex and requires that you know a great deal about the device. Check the documentation to see whether information is provided about key, patch, and channel mapping; if not, call the manufacturer to get the information (first read through this section so that you understand what information you need). Also be aware that the application you use to play the device must be Windows-compatible to take advantage of the settings you create in the MIDI Mapper.

To set up a MIDI device, you need to know whether the device is a base-level or an extended-level synthesizer. *Base-level* synthesizers meet the minimum MIDI requirements; *extended-level* synthesizers can play more notes simultaneously than base-level synthesizers, which produce richer sounds.

Four basic steps are involved in setting up a MIDI device:

1. You must set up the device to receive MIDI messages on multiple MIDI channels. Refer to the device's documentation to learn how to perform this procedure.

2. You must create a key map for both percussion instruments and melodic instruments that play in the wrong key.

3. You must create patch maps for both the percussion and melodic instruments. A patch defines a sound and all of the sound's voices.

4. You must create the channel map for the synthesizer.

Creating key, patch, and channel maps all are similar processes. First, you name the map (if you are creating a map). Then, a table-like chart appears, listing possible specifications. In the left columns, information describes the MIDI source; you cannot change this information. In the remaining columns, however, identified with an underlined letter in the column headings, the information pertains to the destination—the sound device. You can change the settings in these columns. To change the settings, select the box in the same row as the corresponding sound or channel at the left. When you change information in a destination column, you map the instructions going out from the computer to the appropriate sounds on the device.

Creating a Key Map

Create a key map for the synthesizer if the synthesizer doesn't conform to MIDI standards which specify that certain keys play certain sounds or a particular octave. MIDI Mapper provides up to 2,048 key maps for each of 128 patch entries for the 16 allowable patch maps.

If the synthesizer plays certain melodic sounds at registrations different from MIDI standards, you may need to create two types of key maps: a map for percussion sounds and a map for melodic sounds.

To create a key map, follow these steps:

1. Choose the MIDI Mapper application in the Control Panel. (Double-click on the MIDI Mapper icon or press the arrow keys to select the application and then press Enter.) The MIDI Mapper dialog box appears.

2. Select the **K**ey Maps option.

3. Choose the **N**ew button. The New MIDI Key Map dialog box appears, as shown in figure 17.22.

4. In the **N**ame text box, type a name (up to 15 characters) for the new MIDI key map. In the **D**escription text box, type a description (up to 28 characters).

5. Choose OK or press Enter. The MIDI Key Map dialog box appears, as shown in figure 17.23, with the following columns:

Src Key	*Source Key Number.* The MIDI-specified keys; you cannot change these keys.
Src Key Name	*Source Key Name.* The names of the instruments associated with the keys, as specified by MIDI standards; you cannot change these names.

Dest Key	*Destination Key Number.* The key on the synthesizer that plays when you press the source key; you can change this number to any number from 0 to 127.

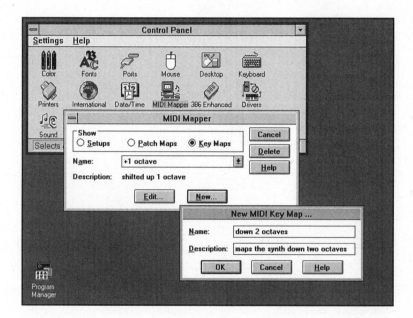

FIG. 17.22

To create a new MIDI map, you must supply a name and description.

6. Select the **D**est Key that you want to change, which causes up and down arrows to appear at the right side of the text box. Click the up arrow to raise the destination key number or click the down arrow to lower the number. You also can press the Tab key to select the existing destination key number and type a new number.

   To show the key you want to change, you may need to scroll the window. Click the up or down arrow in the scroll bar or press PgUp or PgDn.

7. Choose OK or press Enter. A dialog box appears, confirming the changes.

8. Choose **Yes** to confirm or **No** to discard the changes (or choose Cancel to return to the MIDI Key Map dialog box).

9. To close the MIDI Mapper dialog box, choose Close.

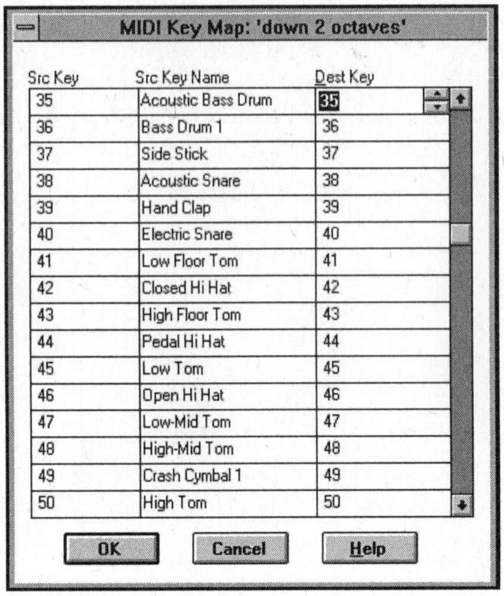

Src Key	Src Key Name	Dest Key
35	Acoustic Bass Drum	35
36	Bass Drum 1	36
37	Side Stick	37
38	Acoustic Snare	38
39	Hand Clap	39
40	Electric Snare	40
41	Low Floor Tom	41
42	Closed Hi Hat	42
43	High Floor Tom	43
44	Pedal Hi Hat	44
45	Low Tom	45
46	Open Hi Hat	46
47	Low-Mid Tom	47
48	High-Mid Tom	48
49	Crash Cymbal 1	49
50	High Tom	50

MIDI Key Map: 'down 2 octaves'

OK   Cancel   Help

FIG. 17.23

The MIDI Key Map dialog box lists the sounds for keys 35 through 81 (the MIDI-specified percussion keys).

Creating a Patch Map

A patch describes a sound, such as an acoustic grand piano or a dulcimer. If the synthesizer uses patches that differ from the MIDI specifications, you must create a set of patches for percussion instruments and for melodic instruments.

To create a patch, follow these steps:

1. Choose the MIDI Mapper in the Control Panel.

2. Select the **P**atch Maps option and choose the **N**ew button. The New MIDI Patch Map dialog box appears as shown in figure 17.24.

3. In the **N**ame text box, type a name (up to 15 characters) for the new MIDI key map. In the **D**escription text box, type a description (up to 28 characters).

4. Choose OK or press Enter. The MIDI Patch Map dialog box appears that contains the following columns:

Src Patch   *Source Patch Number.* MIDI-specified patch numbers; you cannot change these numbers. Some synthesizers number patches 0 through 127; others number from 1 through 128. Select the sequence the synthesizer uses by choosing a button at the top of the dialog box.

Src Patch Name	*Source Patch Name.* Names of sounds or instruments associated with the source patch numbers, specified by MIDI standards; you cannot change these names.
Dest Patch	*Destination Patch.* Patch numbers the synthesizer plays to create sounds described in the Source Patch Name column. If the synthesizer confirms to MIDI standards, these numbers are the same as Source Patch numbers. Otherwise, you must change these numbers.
Volume %	*Volume by percent.* Volume at which the destination plays the sound. The default, 1ØØ, means that the sound plays at 100 percent. To play louder, set a **V**olume % greater than 100; to play softer, set a number less than 100.
Key **M**ap Name	Links the patch to the correct key map—a custom or an existing key map. Selecting this option shows a list of all existing key map names. Several pre-existing key maps exist, such as *–1 Octave*, which you can use to map a melodic patch to an octave lower.

5. If the synthesizer's patch numbers start at 0 rather than 1, choose the **0** Based Patches button; if the numbers start at 1 rather than 0, choose the **1** Based Patches button.

6. To change the destination patch number (the patch number in the synthesizer that maps to the existing source patch number), select the appropriate box in the **D**est Patch column, which causes an up and down arrow to appear at the right side of the box. Click the up arrow to increase the number; click the down arrow to decrease the number; or press the Tab key enough times to select the patch number you want to change and type a new number. If the patch you want to change isn't visible, use the scroll bar to show more numbers or press Tab enough times to scroll to the number you want to change.

7. To change the destination patch volume, in the **V**olume % column, select the volume box in the same row as the patch you want to change. Click the up or down arrow to change the number or select the existing number and type a new number.

8. To map the patch to a different key map, in the Key **M**ap Name column, select the key map name box in the same row as the patch you want to map differently. A list of all existing key maps appears. Select the name of the key map that you want the patch to use.

9. Choose OK or press Enter. A dialog box appears that confirms the changes.

10. Choose **Yes** to confirm or **No** to discard the changes (or choose Cancel to return to the MIDI Patch Map dialog box).

11. Choose Close to close the MIDI Mapper dialog box.

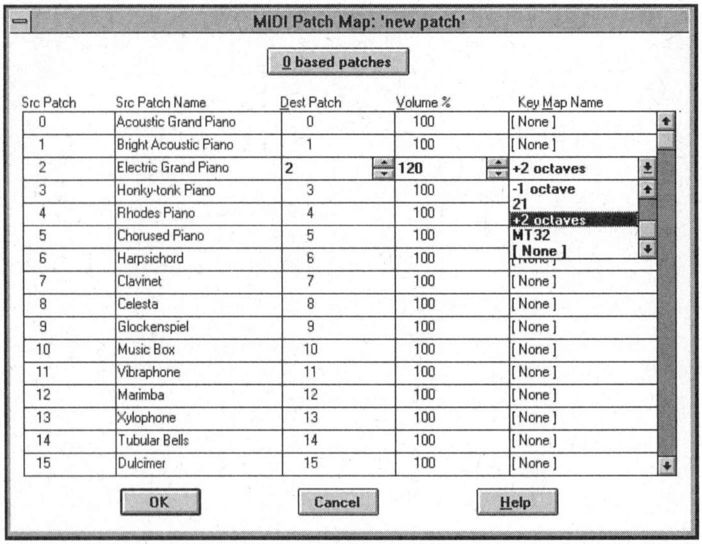

			MIDI Patch Map: 'new patch'		
			0 based patches		
Src Patch	Src Patch Name	Dest Patch	Volume %	Key Map Name	
0	Acoustic Grand Piano	0	100	[None]	
1	Bright Acoustic Piano	1	100	[None]	
2	Electric Grand Piano	2	120	+2 octaves	
3	Honky-tonk Piano	3	100	-1 octave	
				21	
4	Rhodes Piano	4	100	+2 octaves	
5	Chorused Piano	5	100	MT32	
6	Harpsichord	6	100	[None]	
7	Clavinet	7	100	[None]	
8	Celesta	8	100	[None]	
9	Glockenspiel	9	100	[None]	
10	Music Box	10	100	[None]	
11	Vibraphone	11	100	[None]	
12	Marimba	12	100	[None]	
13	Xylophone	13	100	[None]	
14	Tubular Bells	14	100	[None]	
15	Dulcimer	15	100	[None]	

OK   Cancel   Help

FIG. 17.24

The MIDI Patch Map dialog box enables you to create or edit a patch map.

Creating a Channel Map

If the channels on the synthesizer don't map to the standard MIDI channels, you need to create a channel map. Sixteen MIDI channels are available; a base-level synthesizer uses channels 13 through 15 for melodic sounds and 16 for percussion sounds; an extended-level synthesizer uses channels 1 through 9 for melodic sounds and 10 for percussion.

To create a channel map, follow these steps:

1. Choose the MIDI Mapper in the Control Panel.

2. Select the **S**etups option and choose the **N**ew button. The New MIDI Setup dialog box appears.

3. In the **N**ame text box, type a name (up to 15 characters) for the new MIDI key map. In the **D**escription text box, type a description (up to 28 characters).

4. Choose OK or press Enter. The MIDI Setup dialog box that appears contains the following columns (see fig. 17.25):

Src Chan	*Source Channel.* MIDI channels specified by the application; you cannot change these numbers.
Dest Chan	*Destination Channel.* Channel the synthesizer uses to play the sounds in the source channel. If the synthesizer supports the MIDI standard, this channel is the same as the source channel. If not, change the channel number.
Port Name	Port you want the channel to use. When you select a box in the **P**ort Name column, a drop-down list appears that shows all the MIDI device drivers connected to ports in the computer. Select the driver for the channel to use (not all channels must use the same port).
Patch **M**ap Name	Name of the patch map to use with the specified channel. When you select a Patch **M**ap Name box, a list of existing patch map names appears; select the patch you want to use. For melodic source channels, select a melodic patch map; for percussion source channels, select a percussion patch map.
Active	Activates or deactivates the selected port (available only if you selected a **P**ort Name). If you select the **A**ctive option (an X appears in the check box), sound from the channel *is* sent to the selected port; if deselected, sound *isn't* sent.

5. If necessary, change the destination channel by using the **D**est Chan option and selecting the appropriate box in the **D**est Channel column, which causes up and down arrows to appear at the right end of the box. Click the up or down arrow to change the number or select the existing channel number and type a new number. You can press the Tab key to move between the boxes in the **D**est Channel column.

6. If necessary, change the name of the port you want the selected channel to use by selecting from the list that appears when you select a box in the **P**ort Name column.

7. If necessary, select the patch map you want each channel to use. To perform this step, select the box in the Patch **M**ap Name column adjacent to the channel whose patch map you want to change.

8. If necessary, activate or deactivate the port by selecting or deselecting the **A**ctive option.

9. Choose OK or press Enter. A dialog box appears that confirms the changes.

10. Choose **Y**es to confirm or **N**o to discard the changes (or choose Cancel to return to the MIDI Setup dialog box).

11. Choose Close to close the MIDI Mapper dialog box.

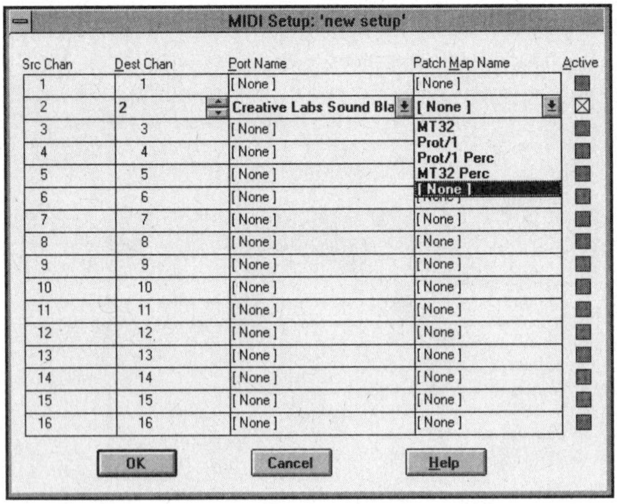

FIG. 17.25

Use the MIDI Setup dialog box to map MIDI channels to the correct channels on the synthesizer.

Editing and Deleting Maps

Besides creating maps, you also can edit existing maps. The process is the same as the methods you used to create a map (see the previous sections), but—rather than choosing the New button—you choose the **E**dit button in the MIDI Mapper dialog box, and you don't have to supply a name or description.

Similarly, you can delete an existing map by selecting the appropriate category from the Show group (**S**etups, **P**atch Maps, or **K**ey Maps), selecting the map name from the N**a**me list, and then choosing the **D**elete button.

For Related Information:

◀◀ To learn more about switching among applications, see "Switching between Applications," p. 58.

FROM HERE...

Chapter Summary

Multimedia is an exciting new technology that turns a PC into a sound-and-video-equipped teacher, research assistant, storyteller, or musician. Your computer can look up information, read you a story, play a tune, or any combination of these activities. Not only can you hear what the PC has to say, you also can see what it has to show. Windows supplies two multimedia applications, Sound Recorder and Media Player.

One way to create custom multimedia presentations is to embed a sound or video object in a document that was created by an application that supports *object linking and embedding*, or OLE. To learn more about object linking and embedding and about using the Object Packager, read Chapter 6.

Using Windows Applets

P A R T

IV

O U T L I N E

Using Microsoft Draw

T he company that manufactures Windows has a vision for the future. This vision, "Information at Your Fingertips," calls for quick and easy access to the information stored on your computer. With multitasking and a consistent graphical user interface shared by all Windows applications, Windows goes a long way toward actualizing "Information at Your Fingertips." Windows goes even further with a new concept—object *linking and embedding*, or *OLE*.

With object linking and embedding, you can use one application within another application, creating a compound document made up of files created by two or more applications. You use a *client* application like Word for Windows to create the initial document, then use a *server applet*, such as Microsoft Draw, to create and edit embedded objects within the compound document. You never have to leave your primary application.

Microsoft Draw is an applet that comes free with Microsoft Word for Windows, Microsoft Publisher, and other applications. As an applet, it is not a stand-alone application like Windows Paintbrush—you cannot start up Microsoft Draw on its own and create a picture. Instead, you must start Word for Windows, or any other Windows application that supports the OLE concept and start Microsoft Draw from within a document. Similarly, you cannot save a Microsoft Draw picture as a separate file—your masterpiece exists only as part of your client document.

The Microsoft Draw applet is a good complement to Windows Paint-brush, which comes free with Windows. Two general varieties of graphics applications are available: object-oriented drawing applications and bit-mapped painting applications. Each type of application has its benefits.

Microsoft Draw, an object-oriented drawing application, creates objects on the screen. Squares, circles, lines, and freeform shapes created with Microsoft Draw can be edited, moved around, and layered on the screen. (See fig. 18.1 for an example of an illustration created with Microsoft Draw.)

In contrast, a bit-mapped painting application, such as Microsoft Paint-brush, works in a single, flat layer on your screen. You can erase and redraw shapes created with Paintbrush, but you cannot edit them.

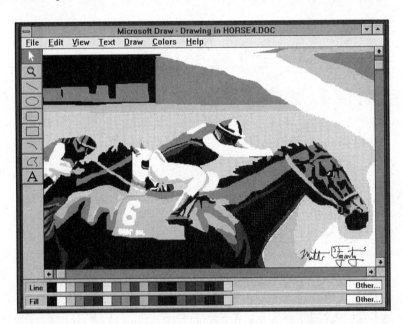

FIG. 18.1

An illustration created with Microsoft Draw.

Although Microsoft Draw is a simple applet that comes free with some Windows applications, it is nonetheless powerful enough that it may be the only drawing application you need. Draw is a valuable business tool that you can use to make letters, reports, and newsletters more interesting and informative. You can use Draw to create anything from a simple line drawing to a complex color composition—and have fun doing it, too.

Object linking and embedding, an important new concept in Windows, furthers the dream of making information easily, quickly, and intuitively

available at your fingertips. Many applications support OLE. You can
embed a Windows Paintbrush painting in a Windows Write letter—or
an Excel spreadsheet in a Word for Windows report. The subject of
object linking and embedding is explored fully in Chapter 6.

 The step-by-step instructions in this chapter are specific to
Word for Windows. Other applications use similar—but not
identical—commands. A chart follows each set of instructions, describing the commands you need to use Microsoft
Draw in other applications.

For Related Information:

◀◀ To learn more about object linking and embedding, see
"Transferring Data with Copy and Paste," p. 223; "Linking Data
between Applications," p. 223; and "Embedding Data into a
Document," p. 233.

FROM HERE...

Starting Microsoft Draw

As an OLE-based accessory application, Microsoft Draw works only
from within a document created in your client application—the application that receives the embedded object. Microsoft Draw is called the
server because it originates the object. Before starting Microsoft Draw,
you need to start Word for Windows or some other application that
supports object linking and embedding; then open a new or existing
document.

To start Microsoft Draw, follow these steps:

1. Open a Word for Windows document or create a new document.

2. Position the insertion point where you want to insert your drawing.

3. Choose the **Insert Object** command. The Object dialog box pops
   up (see fig. 18.2).

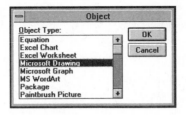

FIG. 18.2

The Object
dialog box.

4. Select Microsoft Drawing.

5. Choose OK or press Enter. Microsoft Draw pops up in a new window on your screen.

Starting Microsoft Draw from Other Applications

Powerpoint   Choose the **File Insert** command. Select Microsoft Drawing from the list of applications.

Publisher   Choose the **Edit Insert O**bject command.

Excel   Choose the **Edit Insert O**bject command.

Ami Pro   Choose the **Edit Insert** command and then select New **O**bject.

Windows Write   Choose the **Edit Insert O**bject command and then choose Microsoft Drawing from the **O**bject Type list.

Since Windows applets are not stand-alone applications, you cannot save the objects they create as stand-alone files. The way you save Draw objects is to update the client document and save that file. When Word for Windows is your client application, you add the Draw picture to your Word for Windows document and then save the Word for Windows file. The way you add a Draw object to a document is to *update* the client document.

FROM HERE...

For Related Information:

◄◄ See "Starting, Using, and Quitting Applications," p. 46.

◄◄ See "Starting an Application from the Program Manager," p. 75.

Updating the Client Document

You transfer your Draw object back into the client document in either of two ways. You can update the document without closing Microsoft Draw, or you can close Microsoft Draw when you update your client document. To save your drawing, you must save your client document after you update the drawing.

To update your Word for Windows document without closing Draw, choose the File Update command in Draw.

To update your Word for Windows document and also close Microsoft Draw, choose the File Exit and Return to document command. A dialog box pops up asking whether you want to update your client document. Choose **Yes**.

To exit Draw without updating the Word for Windows document, choose the File Exit and Return to document command. When a dialog box pops up asking whether you want to update your client document, choose **No**.

Updating the client document is the same no matter which client application you are using.

Remember: updating your client document does not save your drawing. Your drawing exists only as part of your client document. To save your drawing, you must save the client document that contains your drawing.

For Related Information:

◀◀ See "Embedding Data into a Document," p. 233.

▶▶ See "Understanding the Methods of Integration," p. 848.

▶▶ See "Integrating Windows Applications," p. 850.

FROM HERE...

Editing a Microsoft Draw Picture

You can change your Draw picture as easily as you created it. Since it is part of your client document, you must first open the client application and then open the client document containing your Draw picture. Instructions for using Draw's tools to edit your drawing appear throughout the remainder of this chapter. When you finish editing, update your client document as described in the previous section, "Updating the Client Document."

To edit a Draw picture in a Word for Windows document, follow these steps:

1. Locate the Draw picture in your document.

2. With a mouse, double-click on the picture to start Draw, with your picture in its drawing window.

   or

   Select the picture by positioning the insertion point next to it, holding down the Shift key, and pressing the appropriate arrow key to pass the insertion point over the drawing. Then choose the **E**dit Microsoft Drawing O**b**ject command. Draw starts with your picture in the drawing window.

3. Edit your drawing.

4. Update your Word for Windows document.

T   I   P   When you exit Draw and return to your Word for Windows document, you normally see your drawing. If, however, the **V**iew Field **C**odes command is selected, you see a field code in place of your drawing. Choose the **V**iew Field **C**odes command again to turn it off so you can see your drawing.

Editing a Draw Object in Other Applications

Powerpoint	Double-click the object or select the object and choose the **E**dit **E**dit Microsoft Drawing command.
Publisher	Double-click the object or select the object and choose the **E**dit Edit Object command.
Excel	Double-click the object or click the object with the right mouse button to display the Shortcuts menu and choose the Edit Object command.
Ami Pro	Double-click the object.
Windows Write	Double-click on the object or select the object and choose the **E**dit Edit Microsoft Drawing O**b**ject command.

In some applications, you can use Draw to edit pictures that were not created by Draw. Thus, you can do a quick edit on a picture created by an application that does not support object linking and embedding. (You also can use this technique when you don't want to take the time to start the original graphics application or when you don't have the original application.) If you want to try it, just follow the same steps as for editing a Draw object. Be careful, however: after you edit a picture in Draw, it becomes a Draw object.

Understanding the Microsoft Draw Screen

If you have ever used a graphics application before, the Microsoft Draw screen probably looks familiar (see fig. 18.3). Even if you haven't used a graphics application, the screen is intuitive.

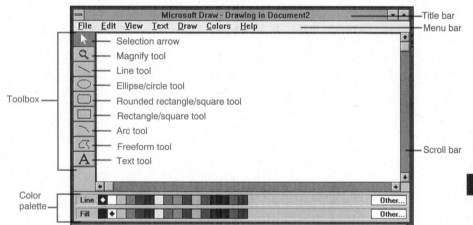

FIG. 18.3

The Microsoft Draw window.

As in every Windows application, the title and menu bars are along the top of the Microsoft Draw window. On the left side is the toolbox: this has the tools you use to create your drawing. On the bottom is a color palette: you use the top half to choose line color and the bottom half to choose fill color. On the right and bottom sides of the screen are the familiar scroll bars that enable you to move around on your drawing (which is a maximum of 22 by 22 inches wide).

The general process for creating a drawing is to select menu options to set frame and fill defaults, select the tool you want to use, select colors from the palette, and draw your picture in the drawing area. You can edit any object after you create it in Microsoft Draw. For details about using the tools, palette, and menu options, refer to the following sections in this chapter.

Although you can operate most Windows applications with either a mouse or the keyboard, you must use a mouse to use Microsoft Draw. Some keyboard techniques and shortcuts are available in the application, but most operations require a mouse.

If you want the Microsoft Draw window to appear full-size on your screen, click the Maximize button at the top right of the Microsoft Draw window. Use Windows techniques to move between the Draw window and the Word for Windows window. To learn more about basic Windows techniques, refer to Chapters 1 and 2.

Scrolling the Drawing Page

Although you can see only a portion of it, the full Microsoft Draw page measures 22 by 22 inches. Use the horizontal scroll bar at the bottom of the screen to scroll left and right and use the vertical scroll bar at the right to scroll up and down.

Although scrolling enables you to view a part of the page that currently is hidden, in the Full Size view (Draw's default), you cannot draw an object larger than the drawing area or select a group of objects that extends beyond the drawing area. To do either of those, you need to use the Magnify tool. (See the section "Zooming In and Out with the Magnify Tool" later in this chapter.)

Working with the Grid and Guides

Before you begin your drawing, you should know about two helpful drawing aids: the grid and the guides.

The *grid* is a magnetic measurement system underlying your drawing. It's like an invisible piece of graph paper with magnetic lines—12 lines per inch both vertical and horizontal. These lines snap your drawing tool to twelfth-inch increments, forcing your drawn objects to conform to the grid. Using the grid is important when you want to ensure accurate sizing and when you want to align objects accurately to one another.

Guides also are helpful for precise drawing. When you turn on this option, two guides appear as intersecting dotted lines in the middle of the drawing area. You can move each guide independently by dragging it with the Selection arrow. As you drag a guide, its distance from the top of the page (horizontal guide) or left of the page (vertical guide) appears at the arrow's location. When you hold down the Ctrl key, the measurement starts from zero at the guide's starting location, making it easy to measure the size of an object. If the grid is turned on, the guides move in the 1/12-inch increments.

Choose the **D**raw Snap to **G**rid command to turn on the grid. To turn on the guides, choose the **D**raw Sho**w** Guides command.

Both the grid and the guides are commands you toggle on and off, using the **D**raw menu. A check mark appears to the left of each command when it's turned on. To turn off the grid or guides, select the command a second time (the check mark disappears).

To move a guide, drag it with the Selection arrow. To measure an object using the guides, follow these steps:

1. Drag the guide to one end or side of the object you want to measure.

2. Hold down Ctrl while you drag the guide with the Selection arrow; watch the measurement that appears on your screen.

Choosing a Frame, Fill, Pattern, or Line Style

Each object you draw with Microsoft Draw is a line or a shape. Lines have only one component: line style. Shapes have two components: a frame (the line around the shape's edges) and a fill (the color inside the shape). You can draw a line in any of several line styles. You can draw a shape that is framed or unframed and filled or not filled. You can choose any line style for a framed shape, and you can choose from several patterns for a filled shape.

You can make these choices from a menu at one of two times. Choices made *before* you draw an object become defaults and apply to any subsequent shapes you draw. Choices made *after* you draw and select an object or objects apply only to the selection.

Remember this rule: if no object is selected, choices you make about frame, fill, pattern, and line style become defaults and apply to future objects you draw. If any object is selected, however, your frame, fill, pattern, and line style choices apply only to the selection. (Selected objects have small black handles at each end or corner.)

Frame, fill, pattern, and line style choices are made through the **D**raw menu. The Frame**d** and **F**illed commands toggle on and off. A black diamond or check mark appearing to the left indicates that the commands are on. A black diamond indicates that Framed or Filled is selected as a default; a check mark indicates that it is selected only for the currently selected object or objects. If two objects with conflicting frames or fills are selected, no mark appears to the left of the Framed or Filled command.

The Pattern and Line Style commands have submenus (see fig. 18.4) from which you can choose a pattern or line style. These commands also toggle on and off, with a black diamond indicating a default choice and a check mark indicating the currently selected object or objects.

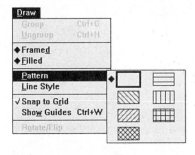

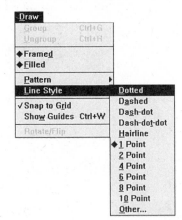

FIG. 18.4

The Pattern and Line Style commands have submenus.

To specify Framed, Filled, Pattern, or Line Style, follow these steps:

1. Make sure that no object is selected if you want all future objects to be framed or filled or if you want to include a pattern or line style in all future objects—in other words, if you want to set a default.

   or

   Select the object or objects for which you want a frame, fill, pattern, or line style.

2. Choose the **D**raw Frame**d** command to frame an object or objects.

or

Choose the **D**raw **F**illed command to fill an object or objects.

or

Choose the **D**raw **P**attern command and select a pattern from the Pattern submenu to fill an object or objects with the pattern.

or

Choose the **D**raw **L**ine Style command and select a line style from the Line Style submenu to frame an object or objects with the line style.

Color is another important component in the drawings you create with Microsoft Draw. Use the Line palette at the bottom of the screen (the palette on the top) to select colors for lines and borders around framed shapes. Fills and patterns appear in the color you select from the Fill palette at the bottom of the screen (the palette on the bottom). To select a Line or Fill color, just click the color you want.

Like other choices you make in Draw, you can choose colors *before* you begin your drawing or *after* you draw and select a line or shape. Colors selected before you begin your drawing become the defaults for any subsequent lines or shapes you draw. Colors selected after you draw and select a line or shape apply only to the selection.

In the color palette, default colors appear with a diamond; colors for the currently selected object appear with a check mark. To learn more about using colors, see "Working with Color" later in this chapter.

For Related Information:

◄◄ See "Getting To Know the Paintbrush Window and Tools," p. 539.

FROM HERE...

Using Microsoft Draw Drawing Tools

Each tool in the Microsoft Draw toolbox has a specific use. Some tools have more than one function. With the Ellipse tool, for example, you can draw an oval or a perfect circle. You can draw a rectangle or a perfect square with the Rectangle/Square tool. Use the Freeform tool to draw a line or a closed polygon.

You first must select a tool before you can use it. To select a tool from the toolbox, click the tool icon in the toolbox. After you select a tool, move the pointer into the drawing area. The pointer changes from an arrow into some other tool. For drawing most objects, the pointer turns into a crosshair.

The next several sections explain how you can use your drawing tool or text tool to create your drawing. Refer to figure 18.3, which shows the nine drawing tools.

Figure 18.5 shows examples of framed and filled shapes created by using a variety of tools, line styles, patterns, and colors.

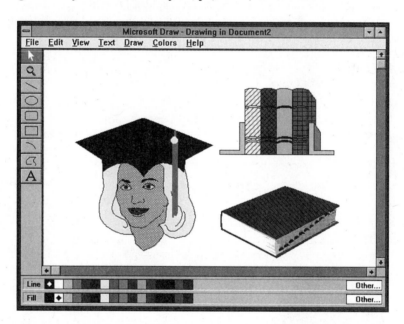

FIG. 18.5

A sampling of framed and filled shapes using a variety of line styles and patterns.

Selecting with the Selection Arrow

The Selection arrow selects text and objects in your drawing, usually so that you can edit them in some way. You can use the Selection arrow in one of two ways. You can point to the object you want to select and click the left mouse button—holding down Shift enables you to select several objects. To select multiple objects in a group, use the Selection arrow to draw a box, or *marquee*, around the group you want to select.

The Selection arrow is particularly important because of one guiding principle that applies in nearly every Windows application: *select and then do.* You first must *select* an object before you can *do* something to it.

To select an object or objects, follow these steps:

1. Click the Selection arrow in the toolbox.

2. Point to the object to select and click the mouse button (hold down Shift to select several objects).

   or

   Drag the Selection arrow in a box around a group of objects you want to select. The box appears as a dotted line while you hold down the mouse button and disappears when you release the mouse button. Be sure to enclose completely each object you want to select.

Many tools in the toolbox revert to the Selection arrow after you use them. After you draw a box and then click elsewhere in the drawing area, for example, the box crosshair turns into the Selection arrow.

Zooming In and Out with the Magnify Tool or View Command

When you first start Microsoft Draw, you see your page in full size—and your drawing is in the actual size it will be when printed. If your drawing is larger than the drawing area, however, you may want to zoom out and see more of the page. You also may want to zoom in and get a close-up look at part of your drawing, particularly if you need to do some detailed editing.

Microsoft Draw offers seven different magnification levels for your picture: 25%, 50%, 75%, Full Size, 200%, 400%, and 800%. You can draw and edit at any magnification. The available magnifications are listed in the View menu. The same choices also are available through the Magnify tool, which offers two advantages. First, the Magnify tool is easy to use—you just point and click. Second, it offers more control—when you point at an object and click the Magnify tool, you zoom in to that specific location on your screen. When you use the View menu, you zoom in to the object you most recently created or edited, regardless of where you want to be.

To magnify your drawing using the Magnify tool, follow these steps:

1. Select the Magnify tool from the toolbox.

2. Position the Magnify tool over the place in your drawing where you want to zoom in or zoom out.

3. Click the left mouse button to zoom in to the next higher magnification.

   or

   Hold down Shift and click the left mouse button to zoom out to the next lower magnification.

4. Click repeatedly to continue zooming in or out.

To magnify or reduce your drawing through a menu, choose the View menu and select 25% **S**ize, **5**0%, 75%, **F**ull Size, 200%, 400%, or **8**00%.

Drawing Lines

The Line tool enables you to draw straight lines. Your line appears in the default Line palette color and in the selected Line Style. Remember that black diamonds are used to indicate the default color and Line Style.

To draw a line, follow these steps:

1. From the **D**raw menu, select the **L**ine Style you want. Select the Line color from the color palette.

2. Select the Line tool from the toolbox.

3. Move the pointer into the drawing area.

4. Position the crosshair where you want to start your line.

5. Click and hold down the mouse button.

6. Drag the crosshair to where you want to end your line.

7. Release the mouse button.

A newly drawn line has selection handles at each end, which you can use to edit the line (see "Manipulating Text and Objects" later in this chapter). When you finish drawing a line, you can click the mouse button anywhere in the drawing area to deselect the line you just drew. Then choose the Selection arrow from the toolbox. Figure 18.6 shows the process of drawing a line.

Two constraint keys, Shift and Ctrl, can help you keep a line straight or enable you to draw a line from the center outwards. To constrain your line to a 45- or 90-degree angle (especially when you want a perfectly horizontal or vertical line), hold down the Shift key as you draw the line. To draw your line from the crosshair outward in both directions, hold down the Ctrl key as you draw.

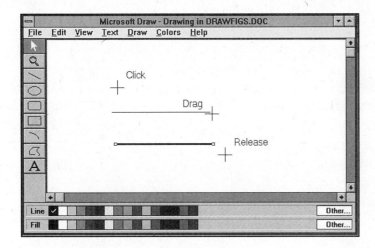

FIG. 18.6

Drawing a line.

Drawing Ellipses, Circles, Rectangles, and Squares

Three tools enable you to draw round and square shapes. The Ellipse/circle tool draws ellipses (ovals) or, when you hold down the Shift key, circles. The Rounded rectangle/square tool draws rectangles with rounded corners or, if you hold down the Shift key, rounded-corner squares. The Rectangle/square tool draws rectangles, or, when you hold down the Shift key, squares. For each tool, holding down the Ctrl key as you draw enables you to draw from the center outward rather than from one corner to another.

You use the same process for drawing ellipses, circles, rectangles, and squares. To draw an ellipse, circle, rounded-rectangle, rounded square, rectangle, or square, follow these steps:

1. From the **Draw** menu, choose the Frame**d** command if you want your shape to have a border; choose the **F**illed command if you want your shape to be filled. Select the **P**attern or **L**ine Style you want. Select the Line color and Fill color you want from the color palette.

2. Select the Ellipse/circle tool to draw an ellipse or circle.

   or

   Select the Rounded rectangle/square tool to draw a rounded rectangle or square.

   or

   Select the Rectangle/square tool to draw a rectangle or square.

3. Move the tool into the drawing area, where it becomes a crosshair.

4. Position the crosshair where you want your shape to start.

   Hold down Shift if you want to draw a perfect circle or a perfect square shape. Hold down Ctrl to draw from the center outwards.

5. Click and hold down the mouse button and drag to draw your shape.

6. Release the mouse button when your shape is correct.

As you can see in figure 18.7, a shape you have just drawn has selection handles at each corner, which you can use to edit the shape. (See "Manipulating Text and Objects" later in this chapter.)

When you finish drawing an ellipse or rectangle, click the crosshair anywhere off the object to deselect the shape tool and select the Selection arrow.

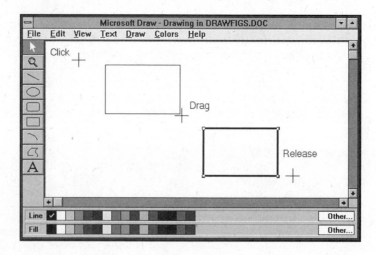

FIG. 18.7

Drawing circles and squares is a similar process.

Drawing Arcs and Wedges

An arc, as drawn in Microsoft Draw, is one quarter of an ellipse or circle. As with all the tools, two constraint keys can help you draw. Hold down the Shift key to make your arc or wedge a quarter of a perfect circle instead of an ellipse. Hold down the Ctrl key to draw your arc from the center rather than from one corner to another.

The process of drawing an arc is similar to that of drawing any shape in Microsoft Draw. To draw an arc, follow these steps:

1. From the **D**raw menu, choose the Frame**d** command if you want your arc to have a border and the **F**illed command if you want to fill your arc. Select the **P**attern or **L**ine Style you want. Select the Line color and Fill color you want from the color palette.

2. Select the Arc tool from the toolbox.

3. Move the tool into the drawing area, where it becomes a crosshair.

4. Position the crosshair where you want to start your arc.

   Hold down the Shift key if you want to draw a perfect quarter-circle arc. Hold down the Ctrl key to draw from the center outwards.

5. Click where you want to start the arc, hold down the mouse button, and drag to where you want to end the arc.

6. Release the mouse button.

As with all tools, you can drag the crosshair in any direction as you draw. To draw an arc that shows the bottom half of a circle or ellipse, drag the crosshair upward.

Drawing Freeform Lines and Polygons

The Freeform tool is one of the most versatile tools in the toolbox. With the Freeform tool, you can draw a curving line, a jagged line, or a closed polygon (see fig. 18.8).

Only one constraint key—Shift—works with the Freeform tool. Holding down Shift while you draw forces line segments to be on the horizontal, vertical, or 45-degree axis. When you're drawing a curved line, holding down Shift still forces each tiny segment of the line to be on one of these axes.

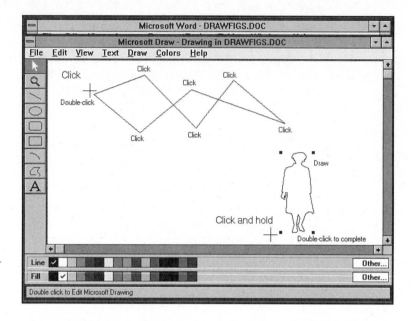

FIG. 18.8

Drawing a polygon is a series of clicks; hold down the mouse button to change the polygon's crosshair to a pencil for drawing freeform lines.

You later can change the frame, fill, pattern, and line style for any freeform object (see the section on "Manipulating Text and Objects"). You can change each segment of a polygon, using the special technique described in "Editing a Freeform Shape" later in this chapter.

To draw a jagged line or closed polygon with the Freeform tool, follow these steps:

1. Select **D**raw Frame**d** for a framed polygon or **D**raw **F**illed for a filled polygon. Select your **P**attern, **L**ine Style, and color defaults.

2. Select the Freeform tool from the toolbox.

3. Move the tool into the drawing area and position the crosshair where you want your jagged line or polygon to begin.

4. Click the mouse button to anchor the first end of the line or polygon.

5. Move the crosshair to the second point on your line or polygon and click again.

6. Continue moving the crosshair and clicking the mouse button to define each point on your line or polygon.

7. Double-click the last point of your line to complete the line.

   or

   Double-click the first point of your polygon to join the last point with the first and create a closed polygon.

To draw a curving line or closed curving freeform shape, follow these steps:

1. Select **Draw Framed** for a framed freeform shape or **Draw Filled** for a filled freeform shape. Select your pattern, line style, and color defaults.

2. Select the Freeform tool from the toolbox.

3. Move the tool into the drawing area and position the crosshair where you want to begin your curving line or freeform shape.

4. Click and hold down the mouse button where you want to start your line or shape. Wait until the crosshair turns into a pencil.

5. Still holding down the mouse button, drag the pencil around in the drawing area to draw your line or shape.

6. When you reach the end of your line, double-click the mouse button.

   or

   To close the shape, double-click the line's beginning point.

Adding and Editing Text

A picture may be worth a thousand words, but sometimes words can help clarify your point. You easily can add text to your Microsoft Draw drawing, selecting its font, style, and size. Later, you can select and edit your text as needed.

You can type just one line of text in Microsoft Draw. If you reach the end of the screen, text does not wrap, and you cannot press Enter to start a new line. To stack lines of text, you must type each line separately and drag each line into place using the Selection arrow. Using Microsoft Draw's Snap to Grid feature (in the **Draw** menu), however, enables you to stack lines of text evenly and easily.

As for any object, Windows' *select and then do* principle applies to text: to change the appearance of your text, first select it. If you don't select the text first, choices you make in the Text menu and the palette become the new defaults and apply to anything you do subsequently.

Moving text is no different from moving other objects. Techniques for moving text are discussed later in this chapter in the section "Copying, Moving, and Deleting Text and Objects."

Typing Text

To enter text in your drawing, follow these steps:

1. Choose your text defaults. If a shape is selected in your drawing, you cannot choose text defaults—unselect the shape. From the Text menu, select any of these commands:

Command	Result
Plain (Ctrl+T)	Plain, with no formatting
Bold (Ctrl+B)	Boldface
Italic (Ctrl+I)	Italicized
Underline (Ctrl+U)	Underlined
Left	Left aligned
Center	Centered
Right	Right Aligned
Font	A different font
Size	A different size

When you choose the **Font** or **Size** command, a list of fonts or sizes pops out to the right of the menu. Select the font or size you want from that list.

Three of the choices in the Text menu—**Bold**, **Italic**, and **Underline**—are style choices, which can be combined. You can type text that is both bold and italic, underlined and bold, or even bold, italic, and underlined. Each style choice selected for the current text has a check mark to its left. To remove all style choices at once, select the **Plain** style.

2. From the Line color palette at the bottom of the screen, select a color for your text.

If the color palette is not visible, choose the **Colors Show Palette** command to display it.

3. Select the Text tool from the toolbox.

4. Move the tool into the drawing area, where it turns into an I-beam. Position the I-beam where you want the left margin of your block of text.

5. Click the mouse button to insert the cursor where you want your text to start.

6. Type the text.

   You can press Shift+Ins to insert text from the Clipboard (even if the text was typed in a different application). Just remember that in Microsoft Draw you can have only one line of text at a time.

7. Press Enter or click the mouse button somewhere off the text to end the text block. The text block and the Selection arrow are selected.

> Colored text sometimes looks best superimposed over a background. To superimpose text, choose one color for your text, draw around the text a shape that is filled with a different color, and then use the Edit menu to send the shape to the back of the text. For best readability, be sure that you have plenty of contrast between the two colors.

T I P

Editing Text

Text must be selected before you can edit it. Text is selected automatically after you type it and press Enter or click outside the text. If the text you want to edit is not currently selected, point to it with the Selection arrow and click the mouse button.

Like any selected object, selected text has selection handles at each of its four corners. The selection handles indicate that you can move or edit the text.

Once text is selected, you can change its style, alignment, font, or size by choosing commands from the Text menu. To change the color of the text, select a different color from the Line palette at the bottom of your screen.

To select text so that you can change its style, alignment, font, or size, follow these steps:

1. Select the selection arrow from the toolbox.

2. Point at the text you want to change and click the mouse button.

Alternatively, you can change the words by deleting, inserting, or retyping characters. To change the words in a text block, you first must move the insertion point inside the selected text. You cannot just click the text to move the insertion point inside it. To move the insertion point inside the text, follow these steps:

1. Select the text block by clicking it with the Selection arrow.

2. Choose the **Edit Edit** Text command.

   or

   Double-click the text block.

   An insertion point appears inside the text block. The insertion point appears exactly where you double-click.

3. Edit the text using standard editing techniques.

   Press the Backspace key to erase characters to the left, or press Del to erase characters to the right. You can select text and retype it, or you can cut, copy, and paste text using commands from the **Edit** menu.

4. Press Enter or click outside the text block to complete the editing process.

FROM HERE...

For Related Information:

◄◄ See "Using the Paintbrush Tools," p. 543.

Working with Colors

If you have a color monitor, you can really enjoy Microsoft Draw's colors. The Line and Fill palettes contain up to 16 solid colors (Windows' limit) and almost limitless *dithered* colors, blended from the available solid colors. You can apply these colors to any object you create—text or shapes. (If you see less than 16 colors, it's because your PC supports fewer colors.)

The color palette at the bottom of the Microsoft Draw window contains colors for Line (top of the palette) and Fill (bottom of the palette). The colors with a black diamond inside them are the defaults. When you select objects created earlier, you may see a check mark inside a color—this means that color is applied to the currently selected object.

You can change your color palette in two ways: by clicking the Other button at the right end of the Line or Fill palette or by using the **Colors** menu. Use either method to add new colors to your palette or to change existing colors. You also can save palettes for use in future drawings, following the techniques described in the next few sections.

To enlarge your screen space, you can hide the color palette. If the palette is displayed and you want to hide it, choose the **C**olors Show **P**alette command. To display the palette, choose the command a second time. The Show **P**alette command toggles on and off; you see a check mark to its left when it's on.

Coloring Text and Objects

The default color in the Line palette is applied automatically to text, lines, the frame around framed objects, and the foreground in any patterned fill. The default color in the Fill palette is applied automatically to the fill in any filled shape and to the background in any pattern fill.

Default color choices apply to any object you create, but you easily can change the Line or Fill color of an object or text created earlier. Simply select the object (or objects) and choose the Line or Fill color you want. Colors change only for the selected object or objects.

To select a Line or Fill color as a default or to change the Line or Fill color for a selected object, follow these steps:

1. If you want to change the default Line or Fill color, make sure that no object is selected. An easy way to do that is to select the Selection arrow; this cancels all previous selections.

   If you want to change the Line or Fill color for one or more specific objects, select the objects.

2. In the top half of the color palette, click the Line color you want.

   In the bottom half of the color palette, click the Fill color you want.

Using Blended Colors

Although your initial color palette contains only up to 16 solid colors, you can add a rainbow of blended colors to your palette. Working with blended colors requires that you use the most colorful dialog box in Microsoft Draw—the Other Color dialog box (see fig. 18.9). The Other Color dialog box offers a rainbow of colors you can add to your palette or apply to the selected objects. (If you access this dialog box through the Colors menu, its title is Add Color.)

When you are blending colors, remember that computers understand color in terms of light—not pigment. Computers use an additive system for blending colors; whereas pigments use a subtractive system. So forget what you have learned about color wheels. In a computer's mind, pure red and pure green combine to make yellow; pure red, pure green, and pure blue combine to make white.

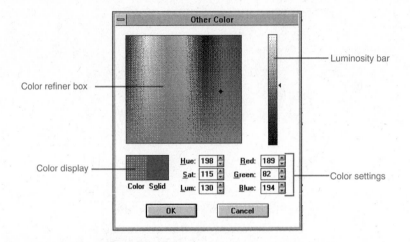

FIG. 18.9

The Other Color dialog box.

You can blend a color using the Other Color dialog box in three ways:

- You can select a color from the Color refiner box (the rainbow-colored box) and a luminosity from the Luminosity bar.

- You can blend your own color by setting its hue, saturation, and luminosity.

- You can blend your own color by setting its levels of red, green, and blue.

In the next section, you learn how you can add blended colors to your palette.

Follow these steps to use the Other Color dialog box to add a color to your objects:

1. Select the objects whose line or fill colors you want to change. Choose Other from the Line or the Fill palette. The Other Color dialog box appears.

2. Use the Color refiner box (the large, rainbow-colored box) to select the color.

   Click the color you like, or, holding down the mouse button, drag the black diamond selection icon onto the color you like. (The color display shows the selected color.)

3. To set your selected color's *luminosity*, or value (lightness or dark-
   ness), use the Luminosity bar (vertical bar to the right of the
   rainbow-colored refiner box).

   Drag the black triangle icon up to select a lighter color, drag down
   to select a darker color, or click the area of the bar you want to
   select. Click the **S**olid box (right side) to select the solid color
   rather than the dithered color.

4. To select a color by *hue* (color), *saturation* (amount of color), and
   luminosity (brightness), select values from 0 to 239 in the **H**ue, **S**at,
   and **L**um boxes. Type the value or select the up and down arrows
   to increase or decrease the value. Values range from 0 (red hue,
   no saturation [black], and no luminosity [black]) to 239 (red hue,
   full saturation [pure color], and full luminosity [pure white]).

5. To select a color by blending hues, select values from 0 to 255 in
   the **R**ed, **G**reen, and **B**lue boxes. Type the value or select the up
   and down arrows to increase or decrease the value. Values range
   from 0 (no hues, or black) to 255 (pure hue, or white).

6. To see the color you have selected, look at the Color/Solid box
   (below the Color refiner box). If it's not one of Windows' 16 solid
   colors, you see a dithered color blended of Windows' 16 colors.

Editing the Palette

You can add blended colors to your initial palette, and you can change
the existing colors and delete colors in your palette. To edit the palette,
use the Colors menu, which accesses the Other Color dialog box
described in the previous section. When you're editing the palette,
however, the dialog box is named Change Color or Add Color. See the
previous section for a description of the Add Color dialog box.

When you edit your palette using the **C**olors menu, you change the Line
and Fill palettes simultaneously.

To change, add to, or delete colors from the palette, follow these steps:

1. Choose the **C**olors **E**dit Palette command.

   The Edit Palette dialog box appears (see fig. 18.10), displaying the
   colors in the current palette as well as many blank spaces where
   you can add new colors. Notice that 100 spots are available for
   colors.

2. Select the existing color you want to change or delete or select
   the existing color you want to use as the basis for a new color.

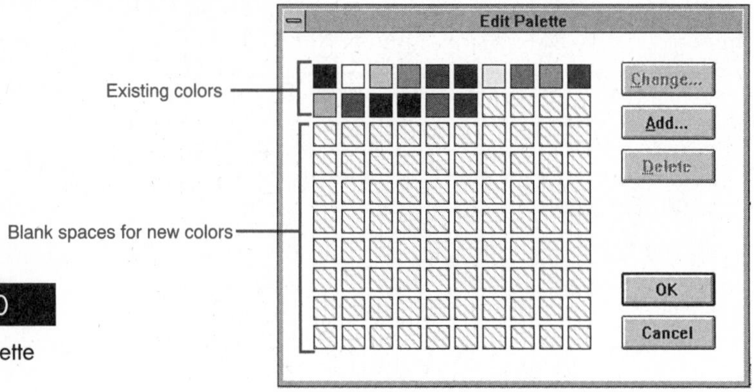

Existing colors ——

Blank spaces for new colors ——

FIG. 18.10

The Edit Palette
dialog box.

3. Choose **C**hange to change the color you have selected, choose **A**dd to add a color to the next available blank space, or choose **D**elete to delete the selected color.

   If you add or change a color, you advance to the Change Color or Add Color dialog box, described in the previous section as the Other Color dialog box.

4. Make your choices in the Add Color or Change Color dialog box and choose OK or press Enter. You return to the Edit Palette dialog box.

5. Choose OK or press Enter.

The Edit Palette dialog box offers a couple of shortcuts. You can double-click the color you want to edit. You also can drag an existing color to a new square in the color grid to rearrange your palette.

As you have seen in the Edit Palette dialog box, you can have up to 100 colors on your palette. If you have more colors than can fit on your screen, scrolling arrows appear at the left and right ends of your on-screen palette. Click those arrows to see more of your palette.

If you have used the on-screen palette to change the color of an object in your drawing, you later can add that color to your palette.

To add an existing object's color to your palette, select the object whose color you want to add to the palette. Choose the **C**olors **A**dd Colors From Selection command.

If your object contains both a new Line and a new Fill color, both are added to your palette. (If your object contains only one new color, it is added to both palettes.)

Saving and Opening Palettes

When you first start Microsoft Draw, the Line and Fill color palette
is displayed at the bottom of the drawing area. It contains 16 solid
colors—fewer, if your PC supports fewer. You also can get a different
palette—Microsoft Draw includes several—or save a palette you have
created yourself, making it available the next time you use Microsoft
Draw. This is the way you can share colors among drawings.

To save your custom palette, follow these steps:

1. Choose the **Co**lors **S**ave Palette command.

2. Enter an eight-character file name. Microsoft Draw supplies the
   extension PAL.

   Microsoft Draw saves the currently displayed color palette in the
   MSDRAW directory by default. You can save it in a different directory if you want, but if you do, your palette will not show up automatically when you choose the **G**et Palette command later.

3. Choose OK or press Enter.

> You can create a palette in Microsoft Draw to use in Windows
> Paintbrush if the palette contains no more than 28 colors. Paint-
> brush uses palettes in the same file format as Microsoft Draw
> (with the same extension), but Paintbrush looks for palette files in
> the Windows directory. If you are creating a palette for Paint-
> brush, save it in the Windows directory.

T I P

To get an existing palette, do the following:

1. Choose the **Co**lors **G**et Palette command. The Get Palette dialog
   box appears.

2. In the **F**iles list box, select the palette you want to open.

   Change the directory if your PAL file is stored somewhere besides
   the MSDRAW directory (a subdirectory under MSAPP).

3. Choose OK or press Enter. The new palette is displayed on your
   screen.

For Related Information:

◀◀ See "Working with Color," p. 575.

FROM HERE...

Manipulating Text and Objects

After you draw objects and type text in Microsoft Draw, you can manipulate your drawing in many ways. Everything you create—even text—is an object you can move, layer, or group with other objects. You can resize, reshape, rotate, and flip shapes or grouped shapes (but not text). With Microsoft Draw's object-editing capabilities, you can produce complex and interesting works of art, like the one shown in fig. 18.11.

By creating and editing objects, you can create complex and interesting works of art.

If you don't like the new look, you can choose the **E**dit **U**ndo command to undo your most recent screen action.

Selecting Text and Objects

Remember: before you can edit any object, you first must select it. When selected, an object has selection handles on its four corners. (Even non-rectangular shapes have four selection handles arranged in a rectangle around the object.) Drag these handles to resize or reshape a selected object.

To review briefly, you can select objects by selecting the Selection arrow and clicking on the object or by drawing a selection marquee around a group of objects you want to select. (For more details, refer to the earlier section "Selecting with the Selection Arrow.") You can select all the objects in your drawing by choosing the Edit Select All command.

Resizing and Reshaping Objects

You can change the shape and size of any selected object, except text, by dragging the selection handles. Two constraint keys apply: Shift to retain proportions and Ctrl to resize and reshape from the center outwards. As you're resizing or reshaping the object, a dotted-line bounding box shows you the object's new size or shape.

To change an object's size or shape, do the following:

1. Select the object.

2. To reshape an object, drag any corner handle to a new shape; release the mouse button when the bounding box shows the shape you want.

   or

   To resize the object and keep it proportional, hold down the Shift key while you drag a corner handle.

> You cannot resize or reshape multiple objects simultaneously unless you first group them (see the upcoming section on "Grouping and Ungrouping Text and Objects").
>
> **T I P**

Copying, Moving, and Deleting Text and Objects

You can easily move an object or a text block—just drag it to its new location. Because you can drag only as far as the edge of the drawing area, you may need to zoom out so that you can move on a larger area of the page. You can move a selected group of objects together by dragging one of the objects.

As you're dragging an object to move it, you see a dotted-line bounding box that represents the position of your speeding object. (The object reappears when you release the mouse button.)

If you prefer, you can use the standard Windows **E**dit **C**ut, **E**dit **C**opy, and **E**dit **P**aste commands to use the Clipboard to copy and move selected objects. This technique is useful when you want to copy or move objects between drawings or between distant spots on the same large drawing. Because you can switch between applications in Windows by sharing the Clipboard, you also can use this technique to copy or move a drawing from Microsoft Draw into another application besides Word for Windows.

To copy or move objects, follow these steps:

1. Select the object or objects you want to copy, move, or delete.

2. To move an object, choose the **E**dit **C**ut command.

   To copy an object, choose the **E**dit **C**opy command.

3. Move to where you want the object moved or copied.

4. Choose the **E**dit **P**aste command.

To remove an object, select it and choose the **E**dit **C**lear command or just press the Del or Backspace key.

Working with Layers

Like most drawing applications, Microsoft Draw enables you to work in layers. That is, you can create two or more objects and stack them on top of one another. Menu commands—and keyboard shortcuts—enable you to bring a selected object to the front or send it to the back of other objects.

Classic examples of layering are a shadow box—usually a white box overlapping a darker box of the same size—and text on a different color background.

To move an object to a different layer in your drawing, do the following:

1. Select the object or objects you want to send to the back or bring to the front of another object.

2. To bring the object to the top layer, choose the Edit Bring to **F**ront command (or press Ctrl+=).

   To send the object to the bottom layer, choose the Edit Send to **B**ack command (or press Ctrl+-).

If you know an object is hidden somewhere behind some other object and you want to find it, choose the **Edit** Select **All** command to select all objects. Then look for the hidden object's selection handles. To reveal the hidden object, you must either move the top object (or objects) to the back of the stack or drag the top object off the object you're trying to find.

Editing a Freeform Shape

You can edit a freeform shape in one of two ways. You can resize or reshape it as described in the earlier section on "Resizing and Reshaping Objects." This technique leaves the freeform object in the same general shape. (When dragging its corner handles, however, you may condense or expand the shape if you don't hold down the Shift key to keep it proportional.)

You also can edit the segments that make up the freeform shape. Use the Selection arrow and then a menu command to display control handles you can use to reshape the freeform shape. While you're editing a freeform object, it appears on-screen as an empty shape with a thin black frame.

To edit a freeform shape, follow these steps:

1. Select the shape by clicking it with the Selection arrow. Four selection handles appear on each corner.

2. Choose the **Edit Edit** Freeform command. Control handles appear at the end of each segment of the freeform shape.

3. Drag any control handle to change the shape of the freeform drawing.

    To add a control handle, hold down Ctrl (the arrow turns into a plus sign inside a circle) and click anywhere on the edge of the freeform shape.

    To remove a control handle, hold down Ctrl and Shift (the arrow turns into a minus sign inside a square) and click any existing control handle.

4. Press Enter or click anywhere outside the freeform shape to hide the control handles.

As an alternative to selecting the freeform shape and then choosing the **Edit** Freeform command, you can double-click the freeform shape to display the control handles.

Editing an Arc or Wedge

You can edit an arc or wedge in two ways. Select the arc or wedge with the Selection arrow and resize or reshape it by dragging the corner handles. Hold down the Shift key as you drag to keep the arc proportional. You also can change the arc's degree by first selecting it with the Selection arrow and then choosing a menu command to display special control handles.

To change a wedge's or arc's degree, follow these steps:

1. Select the arc or wedge by clicking it with the Selection arrow. Four corner handles appear.

2. Choose the **E**dit Edit Arc command. Two control handles appear—one at each end of the arc or wedge.

3. Drag either control handle in a clockwise or counterclockwise manner to change the degree.

4. Click outside the arc to deselect it.

As an alternative to selecting the arc and then choosing the **E**dit Arc command, you can double-click the arc to display the control handles.

Grouping and Ungrouping Text and Objects

If you want to turn several objects into one (to copy, reshape, or move them together easily, for example), you can select and group them. You then can edit the objects as a single object. However, you cannot resize, reshape, rotate, or flip text included in the group. Later, you can ungroup grouped objects. If you have resized a group, the ungrouped objects will be the new size.

To group objects, follow these steps:

1. Select all the objects you want to group. (Either hold down Shift while you click each object you want to select or draw a selection marquee around a group of objects.)

2. Choose the **Draw G**roup command.

To ungroup a grouped object, do the following:

1. Select the grouped object.

2. Choose the **Draw U**ngroup command.

To select a grouped object, you must click on one of the grouped objects using the Selection arrow. You cannot select a group by clicking between the objects.

Rotating and Flipping Objects

You can rotate a selected object (or selected group) in 90-degree increments to the left (counterclockwise) or right (clockwise). You can flip an object vertically or horizontally. You cannot rotate or flip text.

To rotate or flip an object, follow these steps:

1. Select the object.

2. Choose the **D**raw R**o**tate/Flip command and select Rotate **L**eft, Rotate **R**ight, Flip **H**orizontal, or Flip **V**ertical.

For Related Information:

◄◄ See "Editing the Painting," p. 564.

FROM HERE...

Importing and Editing Clip Art and Other Pictures

You can import many types of graphics into Microsoft Draw. Among the most interesting are a series of clip-art images that come with Microsoft Draw, which you can import and disassemble to use in whole or in part. Browse through the various clip-art files to see what's available.

To import a picture, follow these steps:

1. Choose the **F**ile **I**mport Picture command. The Import Picture dialog box appears.

2. Select the file you want to import from the **F**iles box (change the directory if necessary).

Clip-art files are stored in the subdirectory CLIPART, located inside your Word for Windows directory. These files have the extension WMF, indicating that their format is Windows metafile.

You also can import BMP, PCX, and TIF files. If you import object-oriented images, edit them the same way you edit any Microsoft Draw object. When you import bit-map files (such as those created in Microsoft Paintbrush), Microsoft Draw converts the bit maps into objects, which you can resize, reshape, or recolor. To restore a bit-map image to its original size or shape, select it and double-click any corner handle.

Saving Your Drawing

You can copy your drawing into the client document in either of two ways. You can update the client document without closing Microsoft Draw, enabling you to continue working on your drawing. Or, you can close Microsoft Draw when you update your client document.

When updating your client document, choose the **F**ile **U**pdate command to update without closing Microsoft Draw. To update the client file and exit Microsoft Draw, choose the **F**ile E**x**it and Return to Document command. For more details, see "Updating the Client Document" earlier in this chapter.

Remember, however: updating your client document *does not* save your drawing—it merely copies it. To save your drawing, you must be sure to save your client document after you update the drawing.

FROM HERE...

For Related Information:

◄◄ To learn more about object linking and embedding and how it works, see Chapter 6, "Embedding and Linking," p. 207.

Chapter Summary

Microsoft Draw is a simple but very powerful application. You can use Microsoft Draw to create original works of art to illustrate your Windows application document or to edit existing art. You even can use the clip art that comes with Microsoft Draw as the basis for your own drawings.

To learn more about how to use Microsoft Draw with your application, refer to a Que book specifically describing that application. In *Using Word for Windows 2,* Special Edition, you learn how you can move, frame, size, and border pictures in Word for Windows, the Windows word processor. *Using Excel 4 for Windows,* Special Edition, explains how to use Draw with the spreadsheet application Excel.

Using Microsoft Graph

With Microsoft Graph, you can create informative and impressive charts that you can incorporate into all Windows applications that have Object Linking and Embedding (OLE) capability. (For a discussion of OLE, see Chapter 6.) Microsoft Graph is an *applet*, or a small application designed to work with Windows applications that have OLE capability. Applets add features to OLE-capable applications. Microsoft Graph is a separate application that embeds charts in Windows applications, such as Microsoft Word for Windows, Ami Pro, or Microsoft Excel. Microsoft Graph comes free with some Windows applications, such as Word for Windows. After you install Word for Windows, Microsoft Graph can be used with other OLE-compatible applications, such as Windows Write.

Using Microsoft Graph, you can turn an overwhelming table of numbers into a chart that shows important trends and changes. You can relegate the detailed numeric table to a location where this much detail doesn't slow down communication. Figure 19.1 shows a Word for Windows document enhanced by a chart. Microsoft Graph is more than a small charting application; Microsoft Graph has all the charting capability of Microsoft Excel 3.0, the most powerful Windows spreadsheet and charting application. Microsoft Graph can even produce 3-D charts with shaded backgrounds, changeable fonts, and movable text.

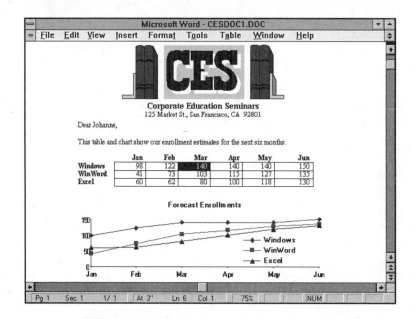

FIG. 19.1

A Word for Windows document enhanced by a chart.

Charts embedded in a Word for Windows document contain both the chart and the data that creates the chart. When you activate Microsoft Graph, the selected chart and the data are loaded so that you can make changes. You cannot save the chart or data separately; both are embedded into the Windows application.

T   I   P   Many tips found in the charting chapters of Que's book, *Using Excel 4 for Windows*, Special Edition, also work in Microsoft Graph.

Creating a Chart

With Microsoft Graph, you can create a new chart in a Windows application in several ways. You can select the text and numbers in the data sheet from a table in a word processing document; you can type data into Microsoft Graph directly; you can copy data from any Windows application; you can import data from Microsoft Excel, Lotus 1-2-3, or a text file; or you can import data from an existing Microsoft Excel chart.

To create a chart within a Windows application, select the place in the document where you want the chart to appear and then follow the instructions for the particular application you are using for inserting a chart. In Write, the word processor included with Windows, for example, you choose the Edit Insert Object command. You then select Microsoft Graph from the Object Type list. In Word for Windows (Version 2.0), you choose the Insert Object command and select Microsoft Graph from the Object Type list.

Microsoft Graph opens in an application window on top of the current application. Microsoft Graph opens with default data in the data sheet and chart (see fig. 19.2). The chart reflects the data in a sample data sheet. (If you select data in a Windows application before you start Microsoft Graph, this data is used.) If you change the data in the data sheet, you change the chart. When you close the Microsoft Graph application, you can embed the chart and the related data into an application.

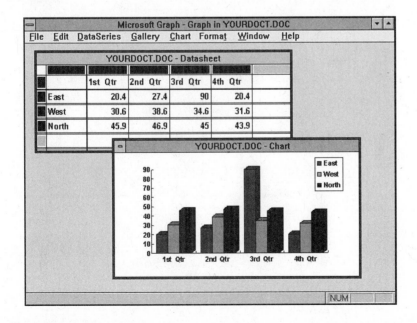

FIG. 19.2

A sample data sheet and chart.

In Microsoft Graph, you can change the data in the sheet in many ways. You also can choose different kinds of charts from the Gallery menu. From the Chart menu, you can add or remove from a chart items such as legends, arrows, and titles. You can change the appearance or position of selected chart items or data in the sheet by using the commands in the Format menu.

Understanding the Data Sheet Layout

The data points from the data sheet are plotted as markers in the chart. Markers appear as lines, bars, columns, data points in X-Y charts, or slices in a pie chart. Microsoft Graph usually uses its default settings when it first creates a chart. A row of data points, therefore, appears in a chart as a series of markers. A series of values appears in the chart connected by a line or as bars or columns that have the same color. In figure 19.3, for example, the row labeled East corresponds to one line in the 3-D line chart.

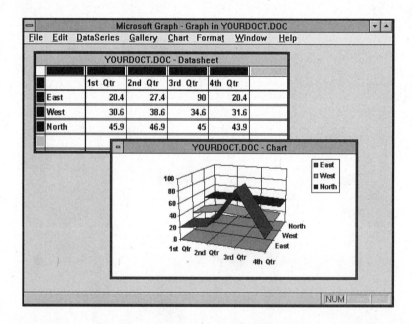

In the default orientation shown in figure 19.3, known as Series in Rows, the text in the first row of the data sheet becomes the category names that appear below the *category (X) axis* (the horizontal axis). The text in the left column becomes the *series names*, which Microsoft Graph uses as labels for the legend. (The legend is the box that labels the different colors or patterns used by each series of markers.) If you change orientation and want to return to the default orientation, choose the **D**ataSeries Series in **R**ows command.

If the data on the data sheet uses the reverse orientation so that each data series goes down a column, you must choose the **D**ataSeries Series in **C**olumns command. The category names (x-axis labels) are taken from the left column of the data sheet (see fig. 19.4). The series names (legend labels) are taken from the top row.

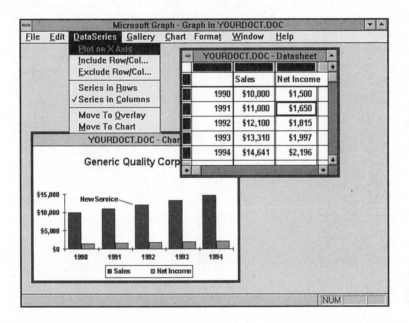

FIG. 19.4

A data series with a column orientation.

When you create a Microsoft Graph chart, be sure that you have text for each series name (legend labels), text for each category label (x-axis), and a number (or N/A to enter a blank data point) for each data point.

Typing Data for a New Chart

To manually create a chart, type over the numbers and text that appear in the default data sheet. When you change the default data sheet, you update the chart.

If you change numbers or text in the data sheet after you open it, you make corresponding changes in the chart. Rows or columns of data you add to the data sheet are included in the chart. Later sections in this chapter describe methods for editing data and for including or excluding rows or columns from the chart.

Creating Charts from a Table in Your Document

In some Windows applications, you can select data in a document from which you want to create a chart. That data is then loaded into the data sheet in Microsoft Graph as soon as it opens. When this happens, the resulting chart reflects the data in the document.

In the following example, a Word for Windows' document contains a table that is quickly converted into a chart. Figure 19.5 shows a table and its subsequent conversion to a chart in a document.

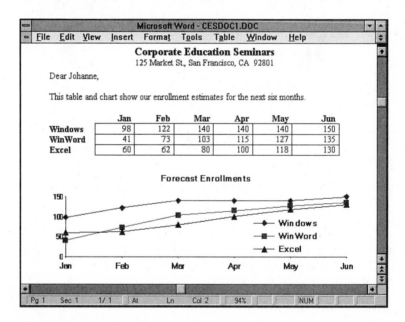

FIG. 19.5

A table and its subsequent chart in a document.

To create a chart from a table in a Word for Windows' document, follow these steps:

1. In the table, enter the data and text in the layout you want to appear in a Microsoft Graph data sheet.

   In Word for Windows, use the Table menu or the Table button on the Toolbar to insert a table.

2. Select the table.

3. Choose the object linking command.

   In Word for Windows, click on the Graph button in the toolbar or choose the **I**nsert **O**bject command.

4. Select Microsoft Graph from the **O**bject Type list and then choose OK.

   Microsoft Graph starts. After a moment, Microsoft Graph will load the table's data in the data sheet. The chart updates.

5. Format, modify, and size the chart and data sheet. If the data series are in columns, you need to choose the **D**ataSeries Series in **C**olumns command.

6. Choose the **F**ile E**x**it and Return to Document command.

7. To embed the chart in the document, choose **Y**es at the prompt.

Microsoft Graph closes. The chart is inserted after the table, with a blank line in between.

Copying Data from Windows Applications into the Data Sheet

You can copy data from applications and paste them into a Microsoft Graph data sheet to create a chart. You can create a chart from a series of text and numbers aligned on tabs in Word for Windows or Write, or you can copy a range of cells from a Microsoft Excel worksheet. (A following section, "Importing a Microsoft Excel Chart," describes how to import a range from Microsoft Excel or use a Microsoft Excel chart as a basis for a Microsoft Graph chart.)

You must separate data and text in a word processing document by tabs for the information to copy into separate data sheet cells. Figure 19.6 shows the same Word for Windows document used in figure 19.5, but the data and labels are separated by right-align tabs. You must arrange data and text as you want this information to appear in the Microsoft Graph data sheet.

To copy data from a document or Microsoft Excel worksheet and create a chart, follow these steps:

1. Select the tabbed data or range of Microsoft Excel cells. Choose the **E**dit **C**opy command.

2. Move the insertion point to where you want the chart and choose the command to start Microsoft Graph and embed an object.

In Word for Windows, click on the Graph button or choose the **Insert Object** command. Select Microsoft Graph from the list and choose OK.

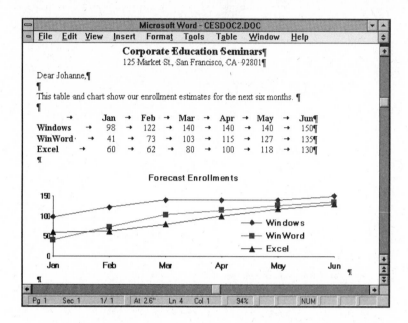

FIG. 19.6

Data and labels
separated by
tabs.

3. Activate the data sheet in Microsoft Graph by clicking on its title bar and then erase all existing data by choosing the **Edit Select All** command or pressing Ctrl+A. Then choose the **Edit Clear** command or press the Del key. When the Clear dialog box displays, choose OK or press Enter.

4. Ensure that the top left cell in the data sheet is selected and choose the **Edit Paste** command or press Ctrl+V.

   The data is pasted into the data sheet, and the chart updates.

5. Format, modify, or size the chart and data sheet as necessary.

6. Choose the **File Exit and Return to Document** command.

7. Choose **Yes** when asked whether you want to update the chart in the document.

The chart is inserted at the insertion point.

Importing Worksheet or Text Data

You may want to use data from an ASCII text file or a Microsoft Excel or Lotus 1-2-3 worksheet to create a chart. You can save time by importing this data directly into the Microsoft Graph data sheet.

To import data into the data sheet, follow these steps:

1. Move the insertion point to where you want the chart in your document and choose the command to start Microsoft Graph and embed an object. In Word for Windows, click on the Graph button or choose the **Insert Object** command. Select Microsoft Graph from the list and choose OK.

2. Erase all unwanted data from the data sheet and select the cell where you want to locate the top left corner of the imported data. If you are importing an entire chart's worth of data, select the top left cell of the data sheet.

3. Choose the **File Import Data** command. The Import Data dialog box appears (see fig. 19.7). Find and select the file from which you want to import data.

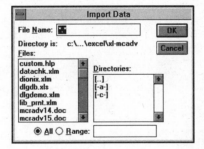

FIG. 19.7

The Import Data dialog box.

4. Specify the amount of data you want imported. To import all data, choose the **All** button. To import a range of data, enter the range or range name in the **R**ange text box.

5. Choose OK or press Enter.

Importing a Microsoft Excel Chart

Microsoft Excel is a powerful worksheet and charting application. With Excel, you can create mathematical models that generate charts. These charts then can be linked to Word for Windows documents. Changing the worksheet changes the chart, which in turn changes the chart in the Word for Windows document. (This concept is described in Chapter 22, "Using Windows Applications Together.")

Importing a Microsoft Excel chart into Microsoft Graph and embedding the resulting chart into your document has advantages over linking a chart. Charts linked back to the original Excel chart change when the Excel data changes; embedded charts don't change. Embedded charts place the chart and chart data in the document so that the document, data, and chart stay together even when copied or moved. Embedded charts can be updated by someone who has Microsoft Graph but doesn't have Microsoft Excel.

To embed a Microsoft Excel chart and the chart's related data into a document, follow these steps:

1. Move the insertion point to where you want the chart and start Microsoft Graph.

   In Word for Windows, click on the Graph button in the toolbar or choose the **I**nsert **O**bject command. Select Microsoft Graph from the **O**bject Type list and choose OK.

2. Choose the **F**ile **O**pen Microsoft Excel Chart command. To overwrite existing data in the data sheet, choose OK when prompted.

   The Open Microsoft Excel Chart dialog box appears (see fig. 19.8).

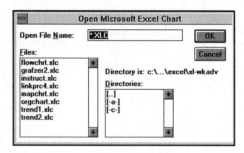

FIG. 19.8

The Open
Microsoft Excel
Chart dialog
box.

3. Select the drive, directory, and file name of the Microsoft Excel chart, and then choose OK. Microsoft Excel charts use the file extension XLC.

   The chart opens in Microsoft Graph, and the associated data appears in the data sheet. Data series found in rows in Microsoft Excel are in columns in the Microsoft Graph data sheet but the **D**ataSeries Series in... command compensates and the chart appears correctly.

4. Format, modify, and size the chart and data sheet.

5. Choose the **F**ile **Ex**it and Return to document command.

6. To embed the chart in the document, choose **Y**es at the prompt.

Editing Existing Charts

Updating existing Microsoft Graph charts embedded in a Windows application is easy. With a mouse, double-click on the chart. With the keyboard, select the chart by moving the insertion point next to the chart, and then pressing Shift+arrow across the chart. After the chart is selected, follow the instructions for editing an embedded object for the application in which you are working. In Word for Windows (Version 2.0), for example, choose the **E**dit Microsoft Graph Object command.

Entering Data for Overlay Charts

Overlay charts overlay one kind of two-dimensional chart onto another. They make seeing the relationships between different kinds of charts or seeing data with widely different scales easier.

Overlay charts consist of a main chart (the underlying chart foundation that uses the Y-axis on the left) and an overlay chart (the overlay that covers the main chart and uses a second Y-axis on the right). You can create an overlay chart by choosing the **G**allery Co**m**bination command. You also can create an overlay chart from existing charts by selecting a data series (line, bar, or column) and choosing the **D**ataSeries Move to Overlay command. The selected series is moved out of the main chart and into the overlay chart.

The **G**allery Co**m**bination command divides the number of data series in half. The first half creates the main chart, and the second half creates the overlay chart. When the total number of series is odd, the main chart receives the larger number of series. If five rows of data existed, for example, the first three rows would be in the main chart and the last two rows would be in the overlay chart.

For Related Information:

▶▶ To learn more about how changing the worksheet changes the chart, which in turn changes the chart in a Word for Windows document, see "Pasting Worksheets and Charts into a Word Processor," p. 855 and "Linking and Embedding Microsoft Excel Data and Charts into Word for Windows," p. 856.

FROM HERE...

Editing the Data Sheet

Working in the data sheet is similar to working in a word processing table or a Windows worksheet. Because the data sheet cannot be printed, the data sheet doesn't have a wide range of font formatting options. Another difference is that you can edit cellular data directly in a cell or within an editing box.

Selecting Data

Moving and selecting cells in the data sheet uses many techniques also used in Microsoft Excel. If you use a mouse, you can use the scroll bars to scroll to any location on the data sheet. Click on a cell to make the selection. To select multiple cells, drag the mouse across the cells. To select a row or column, click on the row or column header. To select multiple rows or columns, drag across the headers. To select all cells in the data sheet, click on the blank rectangle at the top left corner where row and column headings intersect.

Caution   Use care when selecting multiple cells, rows, columns, or the entire data sheet. Selecting the entire worksheet and then pressing Del erases the entire worksheet.

If you are using the keyboard, use the keys shown in the following tables to move the insertion point or select cells and the cells' contents.

To move	Press
To a cell	Arrow
To first cell in row	Home
To last cell in row	End
To top left data cell	Ctrl+Home
To lower right data cell	Ctrl+End
A screen up/down	PgUp/PgDn
A screen right/left	Ctrl+PgUp/PgDn

To select	Press
A cell	Arrow
A range (rectangle) of cells	Shift+arrow or F8 (enters Extend mode); Arrow and then F8 (exit Extend mode)
A row	Shift+space bar
A column	Ctrl+space bar
The datasheet	Shift+Ctrl+space bar or Ctrl+A or Edit Select All
Undo selection	Shift+Backspace or move an arrow key

Replacing or Editing Existing Data

The easiest way to replace the contents of a cell is to select the cell by moving to it or clicking on the cell and then typing directly over the cell's contents. When you press Enter or select a different cell, the edits take effect.

To edit the contents of a cell, select the cell by moving to it using the arrow keys or by clicking on the cell. Press F2, the Edit key, or double-click on the cell. A simple edit box appears and shows the contents of the cell. You can edit the cell's contents as you edit the contents of any edit box. After you finish editing, choose OK or press Enter.

> **T I P**
>
> To break a line chart at one point and continue at another point without dropping to a zero value, enter *N/A* in the appropriate cells in the data sheet. If you enter *0* (zero) in a cell, the line drops to the zero value, but if you enter *N/A*, the line stops and then restarts at the next cell that contains a numeric value.

Inserting or Deleting Rows and Columns

Microsoft Graph expands the chart to include data or text you add in rows or columns outside the originally charted data. If you add rows or columns of data and leave blank rows or columns, Microsoft Graph doesn't include the blank rows or columns as part of the chart.

To insert or delete rows or columns in the data sheet, select the rows or columns where you want to insert or delete and then choose the **Edit** **I**nsert Row/Col or the **Edit** **D**elete Row/Col command. The shortcut keys for inserting or deleting selected rows or columns are Ctrl++ (plus) and Ctrl+- (minus), respectively. A dialog box appears if you don't select an entire row or column and asks you to select whether you want to affect the rows or columns that pass through the selected cells.

The Microsoft Graph data sheet cannot have more than 256 columns or 4,000 rows. If you need a larger data sheet, create the chart in Microsoft Excel or an advanced charting application and link or paste the chart in the application.

Copying or Moving Data

Copy or move data in the data sheet by using normal Windows techniques. Select the cells you want to copy or move and then choose the **Edit** **C**opy or **Edit** **C**ut command. (The shortcut keys are Ctrl+C and Ctrl+X, respectively.) Select the cell at the top left corner of the area where you want to paste the data and choose the **Edit** **P**aste command or press Ctrl+V. The pasted data replaces the original data. To undo the paste operation, choose the **E**dit **U**ndo command.

Including and Excluding Data from a Chart

When you add data or text to the data sheet, Microsoft Graph immediately redraws the chart, even if the data doesn't touch the preceding data. This redraw feature is inconvenient if you want to exclude some rows or columns from the chart.

You can see which rows and columns of data are included because the row or column headings are darkened. Excluded rows or columns are grayed.

To include or exclude a row or column with the mouse, double-click on the row or column heading. The double-click toggles the row or column between included and excluded.

To include or exclude a row or column with the keyboard, select the entire row or column and then choose the **DataSeries** **I**nclude Row/Col or the **DataSeries** **E**xclude Row/Col command.

Changing Data by Moving a Graph Marker

Microsoft Graph enables you to move column, bar, lines, or X-Y markers on 2-D charts using the mouse. As you move the data point, the corresponding data changes in the data sheet. This feature is convenient for smoothing a curve so that the chart matches real-life experience or for *fudging* numbers to fit the results you want.

To change values on the datasheet by moving markers on the chart, follow these steps:

1. Open the data sheet and chart. Activate the chart. The chart must be a two-dimensional column, bar, X-Y, or line chart.

2. Hold down the Ctrl key and click on the column, bar, or line marker you want to change. A black *handle* (a small square) appears at the top of the marker.

3. Click on the black handle and drag the handle to the new position. When you drag the black handle, a tick mark on the vertical axis moves, showing you the value of the new location.

4. Release the mouse when the marker reaches the location you want.

The corresponding data in the data sheet changes.

Sizing Your Chart

You get the best results if you resize the chart in Microsoft Graph rather than in the application in which the chart is embedded. Resizing the chart in the application changes the size but doesn't correct text placement, readjust the scale, and so on. By sizing the chart in Microsoft Graph before updating the chart in the application, you use Microsoft Graph to reposition and resize elements in the chart.

Change the size of the chart as you change the size of any window. Drag the borders or corners with the mouse. With the keyboard, press Alt+- to open the document Control menu, choose the **S**ize command, and then use the arrow keys to resize the window. Make sure that the chart's window is the size you want the chart when pasted into the application.

Although you can change the magnification of the graph, doing so doesn't change the size of the chart when pasted in the document. Magnifying is useful when you format or position text or arrows. To magnify or shrink the view of the chart, select the Window menu and choose a percentage to magnify or shrink.

Changing the Chart Type

When Microsoft Graph first opens, the chart appears as a three-dimensional column chart. Many different kinds of charts are available, but you have to select the appropriate one.

Try to choose the appropriate chart before you begin customizing. To change the chart type after you customize, follow the procedure described in the later section, "Customizing an Existing Chart Type."

Selecting the Original Chart Type

When you build charts, you can use any of the 81 predefined chart formats. The easiest way to create charts is to select the predefined chart closest to the chart you want. You then can customize the predefined chart until it fits your needs. To use a predefined chart, follow these steps:

1. Choose the **G**allery command.

2. From the menu, choose one of the following twelve kinds of charts:

> Area
> Bar
> Column
> Line
> Pie
> X-Y (Scatter)
> Combination
> 3-D Area
> 3-D Bar
> 3-D Column
> 3-D Line
> 3-D Pie

> After you make a choice, the Chart Gallery dialog box appears. This dialog box shows the different predefined kinds of charts. Figure 19.9 shows the gallery available for 3-D column charts.

3. To select a chart type, click on the associated square or type the chart's number and choose OK or press Enter.

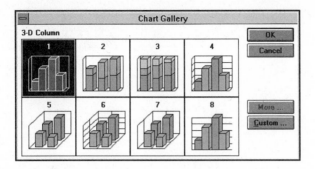

FIG. 19.9

The gallery of predefined formats for 3-D Column charts.

4. If you don't see the kind of chart you want and the **M**ore button is not grayed, choose the **M**ore button to see more formats of this kind of chart.

5. If you want a variation from one of the listed charts, choose the **C**ustom button.

   The Format Chart dialog box appears (see fig. 19.10). Select the desired options to modify the chart. This dialog box is different for each kind of chart.

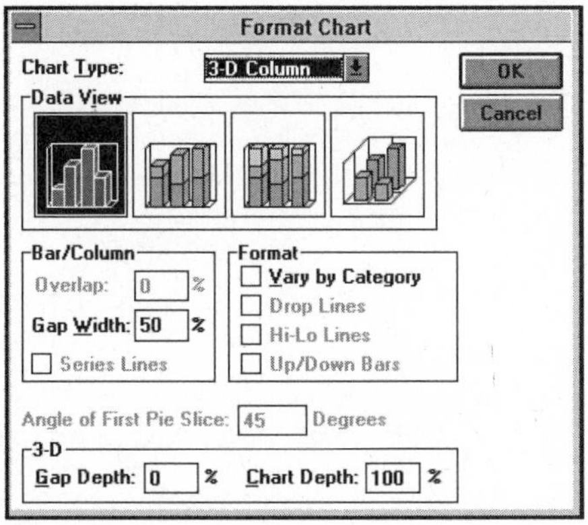

FIG. 19.10

The Format Chart dialog box for 3-D column charts.

6. Choose OK or press Enter.

You can access the customizing options available through the **C**ustom button in step 5 at any time by choosing the Forma**t C**hart or Format **O**verlay command.

T I P   To select the kind of chart you want, double-click the box in the Gallery that contains the chart. This technique selects the type and chooses OK.

The following table describes the two-dimensional chart types available through the Gallery menu:

Chart	Description
2-D Line	Compares trends over even time or measurement intervals plotted on the category (X) axis (If the category data points are at uneven intervals, use an X-Y scatter chart.)
2-D Area	Compares the continuous change in volume of a data series
2-D Bar	Compares distinct (noncontinuous) items over time. Horizontal bars show positive or negative variation from a center point. Frequently used for time management.
2-D Column	Compares separate (noncontinuous) items as they vary over time
2-D Pie	Compares the size of each of the pieces making up a whole unit. Use this chart when the parts total 100 percent for the first series of data. Only the first data series in a worksheet selection is plotted.
X-Y (Scattergram)	Compares trends over uneven time or measurement intervals plotted on the category (X) axis
Combination	Lays one chart over another. These charts are useful for comparing data of different kinds or data requiring different axis scales.

The following table describes the three-dimensional charts available through the Gallery menu:

Chart	Description
3-D Area	Uses 3-D area charts for the same kinds of data as those used in 2-D area charts
3-D Bar	Uses 3-D bar charts for the same kind of data as those used in 2-D bar charts

Chart	Description
3-D Column	Uses 3-D column charts for the same kinds of data as those used in 2-D column charts. You can create 3-D column charts with the columns adjacent to each other or layered into the third dimension.
3-D Line	Uses 3-D line charts for the same kinds of data as those used in 2-D line charts. 3-D line charts also are known as ribbon charts.
3-D Pie	Shows labels or calculates percentages for wedges. Only the first data series from a selection is charted as a pie. Wedges can be dragged out from the pie.

Customizing an Existing Chart Type

You can save work by choosing the kind of chart you want before you customize it. Use the **G**allery command to try different kinds of charts and then customize the kind you decide to use. If you use the **G**allery command to change the kind of chart after customizing, you may lose some of the custom selections.

To change or customize a chart type without losing custom formatting, choose the Forma**t** **C**hart or Forma**t** **O**verlay command and then select from the available options.

The Forma**t** **O**verlay command is only available when the chart is a combination chart.

Forma**t** Chart changes the basic chart type or customizes the main or background chart. Forma**t** Overlay changes or customizes the overlay chart. Figures 19.11 and 19.12 show the Format Chart and Format Overlay dialog boxes that enable you to customize the main or overlay charts. Both use the same options for a given chart type.

Options in the Format Chart and Format Overlay dialog boxes are available only when appropriate for the active chart. For a detailed description of the options available in the Format Chart and Format Overlay dialog boxes, choose the **H**elp command, select Commands and Menus, and then select Format Menu Chart or Format Menu Overlay from the list of topics.

If you didn't choose a combination chart as the first chart type, you still can change the chart to include an overlay. To add data series to an overlay or to create an overlay, select the data series in the data sheet or select the markers in the chart. Choose the **D**ataSeries Move to **O**verlay command. The series you selected will become an overlay.

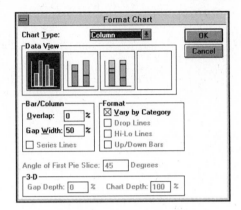

FIG. 19.11

The Format Chart dialog box.

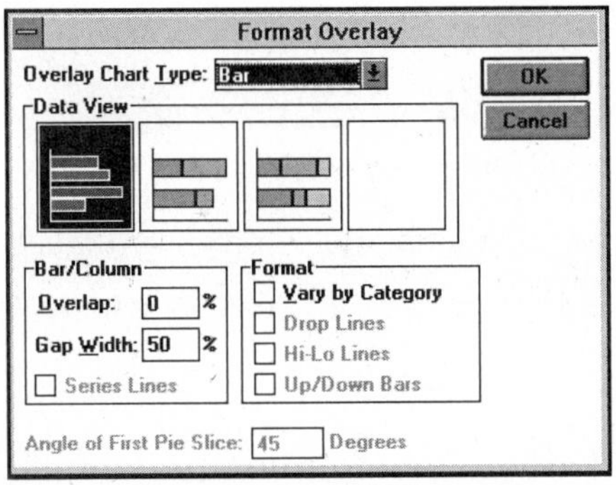

FIG. 19.12

The Format Overlay dialog box.

To remove a data series from the overlay, select the data series or the markers and then choose the **D**ataSeries **M**ove to Chart command. To completely remove an overlay, move the data series in the overlay back to the main chart.

Formatting the Data Sheet

Formatting the data sheet is important for more reasons than making data entry easier and more accurate. The format of the numbers and dates in the chart are controlled by the formatting of the numbers and dates in the data sheet.

Adjusting Column Widths in the Data Sheet

Numbers, when entered in unformatted cells, appear in General format. If the column isn't wide enough to display the full number, the number's format changes to scientific format. 6,000,000, for example, changes to 6E+6 on-screen. When a scientific number is too large to fit in a cell, the cell fills with # signs.

To change the column width with the mouse, follow these steps:

1. Move the pointer to the vertical line to the right of the column heading that you want to widen. The pointer changes to a two-headed horizontal arrow.

2. Drag the column left or right until the shadow appears where you want. Release the mouse button.

To change the column width with the keyboard, follow these steps:

1. Select a cell in the column you want to change. Change multiple columns by selecting a cell in each column that you want to change.

2. Choose the Format Column Width command.

3. Enter the column width as the number of characters.

4. Choose OK or press Enter.

Formatting Numbers and Dates

Microsoft Graph has many predefined numeric and date formats. You can choose from these formats to format the data sheet and chart or to create custom formats.

The format of the first data cell in a series defines the numeric or date format for that series in the chart. You even can enter a date, such as *12-24-92*, as a label for a category axis. You then can format the cell with a different date format (such as *d-mmm*, and the date appears as 12-Dec).

Microsoft Graph uses the same numeric and date formatting methods as Microsoft Excel and the same as many of the numeric and date formatting switches used with Word for Windows' field codes. Graph has all of Microsoft Excel's custom numeric and date formatting capability.

To format data cells, follow these steps:

1. Select the data cell or range you want to format. You can select entire rows or columns at one time.

2. Choose the Format **Number** command.

   The Number dialog box displays a list of different numeric and date formats.

3. From the list, select the numeric or date format you want to apply to the selected data cells.

4. Choose OK or press Enter.

The items in the list may appear strange looking until you understand the symbols used to represent different numeric and date formats. The characters in the list are as follows:

Character	Example	Entry	Result
#	#,###	9999.00	9,999
0	#,###.00	9999.5	9,999.50
$	$#,###	9000.65	$9,001
( )	0.00 ;(0.00)	5.6	$5.60
		-9.834	($9.83)
m	mmm	12	Dec
d	dd	6	06
yy	yy	1991	91
h or m	hh:mm AM/PM	6:12	06:12 AM

is a position holder for commas. Blank values, such as the trailing zeros to the left of the decimal, aren't represented.

0 is a position holder for leading or trailing zeros.

$ displays a dollar sign. Values are rounded when there are no trailing zeros.

( ) parenthesis are used to enclose negative numbers.

m represents months (m = 6, mm = 06, mmm = Jun, mmmm = June).

d represents days (d = 6, dd = 06, ddd = Tue, dddd = Tuesday).

yy represents years (yy = 93, yyyy = 1993).

h represents hours; m following h represents minutes; AM/PM indicates 12-hour clock; no AM/PM indicates 24-hour clock.

Microsoft Graph also enables you to format numbers and dates with a different format for positive, negative, or zero values. A semicolon separates positive, negative, and zero formats. The combination $#,##0.00 ;($#,##0.00), for example, produces different formats for positive and negative numbers, as shown in the following example:

The number	Appears as
89875.4	$89,875.40
-567.23	($567.23)

When a negative format is enclosed in parentheses, the positive format usually has a space between the last digit and the semicolon. This space leaves a space at the end of the positive number to balance the trailing parenthesis on a negative number and helps positive and negative numbers align when a column is right aligned.

Custom Formatting of Numbers and Dates

If you don't find the format you need in the Number Format list, you can create custom formats by typing them in the Format text box. Use the same characters as used in the predefined formats. After creation, a custom format appears at the bottom of the Number Format list for later reuse. Que's book *Using Excel 4 for Windows*, Special Edition, covers creating custom formats extensively.

Adding Items to a Chart

You can add many items to make Microsoft Graph charts more informative and easier to read. Some of the items you add are movable, and some are fixed. Items fixed in position, when selected, appear with white handles at the corners. You cannot move or resize fixed items. You can move or resize items that, when selected, display black handles.

You use the Chart menu to add most items to a chart. For example, you can add titles, arrows, or a legend with this menu. To format an existing item, select the item and use the Format menu.

Adding Titles and Data Values

You can use the Chart menu to add or delete most items from a chart. To add a title to a fixed location on a chart, for example, follow these steps:

1. Choose the **Chart Titles** command. The Attach Title dialog box appears (see fig. 19.13).

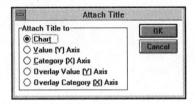

2. Select one of the option buttons.

3. Choose OK or press Enter.

   If you choose Chart or one of the axis options, a default title of Title, X, Y, or Z appears at the appropriate location in the chart.

4. With this default title selected, type the text you want. Press Enter to move to a second line. Edit by using normal editing keys.

5. To finish the text, Press Esc or click outside the text.

To remove fixed text, select the text and then press the Del key or choose the **Edit Clear** command.

To attach numbers or labels that move with the data point in a bar, column, or line chart, follow these steps:

1. Choose the **Chart Data Labels** command.

2. Select the Show **Value** or Show **Label** option. If you are working with a pie chart, you may choose the Show **Percent** option.

   The Show **Value** option labels each data point with its numeric value. The Show **Label** option labels each data point with its category name. The Show **Percent** option labels each slice in a pie chart with its percentage of the total value.

3. Choose OK or press Enter.

The Chart Data Labels command adds labels to all the data points. To remove the labels, select one of the labels and press Del or choose the Chart Data Labels command and select the **None** option. Either method removes all labels.

Adding Floating Text

You can use *floating text*, which you use to add comment boxes or to create boxes for embellishing or covering parts of a chart.

To add floating text, make sure that no other text is selected and then type the text you want to float. The text appears in a floating box surrounded by black handles. To complete the box, click outside the box or press Esc.

The black handles on selected text indicate that you can resize and move the text. To move the text, point to any area between two black boxes and drag the text to the new location. To resize the box enclosing the text, point to one of the handles (the pointer changes to a crosshair) and drag the handle. You can format floating text boxes to include colors and patterns, using the Format menu commands.

To use the keyboard to format the text, press the arrow keys until the text you want formatted is enclosed by black or white handles. You cannot use the keyboard to move floating text.

To edit the text in a floating text box, click on the text to select it and then click where you want the insertion point. Use the normal editing keys (Del and Backspace) to edit the text. To delete a floating text box, select the text and then press the Del key or use Edit Clear.

Adding Legends, Arrows, and Gridlines

To add a legend, choose the Chart Add Legend command. The legend appears. Notice that the legend is enclosed with black handles. To move the legend to a fixed location, select the legend and then choose the Format Legend command. Select one of the position options and choose OK. You also can drag the legend to a new location with the mouse. You cannot resize the legend.

To change labels used in the legend, change the series labels in the data sheet.

To add arrows to charts, make sure that an arrow isn't selected and then choose the Chart Add Arrow command. If an arrow is selected, the Chart Delete Arrow command replaces the Chart Add Arrow command. For resizing and pivoting, there are black handles at either end. To change the length of an arrow, point to one of the black boxes and drag the box to the desired length. To pivot the arrow around the head or tail, grab the appropriate box and move the head or tail to a new location. To move an arrow, drag with the pointer on the arrow's shaft. You can format arrows with different heads, thicknesses, or as a line, using the Format menu commands.

To add gridlines to a chart, choose the **Chart Gridlines** command. The Gridlines dialog box that appears has many check boxes for vertical and horizontal gridlines. To delete gridlines, choose the **Chart Gridlines** command again and clear the check boxes for the gridlines you no longer want.

Formatting the Chart and Chart Items

After you select a predefined chart format and add chart items, you can customize a chart. You can change the colors, patterns, and borders of chart items; the type and color of the fonts; and the position and size of some chart items. By selecting an axis and then selecting a format command, you can change the scale and the appearance of tick marks and labels. You also can rotate 3-D charts and create picture charts, in which pictures take the place of columns, bars, or lines.

Customize charts by selecting an item in the chart and then choosing a format command, as in the following steps:

1. Select the chart item you want to customize by clicking on the item or by pressing an arrow key until the chart item is selected.

2. Choose the Format menu and select the appropriate command to format the item.

3. Select the changes you want to make from the dialog box that appears.

4. Choose OK or press Enter.

T I P   As a shortcut, you can double-click on any chart item, such as an arrow, bar, or chart background, and this item's Pattern dialog box appears. You then can change the item's pattern, border, color, or line weight or choose one of the buttons in the dialog box to move to another dialog box such as Font, Scale, or Text.

Changing Patterns and Colors

To add patterns or colors to an item, choose the Format **Pattern** command and select the colors, patterns, shading, and line widths you want for the item. To display the item's Pattern dialog box with a mouse, double-click on the item.

You can return to the default colors, patterns, and borders by selecting the chart items you want to change, choose the Format **P**atterns command, and then select the **A**utomatic option.

> You are limited to 16 colors, but can blend these colors to create custom colors. To create a custom color palette, choose the Format Color Palette command. After the Palette dialog box appears, select the color you want to replace and then choose the **E**dit button. When the custom palette appears, type new color numbers or click in the palette and choose OK. The custom color replaces the color you previously selected. To return to the original color settings, choose the **D**efault button.

T I P

Formatting Fonts and Text

One font, size, and style are used by the entire data sheet. Each text item in the chart, however, can have a different font, size, or style.

To change an item's font, size, or style, select the item and then choose the Forma**t F**ont command. Select the font, size, or style you want. With a mouse, double-click on the item and then choose the Font button to tunnel through to the Font dialog box. The Font dialog box resembles Font dialog boxes found in most Windows applications but enables you to select different kinds of character backgrounds.

To rotate or align text, such as the text on an axis, select the text or axis and then choose the Forma**t T**ext command. Select the text orientation from the options and choose OK.

Formatting Axes

By default, Microsoft Graph scales and labels the axes, but you can select any axis and change the scale, how frequently labels or tick marks appear, and the orientation and font of text.

Microsoft Graph scales charts to even amounts. To rescale charts, select the axis (vertical or horizontal) and then choose the Format **S**cale command. (A shortcut is to double-click on an axis. When the Pattern dialog box appears, choose the Scale button.) If you select the

Category (X) Axis, you can change tick marks styles and spacing or labels spacing along the horizontal axis. If you select the Value (Y) Axis, you can change the vertical axis' beginning and ending values, the number of increments and the kind of tick marks. Figure 19.14 shows the Format Axis Scale dialog box for the Value (Y) Axis, where you can adjust the end points and increments.

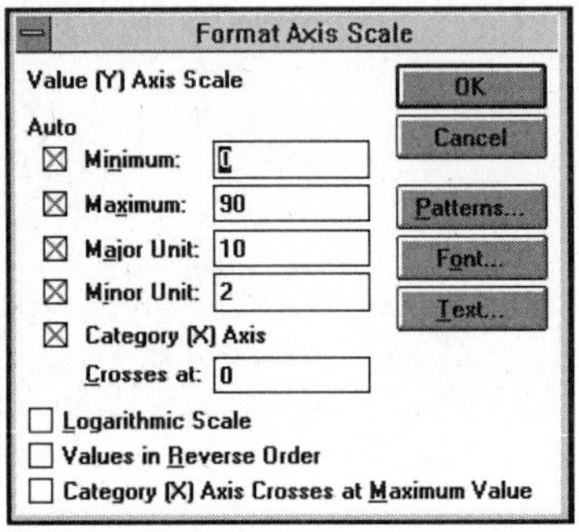

FIG. 19.14

Format Axis Scale dialog box for the Value (Y) Axis.

To thin out the number of tick marks or overlapping labels along the Category (X) Axis, select the axis and then choose the Format **S**cale command. Select the text boxes for either or both Number Of Categories (or Series) Between Tick **L**abels and Number of Categories (or Series) Between Tick Mar**k**s. If you type 5 in a box, for example, every fifth tick mark and label is displayed. Choose OK or press Enter. Figure 19.15 shows the Format Axis Scale dialog box for the Category (X) Axis where you can adjust the frequency of data labels and tick marks.

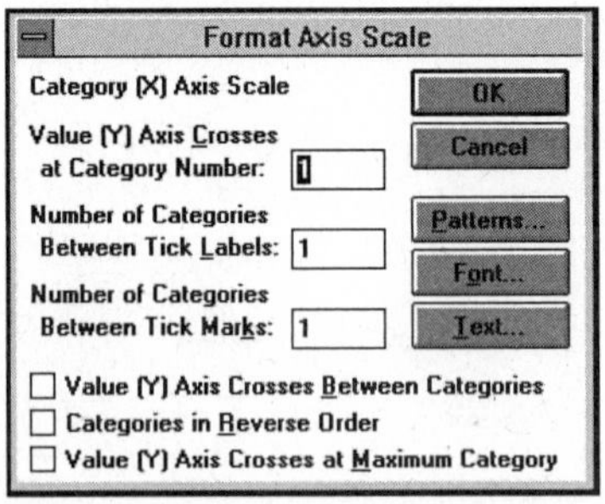

FIG. 19.15

The Format Axis Scale dialog box for the Category (X) Axis.

To change how tick marks appear on an axis scale, double-click on the axis or select the axis and choose the Forma**t P**attern command.

Rotating 3-D Charts

If a 3-D chart appears so that you don't have a good point-of-view to see the entire chart, you can rotate the chart to show the angle you want (see fig. 19.16). To rotate a 3-D chart, follow these steps:

1. Choose the Format **3**-D View command. The Format 3-D View dialog box appears (see fig. 19.16).

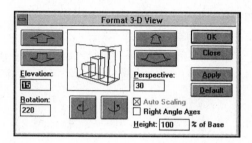

FIG. 19.16

The Format 3-D View dialog box.

2. Change the **E**levation, **P**erspective, or **R**otation by clicking on the appropriate buttons or by typing values. Changing these values affects the wire frame sample chart.

3. When the wire frame sample is oriented so that you can see the chart as you want, choose OK or press Enter.

The **A**pply button enables you to apply the new orientation to the chart and still keep the dialog box open, which helps when you are experimenting. To return to the original orientation, choose the **D**efault button.

Exiting or Updating Graphs

You can keep Microsoft Graph open and update the chart in an application or close Microsoft Graph and update the chart. Updating the chart embeds the chart and that data in the other application. The chart and data cannot be saved separately but must be saved as embedded objects within another application.

To see how a chart or your changes appear in an application, you don't need to close Microsoft Graph. To keep Microsoft Graph open and update the new or existing chart in the document, choose the **F**ile **U**pdate command. You then can use the standard Window's methods for making the application window active. Press Alt+Tab until the application window is selected and then release both keys or press Ctrl+Esc to bring up the Task list, select the application from the list, and choose Switch To.

When you exit Microsoft Graph, you are asked whether you want to update the new or existing chart in the application. To exit Microsoft Graph, choose the File Exit and Return to Document command. If you made changes since the last update, you are prompted to update the chart in the document. Choose Yes to update the chart.

FROM HERE...

For Related Information:

◄◄ To learn more about handling the chart as an embedded object, see "Embedding Data into a Document," p. 233 and "Embedding Data as Packages," p. 238.

Chapter Summary

If you are familiar with charting in Microsoft Excel, use what you learned in Microsoft Excel to learn about Microsoft Graph. For more information about Microsoft Graph, refer to the book *Using Excel 4 for Windows*, Special Edition, published by Que Corporation. Many descriptions, tips, and tricks used in this best-selling book also apply to Microsoft Graph.

Using WordArt

Words do not always function strictly as abstract symbols read for meaning. Words sometimes work as graphics, not only conveying meaning but also attracting attention and creating memorable images. You see examples of words used as graphics every day: logos incorporate words in symbols that you recognize without even reading; decorated words embellish the mastheads in newsletters; special text effects add interest to the covers of record albums. You can add spice to brochures, ads, newsletters, memos, stationery, forms, and cards by using Microsoft WordArt to add shadows and colored backgrounds, stretch and condense letters, angle text, turn words on end, and arrange words in a circle (see fig. 20.1).

WordArt comes free with Microsoft applications such as Word for Windows and Publisher.

Like Microsoft Draw and Microsoft Graph, discussed in the previous two chapters, WordArt is an *applet*, or mini-application that works from within a client application. As an applet, WordArt doesn't exist independently—you can start and use WordArt only from within the client application. For example, to include a WordArt logo in a Word for Windows document, you must start Word for Windows and choose the **Insert O**bject command. After an applet is installed on your computer, you can use it in any application that supports object linking and embedding, including Word for Windows, Publisher, PowerPoint, Ami Pro, Excel, and others.

FIG. 20.1

With WordArt, you can twist and turn your words into more interesting shapes.

Applets offer a big advantage in file management: you can always find the object you create using an applet in the same document where you created the object. Because the object already is located where you use it, you have much less chance of not being able to find it later.

NOTE Throughout this chapter, instructions for accessing WordArt assume that you are using Word for Windows. The commands for using WordArt with other applications are similar; they are listed in a table after the Word for Windows commands. (If your application is not listed, look for a command similar to the one in another application.) The procedures for using WordArt are identical, no matter what your host application.

Starting and Exiting WordArt

WordArt is an application you run from within Word for Windows or other applications that support object linking and embedding. WordArt embeds a WordArt object at the insertion point. See the later section in this chapter, "Editing a WordArt Image," to learn how you can change your image after it is in your document.

To start and edit WordArt, follow these steps:

1. Position the insertion point where you want to embed the WordArt image.

2. Choose the **Insert O**bject command in Word for Windows or a similar command in other applications. The Object dialog box appears (see fig. 20.2).

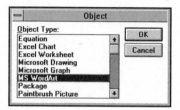

FIG. 20.2

The Object dialog box in Word for Windows.

3. Select MS WordArt and choose OK.

   The Microsoft WordArt dialog box appears. (See the next section, "Understanding the WordArt Dialog Box.")

4. Create your WordArt image. (Refer to "Creating a WordArt Image" in this chapter.)

5. Choose **A**pply to preview your image and to insert the image into your document or update an existing image. If you choose **A**pply, you do not exit WordArt.

   or

   Choose OK to insert your image into your document or to update an existing image. If you choose OK, you exit WordArt.

You can start Microsoft WordArt from other applications:

Powerpoint	Choose the **File Insert** command. Select MS WordArt from the list of applications.
Publisher	Choose the **Edit Insert O**bject command. Select MSWordArt from the Type of **O**bject list and choose OK or click the MSWordArt icon and draw box.
Excel	Choose the **Edit Insert O**bject command and select MS WordArt from the **O**bject Type list.

Ami Pro	Choose the **Edit Insert** command and then select New **O**bject.
Windows Write	Choose the **Edit Insert** Object command and select MS WordArt.

Because your WordArt image exists only as part of the client document, the image cannot be saved by itself. To save your WordArt image, save your client document.

FROM HERE...

For Related Information:

◄◄ See "Starting, Using, and Quitting Applications," p. 46.

◄◄ See "Starting an Application from the Program Manager," p. 75.

Understanding the WordArt Dialog Box

WordArt consists of only one dialog box that you can open, close, and move, but which—unlike a true application—you cannot minimize or scroll. No commands are available in WordArt; only the options displayed in the dialog box. The only menu in WordArt is the Control menu, which provides keyboard techniques for moving and closing the dialog box (see fig. 20.3).

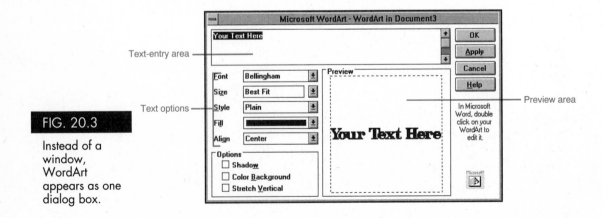

FIG. 20.3

Instead of a window, WordArt appears as one dialog box.

At the top of the dialog box is a text-entry area with text selected. At the bottom right is the Preview screen, which displays a preview of the choices you make. To the left of the Preview screen are options you use to manipulate your text. The Font, Size, and Fill lists enable you to set the appearance of your text; the Style list enables you to stretch, tilt, flip, arch, and stand text on end; and the Align list sets the alignment of text within the text frame. The Options group is below these lists. By selecting choices from the Options group, you can enhance text.

For Related Information:

◄◄ See "Using Menus and Dialog Boxes," p. 35.

◄◄ See "Operating Applications," p. 77.

FROM HERE...

Entering Text

When you are creating a WordArt image, you first must enter the text. When you start the application to create an image, the text-entry area contains the sample words Your Text Here. Type text to replace the selected sample text.

After you insert your text into the text-entry area, you can use any standard Windows text-editing convention. You can select several words or lines by dragging the mouse across the text, for example, or you can select one word by double-clicking. You can click the mouse button to position the insertion point, press the Backspace key to delete text to the left of the insertion point, or press Del to delete text to the right of the insertion point. Pressing Enter ends a line.

You can press Shift+Insert to insert text into the text-entry area from the Clipboard.

The text you enter appears in the font selected in the Font list box. The Font list contains 19 different fonts, from Anacortes to Wenatchee. These fonts are graphic fonts specific to WordArt and are not the same as TrueType fonts or the fonts built into your printer.

The text you enter appears in the font size selected in the Size box. To enable WordArt to select the size that best fits the WordArt frame, select Best Fit from the Size list.

To change the font or size, follow these steps:

1. To change the font, choose the **F**ont list and select the font you want from the drop-down list that appears.

T I P

After you choose the Font list, press the up- and down-arrow keys repeatedly to cycle through the different fonts. Watch the Preview box to see how each font looks.

2. To change the size, choose the **S**ize list and select the size you want from the drop-down list. You also can type the size you want in the Size box.

As you enter text, it appears in the Preview box—unless you are editing existing text. If you edit existing text, you must choose the **A**pply button to see your changes in the Preview box.

Applying Special Effects

WordArt offers many ways to graphically enhance words. You can change the style by arching or flipping the words; you can change the fill or color; and you can align the words to fit the frame in many different ways. You also can add a drop shadow to words, add a colored background, or stretch the words vertically.

To apply effects to text, follow these steps:

1. From the **S**tyle list, select a style. The choices in the **S**tyle list release you from the typical text baseline. These choices include the following:

Selection	Result
Top to Bottom	Stands text vertical, with the first letter on top
Bottom to Top	Stands text vertical, with the first letter on the bottom
Plain	Removes all styles
Upside Down	Flips text upside down
Arch Up	Fits text to the top of a circle
Arch Down	Fits text to the bottom of a circle

Selection	Result
Button	Arches up the first line of text, arches down the third line, and leaves the second line of text horizontal (repeats a single line of text three times)
Slant Up (Less)	Slants text slightly upward
Slant Up (More)	Slants text upward by about 45 degrees
Slant Down (Less)	Slants text slightly downward
Slant Down (More)	Slants text downward by about 45 degrees

2. From the Fill list, select a color for your text.

   If your PC supports the full Windows palette, 16 colors, including black, white, and two shades of gray, are listed. If your PC supports fewer colors, fewer colors are displayed.

3. From the Align list, select a text alignment.

Selection	Result
Left	Aligns text in your WordArt image to the left of the frame
Center	Aligns text in your WordArt image to the center of the frame
Right	Aligns text in your WordArt image to the right side of the frame
Letter Justify	Spaces the letters out to fill the frame (adding space between the letters)
Word Justify	Spaces words equally from the left to right edges of the frame (adding spaces only between words)
Fit Horizontally	Stretches the text out to fill the frame's width

Letter and Word Justify change the spacing, not the appearance, of the text. Fit Horizontally, in contrast, stretches the actual characters, distorting those letters that are smaller than the frame (if the letters are as wide as the frame, you do not see much difference when you select Fit Horizontally). To see the difference of Fit Horizontally, select a small point size for short lines of text.

4. From the Options group, select Shado**w**, Color **B**ackground, or Stretch **V**ertical to add special effects to your WordArt image.

Selection	Result
Shado**w**	Adds a black drop-shadow to text
Color **B**ackground	Includes a colored background. If the text is any color besides white, the background color is light gray; if the text is white, the background color is black.
Stretch Vertical	Stretches the text vertically to fit the frame. (This option is similar to the Fit Horizontally alignment option, except that Stretch Vertical does up and down what Fit Horizontally does side to side.)

Options are selected if an X appears inside the box to the left of the option.

Editing a WordArt Image

You can edit your WordArt image in two ways: you can start WordArt and make changes to the image, using any of the techniques described earlier in this chapter; or you can edit the image in many host applications. For example, in Word for Windows, a WordArt image is the same as a picture. You can select the WordArt image and resize or crop the image by dragging its corner handles; you can add a frame to the image so that you can position it anywhere on the page and wrap text around it; and you can add a border around your WordArt image.

When you edit a WordArt image, the WordArt dialog box appears, displaying the image you want to edit.

To edit a WordArt image in Word for Windows, follow these steps:

1. Double-click the image to bring up WordArt.

   or

   Select the WordArt image and choose the **Edit MS WordArt Object** command.

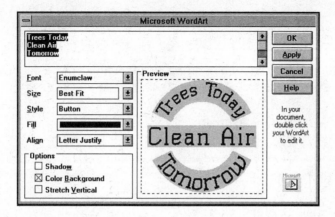

FIG. 20.4

The image you
want to edit
appears in the
WordArt dialog
box.

2. Make changes in the Microsoft WordArt dialog box.

3. Choose **A**pply to apply your changes to the Preview box and the
   Word for Windows document.

   or

   Choose OK to apply your changes and exit WordArt.

You can edit a Draw object in other applications:

Powerpoint	Double-click the object or select the object and choose the **E**dit **E**dit MS WordArt command.
Publisher	Double-click the object or select it and choose the **E**dit Edit WordArt **O**bject command.
Excel	Double-click the object or click the object with the right mouse button to display the shortcut menu and choose Edit Object.
Ami Pro	Double-click the object.
Windows Write	Double-click on the WordArt object or select the object and choose the **E**dit Edit MS WordArt **O**bject command.

FROM HERE...

For Related Information:

◄◄ To learn more about embedding WordArt images in a document, see Chapter 6, "Embedding and Linking." Specifically, see "Embedding Data into a Document," p. 233.

◄◄ To learn about the Microsoft Draw applet, see Chapter 18, "Using Microsoft Draw," p. 751.

◄◄ To learn about the Microsoft Graph applet, see Chapter 19, "Using Microsoft Graph," p. 787.

▶▶ To learn about the Equation Editor applet, see Chapter 21, "Using the Equation Editor," p. 827.

Chapter Summary

Microsoft WordArt is an applet that enables you to change words into pictures. You can rotate, flip, bend, stretch, and tilt words, and you can choose from a wide selection of fonts and styles. You can add a shadow or a colored background to words. WordArt images are great for logos, business cards, signs, and much more.

The logos you create using WordArt exist only as part of your client document. Therefore, you start WordArt from within the host application and save the image as part of that application's document. You cannot start an applet from the desktop in the way you start other applications.

To learn more about using WordArt images in your applications, refer to Que books such as *Using Word for Windows 2*, Special Edition; *Using Excel 4 for Windows*, Special Edition; *Using Powerpoint*; *Using Ami Pro*; and *Using Microsoft Publisher*.

Using the Equation Editor

I f you are a scientist or engineer, you may have longed for an easy way to enter equations into a document so that you are not faced with having to hand-draw equations into an otherwise polished-looking document. The Equation Editor enables you to quickly and efficiently produce professional looking equations that can be included in any application that supports Object Linking and Embedding (OLE).

Like the other mini-applications discussed in this section of the book, the Equation Editor is an *applet* that comes free with some Microsoft applications such as Word for Windows 2.0. The Equation Editor does not come with Windows. However, this applet is available in any application that supports object linking and embedding (to learn more about OLE, see Chapter 6).

NOTE In this chapter, the step-by-step instructions for using the Equation Editor are specific to Word for Windows. Other applications use similar—but not identical—commands. Following each set of instructions you should find a chart describing the commands you need to use the Equation Editor in other applications.

To insert an equation into a Word for Windows document, follow these steps:

1. Position the insertion point where you want to insert the equation in your application.

2. Choose the **Insert O**bject command. The Object dialog box appears, listing all of the OLE-based objects you can insert in a Word for Windows document.

3. In the Object dialog box, select Equation and choose OK.

   When you choose OK, the Equation Editor opens, as shown in figure 21.1.

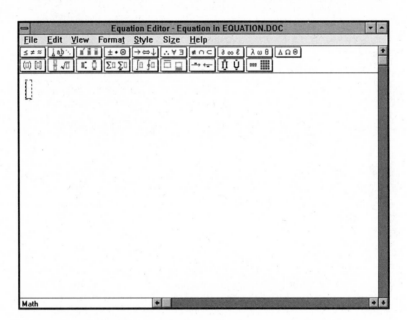

The Equation Editor window.

4. Create the equation in the Equation Editor (see the following sections for detailed instructions on creating an equation).

5. Choose the **File Exit** and Return to Document command to close the Equation Editor and return to your application. You are asked whether you want to save the equation in the application; choose yes.

   or

   Choose the **File Update** command (or press F3) to insert the equation into the document without closing the Equation Editor window.

If you choose to update your equation without closing the Equation Editor, you can return to your document just as you switch to any other application—press Ctrl+Esc to use the Task List or press Alt+Tab until the document window is active.

Starting the Equation Editor from Other Applications

PowerPoint	Choose the **File Insert** command. Select Equation from the list of applications.
Publisher	Choose the **Edit Insert Object** command. Select Equation from the **O**bject Type list.
Excel	Choose the **Edit Insert Object** command. Select Equation from the **O**bject Type list.
Ami Pro	Choose the **Edit Insert** command and then select New **O**bject.
Write	Choose the **Edit Insert Object** command. Select Equation from the **O**bject Type list.

When you first open the Equation Editor, you are presented with a screen containing one *slot* (see fig. 21.1). Slots demarcate the different components of an equation. If you are entering a fraction, for example, a slot is available for the numerator, and a slot is available for the denominator. You move from slot to slot by clicking a slot or by pressing the arrow keys or the Tab key, filling in the slots with text and symbols to create your equation.

The Equation Editor has several tools for simplifying the task of creating an equation. Just below the menu bar are two rows of palettes. The top row includes symbol palettes; the bottom row includes template palettes. To access these palettes, you point to the palette and press and hold down the mouse button. The *symbol palettes* include scientific and mathematical symbols. The *template palettes* contain collections of ready-made templates that enable you to easily create the different components in an equation.

For example, the second palette from the left in the second row of palettes contains a collection of templates for entering fractions and roots (see fig. 21.2). The dotted areas within a template represent the slots into which you enter symbols and numbers. Several template palettes contain a variety of templates for creating fractions, roots, summations, matrices, integrals, and many other mathematical expressions.

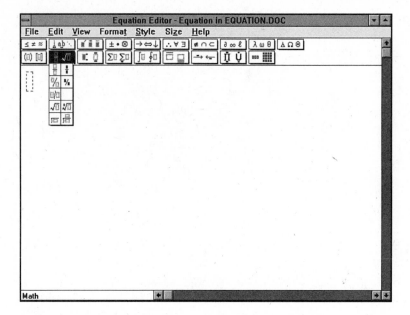

FIG. 21.2

The Equation
Editor with a
template palette
opened.

The Equation Editor also has several palettes for entering symbols,
including math operators, Greek symbols, arrows, and so on. The best
way to become familiar with the template and symbol palettes is to
experiment with them, running through them one-by-one and inserting
the template or symbol to see what it looks like.

Constructing an equation consists largely of using the template palettes
to insert slots, the symbol palettes to insert symbols, and the keyboard
to insert text. You assemble the equation piece by piece. You enter text
and symbols into slots that either stand alone—such as the slot that
appears on-screen when the Equation Editor is first opened—or are
part of a template. The Equation Editor enters text or symbols into
whichever slot contains the insertion point. You use the arrow and Tab
keys to move the insertion point from slot to slot.

The templates take care of most of the positioning and spacing aspects
of equation building, although other commands are available for fine-
tuning spacing and alignment of the components of an equation. Commands also are available for controlling the font and font size of the
various elements in an equation.

Figure 21.3 shows a partially completed equation in the Equation Editor. Notice the slots near the end of the equation into which characters
have yet to be inserted.

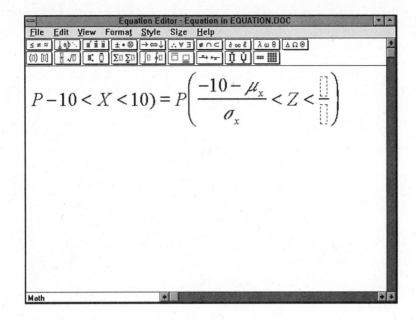

FIG. 21.3

A partially completed equation in the Equation Editor.

Typing Text in the Equation Editor

Typing in the Equation Editor is much like typing in any Windows application, such as Word for Windows, although with some important differences. When you type in the Equation Editor, text is entered into the slot containing the insertion point. You can use the Backspace and Del keys to delete characters as you would in a word processor.

Unless you choose the **Text** style from the **Style** menu, the space bar has no effect. The Equation Editor takes care of the spacing in an equation. When you type an equal sign, for example, the Equation Editor adds spacing before and after the equal sign. If you press the Enter key, you start a new line.

If you want to type regular text, choose the **Text** style from the **Style** menu or press Ctrl+Shift+E. You then can enter text as you usually would, using the space bar to insert spaces. Choose the **Math** style from the **Style** menu or press Ctrl+Shift+= to return to the Math style—the style you normally work with when creating an equation.

Selecting Items in an Equation

You may need to select an item within an equation—to change the point size or reposition the item, for example. To select characters within a slot, use the mouse to drag across characters, or with the keyboard, press the Shift+arrow key combination as you normally would. To select an entire equation, choose **E**dit Select **A**ll or press Ctrl+A.

To select embedded items (items not contained in a slot), such as character embellishments (carets, tildes, prime signs, and so on) or integral signs, hold down the Ctrl key, and the mouse pointer changes to a vertical arrow. Point to the embedded item with the arrow and click to select the item.

Entering Nested Equation Templates

Complex equations involve templates nested within templates. The result is an equation involving many templates that are each nested within the slot of a larger template. To enter a template within an existing equation, follow these steps:

1. Place the insertion point where you want to insert the template.

2. Use the mouse to choose the desired template from one of the template palettes.

   The template is inserted immediately to the right of the insertion point.

   or

   Use one of the shortcut keys listed in table 21.1 to insert the template.

3. Type text or enter symbols into each slot in the template. The insertion point must be positioned in the slot before you begin entering text or symbols.

   To position the insertion point with the mouse, point to the desired slot and click.

   or

   Use the arrow and Tab keys to position the insertion point.

Table 21.1 lists the shortcut keys for inserting templates.

Table 21.1 Shortcut Keys for Inserting Templates

Template	Description	Shortcut Key
(☐)	Parentheses*	(or)
[☐]	Brackets*	[or]
{☐}	Braces*	{ or }
|☐|	Absolute Value	|
☐/☐	Fraction*	F
☐/☐	Slash Fraction*	/
☐	Superscript (high)*	H
☐	Subscript (low)*	L
☐	Joint sub/superscript*	J
√☐	Root*	R
ⁿ√☐	Nth Root	N
Σ☐	Summation	S
∏☐	Product	P
∫☐	Integral*	I
⊞	Matrix (3x3)	M
☐	Underscript (limit)	U

To use many of these shortcuts, press Ctrl+T and then the shortcut key. However, the items marked with an asterisk can be inserted by pressing the Ctrl key and then the shortcut key—you do not have to press T first.

Entering Symbols

Many fields of mathematics, science, and medicine use symbols to represent concepts or physical structures. The Equation Editor can insert symbols into slots with the following procedure:

1. Position the insertion point where you want to insert the symbol.

2. Use the mouse to select the desired symbol from one of the symbol templates.

   or

Use one of the shortcut keys listed in table 21.2 to insert the symbol.

Table 21.2 lists the shortcut keys for inserting symbols. To use these shortcuts, press Ctrl+S and then the shortcut key.

Table 21.2 Shortcut Keys for Inserting Symbols

Symbol	Description	Shortcut Key
∞	Infinity		
→	Arrow	A
∂	Derivative (partial)	D
≤	Less than or equal to	<
≥	Greater than or equal to	>
×	Times	T
∈	Element of	E
∉	Not an Element of	Shift+E
⊂	Contained in	C
⊄	Not contained in	Shift+C

Adding Embellishments

The Equation Editor has several embellishments you can add to characters or symbols, such as prime signs, arrows, tildes, and dots. You add an embellishment by first typing the character or inserting the symbol you want to embellish and then selecting the appropriate embellishment from the embellishment symbol palette—the third palette from the left in the first row of palettes. To add an embellishment, follow these steps:

1. Position the insertion point to the right of the character you want to embellish.

2. Click and hold down on the Embellishment symbol palette (the third palette from the left in the first row of palettes).

3. Drag the mouse pointer down to select the embellishment you want and release the mouse button. The embellishment is added to the character to the left of the insertion point.

or

Use one of the shortcut keys listed in table 21.3 to add an embellishment.

Table 21.3 Shortcut Keys for Inserting Embellishments

Icon	Description	Shortcut Key
	Over-bar	Ctrl+Shift+-
	Tilde	Ctrl+~ (Ctrl+" on some keyboards)
	Arrow (vector)	Ctrl+Alt+-
	Single prime	Ctrl+Alt+'
	Double prime	Ctrl+" (Ctrl+~ on some keyboards)
	Single dot	Ctrl+Alt+.

Controlling Spacing

With the Format Spacing command, you can modify spacing parameters, such as line spacing, and row and column spacing in matrices. To modify the spacing setting used by the Equation Editor, follow these steps:

1. Choose the Format Spacing command.

   A dialog box displaying a scrolling list of dimensions appears (see fig. 21.4).

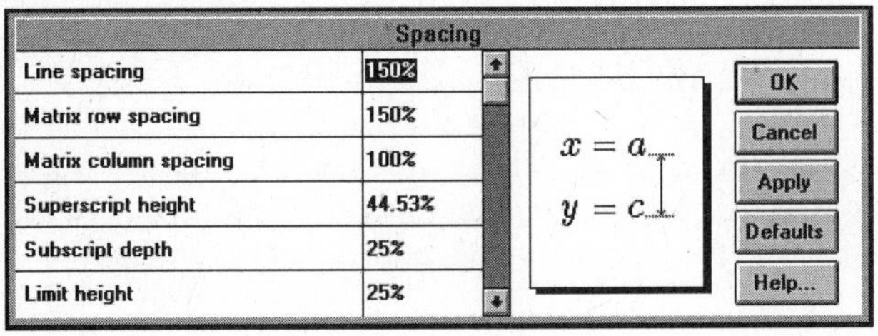

Spacing		
Line spacing	150%	
Matrix row spacing	150%	
Matrix column spacing	100%	
Superscript height	44.53%	
Subscript depth	25%	
Limit height	25%	

$x = a$
$y = c$

OK
Cancel
Apply
Defaults
Help...

FIG. 21.4

The Spacing dialog box.

2. Select the text box next to the dimension you want to modify. Use the scroll bar to move through the list of dimensions.

   The dimension you select is illustrated in the diagram at the right of the dialog box.

3. Type a new measurement; for example, to increase line spacing, erase the default, 150%, and type *200%*.

   Dimensions can be specified as a percentage (of the **Full Size** type, which is set in the Size **D**efine dialog box) or as an absolute value. The default unit of measure is points. You can specify other units by typing the appropriate abbreviation from table 21.4.

Table 21.4 Abbreviations for Units of Measure

Unit of measure	Abbreviation
Inches	in
Centimeters	cm
Millimeters	mm
Points	pt
Picas	pi

4. Choose the Apply or OK button.

   Choosing Apply applies the modified dimension to the current equation and leaves the dialog box open, enabling you to continue modifications. Choosing OK applies any modifications and closes the dialog box.

NOTE   In practice, you probably should specify the spacing dimensions as a percentage of the point size specified for **F**ull size type, which is set in the Size **D**efine dialog box. The advantage to this approach is that if you change the type size, you don't have to redefine your spacing dimensions; spacing always is proportional to the type size.

Unless you are using the Text style, the Equation Editor takes care of the spacing between elements in an equation. You can insert spaces yourself, using the mouse or the keyboard. Four spacing symbols can be used for inserting spaces. These symbols are located in the second symbol palette from the left in the top row or can be accessed with shortcut keys. The spacing symbols and shortcut keys are listed in table 21.5.

Table 21.5 Shortcut Keys for Inserting Spaces

Icon	Function	Shortcut key
ab	Zero space	Shift+space bar
ab	One point space	Ctrl+Alt+space bar
ab	Thin space	Ctrl+space bar
a b	Thick space (2 thin)	Ctrl+Shift+space bar

You can insert as many spaces together as you want. To delete a space, use the Del or Backspace key, as you do with text.

Positioning and Aligning Equations

If you are not satisfied with the automatic positioning of the elements' in an equation, you can fine-tune the positioning of any selected item using the Nudge commands. You first must select the item (see the section on selecting) and then use one of the key combinations in table 21.6 to move the item, one pixel at a time.

Table 21.6 Positioning Items with the Nudge Commands

Keystroke	Function
Ctrl+left-arrow key	Moves item left one pixel
Ctrl+right-arrow key	Moves item right one pixel
Ctrl+down-arrow key	Moves item down one pixel
Ctrl+up-arrow key	Moves item up one pixel

The Equation Editor enables you to horizontally align the lines in an equation, or lines of equations, using the Format commands or the alignment symbol. Lines can be aligned to the left, center, or right, or they can be aligned around equal signs, decimal points, or alignment symbols. You align a group of equations by choosing one of the Align commands from the Format menu. To align lines within an equation, position the insertion point within the lines and then choose one of the alignment commands.

To insert an alignment symbol, position the insertion point and choose the alignment symbol (top row, leftmost symbol) from the Spaces palette (top row of palettes, second palette from the left). The alignment symbols are used as a reference point around which lines of equations or lines within an equation are aligned. They override the Format commands.

Selecting Styles

When you work in the Equation Editor, you normally use the **M**ath style found on the **S**tyle menu. When you use the **M**ath style, the Equation Editor recognizes standard functions and applies the **F**unction style (typeface and character formatting, for example) to such functions. The **V**ariable style is applied otherwise. If the Equation Editor fails to recognize a function, you can select the function and apply the Function style. Styles are a combination of font and character you assign to selected characters or to characters you are going to type. The styles that are available are **M**ath, **T**ext, **F**unction, **V**ariable, **G**reek, Matrix-Vector, and **O**ther. Choose the style you want from the **S**tyle menu. You can modify the font and character formatting (make the font bold or italic) of these styles by choosing the **S**tyle **D**efine command.

To define the font and character attributes for a style, follow these steps:

1. Choose the **S**tyle **D**efine command. The Styles dialog box appears (see fig. 21.5).

2. Select the style you want to define.

3. Select the desired font from the list of available fonts.

4. Select the Bold or Italic boxes, if desired.

5. Choose OK or press Enter.

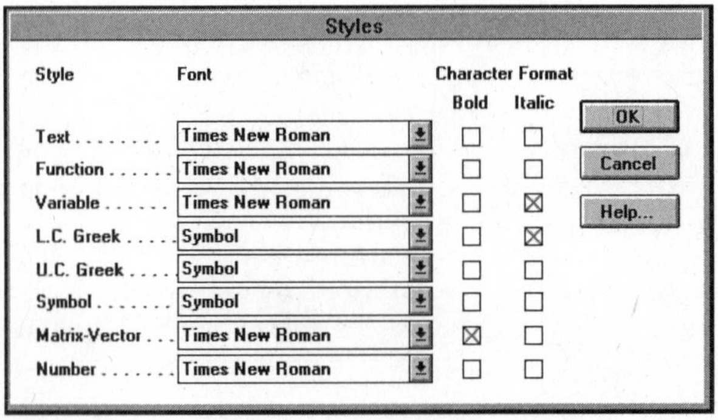

FIG. 21.5

The Styles dialog box.

Use the **T**ext style to type regular text. Selecting this style applies the **T**ext style to the text you type and enables the space bar so that you can enter spaces as normal. With the other styles, spacing is handled by the Equation Editor.

Use the **O**ther style to select a font and character format that is not one of the standard styles. Selecting this style opens a dialog box in which you can select a font and character format for selected characters or for the characters you are about to enter.

T   I   P

Selecting Font Sizes

Just as the Equation Editor provides several predefined font styles, described previously, this applet also provides several predefined font sizes. The **F**ull size is the choice you usually work with when you are building equations. You also have selections for s**u**bscripts, sub-subscripts, s**y**mbols, and sub-sy**m**bols. You can use the **O**ther size option for those cases in which you want to specify a size not defined by one of the standard sizes just listed.

To apply a font size to an equation, follow these steps:

1. Select the characters whose point size you want to modify.

   If you do not select any characters, the size you choose applies to characters you type subsequently.

2. Choose the Si**z**e menu.

3. Select the desired size from the Si**z**e menu. If none of the defined sizes match your needs, select **O**ther and specify a size, in points, in the Other Size dialog box.

You can modify the default settings for each of the sizes listed in the Si**z**e menu by using the Si**z**e **D**efine command, as in the following steps:

1. Choose the Si**z**e **D**efine command.

2. Select the box to the right of the size you want to define.

   When you select a box, the element you are defining is highlighted in the diagram on the right side of the dialog box.

3. Type a new size.

4. Choose OK or press Enter.

To apply a size, select the size from the Size menu and type the characters to which you want to apply the size. To apply a size to characters you already have typed, select the characters and then choose a size.

For Related Information:

FROM HERE... ◀◀ To learn more about TrueType fonts, see "Using TrueType Fonts," p. 309.

Working with Matrices

The Matrix template palette (the last palette in the second row) includes several matrices of predefined size. You also can select one of the template symbols in the bottom row of the palette to open up a Matrix dialog box, in which you can specify the dimensions of the matrix and control several other matrix characteristics.

To insert a matrix template, click on the matrix template palette (the last palette in the second row) and drag the pointer to the desired template. Release the mouse button. Selecting a template from the last row of icons opens up the Matrix dialog box (see fig. 21.6). In the Matrix dialog box, you can specify the dimensions of the matrix and make several other selections. You can specify how the elements in rows and columns are aligned and whether or not the column widths and row heights are equal (if rows and columns are not equal, their width and height are based on widest or highest entry). By clicking in the space between the rows and columns in the dialog box, you can select one of three types of partition lines: solid, dashed, or dotted lines. As you click in the space, you cycle through the three types of lines and then back to no line. Click once to insert a solid line; click a second time to insert a dashed line; click a third time to insert a dotted line; and click a fourth time to remove all lines. The spacing between rows and columns is controlled using the Format Spacing command. After making the desired selections, choose OK or press Enter.

To format an existing matrix, select the entire matrix and choose the Format Matrix command. Make the desired selections from the dialog box. Choose OK or press Enter.

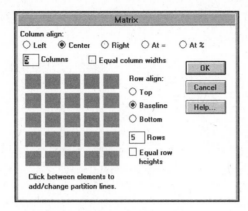

FIG. 21.6

The Matrix
dialog box.

Viewing Equations

You can choose from three different views of the equation in the Equation Editor window. To change the view, open the View menu. To display the equation at the actual size it appears in the document and on the printed page, select 100%. Select the 200% and 400% commands to display the equation at twice and four-times the actual size, respectively. These commands are useful when you want to fine-tune the spacing in an equation or get a close-up look at small items in an equation.

Editing an Equation

To edit an equation, you must return to the Equation Editor from within the client document. To open the Equation Editor in Word for Windows, follow these steps:

1. Double-click on the equation you want to edit or select the equation and choose the **E**dit Equation **Ob**ject command.

2. Make the desired editing changes.

3. Choose **File U**pdate to update the equation without closing the Equation Editor.

or

Choose the **File Ex**it and Return to Document command to close the Equation Editor and return to the document. You are asked whether you want to save the equation in the document; choose **Y**es.

Editing an Equation in Other Applications

Powerpoint	Double-click the equation or select the equation and choose the **Edit Ed**it Equation command.
Publisher	Double-click the equation.
Excel	Double-click the equation.
Ami Pro	Double-click the equation.
Write	Double-click the equation or select the equation and choose the **Edit Edit Equation O**bject command.

Printing Equations

Generally, to print an equation, print the document containing the equation. (You cannot print from the Equation Editor.) To print equations, you need to have a PostScript printer, an HP LaserJet printer that supports downloadable fonts, or a dot-matrix or HP DeskJet printer in conjunction with a font-scaling utility, such as TrueType or Adobe Type Manager. Chapter 8 describes the use of fonts in more detail. The Help facility in the Equation Editor contains extensive information on using printers and fonts with the Equation Editor. To access these Help screens, follow these steps:

1. Choose the **H**elp command in the Equation Editor.

2. Choose Index.

3. Select one of the topics under the Printers & fonts category.

You can obtain a printout of the Help screen by choosing **File P**rint Topic.

For Related Information:

◄◄ See "Starting, Using, and Quitting Applications," p. 46.

◄◄ See "Starting an Application from the Program Manager," p. 75.

◄◄ To learn more about embedding WordArt images in a document, see Chapter 6, "Embedding and Linking." Specifically, see "Embedding Data into a Document," p. 233.

◄◄ To learn about the Microsoft Draw applet, see Chapter 18, "Using Microsoft Draw," p. 751.

◄◄ To learn about the Microsoft Graph applet, see Chapter 19, "Using Microsoft Graph," p. 787.

◄◄ To learn about the Microsoft WordArt applet, see Chapter 20, "Using WordArt," p. 817.

Chapter Summary

The Equation Editor, like all other Windows applets, is a mini-application that comes free with some Microsoft applications such as Word for Windows 2.0. The Equation Editor is not a stand-alone application; you can use it only within an application that supports object linking and embedding. The application from within which you can use applets is the *client* because this application receives the embedded objects; the applet is the *server* because it originates the objects—in this case, equations.

Running Applications

P A R T

V

O U T L I N E

Using Windows Applications Together

One of the most useful features of Windows is its capability to run multiple applications—both Windows and DOS applications—at the same time and to transfer data between those applications. Windows enables you to use different Windows applications as though they were parts of a single application. By integrating applications, you multiply their power, making your work more efficient and your result more professional.

When you link Windows applications, you can work in new ways. While you type a letter in Word for Windows, for example, you can enter a name and address by selecting the name in the letter and then choosing a custom command on the Word menu. PackRat, a personal information manager designed for Windows, finds the correct address and inserts it in the letter using a built-in macro. You never see PackRat working.

Many corporations—especially those companies that want to quickly write reports or analyze or chart database information—use Windows to link Microsoft Excel (the worksheet and charting application) to databases on the personal computer disk, on a SQL Server, or on a mainframe. Microsoft Excel comes with Q+E, an application that enables you to link areas of your worksheet to a database. When you enter sales data into a mainframe or local database, for example, Microsoft Excel can read the information and create reports and charts that show changes against forecast sales. Q+E can operate through commands on Microsoft Excel's menu. You also can control Q+E with macros.

If you use Windows at home, in a small business, or in a corporate division, you can integrate Quicken with Microsoft Excel. Quicken is a popular personal financial manager that tracks multiple check books, credit cards, and personal investments. By linking Quicken to Microsoft Excel, you can perform financial calculations and create charts that surpass those calculations and charts built into Quicken.

Budget and financial reports you create at the end of every month can be updated automatically. You can link or embed numbers and charts from Microsoft Excel into a professional word processor such as Word for Windows or Ami Professional or a presentation application such as PowerPoint. When you change numbers in the spreadsheet, you also change the numbers and charts in the report or presentation.

Windows makes DOS applications more productive, too. You can use DOS applications under Windows to copy budget and report information from an accounting application or 1-2-3 spreadsheet, for example. You then can paste that information into a DOS or Windows application—helpful if you want to copy a column of numbers from Lotus 1-2-3 and paste them into a DOS accounting application. DOS applications can copy and paste data, but they cannot link or embed data.

Understanding the Methods of Integration

You use the following methods of integration with Windows and DOS applications:

- Copying and pasting text or graphics between applications via the Clipboard. DOS applications can receive only alphanumeric (text and numbers) data.

- Transferring text or graphics by saving the file from one application and reading and converting the file into another application

- Linking text or graphics between Windows applications by using a Copy and Paste Link command

- Embedding data or graphics from a server Windows application into a client Windows application so that the data from the server document actually is stored inside the client document

- Transferring data between Windows applications with Dynamic Data Exchange under the control of a macro application

You easily can transfer text or graphics between applications by using the copy and paste procedures common to all Windows applications. You select the data to be copied from one Windows application, choose **Edit Copy**, switch to the other Windows application, position the insertion point, and choose **Edit P**aste. If you are working with DOS applications, additional steps are required, and you can copy and paste text only.

The most common method of exchanging data in DOS applications is to save the file from one application, exit the application, use a second application to convert the file's data and format, exit that application, and import the data into a third application. 1-2-3 for DOS, for example, uses this method with its Translate application, and WordPerfect for DOS uses this method with its Convert utility.

Most Windows applications read or save other file formats and automatically convert or translate the file while the applications read or save. Microsoft Excel, for example, reads and writes text files, 1-2-3 files, and dBASE files. Word for Windows reads and writes files for common word processors such as WordPerfect, WordStar, MultiMate, and the IBM standard, DCA (RFT). PageMaker converts files from Word for DOS, WordPerfect, and other word processors. The translation process is invisible to you. You often can use Windows applications and the DOS applications in the same office.

Some Windows applications can include in their documents all or part of another application's document. In many Windows word processors, for example, you can create a document composed of its own text and pieces of files from other word processors, different spreadsheets, and graphics from different graphic file formats. You can paste these files in or link them to a file on disk. If you link them to a file on disk, you can update the document that contains all the pieces by changing the files on disk.

The greatest level of integration between Windows applications comes with linking and embedding. Linking enables changed data to transfer from the server document to the client document. The changes can be sent automatically or when the user requests an update. Embedding buries one application's data in another application's document. You do not have to copy multiple files or keep track of where information came from. The information is all in one document, even though it retains its original format, and you still can edit it with the original Windows application.

If you are unfamiliar with the concepts or procedures of copying and pasting, you may want to read Chapter 1. Read Chapter 6 to learn about linking and embedding with Windows applications and Chapter 23 to learn how to copy and paste between DOS applications.

For Related Information:

▸▸ See "Responding to an Application Failure," p. 1071.

Integrating Windows Applications

Because Windows applications can operate together, the power of multiple applications is available to work on one task. You can use an application to enhance or analyze data from another application; you aren't limited to the features built-in to the one application you use most frequently. You can use a second or third Windows application without taking days to learn it because Windows applications use similar menus and procedures.

Using Windows applications together produces a more polished and more efficient result than using one application. The following sections demonstrate some of the ways you can use Windows applications together to improve your work efficiency.

Embedding Voice Messages into a Letter

Windows applications that have object linking and embedding capability can include voice messages within a text-based document—such as a letter, worksheet, or database. You easily can attach voice notes to a document. The following list shows some of the ways in which you can use voice messages:

Voice message attached to	May communicate
A letter	A description of the letter's distribution and enclosures
A worksheet	The reasons for a budget discrepancy
A database report	A verbal warning when process control or inventory limits are reached

Before you can record a voice message, you must install a sound board in your personal computer. A sound board, such as the Sound Blaster board, adds sound recording and playback capability. You can record with any high-quality microphone, and playback can be through miniature speakers or any stereo system.

After you install a sound board, use the Drivers program in the Control Panel to install the driver for your board. The driver is the software translator that enables Windows and the sound board to communicate. To install the driver, you need your original installation disks; they contain the different driver softwares. (See Chapter 17 for information on installing a multimedia driver.)

To record a voice message and copy it to the Clipboard, follow these steps:

1. Open the Sound Recorder program in the Accessories group.

2. If you have a previously recorded message, choose the **File O**pen command and open the file containing the message.

   To record a new message, click on the microphone button. Speak your message into the microphone. Click on the stop button to stop the recording.

3. Replay your message to test it. Edit or rerecord it if necessary.

4. Choose the **Edit C**opy command.

When you record your voice message, the Sound Recorder displays your voice's wave form (see fig. 22.1). You can see the elapsed time of your message in the counter on the left. You have up to 60 seconds for a message. Before you copy the recording, you can replay it to hear your message. Use the rewind button, <<, and then click on the play button, >, to hear your message. The square stop button stops the message. You can reposition the message to any point in the recording by dragging the square in the horizontal scroll bar.

To package your voice message so that you can embed it into a word processing letter, a worksheet, or a database, follow these steps:

1. Open the Object Packager in the Accessories group window.

2. Choose the **Edit P**aste command.

   The Appearance side of the Object Packager displays a microphone icon. The Content Description side displays the words "Copy of Sound." (Chapter 17 describes how to change the icon and its label.)

3. Choose the **Edit Copy Pac**kage command.

This procedure copies the package into the Clipboard (see fig. 22.2). The package contains an icon and your voice message bundled as an embeddable object.

While stopped
during playback,
the Sound
Recorder shows
the voice wave.

A copy of your
packaged voice
appears like this.

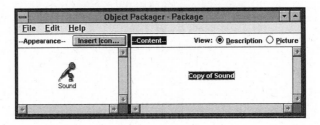

To paste the voice message into a document (Window Write is shown
in this example and in fig. 22.3), follow these steps:

1. Activate the application in which you want to paste the voice
   package.

2. Move the insertion point to where you want the icon to appear.

3. Choose the **Edit P**aste command.

   The microphone icon is pasted at the insertion point.

4. Choose the **File S**ave command to save the document.

When you send someone this document, they can replay your message
if they also have a supported voice board. To replay your message,
double-click on the microphone or select the microphone icon by moving next to it and then holding down Shift while you press the appropriate arrow key to select the icon. To replay the message, choose the
Edit Package Object command and then choose **Activate Contents** from
the cascading menu.

Updating Word Processing Letters with a Personal Information Manager

Windows can improve productivity by linking a personal information
manager, such as PackRat, to a word processor, such as Word for Windows or Ami Pro. Because it is a Windows application, PackRat can
pass name, address, and client data to a word processing letter while
you type the letter.

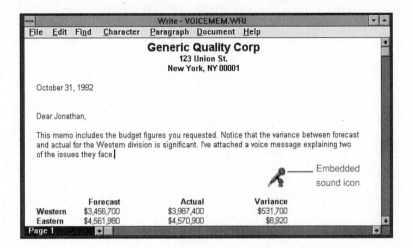

FIG. 22.3

Double-click on
the microphone
icon to hear the
voice message.

Personal Information Managers (PIMs), like PackRat shown in figure
22.4, store your personal information. PIMs are designed to handle
names, addresses, contact dates, priority lists, agendas, and phone
books. Such applications can contain many notes that you can retrieve
by looking for key words in the notes.

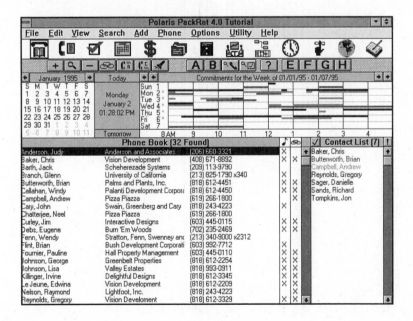

FIG. 22.4

Linking PackRat
to Word for
Windows or Ami
Pro enables you
to easily look up
and enter names,
addresses, and
client data.

PackRat comes with a set of macros that you can load into Word for Windows or Ami Pro. When you load the macros, they attach themselves as new commands in the menus. These new commands enable you to stay in the word processor and retrieve information from PackRat. You can type a name, for example, and then choose a command that looks up the appropriate address from PackRat and inserts the address below the name. You also can generate form letters from a selected group of names and addresses in PackRat.

The following example shows you how to retrieve a forgotten name and address from PackRat and insert it into the letter you are typing in Word for Windows.

To insert a name and address stored in PackRat into a Word for Windows letter, follow these steps:

1. Position the insertion point in Word for Windows where you want the name and address to appear.

2. Type the name and then select it.

3. Choose the **I**nsert Find Name in Pac**k**rat command (see fig. 22.5). (This command is a custom Word for Windows command that PackRat adds to the Word for Windows menu. It comes with PackRat.)

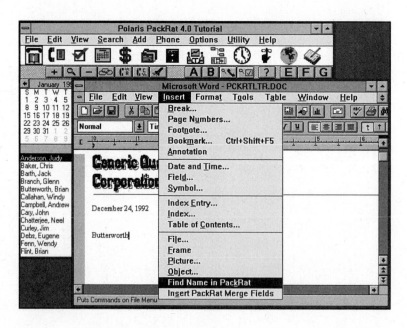

FIG. 22.5

Some applications add custom commands to make integration with other applications easy.

4. If PackRat finds a name that matches, it inserts the address it finds in its files.

   or

   If PackRat cannot find a name that matches, it displays a dialog box from which you can choose the correct name. Select a name and choose OK. PackRat inserts and formats the address.

PackRat searches its phone and address lists to fill in the address for the Word for Windows document.

Pasting Worksheets and Charts into a Word Processor

One of the more frequent uses of copying and pasting between applications is to exchange tables of numbers and charts between Microsoft Excel and other Windows word processors, such as Word for Windows, Ami Pro, or WordPerfect for Windows. Copying and pasting numeric data prevents wasted effort in retyping, eliminates the possibility of typing incorrect numbers, and produces a more professional report by integrating tables, charts, and illustrations into the body text. Figure 22.6 shows a Word for Windows document containing a pasted Excel worksheet.

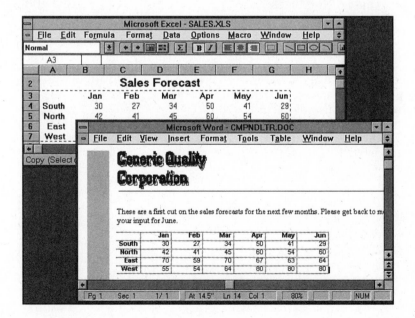

FIG. 22.6

Pasting Microsoft Excel charts and tables into a word processing document ensures that they will not change.

When you paste Excel data into a Word for Windows document, Word for Windows builds a table to hold the data. You can format the cells, cell contents, and borders in a Word for Windows table. You can add single or double underlines and even make each cell a different width.

Follow these steps to copy worksheet data from Microsoft Excel and paste it into Word for Windows to produce a table of data not linked to the worksheet:

1. Activate the Microsoft Excel worksheet.

2. Select the cells to be copied.

3. Choose the **Edit C**opy command.

4. Activate Word for Windows so that its window is the top window.

5. Position the insertion point in the document where you want the data in the cells to appear.

6. Choose the **Edit P**aste command.

The Microsoft Excel worksheet data appears as a table in Word for Windows. This table contains numbers and text as if they were typed into Word for Windows. Because you chose the **P**aste command rather than the Paste **S**pecial command, the data is not linked to Microsoft Excel. (To display the edges of cells as a gray line on-screen in Word for Windows, choose the Table menu and select the Gridlines command so that a check mark appears to its left. Choose the command a second time to hide the gridlines.)

You can use the Forma**t B**order command in Word for Windows to format tables with outlines, double lines, and borders. Choose the **S**hading button from the Border Cells dialog box to apply shading to the table.

When you paste Microsoft Excel worksheet data into some Windows applications, each worksheet cell is pasted in as a cell in a table. In other Windows applications, such as Windows Write, each cell is pasted in as data separated by tabs. To align data separated by tabs, select the rows of data and then create new decimal or right tab settings. (In Write, no right tabs are available; use decimal tabs to align numbers.)

Linking and Embedding Microsoft Excel Data and Charts into Word for Windows

You can link or embed Microsoft Excel worksheet data and charts into Word for Windows in two ways: you can copy and paste a link between an active worksheet and the word processing document, or you can link your Word for Windows document to a Microsoft Excel file. The Word for Windows document shown in figure 22.7 includes a linked Excel chart.

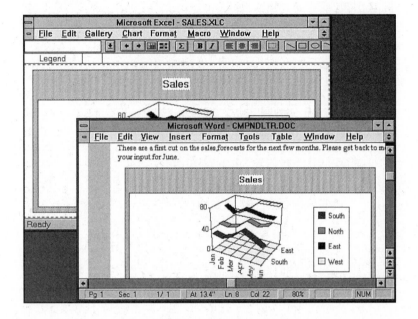

FIG. 22.7

Linking or embedding Microsoft Excel charts or tables into a Windows word processor means changes can be updated.

To link or embed Microsoft Excel worksheet data or a chart into a Word for Windows 2 document, follow these steps:

1. Display in the active window the Microsoft Excel worksheet data or chart.

2. Save the worksheet data or chart with a file name. The link will use this file name to identify the worksheet or chart.

3. Select the worksheet cells you want linked. For a chart, choose the **Chart** Select **Chart** command.

4. Choose the **Edit Copy** command to copy the data or chart into the Clipboard.

5. Start or activate Word for Windows.

6. Position the insertion point in the Word for Windows document where you want the data or chart to appear.

7. Choose the **Edit Paste Special** command.

8. To embed the cells or chart, select Excel Object from the **Data Type** list in the Paste Special dialog box. To link the cells or chart to the Word for Windows document, select one of the other alternatives.

9. Choose the **P**aste button to embed an object. Choose the Paste **L**ink button to link to the worksheet or chart in Excel. A button that is not appropriate for the data type you have selected may turn gray and be inaccessible.

The data or chart appears in the Word document. Chapter 6 describes how to update linked or embedded data.

If you later change the file name of the source worksheet or chart in Microsoft Excel, you will need to change the linked file name in the Word for Windows document. To change or update the links, use the **E**dit **L**inks command as described in Chapter 6.

Microsoft Excel charts linked into a Word for Windows document reflect the size of the chart window in Microsoft Excel. If the chart's window changes size in Microsoft Excel, the chart in the document also will change size. Use Excel to adjust your chart to the size at which markers, text, and legends are correctly positioned (a too-small chart may display truncated text or a jumbled legend). Although you can resize a chart in Word for Windows, doing so will not correct flaws in a chart. To get well-formed linked charts, size all charts in Microsoft Excel. To ensure that no one accidentally changes the chart's window in Microsoft Excel, activate the chart in Microsoft Excel. Choose the **C**hart **P**rotect Document command. In the Protect Document dialog box that appears, select the **W**indows check box and then choose OK. To remove protection, activate the chart and then choose the **C**hart Un**p**rotect Document command.

T I P   When you copy a range of data from a Microsoft Excel worksheet and paste link it into a Word for Windows document, part of the field code that describes the link is a switch, * mergeformat. This switch preserves formatting you apply in Word to the linked data from Microsoft Excel. (You can align cell contents or make text italic without losing this formatting the next time the table updates from Excel.) The * mergeformat switch does not help in situations like figure 22.8, however. In this figure, two titles—Generic Quality Corporation and Five Year Forecast—are centered as long text in an Excel cell, but appear word-wrapped when linked into the Word for Windows document. Use Word for Windows table editing techniques to correct these flaws.

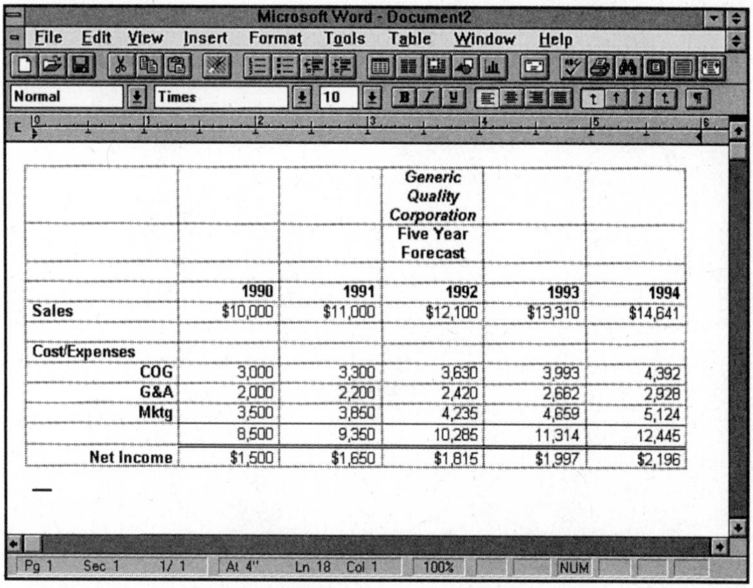

FIG. 22.8

Centered titles do not center when linked from Microsoft Excel into Word for Windows.

You can use the Table Merge Cells command in Word to merge cells adjacent to the title and give the titles enough room to be centered. The * mergeformat switch, however, does not preserve merged cells; when the table is updated, the merge cells return to split cells and force word-wraps again. Instead, adjust the cell widths of individual cells on either side of the titles as shown in figure 22.9 to give the title cells enough width for a centered title. The format is preserved when the table updates.

Linking Microsoft Excel to Databases Using Built-in Commands

Integrating applications enables computer users to combine applications and use them together for new purposes. Many corporations are linking Microsoft Excel to personal computer, SQL Server, or mainframe databases. Instead of waiting until the end of the month to learn how the business is changing, they can see changes every day because changes in the corporate database produce immediate analysis in Microsoft Excel.

		1990	1991	1992	1993	1994
				Generic Quality Corporation		
				Five Year Forecast		
Sales		$10,000	$11,000	$12,100	$13,310	$14,641
Cost/Expenses						
	COG	3,000	3,300	3,630	3,993	4,392
	G&A	2,000	2,200	2,420	2,662	2,928
	Mktg	3,500	3,850	4,235	4,659	5,124
		8,500	9,350	10,285	11,314	12,445
Net Income		$1,500	$1,650	$1,815	$1,997	$2,196

FIG. 22.9

To preserve formatting when updated, adjust the widths of adjacent cells; do not merge cells.

The combination of Q+E and Microsoft Excel enables you to link worksheets to databases that contain accounting, sales, manufacturing, and inventory information. You then can link Microsoft Excel worksheets to selected portions of the database and analyze the data as it changes, as shown in figure 22.10. For long, complex analysis and reports, you can run the work at night using a Microsoft Excel macro that automates the process.

Q+E comes with Microsoft Excel. A more extensive version of Q+E also is sold separately by its manufacturer, Pioneer Software.

Microsoft Excel comes with add-in macros—QE.XLA and QESTART.XLA, stored in the EXCEL\XLSTART\QEMACRO directory—that add commands to Microsoft Excel's **D**ata menu and modify existing commands so that they can handle *external* databases (databases outside the worksheet). These new commands enable you to link to a local or remote database and extract selected data into your worksheet. The process uses the same steps used to extract data from a Microsoft Excel database. The new commands added are as follows:

Paste Fieldnames	Reads field names from the database file so that you can paste them into the worksheet
SQL **Q**uery	Presents a dialog box in which you can write an SQL query that extracts information from a database
Activate Q+E	Activates Q+E if it is running or starts it if it is not running

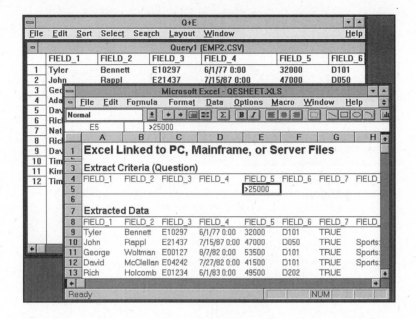

FIG. 22.10

Linking a
worksheet to
local or main-
frame databases
means more
responsive
business
analysis.

Commands that remain on the **D**ata menu but are modified to work
with external databases are the **D**ata Set Data**b**ase and **D**ata Extract
commands. The modified **D**ata Set Data**b**ase command enables you to
connect to database files on the hard disk, on the local area network, or
on a mainframe.

In the following example, data from a dBASE file on disk is extracted
into the worksheet. The extracted data is limited by the query in the
criteria range. The extracted data is only extracted if it meets the conditions found in the criteria range.

To add the new commands to the **D**ata menu, choose **F**ile **O**pen and
open the file QESTART.XLA located in the EXCEL\XLSTART\QEMACRO
directory. Notice that new commands are in the **D**ata menu.

To define which external database will be used, complete the following
steps:

1. Choose the **D**ata Set Data**b**ase command.

2. Select the **E**xternal Database option and choose OK (see
   fig. 22.11).

3. Select dBASEFile from the **S**ource box as the type of file to which
   you are connecting. (If you are connecting to a network or accessing a mainframe, you choose the Sources button.)

4. Select the directory C:\EXCEL\QE from the **D**irectories list. This
   directory is the location of sample files.

5. Select the file ADDR.DBF and then choose OK twice.

Microsoft Excel - Sheet1

| File | Edit | Formula | Format | Data | Options | Macro | Window | Help |

Normal

A3

Set External Database

File name: addr.dbf

Source: dBASEFile   Sources..

OK

Cancel

Files: Directory is: c:\excel\qe

addr.dbf   Directories:
dept.dbf
emp.dbf   [..]
loc.dbf   [-a-]
             [-c-]

Options...

For Help on dialog settings, press F1   NUM

FIG. 22.11

Set the source
and the location
of the external
database.

Before you can query the database, you need to paste fieldnames from the database into the worksheet and create a criteria range. A criteria range is where queries are entered. To paste field names from the ADDR.DBF file into the worksheet, do the following:

1. Select the left cell of where you want to paste the field names.

2. Choose the **D**ata Paste **F**ieldnames command. The Paste Fieldnames dialog box, shown in figure 22.12, appears.

FIG. 22.12

Select the field
names (or all
names) you want
to use from the
external
database.

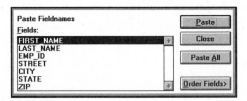

Paste Fieldnames

Fields:

FIRST_NAME
LAST_NAME
EMP_ID
STREET
CITY
STATE
ZIP

Paste
Close
Paste **A**ll
Order Fields>

3. Choose the Paste **A**ll button to paste all names. (To paste names selectively, select each individual field and choose **P**aste.)

   The field names from the database are pasted across the row.

4. Select the field names and the cells underneath each field name and then choose the **D**ata Set **C**riteria command.

The blank cells under the field names are where you enter a description of what you want to retrieve from the database. You may want to put a border around the criteria range so that the criteria range is obvious.

The next step is to create an extract range. The extract range is the area on the worksheet where Q+E copies records from the external database that match your queries. To create the extract range:

1. Select the field names in the criteria range and choose the **E**dit **C**opy command.

2. Select a cell to the left of where you want the extract range to appear and choose the **E**dit **P**aste command.

3. Select the names you pasted and choose the **D**ata Set **Ex**tract command.

You copied the field names to be used as headings for the extract range to ensure that the field names are spelled correctly. Q+E and Excel cannot find data that matches if the field names are spelled incorrectly.

All the records that meet a query are copied under the field names you created. The finished worksheet before data is extracted should look similar to figure 22.13.

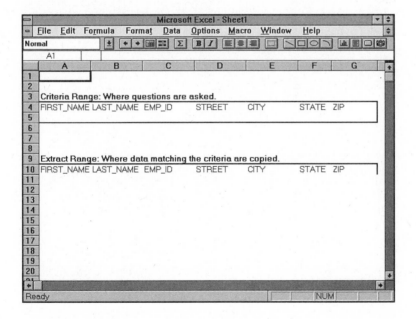

FIG. 22.13

The worksheet before data has been extracted from a database file on disk.

To enter a query of the ADDR.DBF file and extract information that matches, complete the following steps:

1. Type a criteria under the Criteria range field name for which you want to limit data. Type *NC* under the field name STATE, for example, to only extract records from the data file that have the state of North Carolina. To extract all records from the data file, clear all cells under the field names in the criteria range.

2. Choose the **Data Extract** command. A dialog box appears. Choose OK.

   Q+E counts the number of records in the database that match your criteria and displays the number in a dialog box.

3. To link the worksheet data to the file on disk, select **Linked** from the dialog box that appears. To copy the data to the worksheet without links, choose **Unlinked**.

4. Choose the **Paste** button to paste the information extracted from the database into the worksheet.

Figure 22.14 shows a finished extraction.

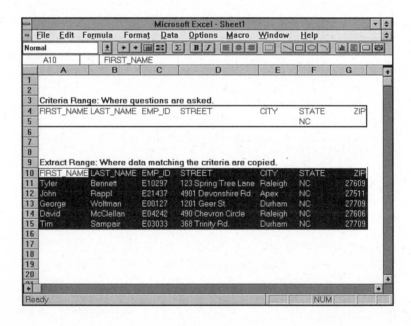

FIG. 22.14

The data appears in the Extract Range in Excel.

To automate the process of linking worksheets to databases, control the Q+E command language with Microsoft Excel's macro language. You can download and analyze database information during the night so that a report filled with charts and tables is waiting for you in the morning.

Controlling Integration via Dynamic Data Exchange Macros

You usually can integrate different Windows applications through easy-to-use copy, paste, and paste link commands. These commands are explained in Chapter 6 and examples are given throughout this chapter. Sometimes, however, a pasted link is not sufficient.

When you link data with a paste link, the link transfers data between the Windows applications with Dynamic Data Exchange (DDE). Sometimes you need more control over when and how the link passes information. The following lists some examples:

- Data should only be received at fifteen minute increments.

- Data should come from first one link and then another.

- Data should be manipulated before being inserted into the worksheet, word processing document, or database file.

- Data should be received at a specific time of night and then reports should be generated from the updated data.

You can handle these types of integrated Windows applications by controlling the DDE with macros. The passage of data is controlled between applications—like a highly structured telephone conversation. Just as both people in a phone conversation must know each other's language, you must know the macro or command language of both Windows applications to program DDE links.

If you know how to name and create a simple command macro in Microsoft Excel, you can create the following Microsoft Excel macro that demonstrates how macros control DDE. This demonstration macro uses the same directory names that are installed when you install Microsoft Excel and Q+E. (Q+E comes with Microsoft Excel and is one of the installation options.)

In this example, shown in figure 22.15, the macro keeps the QETEST.XLS worksheet on-screen at all times. In the background, however, it opens a database through Q+E, requests two columns of information from the database file, and copies those two columns into the Microsoft Excel worksheet.

When combined with an ON.TIME function, this type of macro can extract information from large data files during the wee hours of morning and transfer the information into worksheets. While the rest of the company sleeps, Microsoft Excel can produce analyses, reports, and charts that are there when you walk in with your first cup of coffee.

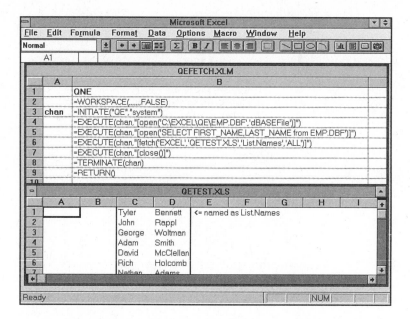

FIG. 22.15

This Excel macro retrieves database information through Q+E and transfers it into the worksheet.

To create this macro, complete the following steps:

1. Make sure that Q+E is installed under Microsoft Excel and the demonstration files are in C:\EXCEL\QE. If Q+E is not installed or you must install Q+E drivers, rerun the Excel Setup disks to install only Q+E and its drivers.

2. Open a Microsoft Excel macro sheet.

3. Name the top cell of the macro by entering *QNE* in cell B1, selecting B1 and choosing the Formula **D**efine Name command. Use QNE as the name and select the **C**ommand option button. Choose OK.

4. Enter the functions exactly as shown in figure 22.15.

5. Type *Chan* in cell A3 as a label identifying the cell to the right. Name cell B3 with the name Chan. Cell B3, Chan, will contain the number assigned to the DDE communication channel for this conversation between Microsoft Excel and Q+E.

6. Save the macro sheet and keep it open.

7. Open a new worksheet. Select a range of cells 2 columns wide and 20 rows deep. Use the Fo**r**mula **D**efine name command to name this range as List.Names. This name is where Q+E will look to place the data.

8. Save the worksheet with the name QETEST.XLS. Keep it open. This specific worksheet name is used within the macro.

To run this macro, make sure that the macro sheet and QETEST.XLS are open. Either sheet can be active and data still will be received. Choose the **Macro Run** command from Microsoft Excel, select the macro name, QETEST.XLM!QNE, and then choose OK.

If Q+E already is running, the data will transfer immediately. If Q+E is not running, a dialog box asks whether you want to run Q+E. Choose OK to start Q+E and transfer the data into the worksheet.

If the macro does not work correctly, check the macro functions for matching quotes, braces, and parentheses, and then check for mis-spelled commands. Check to see whether Q+E loaded. If it did not, en-sure that Q+E is installed underneath the Excel directory. Make sure that the EMP.DBF sample file is located in C:\EXCEL\QE.

The macro sets up the Excel environment, opens a DDE channel to Q+E (starting Q+E if necessary) and then sends Q+E commands down the DDE channel. When the communication is complete, the DDE channel is closed. The number of the DDE channel is stored in cell B3, named Chan.

The WORKSPACE function ensures that DDE communication works by turning off the **I**gnore Remote Requests check box in the **O**ptions **W**orkspace command. The INITIATE function then opens a DDE chan-nel to Q+E. The channel number for this communication channel is returned and stored in the same cell as the INITIATE function. The channel number is used during all DDE communication to specify who is communicating.

The first EXECUTE function sends the Q+E command, OPEN, to Q+E and opens the file named EMP.DBF by using the dBASEFile filter. (You must have the dBASE file filters installed for Q+E for the first EXECUTE func-tion to work.) The second EXECUTE function sends another Q+E com-mand, OPEN, that selects the entire fields named FIRST_NAME and LAST_NAME from the EMP.DBF database.

The third EXECUTE function sends the Q+E command, FETCH, to Q+E to retrieve information from the selection and put it into the worksheet. It *fetches* the selected data back to the application named EXCEL, into the worksheet named QETEST.XLS, into a named range of List.Names, and retrieves all the selected information.

The fourth EXECUTE function closes the Q+E database window. The TERMINATE function closes the DDE channel between Excel and Q+E. Because a finite number of DDE channels exist, you should write your macros to close a DDE channel when the DDE transfer is complete.

This example shows one way you can use DDE to transfer data under macro control. Other DDE macro commands also request and poke information. Each Windows application works differently with DDE.

Some, such as Microsoft Excel and Q+E, are fairly well-documented. Others are inscrutable. You should understand the macro languages used on both sides of a DDE conversation.

Enhancing Charts with a Graphics Application

You can copy and paste charts or graphics from one Windows application into other Windows applications for graphic enhancement or changes. You can copy and paste a chart from Microsoft Excel, for example, into CorelDRAW, Microsoft Draw or one of the other higher level drawing applications. You can add logos, symbols, or gradient shaded backgrounds to a chart as shown in figure 22.16.

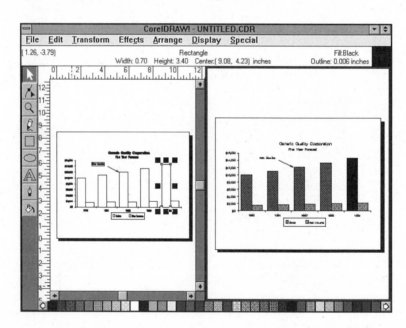

FIG. 22.16

Copy a worksheet's chart into a drawing application to add high-quality enhancements.

To copy a Microsoft Excel chart and paste it into CorelDRAW, follow these steps:

1. Display the Microsoft Excel chart in the active window.

2. Choose the **Chart** Select **Chart** command.

3. Choose the **Edit Copy** command to copy the entire chart into the Clipboard.

4. Start or activate CorelDRAW.

5. Choose the **E**dit **P**aste command to paste the chart into CorelDRAW.

After you paste the Microsoft Excel chart into the drawing application, each piece of the chart becomes a separate object that you can resize or color separately. In some drawing applications, you may need to select an *ungroup* command so that the chart is divided into its component pieces.

Use the professional art capabilities of CorelDRAW to select and change any object on the chart. Each object on the chart—such as a column, an arrow, or a string of text—is a separate object; you can stretch, rotate, resize, or color it. You also can paste in your corporate logo, add clip art, or add a shaded and colored background.

You can see how the right column in the chart on the left side of figure 22.16 has been selected because of the square handles at each of its corners.

For Related Information:

◄◄ To learn more about using multimedia, see "Installing Multimedia Equipment and Drivers," p. 716; "Operating the Sound Recorder," p. 722; and "Embedding Sound and Video in Applications," p. 733.

◄◄ To learn more about object linking and embedding, see "Transferring Data with Copy and Paste," p. 223; "Linking Data between Applications," p. 223; "Embedding Data into a Document," p. 233; and "Embedding Data as Packages," p. 238.

FROM HERE...

Copying and Linking between DOS and Windows Applications

Windows applications and DOS applications can exchange data in two ways: you can copy and paste data between the applications, or you can use a common file format that both applications understand. Copying and pasting data with DOS applications is easier when Windows is operating in 386-enhanced mode. When applications run in Windows in 386-enhanced mode, you can easily switch between applications and select portions of the screen to copy and paste into another application. If Windows is running in standard mode, Windows can copy only the entire screen of data.

DOS applications handle multiple lines of pasted data differently depending on how the application deals with the carriage return at the end of a line. If you paste multiple lines of data into Lotus 1-2-3 for DOS, for example, all lines of text copied into the Clipboard are pasted into the same spreadsheet cell; each line is entered over the top of the preceding line. You therefore should paste cells one at a time in Lotus 1-2-3 for DOS. Word processors accept multiple lines of data and will paste all the copied lines to a separate line. Each line, however, will end with a carriage return.

Capturing DOS and Windows Screens for Documentation

Windows presents you with an excellent set of tools for creating training materials and documentation. In Windows, you can run the software you want to document and the Windows software used to create the documentation simultaneously. To put a snapshot of the screen into the Clipboard, press the Print Screen key, as described in Chapter 6, "Using the Clipboard To Copy and Paste." You then can paste the screen shot into Windows composition software, such as PageMaker, Word for Windows, or Ami Professional. You can use this technique to document Windows or DOS software.

The following technique captures a 1-2-3 for DOS screen and pastes it into PageMaker, Word for Windows, or Ami Pro as shown in figure 22.17. You also can capture screens of Windows applications and easily insert snap shots of application screens into documentation or training materials. To use this technique, follow these steps:

1. Start 1-2-3 and retrieve the spreadsheet you want to document.

2. Start the Windows software that you are using to write documentation. (In this example, you use the page-layout software PageMaker.)

3. Activate the 1-2-3 application. If the application is running in a window in 386-enhanced mode, press Alt+Enter to expand 1-2-3 to full screen.

4. Capture an image of the 1-2-3 screen by pressing PrtScr, the print screen key. (If you are using an older computer, you may need to press Alt+PrtScr.)

Windows stores the image in the Clipboard. This step captures the screen text. If the application is any Windows application, it captures the screen as a graphic.

5. Activate the PageMaker window. Position the insertion point where you want the captured screen to appear.

6. Choose the **E**dit **P**aste command.

   The 1-2-3 screen text appears in PageMaker as though typed. If you captured a Windows or graphics screen, a picture of the screen appears.

7. If the pasted text does not align correctly, select the text and change the font to Courier, a nonproportional typeface. Alternatively, leave the font and insert tab stops on which to align columns.

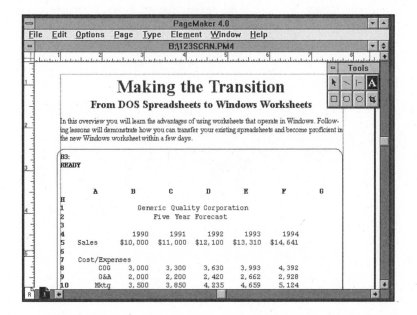

FIG. 22.17

Press the PrtScrn key to capture screens and paste them into Windows applications.

If you paste a graphic screen image into PageMaker, Word for Windows, or Ami Professional, the image appears as a picture that you can resize or crop. These Windows applications also enable you to draw lines and borders around screen images. You can send the resulting documentation to a normal printer for printing or print it to a file so that it can be typeset on a Linotronic typesetter.

Windows makes documentation easier. Because you easily can switch between applications, you can run an application you are writing about and your Windows word processor or page layout application at the same time. All it takes to switch between them is Alt+Tab or Ctrl+Esc.

Copying from DOS Applications into Windows Applications

You can copy text or numbers from any DOS application and paste the copied material into another Windows or DOS application. Figure 22.18 shows how tabbed data is copied from a memo in WordPerfect for DOS and pasted into a Microsoft Excel worksheet. If you copy tabbed data, the data automatically separates itself into cells in the worksheet where it is pasted.

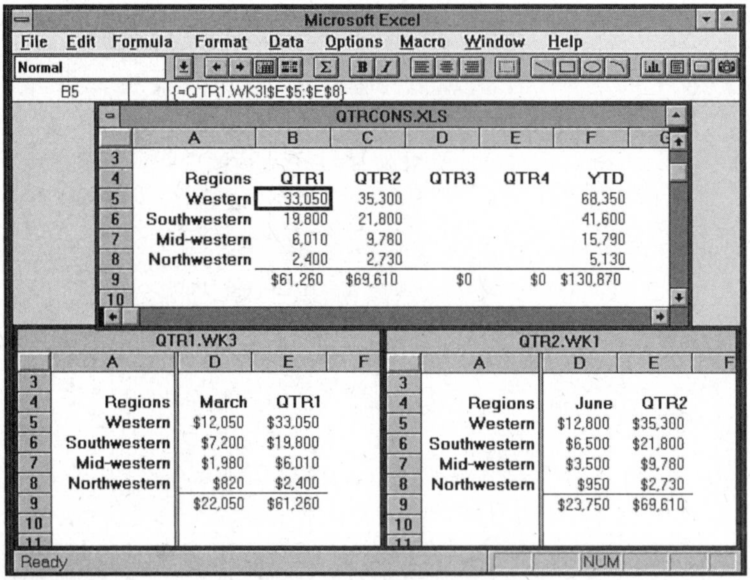

FIG. 22.18

Copy text out of any DOS application and paste into any other application.

Copying from DOS applications usually is efficient only when Windows is in 386-enhanced mode. When Windows operates in 386-enhanced mode, you can copy selected portions of the DOS application screen. When Windows is in standard mode, however, you must copy the entire screen and edit a great deal after you paste the data into another application.

To copy out of a DOS application and paste into a Windows or other DOS application when you are operating in 386-enhanced mode, follow these steps:

1. Activate the DOS application.

2. Press Alt+Enter until the DOS application displays in a Window.

3. Use the DOS application's movement keys to display the data you want to copy.

4. Choose the application Control menu by clicking on the dash icon at the top left corner of the window or by pressing Alt+space bar.

5. Select the **E**dit command and then select Mar**k** from the cascading menu.

6. With the mouse, click and drag across the portion of the screen you want to copy. With the keyboard, move the square cursor to a corner of what you want to select, hold down the Shift key, and press arrow keys to select the area to be copied. The selected area will be highlighted.

7. Choose the document Control menu again and select the **E**dit command and then select the Cop**y** Enter command.

The text and numbers you selected are now copied into the Clipboard. To paste that information into another application, follow these steps:

1. Activate the receiving DOS or Windows application.

2. Move the insertion point or cursor to where you want to paste the text or numbers.

3. If the application is a Windows application, choose the **E**dit **P**aste command.

   or

   If the application is a DOS application, put the DOS application into a window by pressing Alt+Enter. Choose the application Control menu, select the **E**dit command, and then select **P**aste from the cascading menu.

Text and numbers copied from DOS applications are pasted in as a line of text. Each line ends with a carriage return.

Linking DOS Word Processing Files into Word for Windows Documents

You also can link Word for Windows and some other Windows word processors to word processing, spreadsheet, and database files that are on disk. To link a WordPerfect document into a Word for Windows document, for example, follow these steps:

1. Position the insertion point in the Word document where you want the WordPerfect document inserted.

2. Choose the Insert File command.

3. Select All Files (*.*) from the List Files of Type list so that you can see the WordPerfect file names.

4. Select the WordPerfect file from the File Name list.

5. Select the Link to File check box to link the results on-screen to the WordPerfect file on disk.

6. Choose OK.

The file will be read from disk and will appear on-screen with the original WordPerfect format, tables, and pictures. If the WordPerfect file is changed later, you can update the Word for Windows document to reflect those changes by selecting the inserted data and pressing the F9 key.

Linking Lotus 1-2-3 Spreadsheets into Microsoft Excel Worksheets

If you are using Windows, you probably are using Microsoft Excel. Others in your work area, however, may be using Lotus 1-2-3. Because Microsoft Excel can read and write 1-2-3 spreadsheets and read 1-2-3 charts, you can use Microsoft Excel to link or consolidate 1-2-3 sheets or to enhance 1-2-3 reports or charts as shown in figure 22.19.

To link Lotus 1-2-3 spreadsheets into a Microsoft Excel worksheet, follow these steps:

1. Activate Microsoft Excel.

2. Choose the File Open command.

3. Change the File Name pattern to *.WK? and choose OK so that the 1-2-3 file names are displayed.

4. Select the 1-2-3 spreadsheet you want to link. If the spreadsheet has attached graphs, Excel asks whether the graphs should be converted.

5. Repeat steps 2 through 4 until all 1-2-3 spreadsheets are open in Microsoft Excel. (Microsoft Excel reads them automatically. You do not have to convert any spreadsheets.)

When the Lotus 1-2-3 spreadsheets are open, you can link them into Microsoft Excel worksheets. To link an open 1-2-3 spreadsheet into a Microsoft Excel worksheet, follow these steps:

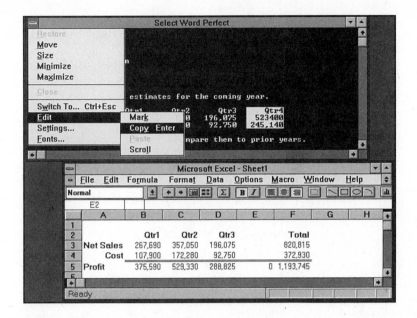

FIG. 22.19

Microsoft Excel
will link to and
consolidate Lotus
1-2-3 for DOS
spreadsheets.

1. Activate the 1-2-3 spreadsheet so that the spreadsheet is the active document in Microsoft Excel.

2. Select the cell or range of cells you want to link.

3. Choose the Edit Copy command.

4. Activate the Microsoft Excel worksheet that will receive the linked data.

5. Select the cell in the Microsoft Excel worksheet at the top left corner of the area in which you want the linked data to appear.

6. Choose the Edit Paste Link command.

The 1-2-3 spreadsheet cells are now linked into the Excel worksheet. If someone changes data in the 1-2-3 spreadsheet, the change is reflected in the Microsoft Excel worksheet.

If you need to consolidate data, for example, combining budgets from many divisions into one, some of your spreadsheets can be Lotus 1-2-3 for DOS, and Excel still will consolidate the data. Use Microsoft Excel's Data Consolidate command to create a consolidation. You can consolidate data located anywhere on the source worksheets from within Microsoft Excel, even when the data has different row or column headings, and each worksheet's data is in a different order.

If you rename or move the 1-2-3 spreadsheets linked to Microsoft Excel, you need to use the File Links command to update the links.

If you make formatting changes, create a chart, or use one of Excel's features that Lotus 1-2-3 cannot recognize, you lose the changes and additions when you save the 1-2-3 sheet back to disk. When you save your 1-2-3 spreadsheet, Microsoft Excel saves the spreadsheet in 1-2-3 format.

FROM HERE...

For Related Information:

▸▸ To learn more about using DOS and Windows applications together, see "Linking DOS and Windows Applications," p. 905 and "Sharing Data through Files," p. 910.

Chapter Summary

Multiple Windows applications can work together and share data. You can link Windows applications together so that data passes between them automatically or under operator control. You or a consultant can build integrated business systems that were never before possible.

At first, it may be foreign to you to consider working with or integrating multiple applications. When you begin working with more than one application at a time, however, you find the concept is natural.

Many businesses now use Windows applications to build information reporting and analysis systems that previously required mainframes. You can download mainframe or widespread data to a network server or to a personal computer, and then applications such as Microsoft Excel or Lotus 1-2-3 for Windows can import and analyze the data. If you save these results to previously used file names, the results are linked into reports created in Word for Windows or Ami Pro. You usually need only recorded macros that make the printing easier to handle.

To learn more about embedding and linking between applications, refer to Chapter 6. To learn more about macros and Dynamic Data Exchange, refer to specific application books by Que. The KnowledgeBase that is part of the Microsoft Connection forum on CompuServe also contains articles on using DDE with different macro languages. (You can access the forum by typing GO MSOFT at the CompuServe prompt.) Search on your application, narrow the search to DDE, and then read or download the articles you find.

Running DOS Applications

When you use Windows, you don't need to give up MS-DOS applications. In fact, you will find that Windows adds new dimensions to MS-DOS applications.

With Windows, you can load more than one application, whether the applications are DOS applications or Windows applications. In 386-enhanced mode, you can run multiple DOS and Windows applications simultaneously. In standard mode, you can run multiple Windows applications simultaneously. You can copy text or graphics from one DOS application and paste the text into another DOS application or paste text or graphics into a Windows application. In 386-enhanced mode, you can run DOS applications in a window just like a Windows application. In 386-enhanced mode, multiple DOS and Windows applications can continue working, even when in the background (not in the topmost window).

NOTE In standard mode, all DOS applications run in a full-screen display; a DOS application cannot run within a window. Windows doesn't try to multitask DOS applications. Instead, only one DOS application is active in memory at any one time. Until closed or until you switch back to Windows, the DOS application receives all the computer's resources. Although constantly monitoring the activities of the DOS application, Windows doesn't interfere with the application's use of computer resources. If you return to Windows without first quitting the DOS application, Windows suspends all further activity within this DOS application until you return to it.

In 386-enhanced mode, Windows can multitask DOS applications. When multitasking, each application that runs shares a portion of computer resources by taking advantage of the 80386 and 80486 processor's capability of making *virtual* computers (or simulating two or more computers within your machine). Each DOS application receives a portion of memory and a portion of processing power. In 386-enhanced mode, the computer has more memory than when running with DOS. In 386-enhanced mode, Windows treats all memory—conventional, extended, and virtual (disk based) memory—as one large pool of memory. When a DOS application makes a request for a block of conventional memory, Windows satisfies this request by giving the application a block of memory from the *pool*. A DOS application running in 386-enhanced mode shares both memory and CPU time with all other active applications and now is one application among many sharing the computer's resources, which Windows governs. You can run DOS applications in 386-enhanced mode in either a window or as a full-screen display.

When you start a DOS application, Windows looks for the Program Information File (PIF) for the application. A PIF is a file that provides Windows with the information needed to run the DOS application. PIFs contain information, such as how much memory the application needs and what video mode is required. If Windows finds the PIF, the information within this file is used rather than the standard settings in the default PIF. Many popular DOS applications can use the default PIF without a problem. By default, PIFs are created for most DOS applications during installation.

If you dislike the configuration used in the default PIF settings, you can use the PIF Editor to create or modify existing PIFs. Chapter 24, "Customizing PIFs," describes how to create and modify PIFs.

Understanding How Windows Handles DOS Applications

Windows manipulates memory, applications, and disk storage to load or run multiple Windows and DOS applications simultaneously. If you understand how this process works, you can get better performance from the computer.

Running DOS Applications in a Window or a Full Screen

Windows runs in two different modes: standard and 386-enhanced. The mode used depends upon the computer processor and available memory. In 386-enhanced mode, Windows runs DOS applications either in a window or full screen. In standard mode, you can run DOS applications only in full-screen display. In standard mode, you can start with one DOS application and switch to another application, but Windows suspends DOS and Windows applications that are not displayed.

In 386-enhanced mode, you can have multiple DOS applications running in separate windows or on full-screen and switch quickly between the applications. Figure 23.1 shows Lotus 1-2-3 Release 3.1 and WordPerfect 5.1, each running in separate windows.

Applications designed for Windows or DOS use memory differently. Windows distributes memory efficiently among Windows applications because Windows applications use memory cooperatively. DOS applications, however, don't have the memory-management capabilities of Windows applications. Most DOS applications, unlike Windows applications, aren't designed for multitasking. A DOS application, due to design, *thinks* that it is the only application running and therefore hogs memory and CPU time and doesn't share data easily. In standard mode, you can multitask (run simultaneously) multiple Windows applications, but DOS applications will be suspended when a Windows application is active, and Windows applications will be suspended when a DOS application is active. Windows in 386-enhanced mode expands the horizons of a DOS application by controlling certain properties of the application, such as memory, CPU time, and video mode, and thereby gives DOS applications multitasking capabilities. In 386-enhanced mode, Windows can have both multiple Windows applications and multiple DOS applications active.

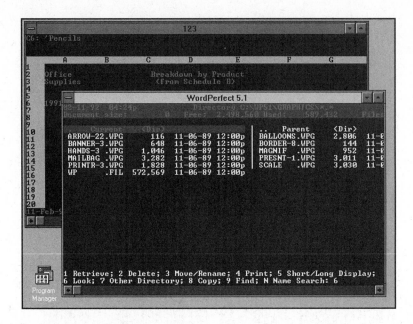

FIG. 23.1

Lotus 1-2-3 and
WordPerfect
in separate
windows in 386-
enhanced mode.

When a DOS application runs in a full screen under Windows, the computer display appears as though only the DOS application is running. Appearances, however, can deceive. Pressing Ctrl+Esc returns you to the Windows Task Manager, and you then can choose a different DOS or Windows application from the Task List. The Windows Task Manager lists all open applications. Windows keeps the DOS application open but shrinks the application to an icon at the bottom of the screen, similar to the icons shown at the bottom of figure 23.2.

If your DOS applications are running in a window in 386-enhanced mode and you press Ctrl+Esc, the Task List appears above the DOS application window. You can always switch to a DOS application by pressing Ctrl+Esc to display the Task List and then selecting the application. You also can press Alt+Tab to switch among applications.

During the Windows installation process, Setup builds Program Information Files (PIFs) for the DOS applications on which Setup has information. This setup information is stored in the APPS.INF file. When a PIF is created by Windows Setup, the file is created with full-screen mode selected as the default. To have a DOS application start in a window (in 386-enhanced mode only), use the PIF Editor to edit the application's PIF. Choose the **W**indowed option from the Display Usage group.

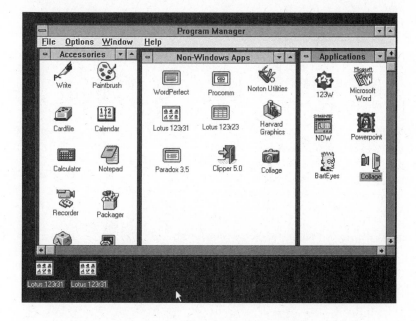

FIG. 23.2

DOS applications minimized to icons when not in use.

T I P

If you are running Windows in 386-enhanced mode and want to switch a DOS application between full screen and window modes, press Alt+Enter. Pressing Alt+Enter at any time toggles the display between full screen and windowed.

Loading More DOS Applications Than Memory Can Hold

In Windows, you can load multiple DOS applications, even if the combined applications use more memory than is available in the computer. In standard mode, when you start a DOS application, Windows creates a *temporary application swap file* for the application. The temporary application swap file is a reserved area on the hard disk for application information too large to fit in memory. When you switch from the application, Windows moves some or all of the DOS applications from memory to the temporary application swap file. This process makes the computer's available memory seem larger. When you exit the DOS application, Windows deletes this swap file.

T I P
You may not be able to load or switch from a DOS application if the hard disk lacks available storage space to create a temporary application swap file for the DOS application you want to load or from which you want to switch.

Windows doesn't use application swap files while running in 386-enhanced mode. Instead, in 386-enhanced mode, you must have sufficient extended memory to run all the DOS applications you load. This memory is necessary in 386-enhanced mode because each DOS application continues to run even when not in an active window. To run, applications must be in memory and not in a swap file on the hard disk. (If you need to run Windows in standard mode on your 80386 computer, start Windows by typing *WIN /S* at the DOS prompt. Chapters 25 and 26 describe special techniques to increase the memory available for DOS applications.

Because Windows in standard mode swaps parts of inactive DOS applications to and from memory and disk, the hard disk must have storage space available for the swap. If you have a fast disk or use SMARTdrive, a disk caching application that comes with Windows, you can significantly improve Windows' performance when running multiple applications. (SMARTdrive and other disk-performance enhancements are described in Chapters 25 and 26.)

DOS applications designed to use expanded memory still require expanded memory when running under Windows. In systems with an 80286 microprocessor, you must provide as much expanded memory as required by the application. You also must use an *expanded memory manager* to use this memory. Usually, you can tell if the computer has an expanded memory manager by looking for a reference to a file with a name such as REMM.SYS or CEMM.SYS in the CONFIG.SYS file.

In systems with an 80386 or 80486 microprocessor, Windows can emulate expanded memory, using extended memory. Because extended memory is much faster and more efficient than expanded memory, you should use only extended memory in 80386- and 80486-based systems. If you are using DOS applications that require expanded memory, use the *expanded memory manager*, EMM386.SYS, that comes with Windows, to emulate expanded memory from extended memory.

NOTE Even when running under Windows, DOS applications use the DOS screen and printer drivers. You must install the DOS application and the print and screen drivers as described in the application's installation instructions. The DOS application doesn't use the printer drivers available in Windows, nor does the application use the special printing features available through Windows, such as the Print Manager or the enhanced formatting capabilities of Windows applications.

Running the DOS Prompt in a Window

To run DOS commands (internal or external) from within Windows, choose the DOS Prompt icon from the Main group window in the Program Manager. The icon appears as the stacked letters MSDOS. Usually, the DOS prompt appears in a full screen when started. Figure 23.3 shows the DOS prompt running in a window. From the DOS prompt, you can issue DOS commands, such as DIR and FORMAT. To quit the DOS prompt, type *EXIT* and press Enter.

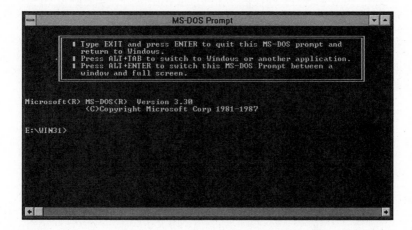

FIG. 23.3

Running the DOS prompt from Windows.

NOTE Never run a DOS command or application that modifies the hard disk while Windows is running, even from the DOS prompt window. Running the DOS command CHKDSK /f, for example, defragments the hard disk. However, this command destroys temporary files used by Windows. Use commands like CHKDSK /f only when Windows isn't running. If your system has DOS Version 5.0 installed, you cannot run CHKDSK /f, so you cannot accidently destroy the files used by Windows.

Running DOS Memory-Resident Applications

Some DOS applications are designed to load into memory simultaneously with other DOS applications. These *resident* applications then can be called up *over the top of* the active DOS application. These applications are referred to as *pop-up* or *terminate-and-stay-resident* (TSR) applications. One of the more familiar DOS TSR applications is SideKick.

DOS TSR applications aren't designed to run with Windows. TSRs were designed before Windows gave you the capability of running multiple applications.

If you must run a DOS TSR, start the TSR directly from Windows. You then can switch to and from the application as you switch between any DOS application. If necessary, create a PIF for the TSR application. (Refer to "Creating PIFs" in Chapter 24 for more information.)

Don't load a DOS TSR before you start Windows. Be aware that your AUTOEXEC.BAT file may load TSRs on start-up. You can use the Windows Notepad to open the AUTOEXEC.BAT file and remove TSRs (by placing the term *REM* at the start of the appropriate batch file lines).

If you load a TSR before you load Windows, you may not be able to access the TSR from the Windows desktop or from any Windows application. You also may be wasting memory. When you load a DOS TSR before loading Windows, the memory that the TSR occupies becomes unavailable to Windows. When you start a DOS TSR and then enter Windows in 386-enhanced mode, Windows reserves memory for the TSR each time you start a new DOS application or DOS prompt, which prevents Windows (and DOS applications) from using a large portion of the memory.

You can start the DOS TSR application by creating a program item icon for the TSR in Program Manager and then double-clicking the icon. You also can setup a PIF for the TSR so that the TSR *pops-up* with the same keystroke that activates the TSR in DOS. Some TSRs require a key combination that Windows reserves (such as Alt+Esc). Here, you must create a PIF by using the PIF Editor and select the Reserve **S**hortcut Keys option for this key combination. After you create the PIF and reserve the shortcut key, pressing this key combination activates the TSR application rather than performing the usual Windows function.

Depending on whether you are operating in standard or enhanced mode and whether you load the TSR from the Program Manager, using a program item icon, or from the DOS prompt, Windows behaves differently.

When you are operating in the standard or enhanced mode and load the TSR from the Program Manager, the TSR is loaded, and Windows displays a message that tells you to press Ctrl+C when you are finished using the TSR (see fig. 23.4). When you press Ctrl+C, Windows removes the TSR from memory and ends that DOS session, returning you to Windows. When you load the TSR from the DOS prompt while operating in standard mode, the TSR is loaded, but no message is displayed. To close the TSR and end the DOS session, you must type *EXIT* at the C: / prompt, which results in the message telling you to press Ctrl+C to return to Windows. When you load the TSR from the DOS prompt while operating in enhanced mode, again, the TSR is loaded but no message is displayed. To close the TSR and return to Program Manager, you must type *EXIT* at the C: / prompt, which immediately returns you to the Program Manager without you having to press Ctrl+C.

You also can switch to a TSR application using standard Windows methods rather than pressing the key combination that usually activates the application. Use the Task Manager to activate a TSR or press Alt+Tab until the TSR is activated and then release the Alt key.

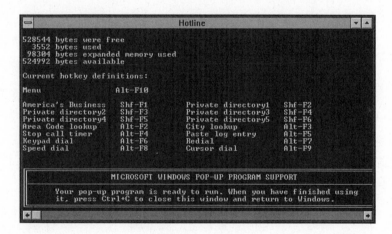

FIG. 23.4

The message Windows displays when a TSR is loaded.

Often, you may want to use a DOS TSR with a specific application, and therefore want the TSR to load only when the application loads. You can do this by creating a DOS batch file that loads the TSR and the DOS application. You then create a PIF that runs the batch file. Use the PIF Editor to create the PIF and put the batch file name in the **Program** filename text box of the PIF Editor.

Loading and Running DOS Applications

You can start DOS applications in four ways:

- Choose an application icon from a group window like the DOS Application group in the Program Manager.
- Choose the application file name from the directory window in the File Manager.
- Choose the application PIF name from the directory window in the File Manager.
- Choose Run from the File menu in the Program Manager or File Manager and then enter the path, file name, and all arguments for the application.

Because Windows must understand the special requirements of some DOS applications, however, Windows needs to use PIFs.

Understanding Why Windows Uses PIFs

When starting DOS application, Windows looks for an application's PIF. A PIF is a *program information file*. A PIF tells Windows how much memory the application requires and how the application interacts with the keyboard and screen. If a PIF cannot be found for an application, Windows starts the application with standard default settings. Most DOS applications run correctly when using these standard settings. Many DOS applications don't need special PIFs. If a DOS application doesn't run correctly or as you prefer when using the default PIF or the PIF created by Windows, then create or modify the application's PIF with the PIF Editor, supplied with Windows.

Usually, you can start a DOS batch file (a file with the extension BAT) as you start any DOS application. Windows also runs DOS applications started and controlled by a batch file. Occasionally, DOS applications may not run when started from a batch file under Windows because the combined memory requirements of the batch file and the application exceed the memory limits set by the application's PIF. Here, create a

PIF for the batch file and increase the memory required in the application PIF to make room for the batch file. If you create a PIF for a batch file, give the PIF the same name as the batch file; for example, call the two files DOWNLOAD.BAT and DOWNLOAD.PIF. See Chapter 24, "Customizing PIFs," for more information on PIFs.

Starting a DOS Application from the Program Manager

You can install DOS applications in Windows during the initial Windows installation process or at a later time. If you install DOS or Windows applications at a later time, you may want to run the Windows Setup application from the Main group of the Program Manager. Running Windows Setup to install applications is described in detail in the appendix.

When you use Setup to install a DOS application and the SETUP.INF file contains information on that application, Setup creates and adds an application icon to the DOS Application group. If a DOS Application group doesn't exist, Setup creates one. Setup also installs a PIF for the application in the WINDOWS directory.

You can start a DOS application from a program group window in the Program Manager by choosing the application icon in the same way you start Windows applications—double-click on the icon or press an arrow key to select the icon and then press Enter. Starting applications from icons is described in detail in Chapter 4, "Controlling Applications with the Program Manager." Figure 23.5 shows the WordPerfect application icon selected in the DOS Applications group in the Windows Program Manager. In this figure, the four DOS applications have different icons. Chapter 4 also explains how to select alternative icons to represent program items you create or modify.

Starting a DOS Application from the File Manager

You can start a DOS application by choosing either the application or PIF from the Windows File Manager. Select the application file (or PIF) and press Enter or double-click on the file name. Application file names are recognizable because the file extensions are COM, EXE, or BAT. Figure 23.6 shows the WordPerfect file name, WP.EXE, in the WP51 directory. The lower directory window shows the PIF that starts WordPerfect, WP.PIF, in the Windows directory. You can start WordPerfect by double-clicking on either the PIF or the WP.EXE file.

Do Not Run Applications That Modify the File Allocation Table From Windows, don't run any utility or application that modifies files or the File Allocation Table (FAT). Utilities you should not use include applications used to unerase or undelete files and those that defragment or compact the disk. When they run, such applications modify temporary files that Windows leaves open for its own use. If these temporary files are destroyed or modified, Windows may freeze, and you may lose data. You may even need to reinstall Windows. Such applications are very useful, but they must be run from the DOS prompt without Windows running.

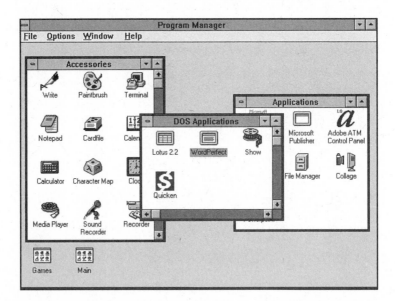

FIG. 23.5

Starting the
WordPerfect
application from
the icon.

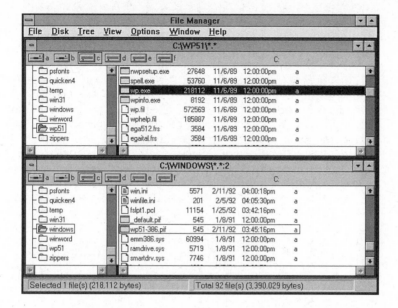

FIG. 23.6

You can start DOS applications from either the filename or PIF in the File Manager.

Customize PIFs To Run Applications with Different Settings

If you start applications by choosing the PIF rather than the application file, you can create a different PIF for different start-up requirements. Each PIF starts the same application but with different Windows or application parameters. Suppose that you want to start WordPerfect 5.1 with the /m-*macroname* parameter so that WordPerfect runs the macro specified by *macroname*. You can type the following command at the DOS prompt:

WP /M-*MACRONAME*

You can enter this start-up command and the argument in the **O**ptional Parameters text box of the PIF Editor when you create the WordPerfect PIF. If you start WordPerfect this way, the *macroname* macro runs when WordPerfect starts. This macro may load documents or change default settings. You also may want to run WordPerfect with large memory limits when working on a book and want WordPerfect to run faster, or you may need to run WordPerfect with minimum memory limits to run WordPerfect alongside other applications in Windows standard mode.

You can create different PIFs to handle these scenarios; to start WordPerfect with one of the sets of options, just select the PIF that contains the desired options. You can create program item icons in the Program Manager for each of these PIFs—making it easy to access the application using the different settings. To learn how to create a program item for a PIF, see Chapter 24.

Controlling DOS Applications

Windows adds a great deal of power to your work, even if you don't run Windows applications. You can run, and switch between, multiple DOS and Windows applications. If you work with DOS applications, this feature enables you to copy a table of numbers from Lotus 1-2-3 and paste them into WordPerfect, or you can copy a number from accounting or checkbook applications, such as Quicken, and paste into Lotus 1-2-3. You can copy and paste information, minimize and maximize the application, and move the window or icon. The time savings you gain definitely makes using Windows with DOS applications worthwhile.

Switching among Applications

Windows uses the same key combinations to switch among all applications, whether they are Windows or DOS applications.

The following table highlights ways in which you can switch among DOS applications:

To switch, press	when DOS applications are...
Alt+Tab	full-screen or windowed. Each application's title bar appears. Releasing keys displays the application.
Alt+Enter	full-screen or windowed. Each windowed or full-screen application appears.
Ctrl+Esc	full-screen or windowed. This displays a Task List of all applications running. Choose the desired application.
Double-click on window	windowed. Click on background window to make window active in foreground.

To switch from an active DOS application to another application, take the following steps:

1. Press and hold down the Alt key and press Tab. Keep holding down Alt and pressing Tab until the window or title bar of the application you want to activate appears.

2. Release Alt.

If the DOS application is running in a window, a blank window or icon with a title appears each time you press Alt+Tab. When the title appears for the application you want, release Alt. By showing only the titles and empty windows as you press Alt+Tab, Windows can switch quickly among applications.

If the DOS application is running in a full screen, a title bar appears at the top of the screen. Each time you press Alt+Tab, the title bar of another application appears. Release Alt when you see the title bar of the desired application. The selected application becomes active.

You also can switch among applications by pressing Alt+Esc. This procedure takes longer if you have multiple applications in Windows. Pressing Alt+Esc immediately activates the next application, which may not be the one you want. Activating this application takes time. After the application is active and the screen is drawn, you must again press Alt+Esc to activate the next application. A faster method is to press Alt+Tab until you see the title of the application you want.

You also can switch to the Task Manager by pressing Ctrl+Esc. After the Task List appears, you can choose the application you want to activate from the list.

Some DOS applications occasionally suspend the keyboard. During these times, using Alt+Tab, Alt+Esc, or Ctrl+Esc may not work. To switch back to Windows, return to the application's standard operating mode (this action may require pressing Esc) and then press Alt+Tab or Ctrl+Esc. If you are displaying a graph in 1-2-3 Release 2.01, for example, press Esc to return to the spreadsheet or menu and then press Alt+Tab.

If you are running Windows in 386-enhanced mode and have DOS applications in windows, you can click the mouse from window to window. Position the windows on-screen so that each window is seen and switch between them.

Printing and DOS Applications

Windows and DOS applications work differently when printing under Windows. When you print from Windows applications and have the Print Manager enabled, scheduled multiple print jobs print without conflict. DOS applications, however, are a different story. Written for a single-tasking environment, DOS applications expect to have exclusive rights to the printer. Furthermore, these applications aren't written for

Windows and therefore don't use the Print Manager. This limitation is no problem if you are running in standard mode where Windows applications are suspended while working in a DOS application. In 386-enhanced mode, however, where you can multitask a mix of Windows and DOS applications, the potential for conflict exists—two or more applications attempting to print to the same printer at the same time.

 NOTE When printing directly to a network printer queue, most of these conflicts are avoided, because the Print Manager is disabled, and the network handles the scheduling of print jobs from both DOS and Windows applications.

Windows handles these conflicts by letting you decide whether printing continues in the Windows application or in the DOS application. If you are in 386-enhanced mode and you try to print from a DOS application—and Windows already is printing—Windows displays a Device Conflict message box. The message box informs you that the applications have conflicted with Windows. You then must assign the printer to Windows or to the DOS application. If you assign the printer to Windows, printing continues with the Windows applications and the DOS application receives a printer not ready message, which prevents it from printing. If you assign the printer to the non-Windows application, the Print Manager suspends printing from the Windows application until you exit the DOS application. The Print Manager then continues from the point where the conflict began.

You can turn off the Device Conflict error message. To turn off the message, open the 386 Enhanced icon from the Control Panel in the Main Group. Select the **N**ever Warn option for the printer communications port you are using. To control device contention, follow these steps:

1. From the Main program group in the Program Manager, open the Control Panel.

2. From the Control Panel, choose the 386 Enhanced icon.

3. From the **D**evice Contention list, select the port that may have a problem (almost always COM1).

4. Select the way you want Windows to handle a device contention:

Option	Description
Always Warn	Displays a message when a problem arises. You are given the opportunity to select which application has priority over the port. Generally, you should select this option.

Option	Description
Never Warn	Enables any DOS application to use the port at any time. This option can cause contention problems.
Idle	Enables the port to remain idle the number of seconds you specify (1 to 999) before the next application can use the port without the warning message appearing. Select if an application pauses between printing, such as a 1-2-3 print macro that prints multiple but separate pages or a communication application that logs onto a database, downloads information, and then logs on a second time for more information.

5. Choose OK.

Using the DOS Application Control Menu

In 386-enhanced mode, all DOS applications have an application Control menu similar to Windows applications. Use the application Control menu to copy and paste information, to minimize and maximize the application, and to control the application's use of system resources.

Whether the DOS application is in a window or full-screen, you can activate the Control menu by pressing Alt+space bar. If the DOS application is in a window, you also can activate the Control menu by clicking on the Control menu bar to the left of the window title. The Control menu is shown in figure 23.7.

If you activate the Control menu when the application is full-screen, Windows puts the application into a window and then brings up the Control menu. The applications don't appear in a standard size window. WordPerfect 5.1, for example, appears in a half-screen window, and Lotus 1-2-3 Release 3.1 appears in a full-screen window.

On the Control menu, you see the commands to Restore, Move, or Size a DOS application window. Of course, because the application is in a window, you also can accomplish these tasks by using the mouse. The Minimize and Maximize commands shrink the application to an icon or expand an icon to a window or full screen. Because the application's icon also has a Control menu, you can restore or move the icon just as you manipulate a windowed or full-screen application. The Close and Edit commands are described in a following section of this chapter.

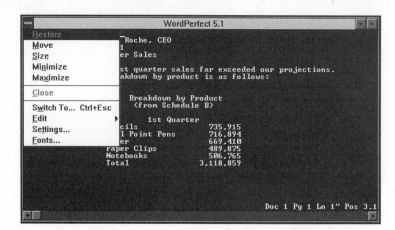

FIG. 23.7

The application
Control menu
for a DOS appli-
cation.

Changing Font Size in DOS Application Windows

You can make a DOS application easier to read by changing the size of
the font used in a DOS application window. To be in a window, you
must run the DOS application in 386-enhanced mode. To change the
font size, take the following steps:

1. Choose the DOS application Control menu by clicking on it or by
   pressing Alt and then the space bar.

2. Select the Fonts command. The Font Selection dialog box appears
   as shown in figure 23.8.

3. From the Font list, select a font size.

   The Window Preview and Selected Font boxes show you how the
   font looks on-screen.

4. To save this size for the next time you run this application, select
   the Save Settings on Exit check box.

5. Choose OK.

Changing the font size doesn't affect how a DOS application prints or
operates but only helps you to make the DOS application more readable when working in a window.

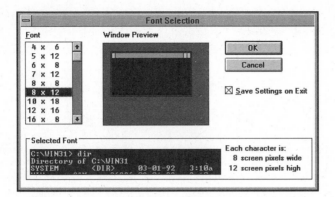

FIG. 23.8

Use the Font Selection dialog box to character size in a DOS window.

Setting Up DOS Applications for 386-Enhanced Mode

When you run Windows in 386-enhanced mode, you can run a DOS application in a window. You can multitask DOS applications with both DOS applications and Windows applications. Some issues may arise, however, when you decide how DOS applications share computer power and communications ports with Windows applications.

Controlling Processor Sharing between DOS and Windows Applications

If you run multiple applications at the same time in 386-enhanced mode and each application uses part of the processor's calculating power, the performance of all the applications diminishes. With the 386 Enhanced program in the Control Panel, however, you can specify how much processor time all Windows applications share in relation to all DOS applications.

To schedule different amounts of processing power between Windows and DOS applications, follow these steps:

1. Open the Control Panel from the Main group window in the Program Manager.

2. Choose the 386 Enhanced icon from the Control Panel. (This icon appears only when you are in 386-enhanced mode.)

The 386 Enhanced dialog box appears (see fig. 23.9).

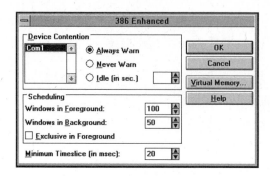

FIG. 23.9

The 386
Enhanced
dialog box.

3. Select one of the following Scheduling options:

Option	Use
Windows in **F**oreground:	Controls proportion of processor resources allocated to Windows applications when a Windows application is in the active window. Type a larger number than in the Window in **B**ackground box for more processing power for the Windows application in the active window. Use a number from 1 to 10,000. Usually, you want this number to be much larger than in the Windows in **B**ackground box so that the active Windows application operates faster and doesn't keep you waiting.
Windows in **B**ackground:	Controls proportion of processor resources allocated to Windows applications when no Windows application is active. Type a larger number than in the Windows in **F**oreground box to add more processing power to the Windows applications in the inactive windows. Use a number from 1 to 10,000. (This selection slows down the performance in the window in which you are currently working.)

Option	Use
Exclusive in Foreground:	Ensures that Windows applications always receive 100 percent of the processing time when a Windows application is in the active window. This selection puts on hold inactive DOS applications.

4. Choose OK.

If you work mostly with Windows applications, and the DOS applications rarely need to work rapidly when inactive, check either the **Exclusive in Foreground** check box or set a high number in the Windows in Foreground box.

In a PIF, you can control the multitasking settings for an individual DOS application. These settings control how the application multitasks with other DOS applications. You control these settings through the Advanced Options Multitasking Options in a PIF. See Chapter 24 for more information on the 386-enhanced multitasking options for an individual application.

Using a Mouse in DOS Applications

If the DOS application supports a mouse and the Windows 3.1 mouse driver is loaded, you can use the mouse normally when the application is running in a full screen. You can do all the things the application usually enables you to do with a mouse—bring up menus, select objects, and so on. If the DOS application is in a window (386-enhanced mode), the mouse is under Windows control, and the application cannot use the mouse to bring up a menu or select objects. You can use the mouse, however, to select areas to copy or to choose commands from the Control menu.

A DOS application that doesn't support a mouse still can use a mouse for some Windows features when the application is running in a window. You can use the mouse to select areas to copy or to choose commands from the Control menu.

Scrolling in DOS Application Windows

While a DOS application is in a window, you can use the mouse as you do with any window, to click on the minimize and maximize buttons at the top right or to resize the window by dragging an edge. When an application is too small to appear on the normal application screen, vertical and horizontal scroll bars appear. You can use keystrokes or the mouse to scroll the window and display the DOS application screen. You cannot scroll to see more than usually appears on a single screen. With the mouse, you also can select areas of a DOS text or graphics screen to be copied.

When you run a DOS application in a window, the Control menu includes a Scroll command. This command enables you to scroll with the keyboard. The Scroll command is a menu choice from the Edit command. You use this command to see parts of the file that cannot fit on-screen. This command scrolls the application's full screen of information in the window. You cannot scroll the window over more information than appears in the application's normal DOS screen.

To scroll with the keyboard, select the Control menu by pressing Alt+space bar, select Edit, and then choose the Scroll command. The window title changes to show that you are in Scroll mode; if you are in WordPerfect and the window title is WordPerfect, the window title changes to Scroll WordPerfect. Now press the arrow keys, PgUp, PgDn, Home, or End to scroll the window. When you finish scrolling, press Esc or Enter to exit scrolling mode.

Copying and Pasting Information between Applications

When you run DOS applications under Windows, you can copy and paste information among applications. Chapter 22, "Using Windows Applications Together," gives examples of how copying and pasting information between applications can be useful and productive. Although you can copy and paste with DOS applications, such as Lotus 1-2-3 for DOS and WordPerfect 5.1 for DOS, you don't have the more powerful features of Windows available, such as a common menu system, linked data, or embedded objects.

DOS applications running under Windows can use the Windows Clipboard. This feature enables you to copy data from a DOS application to a Windows application, from a Windows application to a DOS application, or between two DOS applications. Windows keeps the copied information in the same Clipboard used by all Windows applications; once copied, you then can paste the information into a Windows or DOS application.

> **Copying and Pasting DOS Graphics May Give Varying Results**
> Some DOS applications handle screen graphics in nonstandard
> ways. This limitation may make capturing the contents of a screen
> in graphics mode difficult or impossible. You may find that the
> color palette changes or text characters, for example, disappear
> when copied from a DOS application and pasted into another ap-
> plication. However, you can capture full or partial screens of
> many applications, which then can be pasted into Windows appli-
> cations, such as Windows Write, Ami Pro, Word for Windows,
> Microsoft Excel, Aldus PageMaker, or Aldus Freehand. Most DOS
> and Windows applications can copy and paste text and numeric
> data indiscriminately, if the receiving application is in a mode that
> can receive the text or numbers you type.

Copying or Capturing DOS or Windows Screens

When you are running in 386-enhanced mode, you can copy either a full
or partial screen of text or a full-screen graphic from a DOS application.
In standard mode, you can copy only a full screen of text or a full
graphic. DOS applications can receive pasted text but are incapable of
receiving pasted graphics. Windows applications can receive pasted
text and Windows applications designed to work with graphics can
receive pasted graphics.

Copying or Capturing a Full Screen

To capture a text or graphics screen, press the PrtScrn (Print Screen)
key. The entire display is copied to the Clipboard, and you then can
paste the image into other applications or save the image with the Clipboard Viewer (found in the Main window of the Program Manager).
With some keyboards, you need to use Shift+PrtScrn rather than
PrtScrn to capture the entire display.

If the screen is a DOS text application, such as a Lotus 1-2-3 worksheet
or a WordPerfect document, you capture the information as text characters that you can paste as text into other applications. If the screen is
a DOS graphic or a Windows application, the screen is captured as a
bit-map graphic, which can be pasted into Windows applications that
accept bit-map graphics.

T I P Capture full Windows or DOS application screens with the PrtScrn key and paste them into applications, such as Word for Windows, Ami Pro, or Aldus PageMaker as a way of quickly producing polished documentation or training materials.

To see exactly what you copy to the Clipboard, start the Clipboard Viewer from the Main program group. Maximize the window to see the entire copied contents. As you view the Clipboard contents, notice that all the text from the screen was copied, including text from the application's work area, any displayed menu names and filenames, the cursor position, column letters and row numbers (if you happen to copy a spreadsheet), and any text in the background. Figure 23.10 shows the contents of the Clipboard Viewer after a full screen capture of Lotus 1-2-3 Release 3.1, which was running in a window. Because the full screen was captured, you can see the Program Manager with the program icons in the background.

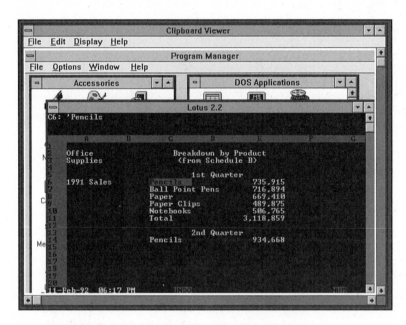

FIG. 23.10

The Clipboard Viewer displays or saves screens that you capture.

Copying or Capturing a Partial Screen

You can capture only the active window in 386-enhanced mode by pressing Alt-PrtScrn. If PrtScrn or Alt-PrtScrn doesn't work, these key combinations probably are reserved as shortcuts in an application's PIF. In standard mode, because you are able to view a DOS application only as a full screen, PrtScrn, Shift-PrtScrn, and Alt-PrtScrn perform the same copy process. See Chapter 24 for more information on PIF reserved keys.

In 386-enhanced mode, to copy a partial screen of text or graphics by using the mouse, follow these steps:

1. Activate the DOS application. If the application doesn't display in a window, press Alt+Enter.

2. Position the application screen in the window to show the information you want to copy.

3. Click on the Control menu at the top left corner and choose the **E**dit **Mark** command.

4. Drag the mouse across the rectangular area you want to copy. Drag past an edge to scroll the window to the limit of the DOS screen.

5. Click on the Control menu at the top left and choose the **E**dit Cop**y** command.

To copy a partial screen of graphics or text characters by using the keyboard, follow these steps (386-enhanced mode only):

1. Activate the DOS application. If the application doesn't appear in a window, press Alt-Enter to make the application appear.

2. Position the application screen in the window to show the information you want to copy.

3. Press Alt+space bar to show the Control menu.

4. Select the **E**dit command and then choose **Mark** (see fig. 23.11).

   A rectangular cursor appears at the top left corner of the application screen. This cursor is used to select the screen area you want to copy.

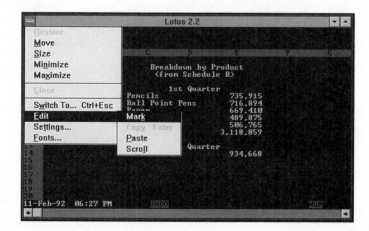

FIG. 23.11

Preparing to mark an area to copy.

5. Press the arrow keys to move the cursor to the top left corner of the rectangular area you want to copy.

6. Press and hold down Shift and press the arrow keys to select a rectangular area that contains the information you want to copy. Figure 23.12 shows a block of cells selected in the Lotus 1-2-3 application.

   You can undo the selection and return to regular Windows operation by pressing Esc.

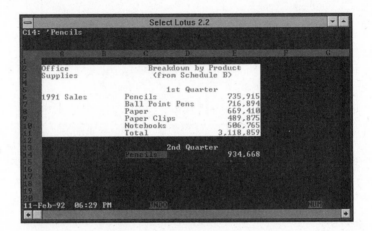

FIG. 23.12

An area marked for copying.

7. Press Alt+space bar again to display the Control menu. Choose the **E**dit **C**opy command.

T I P After you begin making a selection in the DOS application window, the title bar changes to *Select APPLICATION_NAME.* While in selection mode, you cannot paste, enter data, or use this application's menu. To exit selection mode, press the Esc key.

When you finish these steps, you have copied the marked text or graphics into the Windows Clipboard. You can paste text in the Clipboard into any Windows or DOS application when the application is in a mode in which you can type text. You can paste Graphics into Windows applications designed to receive graphics through the Clipboard.

> **Switch DOS Applications between Windowed and Full-Screen Views**
>
> To switch a DOS application between full-screen and windowed views while in 386-enhanced mode, press Alt+Enter. In full-screen view, the application displays as you see the application running under DOS. When the application is in a window, you can use the application as you do in DOS, but you also can change the size of the screen font and use the Windows Control menu to copy and paste.

After you either copy or capture text or graphics to the Clipboard, you can save this image or data as a file. This capability enables you to paste the image or data at a later date or send a file of copied data to an associate. If you don't save the image or data, when you next copy or capture a screen, the new image or data overwrites the current Clipboard contents. When you exit Windows, the Clipboard also is erased. You save the current clipping by starting the Clipboard Viewer from the Main program group in the Program Manager. Choose the File Save As command and enter a filename to save the current clipping. The File Save As dialog box is shown in figure 23.13. Type in the file name under which you want to save this file; note that the file is given the extension CLP. This clipping file can be retrieved by any other Clipboard Viewer so that the contents can be pasted into an application.

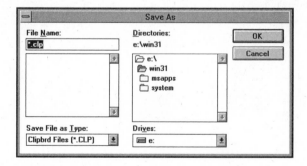

FIG. 23.13

The Clipboard Viewer File Save As dialog box.

Pasting Data into DOS Applications

Now paste the text or graphic from the Clipboard into the Windows or DOS application by following these steps:

1. Switch to the DOS or Windows application in which you want to paste.

2. Move the application's cursor to the location where you want the top left corner of the pasted data. (This is the application's normal cursor.)

3. If the application is a Windows application, choose Edit **P**aste. If the application is a DOS application, press Alt+space bar to display the Control menu and then choose Edit **P**aste.

Figure 23.14 shows the results of pasting a 1-2-3 worksheet into WordPerfect. When pasting text into a DOS application, such as WordPerfect, notice that the space between Lotus 1-2-3 columns is filled with space characters. If the receiving application uses proportional fonts, you may find that columns of text and numbers do not align correctly. If this happens insert tabs to align the columns.

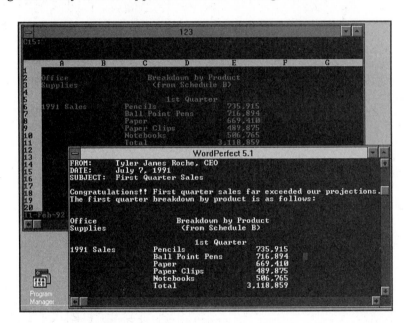

FIG. 23.14

A 1-2-3
worksheet pasted
in a WordPerfect
document.

Copying Clears the Previous Copy from the Clipboard
Making a copy removes the previous copy from the Clipboard. If you don't make another copy or clear the Clipboard, you can paste the information you copied more than once. You can view the Clipboard contents by opening the Clipboard Viewer in the Main program group.

Applications Handle Multiple Pasted Lines Differently
DOS applications handle multiple lines of pasted data differently.
The difference is caused by how the application deals with the
carriage return at the end of a line. If you paste multiple lines of
data into a Lotus 1-2-3 file, all the lines paste in the same cell, each
over the top of the previous line. Therefore, paste one number
into one cell at a time into Lotus 1-2-3 for DOS. This problem, however, isn't true for other applications. When you paste a multiple-
line entry into Microsoft Excel, each line is pasted into a separate
cell. WordPerfect also accepts multiple lines of data. Each line of
data pastes into a new line in the WordPerfect document.

For Related Information:

▶▶ To learn more about the 386-enhanced multitasking options
for an individual application, see "Understanding PIF Editor
Options," p. 926.

FROM HERE...

Linking DOS and Windows Applications

You can exchange data between Windows and DOS applications by
copying and pasting; you also can exchange data by using a common
file format that both applications read or write.

Copying and pasting data with DOS applications is easier when you are
in 386-enhanced mode. In this mode, DOS applications can run in Windows, making switching between them easier, and making possible
selecting portions of the screen to copy and paste into another
application.

Linking Lotus 1-2-3 Spreadsheets to Microsoft Excel Worksheets

You may be using Microsoft Excel for Windows and others in your work
area may be using a DOS version of Lotus 1-2-3. Because Microsoft Excel can read and write Lotus 1-2-3 spreadsheets and can read 1-2-3

graphics, you can use Microsoft Excel to link or consolidate 1-2-3 worksheets or to enhance 1-2-3 printouts and charts.

The advantages of linking 1-2-3 spreadsheets to Microsoft Excel worksheets are many. You can create impressive graphs using Microsoft Excel; you can use Microsoft Excel's automatic database form; or you can create automated systems involving integrated Windows applications.

To link Lotus 1-2-3 spreadsheets to an Excel for Windows worksheet, you start by opening the 1-2-3 files, as described in the following steps:

1. Activate Microsoft Excel.

2. Choose the **File Open** command.

3. Select the directory where the 1-2-3 files are located from the **Directories** list box.

4. Change the filename pattern to *.WK? and choose OK so that you can see the list of Lotus 1-2-3 files.

5. Select the 1-2-3 spreadsheet with which you want to work. If the worksheet has attached graphs, Excel asks whether you also want to convert these files.

6. Repeat steps 2 through 5 until all the Lotus 1-2-3 spreadsheets you want to link are open.

Microsoft Excel opens Lotus 1-2-3 spreadsheets and graphs. Notice that the 1-2-3 spreadsheets appear in a document window in the same way as Microsoft Excel worksheets. 1-2-3 title bars show the WK3, WK2, or WK1 extension, which indicates the files are 1-2-3 spreadsheets.

You can link open 1-2-3 spreadsheets to an Excel worksheet. To link a 1-2-3 spreadsheet to an Excel worksheet, follow these steps:

1. Activate the 1-2-3 spreadsheet (so that the 1-2-3 spreadsheet is the top document window).

2. Select the cell or range of cells you want to link to an Excel worksheet.

3. Choose the **Edit Copy** command.

4. Activate the Microsoft Excel worksheet to receive the linked data.

5. Select the cell at the top left corner of the area where you want the linked data to appear.

6. Choose the **Edit Paste Link** command.

As shown in figure 23.15, the data from the 1-2-3 spreadsheets, QTR1.WK3 and QTR2.WK1, opened in Microsoft Excel can be linked or consolidated into a Microsoft Excel worksheet. When numbers change in the 1-2-3 spreadsheets, the link sends this change to the Microsoft Excel worksheet. After being linked, the 1-2-3 spreadsheets can be open or on disk for the link to remain. If one of the 1-2-3 files is later retrieved, changed, and saved in Lotus 1-2-3, you need only start Microsoft Excel and open the Microsoft Excel worksheet that contains the link for the new 1-2-3 data to be read in.

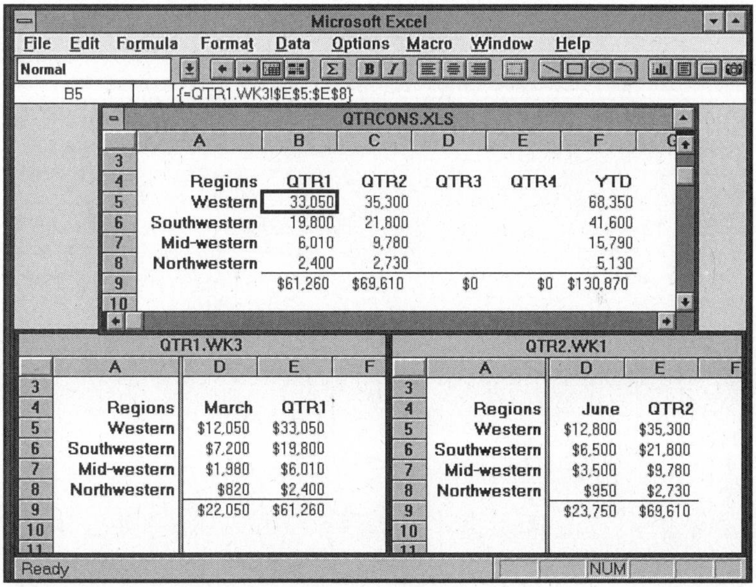

FIG. 23.15

Linking 1-2-3 spreadsheets into a Microsoft Excel worksheet.

Linked cells that contain blanks appear as zeroes (0) in the Microsoft Excel worksheet. You can hide zeroes throughout the Microsoft Excel worksheet by choosing the Options Display command and then selecting the Zero Values check box. Hide zeroes selectively by using a custom numeric format that contains no zero portion of the format, as shown in the following example:

$#,##0 ;($#,##0);

Because no format follows the second semi-colon, zeroes aren't displayed.

Use care if you save the 1-2-3 spreadsheet from Microsoft Excel. Microsoft Excel saves the worksheet back to the original 1-2-3 format. Microsoft Excel cannot save Excel's enhanced charts to 1-2-3 format because 1-2-3 has no equivalent. If you enhanced the 1-2-3 spreadsheet with Microsoft Excel formatting commands or used formulas or functions not available in 1-2-3, you lose these changes when you save the worksheet back to a 1-2-3 file. To keep the formatting and extra features, save the file in Microsoft Excel format by choosing the **F**ile Save **A**s command, choosing the **O**ptions (>>) button, and selecting **N**ormal format. Save the file with the same or with a different name.

Make sure that you either keep the 1-2-3 spreadsheet name the same or save the spreadsheet before you save the Microsoft Excel worksheet that contains the links. By first saving the 1-2-3 spreadsheet, Microsoft Excel knows the name of the spreadsheet that contains the data to be linked.

If you move or rename a linked 1-2-3 spreadsheet so that the Microsoft Excel worksheet cannot find the file, activate the Microsoft Excel worksheet that contains the links. Choose the **F**ile Links command, select the name of the spreadsheet that was moved or renamed, and choose the **C**hange button. Then type or select the name of the new 1-2-3 worksheet to be linked.

T I P   If you need to consolidate (roll-up) multiple Microsoft Excel or 1-2-3 worksheets, make sure that you learn about Microsoft Excel's **D**ata Co**n**solidate command. Data Consolidation enables you to total, average, count, or perform other statistics across ranges on multiple Microsoft Excel or 1-2-3 worksheets. The data on the different sheets can be located in different areas of the sheet, can use different item names, and can even have items in different ordering. Microsoft Excel matches item headings and totals, averages, or counts appropriate items and then builds a table that shows the result.

Linking 1-2-3 Spreadsheets into Word for Windows

Many Windows applications enable you to insert or link data from DOS applications. This capability enables you to incorporate DOS application data into documents from Windows applications. The following example uses Word for Windows to demonstrate how many Windows applications can read and convert files from DOS applications. The receiving Windows application may even be able to link to a DOS application file. Linking enables you to quickly update a Windows document when data in a DOS application file changes.

Although you can use the copy and paste techniques described previously to copy spreadsheet data to a word processor, a better way is available. In Word for Windows, you can link all or a portion of a Lotus 1-2-3 file to a Word for Windows document. When the worksheet changes, the word processing document can be easily updated.

The 1-2-3 file which you want to link to must be on disk. To link 1-2-3 spreadsheet data from disk to a Word for Windows document, take the following steps:

1. In the Word for Windows document, position the insertion point where you want the spreadsheet data to appear.

2. Choose the Insert File command.

3. From the File Name list, select the 1-2-3 worksheet file.

4. In the Range text box, type the range name or range reference (cell addresses) you want to insert.

5. If you want a link to the file so that you can update the data on request, select the Link to File check box. If you want to bring in the data without a link to the file, don't select the Link check box.

6. Choose OK or press Enter.

The 1-2-3 spreadsheet data is inserted into the Word for Windows document.

If you selected the Link check box and the spreadsheet data in the 1-2-3 file changes, you can update the Word for Windows document by selecting the linked data and pressing the Update Field key, F9. Word for Windows rereads and reinserts the spreadsheet data.

Windows applications that have the capability of reading or writing other application files usually require converter or filter files. These files usually are installed during the application installation. If the Windows application doesn't show that it can link to DOS files, check to make sure that you installed the appropriate converters or filters.

Use Nonproportional Fonts To Align Columns from DOS Applications

If you paste text columns from a DOS application into a Windows application, the columns may no longer align. The reason for the misalignment probably is because the DOS applications use nonproportional fonts, and Windows applications use proportional fonts. With *proportional* fonts, different characters have different widths. With *nonproportional* fonts, such as Courier, all characters have the same width.

Repair this problem by using one of two techniques. One method is to insert tabs as needed in the rows and then align the columns on new tab settings. The second method is to format the pasted data in Courier or a similar nonproportional font. Because the characters again are the same width, the columns realign.

Sharing Data through Files

If you have large volumes of data to transport between applications, copying and pasting can be too slow. For large volumes of data, use a common file format to transfer information.

In the first of the following two examples, check-register data is exported from Quicken and imported into Microsoft Excel, where financial analysis can be performed and charts created. In the second example, Microsoft Excel chart is printed to disk to create a graph for use in WordPerfect 5.1 documents.

Usually, DOS applications come with a utility application that converts the data file to other formats. Most Windows applications have conversion capability built-in, but you need to make sure that the correct converters or filters are installed for the Windows application.

The following list shows some file formats. These aren't used as a native format by applications but are used as a *lingua franca*, or common language, for exchanging data between applications from different manufacturers. You often can use a file format, such as DBF for dBASE, that may be understood as a common format by the applications involved. The following table lists some file formats through which DOS and Windows applications can transfer data:

CSV, PRN	Comma Separated Values; commas and quotes separate *fields* of data; used to exchange spreadsheet and database data
DIF	Data Interchange Format; used to transfer text and numeric data between spreadsheets
RFT-DCA	IBM document exchange format; used to transfer word processing documents
RTF	Rich Text Format; used to transfer text and formatting between word processing documents
TXT	Text files; tabs used to separate values; use to transfer data between word processors, databases, and spreadsheets
TXT	Column delimited files; each field of data must be within specified character positions; used to transfer data between databases or databases and spreadsheets

Converting Quicken Checkbook Data into Microsoft Excel Spreadsheets

Certain text-file formats have become accepted as vehicles for transporting text and numeric data between incompatible PC applications, and even between PCs and mainframe databases. The following example shows how to transport data from the DOS version of Quicken, a popular check-register application, to Microsoft Excel where you can analyze or chart the data. This same technique and file format frequently is used to transfer data from a corporate mainframe to Microsoft Excel for analysis.

The file format used as the medium of exchange in this example is *Comma Separated Values* (CSV). CSV is one of the kinds of text files Microsoft Excel reads and directly imports into a worksheet. The file to be imported must end with the extension CSV so that Microsoft Excel knows which converter to use to read the file. In the file, text and numbers are separated by commas. Text or numbers that contain commas are enclosed in quotation marks (" "). The CSV format frequently is used to download mainframe data so that Microsoft Excel can read the file directly.

To create a CSV file from the Quicken application, follow these steps:

1. In Windows or from DOS, open Quicken and use the normal process to prepare a report for printing.

2. After choosing the kind of report you want to print, a line at the bottom of the screen prompts you to press F8 to print. Press F8.

3. Choose the Disk (1-2-3 File) option from the Print Report menu.

4. Type the name for the file. For example, type *QCKN2XCL*. Don't type a file extension.

5. To save the file, press Enter. Quicken saves the file with a PRN extension.

6. Exit from Quicken.

To create a Microsoft Excel file from the Quicken file, follow these steps:

1. Use the Windows File Manager to change the file's name from *QCKN2XCL.PRN* to *QCKN2XCL.CSV*.

2. Activate Microsoft Excel.

3. Choose the **File O**pen command and change to the directory that contains the QCKN2XCL.CSV file. If you didn't specify a directory when you saved the file in Quicken, look in the QUICKEN directory.

4. Change the File **N**ame text box to *.CSV* and choose OK to list all the files in the directory that have the extension CSV.

5. Select the QCKN2XCL.CSV file and choose OK.

   The file opens in a worksheet with each text title in a cell and each number in a cell.

6. Use this worksheet as you use any Microsoft Excel worksheet.

7. Save the worksheet in Microsoft Excel format by choosing the **F**ile Save **A**s command, choosing the **O**ptions button, and selecting Normal from the **F**ile Format drop-down list. Choose OK twice.

Importing Microsoft Excel Charts to WordPerfect

You cannot paste graphics into DOS applications. However, an alternative for transferring graphics from Windows applications to DOS applications is to create a graphics file that the DOS application *can* import. You can create a file that contains a Microsoft Excel chart that a DOS application—such as WordPerfect for DOS—can import.

To create a Microsoft Excel chart that WordPerfect can import, you first must set up Windows as though you plan to print the chart on an HP plotter. Rather than printing the chart to the plotter, however, you use the Control Panel to redirect the printing information to a disk file. The file created is a Hewlett Packard Graphics Language, HPGL, file. You then can import this file into WordPerfect. Setting up for this operation is as easy as adding a printer driver; you have to set up for the operation only once.

Begin by choosing the Printers icon from the Control Panel. Choose the **A**dd button and add an HP 7550A Plotter driver. (Chapter 7, "Customizing with the Control Panel," describes how to add new printers and plotters.) Use the original Windows installation disks to install the driver software. After you add the plotter driver, choose the **C**onfigure button and select *FILE:* from the **P**orts scrolling list. This selection instructs Windows to send the information to print to a disk file rather than to a printer or plotter port. Choose the **S**etup button before you exit from the Printers dialog box. Leave the plotter pen colors at the defaults but clear the **D**raft check box. Choose OK.

To create a Microsoft Excel chart that WordPerfect can import, choose the **F**ile P**r**inter Setup command and select *HP Plotter on FILE:*. Set the page layout and margins and then print. A dialog box appears, asking for a path name and file name for the file. You can give the file any file extension. The file created is an HPGL printer/plotter file. Many kinds of software and printers can read the HPGL file.

Import the Microsoft Excel chart file into WordPerfect for DOS by using WordPerfect's graphics-import procedures.

For Related Information:

◀◀ To learn more about adding printers and plotters, see "Adding and Configuring Printers," p. 277.

▶▶ To learn more about using DOS batch files with PIFs, see "Creating and Using PIFs," p. 915; "Customizing DOS Applications with Multiple PIFs," p. 946; and "Running DOS Batch Files," p. 946.

▶▶ See "Responding to an Application Failure," p. 1071.

Chapter Summary

In this chapter, you learned how to run and switch between DOS applications. The chapter also gave an introduction to how Windows accommodates DOS applications. You learned how to use copy and paste to transfer text and graphics between DOS and Windows applications. In instances where copying and pasting data is not appropriate, you learned how to transfer entire files.

Three chapters important for further understanding how to best run DOS applications under Windows are Chapters 24, 26, and 29. Chapter 24 describes how to modify PIFs to change how a DOS application runs under Windows. Chapter 26 describes methods that improve the performance of DOS applications when they run under Windows. If you have trouble getting DOS applications to run or operate as you suspect they should, turn to the troubleshooting sections in Chapter 29.

Customizing PIFs

A PIF (Program Information File) is a file that provides Windows with the information the program needs to run a DOS application. PIFs contain such information as how much memory the application needs and what video mode is required. Windows creates PIFs for most popular DOS applications. If Windows does not have the information on how to create a PIF for the DOS application, you can create your own PIF using the instructions in this chapter. This chapter also describes how to improve DOS application performance and how to modify PIFs to decrease the use of memory by DOS applications.

Creating and Using PIFs

When you start a non-Windows (DOS) application, Windows looks for a PIF designed for that application. If Windows finds the PIF, the application uses that information instead of the standard settings in the default PIF. Windows uses the default PIF, _DEFAULT.PIF, unless a specific application PIF is located.

You can set up a PIF in three ways:

- Have the Windows Setup application create a PIF for you.

■ Use or modify the default PIF.

■ Use the PIF that came with the DOS application.

T I P   PIFs created by the Windows Setup application are stored in the directory containing Windows. After they are created, you can move the PIF anywhere on disk. For example, you may want to locate the PIF for a particular application in that application's directory to reduce the number of files stored in the Windows directory.

The Windows Setup application creates a PIF for your DOS application when you first install Windows or when you run Windows Setup to install an application. Windows Setup searches your hard disk for the Windows applications and DOS applications listed in the APPS.INF file. Windows can create PIFs for any DOS applications listed in the APPS.INF file.

If an application PIF is not created or if an application does not come with a PIF, Windows uses the default PIF. If settings need to be changed in the default PIF so that the application works correctly with Windows, you can modify the default PIF by using the PIF Editor.

Many DOS applications provide a PIF. For example, when you install Lotus 1-2-3 Release 3.1, a 123.PIF is installed. Generally, you should use the PIF that comes with an application because its settings are optimized.

Creating a PIF with Windows Setup

The Windows Setup application is used when you initially install Windows to find and create PIFs and program item icons for applications on disk. You also can run the Windows Setup program at any later time to install applications you did not originally install. The Windows Setup program item icon is located in the Main group window.

When you use Windows Setup to install a DOS application, it creates and sets up a PIF for that application in the Windows directory (usually C:\WINDOWS). The Setup application searches the drives you specify and lists any applications it finds. Setup lists only the DOS applications that the APPS.INF file provides PIF information on. When you install Windows, APPS.INF is placed on your hard disk in the C:\WINDOWS \SYSTEM directory. APPS.INF contains the recommended settings for many of the most popular DOS applications. If an application is not listed in APPS.INF file, Windows does not provide a PIF for that application when SETUP is run.

NOTE The Windows Setup application reads the APPS.INF when it executes. APPS.INF is located in the SYSTEM directory underneath the directory in which you installed Windows.

APPS.INF contains a series of sections that provide the Windows Setup application with information. One section is the [pif] section. When you open APPS.INF in the Notepad and view the contents of the [pif] section, you see a list of DOS applications for which Setup can create PIFs. Each line in the list includes the name of a DOS application, the name of the application's executable file (EXE or COM), and several other settings. If a DOS application is not in this list, but the application is on your hard disk, Windows does *not* create a PIF for the application when Setup is run.

Windows makes creating PIFs easy if you use the Windows Setup application. Although most DOS applications run well using the default PIF, you may need more memory or a special feature available only if the application runs with a custom PIF. In that case, you can modify the PIF Windows Setup creates by using the PIF Editor.

To run Windows Setup and create a PIF after you have installed Windows, follow these instructions:

1. Activate the Main group window in the Application Manager.

2. Start the Windows Setup application. The Windows Setup dialog box appears.

3. Choose the **O**ptions **S**et Up Applications command.

4. Select Search for applications if you want Windows to search for applications on your hard disk(s).

   or

   Select Ask to specify an application option if you know the path and filename of a particular application you want to set up.

5. If you specified the Search for applications option, select the drive to search or choose to search the current path from the list box. Choose the **S**earch Now command.

   or

   If you selected to specify an application, type the application path and filename, select which program group to add a program item to, and choose OK.

6. If Windows cannot determine the application that matches an EXE or COM filename, you can select the application from a list of possible matches. For example, WP.EXE may be the EXE filename for more than one word processor.

7. When the Setup Applications dialog box appears, select from the list box on the left the DOS applications for which you want PIFs.

8. Choose the **A**dd button to add the applications to the list box on the right. Setup creates PIFs for these applications. Figure 24.1 shows the Setup Applications dialog box with two applications selected for setup.

Using the Setup Applications dialog box to set up applications in Windows.

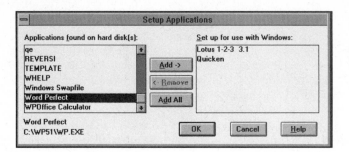

9. Choose OK if you want Windows to create PIFs for the DOS applications in the right list.

10. Close the Windows Setup window.

If you did not have a DOS Application group previously, Setup creates one for you. In addition to the PIF created and stored in the WINDOWS directory, Setup creates a program item icon to match your application.

If you select applications to be set up that already have been set up, you may get more than one program item icon for an application. To delete unwanted program item icons, select them in the Program Manager and press the Del key.

Open the DOS Application group in the Program Manager and run the added DOS application by choosing its program item icon. If the application does not run or does not run with a feature you desire (such as running in a window if you are in 386-enhanced mode), modify the PIF with the procedures described later in this chapter.

Creating a PIF by Dragging and Dropping

One of the easiest ways to create a PIF is through *dragging and dropping*. This easy technique works with DOS application files that Windows recognizes and for which Windows has PIF information.

To create a PIF and program item icon:

1. Arrange the Program Manager and File Manager side-by-side on-screen.

2. In the Program Manager, open the group window in which you want to create a program item icon.

3. In the File Manager, display the DOS application file for which you want to create a PIF.

4. Drag the application's file folder from the File Manager to the group window.

   If more than one DOS application uses that same file name, a scrolling list appears (see fig. 24.2).

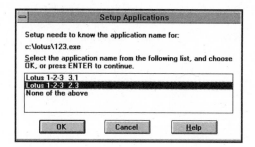

Windows asks you to select the application when applications have the same filename.

5. If the scrolling list appears, select the name of the DOS application and then choose OK.

In the group window where you released the file folder icon, a generic DOS application icon appears. If Windows cannot find an existing PIF for the application, it creates a PIF in the WINDOWS directory.

You can use the process described next to change the generic DOS icon to an icon designed for that application.

From the Program Item Properties dialog box, you can add a specific icon by completing the following steps:

1. Choose the Change **I**con button.

   The Change Icon dialog box appears.

2. In the **F**ile **N**ame box, type the name of the file containing icons and then choose OK. You also can use the **B**rowse button to search for files containing icons.

   Default icons are found in C:\WINDOWS\PROGMAN.EXE. Icons specifically designed for many DOS applications and generic tasks are found in C:\WINDOWS\MORICONS.DLL. Files that contain icons use the extensions EXE (for Windows applications), DLL, and ICO. Not all EXE or DLL files contain icons. You can buy libraries of icons as a file and save them to your WINDOWS directory for use with any application.

When you choose an icon file, the Current Icon list displays the icons available as shown in figure 24.3.

FIG. 24.3

Select application-specific icons from the MORICONS.DLL file.

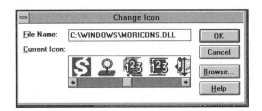

3. Choose an icon from the Current Icon list.

4. Choose OK twice.

If you already have created a program item icon for any Windows or DOS application, you can change the program item icon in the Program Manager by selecting the icon and then choosing the File Properties command. When the Program Item Properties dialog box appears, choose the Change Icon button and follow the previous steps.

Manually Creating a PIF

If you need to edit or create a PIF and want to have control over the settings, use the PIF Editor. The PIF Editor is located in the Accessories group if you installed Windows 3.1 over Windows 3.0. The PIF Editor is located in the Main group if you installed Windows 3.1 as a new application. The icon for the PIF Editor looks like a luggage tag.

T I P   Many popular DOS applications use the default PIF and run without a problem. However, in most cases, you want to create a PIF because the default PIF operates with settings that fit the widest range of applications. Creating a PIF specific to your DOS applications increases the applications' speed and improves their memory use when operating under Windows.

When you start the PIF Editor, a window displays a new, untitled PIF with the standard settings. Every PIF has two sets of options that match the different modes in which Windows runs. When you edit a PIF, you see the options available for the current Windows mode:

■ Standard mode options for running the application in standard mode

■ 386-enhanced mode options for running the application in 386-enhanced mode

Usually, the PIF Editor displays the PIF settings for the current mode in which Windows is running. You may want to select PIF options for a mode that is not the current Windows mode. For example, you may want to create a PIF for an application in standard mode, even though you currently are running Windows in 386-enhanced mode. To switch modes in the PIF Editor, choose the mode you want from the **M**ode menu.

The PIF Editor window changes slightly depending upon which mode is being displayed. Figure 24.4 shows the default settings of the PIF Editor window that appears when Windows is operating in standard mode; figure 24.5 shows the default settings of the PIF Editor window that appears when 386-enhanced is the current mode. The **A**dvanced button on the screen in 386-enhanced mode has a second window available for advanced options, shown in figure 24.6. Most PIF options apply only in the mode in which they are selected. To create a PIF, do the following:

1. Choose the PIF Editor from the Main group window in the Program Manager to start the application.

2. Fill in the appropriate text boxes and options as described in the section "Understanding PIF Editor Options."

3. Choose **F**ile **S**ave, name the file, and save it.

4. Choose **F**ile **N**ew to start a new PIF or choose **F**ile E**x**it to close the PIF Editor.

NOTE Before testing a PIF, close all other applications in Windows. If you encounter a problem, you can restart the computer without losing data in another application. After the application runs by itself, test it while running other applications.

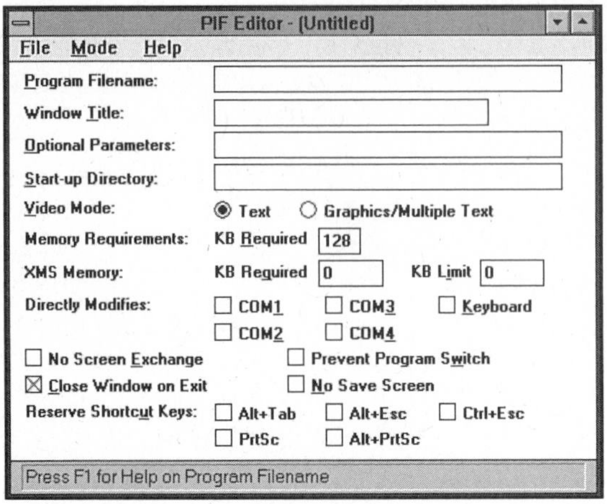

FIG. 24.4

The PIF Editor options and defaults for Windows in standard mode.

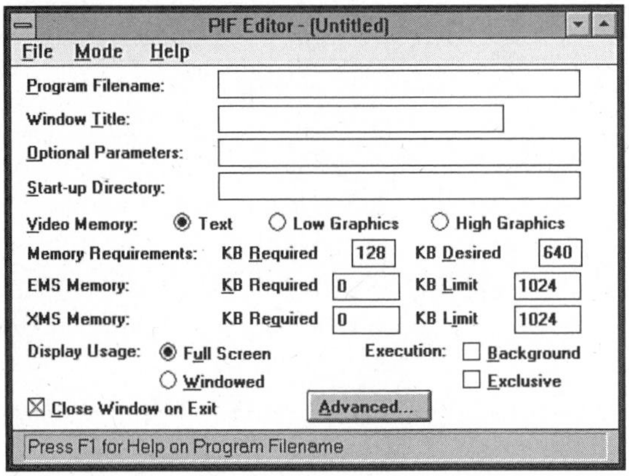

FIG. 24.5

The PIF Editor options and defaults for Windows in 386-enhanced mode.

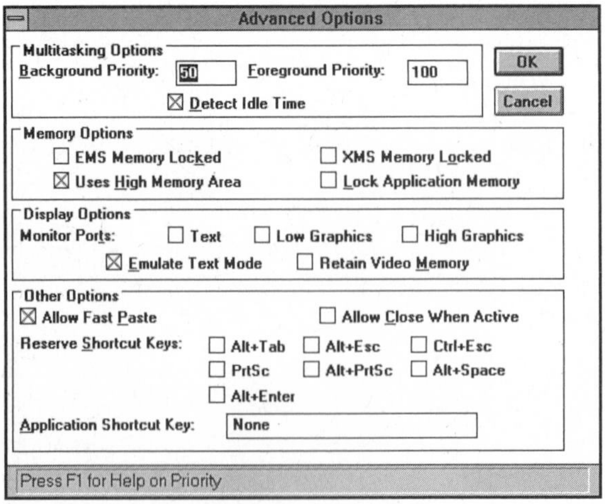

FIG. 24.6

The advanced PIF Editor options and defaults for Windows in 386-enhanced mode.

When you start a DOS application for which Windows cannot find a PIF, Windows starts the application using the default PIF options for the current mode. You can override these default options by modifying the default PIF. The default PIF is named _DEFAULT.PIF and is in the \WINDOWS\SYSTEM directory. For example, in 386-enhanced mode, Windows always starts DOS applications in full-screen mode. You can modify the _DEFAULT.PIF and change the Display Usage option so that applications start in a window instead of in a full screen.

Make sure that you make a backup copy of _DEFAULT.PIF before you modify it. If your new default PIF does not work as planned, you can return to the original default PIF settings by copying your backup file over the modified file.

When you change _DEFAULT.PIF, leave the Windows **T**itle option blank. You must provide a **P**rogram Filename, however, because the PIF Editor checks that this text box is filled before it enables you to save the PIF. Type *DEF.BAT* (you can use whatever program filename you like, but it must have an EXE, COM, or BAT extension) in the **P**rogram Filename box. Type over this program filename when you make a new PIF.

Editing a PIF

You may have to edit a PIF in the following circumstances:

- The application runs using the _DEFAULT.PIF, but it needs operating memory, or speed improvements.

- The application is in a different directory than the one listed in the Program Filename text box of the PIF.

- The Start-up Directory, which specifies the data directory, is different from the directory you want or the directory expected by the application.

- You want to start an application with a special parameter.

- You want to ensure that an application swaps to disk when not in use, freeing more memory for additional applications (the Prevent Program Switch option).

- An application has been upgraded and requires more memory or uses additional graphic memory.

924

Naming and Running Applications from a PIF

Before you edit a PIF, make a backup copy of the original PIF, using an extension such as PAK instead of PIF. If the edited PIF gives you trouble, return to the original settings by renaming the PAK file to PIF.

If you start the application by choosing the application file name from the File Manager or from within a program item, the PIF name must have the same name—WP.EXE and WP.PIF, for example. If the PIF has the same name as the application file name, when you choose an application file name, the corresponding PIF is executed. If you have several WordPerfect PIFs (all for the same version of WordPerfect), each with unique settings, start the application by choosing the PIF or create a program item icon in the Program Manager for each of the PIFs.

NOTE If you start the application by choosing the application file name, Windows looks for the PIF filename that matches the application's name. For example, if you are in the File Manager and click on WP.EXE to launch WordPerfect, Windows looks for WP.PIF. Windows looks for the PIF in two places— the Windows directory and the directory associated with the application (such as WP51 for WordPerfect). Windows does NOT search the directories in your PATH statement.

Editing a PIF

To edit a PIF, follow these steps:

1. Choose the PIF Editor application from the Main or Accessories group.

2. Choose **F**ile **O**pen and change to the directory containing the PIF to be edited.

   Windows Setup stores PIFs in the \WINDOWS directory. The default PIF, _DEFAULT.PIF, is in the \WINDOWS\SYSTEM directory. PIFs have the extension PIF.

3. Select and open the PIF you want to edit. The PIF Editor window appears, showing the current PIF settings (see fig. 24.7). Choose **F**ile Save **A**s and save a backup copy of the PIF with an extension such as PAK.

4. Make changes to the text boxes or selections in the PIF Editor window. If you are in 386-enhanced mode, choose the **A**dvanced button to see additional PIF options.

See "Understanding PIF Editor Options," for a detailed discussion of all the PIF options.

5. Choose **F**ile Save **A**s and name the PIF with a PIF extension.

6. Choose **F**ile **E**xit to quit the PIF Editor or minimize it to an icon so that it is readily accessible for further editing after you test the application.

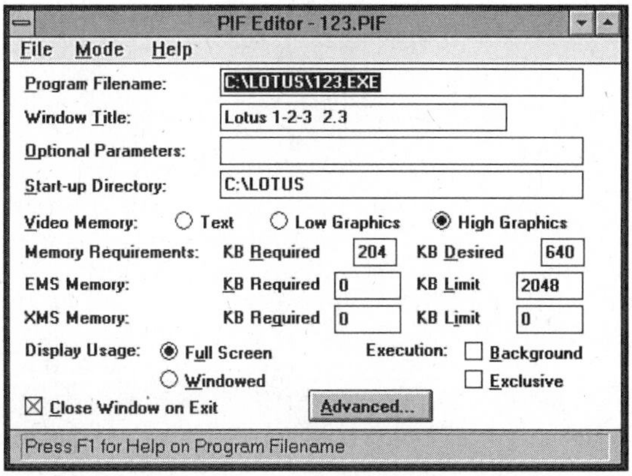

FIG. 24.7

The 123.PIF in the PIF Editor shows the settings for 1-2-3 in 386-enhanced mode.

To get help specific to any item in the PIF Editor window, select the item by clicking on it or by tabbing to the item and then pressing the Help key, F1. A Help window displays information about the item you selected. Press Alt+F4 to close the Help application.

T I P

Starting an Application in a Data Directory
To specify an active directory after the application starts, type that directory name in the **S**tart-up Directory text box in that application's PIF. Because you can have multiple PIFs for the same application, you can make each PIF start the application in a different directory. Be aware, however, that some applications require that the start-up directory be the same as the application's directory. Some applications look in the application directory for additional files needed at start-up so that the application can successfully locate those files; the current directory must be the application's directory.

Understanding PIF Editor Options

The PIF Editor text boxes are nearly the same for standard and 386-enhanced modes, although each mode does have some different text boxes. The boxes also look similar in design.

PIF Options Common to Standard and 386-Enhanced Mode

The following paragraphs describe the PIF Editor text boxes that are similar for the two modes.

The **P**rogram Filename text box entry specifies the name of the application's executable file or start-up file. You type this file name from the DOS prompt to start the application. Type the full path name and application name, including the file extension. Most application file names have the extension EXE or COM. Batch files that run commands or start applications have the extension BAT. For example, an entry for WordPerfect 5.1 would be *C:\WP51\WP.EXE* and an entry for Lotus 1-2-3 Release 2.2 would be *\123R2\123.EXE*.

If you have included the directory associated with the application in your DOS path statement (found in the AUTOEXEC.BAT file), you do not need to enter the complete path in the text box. For example, if C:\WP51 is in your path, instead of entering C:\WP51\WP.EXE, you can enter *WP.EXE*. Generally, however, you should enter the full path name in the PIF Editor.

The Window **T**itle text box entry is the description that appears in the applications window title bar when it displays in a window and the title under the application's icon when it is minimized. Type the name you want to appear in the application window title bar and under the icon. If you leave the Window Title text box blank, Windows uses the application name (for example, WordPerfect), for the window title bar and for the icon name when you minimize the application. The title entered in the Window **T**itle text box is only used if the application is started using the File Run command (using the PIF filename) or if it is started from the File Manager. (If you associate the PIF to an icon, the icon name entered in the Description text box in the Program Item Properties dialog box overrides the description in the PIF's Window Title. The icon description, therefore, appears in the application's window title bar when it displays in a window and as the title under the application's icon when minimized.)

In the **O**ptional Parameters text box, type any parameters you want added to the application when it starts, such as which file to open. These parameters or arguments are the ones you type after the file name when you start an application from the DOS prompt. If you frequently use different parameters, type a question mark in this box, and Windows prompts you for the optional parameter when you run the PIF. Parameters can be up to 62 characters in length.

Some examples of optional parameters follow:

- *templet.let* loads the file templet.let when WordPerfect 5.1 starts.

- */m-macroname* starts the specified macro when WordPerfect 5.1 starts.

- */C* puts Microsoft Word into character mode.

- *filename.set* loads a different set of drivers for Lotus 1-2-3.

If you launch an application by typing the application's file name after choosing **F**ile **R**un from the Program Manager or File Manager, and the PIF has the same name as the application file, any parameters you supply on the **F**ile **R**un command line automatically override those supplied in the Optional Parameters box for this PIF.

The **S**tart-up Directory text box entry defines the drive and directory made current before the application starts. For example, you may keep all your word processing files in a directory called \WPDOCS, but the word processor is located in \WP. If you want the word processor to have \WPDOCS as the file directory when it starts, enter C:\WPDOCS in the Start-up Directory box.

You also can specify a Start-up Directory in a program item icon by entering a directory in the Working Directory box with the **F**ile **P**roperties command from the Program Manager. Settings made in Program Manager override settings made in PIF Editor.

If the application has a default settings file that includes a default start-up directory (like WordPerfect and Lotus 1-2-3), the start-up directory in the PIF or the Working Directory in a program item icon are overruled.

If your application must locate additional files on start-up (as is the case with Lotus 1-2-3), do not enter a Start-up Directory.

PIF Options for Standard Mode

The following sections describe the standard mode PIF Editor settings (see fig. 24.4). The Memory Requirements options specify how much memory the application uses; the Directly Modifies options, Prevent Program Switch option, and No Screen Exchange option affect how much memory is left for other applications to use.

Video Mode

Option	Description
Text	Select this option when the application uses only text mode. This Video mode option tells Windows to set aside only enough memory to save an application's text display so that you can switch back and forth between the application and Windows. The Text option reserves the least amount of memory possible for saving the display. You cannot display graphics screens when this option is set.
Graphics/MultipleText	Select this option when the application displays graphics. This choice causes Windows to set aside more memory for saving the screen because the application is using video data. You should choose this option in most cases.

Memory Requirements

Setting	Description
KB Required	Type the amount of memory in kilobytes required by the DOS application to run. This setting tells Windows the minimum conventional memory that must be available to load the application. The KB Required setting is less than the amount listed in the application user manual because the amount listed includes memory required for DOS and other parts of the system. Usually, you should start with the default setting of 128. Start the application with no other applications running to see whether it

Setting	Description
	starts. If the application does not start, raise the KB Required setting in increments of 64 until the application does run. If you try to start a DOS application and the required amount of memory is not available to the system, you receive an error message from Windows, and you cannot start the application.

XMS Memory

These options tell Windows how much extended memory to use for applications requiring XMS memory specification. Because Windows enables the use of extended memory as long as it is available, you can leave these options at the standard settings of 0.

Setting	Description
KB Required	Type the number of kilobytes of extended memory recommended by the application manual if your application uses extended memory that prescribes to the Lotus/Intel/ Microsoft/AST Extended Memory Specification Version 2.0 or later. This setting is the minimum amount needed to start the application. Unless you are positive that the application you are creating the PIF for uses extended memory, leave this setting at 0. The 0 setting prevents applications from using XMS memory. Few DOS applications use extended memory. For DOS applications that do use extended memory, such as Lotus 1-2-3 Release 3.1, enter *512* and increase the setting as necessary.
KB Limit	Type the maximum amount of extended memory needed by the application. This setting prevents the application from taking all extended memory for itself by setting an upper limit. Leave the setting at 0 to prevent the application from gaining access to any extended memory or set the option to -1 to give the application all the extended memory it requests. Use the -1 setting only if the application requires large amounts of extended memory, because this setting slows the system down significantly.

Directly Modifies

Some applications cannot share resources with other applications. The Directly Modifies settings group defines which resources cannot be shared. You cannot switch back to Windows without quitting the application if you choose these options.

Setting	Description
COM1, COM2, COM3, or COM4	Select one of these check boxes if the application uses COM1, COM2, COM3, or COM4. Selecting an option prevents other applications from using the COM port selected for this application. The application using a PIF with this selection does not swap from memory onto a hard disk, so you cannot fit as many additional applications in Windows.
Keyboard	Select this option if the application directly controls the keyboard.

No Screen Exchange

Select this option to prevent copying and pasting between DOS applications using the Clipboard. If you select this option, you cannot copy screens with the Print Screen or Alt+PrtScrn key. Selecting this option conserves memory.

No Save Screen

Select this option so that Windows does not save the screen information when you switch to another application. When you choose the No Save Screen option, Windows no longer retains in memory the screen information for the application, and the memory becomes available. Use this option only when the application has the capability to retain its own screen information and has a "redraw screen" command.

Prevent Program Switch

Select this option to prevent switching from the application back to Windows. Selecting this check box prevents you from using Alt+Tab, Alt+Esc, or Ctrl+Esc to switch back to Windows. You must exit the application to return to Windows. This option conserves memory.

Close Window on Exit

Select this option to close the window in which the DOS application is displayed when you exit the DOS application.

Reserve Shortcut Keys

Select the Reserve Shortcut Key options to select the key combinations you want to use for carrying out functions in the application instead of for use by Windows.

Setting	Description
Alt+Tab	Select this option to reserve the Alt+Tab shortcut key for this application. Windows uses Alt+Tab to toggle between applications.
Alt+Esc	Select this option to reserve the Alt+Esc shortcut key for this application. Windows uses Alt+Esc to switch to the next application.
Ctrl+Esc	Select this option to reserve the Ctrl+Esc shortcut key for this application. Windows uses Ctrl+Esc to switch to the Task List.
PrtSc	Select this option to reserve the PrtSc shortcut key for this application. Windows uses Print Screen to copy a full screen to the Clipboard.
Alt+PrtSc	Select this option to reserve the Alt+PrtSc shortcut key for the application. Windows uses Alt+PrtSc to copy a full screen (or active Window) to the Clipboard.

PIF Options for 386-Enhanced Mode

The 386-enhanced options appear in two dialog windows (see figs. 24.5 and 24.6). The basic PIF options are similar to the PIF options in standard mode. The advanced options fine-tune the application for running in 386-enhanced mode.

Many of the standard and real mode PIF options are duplicated for 386-enhanced mode. For example, if you set the Program Filename option in standard mode and then use a Mode command to switch to the settings for 386-enhanced mode, Windows duplicates the same settings in 386-enhanced mode. This duplication is especially helpful when you run Windows frequently in standard or 386-enhanced mode and you need to set PIF options for both modes. The most notable exception, however, is the Optional Parameters setting, which you use to supply command-line parameters to an application when you start it. You must set this option independently for each mode.

Use 386-Enhanced Mode if You Have an 80386 Computer and Run DOS Applications

386-enhanced mode enables you to run multiple DOS applications at one time. The advantages of this type of operation are that you can continue processing a mail merge or a database search while you work in a different application. If you run only Windows applications and you have an 80386 computer, performance and memory management are better running in standard mode.

386-enhanced mode gives you greater control over DOS applications. For example, standard mode enables you to run DOS applications only in a full screen; 386-enhanced mode enables you to run most DOS applications in Windows, making switching between windows and copying and pasting portions of a screen much easier. For example, you can copy small sections of a DOS application from a window in 386-enhanced mode. If you run the same application in standard mode, the application runs full-screen; you can copy only the entire screen contents.

Windows and DOS applications view conventional memory very differently. Windows, when running in 386-enhanced mode, treats all memory—conventional, extended, and virtual (disk-based) memory—as one large pool of memory. DOS is a single-tasking operating system, and a DOS application assumes that it is the only application running and that it can use unlimited conventional memory (0K to 640K). When a DOS application makes a request for a block of conventional memory, Windows satisfies that request by giving it a block of memory from the pool. The Memory Requirements PIF settings enable you to specify the upper and lower limits of memory that a DOS application receives.

The previous sections describe the 386-enhanced mode basic options (default settings are shown in fig. 24.5). The following few sections describe the 386-enhanced mode advanced options (default settings are shown in fig. 24.6). The descriptions of Program Filename, Window Title, Optional Parameters, and Start-up Directory are listed in "PIF Options Common to Standard and 386-Enhanced Mode."

Video Memory

These options determine the video mode for the program. Different methods of displaying graphics require different amounts of memory, and these options ensure that Windows sets aside enough memory for the video mode used by the software. These modes are Text, Low Graphics, and High Graphics. Use the lowest memory mode possible so that more memory is available for Windows. If the application does not have sufficient video memory, it does not start, and a warning message appears. If you switch from a graphics mode to one that requires less memory, Windows releases the video memory no longer needed. However, you are prevented from switching back to graphics if another application is using the memory. To ensure that video memory is reserved for your application so that this does not happen, select the High Graphics option and, from the advanced portion of the dialog box, select the Retain Video **M**emory check box. This means that your applications will always be able to switch memory modes, but less memory will be available for other applications.

Setting	Description
Text	Requires the least amount of memory. Graphics will not display. Use this mode if the DOS application will not be displaying graphics. This mode makes more memory available for Windows.
Low Graphics	Low resolution graphics will display.
High Graphics	Requires the most amount of memory. Select this option and the Retain Video **M**emory check box in the Advanced portion of the PIF Editor to ensure that high resolution memory is always available for the application.

Memory Requirements

Setting	Description
KB **R**equired	Type the minimum amount of conventional memory that must be free for the application to start. Windows does not start the application if available memory is less than the amount specified in the KB **R**equired text box. If you are unsure of what to enter, leave the setting at 128. Do not enter the amount of memory recommended by the user manual—this figure is inflated to account for drivers and DOS. Generally, you should use a KB **R**equired setting just high enough to load the application without Windows issuing an insufficient memory error message, but low enough that you can load the application when memory is tight. If the application does not run due to insufficient memory, close all other applications and increase the KB **R**equired setting in 64K increments until the application runs. Enter *–1* to give the application all available conventional memory up to 640K. You should avoid using this setting; in most cases, using a setting of –1 sets aside a full 640K, which is too much for most applications.

continues

Setting	Description
KB Desired	Type the maximum amount of memory you want the application to use if the memory is available. The default 640K is the maximum; most applications use much less. Use -1 to give the application as much memory as possible up to 640K. Most applications run more efficiently with more memory, but remember that Windows shares a pool of memory and you do not want one application taking more memory than it uses. Be frugal with this setting if you know your application will not need the upper limit of 640. If you decrease the KB Desired amount to 512K, you conserve 128K for other applications because this application cannot use more than 512K of memory.

EMS Memory

When running in 386-enhanced mode, Windows uses only extended memory; however, Windows simulates expanded memory for applications that need the memory or that perform better when expanded memory is available.

Setting	Description
KB Required	This setting is the minimum amount of memory required for the application to run. Leave this setting at 0 (no expanded memory) for most applications. Entering a required amount does not limit the amount of expanded memory used, but if less memory is free than what is specified by **KB** Required, the application does not start and displays a warning message.
KB Limit	Enter the maximum amount of expanded memory you want the application to use. Windows gives the application as much expanded memory as it needs, up to the limit you specify in this text box or until no more memory is available. The default setting is 1024. Set to 0 to prevent the application from having any expanded memory. A setting of -1 gives the application unlimited memory, but this setting can slow the performance of other applications.

XMS Memory

These settings configure Windows for an application that uses the Lotus-Intel-Microsoft-AST Extended Memory Specification (XMS). Few applications use XMS; generally, you can leave these options at their default settings. Lotus 1-2-3 Release 3.1 uses XMS memory.

Setting	Description
KB Required	Type the minimum amount of extended memory recommended by the user manual for the application. If the application uses XMS memory, the computer must have the amount of memory specified by this option, or the application does not start. Leave this setting at 0 for most applications.
KB Limit	Type the maximum amount of extended memory you want the application to use. The default setting of 1024 gives the application as much extended memory as it requires, up to 1024K or until no more memory is available. Leave this setting at 0 to prevent the application from using extended memory. Few DOS applications use extended memory. Lotus 1-2-3 Release 3.1 uses extended memory.

Display Usage

Setting	Description
Full Screen	Select this option to start the application in a full-screen display rather than in a window. Running an application in a full screen saves memory and is required for some applications running in high video modes. You can switch between full-screen applications and Window applications quickly by pressing ALT+TAB.
Windowed	Select this option to start the application in a window. Running in a window provides the advantages of easily activating other applications and copying and pasting data portions of a screen.

You quickly can switch from a window to full-screen display using Alt+Enter, and the application reverts to the application set color scheme. You can toggle between windows and the full-screen by pressing Alt+Enter.

Execution

In 386-enhanced mode, Windows is a multitasking environment for DOS applications. Although Windows appears to be running multiple applications, Windows really can run only one application at a time. Windows must share the computer time between each running application by using time slicing. Each application gets a portion of the total processor time. To run multiple DOS applications simultaneously with all of them continuing to run while you are working in one of them, the DOS PIFs must be set up so that one application runs in the foreground, where it is active, and the other application runs in the background. The PIFs that Windows Setup and the installation application create make sure that all DOS applications run in the foreground and background. You can change the proportion of time each application receives by modifying the Execution Settings options in an application's PIF.

Setting	Description
Background	Select this check box to enable the application to run in the background while you use another application. For example, a mail-merge application or database search can run in the background while you complete a letter with a word processor in the foreground. The amount of processor time allocated to the application while in the background is set using one of the Advanced PIF options.
Exclusive	Select this check box to suspend all other applications while this application is in the foreground. All other applications are halted— even if the applications have their Background option selected. This option gives an application all the processor time. Usually, this option can be left unchecked. If you want to run the DOS application exclusively, you can change its exclusive setting while it is running. To do so, select the Settings command from the application window's Control menu and select the Exclusive check box under the Tasking Operations group.

Close Window on Exit

Select this option to close the window when you exit the DOS application.

Advanced

Choosing the Advanced button displays the Advanced Options dialog box for additional 386-enhanced mode PIF options (see fig. 24.5).

Advanced PIF Options for 386-Enhancement Mode

By using the Advanced options in 386-enhanced mode, you can modify a PIF for better memory use and performance for the DOS application. To display the Advanced Options dialog box, choose the **A**dvanced option button at the bottom of the basic PIF Editor window. This button displays only when the PIF Editor is in 386-enhanced mode. Use the Mode menu to switch to the 386-enhanced PIF Editor if the **A**dvanced button does not show. (Although you can edit a 386-enhanced PIF while running standard-mode windows, the PIF options take effect only when operating in 386-enhanced mode.)

Figure 24.6 shows that the Advanced Options window is divided into four segments: Multitasking Options, Memory Options, Display Options, and Other Options. Using these options, you can adjust your PIF for best performance and memory usage.

Multitasking Options

These options control how a DOS application shares processing time with other DOS applications. When you are running two (or more) DOS applications at the same time and one (or more) of them is running in the background, you need a way to control how much processor time each application gets in relation to the other applications. Windows enables you to control this ratio through the Multitasking Options group.

The ratio of processor time between all Windows applications and all DOS applications is set in a different way. Set this ratio by running the 386-enhanced program found in the Control Panel. The settings in the Scheduling group control the ratio of processing time between Windows and all DOS applications.

Setting	Description
Background Priority	Type a value between 0 and 10000 to specify the background priority for this DOS application. The default background priority is 50. This value is meaningful only when compared to Background and Foreground Priority settings for the other running DOS applications.

continues

Setting	Description
	To figure the percentage of processor time allocated to a DOS application, total the Foreground Priority for the active DOS application with the Background Priority for all DOS applications running in background at that time. Divide the priority (Foreground or Background Priority) of an application by the total. For example, the total priority of three applications is 200 (one foreground application with a priority of 100 and two background applications each with a priority of 50). The background activity gets 50 out of a total of 200, or 25% of the processor time allocated to DOS applications. (The ratio of DOS to Windows application priority is set with the 386-enhanced program in the Control Panel.)
	If an application's Execution: Background check box is turned off, the application cannot run in the background. Therefore, any number you enter in the Background Priority box does not have any effect. You can change an application's background or foreground setting while it is running by changing the Settings Priority options in the Control menu of the DOS application's window.
Foreground Priority	Type a value between 0 and 10000 to specify the foreground priority for the application. The default foreground priority is 100. The value has no meaning unless another DOS application is running in the background.
Detect Idle Time	Select this option so that Windows gives processor resources to other applications when this application is idle (waiting for input from you, for example). This option enhances the performance of your computer and should be selected in most cases. If an application is running slowly, deselecting this option may help in some circumstances.

Memory Options

Setting	Description
EMS Memory Locked	Select this option to prevent the application's expanded memory from swapping to hard disk.

Setting	Description
	This setting improves the application performance because the application remains in memory; however, selecting this option can force other applications to swap more frequently and slow down their performance.
XMS Memory Locked	Select this option to prevent the application from swapping memory to hard disk. Selecting this check box improves the application performance because the application remains in memory; however, selecting this option can force other applications to swap more frequently and slow down their performance.
Uses High Memory Area	Select this option to enable the application to use the high memory area (HMA). If HMA is available, each application can allocate its own HMA.
	HMA is used by some memory-resident utilities such as networks. If a memory-resident utility is using HMA when you start Windows in 386-enhanced mode, no other applications can use HMA.
	Select Uses High Memory Area for most applications. This option makes more memory available for the application if needed. If the application does not use the additional memory, HMA is not wasted. The default setting of 1024 gives the application as much extended memory as it requires, up to 1024K or until no more memory is available.
Lock Application Memory	Select this option to prevent conventional memory from swapping to the hard disk. Selecting this option improves the performance of this application but decreases overall system performance. Use the settings previously described to lock EMS and XMS memory.

DOS 5.0 can use HMA. If you are using DOS 5.0 and have the line DOS=HIGH in your CONFIG.SYS file (which enables DOS to use the HMA), the HMA is not available to DOS applications running in Windows. The check box for Uses High Memory Area, therefore, should be turned off.

T I P

Display Options

Some applications directly access the computer's hardware input and output ports to control the display adapter. Windows must monitor the application's interface with the hardware ports to ensure that when you switch applications, the video display is restored correctly. Use the default settings for most applications.

These selections control the amount of memory Windows reserves for the application display when the application starts. Generally, these settings should not be changed. If you change the application's display mode during operation, Windows releases unused memory to other applications if you go to a less memory-intensive mode; Windows attempts to use additional memory if you go to a more memory-intensive mode. If additional memory is not available, the screen image may be lost. Use the High Graphics and Retain Video **M**emory options to ensure that memory is available if you lose the display when you switch graphics modes.

The first three options in the following list are Monitor Ports selections:

Setting	Description
Text	Select this option to have Windows monitor video operations when the application is running in text mode. Few applications require this option.
Low Graphics	Select this option to have Windows monitor all video operations when the application is running in low-resolution graphics mode. Few applications require this option.
High Graphics	Select this option when the application displays graphics in high-resolution graphics mode. EGA and VGA graphics adapters display applications in high-resolution graphics mode. The High Graphics option requires about 128K of memory. Select this option and the Retain Video **M**emory option to make sure that you have enough memory to run any application. Be aware, however, that these selections reduce the amount of memory available to all applications.
Emulate Text Mode	Select this option to increase the rate at which the application displays text. Leave this option selected for most applications. If your application has garbled text, if the cursor appears in the wrong place, or if the application doesn't run, try clearing this check box.

Setting	Description
Retain Video **M**emory	Select this option so that Windows retains extra video memory and does not release it to other applications. Some applications, such as Microsoft Word, use more than one video mode. When Word switches from text to graphics mode, Windows usually releases the memory for the video mode not in use. If memory becomes scarce, Word may not be able to switch back to a previous video mode. Selecting this check box and the correct video memory option ensures that you always have enough memory available to switch back to an application and to view the screen.

The application may lose its display if you select this option under low-memory conditions and then change to a more memory-intensive video display. The display is lost because Windows cannot dynamically free the memory needed for the new display mode. |

IBM's VGA display adapter is not affected by the settings you make in the Monitor Ports options. Any settings made are ignored by these types of display adapters.

T I P

Other Options

These options enable you to customize Windows even further when in the 386-enhanced mode.

Setting	Description
Allow Fast **P**aste	Usually, this option is selected. Most applications can accept information pasted from the Clipboard using the fastest method. If you paste into a DOS application and nothing happens, clear this check box on the application's PIF.
Allow **C**lose When Active	Select this option to enable Windows to close the application without requiring you to use the application's Exit command. Select this option to exit Windows without closing all active DOS applications first. Because you do not have to exit the application before closing the window, no reminder to save work in

continues

Setting	Description
	progress appears. Windows does display a message box asking whether you are sure that you want to close the active application.
Reserve Shortcut Keys	Select the key combinations you want available for an application when it runs in the foreground. Usually, these key combinations are reserved for use by Windows. This option enables you to use special keys in your application that Windows may otherwise reserve for its use. Two more shortcut keys are available in 386-enhanced mode than in standard mode: Alt+Enter, which toggles a DOS application between full screen and windows and Alt+Space Bar, which activates an application's window Control menu.
Application Shortcut Keys	Specify the shortcut-key combination you want to use to activate the application so that the application moves from background to foreground. The shortcut combination must include Alt or Ctrl. You can include combinations of letters, numbers, and function keys. To specify a shortcut-key combination, select this option and press the key combination you want. For example, select this option and press Alt+W. (To remove the current shortcut key, select this option and press Shift+Backspace.)
	Select your shortcut-key combinations carefully. After the application is loaded, the shortcut keys specified activate that application and do not work as shortcut keys for other applications.

Be Careful Selecting the Allow Close When Active Option
Selecting the Allow Close When Active check box can result in loss of data and file damage. This option enables Windows to close an application before the application has the chance to close its open files. The files may be damaged, and you lose any changes made to these files.

This problem occurs most frequently with accounting and database software. These applications keep files open while operating. If you quit the application with Allow Close When Active selected, the open files may be left open—ruining the data files with which you were working.

Changing Settings of a Running Application

Besides using the PIF Editor to define PIF option settings, you can change some PIF options while the application is running in 386-enhanced mode. You can change an application's display option between full-screen and windows. You also can change the percentage of processor time the application receives when it is active or in the background.

To change settings for an application running in 386-enhanced mode, follow these steps:

1. Press Alt+the space bar to quickly access the Control menu.

2. Choose the **S**ettings command from the application's Control menu.

   A Settings dialog box for the application appears (see fig. 24.8).

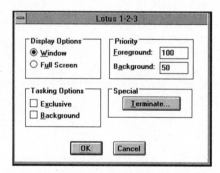

Switching Back to Full Screen

If you press Alt+the space bar while running a full-screen DOS application in 386-enhanced mode, the application is put into a window, and the Control menu appears. To return to full-screen mode from a window, press Alt+Enter or choose Settings from the application's Control menu, select F**u**ll Screen, and choose OK.

Some applications, such as Microsoft Word, use Alt+the space bar for their own purposes. Remember to reserve this shortcut key in the PIF for the application if you want to retain the shortcut key for the application's purposes, and you do not want to return to Windows. If Alt+space bar is used by the application, open the Control menu by pressing Alt+Enter, which puts the application in title bar) to open the Control menu.

3. Select the option you want to change.

The following sections list the options you can change as the application runs.

Display Options

The Display Options change how the application appears. A faster method of switching display options is to press Alt+Enter to alternate between full-screen and windowed modes.

Option	Description
Window	Displays the application in a window
Full Screen	Displays the application in a full screen

Tasking Options

The Tasking Options control how much of the computer's processing power is used. Select either or both of these options.

Option	Description
Exclusive	Puts the processing of other applications on hold while the active application runs. If the DOS application is in a window, Windows applications continue to run, but DOS applications stop.
Background	Runs this application in the background when other applications are active. The application's use of processing time depends upon the advanced 386-enhanced mode PIF settings or the settings in the Priority Options section.

Priority Options

The Priority Options control the priority of processor time when the application is running in the foreground or background. The actual amount of time allocated to the application depends on the priority settings of the other applications. The numeric settings and allocation of processor time between applications are described in detail under the Background Priority option earlier in this chapter.

Option	Description
Foreground	A numeric setting that is the weighted amount of processor time as compared to all running applications
Background	A numeric setting that is the weighted amount of processor time as compared to all running applications

Special Setting

Use the **Terminate** option as a last resort. Choose this option when you cannot exit or quit the application in any other way. **Terminate** closes the application and gives you the chance to return to Windows to save open files in other applications. Save the files in all other applications and then close the applications and exit Windows. If you are unable to exit Windows, press Ctrl+Alt+Del.

If you choose a PIF to start a DOS application but the application does not start or operate correctly, use the PIF Editor to edit the PIF.

Some of the most common problems and their solutions follow:

Problem	Solution Using the PIF Editor
Application file not found	Check the file-name extension in the **Program Filename** text box.
Application file not found	Check the application path name in the **Program Filename** text box.
Associated files not found	Type the application's path name in the **Start-up Directory** text box.
Insufficient memory to start	Increase the KB Required setting. You may need to increase the EMS and XMS KB **R**equired if your application requires EMS or XMS memory.
Add-in applications don't run	Increase the KB **R**equired setting.
Special keystrokes don't work	Reserve keystrokes for the application's use in the Reserve Shortcut Keys group (choose the **A**dvanced button in a 386-enhanced mode PIF to see these options).

Customizing DOS Applications with Multiple PIFs

Sometimes, you may need to start the same DOS application in different ways. You can create a different PIF for each of the ways in which you want the DOS application to run. Assign a different program item icon to each PIF or start each PIF directly from the File Manager. For example, you may want to specify different start-up directories for different types of work, or you may want to specify a different application macro to run for each of the PIFs.

You also may want a different memory configuration for the different times you run the application. You may need to invoke WordPerfect with a large amount of memory reserved.

Another good use for several PIFs is to invoke specific applications parameters. For example, you can name a PIF WP-M.PIF to invoke WordPerfect and run a macro provided in the **O**ptional Parameters by using the /m-*macroname* parameter. You also may have a PIF named WP-F.PIF that has a ? in the **O**ptional Parameters text box so that you can provide a file name to automatically load.

Running DOS Batch Files

You can run DOS batch files from within Windows by creating a PIF for them. Creating a PIF for a batch file is the same as creating a PIF for any application. Although you can run some DOS batch files without creating a corresponding PIF, the following sections illustrate some of the advantages to running batch files from a PIF.

Running a Batch File from a PIF

You can run a batch file from a PIF in the same way you run any DOS application. By creating a PIF to prepare Windows for the batch file, you can set up the Windows environment correctly. For example, you may want to load a terminate-and-stay-resident (TSR) application along with one of your DOS applications.

To run a TSR and then a DOS application in the same DOS session, use the Notepad accessory to create a batch file like the following:

C:*tsrpathname*\\tsr.EXE

C:*application_pathname**application*.EXE

Save this batch file with the extension BAT.

Create a PIF to run this batch file by using the path name and file name of the batch file entered in the **P**rogram Filename box. When the PIF runs, the file first opens a DOS session with the parameters set by the PIF. Then the PIF runs the batch file. The batch file loads the TSR and then loads and runs the application. When you quit the application, the session ends; Windows recaptures the memory; and the window closes, if a window was used.

When you create a batch file to run more than one application, for example a TSR and a DOS application, enter into the PIF the settings for the most demanding application in the batch file. The DOS session started by the PIF has the settings for the most difficult to operate DOS application.

The following batch files illustrate how you can run batch files to do chores or procedures unavailable through the File Manager. This one-line batch file prints a listing of the files and directory names in the current directory to most non-Postscript printers connected to the LPT1 parallel port. After the batch file runs, you need to turn the printer off-line and press the form feed button to eject the page.

Type *DIR>LPT1:* into the Notepad and save the file with the name DIRPRINT.BAT. Open the PIF Editor and choose the **F**ile **N**ew command. Type *DIRPRINT.BAT* in the **P**rogram Filename box. Choose the **F**ile **S**ave **A**s command and enter a name for the file name.

You now can print the current directory by choosing the DIRPRINT.PIF from the File Manager. If you use this command frequently, you may want to use the **F**ile **N**ew command with the Program **I**tem option in the Program Manager to create a program item icon that starts this PIF and prints the directory. When the batch file runs, the DOS session closes, and control returns to Windows.

Keeping a DOS Session Open after a Batch File Finishes

When you run a batch file under Windows, whether from a PIF or not, the DOS screen closes, and control returns to Windows. Windows reclaims the memory the batch file used.

You may want the DOS window or screen to remain open so that you can read results from a DOS application. For example, when you are writing batch files to run from PIFs, you may want to see the batch file operations on-screen to ensure that they have run correctly. If the window or screen immediately closes when the batch file finishes, you probably cannot see what happens.

To make Windows execute the batch commands and then keep the DOS screen open, you must add the line `C:\pathname\COMMAND.COM` as the last line of your batch file (where *pathname* is the directory containing COMMAND.COM). On a network, you can use the variable name *%COMSPEC%* instead. *%COMSPEC%* is a DOS environment variable that stores the location of DOS. Because %COMSPEC% always contains the current location of the COMMAND.COM file, no matter how the system is configured, you will want to use IT as the last line of any batch file for which the DOS screen should remain open.

For example, if you want a batch file to display file names in wide format for the current directory and then keep the list on-screen, the batch file appears as follows:

```
DIR /W
%COMSPEC%
```

T I P   When you run a PIF that keeps the DOS screen open, don't forget to type *EXIT* and press Enter to return to Windows.

Creating a Program Item Icon for a Batch File

After you have created a PIF that runs your batch file, you can assign a program item icon to the PIF so that you can run the PIF by choosing an icon in the Program Manager. To create a program item icon for your batch file, complete the following steps:

1. Activate the group window in the Program Manager in which you want the icon.

2. Choose the File New command.

3. Select the Program Item option and choose OK.

4. Type the label for the icon in the **D**escription box.

5. Type the path and file name for the PIF in the **C**ommand Line box. Use the **B**rowse button to find and select the file if you cannot remember the name.

6. Choose the Change **I**con button.

7. Type the name of the file containing icons in the File Name box. If you do not have a library of icons, enter the name of a file that contains icons that came with Windows. These files usually are

found in C:\WINDOWS\PROGMAN.EXE or C:\WINDOWS\ MORICONS.DLL. Choose OK.

8. From the **C**urrent Icon list, select the icon you want in the Program Manager.

9. Choose OK twice.

Ensuring that Batch File Variables Have Enough Memory

DOS reserves a small amount of memory in which to store names and numbers. This memory is the DOS environment. Usually, the DOS environment stores information such as COMSPEC (the location of COMMAND.COM), PATH (directories in the path), and PROMPT (the appearance of the DOS prompt.) The DOS environment also can store variables used by batch files. Variables are changeable items in a batch. For example, if a batch file asks that you type a number, the number is stored in an environment variable.

The amount of memory available in the DOS environment is important to you if you want to run batch files from within Windows that use a large number of variables. Batch files that create DOS menuing systems, batch files that ask for many user prompts, or batch files that set up networks all need a larger DOS environment than Windows usually sets aside.

One way of expanding the DOS environment is to use Notebook to add a line to your CONFIG.SYS file:

SHELL=C:*pathname*\COMMAND.COM /E:512 /P

This line loads COMMAND.COM with an environment of 512 bytes. If you are using DOS 3.0 or 3.1, use the blocks of memory instead of bytes. To calculate blocks, divide the memory (512) by 16 for an environment parameter of /E:32. The /P parameter indicates that COMMAND.COM is loaded; you must include this parameter.

Because the amount of DOS environment may change, you may want to use the PIF to expand the environment memory and to run the batch file or application. The following modifications to a PIF expand the DOS environment so that it can store variables that may be used by the batch file:

Program filename:	COMMAND.COM
Title:	*filename*.PIF
Optional Parameters:	/E:384 /C C:*pathname**filename*.BAT

These changes create a DOS environment of 384 bytes and then run any application or batch file (COM, EXE, or BAT) that follows the /C. In this case, the batch file *filename*.BAT runs.

Passing Variable Data from a PIF to a Batch File

You can pass variable data from a PIF to a DOS batch file. This enables you to create a batch file that changes how it operates depending upon which variables are passed to it. For example, the same batch file can add different directories to the DOS PATH depending upon which PIF ran the batch file. With this arrangement, you can set up a program item icon tied to each PIF so that double-clicking on an icon adds a new directory to the PIF. You also can create a PIF that prompts you to enter information. The batch file then uses that information to operate. This example is just one way in which you can control DOS from within Windows.

Use Notepad to create a batch file that adds a variable directory name to the current DOS PATH. (By adding a directory to the PATH, any file in the PATH can be run from anywhere on the disk without entering the file's full path name.) Save this one line batch file to the name PATHCHNG.BAT:

        SET PATH=%PATH%;%1

This line tells DOS to attach a directory name stored in the variable *%1* to the current path, stored in the variable %PATH%. The PATH then should be set equal to this new path that includes an additional directory. The variable *%1* stores what is entered in the **O**ptional Parameters line of the PIF that ran PATHCHNG.BAT.

For example, if you occasionally need to add the Paradox 3.5 directory to your DOS path, you can create a PIF with C:\PDOX35 in its **O**ptional Parameters box. The **P**rogram Filename should be PATHCHNG.BAT. When the PIF runs, the optional parameter C:\PDOX35 is stored in *%1* in the DOS environment. The PATHCHNG.BAT batch file runs. The SET PATH line then adds the directory in *%1* to the existing PATH.

You can make this type of PIF more flexible by typing a question mark in the **O**ptional Parameters box. When the PIF runs, Windows prompts you for the **O**ptional Parameter. What you type in the prompt box is stored in the variable for use by the batch file.

You can enter multiple variables in the **O**ptional Parameters box. Separate each variable with a space. Each variable then is passed to the batch file as *%1*, *%2*, *%3*, and so on depending upon the order in the PIF Editor.

Passing Variable Data from a Batch File to a PIF

Just as a PIF can pass variable data to a batch file, a batch file can pass variable data to a PIF. In a batch file, the DOS command SET can store a value in an environment variable. The contents of the environment variable then can be retrieved by using the variable name enclosed in percent signs, *%variable%*. That variable then can be read by a PIF. The **P**rogram Filename, **W**indow Title, **O**ptional Parameters, and **S**tart-up Directory boxes in the PIF Editor can all receive DOS environment variables.

For Related Information:

▶▶ To learn more about fine-tuning Windows to increase memory and performance, read Chapter 25, "Enhancing Windows Performance," p. 955 and Chapter 26, "Enhancing DOS Application Performance," p. 981.

FROM HERE...

Chapter Summary

In this chapter, you learned what a PIF is and how Windows works with a PIF. You learned how to create, edit, and optimize PIFs. You also learned how to use the PIF Editor.

Now that you know how to work with PIFs, you may want to experiment and optimize the performance of your DOS applications. PIFs are one of the keys to making DOS applications run efficiently within Windows.

Customizing and Tuning Windows

P A R T

VI

O U T L I N E

Enhancing Windows Performance

Tips and tricks are available for improving the performance of Windows throughout this book, but the factors that have the greatest effect can be summarized as follows:

- How you use Windows
- Hardware capability (speed of CPU, video adapter, and hard disk)
- Memory optimization
- Hard disk performance

In far too many cases, Windows users begin trying to increase performance by making adjustments in the WIN.INI and SYSTEM.INI files that yield only small improvements in performance. If you want large improvements, start with changes that make the biggest improvements and then work down to the small fine-tuning.

Before you begin optimizing a computer for Windows, check to make sure that you don't have operating habits that drain performance, such as keeping many applications loaded that you aren't using. Honestly evaluate the hardware and upgrade the critical areas, such as meeting an acceptable memory limit of 4M for multiple applications. Next, optimize the performance of the hardware by improving the efficiency of the memory and hard disk. Finally, improve Windows efficiency by conserving resources and making fine adjustments to Windows internal operating methods.

Working Efficiently in Windows

You can follow some common guidelines that help you operate Windows and applications faster and more efficiently. These guidelines don't require any technical adjustments; they only require that you adjust the way you work.

When you run Windows, consider the hardware's capabilities. If you operate a 486 machine with 16M of memory, you can probably run as many applications as you want without worrying about performance. But if you have an 80286 or 386 machine with two or three megabytes of RAM, expect performance to deteriorate if you try to run more than a few large applications at the same time.

Limit the number of loaded or running applications. Even idle applications can use computer resources, slowing the performance of the application you are currently using. Weigh the time an application takes to open against the performance degradation you experience.

Operate DOS applications full screen rather than in a window. Use windowed DOS applications only when you copy and paste between these applications.

Turn off processing for DOS applications that reside in the background and that don't need to use processor time. Chapter 24 describes how to improve DOS application performance.

Use printer fonts and Windows screen fonts for normal work that doesn't demand special sizes or styles. Font scalers, such as Adobe Type Manager and TrueType, give you extra capabilities but are slower than Windows screen fonts.

Limit the display of graphic features in Windows applications. Many Windows applications come with useful graphical features, such as icon bars or special page display options. Although convenient, these features usually degrade the application's performance. If performance is sluggish and the Windows application has a draft mode, use draft mode. If you don't need the graphical features, try turning off these features—performance probably will improve.

Limit the number of open windows on the desktop. These windows occupy the computer's memory and your memory. Too many document windows slow performance and can confuse you. In some applications, such as word processors, document length can affect performance so having multiple short documents rather than one long document is a good idea.

Providing a Good Environment for Windows

The first step in optimizing the system is to verify that the hardware is configured properly and that the system environment is set up to work smoothly with Windows.

Before you install or optimize Windows, be sure that the hardware and operating system are working correctly. Checking these parts of the system may seem obvious, but you can easily spend hours investigating a *problem* in Windows, only to find that the problem is part of the basic computer configuration.

Protect What You Have When You Install Windows

One step you can take prior to changing the system configuration or installing a new application is to prepare a diskette that you can use to boot the system. If the hard disk's AUTOEXEC.BAT or CONFIG.SYS files are incorrectly changed, you can restart the computer from the diskette. This diskette also can be used to copy back the original AUTOEXEC.BAT and CONFIG:SYS files.

Another diskette that contains files for the minimum system configuration is an essential tool for troubleshooting. In a minimum configuration, CONFIG.SYS and AUTOEXEC.BAT files are limited to the command lines needed to run the computer, and nothing else. When you experience a problem with Windows, or any other application, you can use this diskette to start Windows in as clean a configuration as possible. Then, if you can't reproduce the error, you can assume the error may have occurred because of an incorrect line in one of these files. (If you recently installed new application software and Windows suddenly doesn't work, the culprit probably is the new application, which incorrectly modified the CONFIG.SYS or AUTOEXEC.BAT.)

Install the Correct Version of DOS

To ensure that Windows runs smoothly on your computer, verify that the operating system (DOS) is installed and configured properly. You find out which version of DOS is installed by typing *VER* after the DOS prompt and pressing Enter.

Run the manufacturer's DOS. Some computer manufacturers ship a special version of DOS, customized to take advantage of the hardware, with their computers. If the machine came with a special version of DOS, use this version. Windows may not run properly if you run a generic DOS version borrowed from someone else.

Get MS-DOS 5.0. Upgrading to MS-DOS 5.0 is worth the low cost, even if you run only a few DOS applications. DOS 5.0 enables you to configure the system to maximize the memory available for DOS sessions, whether or not you run applications in Windows. Written to work well with Windows, MS-DOS 5.0 offers you the best opportunity for compatibility and includes some useful new utilities.

Installing New Applications

New applications often modify the AUTOEXEC.BAT and CONFIG.SYS files. Try to keep a record of the modifications each application makes in case one application causes problems or is incompatible with other applications.

If you keep backups to the original AUTOEXEC.BAT and CONFIG.SYS files, you can install new applications and then use Notepad to compare the old and new versions of the files to see where changes occurred. Note these changes to see whether they are in an incorrect position or whether they change a setting required by Windows. Changes you don't want to accept can be *commented out* so that they do not work by typing the letters *REM* at the beginning of the line. REM stands for REMark. Adding back a remarked line is easy; just remove the REM at the beginning of the line.

Some changes you must watch for are detailed in the following list:

Unnecessary Drivers	Windows comes with drivers to handle the mouse, memory, monitors, and other devices. Because these drivers were created for Windows, use them rather than third-party drivers. *Comment out* unneeded drivers, leaving only those required by the system, network (if necessary), and Windows. DO NOT remove HIMEM.SYS or SMARTDRV.EXE

from the CONFIG.SYS file. Windows needs these drivers for optimum performance. HIMEM.SYS and SMARTDRV.EXE are discussed in a following section of this chapter.

Terminate-and-Stay-Resident Applications

TSRs (Terminate-and-Stay-Resident applications) are applications that stay in memory until activated by pressing a keystroke combination. TSRs loaded into memory prior to starting Windows consume valuable memory and are incompatible with Windows in some situations. If the AUTOEXEC.BAT contains statements to load TSRs, comment these out by using the REM statement. When needed, you always can load these applications from Windows.

Incompatible DOS Commands

Edit the AUTOEXEC.BAT file to remove or comment out the following commands. Because these incompatibilities are potentially destructive, remove them from the AUTOEXEC.BAT file before you install Windows.

Disable Shadow RAM

Some systems have the capability of loading ROM (Read Only Memory) into RAM to improve performance. RAM is faster than ROM, so this practice results in increased performance on the system. Unfortunately, this practice also consumes conventional memory and may be incompatible on some hardware with Windows. If you run many DOS applications and are tight on conventional memory, run the computer's setup software and disable Shadow RAM before you start Windows.

Set a TEMP Variable

Windows creates temporary files when running. These files act as a temporary working space for applications and windows. (These temporary files are different from the swap files and application swap files described in a following section of this chapter and in Chapter 26.)

From a housekeeping standpoint, specifying where Windows stores temporary files is a good idea. If the computer ever loses power or an application fails and the old temporary files aren't cleaned up by default, you will know where to look for the files so that you can erase them. These temporary files begin with ~ and have the file extension TMP.

| **Caution** | Never erase temporary files while Windows is running. Always exit Windows before erasing temporary files. |

A simple line in the AUTOEXEC.BAT file enables you to set a TEMP variable that specifies where on the hard disk to place temporary files. During setup, Windows inserts this statement for you. If Windows is on drive C, for example, the following line is inserted:

    SET TEMP=C:\WINDOWS\TEMP

You can keep this setting, or you can change the setting by editing the AUTOEXEC.BAT with the Notepad. If you edit the SET TEMP line, you must create the directory named by SET TEMP. Use the MD command in DOS or the File Manager to create this directory.

When choosing a directory for temporary files, keep the following guidelines in mind:

- Pick the fastest drive available.

- Set TEMP to a subdirectory (not the root directory).

- Make sure that 2 to 4M of free disk space is available for the temporary files on the selected drive.

Use the Most Recent Versions of the Windows Drivers

Be sure that you update the AUTOEXEC.BAT and CONFIG.SYS files to include only the latest versions of Windows memory and device drivers. Improvements were made to most of the drivers since Windows 3.0 was introduced, and you cannot substitute an old driver for a new one just because both drivers use the same name. If you install Windows 3.1 over the top of a previous version of Windows, the drivers are automatically updated.

EMM386.SYS and SMARTDRV.SYS, used in previous versions of Windows, were replaced with EMM386.EXE and SMARTDRV.EXE. Usually, you should use the latest version of a Windows driver, regardless of whether the source is a DOS upgrade or a new release of Windows. If you have two copies of the same driver, use the driver that displays the most recent creation date and delete the older driver from the system.

T I P

Many hardware manufacturers introduced upgrades to Windows device drivers. Check with the manufacturer of the equipment to be sure that you have the most recent driver.

Separate Windows and Windows Applications on the Disk

In the past, installation guides for some Windows applications recommended that you install application files in the Windows directory. Microsoft Excel is a good example. The problem with this advice is that no easy way exists to tell which files belong to the application and which files belong to Windows. This kind of installation makes upgrading Windows, or the application, difficult. Most applications enable you to upgrade over an older version in the same directory, but this procedure requires that you trust the installation application to remove old files. Unfortunately, application upgrades can neglect to delete old application files from the system, which subsequently can cause compatibility problems.

You can save work by installing each Windows application in a separate directory on the hard disk. Be sure that you also store data and applications in separate directories, which prevents having to cull the data from the application directory before you delete an outdated application from the disk.

Protect Your Initialization Files

Windows uses two initialization files to store information needed to run Windows on a computer. WIN.INI contains settings that relate to applications and to your preferences for the Windows environment. SYSTEM.INI contains information related to system hardware. In the past, Windows applications made use of WIN.INI to store different types of information, from preferences for screen display to default settings for fonts. Increasingly, Windows applications are being written to make use of their own INI files instead of cluttering the WIN.INI.

Before upgrading Windows, or a Windows application, make copies of the WIN.INI and SYSTEM.INI files. Call them WIN.SAV and SYSTEM.SAV. Sometimes an installation application adds lines to the WIN.INI file without deleting lines its earlier version left behind. Unless you plan to run both versions of an application, you probably don't want both sections in the WIN.INI file. Keeping a copy of the WIN.INI prior to the upgrade will allow you to recognize which sections to remove. In addition, it is sometimes helpful to know just what sections of the INI file an application affects. If you later decide to remove the application, you can edit the INI file to remove unnecessary commands.

Using Memory Efficiently

The performance of Windows is strongly influenced by the way you configure the computer's memory. In many ways, Windows memory management is a balancing act—each time you make use of a disk enhancer, such as SMARTDrive or a RAM disk, you must weigh the enhanced performance against the cost of the memory used. The more memory you have available for applications to use, the more applications you can run in Windows. On the other hand, dedicating portions of the memory to performance enhancement, thereby excluding them from use by applications, will make Windows sessions faster. There is really no single solution.

Memory management techniques are worth exploring, whether the supply of system memory is minimal (2 to 3M) or plentiful (8M or more). The less memory available, the greater the need to manage memory wisely. On the other hand, those with the luxury of plentiful extended memory have more options available for optimizing Windows. In either case, it is important to understand a bit about the memory on the system and how Windows uses it in each of its two operating modes. This section covers the basic concepts of memory, its use by Windows, and some of the tools for managing memory.

Understanding Memory

Figure 25.1 illustrates the areas of Random-Access Memory (RAM) in an 80286, 386, or 486 machine.

The first 640 Kilobytes (K) of memory is known as *conventional memory*. If you run DOS applications, this memory may be the computer's most precious resource. Conventional memory is the original location of the DOS operating system, hardware device drivers, and other system software. Before the advent of 80286 computers, conventional memory also was the only memory available to applications. DOS developers had to write applications that fit in whatever conventional memory remained after DOS and other system software was loaded. Most DOS applications still maintain compatibility with older computers by running within the confines of conventional memory.

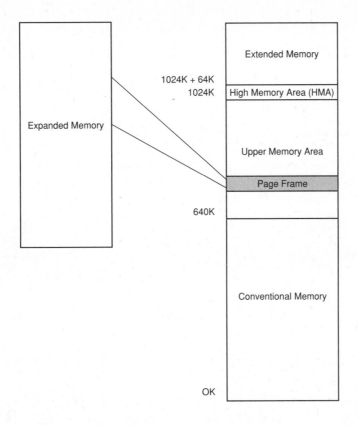

FIG. 25.1

Computer
memory
architecture.

The Upper Memory Area (UMA) is the memory between 640K and 1024K, which traditionally is reserved for use by accessory cards (such as a video adapter), Read-Only Memory (ROM), and the ROM BIOS. In an 80286 computer, this area of memory still is largely unavailable to applications. Using the features of DOS 5 or other memory management software on an 80386 or 80486, your computer can use this part of memory for device drivers and memory-resident applications. (See the section "Configuring Memory under DOS 5.0" later in this chapter.)

Expanded memory (or EMS memory) was designed to get around the 640K memory limit on DOS applications. EMS memory comes as an add-in board you install in the computer, and an Expanded Memory Manager (EMM) enables applications to use the board. Only applications written to work with an EMM can take advantage of expanded memory. EMS memory overcame the problems of being unable to exceed the 1024K memory barrier by redirecting the addresses within the area shown in figure 25.1 as the Page Frame. The EMM works by mapping small chunks of memory in and out of a sliver of memory in the UMA.

These portions of memory are known as *pages,* and the section of UMA is a *page frame*. The application looks at the memory area in the UMA shown as the Page Frame, but the application actually sees an area in the expanded memory. For years, expanded memory was the only additional memory available to application developers and, as a result, a variety of popular DOS applications require expanded memory to work. Because of the technical limits inherent in EMS, Windows doesn't use expanded memory, but you still can run DOS applications that require expanded memory. (See Chapter 24, "Customizing PIFs," to learn how to configure DOS applications to use expanded memory.)

Extended Memory (XMS memory) is the area of memory above 1024K on 80286, 80386, and 80486 computers. Extended memory mounts on the system board of the computer or on special add-in boards you install. Unlike expanded memory, extended memory doesn't need to be mapped in and out of the UMA to work. This advantage makes applications faster and easier for the programmers to write. XMS memory does require the use of an extended memory manager to coordinate its use by multiple applications. Windows doesn't differentiate between conventional memory and extended memory—but combines conventional and extended memory into a single source of memory that it can access directly when this memory is needed.

The *High Memory Area* (HMA) is the first 64K of extended memory above 1024K. If you have DOS 5.0, you load most of DOS in HMA, freeing an additional 45K of conventional memory for DOS applications. (The remaining portion of HMA is used for system resources.)

By using a special area of the hard disk as an extension of RAM, *virtual memory* is a mechanism for increasing the amount of memory available to applications. Using virtual memory, you may be able to run more applications at the same time than is normally possible when using the physical memory on the system.

Virtual memory is available in Windows 386-enhanced mode on 80386 or 80486 machines. When physical memory is tight, Windows begins to move 4K *pages* of code and data from memory to the hard disk to make more room in physical memory. Windows uses a *least-recently-used* technique to move pages of memory to the disk, selecting first the pages of code and data not recently accessed by an application. If an application requires a piece of data no longer in physical memory, Windows retrieves the information from disk, paging other information from memory to make room.

To applications running in Windows 386-enhanced mode, no difference exists between physical memory on the system and virtual memory on the disk. Windows can use up to 64M of memory (16M of physical memory and 48M of virtual memory on the hard disk) with this technique. The use of virtual memory slows Windows operation.

Calculation-intensive applications, such as worksheets, may run significantly slower if virtual memory is used.

Understanding How Windows Uses Memory

A major benefit of Windows is multitasking capability. Although only one application can use the computer processor at a given instant, in Windows, multitasking means that you can run multiple applications at the same time. Windows uses different methods to achieve multitasking in standard and 386-enhanced modes, primarily because standard mode must work within the confines of the 80286 processor.

Memory Management in Standard Mode

In standard mode, Windows applications are multitasking, but DOS applications are single tasking. This means that multiple Windows applications process information at the same time. A DOS application, however, operates in full-screen mode and monopolizes the processor, requiring all other applications to be suspended while the DOS application is active.

Windows applications can use either conventional or extended memory. DOS applications, however, run only in conventional memory. When you start a DOS application, Windows swaps the current application out of memory and writes an *application swap file* to the disk. If Windows and Windows applications are currently running, these applications are moved together to separate swap files on the disk, leaving behind only the portion of code needed to run the Task Switcher.

DOS applications aren't designed to multitask. Because Windows isn't in memory when a DOS application runs, Windows cannot provide multitasking capabilities. In standard mode, the only portion of Windows that remains in memory after a DOS application loads is the Task Switcher needed for Windows to restore itself. The Task Switcher responds to an Alt+Tab, Alt+Esc, or Ctrl+Esc key combination and swaps the active DOS application to disk to make room for Windows and any active Windows application.

When you press Alt+Esc to switch between DOS applications or to Windows, the active DOS application is moved to a separate application swap file on the disk. Each DOS application has an application swap file. Windows and all open Windows applications share one Windows swap file.

By default, application swap files are stored in the directory identified by the TEMP variable in AUTOEXEC.BAT. Swap files begin with a tilde (~) and have the extension, SWP. You can view the files from the File Manager, using the View By File Type command and then selecting the Show Hidden/System Files check box.

Caution   Do not delete swap files while Windows is running.

Memory Management in 386-Enhanced Mode

In 386-enhanced mode, both Windows and DOS applications multitask. Windows uses the special capabilities of the 80386 and 80486 processors to create a virtual machine for each DOS application's exclusive use. The *virtual machine* is a simulation of an 8086 processor and inherits the conventional memory configuration present before you start Windows. In 386-enhanced mode, Windows and Windows applications are contained in one virtual machine (the system VM), and each DOS application is contained in a separate virtual machine.

Imagine these virtual computers, stored end-to-end in the length of conventional through extended memory. Moreover, each virtual machine uses an image of the original conventional memory for DOS and TSRs loaded before Windows 3.1 starts.

This explains why having a well-configured and uncluttered conventional memory area is important. You duplicate this area for each virtual machine used by a DOS application. Clutter and waste becomes clutter and waste multiplied by the number of DOS applications running. If you optimize the use of this memory, loading drivers in upper memory and moving part of DOS to the HMA, you maximize conventional memory available *to every virtual machine*. If you neglect to clear TSRs and unnecessary applications from the AUTOEXEC.BAT, these applications are loaded in the original conventional memory area, and each virtual machine created will include a copy of the TSR. (See Chapters 23 and 26 for discussions on loading TSR efficiently.)

Running Windows 3.1 with DOS 5.0

One benefit of using DOS 5.0 is that you can load most of DOS into extended memory without using a third-party memory manager. If you load the operating system in extended memory, you save approximately 50K of conventional memory. You also can load device drivers and terminate-and-stay resident (TSR) applications in extended memory and therefore save even more conventional memory. This procedure frees more memory for DOS applications running under Windows.

DOS 5.0 is equipped with HIMEM.SYS, an extended memory manager that allows DOS 5.0 to load most of the operating system, and device drivers and TSRs above conventional memory. The significance is that by loading most of the operating system, the device drivers, and TSRs above conventional memory, more conventional memory is available for DOS applications. When used on an 80286, 80386, or 80486 PC, HIMEM.SYS provides HMA and XMS memory to DOS applications that can use it.

HIMEM.SYS opens three areas of memory above the 640K barrier that you can make available to applications:

- Upper Memory Area: (UMA) consists of the memory between 640K and 1024K. DOS 5.0 can load device drivers and memory-resident applications into the upper memory area. UMAs are created only on the 80386 and 80486 families of processors.

- High Memory Area: HMA is the first 64K of memory above 1024K. DOS 5.0 can load a portion of the operating system into the HMA.

- Extended Memory: includes all memory above 1024K.

You load HIMEM.SYS by entering a line, such as *DEVICE=C:\DOS\ HIMEM.SYS*, in the CONFIG.SYS file. Windows usually adds this line for you during installation. Windows uses the same memory manager, HIMEM.SYS, as DOS 5.0. Use the memory manager file that has the most recent date.

After the HIMEM.SYS memory manager loads, another line in the CONFIG.SYS loads most of DOS into the High Memory Area. The line, *DOS=HIGH*, must be in the CONFIG.SYS file *after* the HIMEM.SYS line.

To load device drivers in upper memory, the PC must be an 80386 or an 80486, and you must add device driver commands similar to the following listing to the CONFIG.SYS file, below the HIMEM.SYS statement:

```
DOS=HIGH, UMB

DEVICE=C:\DOS\EMM386.EXE RAM

DEVICEHIGH=C:\DOS\ANSI.SYS
```

The DEVICEHIGH command loads the ANSI.SYS driver in upper memory.

T I P
Many applications require you to load the ANSI.SYS driver before you can type certain characters. You can load this driver in upper memory by using the DeviceHigh command, as shown in the preceding listing, and save valuable conventional memory.

 NOTE
EMM386.EXE is incompatible with Windows running in standard mode. You must remove or disable the DEVICE=C:\DOS\EMM386.SYS RAM command in the CONFIG.SYS file if you run Windows in standard mode.

To load TSRs into upper memory, the PC must be an 80386 or an 80486, and you must include the following line in the AUTOEXEC.BAT file:

LOADHIGH *TSRname*

You must have the statements in the CONFIG.SYS file for loading HIMEM.SYS and EMM386.EXE, and the DOS=UMB statement.

Loading TSRs—whether or not in upper memory—before loading Windows is not recommended. See Chapters 23 and 26 for additional discussions on using TSRs within Windows.

DOS 5.0 installs a file named WINA20.386. This file must be present in the root directory. WINA20.386 is a driver that enables Windows to run DOS 5.0 even if DOS is loaded into HMA via the DOS=HIGH command. This is pertinent to 386-enhanced mode only.

NOTE
If you own an 80386 or 80486 system, DOS 5.0, and Windows, you have many options for controlling memory. But remember that Windows and all Windows applications use extended memory (in standard and 386-enhanced mode). Loading most of DOS, device drivers, and TSRs high will reduce the amount of memory available to Windows. If you are using mostly Windows applications, you should not use the DOS 5.0 memory enhancement commands. If you are using mostly DOS applications, you should go ahead and make use of DOS 5.0 memory management tools and open up as much conventional memory as possible for the DOS applications.

You can load device drivers in upper memory, which enables you to load selected drivers in high memory in the same way a TSR is loaded in high memory. To load a device driver in upper memory, after the

HIMEM.SYS, EMM386.EXE, DOS=HIGH, and UMB lines, add a command in CONFIG.SYS similar to the following line:

DEVICEHIGH=C:*path**devicefile.ext.*

Optimizing Hard Disk Performance

Besides an adequate amount of memory, the hardware resource most responsible for Windows performance is the hard disk. Most people consider the hard disk primarily as a storage area for applications and data. The hard disk, however, performs an additional function, serving as swap space for information that Windows moves to and from memory as needed. Because Windows accesses the hard disk so often, the drive's capability to move information to and from the disk directly affects performance. The most important areas you can change that affect hard disk performance for Windows are shown in the following list:

- Amount of free space
- Regular use of CHKDSK
- Amount of disk fragmentation
- Efficient use of SMARTDrive
- Creation of temporary and application swap files

Increasing Available Space

As Windows works, the hard disk is used to store temporary files, known as swap files. Because Windows frequently reads and writes these files, the efficiency of the hard disk affects Windows performance. If a large amount of storage is available on the hard disk, however, Windows can more easily find available and efficiently located space. Some procedures described in following sections of this chapter, such as creating swap files, are easier to apply if the hard disk has adequate available space.

The easiest step you can take to maximize free space on a hard disk is to delete all unnecessary files. If possible, make a backup of the disk before deleting files. This way, if you make a mistake and delete important files by accident you still can recover the data.

Erase data files and old applications from the File Manager. Any files that you are unsure of or that begin with a ~ (tilde) should be erased from DOS only when Windows is *not* running.

Begin by deleting old applications and data you no longer need. If you do not use the Windows accessories, such as Cardfile, Paintbrush, Calendar, and Calculator, you may want to delete their EXE files and the associated help files from the Windows directory.

Next, delete the *temp files* left behind by applications that terminated unexpectedly. These files usually end in the extension TMP or SWP and begin with a ~ (tilde). (Make sure that you erase these files from DOS when Windows is not running.) If you have one, clean out the TEMP directory. The TEMP directory is identified in the AUTOEXEC.BAT file with the statement SET TEMP=*path*. This directory is where temporary files should be stored. Finally, consider using a tape drive or other storage medium to archive historical data. If you haven't used the data in months, you probably should archive.

Using the CHKDSK Utility

After deleting unnecessary files, use the DOS command CHKDSK to find and recover lost file clusters (also known as *allocation units*). A *file cluster* is the smallest unit that can store a file on the hard disk. When applications terminate unexpectedly, a number of these clusters often are left on the disk, unaccounted for and inaccessible by the applications. As an analogy, these clusters are similar to scraps of paper, as though you started to write a sentence and then left the work unfinished.

CHKDSK finds and links the unfinished ends of lost clusters to other clusters beginnings—converting them to files that you can inspect or delete. Converted clusters appear in the root directory with a file name similar to FILE*xxxx*.CHK. If these files contain text, you may be able to read the contents with the Notepad.

To use CHKDSK, first *exit Windows*. (Never use CHKDSK from within Windows; doing so may destroy applications and data.) At the DOS prompt, type the following line:

    CHKDSK /F

If CHKDSK encounters lost clusters, you are asked if you want these clusters converted to files. Type Y and press Enter to proceed with the conversion. You are then shown how many clusters were found and how much storage space was recovered. Next display the directory of the root for files that end with CHK by typing the following line at the DOS prompt:

    DIR C:*.CHK

Check these files with Notepad for lost data you may want to recover and then delete them.

Defragmenting Your Disk

Information written to a hard disk is not necessarily stored in a *contiguous* (adjacent) block. Rather, fragments of information are more likely spread across the disk wherever the system can find room. The more you use the hard disk, the more fragmented the disk becomes. Obviously, the drive takes more time to hunt for information located in several places than it takes to fetch the same information from a single location. Because of this extra time, disk fragmentation can slow the computer's operation considerably.

Fortunately, a number of applications that compact the hard disk by restructuring files into contiguous blocks and moving free space to the end of the disk are available. A large block of contiguous free storage on the hard disk can be used by temporary and permanent swap files in 386-enhanced mode and by temporary application swap files in standard mode. All of these applications can improve Windows performance.

After you *defragment* the disk, you may want to put the defragmenting utility in the AUTOEXEC.BAT so that it compacts the disk on start-up. This reduces the time for defragmenting to a few seconds. The improved performance of the hard disk is well worth the investment.

Using SMARTDrive To Increase Disk Performance

SMARTDrive is a disk cache, a hard disk enhancement software package that comes with Windows. A *disk cache* works by reducing the amount of work Windows must do to write and read information to and from the hard disk. SMARTDrive sets aside an area of extended memory, known as a *cache*, which acts as a high-speed reservoir of disk information for Windows. When Windows needs a piece of data from the hard disk, Windows first checks to see whether the information is in the cache. Because the cache is electronic memory, the retrieval can be hundreds or even thousands of times faster than a mechanical disk drive.

If Windows doesn't find the needed data in the cache and must read new data from disk, the cache receives a new store of data. SMARTDrive has a good hit rate for guessing which information will be needed next and for storing that information in the cache.

A disk cache also can speed the process of storing information on a disk. Rather than writing information to the disk, Windows writes to the cache, which enables an application to continue a task without taking the time to access the hard drive. When the system has a spare moment, SMARTDrive moves the information from the cache to the disk. Although the increased performance is noticeable, this caching operation may not be noticeable to the user.

As mentioned previously, Windows and MS DOS 5.0 both come with the SMARTDrive disk-caching application. The SMARTDrive application that comes with Windows 3.1 is an improved version of the application that came with Windows 3.0 and DOS, so be sure that you use the most current version.

SMARTDRV.EXE is an application that you can run from the DOS prompt. During Setup, Windows installs SMARTDRV.EXE as the first line in the AUTOEXEC.BAT file. Because of this location in the AUTOEXEC.BAT file, SMARTDrive runs immediately on start-up and is then installed in the CONFIG.SYS file with a line similar to the following command:

DEVICE=C:\WINDOWS\SMARTDRV.EXE

T I P   Do not use SMARTDrive with other disk caching software. DOS disk caching software will not run with Windows. If you use a replacement for SMARTDrive, it must be designed for Windows.

To load SMARTDrive so that you can view the current settings, type *SMARTDRV* or *SMARTDRV /S* at the DOS prompt. When you run with /S SMARTDrive statistics display on-screen. A table similar to the following appears on the screen:

```
Microsoft SMARTDrive Disk Cache version 4.x.xxx
Copyright 1991,1992 Microsoft Corp.

Cache size: 2,097,152 bytes
Cache size while running Windows: 2,097,152 bytes

Disk Caching Status

drive         read cache       write cache       buffering
- - - - - - - - - - - - - - - - - - - - - - - - - - - - - - - - - - - - - - -

  A:           yes              no                no
  B:           yes              no                no
  C:           yes              yes               no
  D:           yes              yes               no
  E:           yes              yes               no

For help, type "Smartdrv /?".
```

Cache size is the size of the SMARTDrive disk cache when Windows is not running. The SMARTDrive application picks a value based on the amount of extended memory in the computer. The performance gains afforded by SMARTDrive tend to drop off after 2M.

The *Cache size while running in Windows* is the minimum size of the SMARTDrive disk cache when working in Windows. In 386-enhanced mode, Windows reduces the SMARTDrive cache to the minimum value and retains use of the extra memory until you exit. In standard mode, SMARTDrive works with HIMEM.SYS to *dynamically allocate* memory to Windows when memory is tight and take back memory for use by the cache when more memory is available.

The *Disk Caching Status* reports the drives on which read and write caching is currently in effect. The read cache holds information read from the hard disk. Information needed by an application can be supplied from the cache instead of being read from the disk. The write cache holds information to be written to the disk. When the computer and Windows are less busy, the information in the write cache is written to disk. By default, write cache is disabled for diskettes.

Double buffering refers to the process of *buffering* information transferred to and from the disk. Using this method, a small amount of memory (the *buffer*) intercepts all information moving to and from the disk. Information is written from memory to the buffer and then read from the buffer to the disk. Double buffering is required in systems with a BIOS chip more than three years old and in systems equipped with an SCSI drive. If, after running SMARTDrive, any of the entries in the buffering column of the SMARTDrive table are *yes*, the following line must be present in the CONFIG.SYS file:

DEVICE=SMARTDRV.EXE /DOUBLE_BUFFER

During Setup, Windows evaluates the system and, if necessary, inserts this line in the CONFIG.SYS file. Windows may insert the line even if you don't need it, resulting in a very slight degradation in performance reading and writing to the disk. If every line in the SMARTDrive column is *no*, you can remove this line from the CONFIG.SYS file.

Increasing Performance with Swap Files and Virtual Memory

Swapping is the process of freeing space in memory by moving information to the hard disk. Nearly all applications use some kind of swapping when working. Swapping, however, encompasses a broad category of operations that involve memory and hard disk space. An application swap file, for example, differs in operation from the swap file used by the Virtual Memory Manager in 386-enhanced mode.

The following definitions may help you to sort out the major uses of swap files and temporary files.

Virtual Memory Swap File	Single file on the hard disk, either temporary or permanent, that is treated by the 386 processor as extended memory. Increases memory recognized by Windows 386-enhanced mode by the amount of disk space allocated to swap file.
Application Swap File	File created for each DOS application running in Windows standard mode. Stored by default in the TEMP directory named by the variable in AUTOEXEC.BAT. Provides appearance of multitasking by providing a space to store inactive applications when other applications are loaded and running in memory.
Temporary Files	Files used by applications to hold information temporarily swapped out of memory. Stored by default in the directory named by the TEMP variable in AUTOEXEC.BAT.

Configuring Virtual Memory in 386-Enhanced Mode

Windows uses disk swapping as a way of expanding the apparent memory of the computer when Windows runs in 386-enhanced mode. Disk swapping occurs when Windows lacks enough RAM to load an application and must move some or all of a Windows or DOS application out of memory and to a hard disk.

> **NOTE** Don't confuse virtual memory swap files used in 386-enhanced mode with *temporary application swap files* used by DOS applications when running in Windows standard mode. These files are different. Temporary application swap files, which aren't used by Windows in 386-enhanced mode, are used by DOS applications and are described in Chapter 26's discussion on improving the performance of DOS applications.

When you run Setup, Windows examines the available space on the hard disk and looks for a large contiguous (single continuous piece) of storage. If Setup finds a large enough contiguous section of storage, a permanent swap file is created. The permanent swap file, 386SPART.PAR, is installed in the root directory of the drive selected by Windows. A small companion file, SPART.PAR, is located in the Windows directory.

If Windows finds no suitable space for a permanent swap file, a temporary swap file is placed on the drive that contains the SYSTEM.INI file. The temporary swap file is known as WIN386.SWP. If insufficient space is available for a temporary swap file, no swap file is created. In this case, Windows performance can become significantly slower.

Swap files are system files and, although you can see these files by displaying hidden files with the View menu in the File Manager, do not delete them. If needed, use the 386 Enhanced application in the Control Panel to remove virtual memory, which is described later.

You can change the type or size of the virtual memory you have. You can increase Windows performance by creating a larger permanent swap file. To make a larger permanent swap file, you need to delete unused files and clean up the hard disk. You also may need to defragment the disk so that the available storage is in a contiguous area.

T   I   P   If you need more disk storage space, you can reduce the size of the permanent swap file, or you can change the file to a temporary swap file. Although this procedure may reduce the performance of Windows, through trial and error, you may find a good balance between adequate disk space and adequate performance.

A permanent swap file is composed of a contiguous (unfragmented) portion of the hard disk where data is stored as a continuous section. Because parts of a permanent swap file are read in a continuous stream, this kind of file may be much faster than a temporary swap file. If you don't have much available storage on the hard disk or if the available storage is dispersed over the disk, then use a temporary swap file. (The permanent swap file is not really permanent on the hard disk and can be removed with the 386 Enhanced program in the Control Panel.)

Before you create a permanent swap file, run a disk defragmenting program. Defragmenting speeds the performance of both temporary and permanent swap files and increases the available space for a permanent swap file.

T   I   P   By default, Windows creates the temporary swap file in the directory that contains the SYSTEM.INI file, which usually is the WINDOWS directory. You can specify, however, a temporary swap file drive and size in the [386Ehn] section of the SYSTEM.INI file. A MinUserDiskSpace line controls the minimum amount of disk space to allocate for the temporary swap file, and a MaxPagingFileSize line controls the maximum size of the temporary swap file. PagingDrive specifies the drive on which to create the temporary swap file. The following example creates a 2M temporary swap file on drive D:

```
[386Enh]
PagingDrive=D
MaxPagingFileSize=2048
MinUserDiskSpace=1024
```

After creating room for a swap file, you can create or change the swap file by selecting the 386 Enhanced icon in the Control Panel from the Main program group. Select the Virtual Memory option button. The Virtual Memory dialog box appears (see fig. 25.2). The Type and Size indicators show the kind and size of virtual memory currently specified.

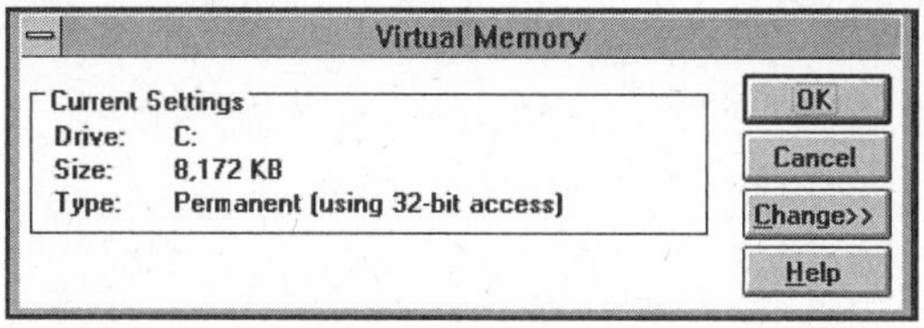

FIG. 25.2

The Virtual
Memory dialog
box.

To change the size, location, and kind of swap file Windows uses, follow
these steps:

1. Open the Control Panel from the Main group window in the Program Manager.

2. Choose the 386 Enhanced program. The 386 Enhanced dialog box
   appears.

3. Choose the **Virtual Memory** button.

   Windows scans the disk for available storage; then the Virtual
   Memory dialog box appears. The current settings appear. If these
   settings are acceptable, choose Cancel twice and don't follow the
   remainder of these steps.

4. Choose the **Change** button.

   The dialog box expands and configuration options for a virtual
   memory swap file appear. Depending upon whether you choose a
   permanent or temporary swap file, the dialog box changes options
   and displayed information.

5. Make the changes and then choose OK twice and close the Control Panel.

After you choose the **Virtual Memory** button, the **Drive**, **Type** and New
Size of swap file currently assigned to 386-enhanced mode are shown in
the New Settings portion of the dialog box. The options and the maximum and recommended size of swap file change, depending upon the
type of swap file you select from the drop-down list. Figures 25.3 and
25.4 show the different views.

If you are setting up a temporary swap file, the New **Size** text box indicates the maximum amount of disk space Windows can allocate to the
swap file during a Windows session. A temporary swap file shrinks and
expands according to demand for memory, and the New **Size** value
indicates the maximum size to which the file can grow. The Recommended Maximum Size (entered by default in the New **Size** text box) is
based on the space available.

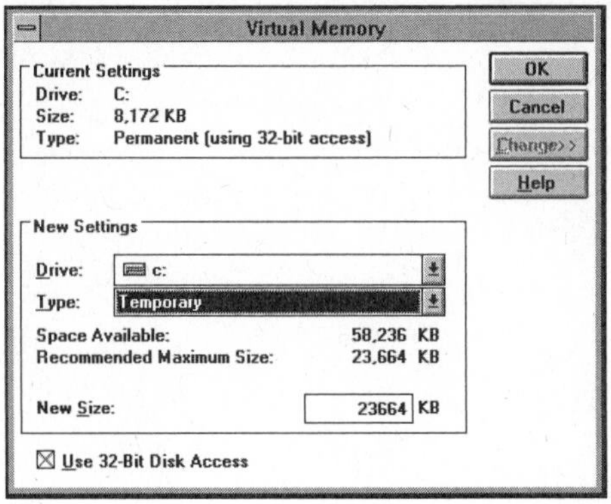

FIG. 25.3

These settings appear when you configure a temporary swap file.

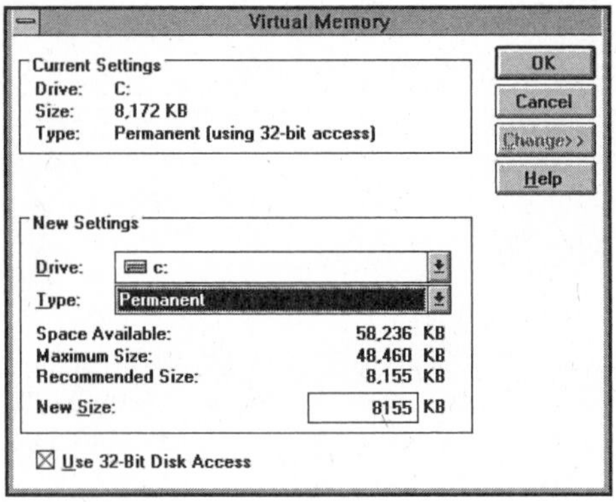

FIG. 25.4

These settings appear when you configure a permanent swap file.

If you are configuring a permanent swap file, the New **S**ize text box indicates the amount of space to allocate to a permanent file on the hard disk. Maximum Size is roughly one half of the contiguous space available on the disk. (Windows displays a warning message if you try to set a larger New **S**ize value). Usually, allocating the largest possible swap file is a good idea, but no more than three or four times the amount of the physical memory. If you have 4M of RAM, for example, allocate a swap file of 16M or less.

Chapter Summary

Windows attempts to make many configuration changes discussed in this chapter when you initially run Setup. If you find the performance isn't adequate, however, you can follow the techniques described here for making more memory available and improving hard disk performance and then reinstall Windows or make manual adjustments.

Windows users who face performance problems find most solutions in the straightforward measures covered in this chapter. If you use an 80286 or 80386SX computer, you should have a minimum of 4M of RAM for adequate performance. With an 80386 computer, you can expect good performance with multiple applications with 4M.

Enhancing DOS Application Performance

E nhancing the performance of DOS applications running in
Windows can be approached in four steps:

1. If you operate in 386-enhanced mode, use normal Windows techniques to make an application faster, such as running it full screen
   or running in Exclusive mode.

2. Use the techniques described in Chapter 25 for enhancing Windows performance overall by increasing memory and disk performance.

3. Customize the application's PIF to clean out settings designed to
   handle worst-case situations, such as high-resolution graphics.

4. Go through a triage that balances certain windows features
   against the memory cost they incur, such as the capability to
   copy a graphic screen.

> **Make Significant Performance Improvements in Two Areas**
> You probably will get the most significant performance improvements by making two improvements to your hardware. For a few hundred dollars, you can add memory to your computer so that it has at least 4M and then set up the SMARTDrive software to increase apparent disk performance.
>
> For even less cost, use disk defragmenting software to compact and defragment your hard disk so that it works more efficiently. After you have defragmented your hard disk, create a permanent swap file if you are running Windows in 386-enhanced mode. These changes, along with increased memory, improved hard disk performance from defragmenting, and a permanent swap file, give you significant performance improvements.

FROM HERE...

For Related Information:

◀◀ To learn more about Enhancing Windows Performance, see "Using Memory Efficiently," p. 962 and "Optimizing Hard Disk Performance," p. 969.

Operating DOS Applications Efficiently

The following list presents a few simple tips on operating DOS applications. These tips should make your DOS applications run faster.

■ In standard or 386-enhanced mode, shut down applications or documents that you are not using. These documents consume memory and may consume computer processing time.

■ Fine tune your system according to the tips in Chapter 25 so that Windows runs faster. In most cases, the small cost to bring your computer's memory up to at least 4M is well worth the significant increase you experience in Windows' performance, and you do not have to perform the arcane manipulations with memory and configuration files.

■ Defragment your hard disk and set up a permanent swap file if you run in 386-enhanced mode. Defragmentation means that all files are in order, and data can be retrieved more quickly than if your data is fragmented. A permanent swap file enables Windows to swap information between memory and hard disk much faster.

■ In 386-enhanced mode, operate DOS applications full screen when possible. Press Alt+Enter to toggle the application between full screen and windows.

■ In 386-enhanced mode, don't operate DOS applications in the background if the application does not need processing while in background.

■ In 386-enhanced mode, if you decide that you need more processing speed in the active DOS application, press Alt+space bar to open the Control menu. Choose the Settings command and then select the Exclusive check box and choose OK. This action gives the application the maximum processor time while the application runs full screen.

■ In 386-enhanced mode, control the ratio of computer time that Windows applications and DOS applications receive. Use the 386 Enhanced application in the Control Panel to change the Scheduling group so that Windows applications receive a lower weighting for computer time while operating in the background. (This change decreases the performance of all your Windows applications.)

Improving Performance with Swap Files

When you start a DOS application in standard mode, Windows creates a space on the hard disk to store that application when you switch away from the application. This space is a *temporary application swap file*. (These files are different from the temporary or permanent swap files used in 386-enhanced mode and described in Chapter 25.)

In standard mode, Windows cannot run a DOS application and Windows applications at the same time as it can in 386-enhanced mode. In standard mode, you also cannot run two DOS applications at the same time. When you have one or more DOS applications open, you switch to an application to use it or switch away from the DOS application when you want to use another application.

When you switch away from a DOS application, the program is copied from RAM to the temporary application swap file on the hard disk. Swapping the DOS program from memory makes memory available for Windows or another application. The number of swap files that can be created on your hard disk is governed by the amount of free space that you have available on the hard disk. When you quit an application, Windows deletes the swap file.

Temporary swap files are hidden and use names starting with ~WOA. Never delete these swap files while Windows is running. Usually, they are put in the TEMP directory specified in the AUTOEXEC.BAT file. If your AUTOEXEC.BAT file does not specify a TEMP file, they are stored in the root directory of the first hard disk. You can define where you want application swap files located by a setting in the [NonWindowsApp] segment of your SYSTEM.INI file. For example, the following line places temporary swap files in the C drive in the directory TEMPSWAP:

    swapdisk=C:\TEMPSWAP

You can use the Notepad to edit the SYSTEM.INI file. Save the SYSTEM.INI file and restart Windows for the changes to take effect.

T I P   Use the swap disk setting in the SYSTEM.INI file to specify the *fastest* hard disk you have as the location for the application swap files. The disk should have at least 512K of available free space.

T I P   Generally, using a RAM disk as a location for the temporary application swap files is not a good idea. Using the RAM as part of SMARTdrive is usually more efficient.

Frequently running a disk defragmenting application increases the performance of your hard drives by making them more efficient. This increased performance enables you to switch between DOS applications more rapidly.

FROM HERE...

For Related Information:

◀◀ To learn more about the temporary or permanent swap files used in 386-enhanced mode, see "Loading More DOS Applications Than Memory Can Hold," p. 881.

Improving Performance by Changing Standard PIF Options

Before changing an option in a DOS application PIF, be sure to read the description of that option in Chapter 24. The PIF options for real or standard modes that help you increase memory follow:

Option	Description
Video Mode	Affects the amount of memory reserved for the application's display. Set this option to Text to reduce the amount of memory set aside for the application and to make more memory available elsewhere. The application must run in text mode and cannot display high-resolution graphics. If you change modes, such as switching from text to graphics mode in 1-2-3, you may not be able to switch from the application to Windows. You must quit the application to return to Windows.
KB Required	Using a number higher than the minimum necessary to get the application started wastes memory. This number specifies the minimum amount of conventional memory required to start the application, not how much memory is allocated to the application. If you receive an out-of-memory warning before the application starts, you do not have sufficient available memory to start the application. Reduce the memory specified by this setting. If the application starts but later displays its own out-of-memory warning, use one of the other techniques to free more memory.
XMS Memory	Affects the amount of extended memory reserved for the application. (Most applications do not use extended memory; Lotus 1-2-3 Release 3 does.) If the application does not use extended memory, set the XMS Memory: KB Required and XMS Memory: KB Limit options to 0.
No Screen Exchange	Affects the memory set aside for screen images copied to the Clipboard when you press Print Screen (PrtScrn) or Alt+PrtScrn. You cannot copy and paste the application's display when this option is active, but more memory is available for the application. If you are not copying and pasting between DOS applications, you can turn this option off to save memory.

continues

Option	Description
Prevent Program Switch	Affects how you return to Windows. This option makes more memory available for the application, but you have to quit the application to return to Windows. This option makes it difficult to switch between applications and basically does away with the advantages of using DOS applications with Windows.

FROM HERE...

For Related Information:

◄◄ To learn more about the PIF option, see "Understanding PIF Editor Options," p. 926.

Improving Performance by Changing PIF Options in 386-Enhanced Mode

Before changing an option in a PIF for operation in 386-enhanced mode, be sure to read the description of the option in Chapter 24. The PIF options for 386-enhanced mode that help you free memory follow:

Option	Description
KB Required	Affects the amount of memory reserved for an application's program code. If the application starts but later runs out of memory, try reducing the KB Required amount to free more memory. If the application uses extended or expanded memory, you may have to increase the XMS Memory or EMS Memory option amounts.
Display Usage	Affects whether the application runs in a window or full screen. Run the application in a full screen to use less memory and operate faster. You also can switch between full screen and windowed mode at any time by pressing Alt+Enter.

Option	Description
Execution	Other DOS applications stop when **Exclusive** is selected and when the application with this setting is in the foreground (active) and full screen. This option prevents simultaneous operation of applications and releases more memory and processor time to the application in the foreground. When Execution is **Exclusive**, set Display Usage to **Full** Screen for maximum benefit; otherwise, Windows uses part of the system resources.

It is not necessary to use EMM386.EXE to emulate expanded memory when running Windows in 386-enhanced mode. In 386-enhanced mode, Windows simulates expanded memory. You may use EMM386.EXE, however, to create upper memory blocks (UMBs) to load device drivers in upper memory. Loading device drivers in upper memory, or loading high, increases the amount of conventional memory available.

T I P

Before changing an option in a PIF for operation in 386-enhanced mode, be sure to read the description of the option in Chapter 24. The PIF options for 386-enhanced mode that help manage multitasking are listed in a following table.

Check the Detect Idle Time Option
If an application is extremely slow, Windows may be assuming that the application is frequently idle; Windows then may be relinquishing the application's share of processor time to other applications. To improve performance, try clearing the **D**etect Idle Time check box under Multitasking Options in the application's 386-enhanced PIF. If this action does not improve performance, select the **D**etect Idle Time check box so that the performance of other applications is not reduced.

Quick Screen Refresh with Windowed Applications

When you run DOS applications in a window in 386-enhanced mode, you may notice a delay in the application's screen refresh. This delay is due to Windows multitasking; Windows gives part of the processor time to all running applications. You can affect the rate at which Windows updates the display of DOS applications running in a window. A setting in the SYSTEM.INI file, WindowUpdateTime, controls the priority given to updating DOS applications running in a Window. If your SYSTEM.INI file does not include a WindowUpdateTime line, you must insert it yourself. Full screen DOS applications are not affected by the WindowUpdateTime setting. The following setting should be added to your SYSTEM.INI file:

```
[386Enh]
WindowUpdateTime=700
```

The WindowUpdateTime is the priority given to updating the windowed DOS applications when Windows has other tasks running in the background. Increasing this setting gives more time to the windowed DOS application. The default is 50. The maximum value allowed is 1000.

Advanced PIF options available to applications running in 386-enhanced mode also make a difference in memory and processor performance. The following list shows the advanced PIF options that you can change to make a difference in performance.

Advanced Option	Description
Multitasking	Affects the percentage of processor time the application receives when the application is in the foreground or background and Execution Exclusive is not selected. The Foreground and Background Priority numbers determine the percentage of processor time given the application as a weighted portion of the time given all the running applications. (Chapter 24 explains this weighting in more detail.) Detect Idle Time should be selected so that other applications can run while Windows waits for input from the user.

Advanced Option	Description
EMS Memory	Affects how Windows emulates expanded memory in 386-enhanced mode. Usually, if you leave KB Required at 0, Windows allocates as much memory as is needed, up to the amount specified in KB Limit. To limit memory use, set the maximum amount of expanded memory in the KB Limit text box. The Locked option prevents Windows from swapping this memory to disk. Locking memory increases application speed by letting this application keep memory. However, this locking memory also limits the memory available to other applications and can slow them down.
XMS Memory	Affects an application's use of extended memory. Few applications require this option, so set KB Required and KB Limit to 0. If an application does use extended memory, you can set the Locked option to increase performance by locking memory so that other applications cannot use it. Locking memory, however, slows the performance of other applications because they cannot use the memory.
Uses High Memory Area	Affects the high-memory area (HMA) of extended memory (the first 64K of extended memory). This option tells Windows that the application is allowed to use high memory. HMA, when available, increases application performance. Set this option unless a network driver or other utility is loaded into HMA before Windows is started. If HMA is in use when you start Windows, no applications running under Windows can use HMA. In 386-enhanced mode, each DOS application can access its own HMA since HMA is duplicated for every DOS session in this mode. Keep this option selected because if HMA is available and the application uses it, more memory is available to the application. If the application does not use HMA, no memory is wasted.
	One of the most significant improvements offered by DOS 5.0 is the capacity to load most of the operating system into extended memory. DOS 5.0, like Windows, has a memory manager, HIMEM.SYS, that enables DOS to access extended memory. Before DOS 5.0 can use extended memory, the HIMEM.SYS

continues

Advanced Option	Description
	memory manager must be loaded with a `DEVICE=C:\WINDOWS\HIMEM.SYS` line and a `DOS=HIGH` line in the CONFIG.SYS file. Note, however, that you should use the Windows HIMEM.SYS, not the DOS Version 5. DOS loads most of the operating system in HMA. When DOS is loaded into the High Memory Area, the HMA is not available to DOS applications running in Windows.
Lock Application Memory	Affects the application by locking it in memory and not allowing the application to swap to the hard disk as long as the application is running. This option increases the performance of the application but decreases the performance of Windows and other applications.
Display Options	Affects the amount of memory reserved for video modes. To save memory, select the Text option and run your application only in text mode. To make additional memory available to the system, clear the Retain Video Memory option. This action may improve speed by increasing available memory, but with most applications, you cannot be in a high-resolution video mode, switch to another application, and then switch back. When you switch back, the screen does not refresh.

NOTE The high memory area is the first 64K of extended memory. You must have the Windows memory manager, HIMEM.SYS, or some other compatible memory manager, loaded to make this 64K available to Windows or any application that requests it. If you do not have a memory manager, no application can access the high memory area. See Chapter 25 for a discussion of HMA.

The speed of DOS applications in 386-enhanced mode is greatly improved by turning off all the Monitor Ports options in the application's PIFs. By default, the High Graphics option is on; the High Graphics option takes up approximately double the memory of the Low Graphics choice. All the Monitor Ports options should be clicked off unless you are having trouble when you switch from Windows to your application.

T I P

For Related Information:

◄◄ To learn more about the PIF option, see "Understanding PIF Editor Options," p. 926.

FROM HERE...

Changing Performance While Running in 386-Enhanced Mode

When you change PIFs, you are making permanent changes to how a DOS application performs. However, you can make some temporary changes even as an application is running in 386-enhanced mode. You can use the **S**ettings command in an application's Control menu to change the Display Option, the processor Priority, and the Tasking Options, all of which affect performance. The **S**ettings command is described in detail in Chapter 24, "Customizing PIFs."

To change performance while an application is running, follow these steps:

1. Choose the **S**ettings command from the Control menu by pressing Alt+space bar and choosing the **S**ettings command.

2. Select one of the options in the following chart to change performance:

Option	Description
Display Option	Select Full for less memory use; select Window for more memory use. (Press Alt+Enter while the application is running.)
Priority	Type a number for the Foreground and Background weighting. The size of this number, relative to the corresponding numbers of other running applications, determines how much processor time the application receives (refer to Chapter 24, "Customizing PIFs").
Tasking Options	Select Exclusive to suspend other applications while this application is in the active window. If this application is in a window, other Windows applications can run, but DOS applications are put on hold. Use the Exclusive and Full Screen display options together to dedicate the maximum amount of computer resources to the active application when it is full screen. Background enables this application to run in the background.

FROM HERE...

For Related Information:

◄◄ To learn more about the Settings command, see "Changing Settings of a Running Application," p. 943.

Balancing Windows and DOS Applications

Getting your system to run Windows applications and DOS applications smoothly is usually a matter of fine tuning the DOS application's PIFs. You also can use settings in the 386 Enhanced application in the Control Panel to balance the computer use between all DOS and all Windows applications.

Windows applications share CPU time equally; therefore, no foreground or background relationship exists among Windows applications. DOS applications, because they were written for a single-tasking system, expect exclusive use of the CPU. By necessity, if you run multiple applications at the same time in 386-enhanced mode and each application uses part of the processor's calculating power, the performance of all the applications diminishes. With the Control Panel, however, you can specify how much processor time all Windows applications share in relation to all DOS applications.

To schedule different amounts of processing power between Windows and DOS applications, follow these steps:

1. Open the Control Panel from the Main group window in the Program Manager.

2. Choose the 386 Enhanced icon from the Control Panel. (This icon appears only when you are in 386-enhanced mode.)

   The 386 Enhanced dialog box appears.

3. Select one of the following Scheduling options:

Option	Use
Windows in Foreground:	Type a large number if you want more processing power for Windows applications than for DOS applications. Use a number from 1 to 10,000. Usually, this number needs to be much larger than the Windows in **B**ackground text box entry so that the active application operates faster and doesn't keep you waiting.
Windows in **B**ackground:	Type a larger number than in the Windows in Foreground box if you want more processing power for the Windows applications in the inactive windows. Use a number from 1 to 10,000. (This selection slows down the performance in the window in which you are working.)
Exclusive in Foreground:	Select this box to ensure that the active applications always gets the maximum amount of the processing time. Applications in the background are left on hold.
Minimum Timeslice	The length of time given to each DOS application is controlled by using the **M**inimum Timeslice setting. This setting determines the amount of time (in milliseconds) that a DOS session or DOS application controls the CPU before Windows may switch to another process. If no other process needs the CPU, the DOS session may have the CPU longer than the **M**inimum Timeslice. Windows always gives the DOS session CPU time at least equal to the **M**inimum Timeslice. The default is 20 milliseconds.

4. Choose OK.

Using WINSTART.BAT To Load TSRs

Windows has a file similar to the AUTOEXEC.BAT file. When Windows loads, it looks for a file called WINSTART.BAT and, if that file is found, runs any commands in that file before loading Windows. This batch file must be located in the Windows directory and executes only if you start Windows in 386-enhanced mode.

If you start a TSR in WINSTART.BAT, the TSR is available only in Windows applications. Any DOS applications you start after loading Windows cannot use the TSR.

If a TSR is loaded *before* you start Windows, that TSR loads every time you start a DOS application or DOS session in Windows. Loading the TSR in each DOS application's memory area like this, whether or not the TSR is needed or wanted, is a waste of memory. Using WINSTART.BAT saves memory.

If you want the TSR to be available to a single DOS application, have the DOS application's PIF run a batch file that starts the TSR and then starts the application. This type of batch file is described in Chapter 23, "Running DOS Applications."

Chapter Summary

Before you begin making subtle changes to PIFs and worrying about minor changes to configuration and system files, examine the big picture. Is your hard disk as clean as possible of unneeded files? Have you run a disk defragmenting application to increase your hard disk efficiency? Can you bring your system up to 4M memory for less cost than the time it would take you to tweak every nuance in the system?

Make sure that you read Chapter 25's descriptions of how to increase overall Windows performance. In addition, when you install Windows, a number of information files are stored in the WINDOWS directory. Read these files using Windows Write, the word processor that comes with Windows. These files are located in the \WINDOWS directory and use WRI and TXT file extensions.

Networking with Windows for Workgroups

Before Windows for Workgroups, the thought of installing a network made most computer consultants cringe, division managers curse, and small business owners cry. In addition to buying the network hardware and software, you had to install a folding cot, sleeping bag, and at least two week's worth of food for the network consultant who came to live with you while the network was installed.

With the release of Windows for Workgroups, networks are within nearly every division or small business's comfort zone. Networks still require installation and setup, but those steps are nearly as easy as installing Windows or most Windows applications. And the advantages of Windows for Workgroups make it a definite plus for small groups of workers.

Understanding Workgroups and Networks

Before you begin to use Windows for Workgroups, you may want to learn a few terms that describe networked computers. Table 27.1 lists some network terms that you hear and use with Windows for Workgroups. The terms are defined here for you.

Table 27.1 Windows for Workgroups Network Terms and Definitions

Term	Definition
Client/Server Network	On client/server networks, one computer is specified as the network server. It takes on all management tasks and network overhead. The cost of this additional computer makes client/server networks more expensive but also makes them faster. Client/server networks usually require that one person be trained as the network administrator. It is this person's job to set up and maintain how resources are shared on the network. This can give a client/server network more structure and manageability.
Log on/Log off	Logging on the network lets the network know that you want to be able to use other resources on the network. If you are using a network password, you are asked for the password when you log on. When you log off, the network resources on the network are no longer available to you.
Network	A network is two or more computers linked by a cable, adaptors, and network software. Each computer is connected to the network via a network adaptor. The adaptor sends signals between computers through the cable. Windows for Workgroups has built-in software that enables people who use the network to exchange files, share printers, and use workgroup applications.

Term	Definition
Password	Passwords are secret words that limit users to certain resources on the network. You can have a password that gives you access to the network or a password into each resource. A network password enters the password for other resources that may require a password from you.
Peer-to-Peer Network	On peer-to-peer networks, the computers in the network share the workload; each is a peer. Each computer on the network manages some of the work, such as sharing and sending files, managing mail, or sharing printers. Peer-to-peer networks are less expensive and easier to install than client/server networks. They are usually slower than client/server networks. In the Windows for Workgroups peer-to-peer network, each user maintains responsibility for the resources they share with the workgroup.
Resource	A resource is the printer or directory and files attached to your computer. You can share the resources you select with others in your workgroup. Workgroup resources are all the resources shared on the network.
Sharing Resources	You must specify which resources, printers, and directories you want other workgroup members to have access to. You can assign passwords to different levels of sharing for different resources. These passwords are useful if you want to allow some people to have full access to the files in a directory and limit others to only reading, not changing, files.
Workgroup	A workgroup is a group of people whose computers are connected on the network. These users are collected under one workgroup name. They share resources and can use such workgroup applications as the Clipbook, Mail, and Schedule+ to improve how the workgroup functions as a unit.

Starting Windows for Workgroups

If Windows for Workgroups has already been installed, as described in Appendix B, you can start Windows for Workgroups. Windows for Workgroups looks and acts very similarly to Windows, but you may be asked to *log on* to the network when Windows starts.

After you install Windows for Workgroups, you can start Windows for Workgroups from the DOS prompt by typing *WIN* and pressing Enter. When Windows for Workgroups starts, you may or may not see the Welcome to Windows for Workgroups logon dialog box shown in figure 27.1, because the options in your Windows for Workgroups may be set to start without logging on the network. (You can log on any time after you start, or you can change options so that you are asked to log on when you start Windows.)

FIG. 27.1

The Welcome to Windows for Workgroups logon dialog box.

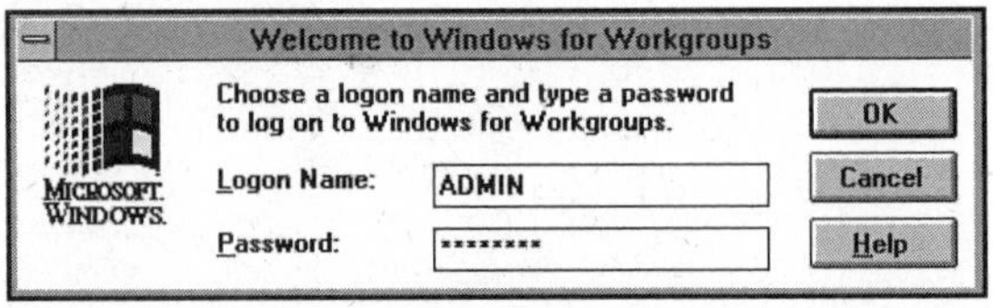

If the Welcome to Windows for Workgroups logon dialog box appears, follow these steps:

1. Select the **L**ogon Name edit box and type the name you have given your computer.

2. Select the **P**assword edit box and type your password.

Logging On and Off the Network

NOTE If you log off the network while others are using your shared directory or printer, the other users could lose data or a print job. Be polite and notify people via the telephone, Mail, or Chat that you will be logging off. To see who is using your resources, use the Net Watch application described in the Windows accessories chapter.

You can log on or off the network at any time. And you or any other person in your workgroup can log on your workgroup from any computer. If you log off your computer, someone else can log back on your computer using his or her computer name. To log on or off, follow these steps:

1. Start the Control Panel from the Main group window in the Program Manager.

2. Double-click the Network icon in the Control Panel or press the arrow keys to select the Network icon, and then press Enter.

   The Network Settings dialog box appears as shown in figure 27.2. Use this dialog box to log on or off the network, and to change names, passwords, network settings, or configurations.

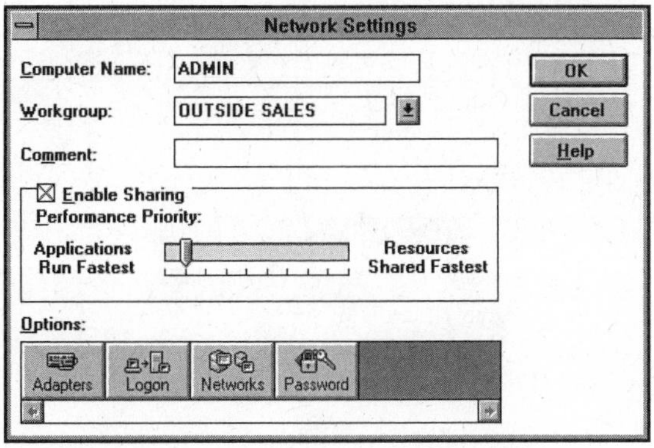

FIG. 27.2

Use the Network Settings dialog box to adjust your network configuration and performance.

3. Choose the **Logon** button at the bottom of the Network Settings dialog box.

   If you are using the mouse, click on the Logon button. If you are using the keyboard, press Alt+O to select the **O**ptions group, use the left- or right-arrow keys to select the Logon button, then press the space bar to choose the Logon button.

   The Logon Settings dialog box appears as shown in figure 27.3. If you are currently logged on the network, the button appears as **Log Off**. If you are disconnected from the network, the button appears as **Log On**.

4. If you are logged on and want to log off, choose the **Log Off** button. As the dialog box in figure 27.4 shows, you are warned that you will lose resources available on the network, such as shared

printers and directories. Others on the network will still be able to use your resources that you have specified as shared.

or

If you are off the network and need to log on, choose the Log On button. The Welcome to Windows for Workgroups logon dialog box displays and prompts you for the computer name and password. Type your computer name and password.

FIG. 27.3

The Logon Settings dialog box enables you to log on or off the network while you remain in Windows.

FIG. 27.4

Logging off makes workgroup resources unavailable to you.

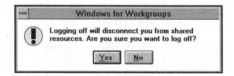

5. Choose OK or press Enter to leave the Logon Settings dialog box.

6. Choose OK or press Enter to leave the Network Settings dialog box.

Sharing Resources

Windows for Workgroups gives you and others in your workgroup the ability to share resources like printers, directories, and the files they contain, and the Clipbook. The Clipbook is like a shared Clipboard, which everyone can use to link to the same graphs, tables, or text.

It can be very useful to share directories within your workgroup. You may have budget files that everyone needs to use. Or you may have a Word or Excel template that everyone shares to create standardized forms, letters, or worksheets. These are much easier to maintain if there is only a single copy that everyone in the workgroup uses. Of course, sharing files over the network also reduces the amount of running down the hall you have to do while clutching a handful of diskettes. To learn about sharing directories and files, refer to the Windows for Workgroup sections in Chapter 5, "Managing Files with the File Manager."

When a company wants to save money in its computer budget while remaining productive one of the first things it should consider is using shared laser printers. Laser printers are mandatory for professional-looking business correspondence and reports, but their expense makes them prohibitive for each user to have one. When you use Windows for Workgroups you can share printers across the workgroup. To learn more about sharing printers, read the Windows for Workgroups portions of Chapter 9, "Using the Print Manager."

When you need to share a common piece of changeable text, graph, or table between members of your workgroup, everyone should read about ways to use linking and embedding with the Clipbook. This information is covered in Chapter 6, "Embedding and Linking."

Changing Settings and Passwords

Workgroups are usually dynamic groups of people sharing a common task or goal. As tasks and goals change, the people within the workgroup may also change, or the workgroups themselves may change their goals or charters. Windows for Workgroups can handle those changes. This section describes how to change workgroup and computer names, how to change your password to ensure its security, and how to specify how you log on.

Changing Your Name or Workgroup Name

The first time you logged on to Windows for Workgroups, you had the opportunity to enter a name for your computer and a name that identified the group of people working together, the workgroup. You can change or create the workgroup name and computer name at any time.

Although your computer name identifies you, you may want to add a comment that appears next to your name in the Connect Network Drive and Connect Network Printer dialog boxes. A comment can help identify you and your job function, or it might serve as a reminder to others in the group. For example, you might want to use a comment such as "Send Sales Reports by 15th of month." to remind others of the date and the person to whom reports should be sent.

You can change or add a new workgroup, change your computer name, and change the comment attached to your name, all within the Network Settings dialog box. To make these changes, follow these steps:

1. Start the Control Panel option from the Main group window in the Program Manager.

2. Double-click the Network icon in the Control Panel, or press the arrow keys to select the Network icon, and then press Enter. The Network Settings dialog box appears (see fig. 27.5).

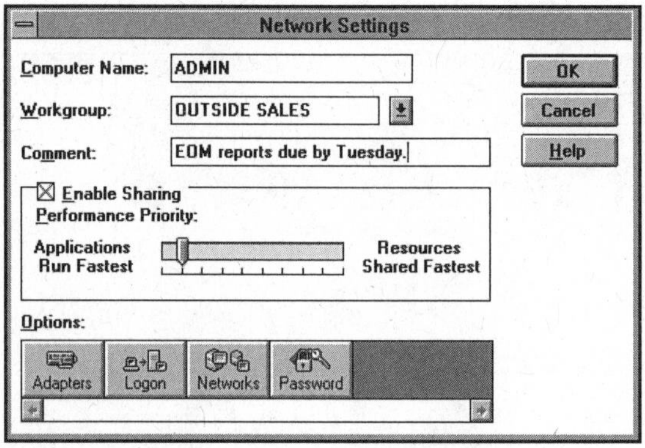

FIG. 27.5

Use the Network Settings dialog box to change workgroup and computer names.

3. If you want a new name to identify your computer, select the Computer Name edit box and type the new name.

4. To create a new workgroup, select the Workgroup edit box and type a new workgroup name. Workgroup names can have up to 15 characters and contain letters, numbers, and the characters ! # % ( ) - . @ ^ _ ' ~

   or

   To change to a new workgroup, select one of the existing workgroups from the Workgroup drop-down list. (Display the list by clicking the down arrow to the right of the list or press Alt+down arrow after selecting the box.)

5. If you want a new description to appear with your computer name, choose the Comment edit box and type a new description.

6. Choose OK or press Enter. The Network Settings dialog box appears on-screen with a warning.

7. Choose **R**estart Windows to quit Windows and start again using your changes.

or

Choose **C**ontinue to save the changes you made but remain in the current session of Windows. Use the **C**ontinue button if other users are sharing resources on your computer.

These changes do not take place until you exit Windows, go back to the DOS prompt and restart Windows for Workgroups. To correctly exit each Windows application and Windows, use an Exit command or Alt+F4. *Do not* turn off the computer or press Ctrl+Alt+Del as a quick way of exiting Windows.

If you change your computer name or move to a new workgroup, use Chat or Mail to let everyone know where you can be reached. (Unless, of course, you don't want to be reached.)

T I P

Changing Your Password

Passwords control who can log on to the network and gain access to resources. Workgroup applications like Mail have passwords to ensure that others cannot read or send your mail unless you have given them your password. Other applications, such as File Manager and Print Manager, have different levels of security that are also controlled by passwords.

When you log on to Windows for Workgroups and enter your computer name and password, you are doing more than logging on to the network. The logon password gives Windows for Workgroup access to a list of all the passwords you use for other workgroup applications like the File Manager. So there is an advantage to logging on with an entry password: you only have to enter a single password.

It's a good idea to change your password on a frequent basis. The changing can help keep your password secure by short circuiting anyone who accidentally found your password and is using it. However, frequently changing your password means that you must be able to remember the new password.

To change your password, follow these steps:

1. Choose the Network option from the Control Panel.

2. Choose the Password button at the bottom of the Network Settings dialog box.

   If you are using the mouse click on the Password button. If you are using the keyboard, press Alt+O to select the **O**ptions group, use the left- or right-arrow keys to select the Password button, then press the space bar to choose the Password button.

   The Change Logon Password dialog box displays, as shown in figure 27.6.

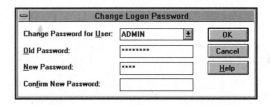

3. Select your computer name from the Change Password for **U**ser list.

4. Select the **O**ld Password edit box and type your current password.

5. Select the **N**ew Password edit box and type the new password.

6. Select the Con**f**irm New Password edit box and retype the new password to confirm that the first did not have typographical errors.

7. Choose OK or press Enter.

8. Choose OK or press Enter in the Network Settings dialog box.

You see asterisks (*) instead of actual characters when you type a password. Your passwords can use upper- or lowercase. The password is not case-sensitive, so you do not need to memorize which letters are capitalized.

> A couple of ideas may help you create new or frequently changing passwords that you can remember. These ideas are based on combining a word that's easy for you to remember with a memorable number that changes. For example, you might use the names of relatives, lovers, or pets and combine that name with a changing number such as your birth month combined with the current month. This could yield passwords, such as HEIDI16 or 14HOBO.
>
> **T I P**

Starting without Logging On and Changing the Default Logon Name

You can tell Windows for Workgroups that you don't want to log on when Windows starts, which enables you to work in Windows without being logged on to the network. You can log on any time you need to.

Any user can log on to the network at any computer by entering his or her computer name and password during log on. But in most cases, a computer is used by the same person, so it's convenient to have each person's computer name appear as the default computer name when the Welcome to Windows for Workgroups dialog box appears.

To change the default logon name that appears when you log on to the network, follow these steps:

1. Start the Control Panel option from the Main group window in the Program Manager.

2. Double-click the Network icon in the Control Panel or press the arrow keys to select the Network icon, and then press Enter.

3. Choose the Logon button at the bottom of the dialog box to display the Logon Settings dialog box.

    If you are using the mouse, click on the Logon button. If you are using the keyboard, press Alt+O to select the **O**ptions group, use the left- or right-arrow keys to select the Logon button, then press the space bar to choose the Logon button.

4. Select the **D**efault Logon Name edit box and type the name to appear in the logon dialog box that appears on startup.

5. Choose OK or press Enter.

To start Windows for Workgroups without immediately requesting a log on or automatically logging on to the network, deselect the Log On at **S**tartup check box. You still have the option of logging on at any time by displaying this same Logon Settings dialog box and choosing the Log On button. Manually logging on and off is described elsewhere in this chapter.

FIG. 27.7

Use the Logon Settings dialog box to change how logon acts when you start Windows.

The new default logon name and the log on at startup do not take effect until you exit and restart Windows.

Optimizing Network Performance

As more people use the Windows for Workgroup network, you may find that workgroup tasks, such as Mail, begin to run more slowly. The sharing of your directories and printers attached to your computer may slow down the performance of applications you use. This degradation may begin to occur when approximately 10 computers are on the network. But you can improve performance.

Improving Performance by Not Sharing Resources

When you need all the power you can grab, you can turn off resource sharing with others in your workgroup. To turn off sharing, follow these steps:

1. Save documents you are working on, and close the applications.

2. Start the Control Panel option from the Main group window in the Program Manager.

3. Double-click the Network icon in the Control Panel or press the arrow keys to select the Network icon, and then press Enter.

   The Network Settings dialog box, shown in figure 27.2, appears.

4. Deselect the Enable Sharing check box.

5. Choose OK or press Enter.

   A message appears asking whether you want to restart Windows for Workgroups.

6. Choose the Continue button if others are using directories or printers attached to your computer. Warn these people that you need to turn off and restart your computer. If no one is currently using resources that you give to the network, then choose the Restart Windows button to restart immediately.

To turn resource sharing back on, repeat the process, but select the Enable Sharing check box.

Changing How Your Computer Shares Its Time

Windows for Workgroups comes with two tools that help you tune your applications while you are logged on. These tools let you control and see the amount of time your computer spends on your applications versus network administration. You can adjust where your computer's time is spent—working on your computer's applications or working on sharing resources with others on the network. It's up to you how you share your computer's power and time.

The WinMeter described in Chapter 16, "Using Desktop Accessories," shows a chart of your computer's processing time. Time spent on your applications appears in one color and time spent on network duties appears in another color.

The tool you use to change how time is spent is the Performance Priority gauge, which is part of the Network Settings dialog box. Figure 27.8 shows the WinMeter in the background window and the Performance Priority gauge in the foreground window. By displaying both at the same time, you may have a better feel for where your computer spends time.

To change how your computer's time is shared, follow these steps:

1. Choose the Network option from the Control Panel.

2. Drag the slide on the **P**erformance Priority gauge to the left to make your applications run faster. Drag it to the right to make shared resources run faster.

3. Choose OK or press Enter.

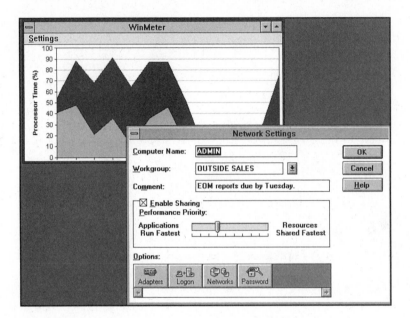

FIG. 27.8

Use WinMeter and the Performance Priority Gauge to change how your computer shares its time.

If you do not have a mouse, you can slide the Performance Priority gauge left or right by pressing Alt+P, and then pressing the right or left arrow keys.

Notice that the Performance Priority gauge is only accessible when the **E**nable Sharing check box is on. This makes sense because if sharing is disabled completely, full priority is given to your applications.

Tips on Improving Performance

In addition to the two previous sections, the following tips may help you improve performance on your Windows for Workgroups network.

■ Read the chapters titled, "Enhancing Windows Performance" and "Enhancing DOS Application Performance," Chapters 25 and 26. The most significant performance increase occurs when you increase the overall speed of Windows through the use of a permanent swap file, SmartDRIVE, and defragmented hard disk.

- Put the Mail Postoffice on the least-used computer or on a computer with a fast hard disk. This precaution reduces the impact of Postoffice traffic on the network. Put the Postoffice on the machine with the largest amount of free disk space.

- If everyone logs on and reads Mail messages at the same time, choose a slightly different time to do yours.

Chapter Summary

You can learn more about the resource sharing and passwords used with specific workgroup applications by referring directly to their chapters. The chapters you may want to read are Chapter 5, "Managing Files with the File Manager," Chapter 9, "Using the Print Manager," Chapter 10, "Using Mail with Windows for Workgroups," and Chapter 11, "Using Schedule+ with Windows for Workgroups." If you are interested in improving the performance of Windows and its peer-to-peer network, look at the major performance enhancements recommended in Chapter 25, "Enhancing Windows Performance" and Chapter 26, "Enhancing DOS Application Performance." Appendix B describes the installation procedure for Windows for Workgroups and may give you some additional insight into the concepts of workgroups and resource sharing.

For in-depth technical information about fine-tuning Windows for Workgroups and making it work with other networks, please look for the Que book, *Connecting Windows 3.1 for Workgroups*, by Doug Bierer.

Networking Windows

This chapter tells you how to install and optimize Windows 3.1 on networks. Most of the comments in the chapter are specific to Novell networks and apply to NetWare Version 2.15C (ELS, Advanced or SFT NetWare), Version 2.2, and 3.11. A brief section at the end of the chapter denotes specifics to Banyan and LANtastic networks. Most concepts, however, apply to networks in general.

In this chapter, you learn how to do the following:

- Install Windows on a network.

- Set up an effective printing environment.

- Set up individual workstations to work with Windows on a Network.

- Install and use the NetWare Windows Workstation Tools.

- Use Windows 3.1 on a LANtastic or NetWare Lite Network.

NetWare Installation Issues

The use of Windows on a network is a hotly debated issue. One school of thought, known as the local school, proposes to run Windows *exclusively* on each workstation's local hard disk. Proponents of the local school claim that running Windows off the file server generates too much network traffic and advise you to set up the local Windows versions so that you can access network programs, map drives, and files. The other school of thought, the network school, claims that Windows runs just fine on the network. This school claims that Windows can be set up as a master where user interfaces are standardized. When changes are made, all users are affected with minimal effort on the part of the System Manager.

The truth lies somewhere between these two philosophies. Windows runs fine on the file server. The Novell server caches and then transmits the files to the workstations, which minimizes hard disk access. Windows opens and accesses a large number of files frequently, however, which generates traffic on the network. The more users using Windows, the faster the Novell server operates relative to the number of users. The server stores frequently used files in the cache. Through the cache, you gain access to these files instead of forcing the server to access the hard disk. Because the cache is accessed in *nanoseconds* (1 billionth of a second), compared to the *millisecond* (1 thousandth of a second) access time of a hard drive, the files are sent over the network quickly.

Installing Windows on a Network

To install a program on a network, you must take the following steps:

- Create a directory for the program files.
- Run the Setup procedure.
- Flag the files if necessary.
- Give users trustee rights.
- Add the directory to the user's search path.

With Windows, you must create one directory to contain the master program files (all the Windows files) and one directory specific to the user or specific to the machine, depending on the style you choose for the network (see the following section, "Standardizing the Master Setup").

Standardizing the Master Setup

Considerable debate exists over whether or not to standardize the Windows Program Manager screen for all users on a network. Arguments in favor of standardization include the following points:

- Makes support easier
- Can make changes globally
- Prevents users from deleting vital elements, such as Program Manager group files

Arguments against standardization include the following points:

- Users like to customize their own Windows desktop.
- Enables individuality
- Users tend to "own" the network to a greater extent.

Standardizing User Setups

Depending on the network environment, you may have to perform one or more Windows installations. Use the following network as an example:

- 10 IBM PS/2s
- 10 Acer Diskless Workstations with Hercules graphics cards
- 10 Compaq Laptops

Assume that volume SYS: contains Windows along with most program files and that volume DATA: contains user data files. The following steps are an overview of the process you need to follow:

1. Create a directory SYS:PROGRAMS.

   - Install the applications (for example, Microsoft Excel, Word for Windows, and so on) under this directory.
   - Put the complete set of Windows files here.
   - Flag the files Sharable Read-Only (FLAG *.* SRO).
   - Create a search drive to the PROGRAMS\WINDOWS directory.
   - Assign RF Trustee Rights (ROS in Version 2.1x).

2. Create a directory DATA:USERS.

   - Create a *home* directory for each user under this directory.
   - Assign each user ALL trustee rights for the home directory.

3. Create a directory DATA:MASTER.

   ■ Create a subdirectory for each kind of personal computer.

   ■ Run SETUP from these directories.

     During login, have the users start Windows from these directories.

     Have the login script redirect users to the appropriate directory.

     FLAG all files in this directory Read Only: FLAG *.* RO.

     Assign RF Trustee Rights (ROS in Version 2.1x).

   ■ Create a file SHELL.CFG in the directory where IPX and NETx are located (see "Workstation Issues").

     Set the Long Machine Type to the proper kind of PC.

After you complete the preceding steps, the directory structure should resemble figure 28.1.

Using Novell Volumes

Be aware that a fundamental difference exists between a volume in NetWare and a volume in DOS. In DOS, volumes are labels for disks. NetWare enables you to subdivide your file server's hard drive(s) into logical volumes. Many networks have only one volume, SYS:. If the network to which you are connected has only one volume, substitute SYS: for DATA: in the following examples.

You can move to another volume in the file server by using one of two methods:

■ To map a drive letter:

   MAP G:=DATA:

■ To change a directory:

   CD DATA:

The *root* of a volume is the same as the root of a hard drive. If you're currently on volume DATA: and want to move to the root, type the following command:

   CD \

```
                              |----- WINWORD
                              |----- EXCEL
SYS: ---        PROGRAMS ---      |----- WINDOWS
                              |        calc.exe
                              |        calendar.exe
                              |        calendar.hlp
                              |        clock.exe
                              |        etc.
                              |----- DOS ---------      |--- V3.30
                                       |               command.com
                                       |               format.com
                                       |               etc.
                                       |               |--- V5.00
                                                       command.com
                                                       format.com
                                                       etc.


                              |----- DOUG
                              |----- SUSAN
DATA: -| ----- USERS----           |----- EILEEN
                              |-----   etc.
       |
       |                      |-----   PS2
       | -----MASTER --            |----- ACER
                              |-----   COMPAQ
                                       win.com
                                       win.ini
                                       system.ini
                                       progman.ini
                                       windows.grp
                                       main.grp
                                       etc.

C: ---|----- NOVELL
      |                       ipx.com
      |                       netx.com
      |                       shell.cfg
      | ----- TEMP
```

FIG. 28.1   A sample directory structure.

Setting Up the Windows Program Directory

When installing all Windows files in the SYS:PROGRAMS\WINDOWS directory, you can use the /A flag in setup. First switch to the disk drive containing the installation diskette (A: or B:). Then type the following:

SETUP /A

Using the /A flag expands and copies all Windows files in the designated directory and also flags the files as read-only by using the DOS ATTRIB command. The read-only status is reflected in the Novell file attributes.

During installation, enter the drive letter and directory where you want to install Windows when prompted. Be consistent and use the same drive letter. In this example, use the disk drive letter F, which is assigned to volume SYS:.

After Setup copies all program files, you are prompted to enter a User or a Group name and the name of your company. You enter this information as a form of copyright protection.

Do not set up applications at this time. You set up applications in the following phase. After all Windows application files are expanded and copied to the application directory, this phase is complete. At this point, exit the Setup program.

You now need to flag the application files as sharable:

FLAG *.* S

Flagging the program files as sharable enables multiple users to use the Windows master program files without conflict.

Setting Up the Master Machine Directories

Now, you can begin setting up a directory for each computer on your system. In the preceding example, you created a directory DATA:MASTER and a subdirectory for each different machine (PS2, ACER, COMPAQ, and so on).

Before proceeding with Setup, you *must* map one and *only one* drive letter to the root of each volume in which you placed programs to enable Setup to search the entire volume. If you do not perform this mapping, Setup limits you to specifying the applications one at a time (very tedious!) or to searching the path.

You should standardize on this mapped drive letter. *You must be consistent.* Each time the user runs Windows on the network, this drive letter must be mapped to the same volume as during Setup.

```
Windows Setup
---------------

Setup has determined that your system includes the following hardware
and software components. If your computer or network appears on the
Hardware Compatibility List with an asterisk, press F1 for Help.

          Computer:          MS-DOS or PC-DOS System
          Display:           Hercules Monochrome
          Mouse:             No mouse or other pointing device
          Keyboard:          Enhanced 101 or 102 key US and Non US keyboards
          Keyboard Layout:   US
          Language:          English (American)
          Network:           Novell NetWare

          No Changes:        The above list matches my computer.

If all the items in the list are correct, press ENTER to indicate
"No Changes." If you want to change any item in the list, press the
UP or DOWN ARROW key to move the highlight to the item you want to
change. Then press ENTER to see alternatives for that item.

ENTER=Continue  F1=Help  F3=Exit
```

FIG. 28.3

The hardware selection screen during setup.

After you complete one or a few master setups and copy the *.INI files, PROGMAN.INI still points to the directory where the setup occurred. After copying, make sure that you go into each PROGMAN.INI file to change it to the proper directory.

Suppose that you have completed the preceding setup for an Acer computer and now want to copy setup files to each user's home directory. The PROGMAN.INI file for the Acer computer setup looks similar to the following:

```
PROGMAN.INI
[Settings]
Window=68 35 580 280 3
[Groups]
Group1=F:\MASTER\ACER\ACCESS00.GRP
Group2=F:\MASTER\ACER\WINDOWS0.GRP
Group3=F:\MASTER\ACER\MAIN0.GRP
Group4=F:\MASTER\ACER\NONWIND0.GRP
```

In this example, you need to change the last four lines to point to the user's home directory on drive G:

During Setup, only drive letters in the DOS path are shown. The drive letter you created, therefore, also must be in the path. The batch file, ADDPATH.BAT, in figure 28.2 illustrates how you can accomplish this task.

```
echo off
echo :          Title:  ADDPATH.BAT
echo :          Date:        12/5/91
echo :          Author: John Jones
echo :          Inputs: 1 = Drive Letter to Create and Add to Path
echo :                      2 = Volume Name
echo :          Notes:  DON'T use colons when using batch file
echo :
echo :          Map Drive Letter %1 to Volume %2
echo :
MAP %1:=%2:
echo :
echo :          Add %1 to PATH
echo :
PATH=%PATH%;%1:.
echo :
echo :          Display Mappings
echo :
MAP
```

FIG. 28

This batc
maps a
letter an
it in the

You must log in from each of these machines in turn and run Setup for the machine. You must verify that the hardware Windows detects during Setup is correct (see fig. 28.3).

Setup then copies certain files to the new directory and creates the WIN.COM file for this computer. Setup then sets up the application programs. Select Search for applications to have Setup automatically compile a list of applications for you.

Setting Up Individualized Users

In the preceding scenario, perform the installation for each different model of computer (three times in the example). Copy the contents of DATA:MASTER\COMPAQ to the home directory of each user, whose PC is a Compaq. This area is where users should have full rights. When modifying the Windows environment, the system enables these users to save the changes they make.

```
PROGMAN.INI
[Settings]
Window=68 35 580 280 3
[Groups]
Group1=F:\USERS\DOUG\ACCESS00.GRP
Group2=F:\USERS\DOUG\WINDOWS0.GRP
Group3=F:\USERS\DOUG\MAIN0.GRP
Group4=F:\USERS\DOUG\NONWIND0.GRP
```

With this arrangement, the user's WIN.COM file is set for only one kind of workstation. If a user logs on at a workstation configured differently from their workstation, the user will experience problems.

> A combined approach—incorporating standardized and individualized techniques—is possible. Indicate the group files that you want read from the directory and the files you want read from the user's directory. Be sure that you limit user's security rights in the Master directory to Read and File Scan (Read, Open and Search in Version 2.15 NetWare). In this way, the user reads some files from the Master directory and the rest from the separate home directory. After users enter Windows, however, a warning message appears that says the group files located in the Master directory cannot be changed.
>
> **T I P**

Assigning Group Security Rights

Users need at least Read and File Scan privileges in each Windows directory set up for each different machine. Because security rights "trickle down," you need only to make an assignment at the next higher level directory. NetWare enables you to assign rights to individual users or groups (a collection of users). Groups are used primarily to make the task of assigning rights easier and are used by some electronic mail packages (DaVinci, for example).

The group Everyone is provided by default. This group consists of all users on the network. To enable all users to read and see files in the Windows program directory, assign the rights as shown in the following line:

GRANT r f FOR sys:programs\windows TO everyone

T I P   Read enables users to open files and Access (read) their contents. File Scan enables users to see a directory listing of the file (the file name, date, time, size, and so on).

Assigning Individualized Setup Security

To customize Windows screens, users need at least Read, Write, Create, Erase, File Scan, and Modify rights in the directory that contains their INI files. These rights are usually granted to users in their respective *home directories*. (These rights correspond to Read, Write, Open, Create, Delete, Search, and Modify in NetWare 2.1x.)

Assigning File Attributes

If you want to use the individualized approach but want to protect certain files (for example, PROGMAN.INI), use the Flag command to change the attributes of selected files without affecting the users' overall rights to the other files. You need to revoke the Modify Trustee Right and use Flag to change the desired file Attributes, as shown in the following example:

    REVOKE modify FROM doug

    FLAG progman.ini RO

This command takes away Modify rights from user Doug and changes the file PROGMAN.INI to a read-only status. Doug has Erase rights but cannot erase or change the file PROGMAN.INI.

A Step-by-Step Installation Procedure

The following steps are involved in the installation process:

1. Create a master program directory:

   ```
   MAP F:=SYS:
   F:
   MD F:\PROGRAMS\WINDOWS
   ```

2. Run the initial setup:

   ```
   A:
   SETUP /A
   ```

3. Enter the drive letter and path to the Windows program files:

```
F:\PROGRAMS\WINDOWS
Enter your user or group name
Enter your company's name
```

4. Create a Search Drive:

```
MAP INS S1:=SYS:PROGRAMS\WINDOWS
```

5. Grant Read and File Scan Rights for Everyone:

```
GRANT r f  FOR sys:programs\windows TO everyone
```

6. Flag the Files as Sharable:

```
FLAG f:\programs\windows\*.*  S
```

7. Create a Directory for the Machine Setups:

```
CD DATA:
MD F:\MASTER
```

8. Grant Read and File Scan Rights for Everyone:

```
GRANT r f  FOR sys:master TO everyone
```

9. For each computer with different requirements, perform the following actions:

- Create a directory:

```
MD F:\MASTER\COMPAQ
```

- Use ADDPATH batch file to map drive letters to each volume and put into PATH:

```
ADDPATH  F  SYS
ADDPATH  G  DATA
```

- Run SETUP on that computer:

```
CD F:\MASTER\COMPAQ
SETUP
```

- Enter the directory to contain the WIN.COM and INI files:

```
F:\MASTER\COMPAQ
```

- Delete unnecessary files:

```
DEL *.EXE
DEL *.HLP
DEL *.DLL
DEL *.SYS
```

■ Delete the SYSTEM directory (not needed):

```
DEL SYSTEM
```

■ In response to the prompt `All files in directory will be deleted! Are you sure (Y/N)?`, type the following:

```
Y
RD SYSTEM
```

■ Flag remaining files as sharable:

```
FLAG  *.*  S
```

10. For *Individualized* Setups, perform the following actions:

■ Copy files from the MASTER directory to the user's home directory:

```
NCOPY f:\master\compaq\*.* f:\users\doug
```

■ Change PROGMAN.INI to correspond to the user's home directory:

```
[Settings]
Window=68 35 580 280 3
[Groups]
Group1=F:\USERS\DOUG\MAIN.GRP
Order= 2 1
Group2=F:\USERS\DOUG\STARTUP.GRP
Group3=F:\USERS\DOUG\APPLICAT.GRP
```

Sample Login Scripts

This section contains sample login scripts that match the installation procedure outlined previously. You may need to make modifications to suit your particular network.

Login Script for the Standardized Setup

This script changes the network user's default directory to the proper setup directory for their machine, based on a variable in their SHELL.CFG file (see the sample SHELL.CFG file in the figure that follows the Login script). The Exit command causes Windows to run. When using the Exit command, the user is at the DOS prompt upon exiting Windows but *still is logged in*. Figure 28.4 shows a standard login script.

```
*
*      Title:      STANDARD.LOG
*      Date:                11/30/91
*      Author:     D. Bierer
*      Notes:      This Login Script takes users to Windows,
*                  and leaves them at the DOS prompt when done.
*
*      Create Drive Letter and Search Drive to Point to
*      the Proper Machine Directory
*
MAP F:=DATA:MASTER\%MACHINE
MAP S1:=DATA:MASTER\%MACHINE
*
*      Create a Search Drive to the Proper Version of DOS
*
MAP S2:=SYS:PROGRAMS\DOS\%OS_VERSION
*
*      Because DOS is now in the PATH, set COMSPEC
*
COMSPEC=S2:COMMAND.COM
*
*      Create Drive Letter for User Home Directory
*
MAP G:=DATA:USERS\%LOGIN_NAME
*
*      Create Search Mappings to PUBLIC and WINDOWS
*
MAP S3:=SYS:PUBLIC
MAP S4:=SYS:PROGRAMS\WINDOWS
*
*      Change Default Drive to Windows Drive and Launch Windows
*
DRIVE F:
EXIT "WIN"
```

FIG. 28.4   A standard login script.

T I P   If you are running different brands of DOS on your network (MS-DOS and PC DOS), you may want to add another level to the subdirectory structure. NetWare provides a system identifier called OS to detect the brand of DOS. Change the line that adds search drive 2 as follows:

```
MAP S2:=SYS:PROGRAMS\%OS\%OS_VERSION
```

Another alternative is to place a copy of the COMMAND.COM file from each machine type in the DATA:MASTER\&MACHINE directory. Set the COMSPEC to this directory.

Sample SHELL.CFG file

The SHELL.CFG file (see fig. 28.5) should be located on the workstation's boot disk (A or C) and should be in the same directory as IPX.COM and NETX.COM. The AUTOEXEC.BAT file should be located in the root directory of the boot disk.

FIG. 28.5

The SHELL.CFG file.

```
;This parameter enables users to move up to the parent directory
;in Windows File-Open menu selections.
SHOW DOTS = ON
;This sets the number of files enabled by the file server
;to be open simultaneously at the user's workstation.
FILE HANDLES = 60
;This parameter is later interpreted by the system identifier
;%MACHINE in the login script.
LONG MACHINE TYPE = MONO
```

Sample Login Script Using DOS Environmental Variables

The following login script assumes that each computer has a DOS variable Machine set in the AUTOEXEC.BAT file (see fig. 28.6). The login script uses this variable to set up the proper exit procedure from the login script into Windows. Look at figure 28.7, which shows a sample AUTOEXEC.BAT file that works with this login script. Note that this login script doesn't leave the user logged in upon exiting Windows. This is accomplished by executing Windows from within the login script (see the line with the command #WIN) or by exiting the login script to a batch file (see the WINBAT.BAT file in fig. 28.8), which calls Windows and then logs the user out.

```
*
*                  Title:        WIN2.LOG
*                  Notes:        Sample Windows Workstation Login Script
*                  Date:                11/30/91
*                  Author:       Doug Bierer
*
*                  Set up Standard Novell Search Drives
*
MAP S1:=SYS:PUBLIC
MAP S2:=SYS:PROGRAMS\DOS\%OS_VERSION
*
*                  Set DOS COMSPEC = Proper Version's Directory
*
COMSPEC=S2:COMMAND.COM
*
*                  Set Search Drive To Windows Program Directory
*
MAP S3:=SYS:PROGRAMS\WINDOWS
*
*                  Set Regular Drive To Master Windows Setup Directory
*
MAP F:=SYS:MASTER
*
*                  Set Drive Letter to User's Home Directory
*
MAP H:=SYS:USERS\%LOGIN_NAME
*
*                  Place User in Windows Directory for Their Machine Type
*
DRIVE F:
*
*                  Check for Certain Machine Types for Targeted Exit, Etc.
*
IF MACHINE="MONO" THEN BEGIN
         MAP F:=SYS:MASTER\MONO
         *
         *                Execute Windows from Login Script
         *
         #WIN /S
         *
         *                Execute a Logout
         *
         #LOGOUT
END
IF MACHINE="EGA" THEN BEGIN
         MAP F:=SYS:MASTER\EGA
         *
         *                Exit to Batch File WIN.BAT
         *
         EXIT "WINBAT"
END
*
*                  All Other Machine Types Exit to Batch File
*
EXIT "WINBAT"
```

FIG. 28.6   A sample login script with DOS variable.

```
echo off
echo :    Title:   AUTOEXEC.BAT
echo :    Date:    11/30/91
echo :    Author:  Doug Bierer
echo :
echo :    Change prompt to reflect directory path
echo :
prompt $p$g
echo :
echo :    Set Machine type via DOS variable MACHINE
echo :
set MACHINE = MONO
echo :
echo :    Set Directory where Windows will store Temp Files to Local Drive C:
echo :
set TEMP = C:\TEMP
echo :
echo :    Novell Login Sequence
echo :
ipx
netx
f:
login
```

FIG. 28.7

A sample
AUTOEXEC.BAT
file.

```
echo off
echo :    Title:   WINBAT.BAT
echo :    Date:    11/30/91
echo :    Author:  Doug Bierer
echo :
echo :    Call  Windows
echo :
WIN
echo :
echo :    Log User Out When Done
echo :
LOGOUT
```

FIG. 28.8

A sample
WINBAT.BAT
file.

Understanding What Happens
When You Limit Rights

In the preceding standardized setup, the users don't have the rights to
change group files or INI files. A message warns of this restriction when
the users enter Windows. The only other effect users may notice is that
program icons cannot be deleted from groups in the Program Manager
and that no option of adding new items to groups is offered.

A user can create group items and add program items to these groups. These changes are lost, however, after the user exits Windows.

The way to change the perceived root of a drive letter is shown in the following command:

MAP ROOT <drive letter>:=[server/]<volume>:[directory]...[/directory]

If you want to *unroot* a map drive, retype the assignment statement without the word "ROOT":

MAP <drive letter>:=[server/]<volume>:[directory]...[/directory]

In a login script, for example, you change the perceived root of a drive letter by adding the following line:

```
MAP ROOT G:=SYS:USERS\%LOGIN_NAME
```

Understanding Other Workstation Issues

This section discusses various configuration files located on the workstations.

Using SMARTDRV.EXE

If you plan to run Windows on each workstation's hard disk and to access local files extensively, place the command to run SMARTDRV.EXE in your workstation's AUTOEXEC.BAT file. Otherwise, don't run SMARTDRV.EXE. The purpose of this utility is to provide temporary caching of disk files in RAM, and NetWare already provides temporary caching. To run SMARTDRV on a workstation is redundant.

Understanding Temporary Files

With Windows, you can control where applications store temporary files, which has a bearing on network traffic. When possible, store temporary files on the local hard disk, not to save storage space but to minimize network traffic. All files are communicated from the workstation to the file server over a common cabling system. Consider the network as a freeway, and the workstations are like entrance ramps. The more traffic on the freeway, the slower everyone must go to arrive safely at their destination.

Placement of temporary files defaults to the directory where Windows was launched (SYS:PROGRAMS\WINDOWS and DATA:MASTER\ machine in the preceding example). To redirect where these files are placed, set a DOS variable known as TEMP. You can use the DOS SET command. The directory indicated by TEMP must exist. You can place this command in the workstation's AUTOEXEC.BAT file by adding the following line:

    SET TEMP=C:\TEMP

Note that SET TEMP=C:\TEMP doesn't work on diskless workstations.

Don't store this command in the user login script because login scripts are individual to the user, not to the Workstation. If a user with a local hard disk logs in on a workstation without a hard disk, Windows cannot operate properly for the user.

Using the SHELL.CFG File

The SHELL.CFG file is an ASCII text file located in the same directory on the workstation as IPX and NETx. This file is the network equivalent of CONFIG.SYS. The commands which are placed in this file affect the workstation's connection with the file server. You can create this file using the Notepad.

The Show Dots command defaults to Off. To turn this parameter on, you need to add to SHELL.CFG a line similar to the following:

    SHOW DOTS = ON

This addition enables you to see the double dots (..) in File Manager. Without this capability, you cannot back up to the parent directory in the directory tree after you change directories.

This problem arose in previous installations where system administrators had removed this command from the SHELL.CFG file, or worse, specified *SHOW DOTS = OFF*. The result was catastrophic when the first Novell shells for Windows were released. When running the BINDFIX utility or MAKEUSER with the *PURGE_USER_DIRECTORY* directive, the operating system deleted not only the unused directories, but also ALL directories in the Network! This bug was eradicated with the 3.02 and later shells.

To check the version of the shells at the workstation's DOS prompt, just observe the message when you run IPX and NETX. The first lines may look like figures 28.9 and 28.10.

```
Novell IPX/SPX  v3.10 (911121)
©Copyright 1985, 1991 Novell Inc. All Rights Reserved.

LAN Option: NetWare NE1000  v3.02EC (900831)
Hardware Configuration: IRQ = 3, I/O Base = 300h, no DMA or RAM
```

FIG. 28.9

An IPX readout.

```
NetWare V3.25 - Workstation Shell (911204)
©Copyright 1991 Novell, Inc.  All Rights Reserved.

Running on DOS V5.00

Attached to server V2
01-06-92   3:01:42 pm
```

FIG. 28.10

A NETX readout.

If you're already logged onto the network, type *NVER* to see the display shown in figure 28.11.

```
NETWARE VERSION UTILITY, VERSION 3.12

IPX Version: 3.04
SPX Version: 3.04

LAN Driver:  NetWare NE1000  v3.02EC (900831) V1.00
             IRQ = 3, I/O Base = 300h, no DMA or RAM

Shell:     V3.22 Rev. A
DOS:       MSDOS V5.00 on IBM_PC

FileServer: VITEK
Novell NetWare v3.11 (20 user) (2/20/91)

FileServer: V2
Novell Dedicated NetWare V2.2(100) Rev. A (02/11/91)
```

FIG. 28.11

A NVER readout.

Another important command is FILE HANDLES, which changes the maximum number of files the workstation can have open on the file server. If you plan to run Windows off the network, expect each user to require a minimum of 15 open files just to have Windows sitting open and running Word for Windows. More open files are needed as the user opens more windows, more documents, and so on. Files used include EXE, COM, DLL, DRV, and FON files, and also document or other personal data files. At least 60 files are recommended. You can accomplish this change by placing the following command in the user's SHELL.CFG file:

FILE HANDLES = 60

Using MS-DOS 5.0, DR DOS 6.0, and NETX

In many installations, you will find a variety of versions of DOS. Often, you will not have the luxury of upgrading every workstation to the latest version of DOS. The best method of dealing with multiple versions of DOS is to create a separate subdirectory for each version. In the login script you can tell the network to detect the version of DOS through the login script variable OS_VERSION. The following line in a login script creates a search drive to the proper version of DOS. This line assumes that you have a directory structure set up as shown in the example described at the beginning of this chapter:

MAP S16:=SYS:PROGRAMS\DOS\%OS_VERSION

Windows runs more efficiently when using DOS 5.0. Microsoft supplies a Novell shell file NET5.CO_ which must be expanded and copied to the proper directory or disk on the workstation.

Novell released a new version of the workstation shell, which is fully Windows compatible and provides support for all versions of DOS, including DOS 5.0. The new workstation shell contains an updated IPX.OBJ file and a NETX.COM file. The NETX file replaces the old NET3.COM, NET4.COM, or NET5.COM. One of the main reasons for this release was to solve problems experienced by NetWare users of Microsoft's DOS version 5.0. Numerous complaints were heard from users, which indicated problems logging in, workstations locking up, and so on when using the NET5.COM file supplied by Microsoft. If you encounter problems of this nature, switch to NETX.COM.

The IPX.OBJ file must replace the existing file on either of the following:

- SHGEN-1 disk or directory for NetWare 2.1x or 3.0

- WSGEN disk or directory for NetWare 2.2 or 3.1x

T I P

You need to rerun the program (SHGEN or WSGEN) to generate IPX.COM for your workstation. This action produces an updated IPX.COM file. You then can copy the new IPX.COM and NETX.COM files to the proper directory or disk for the workstation. Windows copies the latest versions of the workstation shells to the machine directories you set up. The files copied include the following:

- IPX.OBJ
- NETX.COM
- LSL.COM
- IPXODI.COM

Note that the last two are needed only if you plan to use the NetWare ODI shells.

DR (Digital Research) DOS 6.0 recently appeared on the market and is shipping as a promotion with NetWare Lite. In a move to gain greater control over the workstation's local operating system environment (besides market share reasons, of course), Digital Research was recently acquired by Novell. You may be a bit surprised to learn that when using the syntax described previously in this section (MAP S16:=SYS:PROGRAMS\DOS\%OS_VERSION), DR DOS returns V3.31 in place of OS_VERSION. If you need to add DR DOS to your directory structure, be sure that you create a directory V3.31 rather than V6.00, as you'd expect from the name.

Setting COMSPEC

COMSPEC is another DOS variable that needs careful management on the network. If portions of DOS are overwritten, this variable tells programs where to find the command interpreter. Lotus 1-2-3, for example, is notorious for overwriting DOS. Usually, this occurrence is no problem but depending on the program, the version of DOS, and the BIOS (or the DOS and BIOS combination), PCs can be sensitive to this problem.

Symptoms of the problem are immediately evident in Novell. The workstation locks up, and you see the message, `Invalid COMMAND.COM` (see fig. 28.12). When this message appears, you have no choice but to reboot. In Windows, the message appears when you try to access the DOS prompt icon in the Main window.

Even more of a problem is when COMMAND.COM is not in the search path. This situation alone may be enough to interfere with certain operations.

FIG. 28.12

The invalid COMMAND.COM message appears if DOS has been overwritten.

In the directory structure indicated at the beginning of the chapter, each version of DOS has a separate directory. Also, in the sample login scripts, a Search drive is created to point to the proper version of DOS. To ensure proper operation, set the COMSPEC to this search drive.

T   I   P   A technique to deny users access to the DOS prompt is to deliberately set the COMSPEC to a non-DOS directory. This technique, although desirable in some situations for security purposes, is dangerous. Some programs rely on DOS and cause the workstation to lock up if unable to find COMMAND.COM by way of the COMSPEC.

Supporting Multiple Protocols

Novell is moving in the direction of a multiple protocol environment. The Open Data Link Interface (ODI) shells make this advance possible. With the proper drivers, you can communicate with machines running TCP/IP and also Novell servers running IPX. Most versions of UNIX use TCP/IP for the networking protocol. Most federal government, military, and universities also support the TCP/IP protocol suite, which is convenient for the Windows environment because you now can have a window open on a Novell Server and a second window open on a UNIX server.

The Novell ODI shell consists of the following four main files:

■ LSL.COM. Link Support Layer driver. Also serves to direct the proper protocol with the proper LAN card driver.

- NET.CFG. ASCII text file read by LSL.COM, which contains the specifications for the protocols and LAN card drivers and indicates which protocol is associated with which card(s).

- MLID (LAN card driver). Multi-Link Interface Drives. An example is NE1000.COM, a generic driver for an 8-bit Ethernet card.

- Protocol Support Stack. Protocol Driver. IPXODI.COM, for example, is a driver for the IPX (Novell) protocol.

Figure 28.13 illustrates the relationship between the ODI drivers. For those readers familiar with the OSI (Open Systems Interconnection) model, the ODI drivers occupy the network and data-link layers.

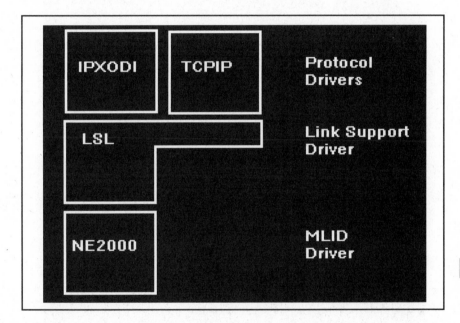

FIG. 28.13

ODI protocol support.

The NET.CFG file (see fig. 28.14) is located in the same directory as LSL.COM and contains specifications for a variety of areas:

- Link Support. Sets aside buffers, memory space, and so on.

- Link Driver. Specifies the Interrupt, I/O Port Address, Base Memory address, DMA Channel, and so on for the LAN card. Also specifies the Frame Type and Protocols to be associated with the driver.

- Protocol. Associates a Protocol (such as IPX) with a LAN card driver (Link Driver). In the case of TCP/IP, this section also is used to assign addressing relevant to the TCP/IP network and routing.

```
Link Support
        Buffers 8 1568
        MemPool 4096
Link Driver NE2000
        INT     3
        PORT    300
        MEM     cc000
        Frame   Ethernet_802.3
        Frame    Ethernet_II
        Protocol IPX     0 Ethernet_802.3
        Protocol TCPIP 0800 Ethernet_II

Protocol IPX
        bind NE2000

Protocol TCPIP
        bind NE2000
        ip_address      130.57.11.213
        ip_netmask      255.255.252.0
        ip_router       130.57.8.254
        tcp_sockets     8
        udp_sockets     8
        raw_sockets     1
```

FIG. 28.14

A sample
NET.CFG File.

```
LSL
NE2000
IPXODI
TCPIP
```

FIG. 28.15

A sample batch
file to load the
ODI drivers.

After the protocols and drivers are loaded, you can run NETX to attach to and log in to the Novell server. To log in to a UNIX machine, you need the appropriate software supplied by the vendor. Note that although the TCP/IP drivers are supplied with NetWare 3.11 for the server, the TCP/IP drivers for the workstation are supplied as a separate package, "LAN Workplace for DOS."

When To Use TBMI

The Task Switched Buffer Manager (TBMI) enables IPX to function in a multitasking environment (such as Windows). A problem arises when you switch between sessions in Windows or when the application makes calls directly to IPX, bypassing the NETX shell. If Windows doesn't function properly on the network, applications hang up, or you experience intermittent problems, running TBMI is recommended.

TBMI is a memory resident application that you must run before you enter Windows. The simplest method of implementing TBMI is to copy TBMI.COM and TASKID.COM into SYS:PUBLIC. In the batch file you invoke to run Windows, or in the user login script, include a command to run TBMI before you run Windows.

If you are in Windows, you must load TASKID in each DOS Window you open. TASKID provides to TBMI a unique ID number for this task. One technique is to include the TASKID command in a batch file to run certain programs.

Assume that you want to use Lotus 1-2-3 and dBASE, and that you switch tasks frequently. Set up the login script to call a batch file to run Windows that loads TBMI first. Batch files can be created to load TASKID before loading Lotus and dBASE. TBMI then can be unloaded after exiting Windows.

Figures 28.16, 28.17, and 28.18 show a login script fragment that exits to a batch file that loads TBMI.

```
*
*      Last 5 lines of a login script
*      Exit to a batch file which loads TBMI
*
EXIT "WINTBMI"
```

FIG. 28.16

The last 5 lines of a login script.

The following batch file loads TBMI and then Windows.

```
echo off
echo :
echo : Title:  WINTBMI.BAT
echo : Notes:  Batch File to Load TBMI, run Windows, and Logout
echo : Date:   12/5/91
echo : Author: Doug Bierer
echo :
TBMI
WIN
TBMI /U
LOGOUT
```

FIG. 28.17

A batch file to load TBMI and Windows.

The following batch file should be invoked from within Windows.

```
echo off
echo :
echo : Title:   123LOAD.BAT
echo : Notes:   Batch file to load TASKID and Lotus 1-2-3
echo : Date:    12/5/91
echo : Author:  Doug Bierer
echo :
echo : Add Search Drive Pointing to Lotus
echo :
MAP INS S1::=SYS:PROGRAMS\123
echo :
echo : Run TASKID and 123
echo :
TASKID
123
echo :
echo : Remove Search Drive
echo :
MAP DEL S1:
```

FIG. 28.18

A batch file to load TASKID and Lotus 1-2-3.

To determine whether you needed TBMI, you can run the diagnostic while in the application. From WordPerfect, for example, you can exit to the DOS shell by pressing CTRL + F1. At the DOS prompt, type *TBMI / D*. Look at the Far Call Usage field. If the number is 0, TBMI wasn't used. If the number is greater than 0, TBMI was needed and used. An update is available for TBMI on NetWire: TBMI2.

Setting Up Diskless Workstations for Windows

Two areas exist where the differences are noticeable when using a diskless workstation: in initial setup and in temporary files.

Initial Setup

The initial setup of a diskless workstation (so that it can log into the network) differs from setting up an ordinary workstation. For more information, consult the appropriate NetWare manual. To perform the initial setup, follow these steps:

1. Create a master boot diskette.

   To create the master boot diskette, you must use a workstation equipped with a diskette drive. Create a diskette with all the files you ordinarily use to boot up a workstation. Files include the following:

   - AUTOEXEC.BAT
   - CONFIG.SYS
   - HIMEM.SYS (or some memory driver)
   - COMMAND.COM
   - IPX.COM
   - NETX.COM
   - Any other files you would like to include

2. Run DOSGEN.

   The DOSGEN program is located in the SYSTEM directory. DOSGEN creates an image file NET$DOS.SYS from the master boot disk in drive A. If the disk is a 360K disk, the image file is 360K or less. If the disk is a 1.44M 3 1/2-inch disk, the image file created is 1.44M or less. DOSGEN doesn't support subdirectories on the master boot disk.

3. Copy NET$DOS.SYS to the login directory.

   NET$DOS.SYS is the file from which the diskless workstation boots. The workstation looks in the login directory for this file.

4. Flag NET$DOS.SYS as sharable.

   The image file must be flagged sharable. If not, only one diskless workstation can boot at a time. To flag this file as sharable, enter the following line:

   FLAG SYS:LOGIN\NET$DOS.SYS S

Temporary Files

Noting that you cannot set the TEMP variable (mentioned in the preceding section) to a local disk drive is important in this case. Unfortunately, you have no choice but to assign TEMP to some directory on the network. This directory must be where the user has a minimum of Write, Create, and Erase trustee rights. The user's home directory is recommended. This setting increases traffic on the network. To set the TEMP variable, use the following command:

> SET TEMP = G:

You can place this line in the AUTOEXEC.BAT file on the Master Boot disk.

Boot Sequence

When a diskless workstation boots up, the following steps are taken:

- The boot PROM on the network interface card seeks the nearest file server
- The file server that responds sends back NET$DOS.SYS
- The workstation creates a RAM disk and loads NET$DOS.SYS
- The workstation boots off the RAM disk and reads CONFIG.SYS
- The workstation loads DOS
- The workstation runs AUTOEXEC.BAT

AUTOEXEC.BAT Limitations

Some limitations exist for the AUTOEXEC.BAT file.

- All calls to change to a subdirectory are ignored.
- After NETX is invoked and you move to drive F, the RAM disk disappears. Here, the message Batch File Missing may appear. Because the RAM drive is gone, AUTOEXEC.BAT can't be completed. What you can do, however, is to copy AUTOEXEC.BAT from the master boot disk to the login directory. In this way, although the workstation cannot complete AUTOEXEC.BAT, the workstation can see the batch file and close properly.

T I P When setting up diskless workstations with different settings, follow the DOSGEN procedure. Rename the NET&DOS.SYS file. Construct an ASCII file (you can use Notepad) called BOOTCONF.SYS. Create a line for each workstation with the network address, node address, and file name. For example:

```
BOOTCONF.SYS file:
0XA100, 8301492F:BOOTDSK1.SYS
0XA100, 83012247:BOOTDSK2.SYS
```

Adjusting the SYSTEM.INI File

Some special considerations must be taken into account when setting up 80386 or 80486 workstations. These computers, with at least 2M of extended RAM, are capable of running Windows in 386-enhanced mode. Therefore, when switching between applications, Windows creates a virtual machine for each application window.

The environment of one virtual window usually is protected from changes made to the environment of another virtual window. Also, changes made to the environment while inside Windows vanish when you leave Windows. In the case of drive mappings, you may not want this effect.

Two parameters can be adjusted from the SYSTEM.INI file that affect how drive mappings are treated: RestoreDrives and NWShareHandles. Both settings must be placed under the [NetWare] heading in the SYSTEM.INI file.

Saving Drive Mappings Created Inside Windows

If you want drive mappings created while in Windows to be saved when you exit Windows, set the RestoreDrives switch in SYSTEM.INI as follows:

    [NetWare]

    RestoreDrives=false

These settings defeat the automatic restore of the drive letters as the letters were before you entered Windows.

Getting Virtual Windows To Share Drive Mappings

The following line, added under the [NetWare] heading enables drive mappings to be shared globally among the different virtual windows:

    NWShareHandles=true

Avoiding Memory Conflicts with Network Interface Cards

The SYSTEM.INI file is the general repository for network-related switches. Under [386Enh] you see a variety of switches that affect how the workstation's network interface card and Windows use memory. NICs usually allocate a buffer in the workstation's memory for transfer of packets of data to and from the network. Occasionally, however, this buffer allocation conflicts with an area of memory Windows wants to use. The EMMExclude switch can be used to block out a range of memory addresses from Windows.

If, for example, the NIC uses the address D000 - D7FF for the communication to and from the network, you can tell Windows not to use this range by entering the following:

[386Enh]

EMMExclude=D000-D7FF

Setting Up Windows NetWare Printing

Before you can set up printing on the network, understanding how Windows prints on the network is important.

If a network isn't involved with printing, then printing follows this process:

- Windows application sends job to Print Manager.

- Print Manager spools job out to printer.

However, with the network involved and Windows setup for a single user, the following events happen:

- Windows application sends job to Print Manager.

- Print Manager spools job out to port.

- Port is connected to file server print queue.

- Print queue receives job from Print Manager.

- Queue sends job to a core printer or a print server.

- Print Server sends job to designated printer.

Using Print Manager

The Windows Print Manager is designed to queue print jobs in the background on a standalone personal computer. Novell NetWare also has a print queue facility. NetWare collects the print job as a file in a subdirectory of SYS:SYSTEM. The server waits until the end-of-job timeout occurs—after the job is entirely collected. The job is then sent to the printer (in the case of core printing) or to the print server.

Having the Print Manager enabled while printing to a Novell network is redundant. Print jobs end up being queued twice. Although not harmful, to increase performance of Windows on the network, disable the Print Manager.

To disable the Print Manager, take the following steps:

1. Open the Control Panel from the Main group in the Program Manager.

2. Open the Printers program.

3. Clear the **U**se Print Manager check box.

Printing Multiple Jobs

If you print a long job from one window, switch to another window, and print another job, what happens? NetWare treats each new print job as a separate item. Each job is assigned its own job number unique to that queue. Each new job is created as a file with a unique file name, in the subdirectory of SYS:SYSTEM designated by Print Queue ID.

In 386-enhanced mode, with windows designated to run in the background, the first job received by the file server is given a file name, and the system collects print information in the file for this print job until the end-of-job timeout occurs. Suppose that you switch to another task in Windows and start a second print job. The server receives the second job and assigns the job a job number. Now two jobs are being collected from one user. The first job to finish spooling, such as the first one to send the end-of-job timeout, is placed in ready mode, ready to be printed.

In standard mode, where Windows doesn't operate in the background, the first job sits idle while the second job starts spooling out to the server. If a Timeout flag was specified in the print configuration (CAPTURE ... TI=nn—where nn = a certain number of seconds, or in your PRINTCON profile), then the server places the first job in Ready mode when it times out. Therefore, a portion of the first job may start printing even before the second job is done. When you return to the first window, assuming that the first job has already timed out, if the personal computer starts to send more print information, the server starts a third job.

Using the CAPTURE Command

You can use Novell's CAPTURE command to set up an initial print queue connection. This command is usually issued in the login script. The parameters can be obtained in your set of NetWare manuals. The two most important parameters for Windows purposes are the Q=, TI= and NT flags.

- Q Flag. Used to establish the print queue.

- TI Flag. Specifies, in seconds, the end-of-job timeout. Be sure to set TI high (30 to 45 seconds) if you have many graphics applications. Some applications, such as PageMaker, even may take as long as 120 to 240 seconds. If the Timeout parameter is too low, you see only partial pages when the job prints out.

- NT Flag. The No Tabs flag defeats NetWare's built-in tab expansion feature. This feature was designed several years ago, with the purpose of aligning columns in reports where the program didn't provide the tab expansions when printing. Since that time, laser printer technology has appeared, and printing is accomplished through dot positioning on a page. If this feature is left on (which is the default), graphic printing jobs come out severely altered for the worse.

T I P When using CAPTURE in a login script be sure that you precede CAPTURE with the # symbol (external program execution). Otherwise, the login script interpreter cannot process the command (see fig. 28.19).

- NB Flag. This flag stops NetWare from printing a banner page. The banner page has, by default, your login name and the name of the file. It is used to separate one print job from the next. NB stands for No Banner.

- NFF Flag. The No Form Feed flag prevents NetWare from adding a blank page at the end of a print job.

- L Flag. This flag is used to designate which local port is to be captured. NetWare accepts L=1, L=2, or L=3. This is reflected if you look at printers in the Control Panel. To set up printing to multiple printers, issue the Capture command up to three times using a different local port number each time.

```
F:\LOGIN>CAPTURE Q=TEMP NB NFF NT TI=10 L=1
Device LPT1: re-routed to queue TEMP on server VITEK.

F:\LOGIN>CAPTURE SHOW

LPT1:   Capturing data to server VITEK queue TEMP.
        User will not be notified after the files are printed.
        Capture Defaults:Enabled Automatic Endcap:Enabled
        Banner :(None)          Form Feed     :No
        Copies :1               Tabs          :No conversion
        Form   :0               Timeout Count :10 seconds
LPT2:   Capturing Is Not Currently Active.

LPT3:   Capturing Is Not Currently Active.

F:\LOGIN>_
```

FIG. 28.19

A Sample capture command issued from the command line.

Using Printdef and Printcon

You use the Printdef utility to create print drivers for devices not supported by DOS-based application programs. In a Windows environment, this utility is of little use except to provide an initial printer Reset.

You can use the Printcon utility to set defaults per user. In a customized environment, you can create Printcon defaults for each user. In the system login script, you only have to issue a command #CAPTURE, which picks up each user's Printcon default.

Using Remote Printers with Windows

Since the first release, the NetWare print server software was greatly improved and streamlined and now works well with Windows. The biggest problem so far is where the print server uses remote printers. Remote printers are printers attached to workstations that run the program Rprinter, which enables the computer's printer to be seen as a network printer.

Rprinter is a memory-resident program of approximately 5K that must be loaded into the workstation's memory before the workstation's printer is shared by other users. As with any TSR (terminate and stay resident program), Rprinter occasionally may conflict with Windows or Windows applications. If this conflict happens, it usually happens while a job is printing through the workstation that runs Rprinter. Typical symptoms include: the workstation hangs up; printing slows down; or the mouse responds slowly.

Three fixes, or workarounds, are available that can be used successfully:

■ Open Rprinter in a Window. If the workstation is running Windows in 386-enhanced mode, open a Window and run RPRINTER in the window. Create a PIF for this process, allocate around 16K of memory, and run Rprinter in background.

■ Use the latest Rprinter patch from NetWire. Novell has released a couple of Rprinter patches for Windows. To access the Novell bulletin board, log onto CompuServe and type *GO NETWIRE*.

■ Use a dedicated print server. A widely used alternative is to dedicate an older workstation (even an XT works!) as a print server. You can attach this PC to the network with the PSERVER software on disk. No more than 512K of memory and a diskette drive are required. You can attach up to five printers to this PC. Alternatively, Intel markets a device known as a NetPort, that really is a print server in a box. NetPort has a network interface card and a parallel and serial port for printer attachments. Hewlett-Packard markets an interface for the LaserJet III laser printer that can attach directly to the network. These printers then appear to the network as print servers.

NetWare Workstation for Windows Tools

As of late summer 1991, Novell began shipping a toolkit for Windows that includes a variety of useful tools to emulate several popular NetWare utilities. As shown in figure 28.20, these tools include the following:

■ Map a new drive letter

■ Capture to network print queues

■ Attach to another file server

■ List users on the network

■ View how much disk space is left on the server

■ Change your password

■ Send messages to users or groups logged in to the network

■ Disable receiving messages

■ Create mapping and print capture scripts

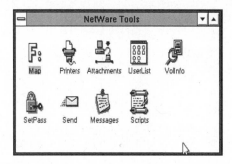

FIG. 28.20

The NetWare
Windows
workstation tools.

Where To Get the Toolkit

New versions of NetWare contain the toolkit. If you purchased your version of NetWare before the summer of 1991, however, you may order the Toolkit from Novell (Novell part number 100-001002-001) or download the toolkit from NetWire on CompuServe. The file name on CompuServe is WINUP2.ZIP, and the size is approximately 360K. Depending on the transfer rate of your modem, allow at least an hour to download, at 2400 bps. You need to use PKUNZIP to decompress the file.

Installation Issues

You may copy all the NW Tools files to the Windows application directory. You must run the Install application, however, from a directory other than the Windows directory (such as from a diskette). The Install application copies the following files to the \WINDOWS\SYSTEM directory:

- NETWARE.DRV
- VNETWARE.386

The remaining files go in the main Windows program directory.

Install also modifies the WIN.INI and SYSTEM.INI files. The WIN.INI file has the following new command:

    Load=NWPOPUP.EXE NWTOOLS.EXE

Any application following the Load= switch is loaded when you first load Windows. The NWPOPUP utility enables Send and Broadcast messages to be received from within Windows. Send and Broadcast are messages generated by the file server (system alerts) or messages sent by other users.

The second item is the toolkit itself. If you don't want the toolkit to load by default, remove this entry from the WIN.INI file.

The SYSTEM.INI file has the following lines added (sections are indicated in square brackets):

```
[boot]
network.drv=netware.drv

[boot description]
network.drv=NetWare Device Driver Version 1.02

[386enh]
network=vnetware.386
device=vpicda.386
```

The line that contains VIPX is deleted. Install also comments out *device=*vpicd* to make this command ineffective. Do not install this patch under Version 3.1. Windows 3.1 was rewritten so that it no longer needs the patch.

When run for the first time, Install updates the NetWare driver files and the DLL files of Novell's C language interface for Windows. Subsequent installs update only the user's INI files. Old driver files replaced are saved with the extension OLD.

Creating Toolkit Scripts

You can use the toolkit to create a series of scripts that users can call up for various situations. The scripts enable you to record different sets of drive mappings and printer connections (see fig. 28.21). The Scripts option of the toolkit enables you to perform any of five actions:

- New. Creates new scripts.

- Edit. For editing existing scripts (see fig. 28.22).

- Delete. To delete a script.

- Take Snapshot. Looks at the existing setup and puts this information into a script that you then can save.

- Apply. Activates the selected script.

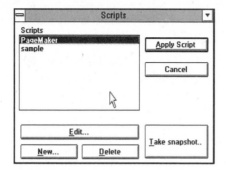

Windows
workstation
toolkit scripts.

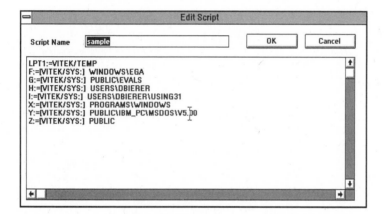

Windows
workstation
toolkit edit script.

Using NetWire To Get Help

NetWire, the Novell bulletin board on CompuServe, is a must for system managers and network installers. To access Netwire while on CompuServe, type *GO NETWIRE*.

NetWire has the following features:

- Forums
- Message boards
- Library of files
- IBM file finder
- Compatibility directories
- Novell press releases

- Novell product list
- Calendar of events

For users who want to obtain the large patches, fixes, drives, and shareware utilities for NetWare. NetWire also is a good source of information on NetWare including technical issues, do's, and don'ts.

Using the NetWire Libraries

Of the most interest to Windows installations are the forums and the Library of Files. You see 17 libraries, located in the Library section. To go immediately to this area at the prompt, type *GO NOVLIB*.

You will see that the libraries are divided according to general categories of products. Separate libraries are available for NetWare Version 2.x and Version 3.x. Also of interest is the New Uploads Library. Besides recent uploads, this library contains the file FORUM.ZIP, which is an archived file that contains a listing of all the files available for downloading. The zipped file is approximately 250K, so—depending on the speed of your modem—expect the download to last from 15 minutes to an hour.

You also may notice that Novell uploads are identified. Also indicated is the number of users who previously downloaded the file. Patches, utilities and fixes that pertain to Windows are liberally sprinkled throughout the Forum. Downloading FORUM.ZIP is advised: this way you can identify the files you need without the expense of spending time on-line, browsing through the libraries.

Using LANtastic and NetWare Lite Networks

A major philosophical difference exists between NetWare 2.2 or 3.11 and LANtastic and NetWare Lite. The former is a file server based technology; whereas the latter two are peer-to-peer networks.

In NetWare 2.2 or 3.11, all information goes from the workstations to the file server and back. NetWare is optimized for fast, reliable file transfers. The file server also is running NetWare, not DOS. A Netware file server can be configured as nondedicated, which means that the file server also can be used as a workstation. Even in this case, however, the workstation is set up with a special DOS process which, like any other workstation, must first talk to the file server.

In a peer-to-peer network, PCs are cabled together with network interface cards and cables, similar to the layout of NetWare. The personal computers also run DOS, as in NetWare. The difference is that any personal computer can be a server, and any personal computer can be a client. A server is a personal computer that enables this computer's hard drive to be shared by clients. These networks enable a single personal computer to be a server and a client.

Using Windows in a Peer-to-Peer Network

You must consider the following issues when you install Windows on a peer-to-peer network:

- Network speed
- Hard disk utilization
- Where is Windows to be installed?

Peer-to-peer networks now are approaching the speed of file server networks. LANtastic, for example, can use Ethernet network interface cards, just like NetWare 2.2 or 3.11. Ethernet cards transmit at a raw rate of 10 million bits-per-second, regardless of who's using the cards. Peer-to-peer networks, however, are not optimized for file transfer. File transfer is dependent on the local operating system—in this case, DOS.

Understanding Disk Use

NetWare caches files and performs other technological tricks to minimize the utilization bottleneck presented by the file server's hard disk is important. None of these tricks are available in a peer-to-peer network. If a peer-to-peer network were called upon to perform as a NetWare network, the hard disk heads would bounce all over the drive in an effort to service requests from users. NetWare caches the file server hard drive(s)' directory entry table and file allocation table. As a result, the server only needs to access the hard drive to save or retrieve files. In DOS, however, the hard drive must be consulted for any operation that pertains to the hard drive.

Disk caching programs are highly recommended when using a peer-to-peer network. SMARTDRV.EXE is an excellent start in this direction. Make sure that the personal computers that you want to use as servers have a good amount of extended RAM that can be set aside for disk caching. Disk caching goes a long way toward improving the speed of the network.

Installing Windows in Peer-to-Peer Networks

The best approach in this kind of environment is to run Windows locally on the hard drives of all machines attached to the network. The network then can be used to share data files and printers.

Here, using the Express option, you can install Windows, which speeds installation considerably. Setting the TEMP files to save to the local hard disk is recommended.

Windows may detect the presence of the network during SETUP. Be sure to change to "No Network Installed."

Establishing Security

The security issues on a peer-to-peer network are similar to the issues on a file server network. If you run Windows locally (highly advised), users' workstations need not be concerned about access rights. To prevent users from changing the INI files, you can use the DOS ATTRIB command to mark the files Read Only. Remember, however, that knowledgeable users can easily change these attributes back to a file that can be edited.

To mark INI files Read Only, type the following commands:

CD \WINDOWS

ATTRIB *.* +R

You may want to establish security for users whose personal computers act as servers. LANtastic and NetWare Lite have a program called NET that can be run. NET is a menu-driven DOS-based program that includes options for establishing *Network Drives* and restricting access rights. NetWare Lite has been criticized for a lack of depth: security rights include only Read, All, or None. LANtastic, however, has an abundance of rights that can be assigned to fine tune desired access.

Before Running Windows

Complete all network related connection activities *before* entering windows. These activities include the following:

- Logging in
- Connecting to network drives
- Connecting to network printers

Drive letters appear as if these letters represented local hard drives. Be sure that you leave plenty of extra drive letters in the local DOS environment, which you can accomplish by assigning, in the CONFIG.SYS file, the last drive to a letter farther down the alphabet:

LASTDRIVE=M:

In the CONFIG.SYS file, this statement enables you to assign up to drive letter M as a network drive.

> The preceding procedure is the opposite of a NetWare 2.2 or 3.11 workstation. Setting the LASTDRIVE reduces the number of drive letters available as file server drives.

T I P

Installing Windows on a LANtastic Network

By default, Setup makes an entry into the SYSTEM.INI file, which reflects the default settings on Artisoft's enhanced 2mbps network interface card. If you changed the settings on the card to other than the default, you also must change the SYSTEM.INI file accordingly. Setup places the settings in the [386Enh] section of SYSTEM.INI. If you aren't using Artisoft's card, you can erase this line in the SYSTEM.INI file, or you can modify the file to suit the card you install.

Certain commands require that the NetHeapSize parameter be set to a value higher than the default. XCOPY is one of these commands. This parameter also is found in the SYSTEM.INI file under the [386Enh] section (see fig. 28.23). The default is 76 for LANtastic Version 3.x and 64 for Version 4.x.

```
[386Enh]
EMMExclude=D800-DFFF
NetHeapSize=64
```

FIG. 28.23

The 386Enh Section of SYSTEM.INI.

When installing and running Windows on a LANtastic Version 4.x network, you must be sure that the file LANTASTI.386 is located in the path.

Printing on a Peer-to-Peer Network

LANtastic and NetWare Lite offer print spooling capabilities. Between the two, again, LANtastic has the more elegant print spooler, which offers considerable capabilities for controlling how and when the print job appears at the printer. Both LANtastic and NetWare offer the capability of deleting jobs from the network queue.

Using the Print Manager is recommended in a peer-to-peer network. Although the network spools the job anyway, holding the job in the local Print Manager queue relieves to a small extent the strain on the network.

When connecting to a network printer, you must select the LPT1.DOS or LPT2.DOS options (see fig. 28.24). This way, the job goes to the network printer, rather than to the local printer (which may not even exist) that was connected before entering Windows.

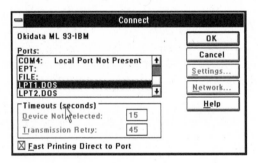

FIG. 28.24

Connecting to LPT1.DOS.

What To Do if the Server Goes Down

Usually, after the server goes down, Windows cannot recover. Program operation continues locally, but the network drives become inaccessible. The best thing to do in this situation is to exit Windows and re-start the server. You can then reissue the NET MAP (NetWare Lite) or NET USE (LANtastic) command to reconnect to the drive. Here, you can reenter Windows. If you were at the DOS prompt or were running a DOS-based program not running under Windows, you would have no problem. Windows, however, prevents DOS from trapping the error and recovering.

Chapter Summary

This chapter outlined some of the more important considerations when installing Windows on a network. When installing Windows on a network, it's important to contact the network vendor and ensure that you receive all updates to network files that you may require for Windows installation and operation. Use the resources in the appendix for contacting the network vendors by telephone or by CompuServe.

After you have Windows operating on the network, tuning both Windows and DOS application PIFs for top performance and the most efficient use of memory is important. Chapters 24, 25, and 26 describe many operating techniques that improve performance and changes you can make to the computer configuratons that improve performance.

Troubleshooting

Windows is a stable operating environment that usually works without a hitch. Computers being computers, however, problems can occur. Often, the solution is simple and quick to implement. At other times, a bit of research may be required to uncover the source of a problem and to devise a solution.

If you encounter a problem, this chapter is a good place to start. The simplest solutions are listed first in each section. Try these solutions first. If a simple solution doesn't solve the problem, go to the next step. Work through the steps until you find a solution that solves the problem. If none of the solutions solve the problem, call Microsoft's technical support line. A technician usually can pinpoint the problem and identify a solution. (The technical support phone number is listed in Chapter 30.)

Although encountering problems may be frustrating, working with any computer problems also can be educational, so consider these experiences a way to learn more about your computer. When the problem next arises, it may not seem so mysterious.

Solving Installation Problems

To install Windows, you typically insert the first of the Windows diskettes in drive A and type *A:SETUP*. Two setup options exist: Express and Custom. Usually, Windows performs the installation flawlessly, gleaning needed information about the computer without asking you any questions. However, if equipment is incompatible or if the computer lacks the correct resources, an installation failure can occur. Several times exist during which an installation failure can occur, so watch the progress of the installation and note when a failure occurs and what message appears.

Correcting a Failure during the DOS Portion of the Installation

The first part of a Windows installation runs in DOS. During this time, the setup application checks the hardware and records information about the equipment for use later in the setup process. If Windows cannot recognize a piece of hardware, the installation may fail, and you must stop the installation.

To solve the problem, first find out exactly what kind of equipment you have in, and attached to, the PC (this investigation may take some research). Write down this information to use during the installation. Restart the installation but this time, insert the disk and, at the DOS prompt, type the following command:

SETUP /I

This command causes Windows to perform a custom installation without detecting the hardware. When prompted by the installation application, you must specify what kind of equipment you have.

If you are unsure of the information you need about the equipment, try the installation even if you aren't sure that you can complete the process. When prompted for information about the equipment, write down the questions and then quit the installation. Try again after you get the needed information.

Correcting a Failure during the Windows Portion of the Installation

When the DOS portion of the installation is complete (during which the files needed by the installation routine are copied on the hard disk), Windows starts, and the rest of the installation runs from Windows. If a failure occurs during the switch from DOS to Windows, quit the installation and try one of the following solutions:

■ Close any memory-resident applications and restart the installation after restarting the computer. If memory-resident applications start up each time you start the computer, you'll have to edit the AUTOEXEC.BAT file (and possibly the CONFIG.SYS file) to remove memory-resident applications that start automatically. You can use the Windows accessory Notepad or a text editor to edit these system files, which are located in the root directory (exit all directories and subdirectories to get to the root directory).

■ Run the installation again and, rather than Custom Setup, choose Express. Then make sure that the hardware descriptions and software settings are correct.

■ Make sure that you have the right version of DOS. You need to have DOS 3.1 or later to install Windows; to check which version you have, type *VER* at the DOS prompt and press Enter. If you have an earlier version of DOS, install a newer version and install Windows.

The Installation Application Keeps Asking for the Same Disk

The Windows installation application prompts you for each diskette, by number, as needed. If you're repeatedly prompted for the same disk, even after you inserted the disk, try one of the following solutions:

■ Make sure that you correctly specified the drive that contains the diskette. Windows assumes that you are installing from drive A. If you are installing from drive B, be sure that you specify drive B in the dialog box that prompts you to insert disks.

■ Disk cache applications on the hard disk can cache a diskette. Remove all lines from the CONFIG.SYS or AUTOEXEC.BAT file that reference a disk caching application (by typing *REM* at the beginning of the appropriate lines) and restart the computer. (You can use the Windows Notepad to edit the CONFIG.SYS or AUTOEXEC.BAT files.) Then try the installation again.

■ If the installation application doesn't recognize that you changed the diskette, you must add a line to the CONFIG.SYS file. This line sends a message to the computer which says that you changed the disk. Add this line to the CONFIG.SYS file if you are installing Windows from drive A, a high-density (1.2MB) drive:

DRIVEPARM=/D:0 /F:1

The /D:0 parameter specifies the drive; to use drive B rather than A, the command reads /D:1; for drive C, the command reads /D:2. The /F:1 parameter specifies the drive type; for a 160, 180, 320, or 360K drive, the command reads /F:0 (zero); for a 3.5-inch 720K drive, the command reads /F:2; for a 3.5-inch 1.44M drive the command reads /F:7; for a 3.5-inch 2.88M drive, the command reads /F:9.

The Installation Application Doesn't List Your Hardware

If you installed hardware on the system that Windows doesn't recognize during the installation, you may need a special driver for the hardware. (First, however, find out whether the hardware is compatible with a similar piece of equipment that may be listed; if the equipment is compatible, choose the compatible equipment during the installation.)

To acquire a driver, call Microsoft Product Support Services and ask whether Windows includes the driver you need (drivers for high-resolution CGA monitors, for example). Ask for a copy of the driver you need (you also can download drivers from CompuServe, GEnie, ON-Line, and some user group bulletin board systems). If the driver you need is not available, contact the equipment manufacturer to see whether they have a Windows-compatible driver available.

You Don't Have Enough Hard Disk Space To Install Windows

Most people use the Express Setup to install Windows. If you lack the space on your hard disk to install Windows, choose the Custom Setup and install only the parts of Windows that you need. You can leave out accessories, for example, such as Windows Write if you use Word for Windows as a word processor. You also may be able to do without Help files.

If you still lack enough space, scour the hard disk for files and applications you can delete (look for big graphic files, which consume a great deal of disk space).

Finally, to get rid of wasted disk space, run a disk defragmentation utility on the computer.

Windows Doesn't Start after Installation

If you cannot start Windows after installation, try one of the following solutions:

- Check whether you installed the wrong hardware. From the DOS prompt, change to the Windows directory. Type *SETUP* and press Enter. Review the hardware settings to be sure that these settings are correct. If incorrect, change the settings.

- Close all memory-resident applications (TSRs). You may have to remove these from the AUTOEXEC.BAT file to prevent the TSRs from starting automatically (see the previous section on "Correcting a Failure During the Windows Portion of the Installation").

- Install Windows again, using the *SETUP /I* command. See the previous section in this chapter, "Correcting a Failure During the DOS Portion of the Installation."

- Windows runs in one of two modes: standard or 386-enhanced. When you type *WIN* at the DOS prompt, Windows starts in the mode that it deems most suitable. Try starting Windows in a specific mode by typing *WIN /S* (to start in standard mode) or *WIN /3* (to start in 386-enhanced mode).

- If Windows won't start in 386-enhanced mode, although you have a 386 or 486 computer, you may lack enough free memory or disk space for WIndows to run in 386-enhanced mode. You need 200K of free conventional memory, 1M of free extended memory, and at least 2M of free disk space.

- If you use an AT-clone computer, the computer's ROM BIOS may not be compatible with Windows. If the computer dates to 1987 or earlier, call the computer manufacturer to find out whether the computer's BIOS is compatible with Windows (if the manufacturer doesn't know, ask for the name of the BIOS and call Microsoft to see whether this BIOS is compatible with Windows). Ask the computer manufacturer whether you can possibly upgrade the computer's BIOS.

Getting the Mouse To Work

If the mouse doesn't work, or behaves strangely, you may have a connection problem, a software problem, or there may be something wrong with the mouse. Two kinds of mice are available: serial and port. A serial mouse attaches to a serial port of the computer; a port mouse attaches to a port on a board that you install inside the computer's system unit.

Getting the Mouse To Work in Windows

A serial mouse must be connected to the COM1 or COM2 port. Although the port you choose doesn't matter, you must make sure that you connect the mouse before you start the computer (reboot if you plugged in the mouse after you started the computer). If the mouse still doesn't work, check the port settings by choosing the Ports application in the Control Panel and choosing **S**ettings to check the COM1 or COM2 settings.

Another reason the mouse may not work is because of an interrupt conflict. Serial devices use *IRQ Interrupts* to communicate with the computer, and only eight IRQ interrupts are available. If two devices are fighting for the same interrupt, a conflict develops. Suspect this problem if you have a lot of equipment attached to the computer. Check the IRQ interrupts for the other devices and make sure that the mouse doesn't conflict. You can change an IRQ Interrupt by choosing the Ports application from the Control Panel, choosing **S**ettings, choosing **A**dvanced, and then selecting a different **I**nterrupt Request Line (IRQ) from the list provided.

Getting the Mouse To Work in DOS Applications

To use a mouse in a DOS application, not only must the mouse be correctly installed in Windows, the mouse must be set up in DOS before you start Windows. The easiest way to get a mouse working in DOS is to make sure that the correct driver is included in the Windows directory and then add a line to the CONFIG.SYS file or the AUTOEXEC.BAT file so that DOS sets up the mouse when you turn on the computer. The Microsoft mouse uses the driver MOUSE.COM, which you set up in the AUTOEXEC.BAT file, or MOUSE.SYS, which you set up in the CONFIG.SYS file by adding the following line:

```
device = c:\windows\mouse.sys
```

If the mouse still doesn't work, Windows may not support this mouse, and you need to purchase a different mouse that Windows supports. (First, check with the mouse manufacturer to see whether the device emulates another mouse that Windows supports; if so, install the mouse with this driver and try again.)

If you use an IBM mouse with IBM mouse driver Version 1.0, you need a newer driver. Contact the dealer where you bought the mouse to get an updated driver and install the driver in Windows using the Windows Setup application in the Main group.

A final reason the mouse may not work is that the monitor doesn't support using a mouse in a DOS application that runs in a window. If you have a 16-color monitor with 800 x 600 resolution, make sure that you use the standard Super VGA driver that comes with Windows 3.1. The driver from earlier versions of Windows needs to be updated. If you have a monitor for which no driver is available in Windows 3.1, check with the manufacturer to see whether an updated driver is available for Windows 3.1.

What To Do If the Mouse Pointer Doesn't Move or Jumps Around

If the mouse pointer appears on-screen but doesn't move, either the wrong mouse driver is selected or an interrupt conflict exists. Suspect first that the wrong driver is installed, because this problem is much easier to fix.

To check the driver, choose the Windows Setup application in the Main group in the Program Manager. A dialog box appears that lists the equipment you installed during the Windows installation. If the mouse doesn't match the equipment settings, choose the **O**ptions **C**hange System Settings command, and from the **M**ouse list, select the correct mouse.

If this procedure doesn't work, check for an IRQ Interrupt conflict. See the previous section, "Getting the Mouse To Work with Windows."

If the mouse pointer moves but jumps around on-screen, the mouse may be dirty, or an IRQ Interrupt conflict may exist. To clean the mouse, you usually can remove the ball easily by following instructions on the bottom of the mouse. Use a solvent to clean and then replace the ball. Don't lose the ball; these parts are almost impossible to replace. If cleaning doesn't work, an IRQ Interrupt conflict is the probable culprit; see the previous section, "Getting the Mouse To Work with Windows."

For Related Information:

◄◄ To learn more about ports, see "Setting Up Communication and Printer Ports," p. 291.

FROM HERE...

Solving General Windows Problems

General Windows problems include difficulties you may have with the Program Manager, the File Manager, or running Windows itself. Following sections in this chapter deal with applications, application failures, printing, memory, communication ports, and networks.

Solving Program Manager Problems

The Program Manager is Windows' hometown. When you first start Windows, you see the Program Manager. When you run an application, you start from this part of Windows.

The Program Manager consists of the Program Manager window, in which group windows exist that contain program item icons. Group icons that represent closed group windows also appear inside the Program Manager. Windows creates some of these group windows as part of the installation process, and you create other group windows. The same is true for program item icons; Windows creates some, and you create others.

Group windows and program item icons are easy to create and to delete. To delete a group window or program item icon, just select the icon and press the Delete key. You can accidentally delete an icon in no time at all. Fortunately, deleting a group or icon doesn't delete applications or files; this action deletes only the group or icon.

If you believe that you are missing a group window or a program item icon, create another window or icon. To create a new group window, choose the **F**ile **N**ew command in the Program Manager and select Program **G**roup.

To create a program item icon select the group where you want the icon, choose **F**ile **N**ew, and select Program **I**tem. In the Description text box, enter a name for the icon; in the **C**ommand Line text box, enter the application's is path and name (choose **B**rowse if you're not sure where the application is located).

Solving Slow or Odd Performance

If Windows begins running slowly after a time, three possible causes exist. One cause may be lack of memory—you may be running too many applications simultaneously for efficient operation. For a temporary fix, run fewer applications. For a better fix, add more memory to the computer (which doesn't cost much, and the speed improvement can be significant).

Windows also may slow down if the hard disk is full; remove some unneeded files.

Another reason for Windows to slow down is that the hard disk has become fragmented. Computers save files in segments on the hard disk, and the segments may not be adjacent. Over time, you end up with a hard disk with pieces of files scattered across the surface of the disk in no particular order, which lengthens the time the computer takes to access these files. A disk defragmentation application can speed up the computer (and usually free some disk space) by moving all fragmented files together.

If Windows suddenly begins behaving unpredictably and you cannot tell why, you may have accidentally erased files that Windows needs. If the problem seems to be with an application, you may need to reinstall the application. If the problem is in Windows, you may need to reinstall Windows. Usually, don't delete files unless you know for sure what the files are (and never delete files with the extension DLL or TMP). Take care not to save the data files in application directories or the Windows directory; this step lessens the chance that you will accidentally delete a file the computer may need.

Recovering Erased and Lost Files

If you erased system or application files that the computer needs, you need to reinstall the application or Windows. If you accidentally erased data files that you need, restore these files from backup copies. What? You didn't make a backup copy? In this case, stop what you're doing—don't do anything else on the computer—and use a file recovery application, such as Norton Desktop for Windows to recover lost files.

If you lose a file through no fault of your own, such as a power outage, then many applications perform an automatic save, which often preserves at least part of your work. Check the application's documentation to see whether the application has the capability of backing up files when a power or application failure occurs. These backup files may have odd names and be located in special directories; the documentation can tell you how to find these files.

Troubleshooting Windows Applications

Sometimes while you use an application, you press a key, and the wrong thing happens. The first thing you should do is to try again. If the incorrect response persists, however, check through this section to see what may be happening.

If the system stops responding altogether, or *crashes*, refer to the section in this chapter on "Responding to an Application Failure."

If you have a performance problem, check Chapters 25 and 26 in this book for many tips on enhancing, respectively, Windows' and the system's performance.

Getting the Wrong Result When You Press a Key

If you press a key in an application—usually a shortcut key—and something happens that you don't expect, a shortcut key conflict probably exists. In many applications, you can assign custom shortcuts to the keyboard combinations. If you inadvertently assigned system-level shortcut keys to an application-level function, when you press the keys, you get the wrong result. (The Ctrl+Alt+Del key combination, for example, reboots a computer. Don't assign this sequence to the function of making selected text bold in the application.) The easiest solution to the problem is to change the shortcut in the application.

You also can change shortcut keys in a DOS PIF or in the Properties dialog box in the Program Manager (select the program item icon and choose the **File Properties** command).

If you press a Windows shortcut key and the Windows function doesn't happen, then a DOS application may be pre-empting the shortcut. Check the DOS application's PIF by using the PIF Editor in the Main group in the Program Manager, or check the DOS program item icon's properties in the Program Manager by choosing the **File Properties** command.

Speeding Up a Slow Application

If the application begins running slowly, the computer lacks enough memory to run the application optimally. You need to free memory by closing other applications or by taking other measures (see the section in this chapter on "Solving Memory Conflicts"). Suspect low memory if the hard disk's light blinks frequently, which indicates that Windows is switching applications between memory and the hard disk because memory is low.

A full hard disk also can cause an application to slow down. If you suspect the hard disk is nearly full, save all work and use the File Manager to remove or back up unneeded files. (Don't put off this step: if the hard disk gets completely full, you cannot save to the hard disk, and the application may freeze.)

If applications slow down when you run multiple applications or open very large files, you may need to set up a permanent swap file. Choose the 386-enhanced application in the Control Panel and choose **V**irtual Memory and **C**hange; change the **T**ype to Permanent.

When you change to a Permanent swap file, Windows may suggest that you defragment the hard disk, which regroups scattered segments of files to make these files contiguous. Defragmenting a hard disk not only saves disk space, but also speeds disk access because files are no longer scattered across the entire disk. You need a utility to defragment a hard disk.

Troubleshooting DOS Applications

DOS applications don't need Windows to run, but you gain many advantages when running DOS applications in Windows. To run DOS applications, Windows uses files that are known as *PIFs*, or application information files. A PIF includes information about the DOS application's location on disk, as well as setup information which is standardized to work on all computers. Although the PIF settings may enable DOS applications to work on the computer, these files may not cause the DOS applications to work optimally on the computer. An entire chapter in this book, Chapter 24, is devoted to optimizing DOS application performance by fine-tuning PIF settings.

Other reasons to edit a PIF include the following:

- The application is in a directory other than the directory listed in the Program Filename text box of the PIF.

- The Start-up Directory, which specifies the data directory, is different from the directory you want or the directory expected by the application.

- You want to start an application by using a special parameter.

- You want to ensure that an application swaps to disk when not in use, freeing more memory for other applications (the Prevent Program Switch option).

- An application was upgraded and requires more memory.

- You want to increase the memory available for an application in order to increase performance.

For more tips about improving DOS application performance, refer to the section in this chapter on "Solving Memory Conflicts."

Installation and Setup Problems

Usually, when installing any software, you need to provide information about the equipment or software. Before you start an installation, find out exactly what equipment you have, how much memory your system has, and what software you previously installed and where on the computer the software is located. Check the application's documentation to see whether you can find a list of information needed during installation. As always, make sure that you have enough hard disk space before you begin the installation process and, if possible, shut down all memory-resident applications. If you have difficulty when installing a DOS application, refer to the application's documentation.

Solving Copy, Paste, and Print Screen Problems

If you cannot copy between a DOS application and other DOS and Windows applications or you cannot print the DOS screen in Windows, open the application's PIF and deselect the No Screen Exchange option.

This option may be selected to save memory. (To edit a PIF, choose the PIF Editor from the Main menu and choose the **File O**pen command to open the PIF for the DOS application you want to change.)

Solving Font and Printing Problems

If you cannot change the font size in a DOS application, the application may be running in graphics mode rather than in text mode. Check the application's documentation to see whether you can switch to text mode.

Some display drivers don't support changing fonts in DOS applications running in a Window. If you use a Super VGA monitor, make sure that you selected the Super VGA driver that comes with Windows 3.1. If this selection doesn't fix the problem, contact the video adapter manufacturer to see if a new driver is available for Windows 3.1.

If you cannot get a driver that supports font switching in DOS applications, try adding the following line to the [NonWindowsApp] section of the SYSTEM.INI file:

```
FontChangeEnable = 1
```

Solving Problems Switching between Applications

If you cannot switch between applications, the DOS application's PIF may be set to prevent switching (which can save memory). If this is the case, the only way to get back to Windows is to close the DOS application. To change this, open the application's PIF and deselect the Prevent Program S**w**itch option. (To edit a PIF, choose the PIF Editor from the Main menu and choose the **File O**pen command to open the PIF for the DOS application you want to change.)

In the PIF Editor, check also the **A**dvanced dialog box and see whether any of the Reserve **S**hortcut Key options are selected. If they are, you cannot use these shortcut keys to switch between applications; try deselecting these options. In particular, deselect the Alt+Tab option.

If when you switch between DOS applications in standard mode and a DOS application's screen does not redraw, edit the application's PIF and deselect the **N**o Save Screen option. This option saves memory by not redrawing the screen but is suitable only for applications that can redraw a screen themselves.

If you are unable to switch from a DOS application, consider the following possibilities:

■ Windows may not have reserved enough memory to save the video image of the application when you switch out of the application. Edit the PIF for that application to reserve a higher video mode. For example, if the current video mode is for text screens, select a graphics video mode.

■ Check the PIF to ensure that the Prevent Program Switch option is cleared (standard mode only).

■ Ensure that the application does not use the Directly Modifies options (standard mode only). Try clearing one or more of these options and rerunning the application.

■ A very few applications take complete control of the keyboard, so Windows cannot receive any keyboard signals. You must quit such an application to return to Windows.

Be Cautious When Changing PIF Settings
When you change PIF settings, do not immediately begin working on important data. Run the DOS application as an experiment to see whether the new PIF setting runs the application and enables you to switch between applications. Some applications require specific PIF settings because of the way they work with the keyboard and video memory. If you cannot find a PIF setting that enables you to switch from that application to another, you must quit that application to return to Windows.

Solving Performance Problems Running DOS Applications

DOS applications running in standard mode usually swap between memory and the hard disk, allowing more applications to fit in memory at the same time. If you assign a serial (COM) port to a DOS application, however, Windows assumes that you are doing so because you want to use the COM port to communicate via a modem. Swapping, however, interrupts modem communication, so Windows doesn't permit a DOS application assigned to a COM port to swap. Therefore, fewer DOS applications can run in standard mode, because saving memory by swapping between memory and the hard disk is impossible. To solve this problem, deselect the COM1, COM2, COM3, or COM4 option in the PIF dialog box. (To edit a PIF, choose the PIF Editor from the Main menu, and choose the File Open command to open the PIF for the DOS application you want to change.)

If the system slows when you're running DOS applications, you may be running a DOS application unnecessarily in the background. In the PIF Editor dialog box, deselect the Execution Background option. (To edit a PIF, choose the PIF Editor from the Main menu and choose the File Open command to open the PIF for the DOS application you want to change.)

In the PIF Editor, type the maximum amount of extended memory needed by the application in the XMS Memory: KB Limit option. This setting prevents the application from using all the extended memory by setting an upper limit. Leave the setting at 0 to prevent the application from gaining access to any extended memory (except in the HMA), or set the option to *–1* to give the application all the requested extended memory. Use the *–1* setting only if the application requires large amounts of extended memory because this setting may slow the system significantly.

Solving Operation Problems Running DOS Applications

If you hear a beep when you try to switch from full screen to a window, the application cannot run in a window. Press Alt+Enter to return to full screen; if this step doesn't work, press Ctrl+Alt+Del to close the application without closing Windows.

If you're stuck in a DOS application after you marked (selected) text or after you scrolled, you still may be in the Windows editing mode, which prevents you from working with a DOS application. You can tell whether this problem exists by looking at the DOS application's title bar: if the bar still reads Select or Mark, a Windows operation still is incomplete. Complete the operation (by selecting text or choosing the Edit Copy Enter command) or press the Escape key to return control to the application.

Capturing the Screen Doesn't Work

If you are unable to capture a DOS screen, check the following solutions:

■ Check the PIF to ensure that the No Screen Exchange option is deselected. Someone may have selected this option to make more memory available, but while No Screen Exchange is selected, this option prevents copying or cutting to the Clipboard.

■ Check the Reserve Shortcut Key option in the Advanced dialog box in the PIF Editor to see whether the Print Screen (PrtScrn) or Alt+Print Screen (Alt+PrtScrn) key combinations are reserved for the application's use. The application may use the key combinations, disabling them for Windows' use.

■ Check the Video Mode if you are running in standard mode or the Video Memory if you are running in 386-enhanced mode. Selecting a higher video mode to make more memory available for the video may enable you to capture screen data.

■ A final reason you cannot capture a screen may be lack of memory. Close some applications to free memory.

Pasting Information Doesn't Work

If you are unable to paste information you have copied or cut into the Clipboard, check the following solutions:

■ Windows cannot paste graphics in a DOS application. Windows can paste graphics in Windows applications that can accept graphics.

■ Copied *text* from a DOS application actually may be graphics that appear as text on-screen. If so, Windows cannot copy the *graphical text* to another DOS application. You may be able to copy and paste the entire screen in the application instead.

■ Some DOS applications cannot handle the fast paste method used by 386-enhanced mode. If you operate in 386-enhanced mode and pasting does not work, modify the advanced portion of the PIF to clear the Allow Fast Paste check box.

Closing DOS Applications

Quit a DOS application with the normal command used to quit the application. If the screen does not return immediately to Windows, press Alt+space bar to display the Control menu and choose Close. You can control how the window or screen for a DOS application reacts when the application closes via the Close Window On Exit setting in the PIF. The application window will remain open if this check box is not checked.

Normally you cannot quit Windows when a DOS application is running. If you try to quit Windows when a DOS application is active, Windows asks you to close the application first unless this PIF option has been selected.

If you are running Windows in 386-enhanced mode and the Allow **C**lose When Active check box is selected in the application PIF, you can close Windows while that DOS application is running. This may result in loss of data and may result in damaged program files. This option should rarely be used.

If you are connected to a network while in a DOS application, disconnect from the network before you quit the application.

If a DOS application running under Windows terminates improperly, it prevents you from exiting the application. When a DOS application crashes, and you cannot exit from the frozen application, you can use the Terminate option in the Control menu to terminate the application. Select the **S**ettings option from the application's Control menu and then choose **T**erminate to close the application. This option should only be used as a last resort.

Responding to an Application Failure

Rarely, the computer encounters an internal instruction that it doesn't understand or that conflicts with another instruction. For this and other reasons, the application may fail, or *crash*. When this happens, sometimes you see a message on-screen advising you that the application has encountered an unrecoverable error. The screen also may freeze and the application may become unusable.

Although crashes occur only rarely, they are the best reason for you to save all important documents frequently. (Earthquakes also happen rarely, but if you live in southern California, being prepared for tremors is a good idea!)

Fortunately, if an application crashes, you may not have lost everything. You often can recover from a crash by shutting down only the crashed application. In many cases, you don't have to turn off the computer or restart Windows. You lose the data in the application that crashed (unless the application has a file-recovery utility, like Word for Windows and other applications), but you may not lose data from other applications running at the same time.

If you encounter a message that advises you that an application has terminated or if the screen freezes, press the following keys:

Ctrl+Alt+Del

A message appears, offering you three alternatives. The first choice is to press the Esc (Escape) key, which exits the message box. If you don't feel the application really crashed, you can try pressing Esc to return to the application. If this step doesn't work (it probably won't), press Enter to exit the application and return to Windows. If this action doesn't work, you have to reboot the computer.

To recover from an application crash, follow these steps:

1. When you see a message advising you that the current application has terminated, press Ctrl+Alt+Delete. (Hold down the Ctrl and Alt keys and then press the Delete key.)

2. To close an application (and lose all changes you made during the current work session), press Enter. If this solution works, you return to Windows. Restart the application and continue working.

3. If you encounter another error message (rather than returning to Windows) press Ctrl+Alt+Delete again to restart the computer. You lose unsaved data in all applications running when the crash occurred.

A crash sometimes occurs for no apparent reason, and you must restart the application to continue. (If the application freezes, rather than simply shutting down, try the Ctrl+Alt+Del technique described previously.) If the system crashes frequently, however, suspect a problem. One problem stems from using an older version of an application not compatible with Windows 3.1. If this is the case, call the manufacturer to see about getting an updated version of the application.

Another problem may be that your equipment is incompatible with Windows. Check first to be sure that you're using the right driver. To learn more about hardware compatibility, use Windows Write to read the README.WRI or SYSTEM.WRI files provided in the Windows directory.

Solving Memory Conflicts

Everything you do on the computer happens in memory, and the computer has only so much memory. Occasionally, memory becomes full. If this problem becomes a regular occurrence, consider adding memory; the cost per kilobyte is far less than in the past, and the improvement in speed can be amazing—especially if you jump from a 2M system to 4M (beyond 4M, the improvements are less noticeable).

Solving Out-of-Memory Errors

If you see an out-of-memory message when you try to start an application, you already have too many applications running. You need to free some memory. If you cannot start a DOS application, try the following suggestions or refer to the following sections on freeing memory in standard and 386-enhanced modes. If you cannot start a Windows application, try the following suggestions:

■ Close any applications you're not using. Close any memory-resident applications. In general, be sure that you really use any of the memory-resident applications that are set to start up automatically. If you don't, modify the CONFIG.SYS or AUTOEXEC.BAT file to remove memory-resident applications.

■ Minimize Windows applications to icons (as icons, applications use less memory).

■ Clear or save the Clipboard contents. From the Main menu, choose the Clipboard Viewer and choose File Save **As** to save the contents or **Edit D**elete to delete the contents.

■ Turn off desktop wallpaper, which uses a great deal of memory. From the Control Panel, choose Desktop; in the Wallpaper group choose None in the **F**ile list.

■ Make sure that Windows has enough disk space available for swap files. If possible, set up a permanent swap file. In 386-enhanced mode, choose the 386-enhanced application in the Control Panel and choose **V**irtual Memory; then choose **C**hange and select Permanent as the swap file **T**ype.

Freeing Memory in Standard Mode

A PIF is an application information file used by Windows to run DOS applications. You can change some of the PIF settings to improve memory management. To edit a PIF, choose the PIF Editor application from the Main group in the Program Manager. Then choose File **O**pen to open the PIF for the application causing the problem.

■ For the Video Memory option, choose Text. This choice reduces the amount of memory Windows reserves for the application.

Close the application before you make this change.

■ In the Memory Requirements KB **R**equired box, reduce the amount of memory required.

■ If the application doesn't need extended memory, set XMS Memory: KB Re**q**uired and KB **L**imit to zero.

■ If you don't plan to use this application to take screen shots, select the No Screen **E**xchange option.

■ If you won't need to switch between applications, select the Prevent Program S**w**itch option. With Prevent Program Switch active, you must exit the application to return to Windows.

Freeing Memory in 386-Enhanced Mode

You can use PIFs to improve memory management in 386-enhanced mode, just as you can in standard mode. Start the PIF Editor as you did in the preceding section and open the PIF for the application causing the problem. If none of the following suggestions helps, edit the PIFs for other DOS applications you may run at the same time you run the one that causes the memory overload.

■ For the **V**ideo Memory option, choose Text. This choice reduces the amount of memory Windows reserves for the application. Close the application before you make this change. Deselect the Retain Video **M**emory option in the **A**dvanced dialog box.

■ In the Memory Requirements: KB **R**equired box, reduce the amount of memory needed.

■ Select the F**u**ll Screen option. Running a DOS application in a window takes more memory.

■ Select the **E**xclusive option to run this application exclusively. With Exclusive selected, you cannot run other applications in the background.

■ Run DOS applications full-screen rather than in a Window to conserve memory. Switch between window and full-screen display by pressing Alt+Enter.

Solving Font and Printing Problems

In the days before Windows, printing was an area likely to cause problems for people. Windows greatly simplifies printing by using a common printer driver and by including the Print Manager to manage printing. Occasionally, however, a problem may crop up in the best of systems.

Getting the Printer To Print

One of the most common problems you may encounter is when the printer simply won't print. Often, this problem is the easiest to fix, because the fault frequently is mechanical. Try one of the following solutions:

■ First, make sure that the printer is plugged in, turned on, and on-line (a light or message on the front of the printer usually gives you this information). Make sure that the printer has paper and that the paper is not jammed. Make sure that the printer lid or case is closed.

■ Make sure that the printer cartridge is firmly plugged in or that the ribbon or print wheel is correctly installed.

■ Make sure that you have the right cable and that the cable is functioning. You can sometimes borrow a cable from an identical printer that you know works to see whether a new cable is all you need.

■ Make sure that you selected the correct printer in the application. Make sure that the settings, such as paper orientation and source, are correct.

■ Make sure that the printer options and port are correct. You can use the Printers application in the Control Panel to check printer settings and connections (see Chapter 7). With the Print Manager enabled, you can use this feature to check settings and connections (see Chapter 9).

■ If you're trying to print on a network, make sure that you're connected to the network printer (see Chapter 9).

■ If you use a switch box to switch between printers, choose the Printers application in the Control Panel and choose **Connect**.

Turn off the **F**ast Printing Direct to Port option. You also can try connecting the printer directly to the computer without the switch box.

■ If a simple solution doesn't solve the problem, test whether the computer and printer are communicating. One simple test is to exit Windows and use a DOS command to copy a small text file directly to the printer (this procedure may work for dot matrix printers and Hewlett-Packard laser printers). Type the following command, for example, at the DOS prompt to print the AUTOEXEC.BAT file to a parallel printer on LPT1:

     copy c:\autoexec.bat > lpt1:

■ For a PostScript printer, try copying the file TESTPS.TXT to the printer. (An Apple PostScript printer is likely to connect to a serial port, such as COM1, rather than to a parallel port.) Use the following command:

     copy c:\windows\system\testps.txt com1

If the file doesn't print when you use the DOS copy command, a problem may exist outside of Windows, such as one of the mechanical problems listed previously. Check the printer's documentation.

Printing from Windows

Make sure that the printer cable is connected and functioning properly. In Windows, all pin connectors must be working (which may not be the case with DOS applications). To test the cable, borrow another cable that you know works.

Windows stores information being processed for printing in a temporary file. If you cannot print from within Windows (but can from DOS) check to see whether a place (a directory) is available for the temporary files and whether enough space exists for the temporary files. To see whether a directory for temporary files exists, at the DOS prompt, type *SET* and press enter. If you see a TEMP= line, then a directory is set. If you don't see a TEMP line, add the following line to the AUTOEXEC.BAT file:

     set temp=c:\temp

Check to make sure that you have a directory named TEMP and make sure that at least 2M of free hard disk space is available on the computer. Then restart the computer and try printing again.

If you still cannot print, try the following possible solutions:

■ If no specific driver exists in Windows for the printer and you selected a driver for a printer that the printer emulates, make sure that you chose the correct printer to emulate. Check the printer's documentation.

■ If you're printing to LPT1, a parallel port, choose the Printers application from the Control Panel, and choose **C**onnect. From the **P**orts list, select LPT1.DOS (or LPT1.OS2) instead of LPT1.

■ If a time-out message appears when you try to print, you can try one of two solutions. The easiest solution is to turn off the Print Manager and print directly (the computer takes longer to print because the file cannot be queued up for printing as usually happens in the Print Manager, but the printer doesn't take longer to print). To turn off the Print Manager, choose Printers from the Control Panel and turn off the **U**se Print Manager Option. Another solution is to increase the printer's time-out settings. Choose Printers from the Control Panel, choose **C**onnect, and increase the value for **D**evice Not Selected or **T**ransmission Retry (these values are the number of seconds before the computer gives up if the printer, or device, is not selected or if a transmission fails in some way).

■ If you have a serial printer, look for an IRQ Interrupt conflict. If another serial device, such as a mouse, is using the same IRQ Interrupt as the printer, one of the devices won't work. See the earlier section in this chapter on "Getting the Mouse To Work in Windows," or refer to Chapter 7.

Correcting Formatting Problems or Garbled Output

If the printed pages are formatted incorrectly, start by using Windows Write to read the PRINTERS.WRI file and see whether you can find pertinent information specific to the printer.

If the PRINTERS.WRI file offers no help, make sure that the printer can print fonts and sizes you specified in the application. Make sure that printer configuration settings are correct. To check, choose Printers in the Control Panel and choose **S**ettings (see Chapter 7). Check all switches on the printer that control settings, such as page length and line feeds, to be sure that all settings are correct (check the printer's manual).

If printed text is garbled, make sure that you selected the correct printer as the default. In the Control Panel, choose Printers and then select the correct printer and choose Set as Default Printer. If the printer contains a cartridge, make sure that you select the correct cartridge. See Chapter 7 or 9 for more information. Try turning the printer off and then on again to clear the printer's memory of text that may be left over from a previous print. Test for a faulty cable by borrowing a cable that you know is functioning correctly.

If you use a serial printer, check the port settings. Choose the Ports application in the Control Panel and choose Settings. Sometimes, choosing a lower baud rate can improve printing.

If the printer doesn't include a driver in Windows, and you're emulating a printer that Windows does include, try emulating a different model.

If nothing else works, try selecting the Windows Generic/Text Only printer driver. Have the Windows disks on hand; then select Printers from the Control Panel; and choose first Add and then Install. Follow screen instructions to install a printer; then choose Connect to connect the driver to the same port to which the printer is connected.

Getting Fonts To Display and Print Correctly

Windows 3.1 comes equipped with TrueType technology, which shows you the same fonts on-screen that you see when you print—no matter what kind of printer you use. Windows comes with four TrueType fonts, and you can easily add more. The four TrueType fonts are Times New Roman, Arial, Courier New, and Symbol.

Because you may have other fonts that you want to use, you also can turn off TrueType. If you don't see TrueType fonts listed in an application's font list, choose the Fonts application in the Control Panel, choose TrueType, and select the Enable TrueType Fonts option. If you see only TrueType fonts in the application's font list but also want to see other fonts you have available, in the same TrueType dialog box, turn off the Show Only TrueType Fonts in Applications option.

If you cannot print TrueType fonts on a laser printer, you may be using an old print driver. Make sure that you use a driver that came with Windows 3.1 or contact your manufacturer for a Windows 3.1 driver.

If you use fonts other than TrueType fonts, what you see on-screen may not match exactly what you see when you print. This can happen when you use printer fonts, for example, for which no corresponding screen fonts exist because Windows substitutes the closest TrueType font for the screen display. To solve this problem, use TrueType fonts for printing or use a printer font for which you have a screen font. In many applications, you can select an option to make only printer fonts available or to show fonts on-screen as they appear when printed. Check the application documentation.

If you installed a cartridge in the printer and cannot print the fonts, check to ensure that you selected the correct cartridge. Choose Printers from the Control Panel, select the printer, choose Setup, and, from the Cartridges list, select the correct cartridge. If the cartridge is correct, try turning off the printer and making sure that the cartridge is properly installed (often firm pressure is needed to insert the cartridge).

If you have trouble printing soft fonts, make sure that you haven't turned off the printer since you downloaded the fonts. If you turned off the printer, you have to download the fonts again. If this action doesn't work, check the font documentation to be sure that you installed the fonts correctly. You also need to download the fonts again if you changed the port connection. If you use many soft fonts at once, try using fewer fonts. Many printers support only a limited number of fonts. The number of fonts you use also is limited by the size of the WIN.INI file, which can be only 64K. If WIN.INI is at the maximum size, use shorter paths for the soft fonts to conserve characters.

Recovering Lost Text

If the printer loses text, the cable or the port may be at fault. If you use a parallel printer (LPT), suspect the cable and try another one that you know is working. If you use a serial printer (COM), change the port settings by choosing the Ports application from the Control Panel and then choosing Settings. Try selecting a lower baud rate from the list. If this step doesn't work, check to see that all settings are the same in DOS, Windows, and on the printer.

If only part of a page prints, the printer probably lacks sufficient memory. Graphics often present this kind of problem because these files are large. If possible, split the graphics so fewer graphic images appear on one page. If you cannot do this, try a lower print resolution. If you run into this problem frequently, find out whether you can add more memory to your printer.

If you know that you have enough memory in the printer, choose the Printers application in the Control Panel, select the printer and choose Setup, and make sure that the correct amount of memory is specified in the Memory list.

Recovering from PostScript Printer Problems

If an out-of-memory message appears when you use a PostScript printer, you may be trying to use too many soft fonts. Try using printer fonts or use fewer soft fonts.

If fonts are not the problem, try making changes in the printer's advanced options. Choose Printers from the Control Panel and then select the printer and choose Setup, Options, and Advanced. In the Send To Printer As list, make sure that Adobe Type 1 is selected. Make sure that the Clear Memory Per Page option is selected, so the printer's memory clears after each page prints. Select the Use Substitution Table option, so the printer substitutes built-in printer fonts for new fonts that you specify in the document (to change the table, choose Edit Substitution Table and make selections for the table).

If a PostScript printer doesn't respond, try increasing the transmission retry setting by choosing Printers from the Control Panel, selecting the printer and choosing Connect, and doubling the value in the Transmission Retry text box.

Correcting Paintbrush Printing Problems

If a Paintbrush picture is printed smaller than normal, check the View Picture command in the View menu to see whether the picture looks okay. If necessary, choose the Options Image Attributes command to change the height and width of the image.

When you print, make sure that the Use Printer Resolution option in the Print dialog box is turned off. Check that the desired scaling is set (if set to less than 100 percent, the picture prints smaller than normal).

FROM HERE...

For Related Information:

◄◄ To learn more about fonts, see "Understanding Fonts," p. 306 and "Understanding How Computers Use Fonts," p. 307.

◄◄ To learn more about printing, see "Printing a File," p. 323 and "Correcting Printing Problems," p. 356.

◄◄ See also "Adding and Configuring Printers," p. 277 and "Adding and Removing Fonts," p. 287.

Solving Network Problems

If you have trouble connecting to a network or using Windows on a network, check this section for solutions. If none of these suggestions helps, read Chapter 28 in this book or read the NETWORKS.WRI file in the Windows directory (use Windows Write to read this file). If the difficulty is with printing, refer to the section in this chapter on "Solving Font and Printing Problems."

Connecting to a Network Drive

If you cannot connect to a network drive, make sure that you use the correct network drivers. Choose the Windows Setup application in the Main group and read the Network line. If the setting is wrong, choose the Options Change System Settings command and choose a different driver from the Network list.

If the driver is correct, try exiting Windows and connecting from DOS. If you still cannot connect to the network drive, the problem is not with Windows, but with the network.

Running a Shared Copy of Windows or an Application on a Network

If you have trouble running a shared copy of Windows, make sure that the personal Windows directory and the shared Windows directory are both listed in the computer's path, with the personal Windows directory listed first.

Make sure that you always use the same letter to indicate the Windows drive when you connect to a network, because the first time you use this drive Windows records the drive letter and always looks for needed files on this drive. (To change the drive letter, you must change the path to match.)

Running Network Software

If you have problems running applications while the network software is loaded into high memory (the first 64K of extended memory) try disabling the network software's high memory area options. For more information, check the network documentation.

If you have trouble running Windows while network software is loaded into upper memory between 640K and 1M, try loading the network software in conventional memory.

If network pop-up messages cause the system to crash, disable the messages. You also may be able to run an application such as WINPOPUP.EXE, to display and dispose of the messages properly.

For Related Information:

◄◄ To learn more about networks, see Chapter 28, "Networking Windows," p. 1011.

Solving Object Linking and Embedding Problems

Object linking and embedding (OLE) enables you to create compound documents made up of objects created by different applications. To create a compound document, the applications must be OLE-compatible.

Creating a compound document involves at least two applications, the primary or client application (into which you embed objects), and the secondary or server application (which you use to create objects to embed in the client application). Some applications can function as either a client or a server. An object embedded in a client application is linked to the server application you used to create the object.

Many Windows applications come with free OLE applications. Word for Windows, for example, includes Microsoft Draw, WordArt, and Equation Editor. Once installed on the computer, these *applets* become available to all other applications that support OLE.

Making the Server Available

When you create, edit, or update an embedded object, the server application used to create the object must be available. If you see a message warning that the server application is unavailable, you must either wait until the application becomes available, or you must switch to the server application and complete or end the current task. You may be able to just choose Cancel to close the warning dialog box and try again later.

If these simple methods don't help, you may need to reinstall the application that includes the applet you want to use as a server. Installing the application registers the applet in Windows.

Opening a Server Application

If you try to insert a new object from within a client application and the server application isn't listed or doesn't start when chosen from the list, try one of the following solutions:

- Make sure that the server application wasn't deleted from the computer.

- If you moved the server application, make sure that the directory where the server application is located is included in the AUTOEXEC.BAT file.

- If you still have an old version of Windows on the computer, along with Version 3.1, the new WIN.INI may not list server applets that you installed before you installed Windows 3.1. Use Windows 3.1 to reinstall the application that contains the applets you cannot open.

Understanding Different Ways of Pasting

When you paste information from one application to another, two different things may happen. If you use certain server applications to create the information, copy the information to the Clipboard, and then paste it in a client application, the information is embedded in the client application, and you can double-click on the information to start up the server application. (For some server applications, you can embed objects only by using a special command.) If, however, you created the information on the Clipboard by using a non-server application, when you paste the data in another application, the information becomes an unchangeable part of the document.

Solving Problems with Linking

When you link an object from one application to another, then to update the link, you must first save all changes made to the original document.

If you are trying to paste and link the contents of the Clipboard into a document, but the Paste Link command is unavailable (grayed out), first save the file you used to create the information as described in the previous paragraph. If the Paste Link command is still unavailable, the application you used to create the information may not be a server application. If not, you can paste, but not link, the information into the document.

For Related Information:

◄◄ To learn more about OLE, see Chapter 6 "Embedding and Linking," p. 207.

Solving Communication and Port Difficulties

Serial communications take place on the four COM ports available in Windows. Serial communications may include printing, faxing, scanning, operating a mouse, and connecting to a distant computer via modem.

Accessing a Serial (COM) Port

If you have trouble using the modem, check to see whether a port conflict exists:

- First check to see whether another application is using the same port. If so, close this application.

- Make sure that the port settings, including the IRQ Interrupt, are correct. To learn more about changing the IRQ Interrupt settings, see the previous section on "Getting the Mouse To Work with Windows." Read the section on ports in Chapter 6 to learn about port settings.

- If the computer crashes when you try to use a serial port, an IRQ Interrupt conflict may exist. COM1 and COM3, for example, often use IRQ4, but COM2 and COM4 often use IRQ3. Some computers can share IRQ interrupts if you add the following line to the [386enh] section of the SYSTEM.INI file:

```
COMIrqSharing = true
```

If you suspect IRQ Interrupt conflicts, check the documentation that came with the serial devices to see what the IRQ Interrupt settings are. These default settings often can be changed so that all applications on the computer can exist harmoniously.

Facilitating High-Speed Communications

Windows enables communication at high speeds of 9600 bps but at this speed, accidents sometimes happen. If you experience problems, try the following solutions:

- If you have DOS applications running in the background, close them or lower the background execution priority of these applications in the PIF Editor (by setting a lower value in the **B**ackground Priority option in the **A**dvanced dialog box).

- Make sure that the computer is running as fast as possible (some computers slow down to prolong battery life). Check the documentation.

- Add a 16550A Universal Asynchronous Receiver Transmitter (UART) to the serial port. The UART buffers the serial port data, which enables the port to run faster. (Windows' own buffering at times conflicts with some versions of UART; in this case, disable the UART's buffering by using the comxfifo setting in the SYSTEM.INI file. You can read about this setting in the SYSINI.WRI file in Windows Write.)

Communicating through DOS

If you use a DOS communications application that uses the Xon/Xoff protocol, you may lose characters if other applications are running and slowing down the system. If this is the case, include the following statement in the SYSTEM.INI file (x is the number of the COM port):

```
COMxProtocol = XOFF
```

Communicating through Windows Terminal

If the modem won't dial the phone number in a Terminal file, first make sure that the hardware is connected correctly. Then make sure that the correct COM port is specified by choosing the **S**ettings Communications command and checking the **C**onnector option.

If the modem dials but doesn't establish a connection, the settings you chose for the remote computer may be wrong. The system and the remote system must use the same baud rate, data bits, parity setting, stop bits, and flow control. You have to contact someone at the remote site to discover the settings of the remote computer. On your system, change the settings to match the settings of the remote computer by choosing the **S**ettings **C**ommunications command and selecting the appropriate options.

If you can dial and connect but cannot send or receive a file, both the computer and the remote computer may not be using the same *handshake protocol* (which is the flow control method). Find out whether the remote system uses Xon/Xoff and whether the remote system uses hardware handshaking. Use the **S**ettings **C**ommunications command to change the **F**low Control settings to match the settings of the remote computer.

FROM HERE...

For Related Information:

◄◄ To learn more about ports, see "Setting Up Communication and Printer Ports," p. 291.

Chapter Summary

Although Windows is a stable operating environment that usually works well, problems can occur. This chapter explained what to do when you encounter common problems. If none of the solutions described in this chapter solve your problem, call Microsoft's technical support line, listed in Chapter 30.

Chapter 30 also identifies other resources that you may find helpful when using and troubleshooting Windows.

Help, Support, and Resources

W indows is one of the most popular software applications ever written. Therefore, a great deal of support is available for Windows. The following resources should help you get the most from Windows.

Telephone Support

Use the following telephone numbers to get technical support or product sales information about Windows or Windows applications.

For questions specific to Windows installation, the Program Manager, the File Manager, or accessories, call Microsoft Corporation's Windows support line at (206) 637-7098.

For technical or sales information regarding a major product, call one of the following support lines:

Manufacturer	Software	Support Line
Microsoft Corp.	Corporate	206-882-8080
	Technical (all software, Publisher, Money, and Project)	206-454-2030
	Windows	206-637-7098
	DOS (pay per call)	900-896-9000
	Microsoft Excel	206-635-7070
	Word for Windows	206-462-9673
Adobe Systems	Corporate	415-961-4400
	Technical (Adobe Type Manager, Adobe Fonts)	415-961-4992
Aldus Corp.	Corporate	206-662-5500
	Technical (PageMaker, Persuasion, Freehand)	206-628-2040
Asymetrix	Corporate	206-462-0501
	Technical (ToolBook)	206-637-1600
Borland	Corporate	408-438-8400
	Technical (ObjectVision)	408-438-5300
Corel	Corporate	613-728-8200
	Technical (CorelDRAW!)	613-728-1990
Intuit	Corporate	415-322-0573
	Technical (Quicken)	415-322-2800
Lotus	Corporate	617-577-8500
	Technical (recordings) (1-2-3 for Windows, Ami Pro, Freelance)	617-253-9130
Lotus	Technical (pay per call)	900-454-9009
Polaris	Corporate	619-674-6500
	Technical (PackRat)	619-743-7800

Manufacturer	Software	Support Line
Symantec	Corporate	310-449-4900
	Technical (Norton Desktop for Windows)	213-319-2020
WordPerfect	Corporate	801-225-5000
	Technical (WordPerfect 5.1 for Windows)	801-228-9907

Support Organizations

Most major cities in the United States have a computer club. Within each club, you usually can find a Windows Special Interest Group (SIG). Clubs usually have meetings monthly, demonstrate new software, maintain a list of consultants, and have free or low-cost training. To contact your local computer club, check newspaper listings under *computer* or call local computer stores.

The Windows User Group Network (WUGNET) is a national organization devoted to supporting its members with information about Windows and Windows applications. WUGNET publishes a substantial journal bimonthly containing tips and articles written by members and consultants. The staff is highly knowledgeable about Windows and Windows applications. Contact WUGNET at the following address:

WUGNet Publications, Inc.
1295 N. Providence Rd.
Media, PA 19063
(215) 565-1861 voice
(215) 565-7106 fax

Computer Bulletin Board Forums

Computer bulletin boards are databases from which you can retrieve information over the telephone line using Terminal, the communication application that comes with Windows. Some bulletin boards contain a wealth of information about Windows and Windows applications. One of the largest public bulletin boards is CompuServe.

CompuServe contains forums where Windows and Windows applications can be discussed. You can submit questions to Microsoft operators who will return an answer within a day. CompuServe also contains libraries of sample files and new printer and device drivers. The Knowledgebase available in Microsoft's region of CompuServe has much of the same troubleshooting information used by Microsoft's telephone support representatives. You can search through the Knowledgebase using keywords. The Microsoft region of CompuServe is divided into many different areas—for example, Windows users, advanced Windows users, Microsoft Excel, Microsoft languages, and sections of each of the major Microsoft and non-Microsoft applications that run under Windows.

After you become a CompuServe member, you can access the Microsoft user forums, library files, and Knowledgebase. To gain access to one of these areas, type one of the following GO commands at the CompuServe prompt symbol (!) and then press Enter.

Type	To access
GO MSOFT	Overall Microsoft area
GO MSUSER	Overall applications and Windows areas
GO MSAPP	Microsoft applications areas
GO MSEXCEL	Microsoft Excel areas
GO WINNEW	New Windows user areas
GO WINADV	Advanced Windows user areas
GO WINVEN	Overall non-Microsoft Windows applications areas
GO WINAPA	Non-Microsoft Windows applications area
GO WINAPB	Non-Microsoft Windows applications area
GO WINAPC	Non-Microsoft Windows applications area

An example of how to log onto CompuServe and enter the Microsoft Windows and applications regions is shown in Chapter 14, "Using Windows Terminal." (You must join CompuServe and get a passcode before you can use the bulletin board.)

For more information, contact CompuServe at the following address:

CompuServe
5000 Arlington Centre Blvd.
P.O. Box 20212
Columbus, OH 43220
(800) 848-8990

For Related Information:

◄◄ To learn more about CompuServe, see "Tailoring Terminal to Your Needs," p. 594.

FROM HERE...

Consultants and Corporate Training

Microsoft Consulting Partners develop and support applications written using Microsoft products for the Windows environment. Microsoft Consulting Partners are independent consultants who have met strict qualifying requirements imposed by Microsoft.

Ron Person & Co, based in San Francisco, has attained Microsoft's highest rating for Microsoft Excel and Word for Windows consultants—Microsoft Consulting Partner. The firm helps corporations nationwide in consulting and developing in-house programming and support skills with the embedded macro languages in Microsoft Excel, Word for Windows, and Microsoft Access. The firm's macro and embedded Basic developer's courses have enabled many corporations to develop their own powerful financial, marketing, and business analysis systems in a minimum amount of time. If your company plans to develop applications using Microsoft's macro or embedded Basic languages, you will gain significantly from the courses taught by Ron Person & Co. For information on course content, on-side corporate classes, or consulting, contact the firm at the following address:

Ron Person & Co.
P.O. Box 5647
Santa Rosa, CA 95402

(415) 989-7508 voice
(707) 539-1525 voice
(707) 538-1485 fax

Installing Windows

The Windows Setup program guides you through installing Windows. If you already have Windows 3.0 installed, you should install Windows 3.1 over the existing version of Windows. This type of installation preserves your current settings, application groups, and custom drivers. Drivers for existing printers are upgraded. Installation should take no more than 20 to 30 minutes.

If you are unfamiliar with computers, you should use Express Setup. This application determines your hardware and software and makes appropriate selections for you. You are asked which type of printer your computer uses and where the printer is connected.

If you are familiar with computers and want to install only parts of Windows or make changes during installation, you should use Custom Setup. Custom Setup enables you to add printers and select hardware that may be different than what is detected by the Setup program. If your hard disk is low on available storage, you may want to use Custom Setup to install parts of Windows rather than the full Windows and all accessories. You can run Setup at any time to add Windows features or accessories that you did not install initially.

Before You Install Windows

For Windows to operate correctly, your hardware and software must meet the following requirements:

- IBM Personal System/2, Personal Computer AT, COMPAQ Deskpro 286, or a compatible computer that uses an 80286, 80386, 80386SX, or 80486 processor

- 1M (megabyte) or more of memory on an 80286-based PC or 2M or more on an 80386 or 80468. (Memory above 640K should be configured as extended memory. Refer to your hardware installation manual for this information.)

- Graphics adapter cards supported by Windows (usually VGA or EGA graphics)

- A hard disk with 5M to 10M of available storage

- At least one 1.2M or 1.44M diskette drive

- MS-DOS 3.1 or higher

To run multimedia applications in Windows, you need a Multimedia Personal Computer (MPC) or an MPC upgrade kit to upgrade your existing computer.

Optional equipment supported by Windows includes the following:

- One or more printers or plotters supported by Windows

- A mouse (highly recommended)

- Pen computer systems (add-in software available with pen system)

- A Hayes, MultiTech, or TrailBlazer (or compatible) modem for communications using Terminal

- Major networks, such as Novell NetWare, 3Com, LANtastic, VINES and LAN Manager

Windows 3.1 can run in two different modes: standard mode and 386-enhanced mode. Standard mode is used on all 80286 computers and 80386 computers with 2M of memory or less. Enhanced mode is used on 80386 computers with more than 2M of memory. Standard mode enables you to switch among multiple applications, but DOS applications that are not *active* (full screen) do not run. These applications are suspended until they are activated again. Enhanced mode enables you to run multiple applications, and DOS applications that are in *background* (in a window behind) can continue to run. Both modes enable Windows applications to run. The computer and memory requirements for these modes are as follows:

	Standard Mode	386-Enhanced Mode
Processor	80286 or higher	80386 or higher
Memory	1M (640K conventional and 256K extended)	2M (640K conventional and 1024K extended)
Storage	5 to 9M hard disk	5 to 10.5M hard disk

When you install Windows, the Setup application checks to see what equipment you have installed and tries to determine the equipment's manufacturer and type. Windows is usually correct, but if you want to confirm the list, use Custom Setup so that you can review the hardware list. To speed the installation process, you may want to make a list of the following information before you install Windows:

■ The drive and directory name that you want to contain Windows

■ Manufacturer and model number of your computer. If you cannot determine your exact computer model and your computer has an MCA bus, choose an equivalent IBM PS/2 model. If your computer has an EISA bus, choose an equivalent COMPAQ model. Most computers have an EISA bus.

■ Type of display adapter. Most 386 and 386SX computers have VGA or SuperVGA adapters.

■ Manufacturer and model of your printer

■ Printer port(s) that your printer(s) is (are) connected to. Most printers connect to the parallel (LPT1 or LPT2) ports. Some older laser printers use a serial port (COM1 or COM2).

■ Communication information, if you are using a serial printer connected to a COM port or if you connect your computer to a phone line with a modem. Include baud rate, number of bits, stop bits, and parity. Find this information in your printer or modem manual, from your dealer, or from the manufacturer.

■ Mouse manufacturer and type (if you have a mouse)

■ Type of keyboard

■ Make and model of multimedia adapters (if you have multimedia capability)

■ Type and version of the network you are on (if you are connected to one). Your system administrator can help you with this information.

If you are uncertain of the manufacturer or type of equipment you use, check your manuals or sales receipts or call your dealer or corporate personal computer support line.

Before you install Windows, you need to make sure that you have 5M to 10M of storage available on the hard disk on which you are installing Windows. Use the DIR command to find the available storage. You can install Windows on any hard drive; Windows does not have to be installed on drive C.

> **T I P** Windows runs faster and, in some modes, switches between applications faster if you prepare your hard disk properly before installing Windows. Because Windows frequently reads and writes information to disk as it operates, the information on your disk needs to be stored as compactly as possible without wasting space. A disk defragmenting or disk optimization application can rearrange files on disk to increase your hard disk performance.

Installing Windows

After you have made a list of your equipment, you are ready to install Windows. If you are unfamiliar with computers, you should use the Express Setup. If you are familiar with computers or need to customize the installation, use the Custom Setup.

Preparing for Installation

Before you install Windows, you may want to prepare for the installation by completing the following optional steps:

1. Protect your original disks from change. On 1.44M (3 1/2-inch) disks, slide open the write-protect tab (a square sliding button). On 1.2M (5 1/4-inch) disks, put a write-protect tab (an adhesive patch) over the square notch on the disk's edge. Copy the original disks onto a set of backup disks and store the originals at a separate site.

2. Complete the registration forms and mail them back to Microsoft while you are waiting for following portions of the installation to complete. Microsoft uses the registrations to send you special offers on related software, to send newsletters containing tips, and to inform you when updates to Windows are available. You may not get discount pricing on upgrades unless you are registered.

3. At the DOS prompt (for example, C:\>), type *CHKDSK /f*. If lost clusters are found, respond Yes to collect and store them.

Caution Do not run CHKDSK /f while Windows is running—it may damage Windows.

4. Run a disk defragmenting or disk optimization application if you have one. This step makes Windows run faster.

5. If you plan to use a memory manager, such as QEMM386, 386Max, or Blue Max, you should be aware of specific setting requirements. Many of these are outlined in two files that come with Windows: README.WRI (a Windows Write file) and SETUP.TXT (a text file). Both are included in the Windows 3.1 directory. You should read these files before using a memory manager. To do that, remark out the DEVICE= line referring to your memory manager before you install Windows. After you read the files, you can make the adjustments necessary to use your memory manager.

Controlling the Setup Options

Express Setup and Custom Setup begin with a DOS segment that uses keyboard controls. The DOS part of the installation process appears in two colors, and characters appear as they do at the DOS prompt (C:\). After the initial software is installed, the setup program changes to a Windows screen. At that point, you can use normal Windows keystrokes or mouse controls.

At almost any time during the installation, you can get Help by pressing F1, the Help key. This key is the same Help key used in Windows and Windows applications. To exit from a Help window, press the Esc key if you are in a DOS screen. If you are in a Windows screen and the Help window is on top, press Alt, F and then X (Alt, **F**ile, E**x**it).

During the DOS segment of the installation, use the following controls. A status line at the bottom of the screen lists available controls.

Move highlight to select next item	Up/down arrow key
Select an option or move to next screen	Enter
Help from a Setup screen	F1
Back up in Help screens	Backspace
Exit the Setup program	F3
Return from Help to Setup	Esc

During the Windows segment of the installation, use the following controls:

Help while in a screen or dialog box	F1
Move between areas in a dialog box	Tab
Select the current item in the dialog box	Space bar
Choose a button (OK, Cancel, etc.)	Click on the button
Select a check box or option button	Click on the check box until an X appears or click on the option button until its center is dark
Scroll through a list and select an item	Click on the up or down arrow to the right of the list. Then click on an item in the list.

The current item in a dialog box is surrounded by dashed lines. A current button, such as OK or Cancel, has a bold border.

To click on something with the mouse, move the mouse until the tip of the mouse pointer, usually an arrow, is over the item. Then gently but quickly press and release the left mouse button.

Starting the Windows Setup

To install Windows, complete the following steps:

1. Start your computer and return to a DOS prompt, such as C:\, if your computer starts automatically with Windows or an application running.

2. Put Disk 1 of the Windows disks in a disk drive and close the door.

3. Type the drive letter, followed by a colon, (for example *A:*) and press Enter to switch to that disk drive.

4. Type *SETUP* and press Enter.

5. Read and follow the on-screen directions. Watch the status line at the bottom of the screen to see what keys to press in response to on-screen directions.

You are given two alternatives for installation, Express Setup or Custom Setup. If you are unfamiliar with Windows or with computers, choose Express Setup. The differences between these choices are described in the following two sections.

If a previous version of Windows is detected, you are given the option of upgrading the older version using the same directory or of installing Windows 3.1 in a new directory. Upgrading an older version of Windows preserves Windows settings, updates printer drivers when necessary, and preserves drivers that Windows does not recognize. Approximately 5M of additional free space on the hard disk are needed to upgrade.

NOTE If you choose to have Windows 3.1 and Windows 3.0 installed at the same time, ensure that the PATH in the AUTOEXEC.BAT does not list both directories at the same time. Listing both directories causes improper operation and may corrupt system files.

At the beginning of the Windows segment of the installation, you are asked to enter your name and company name. You must enter a name. The name is used to notify anyone who reinstalls the software that Windows has been previously installed. Press Tab to move between the two text boxes. Use the arrow keys, Backspace, or Del to edit what you type. You are given a chance to make corrections.

You are asked to insert additional disks as you complete installation steps. Insert these disks as the Setup program requests and then follow the on-screen instructions.

NOTE If you have trouble installing Windows due to a Terminate-and-Stay-Resident program, then remove the TSR load line from CONFIG.SYS and restart your computer so that the TSR does not load. Then restart the Windows installation.

NOTE If you are installing Windows on a network or installing Windows on your own system, which is connected to a network, read Chapter 28 and check with your network administrator for the best method of installing. The file NETWORKS.WRI contains information in a Windows Write format about installing Windows on a network.

When you have finished installing Windows, three large buttons appear: **R**eboot, Restart **W**indows, and Return to MS-DOS. The selections you made during setup do not take effect until you restart your computer by rebooting. To choose Reboot, click on that button or press R.

Rebooting restarts your computer without turning off the power. Memory is erased, and DOS is reloaded. The AUTOEXEC.BAT and

CONFIG.SYS files are reread, which configures your computer with the selections you made during setup. If you chose not to let Windows Setup modify AUTOEXEC.BAT and CONFIG.SYS, Windows may not run correctly even after you reboot. Modify these files as needed.

Installing Windows Using Express Setup

When you begin the Windows setup, you areasked whether you want to do an Express Setup or Custom Setup. If you are unfamiliar with computers, you should choose the Express Setup. The Express Setup uses settings and hardware configuration that the installation application has determined run on your system. These settings and installation configurations can be changed later if necessary (see "Changing the Setup after Installation"). Some of the things that the Express Setup does for you are as follows:

- The AUTOEXEC.BAT and CONFIG.SYS files are automatically modified.

- Windows is installed in C:\WINDOWS unless drive C does not have enough room. In that case, the installation application searches for a drive with enough room. If not enough room is available for a full version of Windows, Express Setup installs a smaller set of Windows and accessory applications.

- If you previously had Windows 3.0 installed, Express Setup reinstalls the same printers. If you did not have Windows 3.0 installed, Express Setup prompts you for which printer and connecting port to use.

- Express Setup searches your hard disk for applications and creates icons and group windows for Windows applications and many DOS applications.

- Express Setup gives you a short tutorial on using a mouse and Windows.

T I P   In most cases, you should use Express Setup. If Express Setup does not work correctly, you can install or reinstall other items or features of Windows at a later time by rerunning Setup.

Setup asks you to select the printers you use and which ports they are connected to. You are given the option of going through a mouse and Windows operations tutorial.

Installing Windows Using Custom Setup

After Setup starts, you have the option of doing a Custom Setup. The Custom Setup enables you to select specifics of how Windows is installed. You can see or select changes as they are made. You should use Custom Setup if you are familiar with computers and want to cross-check the installation process or select different hardware configurations than those automatically selected. Some of the steps that Custom Setup executes are as follows:

- Shows you a list of the hardware detected. You can accept or change the detected hardware, which is useful if the type of mouse or video adapter has been incorrectly detected.

- Shows you the changes Custom Setup will make to AUTOEXEC.BAT and CONFIG.SYS and enables you to edit the changes. You have the option of accepting the modification, rejecting the modifications, or making manual changes.

- Enables you to select the drive and directory name where Windows will be installed

- Enables you to select the Windows components (such as screen savers, wallpaper, and sounds) and accessory applications to be installed

- Gives you full control over installing printers

- Enables you to select which Windows and DOS applications will be set up with icons and windows

- Gives you the opportunity to take a short tutorial on the mouse and Windows

In Custom Setup, you need to make choices from dialog boxes in the Windows screens. If you are familiar with Windows operations, use normal Windows selection techniques with the keyboard or mouse. For example, to select any item in a dialog box, press and hold down Alt; then press the underlined letter in the item you want to select. Release both keys. If you are selecting a group of option (round) buttons, you can move among them by pressing the arrow keys after the group has been selected. The button with the dark center is selected.

To edit text in a name or text box, hold down the Alt key as you press the underlined letter to select that text box. A flashing cursor, the insertion point, appears in the box. Type the text. To edit existing text, move the insertion point with the left- or right-arrow keys and then use the Del key to delete characters to the right, use the Backspace key to delete characters to the left, or type new characters at the insertion point.

During installation, you are asked where you want to install Windows. The default choice is as follows:

C:\WINDOWS

You can edit this path name so that Windows is installed on a different hard drive or directory. To edit, press the arrow keys to move from character to character, the Del (Delete) key to delete to the right, the Backspace key to delete to the left, and the character keys on the main keyboard to type characters.

Windows also asks whether it can make changes to the AUTOEXEC.BAT and CONFIG.SYS files. You are given three choices for these files:

- You can accept all changes. Copies of the old files are saved to backup files.

- You can modify changes. A dialog box shows you the original and proposed file. Use the Tab key to move into the top list and edit the proposed changes. Press the arrow keys to move around in the text and press Backspace or Delete to remove text. Type new text at the insertion point.

- You can reject all changes.

You are given a chance to install printer and plotter drivers, which tell Windows how to communicate with a printer or plotter. You do not have to install printer or plotter drivers at this point, although it is a convenient time. You can install drivers later, using the Control Panel, as described in Chapter 7, "Customizing with the Control Panel."

Select the names that match your equipment and choose Install. Choose Connect to connect your printer to the port where it is physically attached. Choose Setup to change the paper orientation (vertical or horizontal printing), paper size, number of copies, font cartridges, and so on. Choose Set as Default Printer if you want to make a printer the default. These settings can be changed later from an application's printer setup command or from the Control Panel. Don't forget to use the Help information available by pressing F1 (Help).

T   I   P   Each printer has different setup options, and if your printer includes a memory option, be sure to specify how much memory your printer has. (The HP Laserjet III, for example, has a memory option.) If Windows does not know how much memory is available, it may display an erroneous message stating that it does not have enough memory to print.

When you finish installing printers, Windows asks whether you want it to search your hard disk for Windows and DOS applications. If you choose this option, Windows makes a list of all applications on your hard disk. You are given an opportunity to put the names of these applications into a special group window. Each application is represented by a small picture. These pictures, called *icons*, make starting an application easy. You probably should select the applications you recognize and have them put into a group. You can add or remove applications in a group window at any time after Windows is installed. Procedures for using group windows are described in Chapter 4, "Controlling Applications with the Program Manager."

Learning from the Setup Files

At the end of the Windows installation, you are given an opportunity to read files that Setup copied into the WINDOWS directory. You can read the files from the installation application when it asks you to, or you can complete the installation of Windows and read the files with Write, a small word processor that comes with Windows. The names of the files are as follows:

README.WRI	Current updates to the user manual
PRINTERS.WRI	Additional information about configuring printers and fonts
NETWORKS.WRI	Information about installing Windows on networks
SYSINI.WRI	Information about modifying the SYSTEM.INI file (described in Chapter 25, "Enhancing Windows Performance")
WININI.WRI	Information about modifying the WIN.INI file (described in Chapter 25, "Enhancing Windows Performance")

Installing Unlisted Printers

If you cannot locate a printer driver from your printer's manufacturer, Windows offers a temporary solution. One of the choices for a printer driver is Generic/Text Only. Using the Generic/Text Only printer driver enables you to print text and numbers on most printers. However, you cannot print with special capabilities, such as underline, bold, or graphics.

Check with the Microsoft telephone support line listed in Chapter 30 and your printer manufacturer for a printer driver for your printer or for a compatible driver. Windows has hundreds of printer drivers available. Microsoft maintains a Windows Driver Library (WDL) containing device drivers supported by Windows 3.1. You can obtain a copy of this library through Microsoft forums on CompuServe, GEnie, ON-Line, or other public bulletin boards. You also can receive a driver by calling Microsoft. Refer to Chapter 30 for their phone numbers.

When you receive a printer driver to match your equipment, you can install the driver without reinstalling Windows. Use the Control Panel to add the new printer driver. The procedure is described in Chapter 7, "Customizing with the Control Panel."

Running Windows after Installation

After you install Windows and reboot, you can start Windows from the DOS prompt, such as C:>, by typing *win* and pressing Enter. Windows starts in the most efficient mode for your processor and memory configuration.

Windows has two modes of operation, standard and 386-enhanced. You can force Windows to start in either mode (see Chapter 1, "Operating Windows").

If the screen goes blank when you start Windows, you may have installed Windows with an incorrect graphics adapter. To fix this problem, find out what kind of graphics adapter you have (you may need to call the manufacturer) and repeat the installation. Turn off and restart your computer and repeat the installation process, specifying a different graphics adapter.

T I P   If you have any difficulty running Windows, try reading through the text file SETUP.TXT or the Windows Write file README.WRI, located in the Windows 3.1 directory.

Changing the Setup after Installation

After Windows is operating correctly, you can make modifications to the way Windows is installed without reinstalling the entire Windows application. You may want to change the installation, for example, if you have a portable computer running Windows. When you are on the road, you need to use the plasma or LCD screen in the portable, but when you are at the office, you want to use a high-resolution color monitor. Instead of reinstalling Windows to get the new video driver, you can use the Windows Setup program to switch between the drivers you will be using. Windows Setup also is useful when you buy and attach a new keyboard or mouse or when you attach your computer to a network.

The Windows Setup program is located in the Main group window of the Program Manager. To change the setup of the display, keyboard, mouse, or network after Windows is installed, follow these steps:

1. Activate the Program Manager and then activate the Main group window.

2. Choose the Windows Setup icon.

3. From the Windows Setup dialog box, choose the **O**ptions menu and select the **C**hange System Settings command.

   From the Change System Settings dialog box, you can change installation settings without reinstalling Windows.

4. Select the pull-down list of the setting you want to change by clicking on the related down-arrow icon. You also can press Alt+*letter* to select the list and then press the down-arrow key to pull the list down.

5. Select from the pull-down list the type of device you want installed by clicking it or by pressing the up- or down-arrow keys.

6. Choose OK or press Enter.

7. If a special driver is required, you may be asked to insert one of the original Windows disks or a disk sent by the manufacturer of your display, keyboard, mouse, or network.

8. After the new setup has been created, you must restart Windows for the changes to take effect. You are given the choice of restarting Windows or returning to DOS. If you need to change hardware—such as attaching a new keyboard or mouse or connecting a new display—return to DOS, make the new connection, and then restart Windows.

If Windows or a Windows application does not behave correctly after changing the installation, check the Windows Setup dialog box to see whether you have the correct settings. Return to the original settings if necessary or reinstall Windows if appropriate.

Summary

This appendix should help you install Windows and change your Windows installation when you change hardware. If you are a systems administrator and are installing Windows on a network, make sure that you read Chapter 28 and the notes in the NETWORK.WRI file that Windows installs. Performance and enhancement tips also can be found in Chapters 23, 25, and 26. A list of Windows resources, such as computer bulletin boards, telephone hot-lines, newsletters, and training, can be found in Chapter 30.

After you have installed Windows, you may want to begin with Chapters 1 and 2 to get an overview of Windows and to learn why Windows is valuable to any personal computer user. In the first few chapters of this book, you also learn the fundamentals of operating all Windows applications and how to start and exit the application.

Installing Windows for Workgroups

I nstalling Windows for Workgroups is very similar to installing Windows 3.1. But there are a few additional hardware requirements, and you are asked a few additional questions about networks and the names you want to assign to your computer and workgroup.

Read through Appendix A, "Installing Windows," to learn additional tips about installing Windows.

T I P

Working Together with Personal Computers

Most personal computers and their applications are designed to increase the productivity of individuals. Connecting personal computers by network can increase the productivity and enhance communication among a group of people who work together. Windows for Workgroups is designed specifically to give Windows users and Windows applications networking capability beyond what is available in some networks.

Windows for Workgroups needs a name for each individual in the network and a name for each group of people. Each user's name, referred to as a *computer name*, must be unique. Computer names are the unique name used by each computer on the network. Each computer name can have passwords associated with it. These passwords are assigned by each of the other users on the network. The passwords control who has access and what type of access to directories and printers is shared by the workgroup.

Workgroups are groups of people who might perform a common task, have a common goal, or have a common work flow or channel of communication. Workgroup names identify a group of people who share directories, files, printers, applications, and a Mail Postoffice. They can send mail to each other, schedule group meetings, and use Chat to communicate interactively.

Workgroup names must be unique, can be up to 15 characters in length, and cannot be the same as any computer name. For example, you may have two workgroups named Admin and Sales. Within each of these workgroups you can have one or more computer names. But no computer name can be duplicated, not even between workgroups.

System Requirements

Windows for Workgroups has nearly the same hardware and operating system requirements as Windows 3.1. Because Windows for Workgroups has greater capabilities and extra applications that come with it, it does have some additional requirements.

Windows for Workgroups should be installed with MS-DOS 3.3 or later. MS-DOS 5 is recommended. To see which version of DOS you are using, go to the DOS prompt, usually shown as C>, type *VER*, and then press Enter.

Windows for Workgroups runs in two different modes. Each mode has different networking and Windows capabilities. The hardware requirements for Enhanced and Standard mode appear in the following table:

Enhanced Mode	Standard Mode
386SX or better	286 or better
640K conventional RAM	640K conventional RAM
3M RAM or more, 4M minimum recommended	2M RAM or more
diskette drive	diskette drive
9.5M free disk space minimum, 14.5M for full installation	9.5M free disk space minimum, 14.5M for full installation
5-10M free additional for system containing Mail Postoffice	

Computers using 8088 or 8086 (or 80286 computers with less than 1 MB of memory) do not run Windows. They can, however, act as a client that uses shared files and printers on a Windows for Workgroups network. For these computers to work as clients on a Windows for Workgroups network, install Workgroup Connection. Workgroup Connection is a DOS networking component of Windows for Workgroups that enables network-capable DOS applications to use Windows for Workgroup resources.

Installing a Network Card

Windows for Workgroups works with more than 150 different network adaptor cards. Although the Microsoft Windows for Workgroups starter kit comes with the Intel EtherExpress network adaptor, this kit works well with many other network adaptors.

Install your network adaptor card according to the directions that come with it. Most network adaptor cards require that you set small switches on the network card before checking the network card or installing the network.

In most cases, Windows for Workgroups recognizes the type of network card in your computer during the installation process. Windows for Workgroups ships with NDIS network drivers for approximately 100 network cards, including the Xircom external LAN adapter for use on portable and laptop computers. More than 50 additional network card drivers are available in the Windows Driver Library; these card drivers can be downloaded free from the Microsoft forum on CompuServe. CompuServe is a publicly available computer bulletin board and database located in Columbus, Ohio. For information call 1-800-848-8990.

When you run the Windows for Workgroups Setup application, Windows usually recognizes the type of network adaptor you have installed. The program displays a list of available drivers showing the detected driver selected. Windows for Workgroups assumes the adaptor card has been left with its factory set defaults for IRQ interrupt, base I/O port, and base memory address. If you have changed these settings by altering the switches on the network card or with a card setup program, you can change the appropriate settings in Windows for Workgroups during the Windows for Workgroups installation.

T I P On most network adaptor cards, settings for the IRQ interrupt, base I/O port, and base memory address are set using miniature switches or jumpers on the cards and complex setup routines. The Intel EtherExpress LAN adaptor, available separately or bundled with the Microsoft Windows for Workgroups Starter Set, is set up with software. There are no switches or complex manual routines. If there are conflicts with the default settings, the EtherExpress setup software guides you through selecting alternate adaptor settings. The EtherExpress card is very cost-effective and easy to install.

Windows for Workgroups works with all standard network cabling, such as twisted pair, fiber optic, and thin- and thick-net coaxial cabling.

Installing Windows for Workgroups

Installing Windows for Workgroups is fairly simple if you are familiar with computers or if you have installed a previous version of Windows. This next section guides you through the basic installation steps. The last sections in the book describe tips on installing Windows. You should read this section and at least scan the tips sections for topics related to your computer and network.

Getting Started

Before you begin installing Windows for Workgroups, you may want to take a few steps to ensure a trouble-free installation. Read through the installation instructions in this book or the Microsoft manual. If you have Windows Write available under an existing copy of Windows, read the WRI files on the installation disks. These files contain installation tips for specific computers, networks, and printers. The file contents are described in the next section.

If you are currently running Windows 3.1, make backup copies of your WIN.INI and SYS.INI files. Installing Windows for Workgroups should preserve all Windows 3.1 settings, but by keeping your original WIN.INI and SYS.INI files available, you can compare or copy portions of the WIN.INI and SYS.INI if there is an application that does not work correctly. These files are text files, so you can read and edit them with the Notepad application that comes with Windows. These files are described in detail by Windows Write files. The files are copied onto your disk during the installation process, so you can read them using Windows Write.

If you are on a network and run LAN Manager, make backup copies of your \\LANMAN.DOC\PROTOCOL.INI file. Similarly, if you run Novell NetWare, make copies of your IPX.COM and NETX.COM files.

You should fill out the following table. Depending upon the type of installation you choose, you need some or all of this information:

Item	My system has
Workgroup name (unique)	_____
Computer name (unique)	_____
Computer manufacturer	_____
Computer model	_____
Processor type (80286, 80386, or 80486)	_____
Amount of extended memory	_____
Network card brand and model	_____
Network card configuration	_____
IRQ interrupt	_____
Base I/O port	_____
Base memory address	_____
Other networks connected	_____
Printer model and type	_____
Printer connection ports	_____

Getting Additional Installation Help

Windows for Workgroups installation disks and the installed files contain files with additional information about installing and configuring your network. These files are formatted for Windows Write, the word processor that comes with Windows. Chapter 12, "Using Windows Write," describes this word processor.

The files are listed in the following table:

Filename	Description
NETWORKS.WRI	Descriptions of special configuration requirements for some networks.
PRINTERS.WRI	Descriptions of special printer and font setup requirements and configurations.
README.WRI	Updates to the *User's Guide* that comes with Windows for Workgroups.
SETUP.INF	Text file containing a list of terminate and stay resident programs that are incompatible with Windows. Use the Notepad or most word processors to read it.
SETUP.TXT	Descriptions of setup requirements for specific types of hardware. This is a text file and can be read by any word processor.
SYSINI.WRI	Topics for advanced users on how to modify the SYS.INI file with Notepad or a text editor.
WININI.WRI	Topics for advanced users on how to modify the WININI file with Notepad or a text editor.

Entering Requested Information

You have two procedures for installation, Express or Custom Setup. For most situations and users, the Express Setup is recommended. The Custom Setup should be used by people who are more familiar with computers and want to understand what is happening or by people who have special hardware or configuration requirements.

When you run the Windows for Workgroups Setup application, you are prompted for the following information, depending upon whether you choose a Custom or Express Setup:

Table B.1 Installation Alternatives

Setup Procedure	Express Setup (recommended)	Custom Setup (adv. users or special requirements)
Windows modules	All or minimum installation	You select the programs, drivers, and installation options.
Drive and directory	If Windows was previously installed, the new version replaces the existing Windows; otherwise it is the same as Custom Setup.	C:\WINDOWS or you specify.
AUTOEXEC.BAT and CONFIG.SYS	Changed automatically	Displays recommended changes and enables you to accept, reject, or edit changes.
Computer, mouse, keyboard, and monitor	Uses detected hardware.	Shows detected hardware but enables you to make changes.
Network card, IRQ, base I/O port, base memory proposed but changeable	Shows a single detected card and its default settings. You can make changes.	Shows detected cards and default settings. You can make changes and install up to four different cards.
Connectivity with other networks	NetWare and LAN Manager available with Windows for Workgroups. Install additional secondary networks manually.	NetWare and LAN Manager available with Windows for Workgroups Install additional secondary networks manually.
Local or remote printer	Selectable	Selectable
Application detection	Detects and automatically sets up most existing applications. Previous Windows application setups preserved.	Detects and sets up most existing applications. Previous Windows application setups preserved. Enables manual setups.
Virtual memory settings	Automatically configured	Can be edited on 386 or better computers
Computer (user) name	Use a unique name of 6-15 characters to identify the user.	Use a unique name of 6-15 characters to identify the user.
Workgroup name	Use a unique name of 6-15 characters to identify the user.	Use a unique name of 6-15 characters to identify the user.

NOTE Be certain that all computer names and workgroup names are unique. No name on the network should be duplicated. Many people use a computer name created by combining their first name with a few characters from their last name. Workgroups are usually named for the task, function, or communication process for which the group is organized.

Windows can recognize and set up hundreds of the most widely used Windows and DOS applications. Should the Express Setup fail to recognize and set up an application on your hard disk, however, you can manually set up any application with the **O**ptions **S**et Up Applications command in the Windows Setup application. The Windows Setup application is found in the Main group window. Chapter 4, "Controlling Applications with the Program Manager," explains how to use the **F**ile **N**ew command in the Program Manager to create icons. Chapter 23, "Running DOS Applications," and Chapter 24, "Customizing PIFs," describe how to create the Program Information Files needed to optimize some DOS applications running under Windows.

Setup automatically installs the Microsoft NetBEUI. NetBEUI works with most networks. For additional information about network installation, refer to the Windows Write file NETWORK.WRI. You can install additional network drivers and protocols with the Net application found in the Control Panel.

Running the Setup Application

The Windows for Workgroups Setup application asks you a series of questions. For questions like the computer name, you type your answer; for questions like type of printer or network card, you select from a list of choices. Depending upon the choices you make, the Setup application will decompress files on the installation disk and copy those files to your hard disk.

Before you go through the installation process, create backup copies of the installation disks with the DISKCOPY command from DOS or the **D**isk **C**opy Disk command in the File Manager of your current version of Windows.

To run the Setup application, follow these steps:

1. Put the Windows for Workgroups installation diskette labeled *1* in one of your disk drives.

2. After the DOS command prompt, which may look like C>, type the letter of the disk drive containing the installation disk, a colon, and the word SETUP, as shown here:

   A:SETUP

3. Press Enter.

At first, the screen displays instructions using DOS characters. It later changes to a Windows type of display.

Windows is designed to automatically detect your computer's network cards, graphics adaptors, and other types of hardware. For computers using EISA or MCA buses, Windows is usually very accurate; you can accept its recommendations. (The computer bus is how your computer communicates internally with its components. The older style bus is ISA. Newer styles buses are EISA or MCA.) For some computers using the older ISA bus, Windows may not correctly detect your hardware. To bypass automatic detection and be prompted for all hardware and network options, type the following instead of typing SETUP:

   SETUP /I

Then press Enter.

T I P

Once Setup displays Windows-style menus and dialog boxes, use Windows operating techniques to make your selections. Use a mouse to place the tip of the mouse pointer arrow on a menu or option, and then click the mouse button to make the selection. Or, using the keyboard, select a menu or option by holding down the Alt key as you press an underlined letter. Pressing the Enter key is the same as choosing OK to accept your choices and continue. Pressing the Esc key is the same as choosing Cancel to disregard choices and continue. The first chapters of this book describe the basic methods of operating Windows and making menu and dialog box selections.

When you install Windows, you are asked whether you want to run the Windows Tutorial. For those who are unfamiliar with the many ways of operating Windows, this tutorial is excellent. You can run the tutorial during the installation process or any time after installation: choose the **Help Windows** Tutorial from the Program Manager.

Running Windows for Workgroups the First Time

If you have not started Windows for Workgroups previously, you see a Windows for Workgroups dialog box that asks you to enter the computer name, workgroup name, and your personal password. The computer name is the name that identifies your computer and the network resources to which it will have access. The workgroup name is the name that specifies the group of people with whom you will share resources. These names must be unique.

You must enter a unique computer name and workgroup name. You do not have to enter a password. If you do enter a password during installation then you will be asked for that password whenever you log on. If you do not enter a password during installation, no password will be requested when you later start your computer. If you wish to control your computer's access on the network, however, you should log on using the following steps:

1. Select the **L**og on Name edit box and type the name you want to identify your computer.

2. Select the **P**assword edit box and type the password you will use to prevent others from using your computer to get on the network.

The Log on Name is displayed to other operators throughout the network. Other users will identify your computer and you by this name, so choose one that identifies you. (This name can be changed, as described later in this chapter.) Most people use a first name with a few letters of their last name as identifiers, for example, KARENR.

Use a password that is simple but memorable. The password can be up to 14 characters in length, with upper- or lowercase characters (the case of characters is not important). Remember that your password restricts unauthorized users from gaining access to your workgroup resources. You can change your password at any time in the future if you remember it. No one can restore or find a password you have forgotten. Don't lose it or forget it.

Additional Tips on Installing Windows for Workgroups

Installing Windows for Workgroups is usually straightforward. It is definitely the easiest network to install and support if you have industry-standard hardware and network adaptors. The following tips give insight into some of the more advanced installation topics, and aid you with some technical problems.

Preserving Existing Settings and Configurations

Windows for Workgroups can modify two files that DOS uses to start your computer. These are the AUTOEXEC.BAT and CONFIG.SYS files. You may want to copy these two files onto a diskette before you install Windows for Workgroups. These files are usually located in the C:\ directory, the root. Should your computer fail to restart with the modified files, you can put the disk into drive A and restart the computer with the original AUTOEXEC.BAT and CONFIG.SYS files.

To view, modify, accept, or reject changes the installation application makes to the AUTOEXEC.BAT or CONFIG.SYS files, choose the Custom Setup method of installation.

Modes of Operation

Windows 3.1 and Windows for Workgroups run in one of two different modes, 386-Enhanced mode or Standard Mode. The mode in which Windows operates depends upon your hardware and whether you start Windows with a command line *switch* that forces it to operate in another mode. Each mode's effect on Windows applications and DOS applications is described in greater detail in other portions of the book. In general, computers with a 386 or 486 processor and 3M of extended memory will operate in 386-Enhanced mode. Computers with a 286 processor or less memory must operate in standard mode.

For Windows for Workgroups, both modes yield similar capabilities. The major difference between the modes is that computers operating in standard mode are able to access shared files and printers but are unable to share their files and printers with other computers in the workgroup. These computers can share DDE data.

The Windows for Workgroups capabilities for each mode are listed in the following table:

Enhanced Mode	Standard Mode
Windows interface	Windows interface
Automatic network card detection	Automatic network card detection
Mail and Schedule+ operation	Mail and Schedule+ operation
Accesses shared files, printers and DDE data	Accesses shared files and printers
Sharing its files, printers, and DDE data	Shares DDE data

Some additional chapters that describe the differences between modes and how to optimize modes are Chapter 22, "Using Windows Applications Together," Chapter 23, "Running DOS Applications," Chapter 25, "Enhancing Windows Performance," and Chapter 26, "Enhancing DOS Application Performance."

Removing Terminate-and-Stay-Resident Applications

Before you install Windows for Workgroups, you should remove any terminate-and-stay-resident (TSR) applications from memory. You may be familiar with these programs as pop-up applications that display over DOS applications when you press a hot key. Windows may have conflicts with TSRs during its installation process. You can read a list of TSRs that cause Windows problems by reading the text file labeled SETUP.INF, located on an installation disk. You can read this file using any word processor or the Notepad application in Windows.

One of the safest ways to prepare your computer for installation is to create a new AUTOEXEC.BAT and CONFIG.SYS that start your computer without loading TSRs. To do this, you need to modify your existing files to create a minimum configuration so that TSRs are not loaded when you start your computer. Follow these steps:

1. Create a backup copy of these two files onto a diskette. In case you later have trouble with the new AUTOEXEC.BAT or CONFIG.SYS, you will insert this diskette and restart your computer to return to normal. If there is a problem, once the computer is restarted you can copy the original AUTOEXEC.BAT and CONFIG.SYS back to their original directories.

2. Start your computer without Windows and load your AUTOEXEC.BAT or CONFIG.SYS into a text editor or word processor that can open and save text files.

3. Type the letters *REM* before lines that load TSRs. This action makes the line into a nonexecuting remark.

4. Save the new AUTOEXEC.BAT or CONFIG.SYS as text files back to their original location.

5. Remove the diskette containing the backups and restart your computer so it reads the new AUTOEXEC.BAT and CONFIG.SYS files from the hard disk.

6. Run the Windows for Workgroups Setup application and see whether it operates correctly.

7. Remove the REM text a line at a time until you discover the TSR causing a problem.

For additional help on troubleshooting Windows for Workgroups, refer to the Que book *Connecting Windows 3.1 for Workgroups*.

Installing Over Existing Windows 3.1

You can install Windows for Workgroups directly over existing copies of Windows 3.1, and Windows for Workgroups will preserve your application setups and printer settings. If you do an Express Setup, Windows for Workgroups installs over the existing Windows 3.1 in the same directory. If you do a Custom Setup, you have the option to install Windows for Workgroups to a different directory, leaving your original Windows 3.1 intact.

Caution   Microsoft does not recommend operating Windows 3.1 and Windows for Workgroups on the same computer.

Installing Network Printers

Printers on your network require print drivers, which are software interpreters that enable Windows applications to communicate with the printer. Because printers come from different manufacturers and have different capabilities, most drivers are specific to a model of printer.

When you install Windows for Workgroups, you will need to know the types of printers that will be shared on your network. You will be asked what those printers are so that the appropriate drivers can be copied from the installation diskettes onto your computer.

To learn how drivers are installed, refer to the section "Adding and Configuring Printers" in Chapter 7. To learn how to connect and share your printers on the network, refer to the section "Printing on a Network in Windows for Workgroups" in Chapter 9.

Setting Up Mail and Schedule

Most users of Windows for Workgroups want to use Mail, the electronic message passing application, and Schedule+, the appointment and scheduler. The installation of Mail and Schedule+ are described in detail in Chapter 10, "Using Mail with Windows for Workgroups," and Chapter 11, "Using Schedule+ with Windows for Workgroups."

Summary

If you are new to Windows, you may want to read more about how to choose menu commands and options before continuing. Chapter 1, "Operating Windows," shows you the few keys you need to choose commands you use during installation.

To change your network setup, add additional network cards and users, change computer names, workgroup names, or passwords, refer to Chapter 27, "Networking with Windows for Workgroups." For information on sharing directories among members of a workgroup, see Chapter 5, "Managing Files with the File Manager." Chapter 9, "Using the Print Manager," describes how to share printers.

In most cases, Windows for Workgroups runs immediately after installation. However, if you need additional information on installing Windows for Workgroups, operating it with other networks, or enhancing its performance, please read *Connecting Windows 3.1 for Workgroups*, by Doug Bierer, published by Que Corp.

Symbols

H

Q-R

V

W

X-Z

Working with the Program Manager

Working with Group Windows

Task	Keyboard	Mouse
Activate Program Manager	Alt+Tab	Click on window
Select a group window or icon	Ctrl+F6 or Ctrl+Tab	Click on group window or icon
Select and open a group window	Alt, **W**indow, **1**, **2**, **3**, or so on	Select icon, Enter; or double-click on group icon
Quit Windows	Alt+F4; or Alt, **F**ile, E**x**it Windows	Double-click program Control menu
Close active group window	Ctrl+F4; or Alt, hyphen, **C**lose	Double-click group document Control icon

Working with Program Item Icons

Task	Keyboard	Mouse
Select a program item icon	Press arrow keys	Click on program item
Start program	Select program item, Enter	Double-click on program item

Working with the File Manager

Selecting Files and Directories

Task	Keyboard	Mouse
Open File Manager	Arrows to select File Manager, Enter	Double-click on File Manager program item
Change a drive	Ctrl+drive *letter*	Click on drive icon
Select any directory	Activate directory tree, up or down arrows	Click on directory
Open selected directory into a window	Alt, **W**indow, **N**ew Window	Double-click on drive icon
Move between directory and subdirectory	Left/right arrow	Click on desired directory
Select previous/ next directory	Up/down arrow	Click on desired directory
Select previous/ next directory, same level	Ctrl+up/down arrow	Click on desired directory
Select directory one screen up/down	PgUp/PgDn	Click in scroll bar, click on directory
Select root directory	Home	Move scroll box to top, click on root directory
Select last directory	End	Move scroll box to bottom, click on desired directory
Select directory beginning with *letter*	*letter*	Click on directory
Expand selected directory	Plus (+); or Alt, **T**ree, E**x**pand One Level	Click on folder with plus (+)
Collapse selected directory	Hyphen (-); or Alt, **T**ree, **C**ollapse Branch	Click on folder with hyphen (-)
Expand selected directory to all levels	Asterisk (*); or Alt, **T**ree, Expand **B**ranch	**T**ree menu, Expand **B**ranch command
Expand all branches	Ctrl+* (Asterisk); or Alt, **T**ree, Expand **A**ll	**T**ree menu, Expand **A**ll command
Create a directory	Alt, **F**ile, **C**reate Directory	**F**ile menu, **C**reate Directory command
Close the File Manager	Alt, **F**ile, E**x**it	Double-click on the Control menu icon

Working with Files in the File Manager

Task	Keyboard	Mouse
Start a program	Select, Enter	Double-click on program or file icon
Select adjacent files	Shift+F8, arrow keys, Shift+space bar	Shift+click on files to select
Select nonadjacent files	Shift+F8, arrow keys, space bar	Ctrl+click on file to select
Select all items	Ctrl+/ (slash); or Alt, **F**ile, **S**elect All	Click on first file, Shift+click on last file
Deselect all items	Ctrl+\ (backslash); or Alt, **F**ile, **D**eselect All	Click on one file
Search for a file	Alt, **F**ile, **S**earch	**F**ile menu, **S**earch command
Move selected file(s) or directory	Alt, **F**ile, **M**ove	Select and drag to directory on same disk (Shift+drag to a different disk)
Copy selected file(s) or a directory	Alt, **F**ile, **C**opy	Select and drag to another disk (Ctrl+drag to the same disk)
Delete a selected file or directory	Alt, **F**ile, **D**elete or Select, **D**el	**F**ile menu, **D**elete command
Rename a selected file or directory	Alt, **F**ile, **R**ename	**F**ile menu, **R**ename command
Format a disk	Alt, **D**isk, **F**ormat Disk	**D**isk menu, **F**ormat Disk command

Windows Moving, Selecting, and Editing

Moving and Selecting

Pressing Shift while moving selects text or cells being moved across.

Pressing Ctrl while moving enables you to move in larger increments or to select separate objects.

Task	Keyboard	Mouse
Move to previous line or cell	Up arrow	Click on line
Select previous line or cell	Shift+up arrow	Drag across line
Move to next line	Down arrow	Click on line
Select next line or cell	Shift+down arrow	Drag across line
Move to next character	Right arrow	Click on character
Select next character	Shift+right arrow	Drag across character
Move to next word	Ctrl+right arrow	Click on word
Select next word	Shift+Ctrl+right arrow	Drag across word or double-click on next word
Move to previous character	Left arrow	Click on character
Select previous character	Shift+left arrow	Drag across character
Move to previous word	Ctrl+left arrow	Click on previous word
Select previous word	Shift+Ctrl+left arrow	Drag across previous word; or double-click on previous word
Move to beginning of line or row	Home	Click at beginning of line or row
Select to start of line or row	Shift+Home	Drag across line or row
Move to beginning of document	Ctrl+Home	Move scroll box up, click on first line or row
Select to start of document	Shift+Ctrl+Home	Drag across line or row to top
Move to end of line or row	End	Click on end of line or row
Select to end of line or row	Shift+End	Drag to end of line or row
Move to end of document	Ctrl+End	Move scroll box down, click on last line or row
Select to end of document	Shift+Ctrl+End	Drag across end of line or row to bottom
Scroll by line or character	Arrow keys	Click scroll bar arrow
Scroll by window	PgUp, PgDn	Click in scroll bar above or below scroll box
Scroll by percentage		Drag scroll box within scroll bar
Select word	Shift+Ctrl and arrow keys	Double-click on word
Select text insertion point	Shift+move	Press, hold down, and drag over selection
Select picture or graphic object		Click on picture or object

Common Editing Commands

Task	Keyboard	Mouse
Delete character to left	Backspace	Drag across character, Del or Backspace
Delete word to left	Ctrl+Shift+left arrow, Del	Drag across character, Del or Backspace
Delete character to right	Ctrl+Shift+right arrow, Del	Drag across character, Del or Backspace
Delete word to right	Ctrl+Del	Drag across character, Del or Backspace
Delete selected text or object	Del	Drag across character, Del or Backspace
Undo most recent edit	Alt+Backspace; or Edit, Undo	Edit menu, Undo command
Cut a selection to the Clipboard	Shift+Del; or Alt, Edit, Cut	Edit menu, Cut command
Copy a selection to the Clipboard	Ctrl+Ins; or Alt, Edit, Copy	Edit menu, Copy command
Paste a selection from the Clipboard	Shift+Ins; or Alt, Edit, Paste	Edit menu, Paste command

Command Guide

To use this reference card, look in the left column for the task that you want to perform.
In the columns to the right of each task listing are the keyboard and mouse commands
for performing that task.

Operating Programs in Windows

Starting, Quitting, and Switching between Programs

Task	Keyboard	Mouse
Start a Windows or DOS program	Select icon in Program Manager or filename in File Manager, Enter	Double-click on icon or filename
Switch between programs	Alt+Tab; or Alt+Esc	Click on window
Display Task List	Ctrl+Esc; or Alt, space bar, **S**witch To	Double-click on desktop
Quit a program	Alt+F4; or Alt, space bar, **C**lose	Double-click program Control icon

Sizing and Moving Windows

Task	Keyboard	Mouse
Bring program to top	Alt+Esc; or Alt+Tab	Click on window
Bring document to top	Ctrl+F6; or Alt, **W**indow, **1**, **2**, **3**, and so on	Click on window
Move a program window	Alt, space bar, **M**ove	Drag title bar
Move a document window	Alt, hyphen, **M**ove	Drag title bar
Resize a program window	Alt, space bar, **S**ize, press arrow keys	Drag borders
Resize a document window	Alt, hyphen, **S**ize	Drag borders
Minimize a program window to an icon	Alt, space bar **Mi**nimize	Click on Minimize button (right of title, down arrow)
Minimize a document window to an icon (Not possible in some programs)	Alt, hyphen **Mi**nimize	Click on Minimize button (right of doc't title, down arrow)
Maximize a program window to full screen	Alt, space bar, Ma**x**imize	Click on Maximize button (right of title, up arrow)
Maximize a document window to full screen	Alt, hyphen Ma**x**imize	Click on Maximize button (right of doc't title, up arrow)
Restore a program to a window	Alt, space bar, **R**estore	Click on Restore icon (double arrow top right) or double-click on program icon
Restore a document to a window	Alt, hyphen, **R**estore	Click on Restore icon or use keystroke if icon not available

Operating Programs

Working with Menus and Dialog Boxes

Task	Keyboard	Mouse
Select a menu	Alt, underlined menu letter, underlined command letter	Click on menu, click on command
Move between areas in dialog box	Tab or Shift+Tab, or Alt+underlined letter	Click on selection
Select list	Alt+underlined letter	Click on list
Select pull-down list	Alt+underlined letter, Alt+down arrow	Click on down arrow to right of list
Select option button	Tab or Shift+Tab, arrow	Click on selection
Select check box	Tab or Shift+Tab, space bar	Click on selection
Select text box	Tab or Shift+Tab type	Click in box, type
Choose command button	Tab or Shift+Tab, press space bar	Click command button
Choose OK button	Enter	Click on OK
Choose Cancel button	Esc	Click on Cancel

Getting Help and Working with Documents

Task	Keyboard	Mouse
Get help	F1; or Alt, **H**elp	Help menu
Start a new document	Alt, **F**ile, **N**ew	File menu, **N**ew command
Open an existing document	Alt, **F**ile, **O**pen	File menu, **O**pen command
Close a document	Ctrl+F4; or File, **C**lose	File menu, **C**lose command
Save a document	File, **S**ave	File menu, **S**ave command
Save and name	File, Save **A**s	File menu, Save **A**s
Exit the program	Alt+F4; or Alt, File Exit	Double-click program Control menu; or File menu, E**x**it command

Printing

Task	Keyboard	Mouse
Print a document	Alt, **F**ile, **P**rint	File menu, **P**rint command
Select a printer or change print orientation	Alt, **F**ile, Printer Setup	File menu, Printer Setup command

Controlling Printing

Task	Keyboard	Mouse
Open Print Manager	Alt+Tab if printing	Double-click on icon
Stop/start/delete print job	Alt, **P**ause/**R**esume/**D**elete button	Click on **P**ause, or **R**esume or **D**elete
Increase print speed/decrease program speed	Alt, **O**ptions **H**igh Priority	**O**ptions menu, **H**igh Priority command
Decrease print speed/increase program speed	Alt, **O**ptions, **L**ow Priority	**O**ptions menu, **L**ow Priority command
Balance print speed/program speed	Alt, **O**ptions, **M**edium Priority	**O**ptions menu, **M**edium Priority command
Setup Printer	Alt, **O**ptions, **P**rinter Setup	**O**ptions menu, **P**rinter Setup command

Operating DOS Programs

Task	Keyboard	Mouse
Start DOS program	Select icon in Program Manager or file name in File Manager, Enter	Double-click on icon or filename
DOS prompt	Choose DOS Prompt program item icon	Double-click on DOS program item icon
Activate next program	Alt+Tab; or Ctrl+Esc	Click on window if visible
Toggle Windows/full screen	Alt+Enter	Alt+Enter
Program Control menu (386-enhanced mode only)	Alt+space bar; Esc to remove	Click on Control menu (if in Windows)
Copy and paste (standard mode)	• Press Print Screen to capture screen • Alt+Tab activates receiving program • Position cursor • Paste into Windows program—Alt, **E**dit **P**aste into DOS program—Alt+space bar, **E**dit, **P**aste	
Copy and paste (386-enhanced mode)	• Alt+Enter (program into window) • Alt+space bar, **E**dit, Ma**r**k • Select text Drag with mouse or press Shift+arrow, Enter • Alt+Tab or click mouse to receiving program • Move cursor into position • Paste into Windows program—**E**dit **P**aste into DOS program—Alt+space bar, **E**dit, **P**aste	

Change Settings in (386-enhanced mode)	Alt+space bar, Settings
Change Font (386-enhanced mode)	Alt+space bar, **F**onts
Exiting DOS programs	Normal program procedure

Customizing Windows

Task	Keyboard	Mouse
Start Control Panel	From Program Manager, Alt, **W**indow, Main, select Control Panel, Enter	From Program Manager, click on Main, double-click Control Panel
Changing screen colors	Select Color icon Enter, Alt+Color **S**chemes, Alt+ down arrow	Double-click Color icon, click down arrow by Color **S**chemes, click on color scheme
Changing screen background (Desktop)	Select Desktop icon, Enter, Alt+ Wallpaper **F**ile, Alt+down arrow	Double-click Desktop icon, click down arrow by Wallpaper **F**ile, click on wallpaper file name
Change mouse settings	Select Mouse icon, Alt+*letter*, arrow keys	Double-click Mouse icon, click or drag box to change
Installing new printers	Select Printers icon, Enter, Alt+ **A**dd Printer, Alt+ **I**nstall, select	Double-click Printers icon, click **I**nstall, select printer
Changing displays	Select Main group, select Windows Setup icon, Enter, Alt, **O**ptions, **C**hange System Settings, Alt, **D**isplay	Click Main group, double-click Windows Setup icon, click **O**ptions, click **C**hange System Settings, click **D**isplay